CANADIAN
ENTREPRENEURSHIP
AND
SMALL BUSINESS
MANAGEMENT
Seventh Edition

D. Wesley Balderson
University of Lethbridge

James D. Clark
University of Lethbridge

Contributing Author

**McGraw-Hill
Ryerson**

Toronto   Montréal   Boston   Burr Ridge, IL   Dubuque, IA   Madison, WI   New York   San Francisco
St. Louis   Bangkok   Bogotá   Caracas   Kuala Lumpur   Lisbon   London   Madrid   Mexico City   Milan
New Delhi   Santiago   Seoul   Singapore   Sydney   Taipei

Canadian Entrepreneurship and Small Business Management, Seventh Edition

ISBN-13: 978-0-07-096330-6
ISBN-10: 0-07-096330-4

1 2 3 4 5 6 7 8 9 10 TCP 0 9 8

Printed and bound in Canada

Care has been taken to trace ownership of copyright material contained in this text; however, the publisher will welcome any information that enables them to rectify any reference or credit for subsequent editions.

Editorial Director: Joanna Cotton
Senior Sponsoring Editor: Kim Brewster
Marketing Manager: Matthew Busbridge
Developmental Editor: Lori McLellan
Senior Editorial Associate: Christine Lomas
Supervising Editor: Graeme Powell
Copy Editor: Gillian Scobie
Senior Production Coordinator: Madeleine Harrington
Cover Design: Michelle Losier
Cover Image: © Victoria Pearson/Botanica/Jupiterimages
Interior Design: Michelle Losier
Page Layout: Michelle Losier
Printer: Transcontinental Interglobe

Statistics Canada information is used with the permission of Statistics Canada. Users are forbidden to copy this material and/or redisseminate the data, in an original or modified form, for commercial purposes, without the expressed permission of Statistic Canada. Information on the availability of the wide range of data from Statistics Canada can be obtained from Statistics Canada's Regional Offices, its World Wide Web site at www.statcan.ca and its toll-free access number 1-800-263-1136."

Library and Archives Canada Cataloguing in Publication

Balderson, D. Wesley (David Wesley), 1948-
    Canadian entrepreneurship & small business management / D. Wesley Balderson. — 7th ed.

Includes bibliographical references and index.
ISBN 978-0-07-096330 6

    1. Small business—Canada—Management—Textbooks. 2. New business enterprises—Canada—Textbooks.
3. Entrepreneurship—Canada—Textbooks. I. Title.

HD62.7.B34 2008   658.02'20971   C2007-905802-7

Brief Contents

Contents

PART TWO

Preparing for Small Business Ownership. 89

CHAPTER 4

Organizing a Business—The Business Plan 90

CHAPTER 5

Buying a Business 142

CHAPTER 9

CHAPTER 10

CHAPTER 11

CHAPTER 12

CHAPTER 13

PART FOUR

Looking to the Future 399

CHAPTER 14

Managing Growth 400

CHAPTER 15

Managing the Transfer of the Business **414**

Preface

Canadian Entrepreneurship & Small Business Management, seventh edition, is the result of many years of teaching entrepreneurship business classes at the college and university levels; of working closely with numerous owners of small businesses in a consulting role; of direct personal small business management experience; and, of course, of experience with all the previous successful editions. This edition has been improved by making it more current, interesting, and instructional; practical and theoretically sound; and rigorous, yet easy for students to follow and absorb.

To accomplish these sometimes diverse aims, the text incorporates standard small business start-up and management fundamentals and introduces the reader to many Canadian entrepreneurs and their businesses through more than 50 real-life small business incidents and 15 profiles of Canadian entrepreneurs. Each individual profiled started his or her own business on a small scale. All have succeeded, and some have expanded into large businesses.

Numerous cases illustrate the small business management concepts discussed in the text. These concepts are stated at the beginning of each case in the Instructor's Manual to aid in teaching. Each case proceeds in a logical order from start-up of the business, through management of the existing business, and finally to planning for the future.

WHAT'S NEW IN THIS EDITION

The seventh edition introduces several improvements to the previous editions based on professor and student feedback. For instance, dated cases and examples have been replaced with more current information. Specifically, the seventh edition includes the following:

- Three new end-of-part cases

- Sixty-four new incidents

- Seven new small business profiles and updates to existing profiles

- Thirty-seven new or updated figures and tables

- Three new video case examples

- Updates of statistics, examples, charts, information sources, government programs, and taxes

- New information about senior entrepreneurs, female entrepreneurs, community futures organizations, feasibility analysis, feasibility for Internet businesses, customer relationship marketing, multilevel marketing, just-in-time human resources training, selling a business to employees, more on Internet commerce, including blogs.

This text remains appropriate for any entrepreneurship or small business management class at the college or university undergraduate or graduate level. It can also be adapted easily to continuing education classes for those who are thinking about or are currently involved in running their own businesses. In many cases, the text would also be a useful resource book for practitioners outside the classroom setting.

CHAPTER STRUCTURE OF *CANADIAN ENTREPRENEURSHIP & SMALL BUSINESS MANAGEMENT*

Canadian Entrepreneurship & Small Business Management is divided into four parts. Each part covers an essential aspect of starting or managing a small business.

Part 1 provides background information essential to the decision to undertake small business ownership. Chapter 1 reviews the characteristics of small business and its contribution to Canadian society. Chapter 2 covers areas required for a personal evaluation of one's suitability for small business ownership. Chapter 3 presents a systematic procedure for determining whether a small business opportunity is feasible. It includes numerous sources of information essential in carrying out a feasibility analysis.

The four chapters in Part 2 discuss important aspects of starting or obtaining a business. Chapters 4, 5, and 6 review the three methods of establishing a small business. Chapter 4 discusses organizing the small business from scratch, including a special emphasis on the preparation of the business plan. Chapter 5 covers buying a business. Chapter 6 deals with franchising as a type of small business ownership. Chapter 7 discusses financing concerns in starting the business and includes a listing of sources of financing for entrepreneurs.

Part 3 includes six chapters that discuss the fundamental management practices used in operating the already established business. Chapters 8, 9, 10, 11, and 12 cover in detail the small business applications in marketing, e-commerce, finance, internal operations, and personnel management, respectively. Chapter 13 focuses on tax considerations for the small business owner-manager.

Part 4 discusses the future and long-term aspects of the small business. Chapter 14 deals with the principles underlying effective growth management. Chapter 15 discusses methods of terminating or transferring the ownership of the enterprise, with a special emphasis on family businesses.

FEATURES OF THIS BOOK

The Incidents contain current examples of small business and entrepreneurship taken from the business press and discuss relevant issues related to the topic.

INCIDENT 1-3   The BlackBerry

The BlackBerry is a wireless hand-held device designed by Research in Motion (RIM) to meet the organization and communication needs of today's high-tech world. Based in Waterloo, Ontario, RIM employs more than 1,400 people, is worth $7 billion, and has won both an Emmy and an Oscar for outstanding technical product development. However, RIM cannot boast that it became successful overnight. Founder, president, and co-CEO Mike Lazaridis and his partner, Doug Fregin, vice-president of operations, experienced eight or nine failures before developing and launching their greatest wireless triumph, the BlackBerry.

Research in Motion's beginnings were modest. It consisted of two employees, Lazaridis and Fregin, friends since Grade 6. Both share fond memories of their childhood electronics shop teacher, Mr. Micsinszki. Micsinszki ran the local ham radio and amateur television club in the boys' home city of Windsor, Ontario. It was this teacher who encouraged Lazaridis and Fregin's interest in electronics and wireless technology. In fact, Lazaridis remembers Mr. Micsinszki saying, "Don't get too captivated by computers. In the future, the people who put computers and wireless technology together are really going to come up with something."

Both Lazaridis and Fregin attended university to study engineering. During university, the two entrepreneurs took a year off to develop automated television, a technology that allowed information to be transferred over the air. This development was inspired by a transmission method used by ham operators to place call letters on television screens. Both men returned to their studies, but Lazaridis never did complete his engineering education. In fact, he fell short of graduating in 1984 by only one month. The young entrepreneur had difficulty balancing his education and a $600,000 contract he had landed with General Motors. General Motors contracted Lazaridis

The Small Business Profiles demonstrate real-life examples and real person profiles, the epitome of applied learning.

SMALL BUSINESS PROFILE
Linda Hipp
Lija Style Inc.

Linda Hipp was a business development manager for Orca Bay Sports and Entertainment, which owned NBA and NHL teams, when she arrived at the idea of providing more stylish apparel for female golfers. Being an avid golfer herself, Linda recognized what she thought was a market niche which had not yet been met.

Linda had received a marketing diploma from Capilano College in Vancouver. She knew she wanted to work for herself. In addition, her father was an entrepreneur who owned his own engineering firm.

As a result, Hipp extensively researched the statistical trends provided by the U.S. National Golf Foundation and discovered that in the late 1990s younger women were starting to play the game in large numbers. Because of this demographic shift, there was a need and demand for more fashion-forward, stylish yet functional golf apparel for younger women.

This rapid growth allowed her to expand both the Spring and Fall collections by increasing the number of styles and selection. She also began to hire key employees to help with production, finance and marketing. Linda still manages the product development and marketing departments while her partner focuses on sales. The two of them oversee the operations of the business as well as future business development.

In 2004, Linda's company went through a brand and name change due to its notable successes outside the golf industry. HYP Golf became LIJA (pr. Lee-zha), a spin on the word leisure. The new name, which offers broader appeal to both men and women will help the company's future growth into other distribution channels.

In both 2005 and 2006, Linda was recognized as one of Canada's top woman entrepreneurs. In those years, the company was voted number 3 and 5 in

Each chapter contains a Summary that clearly reinforces important chapter concepts covered in the chapter.

Summary

1. The potential advantages of buying a small business include the reduction of risk, time, set-up expense, and competition; capitalization of business strength; possible assistance from the previous owner; and easier planning. Potential disadvantages include problems with physical facilities, personnel, inventory, and accounts receivable; deterioration of the business's financial condition or market; and difficulty in negotiating a purchase price.

2. The common sources for locating a business for sale include classified ads, government departments, real estate brokers, word of mouth, and professionals such as lawyers, accountants, and bankers.

The chapter problems and Web Exercises allow students to use applied and lateral thinking, and to come up with unique solutions to typical small business issues.

Web Exercise

www.
rockymountainsoap.
com

Visit the website for the Rocky Mountain Soap Company and identify possible concerns about purchasing this company.

The numerous chapter cases, end of text cases, and the Comprehensive Case all ensure numerous opportunities for students to apply the theory covered in the text. The Comprehensive Case allows students to build upon the concepts as their course progresses.

Comprehensive Case   *Sid Stevens: Part 3*

Although the numbers Sid had put together indicated that the Ladder Rail business might face several challenges, he decided to devote all his spare time to the venture. This was primarily because of the positive response that he had received from his co-workers, as well as from the local Home Hardware dealer, who thought that the product had a lot of potential. Within two months, this dealer sold five units of the Ladder Rail that Sid had made in his garage. Customer feedback was positive and this was encouraging to Sid.

One of the decisions that Sid is concerned with is whether to build a manufacturing plant or purchase an existing facility. He is aware of a small plant close to his home that is for sale. It has much of the metal-bending equipment that he needs and he could retrofit the plant to suit his purposes for $10,000. However, when he learned that the owner of the plant was asking $200,000 and that its net worth was only $180,000, Sid felt that it was just too much money and was leaning toward building his own plant.

Regardless of how he established the manufacturing facility, one thing that Sid had learned in his small business management class was that he should prepare a business plan. He therefore set to work preparing the plan and had Suzie type it for him. The outline of Sid Stevens' business plan for the Ladder Rail is found below.

CBC videos demonstrate real life situations and how the concepts work in the world of business.

PART ENDING VIDEO CASE & QUESTIONS   *Java Nook**

(Appropriate Chapters—1, 2, 3, 4, 7, 15)

Annette Lavigne and John Welter have started a small café in Toronto. This video example describes the problems associated with a small business start-up. It also illustrates some of the typical weaknesses that entrepreneurs possess that hamper them from successfully establishing an enterprise in a volatile industry. However, in the end Annette and John do realize their dream of owning a small business.

1. What does this example illustrate about the advantages and disadvantages of starting a small business?
2. Evaluate Annette and John's backgrounds and preparation for starting a small business. What could they have done to better prepare for small business ownership?
3. What does this case show about the strains of families starting and operating businesses?
4. How could Annette and John have been more successful in obtaining adequate financing?

*Source: CBC *Venture* #796, running time 13:00.

CBC

INSTRUCTOR AND STUDENT SUPPORT

Integrated Learning System

Great care was used in the creation of the supplemental materials to accompany *Canadian Entrepreneurship & Small Business Management*, seventh edition. Whether you are a seasoned faculty member or a newly minted instructor, you will find the support materials to be comprehensive and practical.

CBC Videos   CBC video segments are available on DVD and VHS tape for instructors and in video streaming for students and instructors from the Online Learning Centre. All segments are tied in by concept to those parts in the text.

Instructor's CD-ROM   The CD-ROM includes electronic versions of the following:

- Instructor's Manual

- Computerized Test Bank

- Microsoft® PowerPoint® Presentations

The Instructor's Manual has been carefully prepared to provide the instructor with helpful information while allowing considerable flexibility. Notes relating to each chapter include the following components:

- Chapter objectives—reproduced from the text chapters

- Summary points—key concepts summarized from text chapters

- Key terms and concepts from chapter material

- PowerPoint® slides

- Answers to end-of-chapter questions

- Case solutions—for end-of-part and comprehensive cases

- Video case teaching notes

The solutions to the supplementary case questions are included toward the end of the Instructor's Manual.

The Computerized Test Bank, Brownstone version, allows instructors to add and edit questions, save and reload multiple test versions, select questions based on type, difficulty, or key word and use password protection. True/false questions test three levels of learning: (1) knowledge of key terms, (2) understanding of concepts and principles, and (3) application of principles.

Microsoft® PowerPoint® Presentations for each chapter are based around the learning goals and include many of the figures and tables from the textbook as well as some additional slides that support and expand the text discussions. Slides can be modified by instructors with PowerPoint®.

Instructors can use this resource to access many of the supplements associated with the text and to create custom presentations. Most of these supplements are also available for downloading from the Instructor's Resource Centre of the Online Learning Centre, located at www.mcgrawhill.ca/olc/balderson

PageOut   McGraw-Hill's unique point-and-click course website tool enables users to create a full-featured, professional-quality course website without needing to know HTML coding. PageOut is free for instructors, and lets you post your syllabus online, assign McGraw-Hill OLC content, add Web links, and maintain an online grade book. (And if you're short on time, we even have a team ready to help you create your site.)

WebCT/Blackboard   This text is available in two of the most popular course-delivery platforms—WebCT and BlackBoard—for more user-friendly and enhanced features. Contact your local McGraw-Hill Ryerson *i*Learning Specialist for more information.

Instructor and Student Online Learning Centres (www.mcgrawhill.ca/olc/balderson) This online learning centre is a text website that follows the text material chapter by chapter. Students will find custom quizzes for chapter content. Instructors will find downloadable supplements.

*i*Learning ADVANTAGE
McGraw-Hill Ryerson

*i***Learning Sales Specialist** Your Integrated Learning Sales Specialist is a McGraw-Hill Ryerson representative who has the experience, product knowledge, training, and support to help you assess and integrate any of the above-noted products, technology, and services into your course for optimum teaching and learning performance. Whether it's how to use our test bank software, helping your students improve their grades, or how to put your entire course online, your *i*Learning Sales Specialist is there to help. Contact your local *i*Learning Sales Specialist today to learn how to maximize all McGraw-Hill Ryerson resources!

*i***Learning Services Program** McGraw-Hill Ryerson offers a unique *i*Services package designed for Canadian faculty. Our mission is to equip providers of higher education with superior tools and resources required for excellence in teaching. For additional information, visit www.mcgrawhill.ca/highereducation/iservices.

ACKNOWLEDGEMENTS

Many people contributed to *Canadian Entrepreneurship & Small Business Management*, seventh edition. I am grateful to the many students and colleagues who have offered input and critical analyses of our small business course over the years. I also appreciate those owner-managers with whom I have had an opportunity to work in a consulting role. They have provided considerable insight regarding the pertinent problems faced by small business owners. Reviewers of the seventh edition and reviewers and users of the previous six editions also provided valuable suggestions. Reviewers include the following:

Michael Piczak, *Mohawk College of Applied Arts and Technology*

Tom O'Connell, *Concordia University*

Terri Champion, *Niagara College*

Richard Wagman, *Saskatchewan Institute of Applied Science and Technology*

Patricia Peel, *University of Guelph and Humber Institute of Technology and Advanced Learning*

Phil Jones, *Algonquin College*

Jonathan Kerr, *York University*

Robert Anderson, *University of Regina*

James Beatty, *George Brown College*

Peter Miller, *Seneca College of Applied Arts and Technology*

Several people made direct contributions to this edition of the text. Research assistants Deborah Steed and Jamie Mann collected data, checked references and permissions, and entered text material into the word processor. Professor Jim Clark, Faculty of Management, University of Lethbridge, wrote the draft of Chapter 9: Small Business and Electronic Commerce. To all of these people I express my gratitude for their valuable contributions.

I thank those who authored some of the cases: Rick Heyland, research assistant, at the University of Lethbridge; Gordon McDougall, Wilfrid Laurier University; Professor Jim Clark, University of Lethbridge, and James Nelson, University of Colorado.

I thank the many authors and entrepreneurs who granted us permission to use diagrams, tables, profiles, and article excerpts to illustrate the text concepts.

I am extremely grateful for the support and assistance the Faculty of Management at the University of Lethbridge provided in allowing computer research and office administration time for this project.

I also thank the staff of McGraw-Hill Ryerson for their encouragement and support.

Wes Balderson

PART ONE

The Decision To Start A Business

The decision to start one's own business is a difficult one. It often involves leaving secure employment to face an uncertain financial future. Such a decision can have far-reaching effects on the physical, emotional, and financial aspects of one's life. To provide a better understanding of the implications and preparation for this decision, Part 1 discusses three topics.

Chapter 1 reviews the role of small business in Canadian society. It examines current trends and the probable future environment for small business.

Chapter 2 describes the characteristics of successful and unsuccessful small businesses, and the personal characteristics that make up the majority of successful entrepreneurs. The chapter also reviews the potential advantages and dangers of operating one's own business. Understanding this information can help one make an informed small-business career decision.

Once an individual understands the relative merits of starting a small business and feels suited to such a career, he or she can do several things in pursuit of the best business opportunity. Generally, a person needs to gather a considerable amount of information to evaluate business opportunities. Chapter 3 presents ideas that can improve information collection and analysis skills for this purpose.

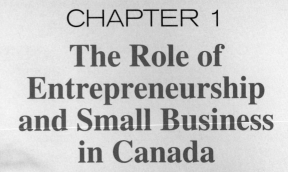

CHAPTER 1

The Role of Entrepreneurship and Small Business in Canada

CHAPTER OBJECTIVES

- To discuss the level of interest and activity in the small business sector

- To review common methods of defining small business and explain why a definition is important

- To understand the current extent of entrepreneurship and small business in Canada

- To discuss the benefits a healthy small business sector can offer society

- To explain the probable future environment for entrepreneurship and the small business community

SMALL BUSINESS PROFILE

Jacqueline Shan

CV Technologies Inc.

Jacqueline Shan had received a Ph.D. in pharmacology from her native China and a Ph.D. in physiology from the University of Alberta when she formed CV Technologies Inc. in Edmonton with her colleague Peter Pang in 1992. With $20 million in government grants and private investor money, their research led to the development of the cold and flu remedy COLD-fX®.

Using a combination of Asian natural preventive techniques and a proprietary extract of North American ginseng, Shan and Pang along with several other research scientists attempted to develop the product and system so that it could become a commercial success. "I believed we had the best product in the world for the prevention and treatment of colds and flu," observed Shan. It had been tried with some professional athletes with positive results.

However they found that marketing the product was not as easy as creating the product. The large pharmaceutical companies were hesitant to adopt the product because it was "natural" and, they felt, not clinically proven to be effective. As a result, the company struggled to make sales and had to lay off most of its scientists. Despite having no management experience, Shan reluctantly took the job as CEO.

Recognizing the importance of "bringing it to the people" proved to be a turning point for COLD-fX. Because the company had little money to spend on advertising, Shan immediately turned to public relations as a way to get the name and performance of the product into the spotlight and recruited such well-known celebrities as Don Cherry. This was aided with the release of results of a significant clinical trial showing COLD-fX was effective in helping reduce the frequency, severity and duration of cold and flu symptoms by boosting the immune system.

Within a short time, COLD-fX had become the #1 selling cold and flu remedy in Canada with sales increasing from $6.4 million in 2004 to $41.3 million in 2006. The company received the Marketer of the Year award in 2006 from Marketing Magazine while Dr. Shan was selected as the Chinese Canadian Entrepreneur of the Year and was inducted into the Canadian Healthcare Marketing Hall of Fame.

As the company has become successful, and growth has continued, Shan has surrounded herself with skilled management experts to help with key areas of administration, finance, and marketing. As she is quick to comment, "Science is still my passion, but business is very interesting." CV Technologies has developed two other natural health products, REMEMBER-fX and CELL-fX, and has recently launched COLD-fX Extra Strength. The company has also launched COLD-fX into the U.S. market. It is in the process of developing new products using the same research principle that has been successful with COLD-fX. The future looks bright for these products and for CV Technologies as it continues to blend together product research and marketing in a winning combination.

Used with the permission of Dr. Jacqueline Shan and CV Technologies Inc.

CV Technologies Inc.
www.cvtechnologies.com

THE ENTREPRENEURIAL REVOLUTION

This chapter provides an overview of the importance of and trends toward small business. The terms "entrepreneurship" and "small business ownership" will be used interchangeably throughout the chapter. Entrepreneurs typically start small businesses but sometimes they establish larger enterprises. At the same time, many small business owners may not be considered very entrepreneurial. The differences between entrepreneurs and small business owners or managers will be discussed in detail in Chapter 2.

Since the mid-1970s a reawakening of interest in entrepreneurship and business ownership has occurred both in North America and abroad. After the Second World War, the philosophy in many circles was that bigger was better in both business and government. As a result, for several years government increased in size and the climate for big business improved.

The critics of "bigness," however, have gathered support because big government and big business have failed to provide the expected panacea for society's economic problems. The result has been that more people and more governments are looking to small business to provide a catalyst for their stagnant economies and to enable faster economic growth. As John Naisbitt has stated in *Global Paradox*, "The entrepreneur is the most important player in the building of the global economy, so much so that big companies are decentralizing and reconstituting themselves as networks of entrepreneurs. Huge companies such as IBM and GM must break up to become confederations of small, autonomous, entrepreneurial companies if they are to survive."[1]

In a recent survey conducted by Ernst and Young, 8 out of 10 influential North Americans indicated that they believe entrepreneurialism will define twenty-first-century business.[2] Many other countries have shared in this growth and increased awareness.[3] This growth trend for entrepreneurial interest and behaviour is also evident in Canada. The Global Entrepreneurship Monitor places Canada third in entrepreneurship progress out of 53 countries studied but second only to the United States among the G-7 countries. Approximately close to 10 percent of Canadian adults are involved in entrepreneurial activity while another 15 percent are employed in entrepreneurial small business, according to the G.E.M. guidelines.[4] While the percentages may seem small, they do not include those who are planning to start small businesses or who work in small businesses not considered to be entrepreneurial. By any measure, however, the trend toward improved entrepreneurial attitude, self-employment growth, and small business formation is all positive in Canada. Starting one's own business is now seen as a preferred occupational alternative for a majority of Canadians. (See Figure 1-1).

This growth in entrepreneurial attitudes, along with the significant growth in self-employment and small business formations, illustrates that entrepreneurship is firmly established in Canada. Except for a brief slowing of this growth from 1999 to 2002, the growth of small businesses has consistently surpassed that of larger organizations and the economy as a whole.[5] This trend is shown in Figure 1-2. As a result, the importance of the small business sector of Canadian society is now more widely acknowledged than ever.

What has fuelled this growth? Throughout this text, we will use many examples of entrepreneurs to illustrate why an increasing number of people are establishing their own businesses. The dream of starting small and developing a successful business, such as Jacqueline Shan's (see the Small Business Profile), is shared by many. However, many individuals have become successful entrepreneurs due to the downsizing of larger organizations. A recent survey found that 22 percent of small businesses are started for this reason.[6]

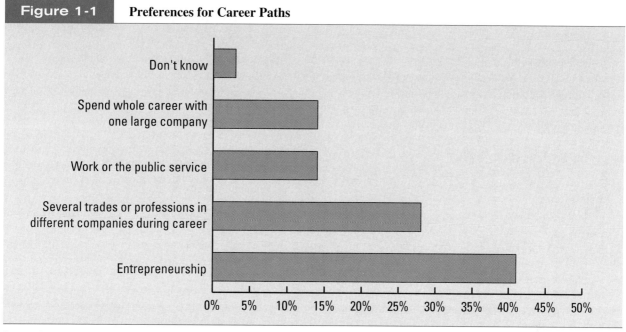

Figure 1-1   **Preferences for Career Paths**

Source: Confidence of Canadians in Companies on Job Creation and Social Responsibilities, Leger Marketing, June 2005.

A description of these situations appears in Incident 1-1. During the past few recessions, and recent downsizings, many individuals who lost their jobs and many college and university graduates unable to secure employment started their own businesses. A recent labour force survey found that 12 percent of self-employed individuals were "pushed" into business ownership because there was no work available.[7] Others chose to leave secure employment and strike out on their own because of a natural interest or a desire for a challenge. Incidents 1-2 and 1-3 illustrate examples of this.

The above examples provide anecdotal evidence of the growth of small business—a detailed discussion regarding the evidence of small business growth follows.

INCIDENT 1-1   Fewer, Deeper, Smarter

Only a week after being let go from an information consultant agency which she helped launch nine years earlier, Clara Angotti started another enterprise in the same sector. In 2002, Angotti founded M Systems Group Inc., a Toronto-based tech consultancy, where revenue grew from $2.6 million in 2002 to $6.1 million last year and is on track to earn $13.5 million in 2004.

Angotti took on a "fewer and deeper" strategy, which serves far fewer clients but serves them far more deeply. M Systems has only three clients: TD Canada Trust, Bank of Montreal, and Scotiabank. These banks are big IT spenders and prefer close and stable relationships with only a few vendors. The "fewer and deeper" strategy lets the company steal share from huge competitors who aren't single-sector specialists.

However, the risk of having only three clients, with 60 percent of revenue coming from TD Canada Trust, is obvious. Angotti is not worried, as she says that losing a division wouldn't mean losing the whole bank. By targeting her clients, Angotti has turned her second attempt of consulting into a success.

Source: Adapted from Jim McElgunn, "Fewer, Deeper, Smarter," *Profit*, November 2004, p. 64.

INCIDENT 1-2   The Gift of Love

Stasia Nawrocki was born with a passion for beauty and has spent her life creating and selling beautiful gifts to enrich the lives of her customers. Nawrocki is the owner of Dansk Gifts in Edmonton and has operated the gift store for 30 years. "Retail was just something I always wanted to do," she says. Nawrocki recognizes that customers come into her store to get ideas and be inspired. She helps them pick out something simple, and then builds a gift around it. She wants customers to leave feeling better than when they came in.

Nawrocki has been very involved in charitable activities in Edmonton over the years. Diane Brisebois, president and CEO, Retail Council of Canada, says, "Stasia represents just one of thousands of small and mid-size store owners across the country who dedicate themselves to raising funds for the much-needed charitable organizations."

Nawrocki believes that the key to surviving is to listen to what your customers want and to put your heart and soul into your work. "To be successful, you've got to put your heart into what you do. You can't do it if you don't love it," she says.

Source: Adapted from Talbot Boggs, "Alberta Retailer Enriches Lives of Customers and Community," *Canadian Retailer*, July/August 2006, pp. 28–29.

INCIDENT 1-3   The BlackBerry

The BlackBerry is a wireless hand-held device designed by Research in Motion (RIM) to meet the organization and communication needs of today's high-tech world. Based in Waterloo, Ontario, RIM employs more than 1,400 people, is worth $7 billion, and has won both an Emmy and an Oscar for outstanding technical product development. However, RIM cannot boast that it became successful overnight. Founder, president, and co-CEO Mike Lazaridis and his partner, Doug Fregin, vice-president of operations, experienced eight or nine failures before developing and launching their greatest wireless triumph, the BlackBerry.

Research in Motion's beginnings were modest. It consisted of two employees, Lazaridis and Fregin, friends since Grade 6. Both share fond memories of their childhood electronics shop teacher, Mr. Micsinszki. Micsinszki ran the local ham radio and amateur television club in the boys' home city of Windsor, Ontario. It was this teacher who encouraged Lazaridis and Fregin's interest in electronics and wireless technology. In fact, Lazaridis remembers Mr. Micsinszki saying, "Don't get too captivated by computers. In the future, the people who put computers and wireless technology together are really going to come up with something."

Both Lazaridis and Fregin attended university to study engineering. During university, the two entrepreneurs took a year off to develop automated television, a technology that allowed information to be transferred over the air. This development was inspired by a transmission method used by ham operators to place call letters on television screens. Both men returned to their studies, but Lazaridis never did complete his engineering education. In fact, he fell short of graduating in 1984 by only one month. The young entrepreneur had difficulty balancing his education and a $600,000 contract he had landed with General Motors. General Motors contracted Lazaridis to produce a display system to communicate messages throughout GM manufacturing facilities. At that point Lazaridis committed to RIM full time.

Fresh out of university, Lazaridis and Fregin sought the business expertise necessary to operate their new company. The next 15 years were a whirlwind of failures and triumphs for the techno-oriented company. By the end of fiscal year 2006, RIM had revenues of almost $2.07 billion and more than 5 million subscibers.

Source: Adapted from Laura Pratt, "Persistence in Motion," *Profit*, May 2001, pp. 18–26; and RIM 2006 Press Release, April 6, 2006, pp. 1–6.

Increases in the Number of Business Establishments

Considerable research has been done to determine the number of new businesses established each year. This has proved a difficult, if not impossible, task because of the many different types of businesses as well as the varied methods of estimating business start-ups. Some indicators of business start-ups that researchers have used are tax returns, new employer registrations, phone hookups, new incorporations, and business registrations.[8]

Figure 1-2 illustrates the number of small businesses in Canada in 2005. Small businesses with few employees constitute the vast majority of all businesses with employees, but small businesses with no employees make up an even larger number. In addition, the number of businesses with fewer than 50 employees has increased substantially over the past decade. Similar trends for the United States show even more increases in small business formations than in Canada.[9] During recent economic downturns, the small business sector has appeared to be more resilient than large business during this time.[10] Statistics Canada has estimated that 97 percent of all existing businesses have fewer than 50 employees.[11] By 2006 there were 2.53 million self-employed persons, representing 18 percent of the total workforce, an increase of 43 percent since 1990.[12] A recent CIBC report indicated that the self-employment growth rate has been double that of the growth in the number of firms with paid employees.[13] Figure 1-3 illustrates this trend. Further, recent Statistics Canada data indicate the growth rate of the self-employed to be 25.4 percent, up from 19.3 percent in 1995.[14]

Statistics Canada
www.statcan.ca

Increases in the Number of Employees of Small Businesses

The number of Canadians employed by small and medium sized businesses has grown substantially in recent years[15] and has been estimated at 56 percent of the total workforce.[16] In addition, there is a marked shift in new job creation from a reliance on big firms and projects to small firms and entrepreneurs. Statistics Canada indicates that more than one third of total job growth in 2006 was due to small businesses.[17] Furthermore, Statistics Canada reports that even the smallest businesses (fewer than five employees), called micro-businesses, accounted for 27.8 percent of new jobs created in Canada in 2006.[18]

| **Figure 1-2** | **Number of Establishments by Employment Size, December 2005** |

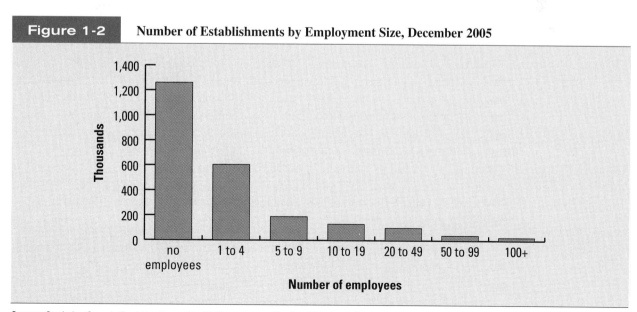

Source: Statistics Canada Register, December 2005, as reported in *Small Business Quarterly*, August 2006, p. 6.

Figure 1-3	Comparison of self-employment growth and the growth of paid employees

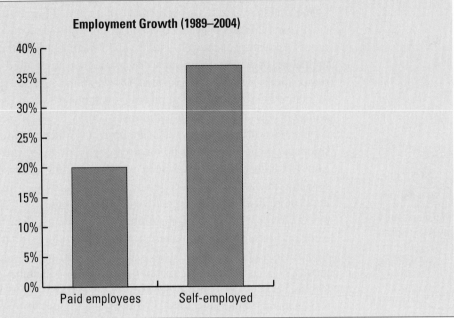

Source: CIBC World Markets Inc. Survey, 2005.

Increases in Government Interest and Programs

The federal government recognizes the vital role that small business plays in the Canadian economy. Small businesses create jobs, they generate wealth, and they provide satisfying careers for a growing number of entrepreneurs. To realize their full potential as an engine for growth, however, they need a favourable environment that allows them to prosper and expand. They also need forms of support that are tailored to helping them meet the challenges of a changing and competitive economy. While extensive assistance is already provided to Canada's small businesses, the government has heard their concerns and it is moving energetically to respond.[19]

As the quotation illustrates, many politicians now recognize the importance of small business to a healthy economy and are beginning to offer various financial and nonfinancial programs to assist the small business owner.[20] The Entrepreneurship and Small Business Office in the Department of Industry Canada coordinates and administers programs designed to aid small business at the federal level. Likewise, all the provinces and territories have departments that perform the same function for small businesses within their jurisdictions. Appendix 3B (see website) gives a complete listing of these agencies.

Increases in the Number of Small-Business-Related Courses at Colleges and Universities

The level of interest in small-business-related courses at Canadian colleges and universities has risen dramatically in the past few years. The trend of increasing the number of entrepreneurship courses in business schools appears to be continuing.[21] Such courses typically were housed in management and commerce faculties and attracted only students of those faculties. However, as a result of the growing general interest in small business in recent years, many nonbusiness majors now take such courses. In addition, a number of entrepreneurship courses are now being taught at the high school level in Canada.[22]

Increases in Entrepreneurial Activities in Large Businesses

Many large, successful companies have developed or altered their organizations to promote creativity, entrepreneurship, and individual initiative.[23] These businesses have realized considerable productivity gains by encouraging this type of intrapreneurship. In their extensive study of successful large companies, which resulted in the best-selling book *In Search of Excellence,* Thomas Peters and Robert Waterman found that one common characteristic of these organizations was their formal encouragement of entrepreneurship within and among departments. These companies were quick to recognize increases in productivity and innovativeness by rewarding employees who engaged in such entrepreneurial behaviour.[24] Canadian companies such as Bombardier and Nortel are examples of companies that have incorporated these practices into their organizations. Other large companies have struggled with the implementation of intrapreneurship because of their size and bureaucratic structure. This difficulty also exists within spin-off entrepreneurial divisions of the main company.[25] This will be discussed further in Chapter 2.

Nortel Networks
www.nortel.com

Bombardier
www.bombardier.com

Increases in the Political Power of Small Business

The small business community is a significant economic force in Canadian society. Several organizations are currently attempting to advance the small business cause through lobbying efforts and educational programs. The largest and most visible organization is the Canadian Federation of Independent Business, which boasts a membership of more than 105,000. Current concerns of CFIB members include the total tax burden, government regulations, and employment insurance premiums.[26] Lobbying has resulted in many government programs and some legislation beneficial to small business. Many industry associations made up primarily of small businesses are also very active in lobbying activities and have influenced the directions of government initiatives.

Canadian Federation of
Independent Business
www.cfib.ca

Improvement in the Image of Small Business

Small business owners and entrepreneurs are viewed more positively today than they were several years ago. An increasing number of Canadians recognize the economic benefits of a healthy small business sector (see Figure 1-4 on the next page). As more and more people recognize the benefits that small businesses provide to society, the occupation of entrepreneur carries more prestige than it previously did. A recent survey carried out by *Business Week* found that small business leaders were more trusted by the general public than leaders of religious institutions, big business, the news media, labour unions, and the government.[27]

WHAT IS SMALL BUSINESS?

What size of business qualifies as a small business? This question is not easy to answer, because most organizations and agencies concerned with small businesses use different definitions. It is essential, however, to understand some of the common characteristics of these definitions to better appreciate what constitutes a small business. These characteristics are outlined in the following paragraphs.

| Figure 1-4 | **Perceptions of Small Business Contributions to the Economy** |

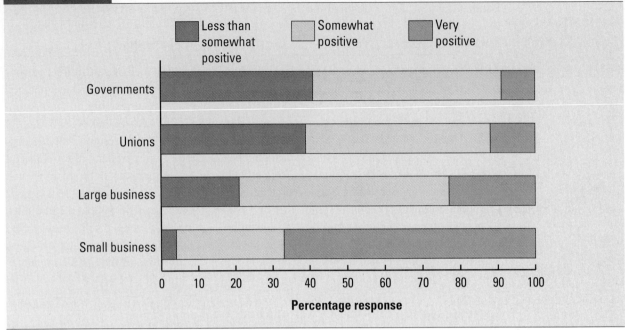

Source: Labourwatch Polls, conducted by Léger Marketing, August 2003.

Comparison and Evaluation

Dun and Bradstreet
www.dnb.ca

To compare the performance of a small business with that of other small businesses, it is necessary to understand the sizes and characteristics used by data collection and dissemination agencies such as Statistics Canada and Dun and Bradstreet. Ensuring that firms are relatively the same size allows a more meaningful monitoring of sales levels, performance, and productivity in relation to other similar firms in the industry. Currently, Statistics Canada publishes operating data for incorporated and unincorporated businesses with average net sales of $1 million or less.

Government Programs

Knowing how various government departments define a small business enables an entrepreneur to take advantage of the tax incentives and other government assistance programs designed for small business. Examples of differences in definitions among government agencies are given below.

Lending Programs

Business Development
Bank of Canada (BDC)
www.bdc.ca

A small business owner needs to know the size of business that lenders require in their lending programs in order to take advantage of favourable small-business provisions. Programs are available to small businesses from the Business Development Bank of Canada (BDC), provincial or territorial government lending agencies, and the chartered banks. Therefore, it is important to understand the criteria commonly used to distinguish a small business from a large one. At least four criteria exist.

1. Number of employees. The Department of Industry, Science and Technology specifies a small business as one that employs fewer than 100 people in a manufacturing industry and fewer than 50 employees in a nonmanufacturing industry. The Ministry of State for Small Business also uses the guideline of 50 employees, while the Business Development Bank of Canada (formerly the Federal Business Development Bank) considers a business that employs fewer than 75 people to be eligible for its Counselling Assistance for Small Businesses program. Other agencies, such as the Small Business Administration in the United States and Statistics Canada, specify much larger numbers of employees, ranging from 250 to 1,500 depending on the industry.[28]

2. Total revenue. Although the limits vary by industry, total revenue is a common basis for defining small business. The Ministry of State for Small Business uses $2 million in revenue as a benchmark. The Small Business Loans Act in Canada applies to firms with revenues of less than $5 million. The Small Business Administration in the United States uses the following revenue guidelines:

Retailing: $3.5 million to $13.5 million
Services: $3.5 million to $14.5 million
Construction: $7 million to $17 million

Canada Customs and
Revenue Agency
www.cra-arc.gc.ca

3. Profits. Canada Customs and Revenue Agency uses operating profits as a guideline to define which businesses qualify for the small business deduction. This special deduction allows a reduced tax rate (the small business deduction is discussed in detail in Chapter 13). This limit is presently set at a net operating profit of $300,000.

4. Type of management-ownership structure. Another criterion used to define small business is the degree to which the owner is also the day-to-day manager of the business. With some exceptions, the majority of small business owners are also the managers.[29] Because the guidelines differ among industries and agencies, the Committee for Economic Development in the United States uses a slightly different and less specific approach in defining a small business. Its definition states that if any two of the following characteristics exist, the business may be classified as a small business:

1. Independent management (i.e., the owner is the manager)

2. Owner-supplied capital

3. Local area of operations

4. Relatively small size within its industry

It is no easy task to define the size limits of a small business. The definition used will depend on the purpose and the agency or program concerned.

CURRENT STATE OF SMALL BUSINESS IN CANADA

Although the size and extent of small business in Canada depends on the definition used, a review of the data compiled by Statistics Canada and Industry Canada illustrates that small business comprises a significant part of the Canadian economy. This is shown in Figure 1-5 on page 12. The pertinent facts derived from this figure show the strong position held by the small business community (percentages are approximate):

- 97 percent of all businesses operating in Canada employ fewer than 50 employees while 78 percent of all businesses have fewer than five employees.[30]

- 56 percent of the labour force is employed in small business.[31] This includes businesses with fewer than 100 employees.

- 50 percent of gross domestic product is provided by small business.[32]

| Figure 1-5 | **Significance of Small Business to the Canadian Economy** |

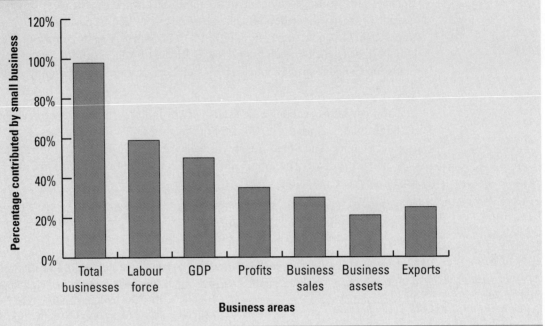

Source: *Small Business Quarterly*, Industry Canada, vol. 2, no. 3, March 2003; and *Small Business Primer*, Canadian Federation of Independent Business, December 2005.

- 32 percent of all business profits are made in small businesses.[33]
- 29 percent of gross sales in Canada are made by small businesses.[34]
- 25 percent of exports are made by small businesses.[35]
- 17.5 percent of all business assets are owned by small businesses.[36]

Young Entrepreneurs

In addition to the large general increases in the number of small businesses in recent years, more small businesses are being started by young people. In 2005, close to 10 percent of the self-employed were under the age of 30 as shown in Figure 1-6. Despite the buoyant employment climate in Canada,[37] starting one's own business is still an attractive career option for many younger Canadians. Further, a recent survey of Canada's fastest-growing small businesses indicated that the average age of the owners was about 40.[38] In recent years, organizations such as the Young Entrepreneurs Association and ACE (Association of Collegiate Entrepreneurs) have been formed in Canada to provide networking and information for these young entrepreneurs. In addition, government and private organizations have recognized the importance of young entrepreneurs in lending programs offered by the Business Development Bank of Canada as well as the Canadian Youth Business Foundation (see Chapter 7). Annual awards are also made to top Canadian youth entrepreneurs by the BDC.

Young Entrepreneurs Association

www.yea.ca

Senior Entrepreneurs

Recently, more senior citizens have become entrepreneurs in Canada. In 2005, Canadians over the age of 55 made up 25 percent of the self-employed, up from 35 percent in 2001.[39] Older entrepreneurs are currently the fastest growing segment in the small business sector

Figure 1-6	Growth and Extent of Self-Employment by Age

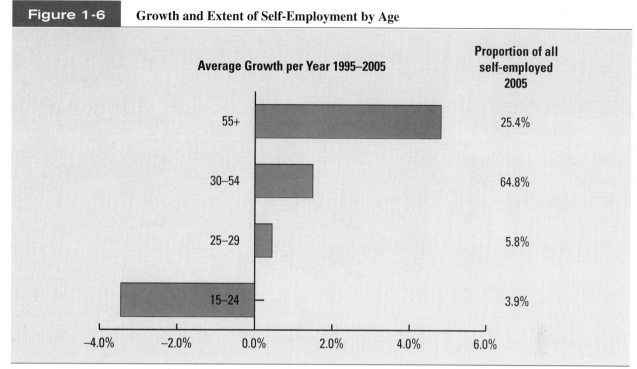

Source: *Small Business Quarterly*, Industry Canada, February 2007, p. 7.

and long-term demographic trends indicate that they will become an even more significant part of the economy in the future. (See Figure 1-6). In addition, a large number of non-retired Canadians are strongly considering working in some capacity after they retire.[40]

A unique characteristic of many older entrepreneurs is that they do not want their businesses to grow. They are content to have a business that will provide some income but allow them to maintain a balance with their lifestyle.

Female Entrepreneurs

Self-employment among women has increased rapidly in recent years. Currently, Canada is home to more than 800,000 women entrepreneurs.[41] In 2000, one in five employed men owned and operated his own business, compared with one in eight employed women. However, for both sexes, the likelihood of being self-employed has grown considerably over the past 20 years, and the rate of growth has been stronger for women (see Figure 1-7). Firms with at least one female owner now account for close to 47 percent of small businesses and employ 2.6 million people.[42]

A Global Economic Entrepreneurship study recently found that in 2005, 43 percent of entrepreneurs starting new businesses were female.[43] Organizations such as Women Entrepreneurs of Canada (WEC) and Women Presidents Organization (WPO) have increased the political power and networking opportunities for female entrepreneurs.

Although the majority of self-employed men and women in 2005 worked in the service sector, 4 in 10 businesses operated by men were in the goods sector, while this was the case for only 2 in 10 self-employed women. This difference mostly reflects the greater concentration of men in the construction industry, since similar proportions of self-employed men (14 percent) and women (12 percent) worked in agriculture.[44]

Canadian Women's Business Network

www.cdnbizwomen.com

Figure 1-7   Self-Employment

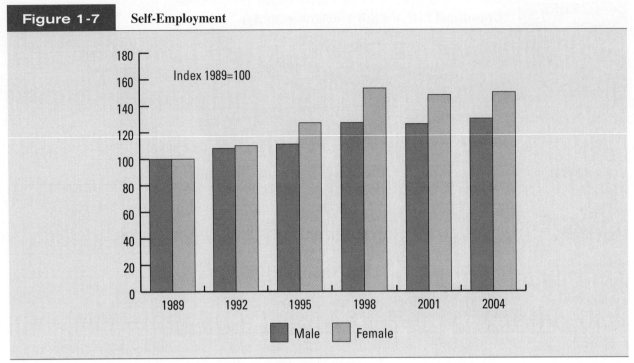

Source: Women Entrepreneurs: Leading the Charge, CIBC World Markets Survey, 2005.

Many females in corporate settings intend to start their own businesses. A recent study of Canadian female managers found that 27 percent intend to leave to start their own businesses. Reasons cited are dissatisfaction and frustrations with their current employment.[45] Increasingly, female entrepreneurs are well educated (24 percent have a university education), and many are over age 55.[46] Many of the incidents and profiles in this text describe the significant contributions of Canadian female entrepreneurs. Incident 1-4 illustrates one example of a successful female entrepreneur.

Immigrant Entrepreneurs

A large number of Canadian entrepreneurs are immigrants to Canada or have parents who were immigrants. More than one in five of the self-employed in Canada are immigrants, almost double the rate observed in the 1980s.[47]

Entrepreneurial Activity by Industry

As in other countries, Canadian small business activity is more dominant in sectors that are not capital intensive, such as the service industry. As noted in Figure 1-7, self-employment is more prevalent in the trades, sales, and management sectors. Furthermore, while the overall number of self-employed workers increased by about 37 percent between 1990 and 2005, the level of self-employment increased by more than double this amount in several service sectors. (See Figure 1-8.)

INCIDENT 1-4   Here, There, Everywhere

Debbie Gracie-Smith, president of Ontario-based Cratos Technology Solutions Inc., can set up a virtual office almost anywhere and so can her 40 global employees. Such savvy use of technology boosts the firm's productivity, attracts top talent and global sales, and generates big cost savings.

Cratos, founded in 1999 by Gracie-Smith and Andrew Wickett, installs and customizes credit-card processing software for major corporations. The company uses technology such as cell phones, Internet, and laptops to issue status reviews, project plans, and for problem solving. This is cost effective and allows the company the flexibility to work from anywhere.

Cratos recently formed an alliance with a large software developer and the firm is also venturing into project management and strategic-planning consulting. Last year, Cratos' sales were 7.2 million, a 2,006 percent increase from the year 2000.

Source: Adapted from Susanne Baillie-Ruder, "Here, There, Everywhere," *Profit*, November 2004, p. 62.

| Figure 1-8 | Proportion of Small Businesses by Sector, December 2005 |

Source: Small Business Quarterly, Industry Canada, August 2006, p. 5.

| Figure 1-9 | **Number of Small Businesses* by Province, December 2005** |

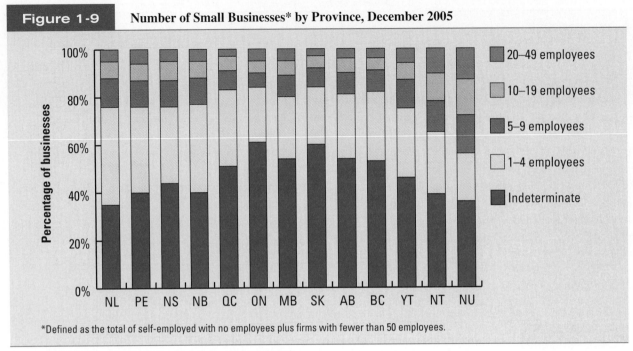

*Defined as the total of self-employed with no employees plus firms with fewer than 50 employees.

Source: Small Business Quarterly, Industry Canada, August 2006, p. 6.

Entrepreneurial Activity by Region

Although small businesses exist in all areas of Canada, some regions seem to be more fertile areas for growth. Figure 1-9 shows that the economies of all provinces are dominated by small business. Manitoba has a slightly smaller percentage of businesses with fewer than five employees, while Newfoundland and Labrador has a slightly higher share. These small businesses make up more than 70 percent of the total share, while businesses with fewer than 50 employees represent more than 90 percent of the total businesses in each province. The regional distribution of growth in self-employment over the past decade shows that Alberta and Ontario have seen the most rapid growth. This trend is predicted to continue.[48]

CONTRIBUTIONS OF SMALL BUSINESS

The size of the small business sector is not the only reason this sector is important to Canada. The following sections discuss other significant benefits of small business to Canadian society.

Labour Intensity

Small businesses are generally more labour intensive than large companies. This means they typically employ more people to produce a certain level of output than a larger business. In addition, small firms accounted for a significant portion of the new jobs created in Canada over the last decade. From 2000 to 2005, small businesses in Canada created over 450,000 new jobs, close to 50 percent of net new jobs in the economy.[49] Most of these new jobs have been created in the trade and services sectors. In this era of concern about employment levels, it is not surprising that current government policy includes incentives to promote the establishment of small businesses.

Innovations and Inventions

Individuals in small businesses have been responsible for a majority of the inventions and innovations that society benefits from today. Many of these inventions were made by Canadian entrepreneurs. Even innovations made within larger companies are often done by individuals who are rewarded for their entrepreneurial creativity. Recent studies show that small and medium-sized businesses do, in fact, invest more money in research and development as a proportion of their revenue than large firms.[50] Incident 1-5 illustrates the innovation of two Canadian entrepreneurs who developed their product after asking customers what didn't work.

Productivity and Profitability

During the twentieth century, the conventional wisdom was that the larger the organization, the greater the opportunity to be more productive and profitable. As a result, both business and government have tended to increase in size. However, the validity of this thinking has been seriously questioned in recent years and shown to be empirically weak.

Large businesses are also recognizing the gains in productivity associated with smallness. Of the eight attributes of success listed by Peters and Waterman in their study of successful corporations,[51] no fewer than six are commonly found in small businesses.[52] These six attributes are:

1. Bias for action. These organizations have found that a preference for doing something— anything, rather than sending an idea through endless cycles of analyses and committee reports—encourages new ideas and creativity. This principle seems typical of most successful businesses.

2. Staying close to the customer. Small businesses learn customer preferences and cater to them. They are generally closer to and have more contact with the customer. Larger organizations spend considerable amounts of money to maintain this closeness.

3. Autonomy and entrepreneurship. Breaking the corporation into small companies and encouraging each unit to think independently and competitively has become a strategy of many large businesses.

INCIDENT 1-5   Poptech Ltd.

Geoff Moss and David Minister, founders of Toronto-based Poptech Ltd., became innovators almost by accident. After fighting a losing battle making baseball hats and t-shirts, the pair decided to look at the point-of-purchase business, where marketers display their gum, sunglasses, chocolate bars etc. close to cash registers in supermarkets, video stores, and drugstores.

After forming Poptech in 2001, Moss and Minister quickly found that most distributors weren't entirely happy with their current suppliers. They discovered that the displays are shipped flat and assembled in store by retail employees, who felt they are just too hard to assemble, and are most often put together incorrectly.

For six months, Moss and Minister worked on a pop-up design and finally came up with a product that assembles itself. Their designs also enabled displays to be folded into smaller sizes, saving on shipping costs.

Poptech now has 10 world patents on its display technologies. KFC, Gatorade, Nestle, and Nintendo are among some of its clients. In 2004, the company achieved sales of $3.3 million, up from $1.3 million in 2002.

Source: Adapted from, "Impudence: Showing Your Elders How to Do Things Right," *Profit*, September 2005, pp. 35–36.

4. Productivity through people. Creating in all employees the awareness that their best efforts are essential and that they will share in the rewards of the company's success is a major goal of successful companies. In small businesses, owner and employees typically share in the rewards of success and the disappointments of failure.

5. Hands on–value driven. Many organizations insist that executives keep in touch with the firm's essential business and promote a strong corporate culture. A popular method of management, known as management by walking around (MBWA), testifies to the realization that management needs to be familiar with the firm's employees and the operation of the business. The successful owner-manager follows this principle faithfully.

6. Simple form–lean staff. Few administrative layers, with few people at the upper levels, is characteristic of many successful businesses. In many small businesses, employees have direct access to the owner-manager. This arrangement increases the flexibility of the organization as well as employee morale.

Flexibility

Small businesses are generally able to respond more quickly than large businesses to changes in the economy, government policies, and competition. In addition, many markets can only be served by small businesses because the areas are too small or too localized for large companies to serve profitably. This situation alone presents countless opportunities for entrepreneurs.

Canadian Ownership

The percentage of Canadian ownership, a major concern of economic nationalists in Canada, tends to be much higher in small business than in large business.[53] Of businesses operating in Canada with less than $2 million in sales, fewer than 1 percent are foreign owned.

Small Business Health as a Link to Economic Growth

Considerable evidence exists that economies that provide the most encouragement for entrepreneurship and small business have experienced the highest growth rates since the 1950s.[54] Recognition of this fact by many centrally planned economies has resulted in more encouragement of entrepreneurship, with the associated potential of rewards for those engaged in this type of productive activity.[55] This recognition may also have contributed to the dramatic changes that have occurred in these countries in recent years. One key finding of the *Second Annual Global Entrepreneurship Monitor*, which examines new and growing business in 21 countries, was that a country has a better chance of achieving economic well-being if it supports entrepreneurial activities.[56]

Social Contributions

Small business owners often have a long-term interest in the communities in which their businesses operate. As a result, they contribute to those communities in nonbusiness ways to a greater extent than an employee of a large corporation might do.

SMALL BUSINESS AND THE FUTURE

An important question for present and future entrepreneurs, as well as for policymakers, is, What effects will future changes in our society have on the small business community?

As mentioned at the beginning of this chapter, the 1970s and 1980s were a period of entrepreneurial revolution. Moreover, the late 1990s determined that change to have been a permanent adjustment to the Canadian business environment.[57] Several developing trends have potentially positive implications for entrepreneurs. At the same time, many of these trends will be advantageous only if entrepreneurs' actions are the result of insight, research, and careful planning.

Some of the more significant factors that will affect the future of small business are discussed briefly in the following sections.

Change

The world is now undergoing a period of rapid change, and this trend is expected to continue. Businesses carry out their various activities very differently today than they will 10 years from now. This means that being flexible will likely continue to be a competitive strength for the entrepreneur.

As the following sections discuss, changes are occurring in technology, consumer demographics and buying patterns, and the competitive aspects of markets.

Technology

Technology has revolutionized the activities of both small and large businesses. Computers allow the entrepreneur to manage large amounts of information as effectively as a larger business. Such advances have signalled significant small business opportunities. Financial management and accounting, marketing research and planning, promotion, and consulting are areas in which small businesses, many of them home based, have succeeded. As computer technology becomes more affordable, more small businesses will take advantage of computer applications in these areas.

New technology has also allowed small businesses to obtain subcontracts of many services from larger businesses and government organizations that are unable or choose not to carry out these activities themselves. Despite these potential opportunities, however, small businesses must be prepared to embrace new technology or face the possibility of obsolescence and lack of competitiveness.

Increased performance in the areas of customer service, marketing, and manufacturing, and improved communications are all benefits an entrepreneur can achieve through the use of technology. Incident 1-6 illustrates how new technology has revolutionized eye surgery. New opportunities are also opening up for entrepreneurs as the Internet and online services become more widely used. This information highway is capable of delivering words, pictures, sounds, and music through the use of satellite communication and compression switches accessed by computers. It also allows users to access libraries and to transmit all forms of business communication to data banks throughout the world. The opportunities for entrepreneurs in both obtaining information and marketing products and services to both domestic and global markets are limitless. Appendix 3A (see Chapter 3) provides a listing of online assistance and Internet addresses that may be helpful to entrepreneurs. More about how small businesses can utilize the Internet is discussed in Chapter 9.

Consumer Demographics and Buying Patterns

The level of retail expenditures is a key to the growth of the small business sector; a 1 percent increase in the growth of consumer spending results in a 0.7 percent increase in small business activity.[58] Canadian consumers are aging and their disposable incomes are growing.

INCIDENT 1-6   TLC Makes Perfect Better

TLC is North America's largest provider of laser eye surgery. When ophthalmologist Jeffrey Machat realized that lasers had the potential to revolutionize surgery, he quickly located business partner Elias Vamvakas and started up the venture. Correcting three common eye problems, myopia (near-sightedness), hyperopia (far-sightedness), and astigmatism has been TLC's specialty since its establishment in 1993.

Combining unfaultering entrepreneurial spirit and technology has resulted in a new use for old technology. Machat developed the Custom Lasik procedure to fix complications from previous eye surgeries and is now using the procedure to maximize the potential of the human eye. Clients willing to pay a third more than standard patient fees receive the chance to acquire vision that is better than 20/20. In fact, 20/15 and 20/10 is the expected eye enhancement for those undergoing the surgery.

TLC is targeting mainly active, athletic clients who are willing to pay about $500 per eye to achieve outstanding vision. Machat began offering the procedure in Toronto in the summer of 2000, but the rest of North America had to wait until more eye surgeons obtained the required training.

After its modest beginning in 1993, TLC experienced an astronomical five-year growth of 28,938 percent. The company has expanded from one Ontario-based laser clinic to over 200 in 2006 as well as numerous associated eye doctors. President and CEO Elias Vamvakas expects to see several clinics a year open their doors. Most of the new clinics will open in the United States, and Vamvakas expects the majority of sales to come from the new Custom Lasik Procedures.

Source: Adapted from Charise Clark, "Better Than Perfect," *Profit*, June 2000, p. 75; and TLC Vision Corporation website, October 2006.

Of particular interest to most businesses is the baby-boom consumer, born between 1946 and 1964. These people are the largest and most significant demographic group, comprising close to one-third of the Canadian population. This group has entered its highest income-earning period, resulting in large expenditures for certain types of goods and services. Although currently few in number, Canadian seniors hold close to 80 percent of personal wealth and are big spenders on travel, health and fitness products, and various services. This age group, however, will represent a large market for entrepreneurs when the baby-boom market moves into this category. In addition, the aging of the population presents implications for self-employment, as the propensity for self-employment rises with age.[59] The larger number of working women has created greater economic clout for females as well as a heavier demand for time-saving products and convenience. All demographic groups in Canada are concerned about the environment and demand quality products at reasonable prices.

Each of these demographic and demand trends represents opportunities for entrepreneurs. Many examples of how entrepreneurs are responding to these trends are presented in the profiles and incidents in this text. Markets will become further fragmented as businesses attempt to satisfy consumer wants and needs. This increase in segmentation should favour small businesses that cater to these smaller, more specialized markets.

Competitive Aspects of Markets

Three major occurrences in the past few years have affected the already intensely competitive environment that most small businesses face. The first is the North American Free Trade Agreement, which has liberalized trade among Canada, the United States, and Mexico. The second is the worldwide movement to global markets, augmented by recent developments in Europe. The third is big business's response to the growth of the small business sector.

The North American Free Trade Agreement (NAFTA). The Free Trade Agreement has gradually removed trade barriers among Canada, the United States, and Mexico, but it has also eliminated protection for certain industries. In general, Canadian small business has been in favour of the agreement because it opened up the large consumer market to the south. With the U.S. and Canadian agreement in 1989 and the addition of Mexico in 1993, market opportunities to more than 380 million consumers were opened to Canadian businesses.[60] The agreement also eliminates tariffs, offers Canadian companies much greater and surer access to government markets in Mexico and the United States,[61] and disallows prohibitions of most services.[62] In addition, Latin American countries such as Chile and Argentina are showing interest in becoming part of NAFTA as they too are working toward the elimination of barriers to trade and investment.[63] Some Canadian entrepreneurs have already successfully penetrated these markets. Many have found, however, that they must overcome other difficulties before they can effectively compete. These problems include higher Canadian taxes and distribution costs.

Free trade with the United States and Mexico has also increased competition, particularly from U.S. firms expanding into Canada. This trend has been most noticeable in the retailing industry. Although there will likely be adjustments in particular industries in the short term, the overall competitiveness of the affected industries is expected to improve.

A recent survey of Alliance of Manufacturers and Exporters Canada members indicated that a high majority of Canadian businesses have benefited from NAFTA.[64]

Global Markets. The world is currently experiencing a major shift to the globalization of markets. The erosion in domestic and international market boundaries means that smaller businesses should have increased opportunities to source, produce, and deliver to international markets. This means that the many small businesses will eventually include an international aspect in their operations. Although the trend toward trade liberalization has been evolving gradually over a number of years, the defeat of communism in the Eastern European bloc countries signalled a number of new opportunities for entrepreneurs. Consumers in these countries have an insatiable demand for Western products and services. As remaining barriers and purchasing power problems are overcome, these areas will offer huge untapped markets.

Another development that will affect Canadian entrepreneurs is the European Union (EU). The EU is an outgrowth of the six-country EEC (European Economic Community), which is adding other European countries in its own free trade arrangements and has established a single currency. Some of the Eastern bloc countries seem likely to join this union, which, although liberalizing trade barriers within the group, may continue with many restrictions to outside countries.

Perhaps the market with the most potential for Canadian entrepreneurs in the future is in Southeast Asia in countries such as Singapore, Thailand, Taiwan, South Korea, India, and, most notably, China. China's population alone of more than 1 billion represents a massive market. These areas are also increasingly receptive to Western goods and services.

Large Business Response. Small businesses have always had difficulty competing with large businesses, particularly for such things as capital, raw materials, and labour. This situation is not expected to change appreciably in some industries. Financing problems continue to plague small businesses. Despite new programs, influence over suppliers by large businesses is strong, and wage rates paid by larger organizations and government are often too high for the smaller business to meet.

In addition to the difficulty of matching wage rates, labour shortages continue. This will increase the competition for competent employees even more. Small businesses will need to find ways to retain top employees through nonfinancial methods. (Chapter 12 discusses this further.) One survey of small business owners indicated that close to half see labour shortages as a major concern for small business.[65]

One positive and often overlooked aspect is that many large businesses and government agencies are increasingly downsizing and subcontracting (outsourcing) the purchase of products and services to small business. It is estimated that close to one-half of small businesses become established through outsourcing with another business (see Figure 1-10). There is also evidence that many small businesses are joining together through such means as industry associations in an attempt to be more competitive. Such a collaborative relationship, however, often runs against the grain of the entrepreneur's independent nature.

Recently, large businesses in some industries have adopted strategies employed by smaller businesses to recoup lost market share. The adoption of entrepreneurial programs in product development (intrapreneurship), the increased attention to customer service, and the addition of some small business operating policies have enhanced the growth and success of smaller enterprises.

The Economy

The performances of many small businesses are directly related to the Canadian economy. During the recession of 2000–2001, the net number of small businesses decreased. This reflects the fact that it is harder for businesses to get established during such times, and the number of failures increases because of lower revenues. The recession of the early 1990s had a similar effect on the performance of the small business sector. There is evidence, however,

| **Figure 1-10** | **Incidence of Outsourcing in Small Business Formation** |

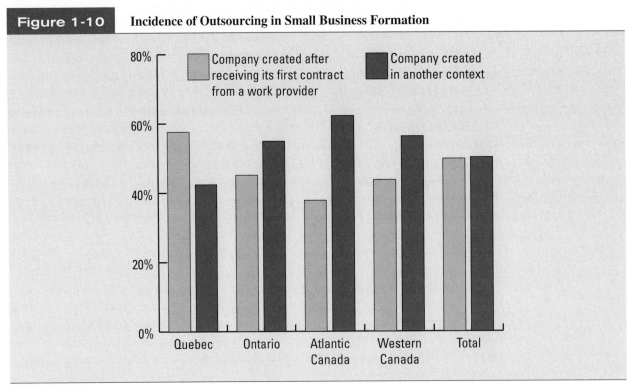

Source: Alain Halley, *A Study of the Outsourcing Activities of Canadian Businesses: A Comparison of the Country's Four Major Regions*, Ecole des Hautes Etudes Commerciales de Montreal (HEC), August 25, 2000.

that those businesses that start during a recession have a greater chance of survival than those that start during expansionary periods.[66] The current recession, the terrorist attacks, the SARS outbreak, the 2003 power failure in southern Ontario, and the BSE (mad cow) crisis are examples of events that have had a significant effect on small businesses. For example, it has been estimated that 8 percent of small businesses in Ontario and 19 percent of small businesses in Alberta were significantly damaged by the SARS and BSE problems, respectively.[67] These events have led to increased costs and decreased customer traffic for some of Canada's key industries and industrial areas. The increase in the value of the Canadian dollar relative to the U.S. dollar has also had an impact on small business. A recent study found that 30 percent of Canadian small businesses have been adversely affected (exporters) by the dollar's rise, and 20 percent of small businesses have benefited.[68] These events have affected business performance and underscore the need for careful planning. Incident 1-7 illustrates how entrepreneurs have been affected by difficult economic times. However, today's economy favours innovation and imagination, creating fertile ground for small and medium-sized businesses with new product and service ideas.

The Political Climate

Over the last decade, the political climate for small business ownership seemed to be improving. This was evidenced by attempts to reduce the burdens of paperwork and provide tax incentives to small businesses. (These efforts are discussed in detail in Chapter 13.) According to the Global Entrepreneurship Monitor, entrepreneurship is fostered as govern-

---

INCIDENT 1-7   Post-SARS Recovery Survey Report

At times, the economy is more affected by a nation's demographics and health issues than anything else. Although the SARS epidemic has definitely played a role in the travel industry, Canada's ability to attract tourists, and Canada's ability to export products, it seems the SARS epidemic has had quite an impact on Canada's small businesses in the local Toronto region.

The SARS health crisis of 2002 had many small business owners in the Toronto area worried that they wouldn't be able to continue business into the next year. The Canadian Federation of Independent Business conducted a poll to determine the effect SARS was having on entrepreneurs in Toronto. The report found that 17.9 percent of Toronto small business owners felt that SARS was having a significant negative impact on their business, while 29.5 percent felt it was having a moderate negative impact. Only 27.7 percent of respondents said it was having no positive or negative impact on their business at all. Overall, this represented a large concern for small business owners in the Greater Toronto Area.

The number one factor contributing to a decline in business according to respondents was the decrease in customer traffic. Other factors included cancellation of sales and orders, disrupted business travel and meetings, and increased costs. The sectors that were hit hardest were hospitality and personal and other services (28 percent), education, health, and social services (17 percent), and retail travel (16 percent). Small business owners also report that in response to the outbreak, they had to offer price discounts, increase their marketing and adverting, and develop a contingency plan. Small business owners feel that the SARS outbreak will continue to have an impact on their business well into the future.

Source: Adapted from Judith Andrew, "Post-SARS Recovery Survey Report," *Canadian Federation of Independent Business*, May 2003. Retrieved from http://www.cfib.ca/legis/ontario/PDF percent20Files/5422.pdf.

ments reduce state involvement in economic activities and instead promote entrepreneurship at the cultural level.[69]

The federal government has attempted to encourage entrepreneurship with incentives for immigrant entrepreneurs to enter the country. Special visas are provided for immigrants who invest in small business. These entrepreneurs have injected considerable capital into the Canadian economy.

Although there is considerable interest in government circles in reducing government involvement in business and encouraging entrepreneurial activity,[70] most small business proponents are still waiting for significant action to take place.[71] A recent CFIB report states that small businesses are especially hard hit by regulation as it takes time and money away from other, more productive, activities. This also puts them at a competitive disadvantage with respect to larger businesses that can afford individuals or whole departments devoted to regulatory compliance.[72] For example, the enactment of the goods and services tax (GST) had a much more severe effect on small businesses than on larger firms. (Chapter 13 discusses the GST further.) Small businesses state repeatedly that some of the major concerns about the business environment are high taxes, regulations and paper burdens imposed by the government, and ineffective government programs.[73] A recent study by CFIB estimates that Canadian businesses spend $33 billion per year to comply with regulations imposed by government.[74] Continued collective lobbying efforts through organizations such as the Federation of Independent Business are required to achieve a political environment more conducive to the establishment and successful operation of the small business.

The Social Climate

Society tends to look favourably on small business and entrepreneurial activities as a legitimate way to make a living. A recent Angus Reid survey indicated that entrepreneurs have the highest level of respect from Canadians (see also Figure 1-4), edging out doctors, police officers, and teachers.[75] More and more college and university graduates are beginning their careers by starting their own businesses, joining the ranks of the many people who left the once secure confines of large business to strike out on their own. Although this trend is expected to continue, adequate preparation and planning will increasingly be required to achieve success following this route. In addition, a structural shift has occurred in Canada, to a strong culture of individualism and self betterment that has resulted in a more accepted and positive attitude toward the small business sector.[76]

The onus is now on entrepreneurs as prospective owner-managers to sharpen their skills in this competitive and rapidly changing society. An owner-manager in today's world cannot survive on guesswork. Numerous programs, courses, and types of assistance are available to allow the owner-manager to acquire this training. The remaining chapters in this book cover the critical areas a prospective owner-manager should be familiar with in starting and operating a successful small business.

Summary

1. The entrepreneurial revolution is evidenced by the growing number of business establishments, employees in small businesses, government small business programs, college and university small business classes, and entrepreneurial activities of large companies.

2. Although defining a small business is difficult, having a definition is important in comparing and evaluating small business as well as in taking advantage of various lending and assis-

tance programs. Some common criteria in defining small business are gross sales, number of employees, profitability, and type of management structure.

3. Small business accounts for 97 percent of all businesses, 29 percent of gross sales, 50 percent of gross domestic product, and 56 percent of the labour force in Canada.

4. Small business can provide jobs, innovations, high productivity, flexibility, a higher proportion of Canadian ownership, and more contributions to a society.

5. The climate for starting a small business should continue to be strong, despite some competitve disadvantages.

Chapter Problems and Applications

1. Why do you think entrepreneurial activity has increased? Do you think these trends will continue? Why or why not?

2. Under what conditions would the various definitions of small business be more appropriate (e.g., the level of profit may be used by the Canada Revenue Agency to determine the small business tax rate)?

3. What is meant by the statement, "Small business is the backbone of the Canadian economic system"? Give evidence to support this statement.

4. The computer-consulting business is becoming more and more fragmented. In data processing, for example, there are hardware versus software consultants, batch versus time-sharing service bureaus, and mainframe versus microcomputer specialists. What effect does this type of industry fragmentation have on the small business community?

5. Ask three small business owners about their projections for the future of small business. What problems and opportunities do they foresee?

6. After reading Incident 1-6, discuss how each factor identified in the chapter as affecting small business in the future might have an impact on this business.

7. Write a short essay discussing your views on the future of small business given currents trends in society *and* in your geographic area.

Web Exercise

www.cfib.ca

Access the Canadian Federation of Independent Business website and read the latest report on the state of small business in Canada.

Suggested Readings

Autio, Erkko, "Gem 2005 High Expectations," Entrepreneurship Summary Report, October 25, 2005.

"Canada's Top 100 Female Owners." *Profit*, November 2003, p. 33.

Bhide, Ancar V. "The Origin and Evolution of New Business." Oxford University Press, New York, 2000.

www.mcgrawhill.ca/olc/balderson

Canadian Imperial Bank of Commerce. "Think Small—Current Trends in Small Business Economic Activity," *CIBC World Market*, March 2003.

Building on Canada's Strength: Small Business Outlook—2003. Canadian Federation of Independent Business, January 9, 2003.

"Canadian Small Business—A Growing Force." *CIBC World Markets*, September 2003.

Chrissman, James J., J. Adam Holbrook, and Jess H. Chua. *Innovation and Entrepreneurship in Western Canada*, University of Calgary Press, March 2002.

"Entrepreneurial Activity," Business Research Newsletter, February 28, 2005, pp. 6–8.

Facts About Small Business—2005. Small Business Administration, Office of Advocacy. Retrieved from http://www.sba.govt/advo/stats.

Luciw, Roma, "Canadian Small Business Owners Getting Greyer," *The Globe and Mail*, September 11, 2006.

Perspectives on Labour and Income. Statistics Canada, Fall 2006, pp. 58–62.

Self-Employment in Canada, Trends and Prospects. CIBC Economics Division, December 2000.

Small Business Profile, An Overview of Canada's Small and Mid-Sized Business Sector, CFIB, December 2005.

Small Business Quarterly. Ottawa: Industry Canada/Statistics Canada, quarterly.

Williams, Geoff. "2001—An Entrepreneurial Odyssey." *Entrepreneur*, 1999, p. 106.

Women Entrepreneurs—Leading the Charge. Canadian Imperial Bank of Commerce, 2006.

CHAPTER 2

The Small Business Decision

CHAPTER OBJECTIVES

- To discuss the advantages and disadvantages of business ownership as a starting point in making the small business decision

- To review the personal and organizational attributes of a successful small business owner

- To explain the reasons some businesses succeed and others fail

- To discuss entrepreneurial development in large business

- To identify the differences between an entrepreneur and a manager

SMALL BUSINESS PROFILE
Peter Van Stolk

Jones Soda

As he tells it, Peter Van Stolk started Jones Soda by accident. In 1987 he was operating a fruit stand in Edmonton called Urban Hand. This business eventually evolved into a western Canada distribution company handling juices and sodas. Through this experience Peter saw a market for new creative sodas that could be marketed to the 12–24 age group. As a result he established Jones Soda which markets such drinks as neon-colored pop with flavours like Chocolate Fudge, Blue Bubblegum, Fufu Berry, and Green Apple, among other lines. Van Stolk seems to have identified a niche alternative market which has company sales growing from $2.4 million in 1997 to $33 million in 2005.

A critical factor for the success of Jones' offbeat products and creative marketing activities that appeal to Generation y'ers is that he obtains market research information directly from consumers. In 1997, Jones Soda launched its own website to provide a forum for ideas. Jones fans log onto the site to chat, enter contests, listen to independent music and share movie reviews in addition to making suggestions for new flavours and products.

Peter Van Stolk acquired his unconventional business approach and understanding of the alternative market while he was a ski instructor and an avid fan of the extreme "X" Games sports. Although he only attended college business programs for a short while at the urging of his psychiatrist father, Peter said it would have helped in starting the venture if he had understood basic business rules. Despite this, Van Stolk creatively competes in the beverage business by building a relationship with his customers.

"The concept about Jones has always been that people are passionate," he says. He realizes that pop is not a necessity. Therefore he has to understand his market and through creative promotion give customers a reason for selecting Jones over the competition. Peter realizes and important lesson which most successful entrepreneurs understand. "We just can't be everybody's soda." One person plays golf; another snowboards. You have to be relevant to your customer base. I've learned that being successful is a personal thing. I've had to define what being successful meant to me. And to me, I feel successful when Jones Soda helps build a school or gives money where it's needed." In the end, he says, "success is about being true to who your are and doing the right thing."

Source: *Costco Connection*, July/August 2006, pp. 17–19.

THE SMALL BUSINESS DECISION: PERSONAL EVALUATION

In contemplating whether to start their own businesses, individuals are well advised to consider the potential consequences of such a move, both for themselves and for their families and friends. Failure to do this can lead to disillusionment, frustration, and an unsuccessful attempt to capitalize on a viable business opportunity. Frequently, the entrepreneur finds that the reasons for continuing in a small business are different from the reasons for start-up (see Figure 2-1). Therefore, a good way to begin this evaluation is to learn the potential advantages and disadvantages of starting and operating one's own business. In addition, understanding the personality characteristics and abilities required of an entrepreneur, as well as an honest self-appraisal of one's own suitability, is essential in making an intelligent small business decision.

ADVANTAGES OF SMALL BUSINESS OWNERSHIP

Running one's own business offers some unique advantages over being an employee. Numerous small business owners cite the following potential advantages:

More Personal Contact with People. Running a small business usually means making contact with a large number of people, including customers, suppliers, and employees. Those who enjoy and are skilled at working with people find such interactions the most rewarding aspect of their business.

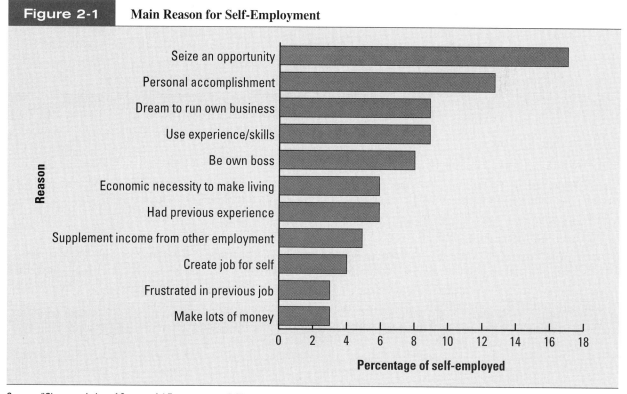

Figure 2-1   **Main Reason for Self-Employment**

Source: "Characteristics of Successful Entrepreneurs," *The Business Link* (Alberta: Canadian Business Services Centres, March 2003).

Independence.   Often, independence is the primary reason for going into business for oneself. This includes the freedom to make one's own decisions without having to ask a superior. One study of successful entrepreneurs indicated that the majority started their businesses to "control their own lives" or to "be their own boss."[1] Entrepreneurs should realize, however, that even though they own their businesses, they must still answer to customers, suppliers, key employees, and creditors. A more recent study found "independence" to be one of the things small business owners like the most about owning their own business.[2] A recent Statistics Canada study found that close to 50 percent of self-employed persons stated that independence was the number one reason for self-employment.[3] Incident 2-1 illustrates this trait. Increased independence allows many entrepreneurs to better balance work and family commitments. A recent study by CIBC World Markets found this to be important to 79 percent of entrepreneurs.[4]

Statistics Canada
www.statcan.ca

Skill Development.   Abilities in many functional areas of management are necessary in running a small business and can be developed during the process. Often, possessing such skills makes an individual more sought after in larger organizations. Today, many progressive and innovative organizations look for employees who have had small business experience.

Potential Financial Rewards.   The higher risk associated with operating a small business offers the possibility of obtaining a higher financial return. Many small businesses are profitable enough to make their owners financially independent. Note, however, that the promise of financial reward is seldom the sole motivating force behind a small business start-up.[5]

Challenge.   Many people start small businesses for the challenge and the feeling of personal accomplishment. A study of Canadian entrepreneurs' perceptions of the "ideal" work showed that work that offers a challenge is the most important factor.[6] Often these people leave larger companies because their positions lack the opportunities and challenges a small business can offer. A recent Angus Reid poll of entrepreneurs indicated that the most common reason for starting a business was "the appeal of doing something interesting and challenging."[7]

Enjoyment.   Most successful entrepreneurs enjoy what they do. In fact, entrepreneurs tend to get their best ideas from their hobbies.[8] The Entrepreneurial Research Consortium found, in fact, that one of the top motivators for starting a business was having a passion for the field.[9] This factor explains in part why financial rewards are not necessarily the prime motivation for establishing a business. Self-employed individuals also score the highest of any occupation on job satisfaction (see Figure 2-2). Indeed, more than 90 percent of Canadian

---

INCIDENT 2-1   Accidental Success

Brad Wallace, president of Nanton Water & Soda Company, has learned to navigate his own boat and not to rely on others. When asked as a young man to buy the company in 1996, Wallace took the challenge and hasn't regretted it for a moment. He had been working at Nanton Water on and off since high school, starting first as a line packer, and working his way up to manger and general manager. In 1997, Wallace was approached about taking the company public. He was told that investors had set it all up and capital would be flowing in. Well, it wasn't, and Wallace learned from this mistake. If you're going to succeed in the business world, you have to drive your own boat. Now Wallace is directly involved in raising capital within his growing business. The company has continued to branch out and market its own soda line, the New Age Division of Nanton.

Source: Adapted from "My Best Mistake," *Alberta Venture*, October 2005, p. 13.

| Figure 2-2 | **Job Satisfaction among Employees** |

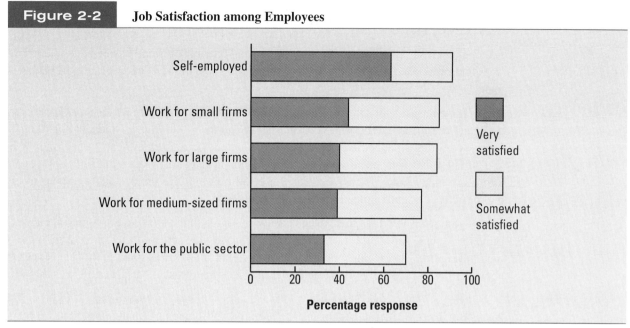

Source: Canadian Federation of Canadian Business, *Small Business Primer*, October 2002, p. 2.

entrepreneurs said they would start their own business again.[10] Further, a recent study of the Canadian Federation of Independent Business has found that flexible workplaces which often exist in small businesses are a key to workplace enjoyment.[11] (See Figure 2-3.)

| Figure 2-3 | **Types of Workplace Practices Available in Small Business** |

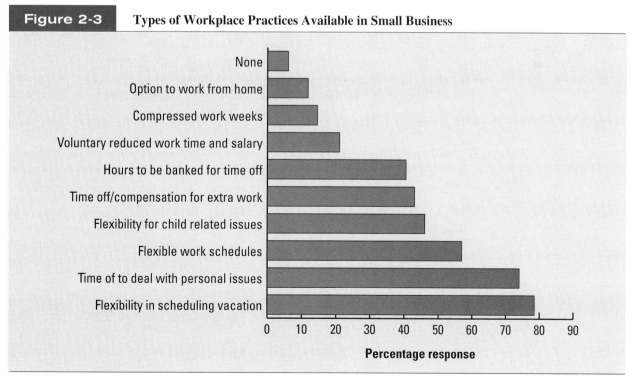

Source: CFIB, *Fostering Flexibility: Work and Family*, September 2004.

DISADVANTAGES OF SMALL BUSINESS OWNERSHIP

Although there are many advantages to owning and operating a small business, there are several often overlooked disadvantages. A discussion of some of these and other disadvantages is found below.

Risk. The failure rate of small businesses is very high. One of the key reasons for Canadians' hesitancy to start a small business is the risk of failure.[12] Bankruptcy statistics for Canada have shown that smaller firms face a greater danger of bankruptcy than larger ones.[13] It is estimated that four out of every five small businesses fail within the first few years. There are many potential reasons for these failures, but the major causes appear to be inexperience and unbalanced management.[14]

Stress. Studies show that small business owners have high stress levels, a high incidence of heart disease, and a high rate of divorce owing to the increased pressures of managing their businesses.[15] In owning a business, it is difficult, if not impossible, to confine concerns about the business to the workplace. Typically these pressures will affect one's personal life and family situation as well.

Need for Many Abilities. Acquiring the required skills, such as accounting, finance, marketing, and personnel management, is a difficult task that many owner-managers never master. This is particularly true for the countless businesses that start out very small. In these situations, entrepreneurs generally cannot afford to hire people with specialized expertise. Failure to acquire these skills, either personally or through recruitment, can seriously hinder the growth of the business.[16]

The Canadian
Federation of
Independent Business
www.cfib.ca

Limited Financial Rewards. Although the possibility of high earnings exists, relatively few small business owners become extremely wealthy. The financial rewards are often very meagre, especially during the first few years. A recent Royal Bank of Canada survey found that while 42 percent of new entrepreneurs expected their income to be higher after starting their business, only 34 percent of them achieved this.[17] Even businesses that grow rapidly are not necessarily as profitable as one might think. The Canadian Federation of Independent Business reports that, although a small number of small business owners do very well financially, the majority earn less than the average paid employee.[18] Statistics Canada also found that median incomes of self-employed individuals were only 80 percent of the median incomes of paid employees' median incomes.[19]

People Conflicts. Because owning a small business tends to require more contact with people, the potential for more conflicts with employees, suppliers, and customers arises. This factor could turn what is often thought of as an advantage into both a disadvantage and a frustration.

Time Demands. At least initially, almost all small businesses require long hours of work. Owner-managers of small businesses often have a much longer workday than if they were working for someone else. Additionally Statistics Canada reports that in 2004, self-employed men worked 41.7 hours per week while male employees worked an average of 35.5 hours per week.[20] Further, small businesses with paid help tended to work 5 to 10 hours longer per week than those self-employed with no employees.[21] The Entrepreneurial Research Consortium found that the main reason entrepreneurs voluntarily stopped operating their own business was that they were working too hard at the business.[22]

| Figure 2-4 | Percentage of Small Business Owners Who Work More Than 50 Hours/Week |

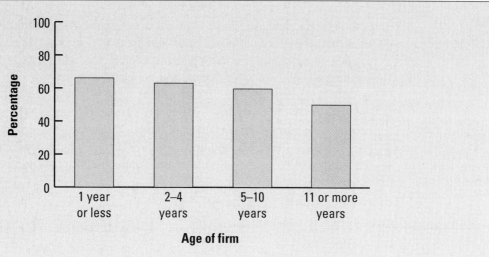

Source: *Canadian Federation of International Business Survey*, 2003; and *BR Newsletter*, vol. 3, no. 6, May 2000, p. 8.

Figure 2-4 illustrates that long hours are part of owning a small business, particularly in the early years of its existence. Another study of 650 small businesses in the service and retail sector found that the most frequently mentioned advice to potential entrepreneurs was to "be prepared to work hard and put in long hours."[23] Incident 2-2 illustrates the time demands for small-business owners.

INCIDENT 2-2   Business vs. Family

Managing both your work and family life can be difficult. This, Ted Degner knows. His goal is to eat supper with his young family every day. That's usually the only time he is able to see his children throughout the day. When the Edmonton-based division that made steel structures was going to be shut down, Degner and a co-worker bought the division and launched Waiward Steel. With only a handful of employees, Degner knew he would have to put in long hours to keep the business running. Because of those long hours, Waiward Steel is now a successful company, and Degner is able to enjoy weekends and vacations with his family. However, it didn't come without a price. Degner admits that his children rarely saw him when he started running his own company and his role of husband and father took quite a hit.

Running your own business can mean 60 plus hours a week and modest paycheques. There is no overtime, no holidays, and no calling in sick. Studies done by Jennifer Jennings of the University of Alberta have explored how entrepreneurs cope in, and away from, the office. "Those who are not letting their role as a business owner become all-consuming are faring better," says Jennings.

Tyler Heathcote, founder of Bio-Synergy Resources, advises entrepreneurs to structure their company so that it is not totally dependent on them, so if you do have to leave, the company will not fall apart in your absence. Degner agrees, and since starting Waiward Steel, he has staffed the company with employees who know the business.

Source: Adapted from Phoebe Dey, "Sorry, Hon, I have a Conference Call," *Alberta Venture*, January/February 2006, pp. 100–105.

DEMOGRAPHIC CHARACTERISTICS OF ENTREPRENEURS

Although entrepreneurs come from all demographic backgrounds, there are some conditions that seem to be correlated with entrepreneurial activity. Entrepreneurs are more likely to come from families in which parents set high standards for their children's performance, encouraged habits of self-reliance, and avoided being strict disciplinarians.[24] A recent significant trend is that the greatest growth of small business start-ups comes from those who have post-secondary education.[25] Statistics Canada reports that the education level of entrepreneurs has risen from 40.1 percent having at least a post-secondary diploma in 1990 to 58.7 percent in 2005.[26] In addition, entrepreneurs tend to be children of parents who owned their own businesses. Some of the relevant demographic characteristics of entrepreneurs are shown in Figure 2-5.

PERSONALITY CHARACTERISTICS REQUIRED BY SUCCESSFUL ENTREPRENEURS

What are the personality traits of the successful owner-manager? In his book *Peak Performers*, Charles A. Garfield estimates that 70 percent of the 1,500 peak performers he studied were entrepreneurs. These individuals exhibited some common characteristics that confirmed the results of previous studies.

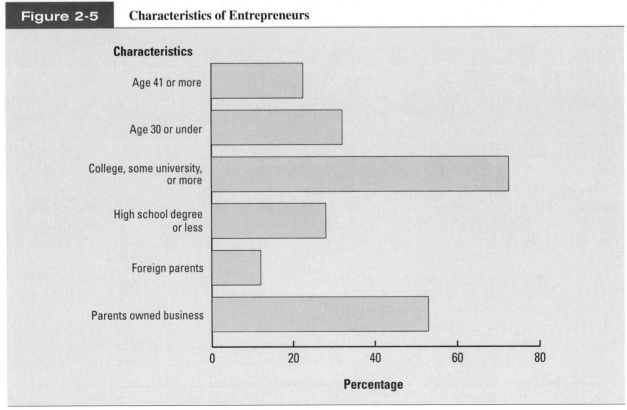

Figure 2-5   **Characteristics of Entrepreneurs**

Source: Arnold C. Cooper, *Entrepreneurship: Starting a New Business* (Washington, D.C.: NFIB Foundation, 1993); Business Development Bank of Canada Survey, 2003, and *Small Business Quarterly*, August 2006.

In discussing the following characteristics, note that Canadian entrepreneurs have many different traits and come from diverse backgrounds. Very few entrepreneurs, if any, possess all the traits discussed, but many possess at least a few of them. However, even possessing such characteristics does not guarantee success in small business.

Individuals contemplating small business ownership would do well to evaluate their own suitability to operate a small business by noting the following personality characteristics. Keep in mind, however, that being an entrepreneur is less about being a type of individual and more about possessing an attitude of "pursuit of opportunity."

Achievement Orientation. Those who place a high value on achievement, competition, aggressiveness, and hard work may be ideal owner-managers. Such people tend to be disciplined goal setters and have a bias for action. Entrepreneurs also tend to possess above-average focus and drive, as well as the initiative to make things happen. Because they are hard workers, they generally strive to maintain good health to sustain this high level of energy.

Risk Taking. As previously mentioned, the very nature of small business suggests that entrepreneurs are risk takers, although they often do not think of themselves as such. Evidence shows, however, that successful entrepreneurs usually do take calculated risks. They do not fear failure but use it as a source of motivation.

Independence, Self-Confidence, and Self-Assurance. Entrepreneurs tend to resent authority and to want to take credit or discredit for their own actions. Karl Vesper, a well-known spokesperson for entrepreneurship, states in his book *New Venture Strategies* that "the entrepreneur … has a basic human appetite … for freedom and power over his/her circumstances."[27] In fact, an American Express survey found that the number one reason that entrepreneurs don't take more time off is because they don't want to relinquish control.[28]

Other characteristics of successful small business ownership strongly correlated with independence are self-confidence and self-assurance. Often these traits are acquired through parents who were also small business owners. A recent study found that 50 percent of Canadian entrepreneurs' parents owned businesses, as was illustrated in Figure 2-5.

Innovativeness. Successful entrepreneurs tend to be creative and willing to try new ideas. They are not afraid to evaluate an idea in a nontraditional way and to ask questions such as "why not?" Such entrepreneurs are sensitive to new trends in society and potential opportunities that result from such trends. Interestingly, the major reason given by Canadian entrepreneurs for starting their own businesses was that they had found an attractive market niche and wanted to pursue it.[29] Entrepreneurs such as Michael Hancock, highlighted in Incident 2-3, tend to be oriented toward opportunity rather than managing a business.

Strong Verbal and Numerical Skills. Successful small business owners are able to communicate their thoughts well. One study of 264 Canadian entrepreneurial companies found that communication skills were judged to be the most important contributor to the success of entrepreneurs.[30] Their numerical skills aid them in solving many of the problems that arise in operating a small business.

Whether or not they have achieved a high level of formal education, successful entrepreneurs have usually acquired the necessary skills and knowledge from various sources. Increasingly, however, the educational background of Canadian entrepreneurs is rising. The CIBC Economic Analysis division recently found that the majority of the owners of small business start-ups had at least some post-secondary education.[31] Statistics Canada has also found that the growth in the number of self-employed persons with graduate degrees was higher than for other educational levels.[32]

Statistics Canada
www.statcan.ca

INCIDENT 2-3   The Brewmaster

Michael Hancock knows how to start up a business. It is the managing of the business that he is not so sure of. Hancock started his one-man brewing operation at Denison's Brewing Co. over 15 years ago, where he does everything from ordering raw materials, to brewing beer, to customer service. "There is nothing I'd rather be doing than brewing beer," says Hancock. As a former engineer and restaurateur, Hancock worked at Molson, first as an engineer and then as a production management trainee. He went from there to become the head brewmaster at Denison's Brewing Co. & Restaurant, where he then decided to start his own brewing company.

Weissbier, the beer made at Denison's Brewing Co., is sold in limited amounts in southern Ontario. Hancock doesn't actually own the brewery, or any of the equipment in it. He doesn't have the million dollar marketing campaign of the big companies so he has hardly promoted the product at all, and marketing efforts have been simple at best. However, Weissbier has proved popular throughout Ontario because of Hancock's established 15-year reputation.

Hancock wants to be able to make more beer, but his lack of management skills prevent him from taking Denison to the next level. He has a great product, but not the wherewithal to expand beyond Ontario. "I'm an engineer, a craftsperson, a details person—perhaps too hung up on the details for my own good, but I'm not a businessman."

Source: Adapted from "The Brewmaster," *Canadian Business*, Fall 2004, pp. 67–68.

Selling Skills.   Most successful entrepreneurs have above-average marketing and selling skills. Selling skills are not only helpful in promoting the business to customers but are also essential for obtaining debt or equity capital, securing suppliers, and maintaining employee loyalty. They are also very valuable in establishing networking contacts or sources of assistance for the operations. Successful entrepreneurs tend to handle rejection well, realizing that when they hear a "no," they can't take it personnally.

Problem-Solving Abilities.   Entrepreneurs identify problems quickly and respond with effective solutions. Typically, they rank above average at sorting through irrelevant details and getting to the heart of a problem. Incident 2-4 illustrates how one Canadian entrepreneur started several businesses to solve various marketplace problems.

Strategic Planning.   Successful small business owners tend to excel at setting business objectives and developing different ways of achieving them. They adapt to change easily and know their industries and products thoroughly.

Perseverance.   Because of the difficulties in starting and operating a small business, successful entrepreneurs tend to have perseverance. They do not quit amid adversity. One study found that successful entrepreneurs "average 3.8 failures before the final success."[33] Incident 2-5 illustrates one example of perserverance. Successful entrepreneurs also tend to have greater self-discipline, as they often forgo paying themselves or taking vacations in the early months of the life of the business.

To assess the suitability of their personalities for starting a small business, entrepreneurs should evaluate their own capabilities in the areas just described. Completing a checklist from a number that are available allows a quantitative evaluation of these characteristics. A simple example of one such checklist appears in Figure 2-6 on page 38. A longer, more comprehensive checklist can be found on The Business Development Bank of Canada website, entitled "Entrepreneurial Self Assessment."

The Business Development Bank of Canada
www.bdc.ca

INCIDENT 2-4   The Cable Guy

Combining a clear view of the present with a vision of the future has led David Campbell of Montreal to become one of Canada's greatest entrepreneurs. After working as a radio operator during World War II, Campbell instinctively knew that radio would spawn an information age. He also knew that the first database of music was records. He immediately saw the potential of a new technology called "long-playing records" and began importing them from the United States to sell in his small store. At the same time, automatic washing machines were becoming popular and Campbell, seeing that low-suds detergent would soon be in demand, set about importing it. Campbell could also see the limitations of TV antennas. He became a cable pioneer, forming Cable TV Inc., a company that delivered cable through underground conduits through Montreal. Campbell saw the possibilities of paging during the 1960s and started Canada's first electronic quote service, delivering stock quotes electronically to brokers.

It didn't end there. When Campbell and his wife became involved in collecting art, they acquired so many works by the Norwegian artist Edvard Munch that they eventually owned the largest collection of Norwegian art in the world. It helped that Norway discovered oil during this time and spent their newfound wealth reclaiming their country's masterpieces. Campbell thought about what he could do with something new, and then considered the benefits of the product to consumers.

Source: Adapted from Doug Steiner, "The Cable Guy," *Report on Small Business*, Spring 2005, p. 10.

INCIDENT 2-5   Amazing Turnaround

Linda Lundstrom, founder of Toronto-based Lundstrom Inc., knows the meaning of determination and perseverance. The company, which produces the latest in women's fashions, had a productive beginning. By 1997, the firm was bringing in sales of $12 million powered by the Laparka, a winter coat. However, the next three years were characterized by declining sales and growing costs, due to an eroding global economy and two warm winters. These changes saw Lundstrom owing creditors over $2 million, as well as being left with only 10 employees. The only options left were bankruptcy or rebuilding. She says, "For about two-and-a-half minutes I considered packing in the company, but that option didn't sit well with me."

Lundstrom's determination allowed her to battle back and help her firm find success. Her action plan included refinancing the ailing firm, trimming its product line, and finally overhauling its manufacturing methods to improve productivity and reduce waste. Lundstrom then called in outstanding receivables and liquidated company assets. The firm suspended production of the fall line, except for Laparka, and retailers were required to pay for orders four months in advance. Still needing capital, Lundstrom received $1 million from a private lender, which allowed her to hire 30 sewers and produce a new clothing line. Moving from batch manufacturing to lean manufacturing became the turning point of the company and inventory costs fell. After only two years of restructuring, Lundstrom's perseverance paid off when the firm finally got out of the red. In 2004, the firm achieved sales of $10.6 million.

Source: Adapted from Deena Waisberg, "Back From the Brink," *Profit*, November 2005, p. 55.

THE SMALL BUSINESS DECISION: ORGANIZATIONAL EVALUATION

It is important not only to evaluate one's personal capabilities to operate a small business successfully but also to investigate what makes some businesses succeed and others fail. The following discussion reviews what some businesses do right and what others do wrong. The potential small business owner should incorporate the things successful businesses do right and avoid the mistakes other businesses have made.

| Figure 2-6 | **Personality Characteristic Checklist** |

1. If the statement is only rarely or slightly descriptive of your behaviour, score 1.

2. If the statement is applicable under some circumstances, but only partially true, score 2.

3. If the statement describes you perfectly, score 3.

Score

1. I relish competing with others. _____

2. I compete intensely to win regardless of the rewards. _____

3. I compete with some caution but will often bluff. _____

4. I do not hesitate to take a calculated risk for future gain. _____

5. I do a job so effectively that I get a feeling of accomplishment. _____

6. I want to be tops in whatever I elect to do. _____

7. I am not bound by tradition. _____

8. I am inclined to forge ahead and discuss later. _____

9. Reward or praise means less to me than a job well done. _____

10. I usually go my own way regardless of others' opinions. _____

11. I find it difficult to admit error or defeat. _____

12. I am a self-starter—I need little urging from others. _____

13. I am not easily discouraged. _____

14. I work out my own answers to problems. _____

15. I am inquisitive. _____

16. I am not patient with interference from others. _____

17. I have an aversion to taking orders from others. _____

18. I can take criticism without feeling hurt. _____

19. I insist on seeing a job through to the finish. _____

20. I expect associates to work as hard as I do. _____

21. I read to improve my knowledge in all business activities. _____

A score of 63 is perfect; 52 to 62 is good; 42 to 51 is fair; and under 42, poor. Obviously scoring high here is not a guarantee of becoming a successful small business owner, since many other personal qualities must also be rated. But it should encourage you to pursue the matter further.

SMALL BUSINESS SUCCESSES

Despite the high risk associated with starting a small business, many small businesses operate successfully today. Numerous examples of these successes appear throughout this book in the incidents and profiles. These examples illustrate many of the characteristics of successful businesses and their owners. The characteristics discussed next are compiled from reviews of successful small businesses.

Alertness to Change. Small businesses that are flexible and plan ahead are able to adapt to changing environmental conditions more quickly and, in many cases, more effectively than larger businesses. The success of many small computer software companies is a good example. The computer industry changes very rapidly, and the new needs that emerge offer many opportunities for small business.

Ability to Attract and Hold Competent Employees. Small businesses tend to be labour intensive. Thus, the value of employees cannot be overstated. Small businesses face increasing competition from large firms and even the government in attracting and holding good employees. Those who have mastered this skill are generally more successful. Many of the owner-managers profiled in this text have retained their good employees by using creative personnel management techniques. John Volken of United Furniture Warehouse has implemented personnel policies that allow the firm to retain its best employees—and have also helped United grow into a successful business.

United Furniture
Warehouse
www.UFW.com

Staying Close to the Consumer. Business owners who have a good knowledge of consumers' wants and needs and are able to incorporate them within the operations of their companies tend to be more successful. This skill involves constant monitoring of and responding to the market. Molly Maid's success can be attributed to the owners' knowledge of consumers' wants and needs. Molly Maid, a maid service franchise, spends $80,000 a year on consumer research and is looking to expand into other areas.

Molly Maid
www.mollymaid.ca

Thoroughness with Operating Details. Successful businesses have a very detailed and highly controlled operating plan, whether in the plant or out in the market. Goals, reports, and evaluations and adjustments are made constantly. College Pro Painters' success can be attributed to the very thorough operating plan the founder, Greig Clark, set up while testing the business concept. Many successful entrepreneurs subscribe to the "management by walking around" (MBWA) technique through which they remain on top of operations details. Also, most successful small business owners have a strong technical background relating to their business.

College Pro Painters
www.collegepro.ca

Ability to Obtain Needed Capital. A potential constraint on the operation and growth of any business is a lack of funds. Businesses destined to succeed, however, often have little difficulty obtaining start-up and operating capital. Their owners are aware of the sources of available financing and are able to make an acceptable presentation of their requirements to both equity and debt sources as the situation requires.

Effective Handling of Government Laws, Rules, and Regulations. Owners of successful small businesses keep abreast of legislation and programs that may affect their operations. They realize that ignorance of certain regulations can cost their organizations not only in a direct financial sense but, and perhaps more important, also in terms of a tarnished reputation or a missed opportunity.

Entrepreneurial Success in Large Businesses

Many individuals may possess the characteristics and desire to be an entrepreneur but find themselves part of an already established company or organization. In addition, many larger organizations realize that to remain competitive, they need to adopt many of the entrepreneurial traits discussed in Chapter 1 and what was referred to as "intrapreneurial" activity.

Because attempts by large organizations to incorporate intrapreneurism are not always successful, the following suggestions have been made to increase the chances of success.[34] These were first developed by management consultant Gifford Pinchot and have been referred to as the "Ten Commandments for Intrapreneur Success."[35] Many large companies have followed these "commandments" to successfully develop and manage products and organizations.

The Intrapreneur's Ten Commandments

1. Do any job needed to make your project work, regardless of your job description.
2. Share credit wisely.
3. Remember, it is easier to ask for forgiveness than permission.
4. Come to work each day willing to be fired.
5. Ask for advice before resources.
6. Follow your intuition about people; build a team of the best.
7. Build a quiet coalition for your idea; early publicity triggers the corporate immune system.
8. Never bet on a race unless you are running in it.
9. Be true to your goals but realistic about ways to achieve them.
10. Honour your sponsor.

SMALL BUSINESS FAILURES

Despite the considerable appeal of operating one's own business, it can also be disappointing if adequate preparations are not made. This section discusses some of the causes of small business failure. It is hoped that prospective entrepreneurs will avoid making the same mistakes as they start their own businesses.

Business bankruptcies have shown a connection with the volatility of the economy and world events in recent years (see Figure 2-7). Situations such as the one described in Incident 2-6 have been increasingly common in recent years. Bankruptcy figures alone, however, do not give a complete picture of business failures. Many businesses are placed in receivership, and other business owners simply close their doors and walk away from their businesses when they fail.[36] Estimates indicate that in 2006 there were 6,747 bankruptcies,[37] but close to 100,000 businesses in Canada actually ceased operations.[38]

Businesses follow much the same life cycle as products do in that both go through start-up, growth, maturity, and decline phases. The majority of businesses that fail pass completely through this life cycle within five years of start-up. Therefore, a small business owner has little time to remedy serious mistakes. Information from Statistics Canada reveals that about 72 percent of businesses are still operating two years after their establishment, 36 percent last five years, and only one in five survives to the tenth year of operation.[39]

Entrepreneurs need to understand the reasons businesses fail so they can avoid making similar mistakes. Both external and internal factors contribute to small business failures. External factors such as economic shifts, competition, and government regulation, although not entirely controllable, may be planned for through extensive research and careful selection of the industry entered. Some of the internal reasons for failing small businesses

Statistics Canada
www.statcan.ca

Figure 2-7	Incidence of Business Bankruptcies

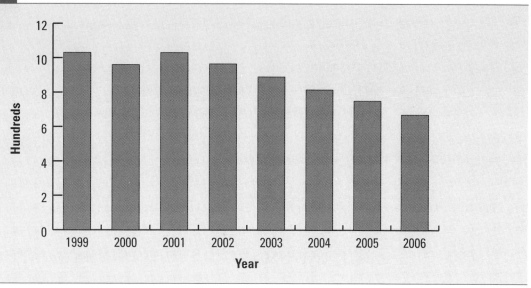

Source: *Small Business Quarterly*, Industry Canada, May 2007, p. 3.

INCIDENT 2-6   Richard Thomas

Daimler Chrysler
Corporation
www.daimler
chrysler.ca

Richard Thomas was optimistic about the new car dealership and gas station he had established in his home town of Kenora, Ontario. He had the only Chrysler dealership in the area and had just received approval from the bank to go ahead with the construction of a new building in an excellent location. He was confident that by offering gasoline at cut-rate prices, he could increase customer traffic, which would eventually lead to sales of other accessories and, of course, automobiles.

Within a few months, however, problems started to surface. The cost of the new building exceeded projections, and Thomas had to use operating funds to complete construction so that he could begin operations. This led to a serious cash shortage. He could not meet operating expenses and service the current debt, which carried a high interest rate. In addition, Chrysler Corporation was experiencing its own difficulties, which were affecting its sales throughout Canada. Finally, although many people stopped to purchase gasoline, few bought anything else at Thomas's business. As a result, a year later Thomas was bankrupt and forced to give up the business that had once looked so promising.

Source: D.W. Balderson, University of Lethbridge, Alberta. Although this incident is based on a real situation, the name and location have been changed.

include budgeting, receivables and payables management, inventory management, fixed-asset administration, high debt load, and marketing. Chapters 8 to 12 are devoted to these principles of management, because failure to follow them contributes to the difficulties unsuccessful firms encounter.

A recent study of failing Canadian small businesses sheds further light on the specific types of management weaknesses that exist. These are shown in Figure 2-8 on page 42.

| Figure 2-8 | **Common Failure Factors for a Small Business** |

1. Poor or nonexistent management information systems (inventory and accounts receivable control)

2. Poor controls on management expenses

3. Overreliance on a few key customers

4. Lack of financial skill (cash flow and profitability management)

5. Company is overleveraged (high debt) and debt is not being reduced

6. Poor cash flow management

7. Company management doesn't ask for help

Source: Julia Geller, "Failure Factors—Seven Signs Your Business Is Sinking," *Profit*, December/January 2003, pp. 31–33.

ENTREPRENEURSHIP AND SMALL BUSINESS MANAGEMENT

Up to this point in the text, the terms *entrepreneurship* and *small business management* have been used interchangeably. However, considerable confusion exists among these two terms, the types of skills they describe, and the type of training required to develop such skills. This section distinguishes between these terms. Understanding this distinction can be valuable in establishing and maintaining a business. Although they differ, both entrepreneurial and managerial skills may be necessary at different stages of the business's life cycle. This is the primary reason that both types of skills and traits were discussed together earlier in this chapter.

Entrepreneurial Skills

Entrepreneurial skills are required to start or expand a business. The specific traits that describe entrepreneurship are creativity, flexibility, innovativeness, risk taking, and independence. Entrepreneurs who have a high tolerance for ambiguity and change tend to think and plan with a long-term perspective. Entrepreneurs are generally idea-oriented.

Those who start their own businesses are known as *founders* of the business and may be found in two types. The first, sometimes called the *artisan* entrepreneur has expertise in the technical or operations side of the business. He or she may have invented the product and tends to be passionate about it and confident of its success. The second is the *promoter*, who identifies a product or service he or she feels has potential and teams up with the founder to assist with initial financing or marketing expertise. Many small businesses are established following this pattern.

Managerial Skills

The skills of a manager are useful in maintaining and solidifying the existing product or service or business. The effective manager knows how to develop strategy, set organizational goals, and develop methods for achieving those goals. Managers require skill and knowledge in several functional areas of a business, including finance, marketing, personnel, network development, research, teamwork development, and operations. Such skills are most valuable after the business has been established.

As can be seen, although the skills the entrepreneur and the manager possess differ, they are nevertheless essential for the long-run success of the business. Entrepreneurial skills

Figure 2-9	**Small Business Skills**		
Type	**Characteristics**		**Appropriate Situations**
Entrepreneurial	Creativity and innovativeness		Generating ideas or solutions to problems
	Independence		Starting new business
	Risk taking		
	Idea-oriented		Expanding or adding new products
Managerial	Develops strategy and goal setting		Reaching performance objectives
	Prefers to know outcomes of actions or activities		Maintaining control of operations
	Is a team player		
	Works through others		
	Has skills in finance, marketing, personnel, operations		

help get the business started, while managerial skills help ensure that the business continues to operate successfully. Entrepreneurial skills may be essential once again to promote the growth of the business. Figure 2-9 summarizes the distinction between entrepreneurial and managerial skills and the situations to which they apply.

A major problem associated with small business is that individuals who have strengths in both areas are rare. Because most small businesses are started and operated by the same person, skills or characteristics that the person might lack must be found in others who are hired or otherwise acquired. Failure to do so may doom the venture. A study by the Harvard Business School found that only one-tenth of 1 percent of the ideas patented and listed in the *Patent Gazette* had actually made money or could be considered successful.[40] This suggests that many of the businesses established to develop these ideas may have lacked the necessary managerial skills. Incident 2-3, discussed earlier, illustrates this problem. Part 2 of this text discusses essential considerations in starting a business (the entrepreneurial side). These chapters refer to the individual as the entrepreneur. Part 3 covers the managerial skills required for the established enterprise (the management side). It refers to the individual as the owner-manager or the small business manager.

Summary

1. There are many advantages and disadvantages to owning a small business. Some of the most common advantages are frequent contacts with people, independence, skill development in many areas, potential financial rewards, challenge, and enjoyment. The possible disadvantages include high risk, higher stress levels, the need for many abilities, conflicts with people, limited financial rewards, and time demands.

2. Certain personality characteristics are associated with a successful owner-manager. These include an achievement orientation, risk taking, independence, self-confidence and self-assurance, innovativeness, strong verbal and numerical skills, problem-solving abilities, strategic planning ability, and perseverance.

3. The major causes of business failure are generally related to incompetent or inexperienced management. Some specific areas in which difficulties are found are budgeting, receivables and payables management, inventory management, fixed-asset administration, high debt load, handling personnel, and marketing problems.

4. Large businesses must develop intrapreneurship activity to retain employees who would otherwise leave to start their own businesses.

5. Entrepreneurs are creative, independent, and idea-oriented, whereas managers possess strengths in problem solving, working with others, and developing strategies.

Chapter Problems and Applications

1. What does your analysis suggest are the most common reasons for small business failure? Investigate the causes of failure for a small business that you are familiar with or for one of the examples in the text.

2. Which characteristic of successful small business owners do you think is the most important? Why?

3. How do managerial skills differ from entrepreneurial skills? When would an entrepreneur's skills be more useful than a manager's? Why?

4. Complete the checklist in Figure 2-6. Do you possess the personality characteristics necessary for successful small business ownership?

5. What characteristics does Peter Van Stolk in the Small Business Profile have? Are these managerial or entrepreneurial characteristics? Explain.

6. Interview a local small business owner about what he or she feels are the advantages and disadvantages of small business ownership.

7. Interview a local entrepreneur, and attempt to identify his or her entrepreneurial characteristics and leadership style.

8. Select a successful small business and discuss the reasons for its success, drawing on the success characteristics outlined in the text (pp. 39–40).

Web Exercise

Look up the website for the profile at the beginning of this chapter and identify some of the reasons for this company's success.

www.jonessoda.com

Suggested Readings

"Chatelaine Top 100 Women Business Owners." *Chatelaine*, November 2000.

Csordis, Mark D. *Business Lessons for Entrepreneurs—35 Things I Learned Before the Age of 30.* Mason, Ohio: Thomson Learning, 2003.

Curran, James and Robert A. Blackburn. "Researching The Small Enterprise." Sage Publications, Thousand Oaks, Calif., 2001.

Debchuk, Don. *Think Big: Nine Ways To Make Millions From Your Ideas.* Entrepreneur Press, Irvine, Ca., 2001.

Dennis, Jeff. "Are Entrepreneurs Born or Bred?," *Profit*, March 2005, p. 20.

Johnson, Cameron and John David Mann. *You Call The Shots. Succeed Your Way In The New Age of Entrepreneurship.* Simon & Schuster, January 2007.

Miller, David C., and James D. Bell. *Profiles in Entrepreneurship.* Mason, Ohio: Thomson Learning, 2004.

Reiss, Bob and Jeffrey C. Cruikshank, *Low Risk, High Reward: Starting and Growing a Business with Minimal Risk.* Toronto: Simon & Schuster, May, 2000.

Spence, Rick. "Nine Hard Truths," *Profit*, September 2005, p. 19.

Tedlow, Richard S. *Greats of Enterprise: Seven Business Innovators and The Empires They Built.* N.Y.: Harper, 2001.

Timmons, Jeffrey A. *New Venture Creation.* 6th ed. Homewood, Ill.: Irwin, 2002.

"The Entrepreneur Test."—www.bizmove.com/other/quiz.htm.

Comprehensive Case   *Sid Stevens: Part 1*

Sid Stevens had worked for a large roofing company in Hamilton, Ontario, for the past 10 years. Although he had moved up in the organization to be a project manager, he was becoming increasingly frustrated with the negative aspects of working for a large company. Things seemed to move too slowly for Sid. He resented the close supervision that the company employed in monitoring his work, and he was often disappointed with the quality of workers assigned to his crew by the company. He preferred to work on his own and not be judged on the quality of work that others did. He was recognized as a dependable, skilled, hard worker. These qualities were instrumental in his promotion to project manager.

Although he was making a good wage, enough to help support his family (his wife Suzie also worked), Sid was certain that he could make more money if he worked on his own. Having grown up with parents who owned their own retail business, he also fondly remembered the freedom that his father had in taking time off to attend Sid's little league games and to take family trips. His father's retail business had been successful and had grown to the point where he was able to hire an assistant manager who could look after things when Sid's dad was away. Sid could not see himself working until retirement for this company or even in the roofing industry. He therefore had been thinking for some time about ideas that could make him rich and allow him to retire early and enjoy himself.

Although Sid had started working right out of high school and had no college training, he had recently taken a night course at a local college about small business management. It was because of this course that Sid had started thinking seriously about leaving his job to pursue an idea he had developed in the past year. Sid's wife, Suzie, was not as excited about his new idea after she realized that it would take much of their savings to get started with no guarantee that the business would succeed. In addition, Suzie wanted to start a family and she knew that this would affect her ability to bring in needed income while the new business was getting started.

Sid had developed a set of rails that could be easily attached to extension ladders to make them more stable and increase their safety. The rails were made of lightweight aluminum bent so that it would attach to a ladder through the holes of the ladder rungs. Figure 1-A shows a sketch of Sid's product, which he intends to call the Ladder Rail. Sid is sure that the product would especially appeal to those in the roofing and construction industry, as well as to homeowners. Sid is confident that he can make the ladder rail in his garage out of lightweight aluminum (the same material that ladders are made from) with metal cutters and benders. He has already made and tested a prototype of the product and uses it on his own ladders. Several workers have commented positively about his invention and have suggested that he start a business to market it.

Sid has shown the Ladder Rail to his boss, hoping that the company would be interested in using it. However, the boss's comment was that he should stick to roofing, not inventing. This reaction angered Sid and was a major factor in his desire to leave the company and start out on his own.

Questions

1. If Sid came to you asking for advice about whether to pursue this idea, what advice would you provide?
2. What aspects of Sid's background and personality traits are suited to owning his own business? What aspects might hinder his success?
3. Briefly discuss aspects of the product and business that may contribute to or hinder the success of the business.

| Figure 1-A | Sketch of the Ladder Rail |

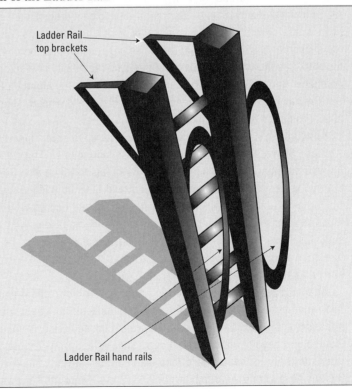

Ladder Rail
top brackets

Ladder Rail hand rails

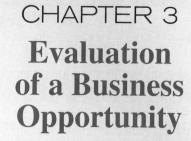

CHAPTER 3
Evaluation of a Business Opportunity

CHAPTER OBJECTIVES

- To review the nonquantitative aspects of evaluating business opportunities

- To introduce the methods by which an entrepreneur can enter a market with a product or service

- To discuss the types of information available to assist in the quantitative analysis of selecting a small business and illustrate how that information can be used

- To discuss ways that an entrepreneur can develop a strategic competitive advantage

- To provide a systematic way to quantitatively assess an industry and evaluate the financial feasibility of a specific small business opportunity

SMALL BUSINESS PROFILE

Linda Hipp

Lija Style Inc.

Linda Hipp was a business development manager for Orca Bay Sports and Entertainment, which owned NBA and NHL teams, when she arrived at the idea of providing more stylish apparel for female golfers. Being an avid golfer herself, Linda recognized what she thought was a market niche which had not yet been met.

Linda had received a marketing diploma from Capilano College in Vancouver. She knew she wanted to work for herself. In addition, her father was an entrepreneur who owned his own engineering firm.

As a result, Hipp extensively researched the statistical trends provided by the U.S. National Golf Foundation and discovered that in the late 1990s younger women were starting to play the game in large numbers. Because of this demographic shift, there was a need and demand for more fashion-forward, stylish yet functional golf apparel for younger women.

Linda quit her job at Orca Bay in 1997 and started her own company, Hyp Golf. She ventured out onto the trade show circuit marketing a small line of women's golf apparel that was influenced by European trends and West Coast style. Sales were slow for the first couple of years while the brand gained momentum. However, within three years performance improved and the company experienced rapid growth of 50 percent per year which has continued since then.

This rapid growth allowed her to expand both the Spring and Fall collections by increasing the number of styles and selection. She also began to hire key employees to help with production, finance and marketing. Linda still manages the product development and marketing departments while her partner focuses on sales. The two of them oversee the operations of the business as well as future business development.

In 2004, Linda's company went through a brand and name change due to its notable successes outside the golf industry. HYP Golf became LIJA (pr. Lee-zha), a spin on the word leisure. The new name, which offers broader appeal to both men and women will help the company's future growth into other distribution channels.

In both 2005 and 2006, Linda was recognized as one of Canada's top woman entrepreneurs. In those years, the company was voted number 3 and 5 in terms of three-year revenue increases.

LIJA clothing is currently worn by a number of professional golfers and is enjoying a rapidly expanding line, sales force and account base in North America. LIJA recently began selling in the UK, Australian, and Asian markets. However, Linda only enters each of these markets after careful research and with a well-developed marketing plan.

Used with the permission of Linda Hipp and LIJA

NONQUANTITATIVE ASSESSMENT OF BUSINESS OPPORTUNITIES

Chapter 2 discussed methods of evaluating one's suitability for small business ownership. Much of this chapter deals with methods of quantitative evaluation. This section examines some nonquantitative factors to consider when selecting a small business opportunity. These factors may influence one's selection and significantly alter the quantitative analysis.

Goals. The individual should examine his or her personal goals regarding income earned from the business. The question to address is, How well will the type of business I choose allow me to achieve not only my financial goals but also my occupational status goals?

Content of Work. The individual should assess his or her suitability for the business's working conditions. What type of work will the business involve? Will the business require hard physical work or considerable contact with people?

Lifestyle. What type of lifestyle will the business allow? Will the hours be long or concentrated in the evenings or on weekends? Will the business allow family members to be involved? Remember that most small businesses take much more time to operate than the owner anticipates before start-up.

Capabilities. In addition to the personal characteristics needed to run a small business that were discussed in Chapter 2, at least three other capabilities are required.

The first requirement is good health. As mentioned earlier, managing a small business usually involves long hours and is often physically and mentally stressful. Good physical health and stamina as well as the ability to withstand high levels of stress are all essential.

The second requirement is expertise in the fundamentals of management, including administration, marketing, and finance. Although numerous courses can provide valuable training, many successful small business managers have acquired expertise in these areas through self-education.

The third requirement is a sound financial base. Except for some types of service businesses, one can seldom start a business with less than $10,000 to $50,000. This amount may, in fact, be only the equity portion, which qualifies the business to acquire the necessary capital.

Experience. Lack of experience and unbalanced experience are two major causes of business failure. One of the best preparations prospective small business operators can make is to acquire knowledge of the type of business or industry they plan to enter. An example of such an approach appears in Incident 3-1. Another benefit of experience is the personal contacts one acquires while working in a particular industry. In addition, some entrepreneurs have received assistance from mentors provided by such organizations as the Canadian Youth Business Foundation and Women's Enterprise. For many entrepreneurs, assistance from such sources can be invaluable in successfully establishing the business.

Many entrepreneurs establish their businesses and work in them part time while holding down another job. This is an excellent way to gain experience and minimize risk. Although such an approach is not possible in some situations, many successful businesses originated from a part-time job. Entrepreneurial ideas come from many other sources. Figure 3-1 illustrates the percentages for such sources in a survey of entrepreneurs carried out by the National Federation of Independent Business.[1]

Canadian Youth
Business Foundation
www.cybf.ca

National Federation of
Independent Business
www.nfibonline.com

INCIDENT 3-1   What a Blast

Doug Adams, president of Pyrotek Special Effects Inc., has one of the coolest jobs in the world. He designs and sets off the explosions, fireballs, and laser blasts that have become a large part of pop concerts. He has handled the special effects for the Grammy Awards for the past seven years and has worked for the music industry's biggest names, such as Metallica, Beyoncé, Prince, Kiss, and Kid Rock, among others.

Adams started out in Quebec as a 17 year old in a rock band. MCA signed him to a record deal. When that didn't work out, Adams ended up working for a sound and lighting company in Ottawa. His boss was doing pyrotechnic effects and Adams found that he enjoyed the work and was good at it. Because of his musical background, he was able to detonate in time to the music and was soon in high demand. His boss didn't want to expand the business to deal with the high demand so Adams decided to buy out the pyrotechnics side of the company and start his own. Adams's career exploded as he left his hard-partying lifestyle and took a disciplined approach to his work. Now, he can pick and choose which big-name artists he will work for. His incredible talent and his ability to outwork his competitors have helped him reach the top of the entertainment industry.

It doesn't end there. Adams recently teamed up with partners to develop a planned community north of Blue Mountain. This development will see 1,000 homes built around a PGA-level golf course and several deer preserves.

Source: Adapted from Jeff Sanford, "What a Blast," *Canadian Business*, April 11–24. 2005, pp. 57–60.

Figure 3-1	**Sources of Ideas for New Businesses**

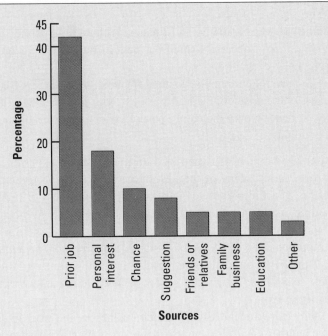

Source: National Federation of Independent Business.

BREAKING INTO THE MARKET

There are three ways an entrepreneur can enter a market. The first is to offer a totally new product to the market. This involves "inventing" a product that meets a need that is not being fulfilled. Thousands of successful products have resulted from an someone's dissatisfaction with existing or a lack of existing products. An example of this type of product appears in Incident 3-2.

Many of the fad or novelty types of products also fit into this category. The needs these types of products satisfy are often emotional or subjective rather than rational. Products such as pet rocks and mood jewellery fit this description. Several periodicals provide product ideas (see Appendix 3A at the end of this chapter). Some companies sell ideas that have received preliminary market testing.

K-tel International
www.ktel.com

A second approach is to offer an existing product to a different market or industry. Phillip Kives, founder of K-tel International, was the master of this type of approach. His company achieved success initially by acquiring products sold abroad and marketing them in North America. Another form of this approach is to offer an existing product or service in the same geographical market but to a different age or income group, or to use the product for a different purpose.

The third way to enter the market is to offer a product or service similar to those already existing in the same market. In this case, the prospective small business owner attempts to obtain some competitive advantage over the existing products or businesses in the industry to maintain viability. Perhaps the market is large enough to accommodate an additional business, or the level of satisfaction with existing businesses or products in the industry is low. Examples of this type of entry into the market include establishing a retail store that stocks brand-name, conventional merchandise and manufacturing a product so that it can be sold at a lower price. This approach is illustrated in Incident 3-3.

INCIDENT 3-2   Learning at Light Speed

For seven years, Bob Vergidis, a software development teacher, had travelled all over Canada, the U.S., and Europe working as a contract instructor for the U.S. military. In early 1998, he began thinking of a more permanent way to use the skills he had learned from years of teaching courses in software development.

His idea was to start a training centre in Edmonton where he would prepare students for the job market. Vergidis believed that there was a market for a training program that graduated students fast enough so that what they learned would still be relevant in the fast-paced computer software world.

In early 1999, after three months of advertising the program, 12 students were enrolled in DevStudios International Inc. (#18). The tuition cost each student $16,500 and the program lasted five months. In the fall of 2003, DevStudios moved to a new 3,251 square metre space in the annex of the Bell Tower, having outgrown its previous 1,657 square metres. Thirty-eight students were enrolled in three program streams; e-commerce development, e-media and design, and 3-D animation and digital compositing. Vergidis' business illustrates how identifying an unmet need in the market can be the key to a successful business.

Source: Adapted from Suntanu Dalal, "Learning at Light Speed," *Alberta Venture*, January/February 2004, pp. 58–59.

INCIDENT 3-3 What's in Store for Healthcare

Founded in 2000 by Dr. Moe Kermani, Bycast Inc. provides high-performance software for healthcare providers that allows for the storage and transmission of large volumes of data. Because the healthcare sector is shifting from paper to e-business, and because healthcare clients need to store and access data for up to 20 years, Bycast enables secure and efficient transmission of this data. The success of the company thus far can be attributed to their persistence and creativity. "We have to mitigate the perception that a smaller company like ours is a risk to clients. I think we do that by offering a capability that the larger players can't deliver right now, such as lower-cost, scalability and protection against technological obsolescence," Kermani says. The company has also joined with larger companies such as HP and IBM, which further strengthens their position on the market.

Source: Adapted from "What's in Store for Healthcare," *BDC Success Stories*, Business Development Bank of Canada, p. 3.

DEVELOPING A STRATEGIC COMPETITIVE ADVANTAGE

An important part of being successful with a start-up business is selecting an industry, a business, or a part of a business that will provide a competitive advantage. A competitive advantage exists when a firm has a product or service that is viewed as better than its competitors'. More will be discussed about the specifics of developing the competitive advantage in the next chapter, as part of preparing the business plan. However, an entrepreneur can save valuable time and energy by identifying the most appropriate area to develop that advantage by selecting (1) the right industry, (2) the right business, and (3) the right aspect of the business to focus on. A brief discussion of each follows.

The Right Industry. Some industries tend to be conducive to small business success and may provide a competitive advantage over larger businesses:

- *Businesses or industries in which the owner's personal attention to daily operations is essential to success.* In a service business, for example, the expertise of the owner-manager is a major factor in generating revenue.

- *Businesses in which owner contact with employees is important to the motivation of staff and the quality of work done.* Specialized or custom-made manufacturing processes or service businesses and other businesses in which employees have direct contact with customers fit into this category.

- *Markets in which demand is small or local, making large businesses generally reluctant to pursue them.* Incident 3-4 illustrates how such a market may offer opportunities for small businesses.

- *Industries that require flexibility.* These include industries with high growth rates, erratic demand, or perishable products.

- *Businesses that are more labour intensive and less capital intensive.* Because of the above points, a business that relies heavily on people rather than machines to provide its product or service may be easier to manage if it is small. The retail industry is a case in point.

- *Industries that receive considerable encouragement from the government in the form of financial, tax, and counselling assistance.* Much of this assistance is directed at

INCIDENT 3-4   Reeling Them In

In an attempt to get her husband to quit using her fishing gear, Terri MacKinnon started up FisherGirl, a company specializing in fishing gear made specifically for women. The rods are smaller, shorter, and lighter than traditional rods, and the reels are lighter. MacKinnon started up the company six years ago. At the product launch at Toronto's Spring Fishing Show, people were banging their heads saying, "Why didn't I think of that?"

Market research shows that various government ministries annually license about 800,000 female fishers in Ontario, and another 17 million in the U.S. Another important statistic is that almost all growth in the fishing industry can be attributed to women taking up the sport. MacKinnon forged ahead with her idea by flying to China where she found a manufacturer after two weeks. FisherGirl products will be showcased at consumer and industry trade shows. Financed with $350,000 by an angel investor, MacKinnon's product line has expanded rapidly and is now sold in WalMart and Home Hardware stores as well as online. In addition, FisherGirl has sponsored professional female anglers as part of Team FisherGirl, a member of which even won the "angler of the year" award in 2006.

Source: Adapted from Laura Bogomolny, "Reeling Them In," *Canadian Business*, October 2005, p. 16.

smaller businesses in the manufacturing, processing, and exporting industries. Such industries represent potential opportunities for small businesses.

The Right Business. To identify a business that may provide a greater chances of success for a small business, the entrepreneur should be aware of those areas that are predicted to grow rapidly in the future. The following are the 10 top Canadian business ventures for the near future as reported by *Small Business Canada*.[2]

The Best Business Opportunities for 2007:

Nutraceuticals—nutrition products

Agritourism—farm vacations and activities

Human Resources Professionals

Personal Memoirs—researchers and writers

Renovation Management

Care Consulting—for seniors

Baby Products

Doggie Daycare Facilities

Financial Planners

Personal Caterers

Source: Susan Ward, "Best Business Opportunities—2007," Small Business Canada website.

The Right Aspect of the Business. Once the industry and type of business are selected, the entrepreneur should decide which aspect(s) of the business he or she will focus on to ensure the company performs better than the competition. Natural advantages for the small business typically are flexibility, innovation, customer service, and product quality. Such aspects as price, selection, and location may also provide a competitive advantage, although they more typically more difficult for the small businesses to achieve. The entrepreneur should be aware of the aspect of the business that is the most important to the consumer and attempt to develop superiority in that aspect of the business relative to competitors. More will be discussed about these areas in the chapter about small business marketing.

COLLECTING INFORMATION

The key to making a wise decision regarding which industry to enter and the type of business to start as discussed above is the gathering and analysis of information. The more relevant the information, the less uncertainty about the results of this decision. One study showed that the overwhelming majority of small business owners do no formal marketing research, although many do informal, unsystematic information gathering.[3] Failure to do adequate or appropriate market research is frequently cited as the most common reason for small business failure.[4] Incident 3-5 illustrates how an entrepreneur was successful because he did some research before starting his business.

Some reasons entrepreneurs commonly cite for not researching and investigating a business are that it is too time consuming, too expensive, too complicated, and irrelevant. Although each of these claims has some substance, there are some simple, inexpensive, but effective methods of collecting and analyzing data available to the entrepreneur.

Sources of Information

The first thing entrepreneurs should be aware of is the many sources of information available to assist them in their investigations. Two general types of information can aid prospective small business owners in selecting the right small business. The first, secondary data, consists of data previously published by another organization. The second, primary data, is data collected by the entrepreneur. The following sections discuss both types of information in detail.

Secondary Data

Secondary data takes the form of reports, studies, and statistics that another organization or individual has already compiled. There is no shortage of secondary data to aid the entrepre-

---

INCIDENT 3-5   Epiphany at 35,000 Feet

While scribbling contracts on a red-eye flight, Ashif Mawji had an idea that led to the launch of what is now Alberta's fastest growing company. Mawji thought how nice it would be to have all his contracts in an electronic format. A larger multibillion dollar company would have thousands of contracts, and keeping track of dates and deadlines of these contracts would be made much easier with an electronic system. After checking around and making sure such a system hadn't already been discovered, Mawji gathered together a focus group, which included clients, friends, and acquaintances. He asked them what they would want in this kind of software. What he got was a list of requirements. Mawji borrowed nearly $500,000 from ISG Group Corp, and then turned to angel investors in the United Kingdom, who provided a multimillion dollar financing package.

Since its launch three years ago, Upside Software has grown from 10 employees to almost 70 and revenues have doubled that pace. Upside Software Inc. is now estimated to be worth $20 billion.

Source: Adapted from Will Gibson, "Epiphany at 35,000 Feet," *Alberta Venture*, January/February 2004, pp. 54–55.

neur, and it is usually inexpensive. A major problem, however, is finding information relevant to one's own situation. The secondary data available may be too general or may not apply to the type of business being established. Also, some reports are out of date and thus will need to be adjusted to make them useful. Such data can be updated by projecting past trends.

Secondary information is inexpensive, which makes it very attractive to the prospective small business owner. Much of the secondary information available in Canada is provided by the federal and provincial governments. However, much valuable secondary information is available from private and semiprivate sources. Appendix 3A at the end of this chapter presents a listing of those sources most relevant for small businesses. Figure 3-2 gives an example of using secondary data to begin the feasibility analysis for a business. This example uses Statistics Canada reports to estimate the market potential for a bookstore in Toronto.

In addition to obtaining published secondary information, entrepreneurs can consult several agencies for counselling in both starting up a business and ongoing operations. The most inexpensive and often most valuable source is the counselling provided to entrepreneurs by federal and provincial governments. The Business Development Bank of Canada can provide start-up counselling as well as analysis of the already operating business. The latter service is offered through the BDC (Business Development Bank of Canada) Consulting Group. The BDC Consulting Group is available to businesses and uses retired businesspeople as consultants. Incident 3-6 provides an example of how this helped a business develop a strategic plan.

Most provincial and territorial governments also employ small business consultants to assist the small business (see Appendix 3B on the website for the addresses of these agencies in each province and territory). Many of these agencies provide start-up and business plan preparation assistance similar to that offered by the federal government.

Statistics Canada
www.statcan.ca

Business Development
Bank of Canada
www.bdc.ca

Figure 3-2	**Assessing Market Feasibility of Opening a Bookstore in Toronto Using Secondary Data**

Problem   To estimate the size of the market for a bookstore in Toronto

Step 1:   Determine the population in Toronto
          Population of Metropolitan Area of Toronto   =   5,200,000
          (Source: Metro Toronto Information, 2005)

Step 2:   Determine the number of families in Toronto
          5,200,000 divided by 3 (average size of
          families in Ontario)
          (Source: Statistics Canada Census information)   =   1,560,000

Step 3:   Estimate total bookstore sales for Toronto
          1,560,000 × $300 (average household expenditures
          on books and magazines)   = $468,000,000
          (Source: *Average Household Expenditures*, 2004,
          Market Research Handbook, 2005)

This shows that a total of $468,000,000 could be expected to be spent in
the Toronto area in bookstores.

Source: *Market Research Handbook,* 2005, Statistics Canada; Metro Toronto Information, 2006; and *Average Household Expenditures, 2005*, Statistics Canada.

INCIDENT 3-6   Strategic Planning

Jim Ochitwa and Mark Bishop know that navigating a company definitely requires a good map. Ochitwa and Bishop are owners of Calgary-based Maryn International Ltd., a leading developer and manufacturer of industrial lubricant additives and finished fluids for all types of equipment. Thanks to BDC Consulting, the company now has a five-year strategic plan in place that will allow the firm to market a full range of products and increase sales. BDC Consulting help the owners to detail clear marketing strategies as well as address target areas such as cash flow, distribution, and succession. "The consultant helped us see where we were performing well and not so well. It's very useful to have an external person pushing you further," says Ochitwa. Their strategic plan allowed Maryn International Ltd. to grow, using a systematic business approach.

Source: Adapted from "Strategic Planning Puts Maryn International Ltd. On the Road to Success," *BDC*, p 4.

Another potentially valuable source of assistance comes from universities and colleges. Many universities have student consulting programs designed to aid the small business owner. Using the expertise of graduating or graduate students, these programs can assist in preparing feasibility analyses or evaluating a business problem for a minimal fee, usually the cost of materials used. (Appendix 3C on the website lists universities in Canada that have such programs; several colleges offer similar services.)

Other helpful counselling sources are lawyers, accountants, or bankers. Some of these sources may be more expensive than government services, however. Numerous consulting firms also specialize in small business operations. Industry Canada has found that small businesses that utilize professional advisors experience sales of 76 percent more than those who don't.[5]

An informal source of valuable information for the entrepreneur that is gaining popularity includes blog websites. Networking with other entrepreneurs on these sites can be an excellent source of ideas and information. Similarly, an increasing number of entrepreneur forums and speaker series such as entrepreneur "igniter" meetings are held in many cities.

In addition to the types of assistance just described, another concept appears to promise considerable help in establishing new enterprises: the incubation centre. The incubation centre consists of an organization—usually a municipal or provincial agency—that provides essential services for new small businesses, either free or at minimal cost. Office space, secretarial services, computer capabilities, and financial and business counselling are examples of these services. One study found that eight out of ten businesses nurtured by incubators were still operating after five years.[6] Incident 3-7 illustrates how business incubators are assisting new businesses and providing employment for Canadian youth.

There are currently more than 500 incubators operating in North America.[7] These include more than 1,000 incubator tenants, and estimates indicate that new incubators are opening at a rate of one per week.[8] In Canada, more than 40 business incubation centres operate across the country,[9] although this recent growth may be difficult to maintain because of cutbacks in funding from government sources. Business incubators allow the small business community to work, individually or collectively, through the chamber of commerce and with municipal (city or town) governments, provincial or territorial governments, universities, and colleges. Statistics show that businesses receiving assistance from incubator centres have a 30 percent greater chance of success.[10] Another organization that helps start-up companies is the Community Futures Development Corporation. This is a not-for-profit organization founded

INCIDENT 3-7   Garrison Guitars

Chris Griffiths has built a solid guitar manufacturing business, but problems such as the rising dollar may cause the booming business to hit a sour note. Garrison Guitars, located in St. Johns, Newfoundland, revolves around the company's patented Griffiths Active Bracing System (GABS), which has revolutionized the process of making acoustic guitars. His high-tech system is a way to make better guitars for a lot less money because it replaces the three dozen wood stabilizing components with one composite molding. This cuts off about two and a half hours of the manufacturing process and makes the guitar sound better and last longer.

But Griffiths wouldn't be where he is today without the help of the Genesis Centre, a public/private sector incubator for high-tech startups in St. Johns. The Genesis Centre provided him with access to marketing, financing, and management expertise in addition to pairing him with a mentor.

Because Garrison Guitars exports about 97 percent of its product to the U.S., the rising dollar has become a concern for the company. However, Griffiths' business is not alone, as almost 30 percent of Canadian businesses share this concern. To combat the rising dollar, Griffiths has made productivity improvements as well as off-shoring production to other countries such as China.

Source: Adapted from Andy Holloway, "Between the Rock and a Hard Place," *Canadian Business*, January 2005, pp. 69–71.

in 1985 with funding from the federal government and several other public and private agencies. Community Futures offices are located throughout the country in rural communities. They assist entrepreneurs and small businesses by offering businesses grants and loans, as well as training, mentoring, and planning services. Additional components of the program include start-up grants and loans, business plan development, and export support. Incident 3-8 describes how this worked for an Ontario business.

Primary Data

Primary data is information collected through one's own research. Although usually more costly to obtain than secondary data, it can be more relevant to one's business and more current. Primary research is essential if secondary sources do not provide the information

INCIDENT 3-8   Braver Than the Banks

When Michelle Pammenter, president of Jelly Bean Garment Company, wanted to start her business, she went to various banks looking for a loan. However, she found the banks less than welcoming and even though she had a detailed plan outlining her high-end baby products, they turned her down. It was then that the Community Futures Development Corporation stepped in with a business start-up grant. To receive it, Pammenter had to present her business to the volunteer CFDC board and is also required to provide the board with monthly status reports on her business.

Pammenter also took several business courses trough the agency to top up her business skills. The agency also stepped in to help when Pammenter wanted to expand her business and the banks once again turned her down. Just as Pammenter predicted, The Jelly Bean Garment Company is turning a profit, thanks to the start-up help from CFDC.

Source: Adapted from Paul Lima, "Braver Than the Banks," *The Costco Connection*, July/August 2004, p. 24.

required for the feasibility analysis. It may also be beneficial to supplement the information obtained from secondary sources. Despite these advantages, small business owners have traditionally hesitated to do much primary research because of their lack of knowledge about how to do it and its relatively high cost.

Some research methods, however, are not complicated and can be of great value to the entrepreneur in evaluating the feasibility of a potential business opportunity. Three general methods that can be used to collect information through primary research are observation, surveys, and test marketing.

1. Observation. Observation involves monitoring the who, what, where, when, and how relating to market conditions. For the small business, this method might involve observing auto and pedestrian traffic levels or customer reactions to a product, service, or promotion. It may also entail simply observing sales or expenditure levels. The observation method may be fairly expensive, as it requires that time be spent monitoring events as they occur. Another limitation of observation research is that it only allows one to make inferences about the reasons people respond in certain ways. There is no two-way interaction with the subject of the research that might shed light on such motivations.

2. Surveys. To obtain more detailed information from potential consumers and to better understand their motivations in purchasing a product or service, a small business owner can carry out a survey. The entrepreneur should clearly define the objectives of the research before questionnaire construction and ensure that each question addresses one of the objectives. Usually, it is not possible to survey each potential customer or the total market; therefore, only a part of the market is surveyed. It is essential, however, that the responses obtained be representative of the total market. Figure 3-3 illustrates a simple but accurate method for determining a representative sample for a research project for a small business. Such a survey might give the entrepreneur a general indication of the extent of demand for a new business. Of course, more detailed research should be carried out before a decision

Figure 3-3	Calculating a Representative Survey Sample for a Small Business

Step 1: Use the following chart to determine the number of surveys that should be completed to achieve a 95 percent confidence level at .05 degree of precision.

Population Size	Sample Size
50	44
100	80
500	222
1,000	286
5,000	375
10,000	385
100,000 and over	400

Step 2: Choose the respondents. If a phone survey is being conducted, there are two ways to choose the respondents. The first is to use the phone book and choose every *n*th individual. The second is to use a random number generator to come up with the phone numbers. Both of these methods have advantages and disadvantages, but both allow the surveyor to obtain a representative sample.

to start the business is made. Many businesses have failed because the owners acted on their own feelings or the opinions of a few acquaintances. In some cases, these responses do not represent the opinions of the total market. Incident 3-9 illustrates how a lack of representative information from the market created a difficult problem for a small agricultural machinery manufacturer.

Occasionally, through design or necessity (e.g., limited funds), a nonrepresentative group of people is surveyed as part of the primary research project. This could involve surveying only experts or knowledgeable people in an industry rather than an equal cross-section of consumers. This method is also often used in surveying shopping mall customers. The most obvious drawback is that the findings may not be representative of the total market.

Three types of surveys are used to collect market information: mail surveys, telephone surveys, and personal interviews.

Mail and Internet Surveys. These surveys are most appropriate when

- Only a small amount of information is required.

- Questions can be answered with "yes–no" or "check the box" answers, or brief responses.

- A picture of the product may be required.

- An immediate response is not required.

One problem with mail and Internet surveys is their poor response rate—typically well under 50 percent—and the lack of control over who fills out the questionnaire. Also, the preparer needs to make sure that the survey is not too long or too complicated. Figure 3-4 on page 60 shows such a survey, carried out for a small business to assess initial demand for a Japanese restaurant.

Telephone Surveys. Telephone surveying has become the most popular survey method in recent years, most likely because of its low cost and quick response time. However, it is even more restricted than a mail survey in the amount and detail of information one can obtain.

INCIDENT 3-9   Kirchner Machine Ltd.

Kirchner Machine Ltd. is a well-known farm machinery manufacturer in Lethbridge, Alberta. It manufactures many successful tillage and haying implements and has built a solid reputation as a well-run small manufacturer in the farm machinery industry. In 1991 several farmers expressed concern to Kirchner about their inability to handle and transport large, round hay bales. These bales, commonly weighing about 500 kg, had become very popular with farmers and ranchers throughout North America. However, they had to be moved to the stack or a larger truck one at a time, which was quite time-consuming.

In response to this concern, Kirchner designed and manufactured a bale hauler that could be pulled six at a time by a tractor. Named the Big Bale Fork, it was expected to be another successful product in Kirchner's line. Unfortunately, sales were disappointing. Although those who purchased the Big Bale Fork were satisfied, sales were too few and far between. One reason was that the firm had not carried out market research to assess total market potential for the product. Those who had purchased the hauler were too small a part of the market to make it economically feasible. Those who had suggested that Kirchner manufacture the Big Bale Fork were unrepresentative of the total market.

Source: D.W. Balderson, University of Lethbridge.

| Figure 3-4 | **Mail or Internet Questionnaire: Japanese Family Restaurant** |

1. Approximately how often does your family eat at a restaurant or dining lounge in the city of Oakville?*

    a. _____ Less than once per month
    b. _____ Once per month
    c. _____ Once every two weeks
    d. _____ Once per week
    e. _____ Two to three times per week
    f. _____ More than three times per week

2. Approximately how much do you normally spend per family when you eat out at a restaurant or dining lounge?

    a. _____ Less than $25
    b. _____ $25–$50
    c. _____ $50–$75
    d. _____ $75–$100
    e. _____ Over $100

3. Are you familiar with the difference between Japanese and Chinese cooking?

    _____ Yes
    _____ No

4. If a family restaurant specializing in Japanese food was opened in Oakville, would you

    a. _____ probably never go?
    b. _____ definitely try it?
    c. _____ patronize it regularly if food, service, etc., were adequate?

5. Where would you prefer such a facility to be located?

    a. _____ Downtown
    b. _____ West Oakville
    c. _____ South Oakville
    d. _____ North Oakville
    e. _____ Does not matter

Thank you very much for your time and cooperation.

* Name of the city has been changed.

Source: Academy Management Services, Lethbridge, Alberta.

The telephone interviewer should follow a survey guide to ensure consistency. Figure 3-5 offers an example of a typical phone survey guide. As with the example of the mail survey, this phone survey might give the entrepreneur an indication of the acceptance of the concept. Further research and analysis would be required before a decision could be made.

| **Figure 3-5** | **Telephone Questionnaire Guide: Sporting Goods Rental Store** |

A sporting goods store, located in a city of approximately 65,000 people, wanted to start renting summer sports equipment. The following survey was designed to determine consumer demand for such a rental business.

Survey number: Phone number:

Hi, my name is _____; I am presently conducting a survey to determine people's summertime leisure activities in the city. A few moments of your time to answer the questions would be greatly appreciated.

1. Can you tell me if you participate in any of the following activities during the summer? List the equipment…and the responses.

2. A lot of people ski in the winter because ski equipment can be rented at a fraction of its retail price. Are there any summer activities you would participate in if the equipment was available on a similar basis?

   a.

   b.

3. Are you older than 18 years of age?

   Yes (   ) No (   ) If no, please record the age and stop doing this survey.

4. Would you consider renting the following equipment if available at reasonable prices?

   Please indicate if you have the item.

   List equipment

5. Male (   ) Female (   ) Fill in for all respondents

6. Age: 18–25   (   )

                 26–35   (   )

                 36–50   (   )

                 > 50   (   )

7. Income: Less than $20,000   (   )

                 $20,000–$40,000   (   )

                 $40,000–$60,000   (   )

                 $60,000+   (   )

Thank you very much for participating in this survey.

Source: Student Consulting Project, University of Lethbridge.

Personal Interviews. The most expensive type of survey is the personal interview. Although this method generally costs more and requires greater expertise, it is the best approach for obtaining more detailed information and opinion-oriented responses. Since the number of people surveyed typically is smaller than in mail or phone surveys, this method is more suitable for interviewing knowledgeable people in an industry as opposed to surveying a cross-section of potential consumers. This type of research is known as customer focused research, or CFI. Personal interviews may involve surveying one individual at a time or, as many companies do, surveying several people together in what is called a focus group. The personal interview may be used for purposes such as testing a new product concept or advertisement or evaluating a company's image.

Entrepreneurs are often unsure about what types of questions to use in a survey. Some areas in which information should be obtained are the following:

- Respondents' reactions to the product or service
- The price respondents are willing to pay for the product or service
- Respondents' willingness to purchase the product or service (answers to such questions are often overly positive and should be adjusted downward by as much as 20 percent)
- Frequency of purchase
- Level of satisfaction with current product or service
- Demographic characteristics of respondents

3. Test Marketing. Test marketing involves an attempt to simulate an actual market situation. For an inventor, it may mean letting a number of people try a new product and then finding out their reactions. For a business, it may mean marketing a product on a limited basis and observing sales levels, or surveying to find out the level of satisfaction with the product or service. This method is fairly costly in that the product must be developed and marketed, albeit on a limited basis. The main advantage of experimental research, or test marketing, is that it measures what people actually do, not just what they say they will do, concerning the product. Small businesses have successfully used this method when taking prototype products to tradeshows, exhibitions, or potential customers to assess potential acceptance. Test marketing is especially appropriate where little capital investment is required, such as with a small service business or online marketing to other businesses and consumers.

The proper collection of secondary and primary data can be invaluable to entrepreneurs as they assess business opportunities. It can provide a base of data that, if analyzed correctly, may allow for the capitalization of a successful opportunity or the avoidance of a disaster. The types of market research just described require an investment in time and money, but many successful entrepreneurs are convinced research is a worthwhile investment.

Although owner-managers often use these information collection methods before starting their businesses, they can and should use them on an ongoing basis after the businesses have been established to stay abreast of changes in market conditions. Many successfully established businesses have become complacent and, as a result, have eventually failed because they lost touch with consumers or market conditions. To avoid this, the small business should set aside the effort and money required to regularly collect and use relevant market information. Chapter 8 discusses this subject further.

QUANTITATIVE ASSESSMENT OF BUSINESS OPPORTUNITIES

Preparing the Feasibility Analysis

Once the entrepreneur has collected the relevant information about the market, the next step is to use this information as quantitatively as possible to assess the financial feasibility of the proposed venture. The purpose of this assessment is to determine whether the business will earn the income the entrepreneur desires. The financial feasibility analysis as described in this section is most appropriate for starting a new business from scratch, but much of it could be applied to the purchase of an existing business or the operation of a franchise. The first step in doing a feasibility analysis for a small business is to prepare a sales or revenue forecast. This is a very important estimate as it will become the foundation for the projected income and cash flow statements, which will ultimately indicate the feasibility of the venture.

There are two methods of forecasting sales. Both secondary and primary information may be required to follow either method. The first is the build-up method. To use this method of forecasting, the entrepreneur identifies each target market and estimates potential daily sales to each. This estimate may be obtained by observation of similar businesses, from industry experts, suppliers, or government sources. The daily sales estimate is then projected to compose an annual amount.

The second method of sales forecasting is referred to as the breakdown method. When choosing this method, the entrepreneur may not be as familiar with the specific target market and so begins with the total population and "breaks down" this large market by eliminating demographic or buyer markets who would be less likely to purchase. Figure 3-2 showed an example of a breakdown method of sales forecasting using secondary information only.

The procedure and example that follow are more similar to the breakdown method of sales forecasting than to the build-up method. Keep in mind that the following and accompanying example is simplified to allow the entrepreneur to follow more easily. Difficulty in obtaining relevant data and rapidly changing market conditions can increase the uncertainty of the result.

Three steps are required to estimate the financial feasibility of a proposed business venture. The first step is to determine potential revenue (demand) for the total market. The second is to estimate the share of total market revenue that the new business might obtain. The third is to subtract the associated expenses from the revenue estimate to arrive at a projected estimated net income for the prospective business. A more detailed explanation of the steps in calculating a feasibility analysis is presented next. A detailed example of such an analysis is given in Figure 3-7 (see pages 68–72). In carrying out the feasibility analysis, one should remember to be conservative with all estimates. See Incident 3-10 on the next page for an illustration of a small business that failed to do this.

Step 1: Calculate Market Potential

The purpose of this step is to arrive at a dollar or unit sales estimate for the total market. It may involve three substeps:

1. *Determine the market area and its population.* Delineate the geographic area or target market the business will serve. This can be done by obtaining a map and marking off the size of the market. Then estimate the population (numbers) within that market that might conceivably purchase the type of product or service to be offered. This process yields an estimate of the size of the target market.

2. *Obtain revenue (sales) statistics for this market area for the product type or service.* Usually federal, provincial or territorial, or municipal governments have this information for many standard types of products or businesses. For example, Statistics Canada publishes retail expenditure and manufacturing data for many products and services. If total revenue or sales figures are not available for the proposed type of business or product, but per capita or per family expenditures are obtainable, simply multiply this figure by the population estimate obtained in substep 1 (population of market $\times$ per capita expenditures).

Statistics Canada
www.statcan.ca

INCIDENT 3-10   Crazy Plates

When Crazy Plates frozen meals flopped, their inventors started over, but this time they used a recipe. Crazy Plates had high expectations, with the meals being an extension of two of the most successful Canadian cookbooks ever—*Crazy Plates* and *Looneyspoons*, written by Janet and Greta Podleski. The team behind the meals also included David Chilton, author of *The Wealthy Barber*.

Chilton and his team had made the all-too-familiar error of creating a product for themselves rather than for the researched market. "Almost all of them (problems) came about because we didn't research our market," says Chilton. The meal kit could feed a family of about four or five for about $14. However, research could have told them that 85 percent of frozen food is marketed to feed two people for less than $10. The packaging was also a problem because the boxes contained too much visual clutter and had no wax coating, making the box look cheap and fragile.

The team decided to start again, and, using market research, reformulated the meals and redesigned the packaging. Chilton also created a 24-page business plan that outlined what exactly went wrong. After only a year, the sales of Crazy Plates were up 400 percent over those of the old product. "The real lesson is you can't replace solid research with pure instinct," says Chilton.

Source: Adapted from Lee Oliver, "Appetite for Resurrection," *Profit*, November 2003, pp. 19–20, and Crazy Plates website, 2006.

If the product or service is new and no secondary data are available, use secondary data about a similar product. If there is no similar product, primary research—in the form of a survey, for example—may be used to assess consumer acceptance of the concept. If the results of such a survey indicate that a certain percentage of the market shows a purchase interest, multiply that percentage by the size of the market to obtain the market potential estimate.

Many entrepreneurs have started Internet businesses. Obtaining an estimate of market potential for this type of business may be difficult because many markets are untested and hard to define. There are some methods, however, that can be helpful in determining the size of the market for an Internet business. Data are emerging which indicate Internet usage for various types of products and services. This information can be used to help attain market revenue estimates as described above, although the geography for the market size may be more difficult to estimate. Figure 3-6 provides an example.

3. *Adjust the market potential total as necessary.* If one is able to obtain actual revenue statistics for the market, usually the only adjustment needed is to update the data. As mentioned previously, secondary data are typically a year or two out of date. A simple way to update sales and expenditure data is to increase the amount of sales by the annual rate of inflation for the years involved. This might also include a forecast of trends that will affect demand in the future. Such trends could be included in the estimate.

If national averages of per capita expenditures are used, adjustments for local shopping patterns must be made. A common adjustment in this regard is to adjust for those living in the market area who purchase outside the market, and vice versa. For example, if it is estimated that 20 percent of the market buys the product or service outside the market area, reduce the market potential by 20 percent.

Projections should include one-year and five-year estimates to reflect trends that may exist in the industry. Projections should also include trends with respect to growth of the competition that might affect future market share.

Figure 3-6	Estimating Market Potential for a Ski Resort Booking Website in British Columbia

Background: An entrepreneur wants to estimate the market potential for a website that provides information and booking services for the 60 ski areas in the province of British Columbia.

Step One: Using the Internet, the B.C. Skiers Profile 1993–94, and Ski Market Study 1997 were located. These studies indicated that 4.5 million skiers visited ski areas in B.C. annually.

Step Two: Using the Internet, the Travel Activities and Motivation Study (Government of Ontario) indicates that 78 percent of U.S. and Canadian skiers and snowboarders used the Internet for research and 36 percent of those used the Internet to book their latest trip.

Step Three: Using the information collected in steps one and two above, the flowing estimate can be made.

$$4,500,000 \times 78\% \times 36\% = 1.26 \text{ million}$$

The market potential estimate is 1.26 million customers. Of course, adjustments should be made to this estimate to update the data, using skiing trends as well as adjustments to reconcile natural and B.C. skiing differences. However, the estimate provides a good starting point for the analysis.

Step 2: Calculate Market Share

The purpose of this step is to estimate the percentage of the total market potential the proposed business will obtain. Because the method of calculating market share differs significantly depending on the type of business, market share calculations for retail, manufacturing, and service firms are illustrated separately.

It is important to remember that the market share calculations as described below are preliminary estimates only. They serve as a simple starting point from which significant adjustments must be made. Some of the required adjustments may be difficult to arrive at due to lack of current information and their possible subjective nature. Collecting the information to make these adjustments typically requires primary information with qualified sources, such as industry experts and personal experience. The amount of the required adjustment may also be difficult to establish. However, the fact that one arrives at a quantitative and objective initial market share percentage and recognizes that appropriate adjustments are necessary will lend confidence to the entrepreneur and credibility to the outside observer.

Retail Firm

1. *Estimate the total amount of selling space in the market devoted to the merchandise the new business will sell (usually in square feet or metres).* This involves taking an inventory of space of competing stores (specialty and department stores) devoted to this product. This estimate may be obtained informally by observation or by asking the owners. In some areas, secondary information about retail selling space may be available through the municipal or city government or department.

2. *Estimate the size of the proposed store (in square feet or metres).* It is likely that the entrepreneur will have a good idea of the size of the proposed store. The actual size, of course, may depend on the availability of outlets.

3. *Calculate the market share based on selling space as follows.* The information collected in steps 1 and 2 is now integrated in the following formula:

$$\frac{\text{Proposed store selling space}}{\substack{\text{Total market selling space} \\ \text{(including proposed store)}}} = \text{Percentage market share}$$

4. *Make adjustments to reflect any competitor strengths and weaknesses regarding the proposed store.* Typical adjustments might include the following:

   a. Decrease percentage share if the competition has a better location, is larger in size, or has considerable customer loyalty. A decrease in the percentage should also be made, because the proposed store is new and will take time to build customer loyalty.

   b. Increase percentage share if the proposed store will offer unique products, services, location, advertising, or other advantages over the competition.

   The amount of the adjustments may be arbitrary and somewhat subjective, but typically they are fractions of a percentage of the market share.

5. *Multiply the revised market share percentage by the market potential estimate obtained in step 1.* The result is a dollar revenue estimate for the proposed business for the first year of operations. By applying market trends to this figure, a one- to five-year estimate can be obtained, if required.

Manufacturing Firm

1. *Estimate the total productive capacity in the market for the product to be manufactured.* Typically this will be calculated in units, but it may be in dollars. This will involve estimating the production size of competitors (both domestic and foreign).

   If the product is a new innovation and no competition exists, market share obviously is the same as the market potential calculated previously.

2. *Estimate the productive capacity of the proposed manufacturing plant.*

3. *Calculate the market share based on productive capacity.* The information obtained in steps 1 and 2 is integrated into the following formula:

$$\frac{\text{Production capacity of proposed business}}{\substack{\text{Total production capacity} \\ \text{(including proposed business)}}} = \text{Percentage of market share}$$

4. *Make adjustments to reflect competitive strengths and weaknesses that the proposed plant may possess.* The market share percentage estimated in step 3 will likely need to be adjusted. The strengths and weaknesses of competitors should be determined and compared with the proposed business. Often primary research may be required to obtain this type of information.

   Generally, a higher market share can be obtained in industries in which competitors are smaller in size, the product can be differentiated from competitors' products, and primary research shows a particular level of dissatisfaction with existing products.

   Market share will tend to be smaller if the industry is made up of a few large and powerful competitors who hold key contracts or where consumer satisfaction with the existing product is determined to be high.

   Even though the existing market may look formidable, some sectors of the economy look favourably on purchases from small businesses. The federal government, for example, is a very large potential purchaser that should not be overlooked. These types of markets are discussed in Chapter 8. For a manufacturing firm, success at obtaining key contracts may provide the certainty required to calculate the market share and bypass some of these calculations.

5. *Multiply the estimated market share percentage by the market potential estimate obtained in step 1.* This figure projects estimated dollar sales for the first year of operations. As in the retail example, industry trends can assist in estimating this figure for more than one year.

Service Firm

1. *Estimate the total capacity of the service available in the market area.* The base used to calculate capacity will vary depending on the type of service being offered. For example, restaurant capacity may be measured by number of seats, tables, or square footage; motel capacity by number of rooms; and beauty salon capacity by number of employees or number of workstations. It is important to determine which base most accurately reflects the service capacity. This estimate can be obtained by observing existing businesses or talking to owners.

2. *Estimate the service capacity of the proposed business.* This involves projecting the size of the proposed business in terms of service capacity.

3. *Calculate market share based on the capacity base.* The information obtained in steps 1 and 2 is integrated into the following formula:

$$\frac{\text{Proposed business service capacity}}{\substack{\text{Total production capacity} \\ \text{(including proposed business} \\ \text{service capacity)}}} = \text{Percentage of market share}$$

4. *Make adjustments similar to those made for a retail store.* The adjustments in the service industry tend to be more significant than in retailing. The opportunity to differentiate from competitors in the service industry is much greater than in retailing, which tends to deal with more standardized products. Therefore, the percentage adjustments may be larger for service industry market share calculations.

5. *Multiply the estimated market share percentage by the market potential estimate obtained in step 1.* This figure projects estimated dollar sales for the first year of operations. As in the retail example, industry trends can assist in estimating this figure for more than one year.

Step 3: Calculate Net Income and Cash Flow

1. *Using the market share revenue figure obtained in step 2 as the starting point, calculate the expenses expected to be incurred for the business.* Most of these figures should be obtained by checking with suppliers and other similar businesses. However, some secondary sources, such as those provided by Statistics Canada, provide typical operating statements for many types of small businesses. Often these statements express expenses as a percentage of revenue and thus can be easily adapted to the proposed business. Some of the more important required expenses are as follows:

   • Cost of goods sold and gross profit percentages—these can be obtained from secondary data but should be confirmed with suppliers.

- Cash operating expenses, such as rent, wages, utilities, repairs, advertising, and insurance—these expenses can also be obtained from secondary sources but should be verified by checking with vendors of these services, as they may differ for the market area of the proposed business.

- Interest and depreciation—a list of the costs of capital items (i.e., building and equipment) and total start-up costs will need to be made so that yearly depreciation and interest expenses can be calculated. Chapter 7 presents information on determining start-up costs and the subsequent interest calculation.

One should remember that only the portion of these assets estimated to be used during that period should be included as the depreciation expenses. Using these start-up costs as a basis, an estimate of the amount of debt and annual interest costs using current rates should be determined.

2. *Subtract expenses from revenue to determine the projected net income from the proposed business in the first year and subsequent years, if required.* Once a projected income figure is calculated, the prospective entrepreneur is in a position to evaluate and compare this result with other types of available investments. Return (income) as a percentage of investment (funds put into the venture) can be compared with other types of businesses or safe uses of money, such as the return obtained by placing the funds with a bank. The rate of return of the business should be higher than bank interest, however, to compensate for the risk factor that accompanies a new business.

It is conceivable—and not uncommon—that the projected income for the new business will be negative, at least in the first few years of operation. Usually the entrepreneur is taking a long-term view of the business, and thus long-term projections may be required to evaluate financial feasibility. In addition to a net income projection, many feasibility analyses include a projected cash flow statement. This document is of particular interest to potential lenders and investors. The cash flow simply describes the cash in minus the cash out on a chronological basis. Usually cash flow statements are shown monthly (see Chapter 7). The sample cash flow in Schedule 4 of Figure 3-7 is shown on a yearly basis for simplicity.

A quantitative financial feasibility analysis for a retail pharmacy is presented in Figure 3-7, which follows. This example illustrates the steps described in the preceding sections.

Figure 3-7	**Feasibility Analysis for a Pharmacy in Lethbridge (approximately 300 square metres)**

Step 1: Calculate Market Potential

1. *Market area.* The market area is the population of Lethbridge plus outlying regions. This region includes towns within a 100 km radius of Lethbridge. The population of this total market area is about 170,000. (Source: *Lethbridge Community Profile*, 2005–2006 edition, published by the city of Lethbridge.)

2. *Sales for market area.* The per capita sales for pharmacies in the market area can be determined through two sources. First, the actual sales figures may be published and available from the municipality concerned. Second, if that information is not available, find the per capita sales by taking Canadian or provincial sales of pharmacies divided by the respective population. This information is available from Statistics Canada.

$$\frac{\text{Pharmacy sales for Canada (2005)}}{\text{Population Canada (2005)}} = \text{Per capita pharmacy sales}$$

$$\frac{\$23,950,000,000}{33,000,000} = \$725$$

Once per capita sales have been determined, this number can be applied to the market area population.

$$\text{Lethbridge} = \text{Population} \times \text{Per capita sales}$$

$$= 77,000 \times \$725$$

$$= \$55,825,000$$

$$\text{Outlying area} = \text{Population} \times \text{Per capita sales}$$

$$= (170,000 - 77,000) \times \$725$$

$$(\text{Total market} - \text{Lethbridge})$$

$$= 93,000 \times \$725$$

$$= \$67,425,000$$

Since only 30 percent of people in the outlying area made their purchases in Lethbridge (primary research), multiply this figure by 0.3:

$$\$67,425,000 \times 0.3 = \$20,227,500$$

$$\text{Total market potential} = \$55,825,000 + \$20,227,500$$

$$= \$76,052,500 \text{ (rounded to } \$76,000,000)$$

3. *Adjustments.* Typical adjustments might include updating secondary information regarding population and purchases by applying past trends.

Step 2: Calculate Market Share

1. *Estimate selling space in market.* There are a total of 35 pharmacies and pharmacy departments in Lethbridge, with a total estimated size of 16,000 square metres. (Primary research collected by observation.)

2. *Size of proposed store.* The size of the proposed pharmacy is 300 square metres.

3. Calculation of market share. Percentage share of the market:

$$\frac{\text{Proposed store selling space}}{\substack{\text{Total market selling space} \\ \text{(including proposed store)}}} = \frac{300 \text{ m}^2}{16,000 \text{ m}^2 + 300 \text{ m}^2} = 1.8\%$$

4. *Adjustments.* The percentage of market share would probably have to be decreased slightly, because the proposed pharmacy is new and would not have built up clientele and the reputation of an existing store.

Based on the above factors, market share has been adjusted to 1.5 percent.

5. *Multiply market share percentage by the market potential.*

Market share × Market potential = Estimated market share

1.5% × $76,000,000 = $1,140,000

Therefore, market share is approximately $1,000,000.

Step 3: Calculation of Net Income and Cash Flow

NEW PHARMACY
Projected Income Statement
For the Period Ended December 2007

		Percent of Sales	**Source of Information**
Sales	$ 1,000,000	100. 0	From calculation in step 2
Less: Cost of goods sold	720,000	72.0	Dun and Bradstreet Key Business Ratios (2005)
Gross margin	280,000	28.0	
Expenses:			
Manager's salary	60,000	6.0	Primary information (talked to owners)
Employee wages (Schedule 1)	150,000	15.0	Schedule 1, primary information
Fringe benefits	7,500	0.75	Stats Canada operating results for pharmacies (2002)
Rent	35,000	3.5	Primary and secondary operating results (talked to owners and Stats Canada 2002)
Utilities and telephone	15,000	1.5	Primary (talked to owners)
Accounting, legal, taxes and licence	6,500	0.65	Primary (checked with agencies)
Insurance	6,500	0.65	Primary and secondary (operating results, etc.)
Repairs and maintenance	6,500	0.65	Stats Canada (operating results, etc.)
Advertising	6,500	0.65	Stats Canada (operating results, etc.)
Bad debts	2,500	0.25	Primary and secondary (talked to owners and Stats Canada)

Depreciation (Schedule 2)	20,000	2.0	Stats Canada (operating results, etc.), Schedule 2 and Schedule 3
Interest, exchange, and bank charges	5,200	0.52	Schedule 3
Office and store supplies	5,000	0.5	Stats Canada (operating results, etc.)
Contingency	5,000	0.5	Stats Canada (operating results, etc.)
Total expenses	331,200	33.0	
Net income (loss) before tax	(51,200)		

Schedule 1 (obtained through primary research)

Employee wages

1 Full-time pharmacist	50,000
1 Part-time pharmacist	30,000
1 Full-time cashier @ $20,000	20,000
2 Part-time cashiers @ $10,000	20,000
1 Bookkeeper	15,000
1 Marker/receiver/delivery person	15,000
Total	$150,000

Schedule 2 Depreciation Schedule

Equipment cost = $80,000 Capital cost allowance (CCA) = 20% (obtained from Master Tax Guide)

Year	Undepreciated Amount	×	CCA	=	Depreciation
2003	$100,000	×	0.20	=	$20,000.00
2004	80,000	×	0.20	=	16,000.00
2005	64,000	×	0.20	=	12,800.00
2006	61,200	×	0.20	=	12,240.00
2007	40,960	×	0.20	=	8,192.00

The above process is continued until the entire item is depreciated.

Schedule 3

Interest schedule

Amount borrowed = $70,000

Interest rate = 6.9%

Interest 2005 = 70,000 × 6%	=	$ 4,200
Estimated bank and service charges	=	$ 1,000
Total		$ 5,200

Schedule 4

Calculation of Cash Flow
NEW PHARMACY
Projected Cash Flow Statement
For Period Ended December 31, 2007

Cash inflow		
Beginning cash	$ 30,000	
Bank loan	70,000	
Cash sales	1,000,000	
Total cash inflow	1,100,000	
Cash outflow		
Start-up costs	100,000	
Merchandise purchases	770,000	(0.72 of sales plus $50,000 inventory on hand and paid for)
Manager's salary	60,000	
Employee wages	150,000	
Fringe benefits	7,500	
Rent (including deposit)	35,000	
Utilities and phone (including deposit)	15,000	
Accounting, legal, etc.	6,500	
Insurance	6,500	
Repairs and maintenance	6,500	
Advertising	6,500	
Interest and bank charges	5,200	
Office supplies	5,000	
Other expenses	5,000	
Total cash outflow	$1,178,700	
Net cash flow	$ (78,700)	

Another potentially important part of the feasibility analysis, particularly for the manufacturing firm, is to estimate the level of production and sales required to break even financially. A detailed discussion of break-even analysis is included in Chapter 10. Once the feasibility analysis is completed, the prospective entrepreneur should have enough information to decide whether to pursue a particular business opportunity. The areas covered up to this point can be used to make this decision. Figure 3-8 presents a checklist for personal and opportunity evaluation.

Figure 3-8	**Self-Assessment for a Small Business Opportunity**

Personality: Do I possess most of the personality characteristics of successful entrepreneurs introduced in Chapter 2?

Nature: Does this business opportunity meet my occupational and lifestyle goals and interests?

Abilities: Do I have the expertise in the fundamentals (financial, marketing, personnel, production) needed to manage this business opportunity? If I do not, am I able and willing to acquire or hire such expertise?

Experience: Do I have experience with the business or industry? If not, am I able and willing to obtain it or find someone who can help me get started?

Financial base: Do I currently have or can I obtain, the necessary funds to finance the venture?

Feasibility: Does the financial feasibility of the business opportunity meet my expectations and financial goals?

Summary

1. Before deciding which small business opportunity to pursue, the entrepreneur must consider some nonquantitative factors such as his or her goals, the content of the work, the lifestyle the business offers, and his or her capabilities and experience.

2. There are three ways to enter a market with a new product or service. The first method is to offer a totally new product. The second is to offer an existing product to a different market or industry. The third is to offer a product or service similar to those that already exist in the same market.

3. Two general types of information are available to aid a potential small business owner in selecting a business opportunity. The first and most inexpensive method is to collect secondary data about a potential market. Many government documents and other sources can provide valuable secondary data. When little current secondary data is available, prospective small business owners can collect primary data to help determine the feasibility of their businesses. Primary data is information collected through one's own research. Although usually more costly than secondary data, it can be more relevant and current to the analysis. Three general methods of doing primary research include observation, surveys, and experiments. Surveying usually is the most effective method for a small business.

4. An entrepreneur can develop a competitive advantage by choosing the right industry to enter, the right kind of business to pursue, and the right aspect of the business to focus on.

5. There are three steps in estimating the financial feasibility of a proposed business venture. The first step is to determine potential revenues for the total market. The second step is to estimate the proposed business share of that total market. The third step is to subtract the associated expenses from the revenue estimate to determine an estimated net income for the prospective business.

Chapter Problems and Applications

1. Briefly explain the ways of entering a market. List examples that fit these methods other than those mentioned in the text.

2. J&J Inc. is thinking of developing a new coin laundry. The firm first needs to do some market research to determine the demand for the product. What kind of information should it collect?

3. What could Kirchner Machine Ltd. (Incident 3-9) have done to properly develop a financial feasibility analysis for the Big Bale Fork?

4. Why is it important to make adjustments in market potential and market share figures?

5. For a small business opportunity of your choice, show how you would evaluate the nonquantitative factors such as goals, experience, lifestyle, and content of work.

6. Design a simple mail questionnaire to assess demand for a carpet-cleaning business in your city.

7. From Statistics Canada Small Business Profiles (see Appendix 3A), find the Return on Sales, Gross Profit, and Current Ratios for a jewellery store, a clothing manufacturer, and a grocery store.

8. The new bakery in Web Exercise 1 has a proposed selling space of 50 square metres. The total amount of selling space devoted to bakery products in the city is 850 square metres. From the market potential estimated in Web Exercise 1, find the market share in dollars for the new bakery.

9. Discuss the difficulties of preparing a feasibility analysis for an e-commerce business.

10. Contact an entrepreneur of your choice and ask what he or she feels his or her competitive advantage is.

Web Exercises

1. Using information obtained from the Internet and from Figure 3-2, develop a market potential analysis for a bakery.

2. Access the website for the Small Business Profiles (federal government) (see page 79). What information is given for a small restaurant?

APPENDIX 3A

Small Business Reference Books and Sources of Information

ABC Assistance to Business in Canada, Business Development Bank of Canada, 204 Richmond Street West, Toronto, Ontario, M5V 1V6. http://www.bdc.ca/en/home.htm

Canadian Industrial Innovation Centre, Waterloo, Ontario. Provides assessment of new product, service or process ideas by marketing experts and engineers. http://www.innovationcentre.ca

Canadian Small Business Guide, CCH Canadian Ltd., 90 Sheppard Avenue East, Suite 300, Toronto, Ontario, M2N 6X1. http://www.cch.ca/

Canadian Federation of Independent Business, Willowdale, Ontario. Has several publications and statistics on small business. http://www.cfib.ca

CIBC Guide to Business Planning, Canadian Imperial Bank of Commerce. Provides a business planning workbook to assist in development of the business plan. http://www.cibc.com/ca/small-business

Compusearch Micromarketing Data and Systems provides information on population segments by lifestyle, 1,000 product categories, and locations of 650,000 businesses. For a free database catalogue, call 1 (800) 268-DATA.

Handbook of Canadian Consumer Markets, The Conference Board of Canada, Suite 100, 25 McArthur Road, Ottawa, Ontario, K1L 6R3. This book includes data on provincial, rural, marital populations, and so on; employment; income; expenditures; production and distribution; and pricing. http://www.conferenceboard.ca

Handbook of Assistance Programs, CCH Canadian Ltd., 90 Sheppard Avenue East, Suite 300, Toronto, Ontario, M2N 6X1. http://www.cch.ca/assistance/?tid=127

How to Succeed in Your Home Business, Toronto Dominion Bank.

Index to Federal Programs and Services, Supply and Services Canada, Ottawa, Canada. http://www.servicecanada.gc.ca

Industry, Science, and Technology Canada. Provides several services for small businesses across the country. ISTC business service centres contain publications, videos, and computer databases, networking sources as well as counselling personnel. http://www.ic.gc.ca

Key Business Ratios, Dun and Bradstreet Canada Ltd., P.O. Box 423, Station A, Toronto, Ontario. Contains key business ratios for more than 800 different types of businesses. Also, the U.S. affiliate of Dun and Bradstreet publishes "typical" balance sheets, income statements, and "common-size" financial figures. http://www.dnb.ca

Kryszak, Wayne D. *The Small Business Index,* Grolier, Inc., Sherman Turnpike, Danbury, Connecticut, U.S.A. 06816. This book is an index to American and Canadian books, pamphlets, and periodicals that contain information on starting and running a small business.

Management Tips—A Guide for Independent Business, Royal Bank of Canada. This series of books offers guidance on starting and running a business. Topics covered include "How to Finance Your Business," "Pointers to Profits," and "Good Management—Your Key to Survival." http://www.rbcroyalbank.com/index.html

Managing for Success Series, The Institute for Small Business Inc., 1051 Clinton Street, Buffalo, New York, U.S.A. This series contains 16 self-tutorials in business procedure written expressly for the independent business owner. It discusses important business topics such as financing, a do-it-yourself marketing plan, planning and budgeting, and advertising and sales promotion. It provides illustrative case studies, detailed examples, and workbook and checklist pages that let you work out your business details along the lines given in the text.

Market Research Handbook, Statistics Canada, Ottawa, Ontario. http://www.statcan.ca/english/ads/63-224-XPB/index.htm

Minding Your Own Business, Business Development Bank of Canada, Management Services, P.O. Box 6021, Montreal, Quebec, H3C 3C3. This is a series of guides to starting and running a small business. The guides provide information on areas such as forecasting for an existing business, managing your current assets, retail pricing, attracting and keeping your retail customers, and buying a franchise. The Business Development Bank also publishes workbook case study pamphlets, which are used in training seminars for entrepreneurs. Some of these topics are "Total Quality Control," "Developing a Financial Forecast," and "How to Prepare a Market Study." http://www.bdc.ca/en/home.htm

Periodicals and trade magazines particular to the type of business involved. For example, one would consult *Restaurateur* if opening a new restaurant. These magazines often provide typical start-up and operating costs for a business. In addition, there are several general small business periodicals, such as *Entrepreneur, Venture,* and *INC.,* that provide valuable ideas on starting a business.

Planning for Success, Business Development of Canada (BDC). Designed to teach entrepreneurship to youth and adults. Brochures and CD format. http://www.bdc.ca/en/home.htm

Provincial and territorial small business departments. These offices can be very useful to someone who operates or plans to open a small business. They can provide information on sources of financing for small business, and so on. In Alberta, for example, the government publishes pamphlets on many aspects of running a small business, as well as "Kind of Business Files" (KOB), which contain data on 100 types of small businesses such as financial ratios, market trends, and so on.

Research and Retrieval, Business Research Newsletter, G.D. Sourcing, Toronto, Ontario. http://www.gdsourcing.com

Small Business Problem Solver, Bank of Montreal. Fourteen pamphlets covering various management topics. http://www4.bmo.com

Small Business Quarterly, Entrepreneurship and Small Business Office. Provides a quick and easy-to-read snapshot of recent performance of Canada's small business sector. 235 Queen Street, Room 505A, Industry Canada, Ottawa, K1A 0H5. http://www.strategis.ic.gc.ca

Small Business Source Book, John Ganly, Diane Seialtana, and Andrea Pedolsky, editors. Gale Research Company, Book Tower, Detroit, Michigan, U.S.A. 48226. This book was designed as a first step toward finding information for anyone who is considering starting a small business. The book lists 100 companies as well as associations, sources of supply, statistical sources, trade periodicals, franchises, educational programs, tradeshows, and conventions.

Statistics Canada, Head Office, R. H. Coats Building, Tunney's Pasture, Ottawa, Ontario, K1A OT6.

1. *Operating Results.* This report presents typical expenses, cost of goods sold, inventory, and net profit as a percentage of sales for many types of businesses. It presents results for both incorporated and unincorporated businesses and gives both mean and median results. Data is provided by both level of sales and province or territory.

2. *Market Research Handbook.* This book presents data on selected economic indicators, government revenue, expenditures and employment, merchandising and services, population characteristics, personal income, and expenditures.

3. *Family Expenditure in Canada.* This report provides information on family expenditures in Canada for a very detailed list of items.

4. *Census Data.* This can be obtained from local city halls. Census data provides information on population growth rates, income level of schooling, and other facts. Census tracts for large centres can also be obtained from Statistics Canada.

5. *Small Business Profiles.* These provide complete financial operating reports for many small businesses.

TD Business Planner, Toronto Dominion Bank. Includes step-by-step financial and business plan preparation.

The Financial Post Canadian Markets, Maclean Hunter Ltd., 777 Bay Street, Toronto, Ontario, M5W 1A7. This book provides complete demographics for Canadian urban markets. It looks at 500 municipalities across Canada with populations greater than 5,000. It includes data on demographics; income; manufacturing activity; television, radio, and newspaper statistics; other economic statistics; average and annual growth rates of the population; and future population projections.

Suggested Periodicals for Small Business

Entrepreneur
Chase Revel
2311 Pontius Avenue
Los Angeles, CA 90064
http://www.entrepreneurmag.com

Home Business Report
http://www.homebusinessreport.com

In Business
Jerome Goldstein, Publisher
Box 351
Emmaus, PA 18049
http://www.jgpress.com/inbusiness.htm

INC.
Bernard Goldhirsh, Publisher
38 Commercial Wharf
Boston, MA 02110
http://www.inc.com

Journal of Small Business and Entrepreneurship
Faculty of Administration
University of Regina
Regina, SK S4S 0A2
http://www.ccsbe.org/jsbe

N.E.D.I. Notes
National Entrepreneurship Development
Institute
Edmonton, AB
http://www.nedi.ca

Profit—the Magazine for Canadian Entrepreneurs
CB Media Ltd.
70 The Esplanade, 2nd Floor
Toronto, ON
http://www.rogersmagazines.com/profit.htm

Profits
Business Development Bank of Canada
BDC Building
5 Place Ville Marie
Suite 400
Montreal, QC H3B 5E7
http://www.bdc.ca

Small Business Canada
P.O. Box 1684 Station Main
Holland Landing, ON L9N 1P2
http://sbinfocanada.about.com/

Success
Lang Communications
230 Park Avenue
New York, NY 10169
http://www.successmagazine.com

Venture
Schofield Media
303 East Wacker Drive
23rd floor
Chicago, Il 60601
http://www.venture-magazine.com

Online Sources of Assistance for Small Businesses

Alberta Business Advantage—http://Albertafirst.com—online source for small business profiles.

American On-line—largest commerical online service for business.

Atlantic Canada Opportunities—http://www.acoa.ca—business opportunities and information for the Atlantic region.

Bank of Montreal Entrepreneur Site—http://www.bmo.com—provides information on management aspects of running a small business as well as interaction with other entrepreneurs.

Business Research newsletter—http://www.gdsourcing.com—reference for government and industry information about small business sector.

Business Development Bank Information Site—http://strategis.ic.gc.ca

Canada Business Service Centres—http://www.cbsc.org—information for government services, programs, and regulations for business.

Canada E-book (yearbook)—http://www43.statcan.ca—social trends and the economy

Canadian Chamber of Commerce—http://www.chamber.ca—information on public policy on business issues.

Canadian Industry Profiles—http://www.hrsdc.gc.ca

Canada One—http://www.canadaone.com—provides useful business tools to start, run, and grow a successful small business.

Canadian Federation of Independent Business—http://www.cfib.ca

Canadian Youth Business Foundation—http://www.youthbusiness.com

CANSIM Main Base Series Directory—index to latest census—http://cansim2.statcan.ca

Census Data (2006 Census)—http://www12.statcan.ca/english/census

Entrepreneur—http://www.Entrepreneur.com—general information about small business.

Export Development Corporation—http://www.edc.ca—provides information about exporting.

Export Source On-line Services—http://exportsource.gc.ca/—step-by-step guide to exporting for small business.

Government of Canada—http://www.businessgateway.ca—access to all government services to start a small business.

A Guide for Canadian Small Business—http://www.cra-arc.gc.ca/E/pub/tg/rc4070—federal government website to help small businesses.

Free Management Library—http://www.managementhelp.org

Inc. Magazine—http://www.Inc.com

International Consortium on Entrepreneurship (ICE)—http://ice.foranet.dk

On-line Small Business Workshop—http://www.gov.bc.ca—provides guides for planning a business through to functional management of the ongoing business.

Market Research Handbook—http://www.gdsourcing.ca/MarketResearchHandbook.htm

Profit—http://www.canadianbusiness.com/entrepreneur/index.jsp—articles and newsletters for entrepreneurs.

RegWatch—http://www.scc.ca—information about standards provided by Standards Council of Canada.

Small Biz Canada—http://microsoft.com/canada/smallbiz—provides news and research articles on the benefits of technology and on issues related to marketing, financing, and general business.

Small Biz Manager—http://smallbizmanager.com—reviews, screens, and recommends business services, products, advice, and so on.

Small Business Advancement National Centre—http://www.sbaer.uca.edu/—research, training, consulting, and information library.

Small Business Desktop—http://www.canadapost.ca/business/intsol/sb/default-e.asp—Canada Post's assistance for small business to reach customers.

Small Business Information—http://sbinformation.about.com—a comprehensive small business website on e-commerce start-ups.

Small Business Information Seminars—http://www.cra-arc.gc.ca/business—provides information on your responsibilities regarding customs, income tax, GST/HST, and so on.

Small Business Profiles—http://strategis.ic.gc.ca/epic/internet/inpp-pp.nsf/en/pm00019e.html—free profiles and statistics for various types of small businesses.

Small E-Business Information Toolkit—http://www.toolkit.cch.com

Small-Office and Home-Office Business Links—http://www.soho.ca

Statistics Canada—http://www.statcan.ca/english/dai-quo—up-to-date information on releases by Statistics Canada.

Trade Commissioner Service website—http://www.infoexport.gc.ca—assistance for small business in identifying markets, contacts, and so on.

Western Economic Diversification Canada—http://www.wed.gc.ca—business opportunities and information for the Western region.

Young Entrepreneurs Association—http://www.yea.ca

Organizations and Trade Associations That Assist Entrepreneurs

Alliance of Independent Business Associations Canada

Canadian Venture Capital Association
http://www.cvca.ca

Association of Collegiate Entrepreneurs (ACE)
Simon Fraser University
http://www.acesfu.ca

Directory of Associations in Canada
1-800-387-2689 ext. 4397

Encyclopedia of Associations
http://library.dialog.com/bluesheets/html/
bl0114.html

Entrepreneurship and Small Business Office
235 Queen Street
Ottawa, ON K1A 0A5

Business Development Bank of Canada (BDC)
BDC Building
5 Place Ville Marie, Suite 400
Montreal, PQ H3B 5E7
http://www.bdc.ca/en/business_solutions/
consulting_group/default.htm

Business Information Centre
Business Development Bank of Canada
204 Richmond Street West
Toronto, ON M5V 1V6
http://www.bdc.ca/en/home.htm

Canadian Association of Business Incubators
http://www.cabi.ca

Canadian Association of Family Enterprise
http://www.cafemembers.org

Canadian Association of Home-Based Business

Canadian Association of Women Executives and Entrepreneurs
http://www.cawee.net

Canadian Chamber of Commerce
120 Adelaide Street West, Suite 2109
Toronto, ON M5H 1T1
http://www.chamber.ca

Canadian Council of Better Business Bureaus
2180 Steeles Avenue West, Suite 219
Concord, ON M6P 4C7
http://www.ccbbb.ca

Canadian Federation of Independent Business
4141 Yonge Street, Suite 401
Willowdale, ON M2P 2A6
http://www.cfib.ca

Canadian Franchise Association
http://www.cfa.ca

Canadian Council for Small Business and
Entrepreneurship
204 Richmond Street West, 5th Floor,
Toronto, ON M5V 1V6
http://www.ccsbe.org

National Association of Home-Based Businesses
(NAHBB)
http://www.usahomebusiness.com

National Entrepreneurship Development
Institute
Edmonton, Alberta
http://www.nedi.ca

National Small Business Institute
1070 West Broadway, Suite 310
Vancouver, BC V6H 1E7
http://www.smallbusinessinstitute.org

Small Business Network
52 Sheppard Avenue West
Willowdale, ON M2N 1M2
http://www.businessknowhow.net

Women Entrepreneurs of Canada
http://www.wec.ca

Young Entrepreneurs Association of Ontario
http://www.yea.ca

Suggested Readings

Baille, Susan, Dee VanDyk, and Kallie Pearson. "The Best Businesses To Go Into Now." *Profit*. December–January 2003, pp. 18–28.

Business Entrepreneur Centres—www.ontario-canada.com/mtcdn/enexpanding/ex_sm_busent_ct.jsp.

Canada Business website—Small Business Tools—CanadaBusiness.gc.ca/businesstools

Canada Entrepreneur website—http://canadaentrep.ca

Entrepreneurial Centre—www.entrepreneurship.com

Goodman, Carla. "Sparking Your Imagination." *Entrepreneur*. September 1997.

Gray, Douglas A., and Diane L. Gray. *The Complete Canadian Small Business Guide 3rd Edition*. Toronto: McGraw-Hill Ryerson, 2000.

Guide for Small Business—www.cra-arc.gc.ca

Researching a Small Business 2005—A Practical Guide to Small Business Research in Canada, Toronto: G.D. Sourcing. (Access through website—http://www.gdsourcing.com)

Skinner, James R. *Success Plan To Business Reality*. Toronto: Pearson-Prentice Hall, 2003.

Comprehensive Case   *Sid Stevens: Part 2*

Following the negative reaction from his company regarding the Ladder Rail, Sid was more determined than ever to start his own business. He felt that his invention had great potential. This had been confirmed by several of his co-workers. He discussed the possibility of becoming an entrepreneur with his wife, Suzie. Although she had reservations, she agreed that Sid should at least do some research on the feasibility of the product. Sid had learned in his small business management class that he needed to collect some information to find out whether the Ladder Rail could provide a large enough income so he could quit his job and make a living at it.

Sid felt that the primary market for the Ladder Rail would be construction and home renovation companies. He also wondered whether homeowners would buy the Ladder Rail. This market would likely purchase ladders at their local hardware stores, such as Canadian Tire, Home Depot, or Home Hardware. Sid estimated that the overall market for the Ladder Rail would be all of Canada, although he knew that if the market were that large he would have to build a plant to manufacture such large quantities. Sid thought that he should start small by attempting to market the product initially in the Hamilton area.

Sid went to the local library and obtained some data regarding construction, population, households, and expenditures for Canada and for Hamilton. The information that he collected is found in Figure 2-A below.

| Figure 2-A | Sid's Market Research |

	Canada	Ontario	Hamilton
Population	31,413,990	11,410,046	662,401
Households	11,552,010	4,302,710	260,968
Household expenditures (Hardware tools per annum)	$1,655	$1,928	$1,848

Sid wasn't quite sure what to do with this information or what additional information he would need. He was aware that the company he worked for had 20 ladders and employed 100 people, so he estimated that 1 ladder was purchased per 5 employees in a construction or roofing company. Sid estimated that 1 out of 10 households would buy an aluminum ladder for such things as roof repairs, TV antennae adjustments, and putting up Christmas lights. He thought that at least 20 percent of these ladder owners would be interested in the Ladder Rail. It cost Sid about $10 to make the standard Ladder Rails and he estimated that he could sell them for about $40. A breakdown of his costs is shown in Figure 2-B. He felt that he could surely get 1 percent of the market. If so he would be a rich man.

| Figure 2-B | Manufacturing Expenses for the Ladder Rail |

Metal	$7 per unit
Labour	$2 per unit
Overhead	$1 per unit

Questions

1. What positive things has Sid done in investigating the new business?
2. What additional information should Sid obtain before completing his feasibility analysis?
3. With the information provided, prepare a feasibility analysis for the homeowner market.
4. What other information would make this calculation more accurate?

Video Cases for Part 1

Java Nook   Bright Lights, Deep Water

PART ENDING VIDEO CASE & QUESTIONS *Java Nook**

(Appropriate Chapters—1, 2, 3, 4, 7, 15)

Annette Lavigne and John Welter have started a small café in Toronto. This video example describes the problems associated with a small business start-up. It also illustrates some of the typical weaknesses that entrepreneurs possess that hamper them from successfully establishing an enterprise in a volatile industry. However, in the end Annette and John do realize their dream of owning a small business.

1. What does this example illustrate about the advantages and disadvantages of starting a small business?

2. Evaluate Annette and John's backgrounds and preparation for starting a small business. What could they have done to better prepare for small business ownership?

3. What does this case show about the strains of families starting and operating businesses?

4. How could Annette and John have been more successful in obtaining adequate financing?

*Source: CBC *Venture* #796, running time 13:00.

PART ENDING VIDEO CASE & QUESTIONS *Bright Lights, Deep Waters**

(Appropriate Chapters—1, 2, 3, 7, 8)

Scientist turned entrepreneur David Green has a multimillion dollar idea for solar-powered marine lighting. Now all he has to do is get the product to market before his competitors do.

1. Discuss the difference between an entrepreneur and a manager using David Green and Carmanah Lights as examples.

2. What dangers of obtaining equity financing are illustrated in this example?

3. How does demand for this product differ from a consumer product advertised through the media?

*Source: CBC *Venture* #780, running time 9:58.

Cases for Part 1

Bookworms Inc.   Petite Shop (B)
Petite Shop (A)   Big D's Painting Company

BOOKWORMS, INC.

James Nelson, *University of Colorado*

Late one August morning, Nancy Klein, co-owner of Bookworms, Inc., sat at her desk near the back wall of a cluttered office. With some irritation, she had just concluded that her nearby calculator could help no more. "What we still need," she thought to herself, "are estimates of demand and market share … but at least we have two weeks to get them."

Klein's office was located in the rear of Bookworms, Inc., an 1,800-square-foot bookstore specializing in quality paperbacks. The store carries more than 10,000 titles and sold more than

$520,000 worth of books last year. Titles were stocked in 18 categories, ranging from art, biography, and cooking to religion, sports and travel.

Bookworms, Inc. was located in a small business district across the street from the boundary of Verdoon University (VU). VU currently enrolled about 12,000 undergraduate and graduate students majoring in the liberal arts, the sciences, and the professions. Despite national trends in enrollment, the VU admissions office had predicted that the number of entering students would grow at about 1 percent per year through the 2000s. The surrounding community, a city of about 350,000, was projected to grow at about twice that rate.

Bookworms, Inc., carried no texts, even though many of its customers were VU students. Both Klein and her partner, Susan Berman, felt that the VU bookstore had simply too firm a grip on the textbook market in terms of price, location, and reputation. Bookworms also carried no classical CDs, as of two months ago. Klein recalled with discomfort the $15,000 or so they had lost on the venture. "Another mistake like that and the bank will be running Bookworms," she thought. "And, despite what Susan thinks, the copy service could just be that final mistake."

The idea for a copy service had come from Susan Berman. She had seen the candy store next door to Bookworms (under the same roof) go out of business in July. She had immediately asked the building's owner, Ed Anderson, about the future of the 800-square-foot space. Upon learning it was available, she had met with Klein to discuss her idea for the copy service. She had spoken excitedly about the opportunity: "It can't help but make money. I could work there part-time and the rest of the time we could hire students. We could call it 'Copycats' and even use a sign with the same kind of letters we do in 'Bookworms.' I'm sure we could get Ed to knock the wall out between the two stores, if you think it would be a good idea. Probably we could rent most of the copying equipment, so there's not much risk."

Klein was not so sure. A conversation yesterday with Anderson had disclosed his desire for a five-year lease (with an option to renew) at $1,000 per month. He had promised to hold the offer open for two weeks before attempting to lease the space to anyone else. Representatives from copying-equipment firms had estimated that charges would run between $200 and $2,000 per month, depending on equipment, service, and whether the equipment was bought or leased. The copy service would also have other fixed costs in terms of utility expenses, interest, insurance, and the inventory (and perhaps equipment). Klein concluded that the service would begin to make a profit at about 20,000 copies per month under the best-case assumptions, and at about 60,000 copies per month under the worst-case assumptions.

Further informal investigation had identified two major competitors. One was the copy centre located in the Krismann Library on the west side of the campus, a mile away. The other was a private firm, Kinko's, located on the south side of the campus, also one mile away. Both offered service while you wait, on several machines. The library's price was about ½ cent per copy higher than Kinko's. Both offered collating, binding, colour copying, and other services, all on a seven-days-a-week schedule.

Actually, investigation had discovered that a third major "competitor" consisted of the VU departmental machines scattered throughout the campus. Most faculty and administrative copying was done on these machines, but students were allowed the use of some, at cost. In addition, at least 20 self-service machines could be found in the library and in nearby drugstores, grocery stores, and banks.

Moving aside the stack of books on her desk, Nancy Klein picked up the telephone and dialed her partner. When Berman answered, Klein asked, "Susan, have you any idea how many copies a student might make in a semester? I mean according to my figures, we would break even somewhere between 20,000 and 60,000 copies per month. I don't know if this is half the market or what."

"You know, I have no idea," Berman answered. "I suppose when I was going to school I probably made 10 copies a month—for articles, class notes, old tests, and so on."

"Same here," Klein said. "But some graduate students must have done that many each week. You know, I think we ought to do some marketing research before we go much further on this. What do you think?"

"Sure. Only it can't take much more time or money. What do you have in mind, Nancy?"

"Well, we could easily interview our customers as they leave the store and ask them how many copies they've made in the past week or so. Of course, we'd have to make sure they were students."

"What about a telephone survey?" Berman asked. "That way we can have a random sample. We should still ask about the number of copies, but now we would know for sure they would be students."

"Or what about interviewing students in the student union cafeteria? There's always a good-sized line there around noon, as I remember, and this might even be quicker."

"Boy, I just don't know. Why don't I come in this afternoon and we can talk some more?"

"Good idea," Klein responded. "Between the two of us, we should be able to come up with something."

Questions

1. What source of information should Klein and Berman use?
2. How should Klein and Berman gather data?
3. What questions should they ask?
4. How should they sample?

PETITE SHOP (A)

D. Wesley Balderson, *University of Lethbridge*

Alice Wood was concerned. She had worked in a women's clothing store for several years and was now considering opening a store of her own. Her investigations had yielded considerable secondary information, but she was not sure how to go about estimating the potential for another women's clothing store in Prince George, British Columbia. Prince George was a city of 86,100 surrounded by a large trading area. Presently it had 17 clothing stores and five department stores that retailed women's clothing. During the past few years, Alice had been saving her money and learning all she could so that her Petite Shop ladies' wear store would be a success.

In anticipation of starting her own store, Alice had enrolled in a small business management course at a local college. The instructor had stressed the importance of market research and mentioned several sources of secondary information that could assist in determining market potential for a new business. Alice had obtained the reports she felt were relevant to her pro-spective business from the Provincial Department of Small Business, Statistics Canada, and the city hall in Prince George. This information is presented in Figures 1 and 2.

Now that Alice had this information, however, she was not sure how to proceed. She did not want to retail all kinds of ladies' clothing but planned to cater to the "petite" woman who wore dress sizes 3 to 9. Alice herself was petite (1.55 metres), and she felt she understood the difficul-ties women of her size had in shopping for clothing. From her retailing experience, she estimated that about 60 percent of all clothing sales were in womens' clothing and 20 percent of all women fit in the size 3 to 9 category. She arrived at her decision to select a store directed at the petite woman after she visited all of the 17 clothing stores in Prince George and the clothing depart-ments of the city's five department stores. She estimated that only about 10 percent of clothing stores' stock was sized 3 to 9, and the five department stores devoted only about 6,500 square feet of selling space to this size range. She believed a small shop of about 1,000 square feet could provide a much better selection to this market than those outlets presently provided.

Figure 1	Selected Data for the City of Prince George
Population	86,100
Number of families	29,200
Per capita income	$15,000
Retail sales	$737,700,000
Per family expenditure on women's clothing	$1,000

Source: *Financial Post Canadian Markets and Urban Family Expenditure Report*; and *Market Research Handbook, 2005,* Statistics Canada.

Figure 2	Estimated Retail Space for Selected Retail Establishments (in square feet) City of Prince George
Food stores	1,200,000
Apparel stores:	
Men's clothing stores	145,000
Women's clothing stores	180,000
Hardware stores	600,000
Department stores	1,650,000

Source: City of Prince George; and *Market Research Handbook, 2005,* Statistics Canada.

Questions

1. Using the information provided, prepare an estimate of the market potential for the target market at which Alice Wood is aiming.
2. What portion of this market potential could Alice expect for Petite Shop's market share?
3. What nonquantitative considerations should be brought into this analysis?

PETITE SHOP (B)

D. Wesley Balderson, *University of Lethbridge*

Now that Alice Wood had a better idea of market potential and market share for her proposed retail store, she wanted to be satisfied that the Petite Shop would provide an adequate return on her savings of $25,000. She began investigating the typical costs she would incur in operating the store. Alice thought she could operate her new store with one other full-time person and some part-time help at the estimated monthly cost of $2,000. In looking at potential rental costs, she came across a retail outlet for lease on a busy street in the central business district of Prince George that seemed ideal for the Petite Shop. She learned that the site leased for $20 per square foot, with no royalty payments except $550 per year to cover municipal taxes. The estimated utility expenses the owner provided were $300 per month, and the insurance for the retail shoe store that had previously been located there was $1,500 per year.

Although Alice was excited about the potential of this site, she estimated she would need to spend approximately $12,000 for leasehold improvements, of which $8,000 would be depreciable items (20 percent). When obtaining the secondary information from the Prince George city hall, she learned that the business licences would be $100. Alice estimated all miscellaneous expenses such as stationery, bad debt expense, credit expense, and telephone to be about $5,000 per year. These figures were based on her experience in the store she currently worked in.

Alice knew she would have to borrow some money to purchase inventories. She visited her local bank and found out that the interest rate for a business loan was 10 percent. She also learned that until she had a more concrete proposal, her banker was not interested in considering her for a loan. He mentioned that in addition to leasehold improvements, she would need one-fourth of the year's cash expenses as operating funds. Although a bit surprised at the bank's reaction, Alice was determined to prepare such a proposal. She knew the new store would need to be promoted, but didn't know how much she should spend on advertising. The banker had suggested the average for ladies' clothing stores was about 2 percent of sales and had given her a copy of a recent Dun and Bradstreet financial ratio sheet to assist her (see Figure 1).

Alice now found herself in the same dilemma she had been in when determining market potential and market share. She had a lot of information, but was not sure how to proceed.

Figure 1	Key Business Ratios, Canada—Corporations

Line of Business Clothing, Women's	
(Number of concerns reporting)	(2,323)
Cost of goods sold	58.40%
Gross margin	41.60
Current assets to current debt	1.4
Profits on sales	2.7
Profits on tangible net worth	15.6
Sales to tangible net worth	5.9
Sales to inventory	5.7
Fixed assets to tangible net worth	63.6
Current debt to tangible net worth	127.6
Total debt to tangible net worth	177.3

Questions

1. Using the information presented in "Petite Shop (A)" and this case, prepare an estimated income statement and return on investment calculation for the Petite Shop's first year of operation.
2. What areas has Alice overlooked in her investigation?
3. Given your analysis, what would you recommend to Alice?

www.mcgrawhill.ca/olc/balderson

BIG D'S PAINTING COMPANY

D. Wesley Balderson, *University of Lethbridge*

Dave Valdon lives in Maple Ridge, British Columbia, and is contemplating starting his own painting business. Having worked for a national painting franchise during his summers while attending college, Dave feels that he has the experience and skills necessary to be successful with this venture. Because he knows the area, he would like to establish the business in Maple Ridge and the surrounding communities of Pitt Meadows, Port Coquitlam, and Coquitlam. He will concentrate on providing professional and high-quality residential painting services. He intends to base the business out of his home and to set up a home office, as his work will be done at the site of the homeowner. In addition to that, Dave has been told that part of his home expenses (utilities, rent, insurance, etc.) can be deductible business expenses if he does this.

Although Dave is pretty sure that a viable opportunity exists, he knows that he should prepare an estimate of income for the first year of operations. From his industry experience, he has estimated that an average painting job for a residential project is about $1700. His main concern is whether he will be able to obtain enough of these projects to make this a financially viable business. To that end, he has collected some information from outside sources as well as from his experience working in the industry. This information is found below.

Homes in the Market Area

Maple Ridge	19,865
Pitt Meadows	3,496
Port Coquitlam	27,134
Coquitlam	15,828

Dave feels that one-third of all homeowners initiate painting projects each year in his area. He is not sure how to verify this percentage however.

Dave has estimated that there are 100 painting companies in his intended market area. He feels that all will be his competition. He has also made the following estimates concerning his operating expenses for his first year.

Wages (he and 1 other employee)	$60,000
Utilities/phone	1,500
Licence/accounting/insurance	3,000
Vehicle expense	3,000
Advertising	4,000
Equipment/supplies	5,000
Rent	2,500
Contingency	1,000
Total	$80,000

Questions

1. Using the information provided, prepare an estimate of total market revenue and Dave's share of market revenue for the first year of operations.
2. What adjustments should Dave make to the above information to be more accurate with total market revenue?
3. What adjustments or additions should be made to the information to be more accurate with the market share and projected income statement for the first year of operations?

PART TWO

Preparing for Small Business Ownership

Once the entrepreneur has assessed an opportunity, the next important consideration is selecting from among three methods of assuming ownership of the business: organizing the business from scratch, buying an existing business, or signing a franchise contract. Chapters 4, 5, and 6 provide information to help evaluate each of these methods. The last, but equally important, start-up consideration is obtaining financing. Chapter 7 discusses the critical factors the entrepreneur should consider in obtaining the financing needed to establish and operate the venture.

CHAPTER 4

Organizing a Business—The Business Plan

CHAPTER OBJECTIVES

- To describe the advantages and disadvantages of organizing a business from scratch compared with purchasing a business or becoming a franchisee

- To discuss the importance of formulating and following a business organizational plan

- To review the essential components of a small business plan

SMALL BUSINESS PROFILE

Christine Magee

Sleep Country Canada

A Toronto native, Christine Magee began her working life in banking after graduating from the University of Western Ontario with a business administration degree. She spent the next 12 years with two major banks, specializing in corporate and commercial lending.

In 1994 Magee teamed up with Stephen Gunn and Gordon Lownds, whom she had met during her days in banking. The three partners all saw a promising niche for a mattress chain offering value and first-class service. Their analysis of the industry indicated a lack of focus and attention to the category. The industry showed steady and stable growth, which greatly aided the trio in their planning and forecasting. To develop their concept they used the results of this research and carefully developed a thorough business plan.

Christine and her partners then chose to validate their business plan and approach by visiting mattress retailers and dealers across the United States to see whether they could learn from someone who was already doing what they wanted to do. In Seattle, the partners discovered a 13-store family business called Sleep Country USA. They liked its name, its commitment to service, its bright, airy stores—even its jingle, which asked, "Why buy a mattress anywhere else?" So, the Canadians licensed the rights to the name and jingle, while incorporating many of Sleep Country USA's best practices.

In 1994, Magee and her partners decided to open their business in Vancouver as the market was very strong and the right scale for their initial expansion, whereas the much larger Ontario market was feeling the effects of a slowdown. The trio launched Sleep Country Canada, opening their first four stores at the same time in the Vancouver area, a strategy that allowed the company to quickly heighten its profile and to support advertising expenditures.

Sleep Country now boasts 119 stores and ten distribution centres in British Columbia, Alberta, Manitoba, and Ontario and has become the number one mattress retailer in the country. The keys to its success were thorough research and forecasting and the development of a sound business plan, which helped Christine and her partners identify and service a viable niche in the market.

Used with the permission of Christine Magee and Sleep Country Canada.

Sleep Country Canada
www.sleepcountry.ca

GETTING STARTED: ESTABLISHING THE BUSINESS

Once the entrepreneur has assessed the feasibility of a business opportunity and found it to be favourable, the next step is to select the method of establishing the business. There are essentially three methods from which to choose. The first is to organize a business from scratch, the second is to purchase an existing business, and the third is to become a franchisee. This chapter discusses the essential steps in organizing a business from scratch and details the steps in creating a business plan. Chapter 5 deals with purchasing an existing business, and Chapter 6 covers franchising. Although the topics covered in Chapters 5 and 6 are treated separately, many aspects of business plan preparation covered in this chapter are applicable to the following two chapters.

Organizing a business from scratch gives an entrepreneur greater independence in the establishment and operation of the business, but it also poses more risk. Figure 4-1 illustrates this concept.

Statistics Canada
www.statcan.ca

The option to organize from scratch is often chosen by an entrepreneur who wants the satisfaction of creating a business and adding his or her personal touch to all its aspects. It may also be the preferred route when few suitable businesses are for sale or there is little chance of obtaining a franchise for the market area. A recent survey of small business owners by Statistics Canada indicates that about two-thirds of them started their business from scratch.[1] In making this decision, the entrepreneur should be aware of the advantages of organizing the business from scratch as well as the potential drawbacks.

Figure 4-1	Independence versus Risk		
	Organizing	**Buying**	**Franchising**
Level of independence	Higher	Medium	Lower
Level of risk	Higher	Medium	Lower
Chance of survival	20%	70%	90%

Advantages of Organizing a Small Business from Scratch

Organizing a business from scratch offers several advantages. First, this option allows the small business owner to define the nature of the business, the competitive environment in which the business will operate, the appropriate market, and the size and extent of operations.

Second, the owner can obtain the exact types of physical facilities—building, equipment, and location—preferred. Buildings and equipment can be tailored to meet requirements precisely. The owner can also choose the most appropriate location for the market, a very important competitive tool in retailing.

Third, the owner can obtain fresh inventory tailored to the target market. Thus, the risk of products becoming obsolete or difficult to turn over is minimized.

Fourth, the owner can personally select and train employees for the business rather than having to rely on the existing personnel of an established business.

Finally, the owner can develop his or her own information systems such as the methods used for bookkeeping and for evaluating the operation. The owner also can take advantage of the latest technology in equipment and materials.

Disadvantages of Organizing a Small Business from Scratch

Starting one's own business also carries substantial risks. First, the owner lacks historical information on which to base future plans. This can be a drawback if the owner has uncertainties regarding market demand, supplies, and operations. It is also generally more difficult to obtain financing if projections are based on estimates rather than on the extension of trends from existing operations.

Second, the advantage of personally assembling physical facilities can become a liability because of the time required. In some industrial situations in which prompt establishment is critical, purchasing a business or signing a franchise contract may be more advisable.

Third, a new business always has start-up problems or bugs that have to be worked out. Incident 4-1 illustrates some of the problems experienced because of a poorly researched plan.

Fourth, establishing outside relationships with financial institutions, suppliers, and other key professionals is often time-consuming. For example, new small businesses typically are not granted trade credit initially, whereas an existing business or franchise has far less difficulty. The savings in interest costs can be substantial.

Finally, the owner faces the risk that there will be insufficient demand for the product or service. Even if a feasibility analysis is to be carried out before business start-up, some uncertainty regarding the extent of the market may remain.

THE SMALL BUSINESS PLAN

morebusiness.com
www.morebusiness.
com

Regardless of whether an entrepreneur starts the business from scratch, buys an existing business or signs a franchise contract, a business plan is essential. The data point to the crucial need for entrepreneurs to formulate business plans, not just for raising capital, but for organization and classification of long- and short-term goals. A business plan is a vital tool for entrepreneurs—a blueprint to be referred to again and again to keep business growth on course.[2]

INCIDENT 4-1   Grounded

Vancouver's David Ho had high hopes for Harmony Airways—gourmet meals, roomy seats, and even cheap tickets. Harmony started flying in 2002 with two Boeing 757s and eventually added two more. The flight plan was to link Vancouver with vacation hotspots like Vegas and Hawaii and then expand into China. However, what Ho didn't plan for was the increasing price of fuel, which more than doubled during Harmony's four years in business. Even worse, expansion into China stalled, thanks to government delays on both sides of the Pacific. As well, the 757 wasn't equipped for long-haul flights and Harmony couldn't invest in long-range planes until it had secured the Asian routes.

In an attempt to compensate, the company tried new routes closer to home (Vancouver to Toronto). Competition from major airlines such as Air Canada and WestJet resulted in Harmony's flights running at about 20 percent capacity. After being advised to shut down the company, Harmony continued to fly for a few weeks but ended up having to lay off most of its 350 employees. This situation shows the effects of a poorly prepared business plan.

Source: Adapted from Nicholas Dinka, "Grounded," *Report on Small Business*, Summer 2007, p. 31.

The use of business plans by Canadian entrepreneurs is increasing. A recent study of 100 successful Canadian small business owners found that 53 percent utilized full-scale plans—91 percent had a timeframe, and 98 percent were written down. Only 4 percent of Canadian entrepreneurs did not prepare a business plan.[3] Incident 4-2 illustrates the value of a detailed plan. As Joe Mancuso says in the quotation above, the business plan may serve both internal and external purposes. From an internal perspective, the business plan provides a blueprint for the business that can assist in maintaining a focus essential to success. The plan can assist the entrepreneur in a business start-up as well as serve as a reference document to assist in the management of the ongoing business. A business plan can also assist the entrepreneur by providing a vehicle to evaluate the performance of the operation over time. Business plans should contain both short-term and long-term or growth components for the business. A business plan may also serve an external purpose in that lenders and investors generally require one before lending or investing capital in the venture. There are several other reasons why a business plan should be developed. A business plan provides a sense of direction for the business, a test of the idea's viability, assistance in achieving financing, and a clear-cut implementation plan.

The format and emphasis of the business plan vary depending on the user. A plan prepared for a lender should emphasize the entrepreneur's security or collateral position and the cash flow statement. It should show how the loan will be serviced in addition to the other areas. A plan prepared for a potential investor generally requires more detail to compensate for greater risk and a thorough description of the manager's or management team's capabilities, with emphasis on the projected rate of return. A venture capitalist will be interested in knowing the above items as well as in knowing how to liquidate ownership interest in a few years. (More is said about venture capital firms in Chapter 7.)

INCIDENT 4-2   A Piece of Cake

Mandy Kan began fooling around in her kitchen when she was only seven. By the time she graduated from the University of Toronto with a degree in commerce, Kan knew she wanted to open her own business involving food. She had worked in a number of professional kitchens, but in order to give herself an edge, she attended the French Culinary Institute of New York and became a professional pastry chef.

While working as a pastry chef for a high-end grocer, Kan began to put together a comprehensive business plan for her own shop and began shopping for a location that would support her business. After a year of looking, Kan found the right spot in Toronto's trendy Yorkville neighbourhood.

After total start up costs of $105,500, Kan's store, named "The Dessert Lady," became an instant hit. Kan relied on repeat customers to spread the word and didn't spend a cent on marketing. In order to lure customers in, a staff member usually stands outside the store with samples.

The reality of running a business has finally sunk in. "I go for a month without a single day off sometimes," she says. Kan also realizes that the bakery business is seasonal, so during holidays you've got to work really hard and plan for those times.

The pleasure Ms. Kan brings to her customers makes all the hard work pay off. "I love making each customer's day, and seeing them smile after they've tried my products."

Source: Adapted from Rasha Mourtada, "A Piece of Cake," *The Globe and Mail*, www.theglobeandmail.com, August 30, 2006.

COMPONENTS OF THE PLAN

Interactive Business
Planner, Government
of Canada
www.cbsc.org/ibp

Although each user of the plan may require a different format or emphasis, the basic components in creating a business plan are as follows:

- Prepare a table of contents.

- Prepare a synopsis of the plan in an executive summary and background statement. This should include a mission statement indicating in general what type of business it is and what it is going to do.

- Describe the management team.

- Establish business objectives.

- Plan the marketing approach.

- Describe the selection of the location.

- Determine the physical facilities.

- Plan the financing.

- Plan the personnel.

- Investigate the legal requirements.

This chapter gives a brief overview of these components. Chapters 8 through 12 discuss the operating aspects of these areas in detail and should be consulted before preparing a business plan. Appendix 4A at the end of this chapter presents a checklist for a small business plan, and Appendix 4B shows two actual business plans following this format. In addition to the business plan outline provided in the appendix, several other business plan templates are available online. Examples are the Canadian Business Service Centres' "Interactive Planner," The Entrepreneurship Centre Business Plan, and the Business Development Bank of Canada's "Business Plan." The websites for this information are found in Appendix A of Chapter 3. Note that a business plan may also be critical when purchasing a business, obtaining a franchise, acquiring financing, and performing other essential activities of the business. The format of the business, however, may vary depending on whom the plan is intended for.

Prepare a Table of Contents

This is mainly for the benefit of outside users of the business plan. It not only provides an overview of what is included in the plan, but it also provides quick access to various parts of the plan.

Prepare a Synopsis of the Plan in an Executive Summary and Background Statement

The executive summary, written at the conclusion of the preparation of the business plan, provides a short summary of the highlights of the plan for the reader. The background statement provides a history of the project or business, as well as a general statement regarding the intended mission of the venture. This mission statement is a general expression of the organization's future direction. It will identify the market, environment, strengths, and management preferences.

Describe the Management Team

This section should describe the background of the entrepreneur and the management team. For the smaller business it may simply include a résumé. The qualifications relating to the experience and education of the owner-manager are important aspects.

Establish Business Objectives

Have clearly thought-out and formally written objectives for the business. The objectives identify goals to be met in order to achieve the mission of the enterprise. The mission of the business indicates in a general, long-term way what the business is and what it intends to do. To be effective, an objective must be specific. Specific and quantitative objectives allow meaningful evaluation of the business's performance. Objectives can be set in the following areas for the initial year and for a few years following start-up:

- *Business size.* This includes the size of the physical facilities, financial commitments, and number of employees.

- *Production levels.* The plan should include the number of products, product lines, and unit production anticipated.

- *Performance levels.* Sales, market share, and profit level should all be estimated and may form part of the plan.

Plan the Marketing Approach

The next step in the business plan is to develop a marketing plan. Considerable information regarding the calculation of market potential and market share, both essential parts of the marketing plan, is provided in Chapter 3. The following additional key aspects of a marketing plan should be investigated before starting the business.

Have a Clear Concept of the Target Market. It is important that the prospective small business owner have a clear idea of who the target customer is and have a well-developed customer profile. This profile should include such demographic information as age, income, occupation, and social class, as well as certain personality and lifestyle characteristics.

After determining the target market, the owner can perform the steps discussed in Chapter 3: determining market area, market area population, market potential, and market share. Sometimes this information can be obtained using secondary data alone, but often primary research will be required. Chapter 8 illustrates a more detailed target market profile.

Understand the Target Market's Needs, Wants, and Purchasing Habits. Understanding the target market's needs, wants, and purchasing habits is essential in formulating a marketing strategy. Answers to the following questions may prove valuable:

- Where do, or where will, the target customers purchase the product or service?

- When do, or when will, they purchase it?

- What product or service attributes influence the purchase decision?

- In what quantities will purchases be made?

- Most important, why do customers, or why will they, purchase the product or service?

Once again, the answers to some of these questions may be obtained using secondary data, but primary research may be required. Incident 4-3 illustrates how one entrepreneur recognized an unmet need in the market and translated it into a business by setting objectives and planning.

Be Aware of Any Uncontrollable Factors That Might Affect the Marketing of the Product or Service. Several factors external to the business can affect the marketing plan and should be investigated, including the following.

Business Gateway
www.
businessgateway.ca

Exisiting or Pending Legislation Relevant to the Business. New laws relating to marketing practices such as advertising, pricing, and manufacturing can have a significant impact on the business and cannot be ignored. This information may be obtained from an office of the federal government or the equivalent provincial agency.

State of the Economy in the Market. The prospective small business owner should investigate whether the state of the economy is in a recovery or recessionary period. This trend also can influence the effectiveness of the marketing plan. Statistics Canada and private reports can provide this information.

Extent and Strategies of the Competition. The entrepreneur should attempt to evaluate the competition and look for competitive strengths in the prospective business. A recent study found that 33 percent of Canadian entrepreneurs omit this important aspect from their business plans.[4]

Cultural Norms of the Market. The entrepreneur should ensure that the new business conforms to the social and cultural norms of the market. This is especially important for exporters and for companies moving into new markets. An important aspect in this area relates to social responsibility. A code of ethics should be established for the organization's operations.

New Technology That Might Affect the Business. New technology should be reviewed and monitored regularly as it can represent either opportunities for the business or detrimental

---

INCIDENT 4-3   Agent of Change

Trafford Publishing is an excellent example of a business that was developed based on an observed need. Unlike other publishers, Trafford Publishing will publish any book, novels, memoirs, diatribes or software manuals as long as the author is willing to pay the cost, and the material is not hateful, pornographic, or libelous in any way. This allows anyone to see their words in print.

Trafford's president and CEO, Bruce Batchelor, started the firm in 1995, along with his wife Marsha and two partners, John Norris and Steve Fisher. Batchelor, a communications consultant, says the company found a niche in exploiting the combination of two technologies: the Internet and high quality print-on-demand equipment. As Trafford has rewritten the rules of North American publishing, Batchelor considers his firm a change agent in the publishing industry. Batchelor is now taking his model overseas, as he sees growth potential in Europe. He has offices in England, Ireland, and Spain.

Source: Adapted from Charles Mandel, "Agent of Change," *Profit*, June 2004, p. 51.

competitor strategies. Trade magazines and competitor strategies are good sources of information concerning new technology.

Plan the Marketing Program. After collecting the above information, the entrepreneur can formulate a marketing program. The essential aspects of the marketing program are as follows:

- *The product or service.* This includes such information as how the product or service is developed, sources of material, and level of quality, variety, and packaging.

- *The distribution system.* This includes determining the path the product or service will take to reach the consumer or ultimate user and may involve selection of wholesalers and retailers.

- *Promotion.* This involves decisions regarding promotion budgets and advertising versus personal selling, and developing appropriate communications.

- *Pricing.* The development of pricing policies, including the calculation of specific price levels, should be planned. These elements of the marketing program are discussed in more detail in Chapter 8.

Describe the Selection of the Location

The next component of a business plan is selecting the location for the business. In setting up a new business, the prospective owner needs to determine the trading area or city in which to locate. Then the owner selects the specific site within the trading area. New Internet services such as Google Maps may be helpful in identifying and selecting suitable locations.

The Trading Area. Several criteria are commonly used to select the trading area. Choosing the general trading area is often more critical for manufacturers than for retailers or service firms, whereas the selection of a specific site within the trade area is generally more important for retailers. The following information is valuable in selecting the trading area.

Economic Base. Information on population, employment levels, income levels, retail sales, and house values within the trading area may be needed. These elements help small manufacturers determine the availability of employees and expected pay scales. For retail and service firms, they indicate the potential for future sales. One should also examine the trends relating to these key indicators. Most of this information may be obtained from secondary data such as the government sources listed in Appendix 3B on the website.

Attitude of Trading Area toward New Businesses. Many communities are eager to attract new industry and offer various kinds of incentives for new businesses. Although this benefit is usually more important for manufacturers, any small business owner should contact the local city administration or chamber of commerce regarding incentives. Often these agencies are aware of specific types of businesses their communities need.

Competition. Competitive firms in a trading area should be noted. A retail or service firm with a fixed geographic market should evaluate various trading areas on the basis of saturation levels for the type of outlet it will establish. There are many methods of calculating the saturation index. A method commonly used in the retailing industry is to divide retail sales of all competitors by the selling space of the trading area:

$$\text{Saturation} = \frac{\text{Competing retail sales}}{\text{Competing retail space}}$$

The saturation index can be compared with other trading areas or industry norms. The higher the index, the more attractive the opportunity. The statistics needed to compute a saturation index can be obtained from city and provincial or territorial licence and tax records, Statistics Canada reference books, or personal visits.

Costs. Obviously a key consideration in selecting a trading area is the cost of land and buildings. Another is the cost of required services and expenses once the business is operating. These include such items as utilities, business taxes, and insurance.

The trading area decision can be quantified to allow evaluation among several alternatives. Figure 4-2 shows an example of such a calculation.

The Site. After selecting the trading area, the prospective owner should investigate the following items in selecting the specific site.

Accessibility. For the manufacturer, this means accessibility of transportation services for incoming supplies and materials, as well as ease of shipping the finished product. It might also include the site's accessibility to necessary services, employees of the business, and protection services such as the fire department.

For the retailer, proximity to major arteries and transit lines and availability of parking is important to ensure maximum customer traffic. Assessing traffic patterns, both pedestrian and vehicular, may be critical to success, especially for retailers of certain types of merchandise (Chapter 8 further discusses the location considerations for retail goods). Often the chamber of commerce can provide information on traffic flows.

Site Costs. The costs of sites within a community usually vary considerably. Generally the higher-traffic areas are more expensive to buy or lease. One should also investigate other possible costs such as utilities, taxes, and licences.

Restrictions. When evaluating a site, any restrictive ordinances such as zoning by-laws should be investigated. Such restrictions may hinder current operations as well as future expansion.

Site History. The prospective owner should find out whether the site has had several tenants or owners over the years. If this is the case, he or she should investigate the reasons for the turnover before proceeding to purchase or lease the site.

Proximity to Other Businesses. Will the surrounding businesses have a positive or negative influence on the business? Levels of competitiveness and complementarity are two signifi-

Figure 4-2	Evaluation of a Trading Area	
1 = Poor; 5 = Excellent		
Criteria	**Trading Area A**	**Trading Area B**
Economic base		
Attitude		
Competition		
Costs		
Other		
Total		

cant factors. Figure 4-3 gives examples of the positive and negative effects of these factors for both noncompetitive and competitive businesses.

Physical Characteristics. Size, frontal footage, external facade, contour, and shape are all important considerations in site selection. The business should blend in with surrounding businesses, but it should also be distinctive.

The evaluation form shown in Figure 4-4, similar to that for the trading area analysis, might be used in making the site selection decision.

The Buy-or-Lease Decision. In selecting the specific site, a major consideration is whether to own or lease the premises. Because ownership is generally more expensive, most small businesses find that to reduce the already high risk at the initial stages, leasing is the more attractive option. The small business owner should investigate several factors before signing a lease contract.

Cost of the Lease. The owner-manager should investigate the cost of the lease, how the rent is calculated, when the payments are due, and what taxes and utilities apply. Most leases are calculated on a per-square-footage basis. In retailing, a percentage of gross sales is often added to the cost of the lease in the form of royalties.

Figure 4-3	Influence of Neighbouring Businesses
Positive Influence from Neighbouring Businesses	**Negative Influence from Neighbouring Businesses**
Complementary—for example, a pharmacy by a doctor's office	Uncomplementary—businesses such as a mortuary, tavern, and factory
Competitive—could be positive for shopping goods such as clothing, automobiles, and motels	Competitive—for nonshopping goods such as convenience stores

Figure 4-4	Evaluation of the Actual Site	
1 = Poor; 5 = Excellent		
Criteria	**Actual Site A**	**Actual Site B**
Accessibility		
Costs		
Restrictions		
History		
Effect of other businesses		
Physical characteristics		
Other		
Total		

Length of the Lease. Questions concerning the length of the lease include these: How long is the contract for? Is there a provision for renewal at the end of that time? What notice is required for renewal, termination, or rent increase?

Restrictions. Potential restrictions on the use of the property should be investigated. Can the site be subleased to someone else? Does anyone have the right to use a part of the property? Are there certain services or products that cannot be sold or manufactured at the site?

Repairs and Leasehold Improvements. Who is responsible for any repairs and improvements required? When the lease expires, who will own such improvements?

Insurance Coverage. What insurance does the lessor have on the property? What about liability insurance coverage? What insurance coverage will be required by the lessee?

Running the Business from One's Home. The final important consideration in site selection is the possibility of operating the business out of one's home. A recent study found that home businesses were operated in 2.8 million Canadian households, a 33 percent increase from 1995 (see Figure 4-5) and that 44.6 percent of Canadians who work at home are self-employed.[5] A recent estimate pegs the percentage of small businesses that operate out of the home at 53 percent.[6] And estimates are that soon two out of every three households will be running either a part-time or full-time business.[7] Some of the best home-based businesses are business services and consulting, computer-related services, marketing and public relations, alternative medicine, independent sales, and online sales. A primary reason for the increase in home-based businesses is the utilization of computer technology. Such equipment allows the entrepreneur access to information and communication capabilities on par with larger businesses.[8] Incident 4-4 provides an example of the establishment of a home-based business.

| **Figure 4-5** | **Growth in the Number of People Working from Home** |

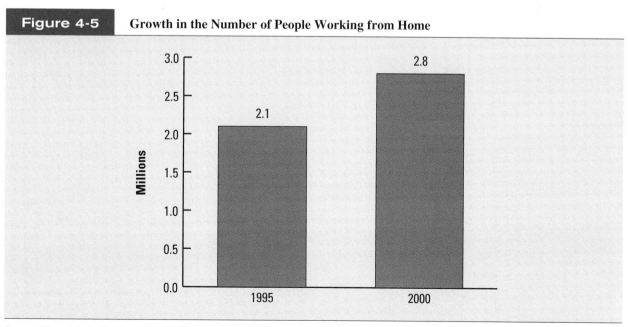

Source: "Growth in the Number of People Working from Home" adapted from the article "Evolution of the Canadian Workplace: Work from Home," published in the Statistics Canada publication *Perspectives on Labour and Income*, Catalogue 75-001, Vol. 2, No. 9, September 2001.

INCIDENT 4-4 Toying with Success

At age 23, Steve Nichols is the founder and sole employee of SteveToys Custom Toy Co. Even though he considers himself the sole employee, Nichols has friends who help him out when the orders start piling up. The idea for the business came to him several years ago during the Christmas season when he was strapped for cash but he wanted to give Christmas presents to his family. He bought some material and proceeded to make customized clay figures for each person in his family. The family loved the gifts which confirmed Nichols' idea to start the toy business. Now this young entrepreneur designs custom clay toy figures from his home in Edmonton.

Nichols invested $4000 to set up his home-based office in October 2002. Since then, his business has been growing rapidly. Although he was confident in his business ability, he kept his day job in the beginning to help him remain financially stable. His appearance on a morning talk show during the 2002 Christmas season really helped him launch his product into the Edmonton community. He began receiving so many orders that he had to turn people down. Since then, he has realized that the business has more potential than as just a side hobby so he quit his job as a property owner to manage the company full time. He has committed himself to developing and implementing a more comprehensive marketing plan for his home-based business. Currently, he realizes profits of about $5000 per month.

Source: Adapted from Tracy Hyatt, "Toying With Success," *Alberta Venture*, April 2003, p. 16.

Some situations are particularly suitable for a home-based business. First, if the business is started on a part-time basis, as many are, the costs associated with establishing a home office are minimal. Second, the lower costs associated with starting a business in one's home reduce the financial risks of a venture that may already carry a high degree of risk. Thus, a home office can serve as a temporary office until the business is more firmly established. Third, a home office is suitable for many businesses for which location is of minimal importance. Many service and some small manufacturing businesses fit in this category. Fourth, locating the business in the home offers several tax-related advantages. Chapter 13 gives more details on such advantages.

Determine the Physical Facilities

In preparing the feasibility analysis outlined in Chapter 3, the entrepreneur should already have prepared a detailed estimate of the total capital needed to acquire the building, equipment, furniture, fixtures, and possibly initial inventory. The size of investment in buildings and equipment is typically larger for a manufacturing firm, while the investment in inventory tends to be larger for the retail firm.

Before constructing buildings and purchasing equipment, the relevant building codes and construction standards should be investigated and required permits obtained.

In addition to these capital requirements and standards, a plan should be made of the operations flow within the business. This includes such factors as purchasing, inventory control, the production process, the interior layout, and distribution of the finished product. Chapter 11 discusses all these items in detail.

Insurance. Small businesses face several risks. Figure 4-6 illustrates four ways that an entrepreneur can deal with risk. The entrepreneur should analyze the extent of such risks and determine whether they threaten the existence of the company. Generally, entrepreneurs transfer risk by buying insurance when the loss would be serious. Insurance coverage for such risks should be purchased before the start-up of the business.

Figure 4-6	**Ways to Manage Risk**

Method	Type of Risk
Self-insurance	Cover losses out of cash flow (asset values small)
Prevention	Burglar alarms, inspections, education, hiring practices
Avoidance of risk	Leasing, incorporation
Transfer of risk	Purchasing insurance (asset values large)

Types of Insurance. Common insurable risks for a small business include the following:

Loss or damage of property. This type of coverage protects the business in the case of fire, theft, and similar occurrences.

Business interruption. If one of the above problems occurs, this type of insurance protects the earning power lost due to the occurrence for a short period of time.

Liability and disability. This coverage includes bodily injury to employees or customers and could include liability coverage for company officials such as members of the board of directors of the company.

Life insurance. This insurance is usually bought in the form of a group insurance plan or occasionally key employee life insurance. Partners of a business may also desire to purchase life insurance for the other partner(s).

Insurance Decisions. The entrepreneur faces three insurance-related decisions:

1. What kind of insurance to purchase
2. How much coverage to take out
3. From whom to purchase the insurance

In making these decisions, the following rules of thumb commonly used in the insurance industry are helpful. The first and most important rule is, Don't risk more than you can afford to lose. In other words, if the prospective loss will put the business into bankruptcy or serious financial difficulty, insurance should be taken out. Usually the probability of these losses occurring is low, and the associated insurance premiums are also low. The maximum sustainable loss will, of course, vary across firms and times in a particular business.

A second rule of insurance management is, Don't risk a lot for a little. In implementing this second rule, the premium should be related to the potential loss and treated as savings or costs. For example, if comprehensive physical damage insurance on a $14,000 automobile costs $350 per year, the savings or return if the insurance is not purchased and the risk is assumed equals 350/14,000, or 2.5 percent. The owner is exposing a $14,000 investment to possible loss or damage for a 2.5 percent return, and that is risking a lot for a little. Conversely, a driver who pays $150 a year for auto collision coverage with a $50 deductible, when the same coverage with a $100 deductible would cost only $125 per year, is paying a cost of $25/$50, or 50 percent for the second $50 of coverage. Here, from a cost point of view, the car owner is paying dearly for a small return. In the first case, the purchase of insurance is consistent with the rule; in the second, it is not. For this reason, it is usually advisable to purchase the largest deductible the business can afford. This can result in substantial premium savings.

The third rule is that insurance should be taken out only when absolutely necessary. Insurance always costs more than the expected value of a loss because the premium must also include the insurer's administration and selling costs, plus profit. This insurance is economically feasible only when the probability of loss is low and the severity of a potential loss is high. Therefore, in the opposite situation, the best approach may be to take preventative measures and build these losses into the cost or expense structure of the business.

The fourth rule is to buy adequate coverage. The reason is that all property insurance contracts contain a co-insurance clause. The co-insurance clause states that if the amount of insurance purchased on the property is less than some stated percentage (usually 80 percent), the insured will share all partial losses up to the face value of the policy. The purpose of co-insurance is to encourage the small business owner to buy adequate insurance coverage for the business. For example, if a small business owner has a building with a current replacement value of $110,000 and a policy containing an 80 percent co-insurance clause, $80,000 of insurance is required for collecting on partial losses. If only $60,000 of insurance were purchased and a $10,000 loss occurred, the insurance company would pay only $60,000 (coverage)/$80,000 (co-insurance), or $7,500 of the loss.

The last insurance purchasing rule involves adequately investigating both the insurance company and the agent. Choosing an insurance company with financial stability, satisfactory claims service, and competitive premiums is important, and the selection of the agent may be even more critical. The agent should have a thorough knowledge of insurance, be located where he or she can provide prompt service on claims and enquiries, and possess a genuine interest in clients' needs. The agent should be questioned regarding the claim settlement procedures, cancellation procedures, and premium rates. Many insurance companies now have special policies tailored to small businesses.

Care should be taken to ensure that coverage is current. As replacement costs rise, the level of coverage should increase. Most insurance companies now adjust policies for inflation automatically.

Plan the Financing

Four major financial aspects of the new business should be planned in advance of opening.

Establish Capital Requirements and Make Feasibility Projections. As indicated previously, these calculations are made when preparing a feasibility analysis. The results of these calculations form an integral part of the projected income statement for at least the first year of operations and in some cases five years into the future. Although making financial projections involves considerable uncertainty, using average industry financial benchmarks and ratios can increase the reliability of these estimates. These benchmarks and ratios are available through Statistics Canada, Industry Canada, Dun and Bradstreet, and some provincial or territorial government economic development departments. The website addresses for these are found in Appendix 3A and further explanation of the use of these numbers is made in Chapter 10. In conjunction with the income statement projection, enough information would have likely been obtained to prepare a projected balance sheet and cash flow statement. Although these statements are described fully in Chapter 10, Figure 7-3 in Chapter 7 shows the format of a cash flow that would be required in a business plan. It may be advisable for the entrepreneur to enlist the services of an accountant in completing these financial statements. Proper preparation of this financial data is key to obtaining funding from investors and lenders.

Determine Sources of Funding. The projections discussed above provide an estimate of the funds required to get started and to operate the business. After calculating the required funds, the owner will need to determine a balance between his or her own funds (equity) and borrowed funds (debt). Because raising funds is such a critical area for the small business, Chapter 7 is devoted entirely to the types of funds required, sources of funding for the small business, and methods of evaluating those sources. Sufficient start-up funding is of critical importance to a new small business.

Plan the Accounting and Bookkeeping Systems. An essential part of any business is record keeping. Bookkeeping is the recording and classifying of the internal and external transactions of the business. This may be an area that requires professional advice. Chapter 10 reviews the types of financial records kept and the different types of bookkeeping systems used by small businesses.

Determine Financial Evaluation Measures. One area crucial to the success of the small business is the financial evaluation of operations. To perform this evaluation, the owner should determine the key indicators of the financial health of the business. These indicators include profit margins, return on investment, and inventory turnover. The owner should also set up a system of regular monitoring and reporting of these areas. This system may also require professional assistance to establish and is discussed in detail in Chapter 10.

Plan the Personnel

Chapter 12 discusses the operating details of personnel administration for a small business. The following are the major considerations in organizing for the management of personnel.

Administrative Structure. This involves setting up the responsibility and reporting procedure for all employees of the business. If there are only two owners, the administrative structure takes the form of a clear division of responsibilities. A business with several employees might require an organizational chart.

Employee Recruitment and Training. The plan for hiring, training, and managing those who will work in the business should be determined.

Personnel Policies. Operating policies affecting employees should be stated explicitly and be formally prepared before the business begins operations.

Investigate the Legal Requirements

A small business can be significantly affected by the legal environment in which it operates. Considerable legislation in Canada applies to the ongoing management of the business. Typical areas covered are advertising and promotion, credit, sales contracts, pricing, distribution channels, personnel, record keeping, and financial relationships. Legislation pertaining to each of these aspects of managing the ongoing business is covered in later chapters.

This section discusses the legal requirements relating to the establishment of the business that should be included in the business plan. Some of the most important aspects are selecting the legal structure, investigating which licences are required, and filing for patent protection if necessary. The legal information provided here and in later chapters is intended not to replace the advice and direction of a lawyer but merely to provide a background against which the entrepreneur can work with such professionals more knowledgeably. Care should be taken in the selection of a lawyer. References from business acquaintances or a lawyer referral service could ensure that you enlist the services of a lawyer who has small business experience and expertise.

Legal Structure. The owner must decide under which legal structure the business will operate. Five types of legal structures can be used.

1. Sole proprietorship. In a sole proprietorship, the business is owned by a single individual. The proprietor has perfect freedom of operation; when business decisions are made or when actions are taken, it is not necessary to get anyone else's consent. Similarly, all profits are the property of the owner and need not be shared with anyone else. There are, however, certain disadvantages to the one-owner organization. Limited personal assets, for example, do not encourage lenders and cannot always provide the capital needed to meet the needs of the business. But perhaps the biggest disadvantage is the proprietor's personal liability for business debts; in case of business failure, the owner's home, automobile, stocks, cash, and other personal assets may be seized by creditors to satisfy the debts of the business. Registration with the provincial or territorial government is normally required and can help protect the name of the business. Figure 4-7 lists the advantages and disadvantages of a sole proprietorship.

2. Partnership. In most ways, partnerships are similar to sole proprietorships except that partnerships include two or more partners. Partnerships typically provide increased resources and complementary abilities, but they also increase the possibility of conflict (see Incident 4-5). It is therefore essential to have a buyout clause built into the agreement. (See Incident 4-6.) Figure 4-8 (on page 108) summarizes the advantages and disadvantages of partnerships. There are two kinds of partnerships a small business might use:

1. *Limited partnership.* In a limited partnership, one or more partners obtain limited liability in exchange for not taking an active part in the day-to-day management of the business or acting on behalf of the company. These partners, often called silent partners, usually provide only the financial investment as their part of the ownership interest. Small businesses are increasingly using this form of ownership because silent partners constitute an important source of equity funding. In addition, limited partnerships offer some tax advantages for the silent partner while retaining the positive aspects of sole proprietorship for the entrepreneur.

Business Gateway
www.
businessgateway.ca

2. *General partnership.* When the partners share in the management or control of the business, it is referred to in legal terms as a general partnership. The most obvious advantage to this form of organization over the proprietorship form is that added capital is made available by combining the assets of the partners, and money is usually easier to borrow because the partners share debts. Similarly, the personal abilities of the partners

Figure 4-7	Advantages and Disadvantages of a Sole Proprietorship	
	Advantages	**Disadvantages**
	1. Simple and inexpensive to start	1. Unlimited liability
	2. Offers individual control over operations, profits, and so on	2. Often more difficult to obtain financing
	3. Fewer forms and reports to fill out	3. The personal tax rate may be higher than the corporate rate
	4. Some tax advantages	4. The life of the business terminates on owner's death

---

INCIDENT 4-5   Skateboard Haven

Mark van der Zalm, a skateboarding park designer, and Kyle Dion, an avid skateboarder, first met in 1999 because Dion thought van der Zalm did a sloppy design job on a skateboarding park. At first, van der Zalm was annoyed with Dion's criticisms, but he soon realized that Dion was right on the money. The two formed a joint venture to design and build skate parks.

Located just outside of Vancouver, van der Zalm + Associates leads the overall park design while Dion's New Line Inc. Skateparks looks after construction and ironing out the rough edges. Clean-cut van der Zalm and tattooed Dion have very different personalities and skills, but that actually helps in many aspects of the business.

The company is experiencing rapid growth across the country as interest in skate parks rises across the Prairies and in Ontario. Because of this growth, the duo no longer has as much time to review strategy together. "We used to travel everywhere together. That's just impossible now," says van der Zalm. It still takes a lot of face time together to get a project up and running, though. Public consultations with residents, design discussions with teenagers and parents, and crews flown out to build the park all have to be done as quickly as possible.

The success of the company is based on the pair's ability to do good work on select projects, instead of gobbling up every single project available. The partners are also focusing on more permanent, high-margin opportunities such as concrete skate parks, or wood or steel ramps for towns that can't afford concrete. The pair also plans to renegotiate their joint venture soon.

Source: Adapted from Gabrielle Giroday, "Dude, How Do We Handle All These Orders?" *Report on Small Business*, Fall 2005, pp. 22–25.

INCIDENT 4-6   Their Work Is All Play

Childspace Playgrounds Ltd., based in Olds Alberta, got its start under rather unusual circumstances. In 1980, Mountain View Association for the Mentally Handicapped was looking for potential employment for its clients. It was decided that playgrounds would be an option because the manufacturing process required only a number of easily learned skills. Because Chris Whittaker, a former shop teacher, was on the committee, he was put in charge. Childspace Playgrounds was established in 1981.

Childspace continued its affiliation with Mountain View until 1995, when the organization felt that it no longer needed it association with Childspace because attitudes about employing disabled people had changed. Chris decided it was either buy the company or clean out his desk so he and the former sales manager put up an offer.

In the summer of 2004, Chris and his son Andrew bought out the partner and today the company is doing very well. Andrew is now general manager and oversees about 30 employees. The company posts annual revenues between $2 and $4 million and has shipped playground equipment as far away as Bermuda, Haiti, and Hong Kong.

Source: Adapted from Natasha Mekhail, "Their Work is All Play," *Alberta Venture*, July/August 2005, p. 11.

---

are complemented, and they may succeed together when neither could alone. However, each partner by law is equally responsible for all the debts of the partnership, regardless of the amount of capital contributed and regardless of any agreement among them to the contrary. Also, any one partner can bind the entire partnership in a business arrangement, even if it is contrary to the wishes or judgment of the majority. The general partnership has other disadvantages as well, such as the termination of the business by the death or withdrawal of any one of the partners and the inability of a partner to sell or

Figure 4-8	Advantages and Disadvantages of a Partnership

Advantages	Disadvantages
1. Simple and inexpensive to start	1. Unlimited liability
2. Pooling of financial and skill resources	2. Death of a partner terminates the partnership unless a provision to the contrary is specified in the partnership agreement
3. Tax advantages (i.e., income splitting)	3. Greater possibility for disagreements (buy-sell agreements should be drawn up in the event that a partner wants to leave the business)

assign his or her interest in the partnership without the consent of all the other partners. However, both of these conditions or eventualities can be circumvented by appropriate provisions in a written partnership agreement, which should be prepared with the consultation of a lawyer. Although not legally required in order to form a general partnership, such an agreement is nonetheless advisable, even among relatives and close friends. At a minimum, it should specify the following:

1. Duration of the partnership.

2. Administrative responsibilities and authority of each partner.

3. Withdrawals and salaries of the partners.

4. Provision for the arbitration of policy disputes among the partners.

5. Provisions for the withdrawal of partners or the admission of additional partners.

6. Amount of capital invested by each partner.

7. Division of profit or loss. (Regardless of the amount of capital invested, general partners must share profit or loss equally unless there is an agreement among the partners to the contrary.)

8. Distribution of assets in the event of dissolution. (As in the case of profits or losses, this distribution must be on an equal basis unless otherwise agreed on in writing.)

9. Settlements in the event of death or disability of a partner. This might include a buy-sell agreement funded with business life insurance in amounts equal to the interest of each partner; thus the surviving partner(s) would be assured of full title to the business, and the deceased partner's estate would be assured of receiving the full value of his or her share of the business. In the absence of such an agreement, the business might well be forced into liquidation to satisfy demands of the deceased partner's estate.

In a general partnership, unlimited liability applies to all partners.

3. Cooperative. The cooperative is used infrequently by small businesses. In most respects, its strengths and weaknesses are similar to those of a corporation (see Figure 4-9). The distinguishing feature is that in a cooperative (which needs a minimum of six members), each member has only one vote, whereas in a corporation each voting share has a vote.

| **Figure 4-9** | **Advantages and Disadvantages of a Corpriation** |

Advantages	Disadvantages
1. The continuity of the business exists even if the owner dies.	1. The cost to incorporate generally ranges from $800 to $1,200.
2. The owners have limited liability.	2. There is a greater reporting requirement by government.
3. The business may have a manager with professional training or expertise.	3. Flexibility may be reduced because of the binding provisions of the corporate charter.
4. It's easier to raise funds, as lenders and equity investors usually look more favourably on incorporated companies.	4. Losses cannot be deducted from other personal income of the owner.
5. The corporate tax rate on small businesses (see Appendix 13B on the website) can be lower than one's personal rate.	5. Lenders often require a personal guarantee, negating the advantage of limited liability.
6. Incorporation can assist in establishing commercial credibility.	
7. Liability insurance may be less expensive.	

4. Corporation. The corporation, or limited company, is becoming an increasingly popular form of structuring a small business. Industry Canada reports that more than 67 percent of all self-employed businesses with paid help and 24 percent of small business without paid help in Canada were incorporated in 2001.[9] Moreover, Statistics Canada reports that incorporated companies grew at an annual rate of 3.9 percent compared to 1 percent for unincorporated businesses.[10] The corporation is a legal entity that is separate and distinct from the shareholders of the business. The chief advantages of the corporation are (1) continuity in existence (2) easy transferability of ownership interest, and (3) limited liability of shareholders. The corporation is long-lived, being able to continue in existence up to the time limit granted in its charter, which may even be granted in perpetuity, whereas other forms of organization may cease abruptly with the death of the proprietor or a partner. Ownership in a corporation is easily transferred merely by the sale or exchange of stock; permission of other shareholders is not required. Care should be taken in drafting a shareholder agreement in order to facilitate the smooth transition of the ownership of the company in the event that a key owner leaves the business. Legal liability of owners or shareholders for suits for personal injury or other activities connected with operating the business is limited to the amount of funds invested in the business. The corporate form of business organization is also more attractive for raising equity capital, because capital can be more readily obtained from many more sources and because of the legal limited liability of corporate shareholders. A corporation has certain disadvantages, however. Its activities are limited to those specifically granted in its charter. Similarly, its geographical area of operations is limited to the province or territory granting its charter until permission is secured from each of the other provinces or territories in which it desires to operate; this means that additional filing fees must be paid and additional legal requirements observed. The corporation must make numerous reports for taxation and other purposes in each jurisdiction in which it does business; not only has federal and provincial or territorial regulation of corporations been increasing for some time, but the paperwork required also increases greatly as the corporation grows in size.

The day-to-day operations of a corporation are handled by a manager who is appointed by and reports to a board of directors. The board of directors is elected by the shareholders. Often in very small businesses the manager, director, and major shareholder are the same person. Many small businesses have found it valuable to enlist the services of lawyers, accountants, and other noncompeting businesspeople to serve on their boards of directors.

The vast majority of incorporated small businesses are private companies. For a business to qualify as a private company, the following conditions must exist:

- The right to transfer shares is restricted, usually requiring the approval of the board of directors.

- The number of shareholders is limited to 50. The company cannot sell new shares publicly.

Figure 4-9 (on the previous page) summarizes the advantages and disadvantages of a corporation.

Steps in Incorporation. Most entrepreneurs regard incorporation as a very complex process that requires a lawyer's assistance. Although it is advisable for a small business to enlist the services of a lawyer to assist in incorporating the business, some entrepreneurs with relatively uncomplicated businesses have incorporated their businesses successfully on their own. Recently, incorporation software has been developed to assist entrepreneurs with self-incorporation.[11] Incorporating a business involves four steps:

1. *Selection of a name for the business.* This name must be submitted to and approved by the provincial or territorial government department that handles incorporations (see Appendix 4C on the website). The selection can be facilitated by doing a computer search to ensure that no similar names are currently being used.

2. *Development of the share structure, directors, restrictions on share transfers, and so on.* The owner must determine the number of shares to authorize, the number of shares to issue, the number of directors, the timing of meetings, and approvals required for shares to be bought or sold.

3. *A description of company operations.* This section describes what the business can and cannot do.

4. *Acquisition of the necessary supplies.* This includes such items as the corporate stamp, the minute book, and the necessary journals and ledgers.

5. *Joint Ventures.* A joint venture is an agreement between one or more sole proprietors, partnerships, or corporations to participate in a business venture. Although similar to a partnership in many ways, this increasingly popular form of business allows for individual ownership of assets in the venture. Items such as capital cost allowance can be used by either party, depending on the need. Other advantages and disadvantages are similar to those in a partnership (see Figure 4-8 on page 108).

Licences and Taxes. Before starting a business, the prospective owner should investigate the required licences and the taxes that may be payable to the government. Licences and taxes can be levied by federal, provincial or territorial, and municipal governments, and these requirements differ among various industries. The following are the most common licences and taxes that apply to the small business. For a more detailed listing, see Appendix 4D on the website.

Federal Government

1. *Income tax.* The income tax is a tax on both companies and individuals earning income from a business operating in Canada. The rates vary by province or territory and by industry (see Chapter 13). Although the income tax payments are made to the federal government, part of this amount is transferred to the province or territory in which the business earns income. Some provinces and territories now collect their own business income tax.

2. *Goods and services tax.* The goods and services tax (GST) is a value-added tax levied on many sellers of goods and services by the federal government. The tax, which currently is 6 percent of the sale price, is collected from the purchaser by the seller and remitted to the government quarterly. Although the GST has met with considerable resistance from business and consumers, it has been an effective method for increasing government revenues. Certain exemptions from the GST, relating to the size of the business and type of merchandise sold, are available. The small business owner should consult Canada Revenue Agency (CRA) for the information about how the GST applies to his or her business and for information about obtaining the GST remittance number.

3. *Excise tax.* The excise tax is an extra tax imposed on certain goods sold in Canada. Payment is made by the manufacturer and is a hidden component in the cost of purchasing those goods.

Provincial or Territorial Government

1. *Income tax.* A percentage of federal income tax payable is assessed by the provinces and territories. Some (Ontario, Quebec, and Alberta) collect this tax. In other provinces and territories, the federal government collects the tax and remits a portion to the province or territory.

2. *Licences.* Many types of businesses require a provincial or territorial licence to operate. Some of these businesses may also require bonding.

3. *Sales tax.* Most provinces and territories levy retail sales taxes on tangible property sold or imported. This tax is collected by the retailer from the purchaser at the time of the sale and remitted to the government in much the same manner as the goods and services tax. Many businesses have found the administration of the sales tax more difficult since the introduction of the GST.

Municipal Government

1. *Licences.* Municipalities (cities) are authorized to license all businesses operating within their boundaries.

2. *Property taxes.* Municipalities are also authorized to levy property taxes on the real estate on which a business operates.

3. *Business taxes.* Other taxes levied on businesses by a municipality might be for water use or other services.

Intellectual Property Protection. As many entrepreneurs create new products or processes, a critical measure for ensuring their success is to secure legal protection. This protection could be required for a patent, trademark, industrial design, or copyright. Copyrights are for literary, artistic, musical, and dramatic works. Industrial designs include shapes, patterns, or ornamentation of an industrially produced object. Trademarks are words, symbols, or slogans that represent origins of goods and services. A patent, the most commonly obtained protection for a small business, is a right granted by the government to an inventor to exclude others from making, using, or selling his or her invention in Canada for 17 years.

It is important for the inventor to record the date of the invention and file for the patent as soon as possible. Registration of a patent may be made through a Consumer and Corporate Affairs office or the Commissioner of Patents, Ottawa-Hull, Canada, K1A OE1. Other helpful information about intellectual property protection may be obtained through the Strategis website listed on the website. In Canada, if the patent has been used publicly or sold within the previous two years, it may not be granted. A patent agent or lawyer can provide valuable assistance in the patenting process and may be essential if infringement on the patent occurs later. Careful screening to ensure that the invention is new, useful, and a result of inventive ingenuity is used in the patent approval.

Two steps are required to register a patent:

1. Conduct a search at the patent office to ensure that the idea is not already registered.

2. File an application—the formal request for the patent, which includes a description of the idea.

A patent application may take from one to three years to receive an approval. Nearly 29,000 patent applications are received each year in Canada, and approximately 24,000 are approved. A listing of patents is available for public perusal at most public libraries. Similar procedures for obtaining patents are followed in registering trademarks, industrial designs, and copyrights. Applications for these items are also obtained through Consumer and Corporate Affairs or the Commissioner of Patents.

Summary

1. Organizing one's own business has several advantages and disadvantages. The advantages of having a hand in determining the type of business, equipment, employees, inventory, and market are balanced against the disadvantages of uncertainty concerning demand, unforeseen problems, and the time required to establish the business.

2. A business plan provides a sense of direction for the business, determines the viability, assists in obtaining financing, and helps the owner to evaluate progress.

3. The basic steps in preparing a business plan are preparing a table of contents and synopsizing the plan in an executive summary and background statement (best done when the plan is complete), setting the overall mission of the business, establishing business objectives, planning the marketing approach, selecting the location, determining the physical facilities, planning the financing, planning the personnel, and researching the legal requirements.

Chapter Problems and Applications

1. Investigate a small business that is for sale. What are the advantages and disadvantages to you of buying this business as opposed to starting a similar one from scratch?

2. You are thinking of opening up a small business consulting company. What uncontrollable factors might affect your decision? Explain.

3. The saturation index is useful to a prospective small business owner in selecting a trading area.

   a. Using the information in the following table, which trading area would you recommend to the prospective owner?

Location	1	2	3
Number of customers for the store	100,000	50,000	25,000
Average purchase per customer	$5	$7	$9
Total square footage of the drugstore (including the proposed store)	20,000	15,000	10,000

   b. If you excluded the proposed store (3,000 square feet), which area would you select?

   c. Which index of saturation is more accurate—the calculation with the proposed store square footage or the calculation without it? Why?

4. Which variables are important in site location for a pharmacy? Note: In answering this question, consider the variables in Figure 4-4 and rank them from 5 (most important) to 1 (least important). Justify your ranking on each variable.

5. Interview a small business owner about the details of his or her start-up plan. Find out what aspects were omitted from the plan that should have been included.

6. Choose a specific type of small business and obtain advice from an insurance agent on the types of insurance needed and the precise costs. Write a short report on your findings.

7. Visit the Canadian Intellectual Property Office (CIPO) website and find out the requirements for registering a patent.

8. Briefly discuss the differences in the development of a business plan between an e-commerce business and a retail store.

Web Exercise

www.bdc.ca

Access the BDC website and compare the components of the suggested business plan with that provided in the text.

APPENDIX 4A

Checklist for a Small Business Plan

Introduction

1. Have a table of contents, executive summary, and description of the management team been prepared?

Business Objectives

1. Have specific business objectives been set? At the end of one or five years, what will the size of the business be in gross sales? in production level? in number of employees? in market share? in profit?

Market Approach

1. Who is the target market in terms of occupation? income level? education? lifestyle?

2. What is the target market's purchasing behaviour for this product or similar products? Where are purchases made? When are purchases made? What quantities are purchased?

3. Why does the target market purchase this product or similar products? Which characteristics are preferred? What other factors influence the purchase?

4. What external constraints will affect the business? existing or pending legislation? state of the economy? competition? social or cultural trends? new technology?

5. Which product characteristics will be developed? quality level? amount of depth? type of packaging? patent protection? extent of warranty protection? level of service?

6. How will the product get to the consumer? What channel of distribution will be used? length of the channel? intensity of channel distributors? legal arrangement within the channel? type of physical transportation?

7. How will the product be promoted? What are the promotional objectives? Which media will be used? How much will be spent on production? Who is the target of the promotion? What is the promotional theme? What is the timetable for promotion?

8. What price levels will be set for the product? Which pricing policies will be instituted? What factors will influence pricing? How important is price to the target market?

Location

1. Has the location been selected?

2. In what trading area or community will the business be established? What is its economic base? its attitude toward new businesses? its saturation level in terms of competing businesses? its costs?

3. What specific site will be selected? Is it accessible to suppliers, employees, and the target market? What is the site cost? What restrictions on site use exist? What is the history of the site? What are the neighbouring businesses? What are the physical characteristics of the site?

Physical Facilities

1. Have the physical facilities been determined?

2. What building, equipment, and start-up supplies will be needed? What are the costs? What are the depreciation rates of the fixed assets? Which building codes or standards are relevant? Which permits are required? What insurance is required?

3. How will the physical facilities be organized? Is the production process efficient and safe? Has the interior layout been carefully planned? Is the exterior facade attractive?

4. How will inventories be managed? What initial inventory is required? How will inventory levels be monitored? How will inventory be valued? What method will be used to order inventory?

Financial

1. Has a financial plan for the business been made?
2. What are the financial requirements of the business? What are the start-up costs? ongoing operating costs? What are projected sales, expenses, income, and cash flow?
3. Which sources of funding will be used? how much equity? how much debt? Which sources will be used? private? commercial? government?
4. What bookkeeping system will be instituted?
5. How will the financial information be used? Which accounts will be evaluated? how often? by whom?

Personnel

1. Has a personnel plan been developed?
2. What is the administrative structure? Is there an organizational chart? a responsibility and reporting procedure? Have job descriptions and specifications been developed?
3. Have personnel policies been developed? What are the hours of work? pay levels? employee benefits? conditions and standards of employment? grievance procedures?
4. How will the business recruit employees? Where will employees be found? How will they be screened? What guidelines will be used in selection? How will employees be trained?

Legal Requirements

1. Have legal requirements been investigated?
2. Has the legal structure for the business been determined?
3. Have the relevant licences and taxes been researched?
4. Has patent protection been obtained, if necessary?

APPENDIX 4B

Sample Business Plans

BUSINESS PLAN 1—RETAIL STOCKING STORE, THE SOCK HOP

Table of Contents

Market Approach

Location

Physical Facilities

Financial

Personnel

Legal Requirements

Executive Summary and Background

The Sock Hop is a store totally devoted to socks. The product is in the medium price range, and emphasis is on variety and quality. The Sock Hop will be located in the new Park Place Mall, Lethbridge, Alberta, which is close to the downtown core. The mall, which opened in August 1988, has a variety of products and services. It contains beauty salons, shoe repair shops, movie theatres, one anchor store (Sears), jewellery stores, men's apparel, ladies apparel, children's stores, toy stores, a food fair, as well as many other specialty stores.

The majority of the customers of The Sock Hop will be between the ages of 15 and 64, both male and female. The 2005 city census indicates that there are 48,436 people between the ages of 15 and 64.[1]

The feasibility analysis shows that The Sock Hop could be a viable business within five years as it becomes well known and builds a clientele.

Description of the Management Team

The owner-manager of The Sock Hop is Sharon Stockwell. She holds a management degree from the University of Lethbridge and has eight years of experience working in the retail clothing industry full and part time. She has prepared this business plan to assist in the start-up of this venture.

Business Objectives

The Sock Hop's business plan consists of a number of objectives. The first objective relates to opportunity costs for the owner-manager. The owner would like to obtain returns that would exceed that of a salary obtained through alternative employment and the cost of capital on her equity investment in the business. Therefore,

> Salary at The Sock Hop ($24,000) + Additional profits > Salary if working for someone else + Cost of capital on equity

It should be noted that the cost of capital on equity investment is included because had the person placed her life savings in a savings account, it would have been earning a stated interest amount. Thus, for the owner-manager to remain in the business, the total tangible benefits derived from the business must be greater than they would have been without the business. This objective should be met in approximately five years.

The second objective is based on performance. Market share should increase from the present adjusted 22 percent to 33 percent within five years (medium-term goal). It is hoped that as the business grows, it will have a loyal following of customers along with a good business reputation to overcome some of the weaknesses.

---

[1] City of Lethbridge Census, 2005.

As a result, the sales and profits should also increase. The sales per square foot should increase from the present estimate of $278/sq. ft. As a way to increase overall profit, a minor objective is to increase the efficiency in selling the merchandise.

A third objective is a five-year long-term goal for future expansion. By the year 2011, the owner hopes to be able to work out a system to franchise The Sock Hop in Western Canada. By then, the bugs should be worked out of the system and a franchising plan can be established. This is dependent on the Lethbridge prototype store being successful.

A fourth (short-term) objective involves the method of financing the business. The owner-manager of The Sock Hop will not be the sole contributor of equity capital to the business. However, she wants to retain as much independence and control as possible while spreading the risk. Thus, even when equity capital is obtained, the owner-manager will retain in excess of 51 percent of the control, and there will be an option for the owner-manager to buy out other equity investors.

Market Approach

Description of the Target Market. The geographic market area for The Sock Hop is Lethbridge. However, this must be further defined into a demographic target market, since a consumer-oriented marketing strategy is to be adopted by The Sock Hop.

For The Sock Hop, the target will be anybody between the ages of 15 and 64 who lives in Lethbridge. Income level, occupation, social class, and education are relatively irrelevant for this necessary product.

The fact that this target market will be interested in quality socks at a moderate price is important. Furthermore, The Sock Hop is targeted at those who are looking for variety and fashion in socks. In addition, a good part of inventory will be devoted to high-quality socks, catering to the business community.

Uncontrollable Factors. There are four uncontrollable factors that the small business owner must understand. The owner must gather information about these uncontrollables, predict or monitor trends, and adjust the internal operations to them.

Economy. At this point, the economy in Lethbridge is positive. The type of merchandise that The Sock Hop is selling, however, tends to be recession proof. Because socks are not a high-cost item, the market should remain steady. The economic environment will be continually monitored, however, with respect to its effect on this business.

Competition. There are several stores in Lethbridge that sell socks. A lot of these stores have built up their reputation and convenient location as strengths. Reputation is one of The Sock Hop's weaknesses. However, its main strength is greater variety, particularly in fashion socks.

The Sock Hop plans to monitor the competition closely through primary observation and by reviewing industry reports on a regular basis. Competitor reactions to its entrance into the market will also be noted.

Legal Restrictions. The specific legal restrictions are discussed in the legal section of this paper. Keeping abreast of new and existing laws that affect retailers and the sock industry is important. Talking to intermediaries in the industry and reading association magazines and newspapers are effective ways to monitor legal effects.

Social/Cultural Trends. Since The Sock Hop has decided to adopt a consumer-oriented marketing strategy, it is imperative that new trends be monitored. Because the product is very fad-oriented at times, trends are going to be vital, especially to the portion of the target market that is young and attracted by the fashion stock. To keep up with these trends, industry and fashion magazines, social statistics, and government reports will be of particular help. Furthermore, observing the competition and the general surroundings will help to keep The Sock Hop management up to date on lifestyle trends, demographic changes, and purchase patterns.

Marketing Strategy

Product. The product strategy for The Sock Hop involves offering a product that can be differentiated from the competition and that will ensure a reasonable profit, anticipating the market's changes in preference and continuing product innovations.

The product will be differentiated by being more fashion-oriented. There will be more variety, greater selection, and better services offered at The Sock Hop than are found with competitors. The customer will be able to choose socks from both the fashion stock and the basic stock. There will be a full money-back guarantee to complete this total package offered to the customer—a package that will sway the consumer's choice toward The Sock Hop.

Distribution. It is an advantage that The Sock Hop is located close to other stores that carry socks, since it aids comparison. The Sock Hop is small and new and thus will have some disadvantages compared with department stores and chains. For this reason, it would be best for The Sock Hop to take part in a buying group. There are a lot of sock stores in Calgary and Edmonton, and many are operated as small businesses. The Sock Hop intends to investigate joining a buying group. In this way, it can obtain volume discounts, pass the savings on to customers, and thus remain competitive. Purchasing with a buying group will help keep a lower inventory, as slow-moving items can be purchased in minimum quantities.

In addition, The Sock Hop will use a more direct channel for purchasing, in accordance with the belief that the fewer the number of intermediaries, the higher the profit margin available to the retailer. It will use a manufacturer/supplier in Canada, if one with a good reputation for quality and dependability exists. The Sock Hop will avoid foreign suppliers, if possible, since it is The Sock Hop's policy to buy Canadian.

Pricing. Price is not the means of differentiating The Sock Hop from the competition. The Sock Hop is competing on the basis of selection, quality, service, and specialization.

Sales will be held at various times of the year to improve overall profit, to promote certain items, to counter competition, to dispose of excess inventory of inactive stock, and to improve cash flow. However, in the long term, pricing based on the full cost will be used. The economic situation, competition, market demand, and price sensitivity of the customers also have to be taken into account when establishing a markup percentage.

Promotion. The objective here is to inform, persuade, and/or remind the target market. Five percent of sales has been devoted to advertising for the first year. This is in spite of the fact that the Dun and Bradstreet average for small businesses for advertising is 1.5 percent. Extra advertising support is needed in the first year of business because sales will not be large compared with those of other clothing stores, and the public needs to be informed about The Sock Hop and its total offering. In the next four years, advertising will be reduced to 3 percent of sales, but it will still be above the Dun and Bradstreet average.

A variety of advertising methods will be used. The normal outlets such as newspapers, radio, television, and the Yellow Pages will be used. A door-to-door flyer campaign will be considered, as Lethbridge is relatively small. For television and radio, The Sock Hop hopes to be involved in any promotional efforts in conjunction with the Park Place Mall.

At the start of the business, various contests can be held to get ideas on new designs for socks, which will help renew the product life cycle. In addition, sponsoring sock hops at the local high schools will improve public relations. This will be especially advantageous since the younger, fashion-conscious portion of the target market are high school youth.

Moreover, a lot of these youngsters are innovators and thus have the power to influence a major portion of the target market.

Finally, price promotions can be used in busy months such as January, when clearances are usually held, during August and September, when it is back-to-school time, and during November.

Location

Trading Area

Economic Base. The City of Lethbridge's economy is strongly based on agriculture. The agricultural economy is supported by the food processing, packaging, distilling, and brewing industries. The city has good road and rail connections to various markets as well as to producers, and these have been important in maintaining Lethbridge's economic position. In addition, Lethbridge is in a prominent position in its region, and growth is expected in the area.

Competition. In terms of general retail and service competition in the trading area, there are 36 major retail/service clusters in Lethbridge, and they have been evaluated at a total of 3,479,000 square feet of retail and service space in addition to the square footage covered by Park Place.[2] The 3,479,000 square feet are allocated in the trading areas as follows:

2,650,000 sq. ft.	in the city of Lethbridge
829,000 sq. ft.	in the surrounding area, which composes the trading area
3,479,000 sq. ft.	

Attitudes of the Trading Area toward Having a New Business. The new mall has increased the trading area and has shown a positive attitude toward development of the area. Lethbridge is moving ahead, and as a result most of the community is anxious for new businesses.

Specific Site

Accessibility. Park Place Mall is centrally located in the city of Lethbridge, north of the cental business district (CBD). There are major roads on all sides with good connections to the city. Careful consideration to traffic flows was given by the city before construction of the mall took place. Lethbridge is also well served by the major highway system serving Southern Alberta. Therefore, vehicular traffic is facilitated both in and around Lethbridge. The transit system facilitates customers who don't own vehicles. There is a major transit station downtown within walking distance of the mall. A proposal to move the station north of Galt Gardens has also been considered, which would bring this station to the street facing this mall. In addition, bus routes include the mall.

Thus, all customers will have good access to the site, which is fairly visible from the major thoroughfares (Stafford Drive, Crowsnest Trail, First Avenue).

Site Costs. The specific site costs (information obtained from Park Place Mall administration and the city of Lethbridge) include the following:

Rent	$20–$30/sq. ft. per year
	($30 × 400 sq. ft. = $12,000 per year)
Utilities	$5–$10/sq. ft. per year
	($10 × 400 sq. ft. = $4,000 per year)

[2] *Lethbridge Community Profile, 2005–2006.* City of Lethbridge, Economic Development Department, October 2006.

Business taxes	4.2% of fair rental value
	$[4.2\% \times (400 \times 30)] = \$504$
City business licence	$53 per year
Business Revitalization Zone fees	$3.78 per month–$45.36 per year
	(0.75% of business tax)
Insurance	$87.39 per year

The total site and operational costs add to $16,689.75.

Total rent of The Sock Hop will be $12,000 per year. In addition, the mall offices generally set a break-even point for the store, and once this point is reached by the store, a royalty of 5 percent to 8 percent of sales in excess of the break-even point is charged in addition to the normal rent.

The typical term of this lease is between 5 years and 10 years. Since this aspect of the lease is negotiable, an attempt should be made to have the term reduced. In addition, advance rent of two months is required by the mall administration. In terms of recharges, the total cost of utilities, electricity, and upkeep of the common area is $4,000 ($10.00 × 400 sq. ft.).

Insurance for The Sock Hop covers the business contents such as merchandise, fixtures, furniture, and equipment. The insurance also applies to the actual business loss sustained by the owner and the expenses incurred to resume normal business operations. Thus, the insurance provides coverage when the damage caused by an insured peril results in the interruption of business. The money and securities are also covered against loss by robbery, safe burglary, and theft from a night depository in a bank or from the custodian. The insurance further covers liability for bodily injury and property damage claims arising out of the maintenance and use of premises.

Total insurance per year is equal to

$$\$3.70 \times (\$23,618.77/\$1,000) = \$87.39$$

It should be noted that the mall administration insures the common area. (The various taxes and licences will be covered in the final section of this business plan.)

Proximity to Other Businesses. Park Place Mall has many products and services. This is advantageous in that it will generate customer traffic essential to the success of the business. Socks are defined as a shopping good, which means that consumers will usually shop around and compare before making the final purchase decision. Therefore, by locating close to competing businesses (see Figure 1 on page 127), consumers will be able to compare and choose the superior product. The Sock Hop offers good quality socks at a reasonable price, which, when compared with other stores, will draw a loyal following.

Furthermore, other stores will be selling complementary articles of clothing (shoes, pants), which will generate customer traffic for The Sock Hop by creating a need for socks. Other than the businesses in Park Place Mall, there are no other stores offering socks in the immediate vicinity of the site.

Physical Facilities

Start-up Costs. The start-up costs for a retail store are made up of two things—capital assets and inventory. The following is a detailed breakdown of the physical items required to furnish the store. (This list was obtained from Roll-It Catalogue, National Signs, and Consumers Distributing.)

Item	No.	Each	Total Value
Furniture and Fixtures			
Multimerchandiser (48″ × 54″)	6	$ 507.00	$ 3,042.00
End frame pegboard (48″ × 66″)	4	146.65	587.00
Miscellaneous hardware (pegs)	1	1,000.00	1,000.00
Used bargain bunk	1	200.00	200.00
Counter	1	500.00	500.00
Sign	1	500.00	500.00
Filing cabinet (4 drawer, legal 24″ deep)	1	190.00	190.00
Desk (30″ × 60″, steel)	1	250.00	250.00
Swivel chair	1	50.00	50.00
Equipment (obtained from Cypress Business Equipment, AGT Business Office, Office Depot, General Fasteners)			
Software (Bedford)	1	$ 300.00	$ 300.00
Computer and printer (IBM clone)	1	2,000.00	2,000.00
Cash register	1	1,200.00	1,200.00
Telephone installation	1	40.00	40.00
Adding machine	1	75.00	75.00
Pricing gun	1	80.00	80.00
Vacuum cleaner	1	280.00	$ 280.00
Total			$10,294.00

Initially The Sock Hop will invest about 15 percent of projected sales in inventory. This is standard.

Inventory = Sales × 15%

$13,324.70 = $88,831.33 × 15%

Layout. In the case of The Sock Hop, the layout is designed to display the merchandise effectively. Although browsing is somewhat encouraged by the multimerchandisers, there isn't enough selling space to encourage a lot of creativity in layout (see Figure 2 on page 134).

Financial

Feasibility Analysis

Target Market and Trade Area. Geographically, the trade area for Lethbridge is delineated. The competitive influence of retail and service facilities in the city of Calgary limit the extension of the trade area to 70 kilometres to the north. To the east, competitive retail facilities in the city of Medicine Hat limit the trade area to 95 kilometres. In the south, the trade area extends some 80 kilometres to the Canada–United States border. The trade area to the west extends 130 kilometres from Lethbridge. Here, it is primarily limited by the distance and driving times and is bounded by the Alberta–British Columbia border. The study by Larry Smith and Associates Ltd. indicates that Park Place Mall expects to derive the majority of its sales volume (80 percent to 95 percent) from this area. The remaining 5 percent to 20 percent of market support normally reflects customer shopping derived from visitors, tourists, or people working in Lethbridge but not residing in the delineated trade area.

Market Potential

- Total 2005 Lethbridge retail apparel and accessories sales were $32,260,000 (*Lethbridge Community Profile*, 2005–06). At an inflation rate of 4 percent per year (Alberta Retail and Service Trade Statistics), the retail sales for 2007 will be

$$\$32,260,000 \times (1.04)^3 = \$36,288,113$$

- The 2006 population of Lethbridge is 66,500 (city statistics).

- The 2006 population for the trade area excluding Lethbridge is 88,250 (city statistics).

- The amount of the regional population that shops for socks in Lethbridge was estimated by clothing retailers to be 33 percent.

- It is estimated by clothing retailers and the personal experience of the owner-manager that between 3 percent and 5 percent of the expenditures on clothing are for socks. However, 3 percent may be on the high side for a low-price item like socks, so a more conservative figure would be 2 percent. Based on these figures, the 2006 Lethbridge per capita socks sales figure can be calculated as follows:

$$\frac{\$36,288,113 \times 2\%}{[66,500 + (88,250 \times 33\%)]} = \$7.59$$

The market area for The Sock Hop can be safely defined as Lethbridge. Thus, in the remaining calculations, Lethbridge population figures will be used. Total market potential calculations:

- 2006 per capita socks sales in Lethbridge is $7.59 (as calculated above).

- 2006 population for Lethbridge is 66,500 (see above).

Therefore, the 2007 unadjusted total market potential figure for The Sock Hop can be calculated as follows:

$$\$7.59 \text{ per person} \times 66,500 = \$504,735$$

An adjustment must be made to this figure in order to take outshopping into account. Outshopping is the result of a consumer in a particular market area going to another area to make purchases. Based on interviews with store managers, the outshopping figure was said to be 20 percent. This is quite conservative, since the presence of Park Place Mall has two implications. Thus, the adjusted 2007 total market potential for Lethbridge will be

$$\$504,735 \times 0.80 = \$403,788$$

This figure is the most accurate market potential figure. It takes into account inflation, outshopping buying habits (figure determined by primary research), and 2006 population figures.

Market Share. No statistics were available on the amount of retail space devoted to socks. Therefore, estimates were obtained through primary research (see Appendix 2). The proposed store will have an area of 400 square feet, with 300 square feet devoted to selling space. Based on these figures, the unadjusted market share of The Sock Hop should be the following:

$$\frac{320 \text{ sq. ft.}}{872 \text{ sq. ft.} + 320 \text{ sq. ft.}}$$

This figure represents the unadjusted market share available to The Sock Hop. To adjust the figure, the strengths and weaknesses of the various aspects of the business must be considered.

The major weakness of The Sock Hop is that it is a new store. It does not have a loyal customer following, has no reputation, and has plenty of established competition. In addition, this specialty store will more than likely have higher prices than some of the discount department stores selling socks.

The major strength of The Sock Hop is its location. It is going to be located in a new major shopping mall, Park Place Mall. The customer traffic in the mall is above average. The store will be in an attractive setting with good exposure. Furthermore, there is a vast amount of parking space available for the satisfaction of the consumers. The Sock Hop provides a variety of socks in one location that is convenient and pleasant for consumers. Another area of strength is the growing trading area. The outlook is very positive for the Lethbridge economy, and this can only aid The Sock Hop.

Based on this analysis, the adjusted market share can be said to be a very conservative 22 percent. This is based on present conditions. In the future, the owner-manager hopes that this percentage will increase as the business becomes more established.

Projected Income. The projected income statements for the next five business years are in Figure 3 on page 135. The figures have been derived through primary and secondary research. The revenue figure was calculated by multiplying the adjusted market potential and the adjusted market share figures together:

$$\$403,788 \times 22\% = \$88,833.36$$

Financing. This section pertains to the financing plan for The Sock Hop. Business start-up costs are needed to determine the financing needed. These costs are made up of the following:

CASE program	$ 400.00
Inventory	13,324.77
Incorporation fees	1,000.00
Physical facilities	10,294.00
Rent (last 2 months of lease + 1 month rent)	3,000.00
Total	$ 28,018.77

Most lenders require the borrower to prepare a financing proposal. This will provide answers to questions the lender will have about the owner and about the proposed business.

www.mcgrawhill.ca/olc/balderson

In order for the lenders to know how a loan will be repaid, they need to look at income and cash flow projections for evidence of earnings that will support the loan. These are shown in Figures 3 and 4 (on pages 135–136).

Sources of Financing. The Business Development Bank of Canada (BDC) offers term loans to allow small business owners to acquire fixed assets such as land, building, machinery, and equipment. The loans are offered at floating rates or at fixed rates. BDC may also provide assistance through its CASE program. CASE is a counselling service offered exclusively to small- and medium-sized businesses. This program employs experienced counsellors who advise the small business owner on any aspect of business.

The interest rate for the loan is approximately 8 percent with a minimum repayment period of four years.

The term of the amount borrowed must match the actual lifetime of what is being financed. Thus, the inventory portion will be financed by an operating loan with a term of two years. This will be financing from a chartered bank. It should be noted that although $13,325 is being borrowed for this purpose, a lesser amount will be needed. This is because The Sock Hop will endeavour to finance a good portion of inventory from suppliers who, because of competition in the industry, are willing to market their products through new outlets. The remaining $7,500 will be borrowed from BDC on a term of five years. The equity investment will thus be $7,500.

Accounting System. Rather than employ a bookkeeper, the manager of the business will record on a computer all transactions that occur every day. The Bedford accounting software will be used, which is priced at less than $300 (quote from computer dealer). The computer and a suitable printer priced at $2,000 will also be used.

The Bedford accounting software is a fully integrated package for the small business. It is easy to use and very user friendly. It consists of the General Ledger, Payroll, Receivables, Payables, and Inventory modules that are all posted, as applicable, through single entries. It is very versatile and easily adaptable to small business needs. It produces full audit trails and a number of other management information reports. The vendors have a good track record of maintenance and support. Computing magazines such as *PC Magazine* and *InfoWorld* have given good reviews to this software.

The services of a public accountant (CA or CGA) will be utilized for annual reviews, for tax advice, and on special occasions when necessary. The business will follow Generally Accepted Accounting Principles in maintaining the financial records.

Credit Policy. The Sock Hop does not intend to allow any credit to customers, since it is not a practice in the industry. It does not intend to start a trend in this area, as the volume per customer would not justify it. However, it will accept all major credit cards (VISA, MasterCard, American Express, etc.). With this facility to customers, there would be no need to extend direct credit, which, in any case, would entail taking some risk on the part of The Sock Hop.

Financial Evaluation. Monthly financial statements will be prepared and reviewed by the owner-manager in an effort to monitor and evaluate progress. Several financial ratios will be calculated and compared with similar businesses as well as with previous performance.

Personnel

Administrative Structure. Since The Sock Hop is not a big store, initially the number of staff employed will be limited.

Store hours for The Sock Hop will be as follows:

Monday–Wednesday, 9:30 a.m.–5:30 p.m.

Thursday and Friday, 9:30 a.m.–9:00 p.m.

Saturday, 9:30 a.m.–5:30 p.m.

Thus, the basic salary and wage expenses will be

Store manager	$24,000.00
1 full-time clerk ($8.00 × 35 h/week)	13,440.00
1 part-time clerk ($7.00 × 10 h/week)	3,360.00
Total salary and wage	$40,800.00

With this staffing plan in mind, the organizational chart will be as follows:

Owner-manager

Full-time clerk   Part-time clerk

Employee Recruitment and Training

Job Descriptions. A typical job description is as follows:

Duties: Greets and helps customers, keeps shelves organized and stocked, rings up sales and bags items, opens and closes store when manager is away, cleans counters and vacuums

Responsible to: Store owner/manager

Requirements: Must have previous sales experience, be available to work nights and weekends, be able to use a cash register, be able to learn store procedures

Personal: Must be friendly, appropriately dressed and groomed, punctual, and reliable

Recruitment. The channels of recruitment utilized by The Sock Hop will include write-ins (applicants), walk-ins, want-advertising, and educational institutions. Job application forms will be used to collect information about recruits. These application forms will attempt to gather information pertaining to personal data, employment status, education, skills, work history, memberships, awards, hobbies, and references.

Evaluation. The first three months of employment are a period of observation for the employee as well as the owner-manager. The employee will receive professional sales training and will be taught the basics of The Sock Hop store procedures.

Beginning at the end of week three of employment, the owner-manager will initiate a coaching discussion. The employee's job performance will be evaluated, and discussions will be held to help the employee understand the job. In addition, any questions the employee has will be answered.

Training. Training will be carried out by the owner-manager and will consist of three general areas. First, the employee will be provided with information about the business and its philosophy and goals. Second, the employee will receive training about the merchandise, including such things as the material they are made of, washing instructions, and so on. The third area of training involves the teaching of specific selling skills—such things as approaching the customer, presenting the merchandise, closing the sale, and suggestion selling.

Policies. The following policies will be followed by The Sock Hop employees:

- An employee is assigned an identification number consisting of four digits to be used for all cash register operations.

- Work schedules will be posted at least one week in advance.

- Scheduling conflicts are to be reported to the manager as soon as possible.

- The wages for regular full-time clerks will consist of an hourly rate of $7.00 plus a 2 percent commission on sales.

- Similarly the wages for part-time clerks will be an hourly rate of $7.00 plus a 2 percent commission on sales.

- An employee who has completed six full months of continuous service by June 30 will be entitled to one week's vacation during the summer vacation period.

- Any employee who has completed one full year of continuous service with the company by June 30 will be entitled to two weeks or 4 percent of earnings as vacation pay (whichever is greater).

- Employees who have completed less than six months service with the company by June 30 must be paid 4 percent of their gross earnings from the date of hire until the last pay period in June.

- All full-time employees must receive vacation pay in the last pay period before leaving for their vacations.

- The employee will be expected to have a professional appearance. This includes proper grooming, clean and pressed clothing (no jeans), name tags, clean and proper footwear, and above all else, a smiling pleasant attitude.

- The Sock Hop emphasizes customer satisfaction. Therefore, the employee should ask all customers to retain their sales receipts. The Sock Hop will provide a full cash refund or merchandise exchanges on all returns with receipts.

- All staff will be entitled to a 20 percent discount on purchases from The Sock Hop.

- All purchases by staff members must be handled by the owner-manager. At no time is the staff member to "key in" their own purchases. These purchases are to be conducted during breaks or at the end of shifts.

- The phone is to be answered promptly, giving the store name and the employee's name. It is important that the employee be cheerful, helpful, and courteous.

- Personal calls are to be kept to an absolute minimum!

- The employee should practise the following prevention activities: (1) approach and greet all customers promptly and never leave the sales floor without coverage and (2) be aware of customers carrying merchandise from one location to another.

Legal Requirements

It has been decided that The Sock Hop will be an incorporated business. This decision was made after looking at the relative pros and cons of incorporation. The main reason for incorporating is the limited liability of shareholders. Thus, the owner is protected should the business fail. By incorporating, the owner is not risking her life savings. She is only liable for the amount invested in the business.

Regulations. Since The Sock Hop is a retail store, the regulations that apply to it are those common to any regular small business in Lethbridge. The municipal government requires that the small business owner hold a business licence ($53 per year). In addition, the city requires building and electrical inspections after renovations have been made. Municipal taxes include a business tax of about $504 per year and a Business Revitalization Zone (BRZ) fee of $45.36 per year, since the mall is within the BRZ. In addition, the small business is required to pay various taxes. The federal and provincial government require the filing of yearly income tax returns. The federal GST will need to be collected on sales and remitted to the federal government. Provincial sales tax is not charged in Alberta.

| Figure 1 | **Selling Space in the Market** | | |

Store	**Number of Stores**	**Total Square Feet**
Zellers	1	323
Safeway	3	22
Wal-Mart	1	161
Smart Set	2	11
Reitmans	2	11
Winners	1	54
Sears	1	75
Shoppers Drug Mart	1	32
Tip Top	3	32
Jack Fraser	2	22
The Bay	1	32
Mariposa	3	11
Error factor	00	237
Total		1,023

Figure 2	Selling Space

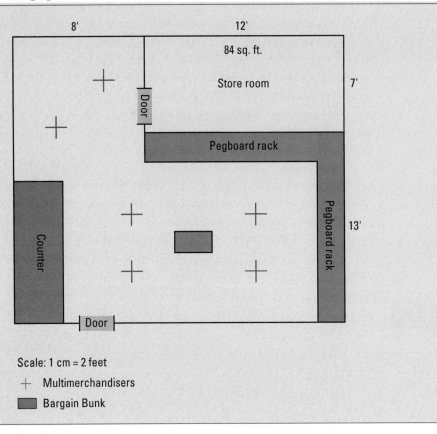

Scale: 1 cm = 2 feet
+ Multimerchandisers
▮ Bargain Bunk

Figure 3	Projected Income Statement for Five Years (in dollars)

	2007	2008	2009	2010	2011
Sales	$ 88,832	$133,248	$173,222	$207,866	$228,654
Cost of goods sold	44,416	66,624	86,611	103,933	114,327
Gross margin	44,416	66,624	86,611	103,933	114,327
Less expenses					
Rent	12,000	12,000	12,000	12,000	12,000
Staff wages	16,800	17,268	17,911	18,579	19,274
Owner's salary	24,000	24,000	24,000	24,000	24,000
Employee benefits	3,960	4,007	4,071	4,138	4,207
Advertising	4,442	3,997	5,197	6,236	6,860
Licences and taxes					
Business licence	53	53	53	53	53
Business tax—4.2% of rent	504	504	504	504	504
BRZ fees	45	48	48	48	48

Credit card discounts	213	360	433	520	572
Repairs and maintenance	711	1,066	1,386	1,663	1,829
Utilities and occupancy costs	4,000	4,000	4,000	4,000	4,000
Professional fees	622	933	1,213	1,455	1,601
Office and store supplies	888	1,332	1,732	2,079	2,287
Telephone—Rent	115	120	124	129	135
Estimated toll chgs	600	624	649	675	702
Insurance	87	91	95	98	102
Interest expense	2,593	1,594	1,396	398	199
Depreciation	2,059	2,059	2,059	2,059	2,059
Other expenses	1,777	2,665	3,464	4,157	4,573
Total expenses	74,269	75,521	79,135	81,591	83,805
Net income (before income taxes)	(29,853)	(8,897)	7,476	22,342	30,522
Income taxes	0		0		1,500
4,468	6,104				
Income after income taxes	$(28,653)	$ (7,697)	$ 5,776	$ 16,674	$ 23,218

Figure 4	**Projected Cash Flow for Five Years (in dollars)**

	2007	2008	2009	2010	2011	Totals
Cash in						
Net income	$(29,853)	$(8,897)	$7,476	$22,342	$30,522	$18,138
Add noncash items:						
Depreciation	2,059	2,059	2,059	2,059	2,059	10,294
Cash flows from operations	(27,794)	(6,838)	9,535	24,401	32,581	28,432
Equity contribution	35,000	15,000				50,000
Loan receipts —Operating	13,325					13,325
—BDC	7,500					7,500
Total cash inflows	28,031	8,162	9,535	24,401	32,581	99,257
Cash out						
Loan repayments—Operating	0	6,662	6,663	0	0	13,325
—BDC	0	1,500	1,500	1,500	1,500	6,000
Return of equity	0	0	0	20,000	30,000	50,000

| Figure 4 | (continued) |

	2007	2008	2009	2010	2011	Totals
Start up costs						
Legal	1,000					1,000
CASE counselling	400					400
Furniture and fixtures	10,294					10,294
Inventory	13,325					13,325
Two months' advance rent	2,000					2,000
Total cash outflows	27,019	8,162	8,163	21,500	31,500	96,344
Net cash flows	$ 1,012	$ (0)	$1,372	$ 2,901	$ 1,081	$ 2,913

BUSINESS PLAN 2—QUALITY CUTS

Table of Contents

Executive Summary and Background

Quality Cuts is a new beauty salon located in the city of Lethbridge, Alberta. It will operate from the College Value Mall in south Lethbridge, will employ five full-time hairdressers, and will be managed by Sue Holland. Quality Cuts will provide haircuts, styles, perms, and colour, as well as hair products supplied by well-known manufacturers. It will also provide cosmetic and manicuring services. Quality Cuts will attempt to target the middle- to older-aged women in the Lethbridge area, which is currently the most rapidly growing part of the market. Quality Cuts will utilize a computer database to build knowledge of customers and improve customer service. The feasibility analysis and business plan projections show that Quality Cuts will be a viable entry to the beauty salon market.

Description of Management Team

Quality cuts will be owned and operated by Sue Holland. She has her hairdressing certification from the Alberta School of Hair and Beauty Design and has worked as a hairdresser for 10 years in the Lethbridge area. Before leaving her current employment to plan the establishment of Quality Cuts, Sue was supervising four other hairdressers. Sue will be assisted in the financial and computer management aspects of the business by her husband, who is a chartered accountant. Preliminary consultations indicate that a high percentage of Sue's current clients will continue with her in the new business.

Business Objectives

The objectives for Quality Cuts are as follows.

The first objective is to have a positive cash flow for the first year of operations. Cash flows consist of receipts and payments attributed to operating, investing, and financing activities. As can be seen from the cash flow statement on page 137, it is estimated that there will be a positive net cash inflow for each of the four sectors of the first year of operations.

A second objective deals with the prices charged to the customers of the business. The prices will be competitive with other salons. Each hairdresser will have some input into prices charged for his or her clients to ensure that pricing is competitive.

A third objective is to achieve a market share of at least 3 percent by the end of the first year of operation, moving up to 5 percent within five years.

Market Approach

Description of Target Market. The target market geographically consists of the city of Lethbridge and some of the surrounding trade area. Lethbridge is an agricultural service centre with a high market draw for many smaller communities within a 48-kilometre radius.

The demographic characteristics include middle- to older-aged women in the middle- to higher-income classes. Approximately 80 percent of Sue Holland's current clients fall into this range. The location of Quality Cuts is ideal for this market because the College Value Mall is adjacent to some very large seniors' apartment buildings and upscale housing projects. It is located on the south end of Lethbridge where new housing developments are being built. The purchase characteristics for this market include concern over quality and service in a clean and friendly atmosphere.

Uncontrollable Factors. There are two uncontrollable factors that would most affect Quality Cuts. The competition is the first. There are currently 35 other beauty salons or shops in the city employing 150 hairdresser/stylists. Because this is a personal service industry, customer patronage is determined to a large extent by the quality of the service provider and the level of confidence the client has in the hairdresser. Quality Cuts has determined that they will attain a competitive edge through careful hiring and training of their employees. Proximity of competitors may be a secondary factor to customer patronage, and Quality Cuts will be the only beauty salon in the College Mall, which should be an advantage.

The second relevant uncontrollable is the social/cultural factor. Concern over one's looks is a major trend in North America. This suggests a continued and growing use of beauty salons. In addition, the Lethbridge market is an aging one. Both of these should be a positive influence on Quality Cuts's performance.

www.mcgrawhill.ca/olc/balderson

Product. The product that makes up a beauty salon comprises three distinct parts: hair service, manicures and cosmetic work, and hair products. The hair service side is by far the most important, as it includes things such as haircuts, styles, perms, and colours. This will make up 80 percent to 90 percent of the entire revenue of the beauty salon. Selling hair products and providing cosmetic and manicure services, although less important, are still vital as they may serve as a draw for passing consumers. The products include things like gels, shampoos, conditioners, moisturants, hair-repair treatments, protectors, sculpting lotions, and hairsprays. These type of products are available to the consumer in pharmacies but the quality of the professional products that are only found at beauty shops makes them attractive, even if the price is slightly higher. The brands that will be stocked include Paul Mitchell, Matrix, Lanza, Zotos, and Mahdeen. Because hair grooming is a service, Quality Cuts will emphasize superior customer service with its clients. Frequent follow-up communications with consumers will be maintained through computer tracking and database programs.

Pricing. Prices will be set close to competitors' prices during the first year to ensure the transfer of existing clients with their hairdresser. Price will eventually rise to 5 percent to 10 percent above the competitors' as the clientele of the business stabilizes. This in turn will be in harmony with the image Quality Cuts wants to project. Markups on the products will be 50 percent of retail selling price.

Promotion. Advertising will take place at approximately the average for hair salons in Alberta. This amount will be 1.9 percent of sales, or approximately $2,836 for the first year of operations.

In addition to this amount in the first year, there will be extra "opening" advertising that will be conducted for the first month. This is to get the name of the business out to the public and to let the hairdressers' old clients know where their hairdressers have moved. The cost of this opening advertising will be an additional $500, making the total advertising budget for the first year $3,336.

This advertising will take a couple of forms. First, the Yellow Pages is a must as it is an easy way for the public to see where certain salons are located. There are currently seven pages full of advertising just for beauty salons, with the average large advertisement occupying approximately 26 square centimetres.

The TV guide within the Friday edition of the *Lethbridge Herald* is also a favourite place for beauty salon advertising.

Business cards and extensive use of single-sheet advertising will also be used. These printed sheets of paper will be slid under the doors of apartments in neighbouring buildings, containing information and possible coupons to attract new customers. As mentioned previously, a sophisticated tracking system will be set up on computer to monitor customers' purchases and improve customer service efforts.

Distribution. There are four main suppliers that Quality Cuts will be dealing with, three from Calgary and one from Lethbridge. They are the following:

Emerald Beauty Supplies (Lethbridge)

Monarch Messenger Beauty Supplies (Calgary)

Consolidated Beauty Supplies (Calgary)

Obsco Beauty Supplies (Calgary)

All these distributors can supply within two days. Quality Cuts will attempt to take advantage of quantity and cash discounts where possible.

Location

Trading Area. Lethbridge has a fairly stable population into which many older people from the surrounding areas retire. The socioeconomic level of the community is above average. Both of these factors will have a positive effect on Quality Cuts's performance.

Specific Site. Quality Cuts will be located in the College Mall in the southeast corner of the city. The exact location in the mall will be where North West Trust is currently located, as it is moving to a different location within the mall.

Accessibility. This location has access from within the mall and private access from outside. It also allows for a neon sign on the outside of the mall to help attract customers. Traffic flow should be quite high as Wal-Mart is not too far away.

Site Costs

Item	Cost ($)	
Rent	18.50	per square foot (includes property tax)
Utilities	3,000	per year (plus $150 deposit)
Telephone	540	per year
Insurance	605	per year
Business taxes	420	per year
Licences/permits	113	per year

Proximity to Other Businesses. There are no other beauty shops within the mall, but there are many businesses that draw traffic and would be complementary to Quality Cuts.

Physical Characteristics of the Site. The store size is 1,200 square feet. It has the front opening into the mall and a side door open to the outside.

Physical Facilities

Equipment, fixtures, and supplies are an integral part of the business, and a list of these items is included below. The costs have been obtained from prospective suppliers.

Item	Cost ($)
9 hydraulic chairs	4,500
9 styling stations	2,997
10 hair dryers	2,490
10 dryer chairs	1,480
4 shampoo chairs	592
4 sinks	1,476
9 mirrors	1,350
washing machine	650
dryer	450
2 neon signs	3,000

www.mcgrawhill.ca/olc/balderson

4 lounge chairs	400
computer system	2,000
air exchanger	5,000
reception desk	300
layout additions	3,000
shelving	500
miscellaneous supplies (includes start-up product)	6,000

Layout. The layout of the shop is shown in Figure 1 (see page 140). The layout diagram shows that the shop contains three areas. The first is the reception area, which houses the reception desk, the shelves of products, the coat rack, and the waiting chairs. The second contains the hair salon itself, with the 9 stations, 4 sinks, 10 dryer stations, and coffee area. The third section is at the back of the location and includes a bathroom, washer/dryer area, and an 18 foot by 18 foot office/lunchroom/storage area.

The salon is set up in a way to accomplish three goals. These are to utilize the space, to be convenient for the patron, and to be pleasing to the eye. The image projected will be one of cleanliness and class, as appropriate for the target market.

Financial

Feasibility

Market Potential. The estimate of average family expenditure on hair grooming for Alberta in 2005 was $375 (Source: Statistics Canada Catalogue 62-555). It is also estimated that 45.5 percent of this amount is for women's hair grooming (Source: Statistics Canada Catalogue 63-555). Using a percentage of 50 percent should be conservative as Quality Cuts's revenue will also include sales of hair care products and cosmetic/manicuring services as well as some haircuts to male customers. The population for the target market includes approximately 20,000 households (Source: Lethbridge Community Profile 2005–06). Market potential estimate is as follows:

Households × household expenditures × percent of expenditures for target market
= 22,000 × 375 × 0.50 = $4,125,000

Market Share. The number of beauty salons and hairdressers/stylists in the market area were obtained through calls to all the shops. This totalled 35 shops and 150 hairdressers/stylists. An estimate of Quality Cuts's proposed market share is shown below.

$$= \frac{6 \text{ hairdressers/stylists (Sue + 5 employees)}}{6 + 150}$$

$$= \frac{6}{156} = 3.8\%$$

This share should be decreased to 3.6 percent because of the fact that the business is new and will take some time to build sales. The start-up delay should not be significant, however, because all five hairdresser/stylists are currently working in the market area and will bring the majority of their clients to the new business.

$$\text{Projected share in revenue} = \text{market share} \times \text{market potential}$$
$$= 3.6\% \times \$4,125,000 = \$148,500$$

Projected Income.   Below are the projected income statements for the first five years of operation. Revenue figures from above are used as the basis behind this information. Amounts and sources of expenses are as follows:

Cost of Goods Sold 10% (Statistics Canada Small Business and Special Surveys Division, confirmed by primary research)

Wages and Salaries 53.5% of sales (Alberta Business Profile, *Barber & Beauty Shops*, July 2006)

Depreciation   See schedule for calculation

Repairs and   0.8% of sales (Alberta Business Profile, *Barber & Beauty Shops*,
  Maintenance   July 2006)

Utilities $3,000 per year, 5% increase yearly (Primary information from College Mall management)

Phone $540 per year, 5% increase yearly (Primary information from phone company)

Rent $10.00 per sq. foot flat rate for first 2 years, $11.00 for years 3 and 4, $12 for 5th year. $8.50 per sq. foot variable rate, 5% increase yearly (Primary information from College Mall management)

Interest Expense   See table for calculation

Legal Fees   0.7% of sales (Alberta Business Profile, *Barber & Beauty Shops,* July 2004)

Advertising   1.9% of sales (Alberta Business Profile, *Barber & Beauty Shops,* July 2004)

Insurance   See legal section for details

Licences/Permits   See legal section for details

Business Taxes $0.35 per sq. foot (City of Lethbridge Taxation Department)

Other Expenses   1% of sales (Statistics Canada Small Business and Special Surveys Division)

The projected income for Quality Cuts is found below.

	Year 1	Year 2	Year 3	Year 4	Year 5
Sales	$148,500	$156,702	$164,537	$172,764	$181,402
Cost of Goods Sold	14,850	15,670	16,454	17,276	18,140
Gross Margin	$133,650	$141,032	$148,083	$155,488	$163,262
Expenses:					
Wages and Salaries	$ 79,448	$ 83,836	$ 88,027	$ 92,429	$ 97,050

Depreciation	1,749	1,749	1,749	1,749	1,749
Repairs and Maintenance	1,188	1,254	1,316	1,382	1,451
Utilities	3,000	3,150	3,308	3,473	3,647
Phone	540	567	595	625	656
Rent	22,200	22,710	24,444	25,008	26,796
Interest Expense	1,894	1,056	829	578	303
Legal Fees	1,040	1,097	1,152	1,209	1,270
Advertising	2,822	2,977	3,126	3,283	3,447
Insurance	605	635	667	700	735
Licences/Permits	113	113	113	113	113
Business Taxes	420	420	420	420	420
Other Expenses	1,485	1,567	1,645	1,728	1,814
Total Expenses	$116,504	$121,131	$127,391	$132,697	$139,451
Net Income	$ 17,146	$ 19,901	$ 20,692	$ 22,791	$ 23,811

Depreciation Schedule

Assets	Capital Cost	Life (years)	YEARS			
			1–5	6–10	11–15	16–20
Equipment:						
Hydraulic chairs (9)	$4,500	20	$1,125	$1,125	$1,125	$1,125
Workstations (9)	2,997	20	749	749	749	749
Hair dryers (10)	2,490	20	623	623	623	623
Dryer chairs (10)	1,480	20	370	370	370	370
Shampoo chairs (4)	592	20	148	148	148	148
Sinks (4)	1,476	20	369	369	369	369
Washing machine	650	10	325	325		
Dryer	450	10	225	225		
Computer system	2,000	5	2,000			
Air exchanger	5,000	20	1,250	1,250	1,250	1,250
Fixtures and furniture:						
Shelves	500	20	125	125	125	125
Neon signs (2)	3,000	20	750	750	750	750
Lounge chairs (4)	400	10	200	200		
Mirrors (9)	1,350	20	338	338	338	338
Reception desk	300	10	150	150		
Total			$8,747	$6,747	$5,847	$5,847

Financing. Start-up costs are found below.

Item	Cost	Source
Initial equipment and fixtures	$30,185	See Physical Facilities section
Miscellaneous supplies and product (includes opening inventory)	6,000	See Physical Facilities section
Rent (one month)	1,850	See Location section
Utility deposit	150	See Location section
Business licences and permits	113	See Legal section
Legal fees	754	See Legal section
Advertising and promotion (first month)	500	See Promotion section
Insurance (first quarter)	151	See Legal section
Total start-up costs	$39,703	

A cash flow statement has also been calculated to determine the cash situation that might arise during the first year of operations. This is shown below.

Quarter ending	Mar 31	June 30	Sept 30	Dec 31
CASH INFLOWS:				
Sales	$29,848	$37,310	$37,310	$44,772
Bank Loan	37,000	0	0	0
Equity Investment	5,000	0	0	0
Mall Payback	25,000	0	0	0
TOTAL CASH INFLOW	$96,848	$37,310	$37,310	$44,772
CASH OUTFLOWS:				
Equipment and Supplies	$36,185	$ 0	$ 0	$ 0
Inventory	2,985	3,731	3,731	4,477
Wages and Salaries	15,969	19,961	19,961	23,953
Advertising	1,334	834	834	834
Licences/Permits	113	0	0	0
Business Taxes	0	0	0	420
Insurance Expense	151	151	151	151
Interest Expense	925	323	323	323
Legal Fees	209	261	261	313
Rent	5,550	5,550	5,550	5,550
Repairs and Maintenance	239	298	298	358
Utilities	900	750	750	750
Telephone	135	135	135	135
Loan Repayment	24,075	788	788	788
Other Expenses	$ 298	$ 373	$ 373	$ 448
TOTAL CASH OUTFLOW	$89,068	$33,155	$33,155	$38,500
NET CASH INFLOW	$ 7,780	$ 4,155	$ 4,155	$ 6,272

Financing. Sue will require approximately $40,000 to finance Quality Cuts. She intends to invest $10,000 of her own money and will borrow $30,000 from the Royal Bank. Current interest rates are 8 percent and the term of the loan is five years. The loan repayment schedule is shown below.

Year	Payment	Principal	Interest	Balance
1	$28,333	$25,933	$2,400	$4,067
2	1,340	1,014	326	3,053
3	1,260	1,015	245	2,038
4	1,180	1,016	164	1,022
5	1,104	1,022	82	0

Bookkeeping/Accounting System. The computer system that will be purchased will take care of all aspects of a beauty salon, including the financial aspects. The ACCPAC software program for small businesses will be utilized to monitor and evaluate performance. Monthly financial statements will be prepared and reviewed by Sue and her husband.

The credit policy for the shop is quite simple: cash, cheque, or charge. There will be no credit granted, except for clients in very good standing and then only with Sue's approval. Cheques will be accepted with identification for unknown customers. Also, major credit cards like Visa, MasterCard, and bank debit cards will be accepted.

Personnel

Quality Cuts will begin operations with five hairdressers and Sue Holland as owner-manager. The organizational chart for the staff can be seen below.

The salon hours will follow that of the mall: 9:30 a.m.–5:30 p.m. Monday to Wednesday and Saturday; 9:30 a.m.–9:00 p.m. Thursday and Friday. It will not be open on Sundays or extend its hours such as during the Christmas season.

Hairdressers work on commission, so the estimate of wages paid out over a year will make up a percentage of total sales. As stated earlier in this plan, secondary data suggests that this percentage averages 53.5 percent of total sales in Alberta, which is used to calculate the wages and salaries paid out over the first year of $79,844.

Hairdressers will work 16 to 24 hours per week. This is in accordance with industry averages as most hairdressers/stylists prefer to work part-time. A work schedule will be drawn up at least one week in advance and will accommodate client preference for certain hairdresser/stylists.

Employee Recruitment and Training. Skill training will be limited in this field of work as hairdressers have to attend a qualified beauty school and earn their certificate. However, Quality Cuts will devote extra effort to stressing to each employee the importance of customer service and projecting the right image. Explanation of company procedures and the commission payment plan will also be a part of the training.

Recruitment will also stress that the workers project the image that the beauty salon itself projects. Sue has already made contact with three hairdresser/stylists who fit the Quality Cuts image and have agreed to work for her. Interviews will be held to select the remaining employees. This should lead to the hiring of those who work well with the customers and other hairdressers.

Policies. The following policies will be in effect at Quality Cuts:

1. Employees must appear neat and clean.

2. No smoking is allowed in the customer area of the shop.

3. The approved uniform top must be worn at all times.

4. No food or drink is allowed in the customer area.

5. Employees will receive a 20 percent discount on all hair care products.

6. The customer is always right.

Evaluation. Employees' performance will be evaluated monthly on the basis of revenues generated, referrals, sales of hair care products, customer complaints, and progress toward employee objectives. As mentioned previously, employees' pay will be based partly on commissions of appointments as well as other sales.

Legal

Legal Structure. Quality Cuts will operate as a sole proprietorship. This will allow Sue to maintain flexibility and control of operations in the first few years.

Licensing. The licences necessary to operate this business are as follows:

Development application	$ 31.00
Occupancy permit	20.00
Business licence	62.00
Total licensing costs	$113.00

Insurance. Insurance is a legal necessity for this business. The breakdown of insurance is as follows:

Commercial general insurance (covering stock and building)	$190.00
Money and security insurance	75.00
Employee dishonesty bond	150.00
Malpractice insurance	190.00
Total insurance (for the first year)	$605.00

Figure 1   **Shop Layout**

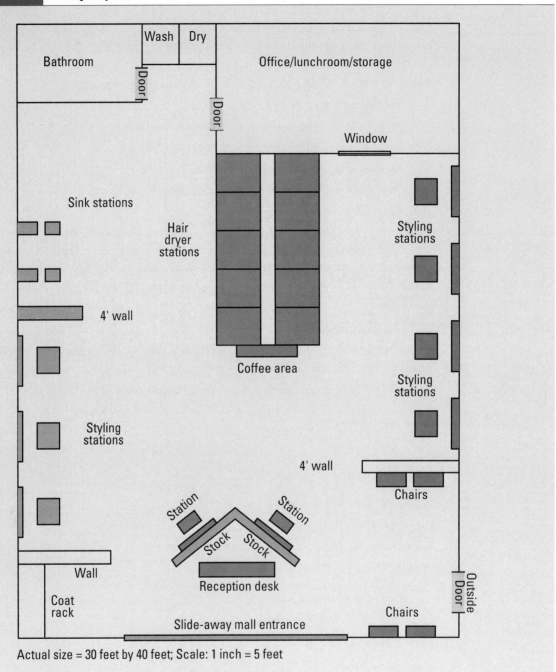

Actual size = 30 feet by 40 feet; Scale: 1 inch = 5 feet

Suggested Readings

Business Development Bank of Canada Business Plan Templates—www.bdc.ca

Business Plan Archive—www.businessplanarchive.org

Business Resource Finder—Aids in developing business plans and cost estimates, http://www.gdsourcing.ca

CBSC Interactive Planner website—Contains sample business plans—www.cbsc.org.osbw/session4/sample.cfm

Canadian Federation of Independant Business website.

CCH Business Owners Toolkit—www.toolkit.cch.com/tools/buspin_m.asp

CIBC. *Your Guide to Business Planning.* Canadian Imperial Bank of Commerce, 1995.

Directory of Home Based Businesses—http://www.homenetpro.com

Dunnett, Paul. "Entrepreneurs Can't Afford to Forgo Insurance." *The Globe and Mail,* January 13, 1999, p. B12.

Entrepreneurship Business Plan Outlines—www.entrepreneurship.com/tools/businessplanworkbook.asp

Gray, Douglas A., and Diana L. Gray. *The Complete Canadian Small Business Guide, 2nd Edition.* Toronto: McGraw-Hill Ryerson, 2000.

———. *The Canadian Home Based Business Guide.* Toronto: McGraw-Hill Ryerson, 1994.

———. *Home Inc.*, 2nd ed. Toronto: McGraw-Hill Ryerson, 1994.

Home Based Business—www.cbsc.org/english/search/display.cfm?

Morse, Dan. "Many Small Businesses Don't Devote Time to Planning." *Wall Street Journal,* September 17, 1999.

Palo Alto Software—Sample Business Plans—www.bplans.com

Patents Questions and Answers. Ottawa: Consumer and Corporate Affairs, 1996.

Skinner, James R. *Business Plan to Business Reality.* Toronto: Pearson-Prentice-Hall, 2003.

Small Business Guide to Federal Incorporation. Corporate Directorate, Industry Canada, February 28, 1998.

Small Office Home Office Business Plans—www.soho.suite.com

Starting A Home Based Business: A Manual For Success. Government of Canada & B.C., June 2002.

Van Hoesellar, Russ. "A Treasury of Home Based Business Opportunities," Ontario Business Service Centre, 2006.

Ward, Susan. "Six Steps To Starting A Home Based Business," Small Business Canada website, October 2006.

www.mcgrawhill.ca/olc/balderson

CHAPTER 5
Buying a Business

CHAPTER OBJECTIVES

- To review the advantages and disadvantages of purchasing an ongoing business compared with the other methods of small business ownership

- To describe the sources of businesses that are for sale

- To explain how to evaluate a business that is for sale

- To review the methods used in determining the price to pay for a business

SMALL BUSINESS PROFILE

Karina Birch and Cameron Baty

Rocky Mountain Soap Company Inc.

Karina Birch and Cameron Baty purchased Rocky Mountain Soap Company in January 2000. This company, located in Canmore, Alberta, just beside the beautiful Rocky Mountains, had been in existence since 1995 and had established a small niche in the natural handmade soap products market with gross sales of $90,000 annually.

Although the business was successful before the purchase, Birch and Baty realized that there was potential to substantially expand the business after they attended a tradeshow in the United States. They saw a growing market that was virtually untapped by Canadian manufacturers and that had not been recognized by the previous owners of the company.

The pair bought the business and set plans in motion to expand all phases of the business. Taking the business to the next level required updating their processes, buying specialized equipment, and learning to become more efficient with the staff they had. A key to the successful purchase and growth strategy involved carrying out extensive research with similar companies in the United States. By doing this, they were able to find out what these companies were doing in the areas of manufacturing, marketing, and distribution.

Their efforts have paid off: Annual sales have reached $2.5 million. This increase in volume of production and sales required Rocky Mountain Soap to farm out packaging the product to local residents, at the same time improving the marketing and packaging of the product. The progress that Birch and Baty have made illustrates how effective research and planning can make purchasing an existing business a viable alternative for entering the small business sector.

Used with the permission of Karina Birch and Cameron Baty.

Rocky Mountain Soap Company
www.rockymountainsoap.com

PURCHASING AN EXISTING BUSINESS

An alternative to organizing a business from the ground up is to purchase an existing business. Many entrepreneurs prefer this method of becoming small business owners. Thirty-eight of Canada's fastest-growing companies have acquired other firms in recent years. Of these, 22 firms can attribute more than 20 percent of their growth to mergers and buyouts.[1] Incident 5-1 describes a company that bought a competitive business after a careful and thorough evaluation.

Advantages of Purchasing

The following are some reasons that buying a business may be an attractive alternative.

Reduction of Risk. Chapter 2 mentioned that high risk is associated with starting a small business. Much of this risk can be reduced by purchasing an existing business. Uncertainty about the extent of consumer demand can be eliminated to a certain degree by examining past results of an existing business. Therefore, with proper investigation, the risk associated with purchasing a small business should be less than with a business organized from scratch.

Reduction of Time and Set-up Expenses. In an existing business, physical facilities such as building and equipment are already in place. The product or service is already being produced and distributed. Financial relationships and other important contacts have also been established. Each of these areas not only takes time to plan and organize but can be costly if unforeseen circumstances arise. Examples of such circumstances include lack of demand for the product or service, construction problems, production difficulties, and legal complications. Purchasing an existing business can minimize these potential problems.

Reduction of Competition. Purchasing an existing business can eliminate a potential competitor. This motive may be an especially important consideration in a fairly stable market

---

INCIDENT 5-1   Buying a Franchise

Bryan Gerber is the man with the tools. The 35-year-old owner of Kitchener's Home Hardware franchise says that the key to building a successful business is to focus on something that differentiates your business from the competition. Gerber's Home Hardware focuses on paint, and his efforts are paying off—paint sales are up 150 percent from last year.

Gerber and his partner decided to buy an existing Home Hardware in Kitchener. They found an owner who was ready to retire, bought his business and ran it while they built a new factory. The made-in-Canada chain is a co-op and for $10,000 to $20,000 you become part-owner of the company, with full rights to the Home Hardware name and logos. Home Hardware also helps the potential dealer develop a good layout for the store, because it gives members information on everything from accounting to regional demographics.

Gerber has a trained staff of 19, who frequently attend seminars to beef up their hardware knowledge to give quality help to customers. The small business owner has had to put in long days and has worked hard to get the business running. "I'm the accountant. I'm the human resources department. I'm the guy cutting keys," Gerber says. Gerber also says it's his passion, so it doesn't feel like work at all.

Source: Adapted from, "How to Open Your Own Hardware Store," *Report on Small Business*, Summer 2005, p. 32.

with only a few well-established competitors. Breaking into such a market with a totally new business may be difficult, and the potential small business owner should investigate the possibility of purchasing rather than organizing. Incident 5-1 illustrates this motivation for a Canadian company.

Capitalization of Business Strength. Often a business for sale has a competitive strength that would be difficult to duplicate with a new firm. For example, the location of the business, a very important consideration in the retail and some service industries, may be excellent. Personnel, technology, or even the physical facilities of the business may be superior to those of competing firms. In such situations, buying a business that offers these advantages may be an attractive alternative. Incident 5-2 provides an example of a company that increased its competitiveness through acquisition.

Possible Assistance from the Previous Owner. The previous owner may be willing to work for the purchaser of the business, or at least to provide some assistance for a short time following the purchase. This type of help can be invaluable to the new owner.

Easier Planning. Financial and market planning for a business is much easier when historical records are available. This information is not available for a start-up business. When approaching lenders or investors, projections from actual results of an existing business may generate more confidence than untested estimates.

Disadvantages of Purchasing

A prospective purchaser should also be aware of the potential disadvantages of purchasing a business. Many of these problems concern the condition of the assets and other aspects of the business.

Physical Facilities. The building and equipment may be old, obsolete, or below current standards. In addition, they may not be completely paid for or may have charges or liens

---

INCIDENT 5-2   Buying a Business

When starting a business, you must consider whether to buy an existing one or start one from scratch. As an experienced entrepreneur, Jerry Harb has seen both sides. Harb was a former senior operations executive for Pizza Pizza and for the Cultures Fresh Food Restaurants chain but left in 1986 to start a restaurant of his own. After looking at more than 100, he bought Lakeview Restaurant, a Toronto landmark diner founded in 1947. He changed the name to Jerry's and, after other modifications, the diner became popular as a Hollywood movie set. Due to this newfound popularity, Harb was able to sell the restaurant at a profit.

Harb suggests that when buying a business, it is important to get one at the right price, that is established but struggling, rather than starting one from scratch. It has been shown that 50 percent of businesses fail within two years and 80 percent within five. The chances of owning a successful business are much better when buying a franchise (many have success rates greater than 80 percent). The success rate of buying a business is much better than starting a new one as established businesses already have a respected name, with clientele, suppliers, and employees already in place.

Source: Adapted from "No Assembly Required," *Report on (Small) Business,"* Fall 2005, p. 13.

against them. If the prospective buyer is unfamiliar with how to evaluate the condition of such facilities, he or she should enlist the services of a professional appraiser.

Personnel. The business's employees may be incompetent or unmotivated. They may also resist the new ownership and reduce their productivity or even quit once the transfer of ownership is completed. The potential buyer is well advised to visit with current employees to ascertain their attitudes toward change.

Inventory. The inventory may be obsolete or hard to sell. This factor may be especially critical in a retail store or a high-technology firm. The age of inventory can often be determined through internal records or by price-tag coding.

Accounts Receivable. The outstanding accounts may be uncollectible or at least costly and time consuming to collect. An evaluation of the length of time these accounts have been outstanding can be helpful in evaluating this potential problem.

Financial Condition. The financial health of the business may be deteriorating or less positive than it appears in the financial statements. An in-depth evaluation of the firm's financial condition should always be conducted before purchase.

Market. The market for the business's product or service may be deteriorating, or a strong, new competitor may be about to enter the market. In addition, such factors as the economic state, interest rates, or government policy could adversely affect the market.

Decisions about Price. The prospective owner may have difficulty negotiating a price to pay for the business or evaluating the fairness of the listed price.

Many of the above potential problems associated with buying a business can be uncovered through a detailed investigation of the operations of the business before purchase. Some of the key evaluation areas are discussed later in this chapter.

SOURCES OF BUSINESSES FOR SALE

Where can the entrepreneur who has decided to purchase a business find out which businesses are for sale? The following are common sources.

Classified Ads. Classified ads are found in local newspapers or financial or business publications. Figure 5-1 gives an example. Although numerous opportunities are publicly advertised, many of the best businesses to buy have been sold before they are advertised in the print media.

Figure 5-1	**Classified Ad for a Business Opportunity**

Lucrative Business for Sale

Manufacturer of picture frames and artists' supplies. Wholesaler to photo shops, artist stores, and craft shops. Growing business with established clientele, situated near Vancouver. Excellent investment potential. $150,000 negotiable. Please reply to

National Post
300–1450 Don Mills Road
Don Mills, ON M3B 3R5

Canada Business
Service Centres
www.cbsc.org

Government Departments. The small business or industry department in most provinces and territories is usually aware of businesses for sale. They may also know of communities that want to attract a particular type of business to locate there.

Trade Journals. Trade journals frequently carry listings of businesses that are for sale in that industry. This may be a more effective source than more general classified ads.

Real Estate Brokers. Many entrepreneurs purchase their businesses with the assistance of a broker whose job is to get buyers and sellers together and help negotiate the sale. If the prospective purchaser knows a certain broker fairly well, he or she might request that this individual be on the lookout for the type of business desired. Brokers are aware of most businesses that are, or soon will be, for sale, and some brokers even specialize in businesses.

Other Professionals. Other professionals such as lawyers, accountants, business appraisers, and bankers often know of businesses for sale. Some prospective purchasers have found excellent opportunities by sending these professionals letters requesting information about businesses for sale. In addition, organizations such as a chamber of commerce may offer match-up services. One example is COIN (Canadian Opportunities Investment Network).

Word of Mouth. In their association with businesspeople, entrepreneurs often learn about business opportunities through word of mouth. Executives of industry associations often hear about owners who want out of their businesses, and prospective buyers can contact these sources.

EVALUATING A BUSINESS FOR SALE

A wise purchase decision may require considerable investigation. The prospective buyer should look into several key areas of a business before making a decision to purchase.

Industry Analysis

The entrepreneur should be well informed about the industry in which the business operates. Ideally, this information should come from an extensive background or experience in that industry. Some specific areas to investigate are the following:

Sales and Profit Trends of the Industry

- The degree of competition, the number of competitors entering or leaving the industry, and the nature of competitors' strategies

- The state of the economy in the market area and the extent to which changes in the economy affect the industry

- Legal restrictions currently affecting the operations of the business, as well as relevant pending legislation or political pressure

- Social concerns that may adversely affect the industry in the future

One or more of these areas could be significant in determining the future success of the proposed purchase. As a result, each should be thoroughly investigated unless the buyer has considerable experience in the industry.

The Previous Owner

The entrepreneur should ask the following questions about the previous owner of the business:

- Why is the previous owner selling the business? The often advertised reason, "because of poor health," may refer to financial rather than physical health.

- Is the previous owner a well-known and respected member of the community? Has this reputation contributed significantly to the success of the business? Will this success continue once that individual is no longer associated with the business?

- Will the previous owner be available—temporarily, at least—to provide assistance and advice to the new owner? This help can be invaluable, especially to a purchaser who lacks experience in the industry or market.

- Is the previous owner willing to finance the purchase by spreading it over a number of years? This may be helpful to the purchaser and advantageous tax-wise to the seller.

- What will the previous owner do after he or she sells the business? To guard against the previous owner starting a similar business in the same market area, the prospective purchaser might insist that a noncompetitive clause be included in the sales agreement.

Financial Condition of the Business

The financial condition of a prospective business is perhaps the most important area to evaluate. Care should be taken in evaluating the financial statements and assessing their validity. It is advisable to review not only the most recent year's financial statements but also those for past years. This process can reveal any trends and extraordinary circumstances. For instance, a general negative trend in profits during the past several years might suggest a lower value for the business, or at least the need for further investigation by the prospective buyer.

If the prospective buyer lacks a basic knowledge of accounting and an understanding of financial statements, it would be wise to enlist an accountant to assist in the financial evaluation. Some specific items to investigate, either by oneself or with the help of an accountant, are the following.

Validity of the Financial Statements. Since some flexibility is allowed in preparing financial statements, and a wide range of bookkeepers and accountants may be preparing them, the entrepreneur should assess the validity of the financial information obtained from the business. This can be done by obtaining audited statements and reviewing the methods used in recording such items as depreciation, inventory value, extraordinary items, repairs, owner's salary, and the treatment and terms of debt.

The prospective buyer should also investigate whether any potential hidden liabilities, such as liens or lawsuits, exist. Some industry experts recommend that if there is a possibility of such a liability but the amount is unknown, the purchaser should buy only the assets of the business. By doing this, the potential liability will accrue to the business itself rather than to the new owner.

Another task in assessing the validity of the statements is to review the income tax returns and bank deposits of the business. In addition, many prospective purchasers insist that the financial statements be audited to ensure their accuracy.

Evaluation of the Financial Statements. Once the prospective buyer is satisfied that the financial statements are complete and accurately portray the operations of the business, he or she can evaluate the performance of the business as described in these statements. Sales, expenses, profit levels, assets, liabilities, and cash flow position are important items. Application of various financial ratios can help in comparing the performance of the business with that of other firms in the industry. Chapter 10 gives a detailed discussion of ratio analysis and other financial evaluation measurements. Appendix 10A illustrates the financial evaluation of a small business.

Naturally, one would hope the business is strong financially and profitable in its operations. In some situations, however, a business may be a good purchase even if it is unprofitable or has a negative reputation at the time of evaluation. This is illustrated in Incidents 5-3 and 5-4. Such situations might be the following:

- The current owner is incompetent or lacks knowledge about the industry, and the purchaser has the competence and knowledge to turn the business around.

- The industry is, or will shortly be, in a growth position that might improve the firm's profitability or resale value.

- The major contributor to the firm's unprofitability is lack of capital leading to high interest costs, and the purchaser has the needed capital to inject into the business.

Condition of the Assets

Several assets of a business may require thorough inspection and, for nonliquid assets, possibly an appraisal by an independent appraiser. The fee for this service is generally reasonable and may be well worth it. Assets to value in this manner are the following.

Liquid Assets (Cash and Investments). An important question to a prospective purchaser concerns how easily the liquid assets can be converted to cash. There may be special terms or conditions with respect to these assets, for example, the period on a term deposit.

INCIDENT 5-3   Canadian Small Business of the Month

Karen Fegarty, owner of MailWorkZ in Bedford, Nova Scotia, will tell you that her biggest hurdle when she started her business was trying to rid herself of the negative reputation that the previous owners had left behind. Fegarty had purchased the company, which had developed a product called Broadcast. Broadcast allows the user to quickly create, manage, and send personalized marketing campaigns.

After buying the company, Fegarty came to realize that the previous owners had a very bad track record. As Fegarty recalls, buying a business with a bad reputation was like having "a business that was essentially dead." Customers had complained about a lack of customer service and support among many other things, forcing Fegarty to win back old customers while at the same time trying to impress new ones.

Perhaps Fegarty should have done a little more research and evaluation before buying the business. Chances are that if she had looked at aspects such as the financial condition of the business, the asset conditions, such as goodwill, the external business relationships, the customer lists or other records, and most important, the previous owner, she would have had a better idea of what to expect. One thing remains certain: When you buy a business with bad customer relations, you have your work cut out for you.

Source: Adapted from "Canadian Small Business of The Month—Part 1: Karen Fegarty: MailWorkZ Emphasizes Customer Service," Small Business Canada website, http://sbinfocanada.about.com/library/weekly/aa033101a.htm, July 10, 2004.

INCIDENT 5-4   Wheeling and Dealing

In 2000, Jason Gordon was working at a skate shop in Calgary when he learned that Social Industries, a Cochrane-based company and one of his suppliers, was looking to sell. Backed by private financing, Gordon jumped at the opportunity and with a wood press, the store's existing inventory, and a customer list, he set about making the business profitable. Within a year, Gordon had burned through $1 million while fighting an uphill battle. But four years later the business had turned around completely, after Gordon re-engineered Social Skateboards Inc. to supply boards to hardware stores and skate shops. This method proved to be far more profitable than selling to individual customers. Gordon has sold more than 100,000 boards to shops across Canada, the U.S., Australia, and England, with sales exceeding $1 million. The rise of the loonie also aided in the business's success, because Gordon buys his wood from Wisconsin. However, trouble is brewing among skateboard manufacturers: several companies have formed an association to combat the growing number of North American manufacturers outsourcing labour to Asia. Gordon has dismissed the idea of hauling his business overseas. Through entrepreneurial tactics, he has turned a struggling strip mall store into one of Calgary's largest skateboard manufacturers.

Source: Adapted from "Wheeling and Dealing," *Alberta Venture*, May 2004, pp.11–12.

Accounts Receivable. Have accounts receivable been aged? How many may be uncollectible? (Accounts receivable aging is discussed in detail in Chapter 10.) Enlisting the services of a professional accountant to assist in this regard may be well worth the cost.

Inventory. Is any inventory old, obsolete, or damaged? A detailed evaluation of inventory should be done by someone with knowledge and experience in this area.

Building and Equipment. Are the buildings and equipment old or obsolete? Are they comparable to competitors' facilities? Are there any liens against them?

Real Estate. What are the land taxes and service costs? If the premises are leased, is the lease transferable? What are the terms and conditions of the lease? Has the location experienced a high turnover of businesses in the past?

Goodwill. What value does the owner place on goodwill? Goodwill is the intangible value of such things as reputation, past experience, expertise, and prominence in the industry or community. Is this value realistic and reasonable? Generally, goodwill costs should not exceed 20 percent of the cost of the assets, even for well-established businesses. Further assistance to evaluate the value of the assets and even the value of the entire business may be obtained by enlisting the services of a qualified chartered business evaluator.

Quality of Personnel

The prospective purchaser should evaluate the efficiency of the business's personnel. How do they compare with employees in other, similar businesses? An important factor is personnel reaction to the new owner after the purchase. It may be wise for the buyer to meet with key personnel to better evaluate their reaction to the sale of the business. What is the staff turnover?

External Relationships of the Business

The investigation should include a review of those organizations or agencies currently essential to the operations of the business. Will these relationships continue, and if so, under what terms or conditions? Some organizations to contact include suppliers, financial institutions, and key customers.

Condition of the Records

Other records to review are credit files, personnel files, sales reports, contracts, and customer lists. These items can be very valuable to the operations of the business and should be included with the business when it is purchased.

Appendix 5A at the conclusion of this chapter presents a comprehensive checklist of considerations in purchasing a business.

DETERMINING THE PRICE OR VALUE OF A BUSINESS

If the preceding evaluation of the business shows positive results and the prospective purchaser decides to buy the business, he or she must make a decision concerning the price to pay for it. Is the asking price reasonable? Should a lower counteroffer be made? Several methods can be used to arrive at a price for a business.

There are four approaches to valuing a business. The first is by market value. The second relies heavily on asset value. The third uses the earnings potential of the business as a basis for determining value. The fourth uses a combination of asset value and earnings potential. Each method can help the entrepreneur make a general estimate of the purchase price. It should be kept in mind, however, that the buyer, the seller, or the business may possess unique characteristics that cannot be incorporated into a formula. Such situations will require adjustments to a formula-determined price. A more detailed coverage of the financial terms used in price determination is found in Chapter 10.

Market Value

In a free market, the right price is the one on which the purchaser and seller agree, or, in other words, where demand and supply meet. When applied to a business purchase, this price is called the market value. To use the market value method effectively, the prospective purchaser must collect data on the market values of many similar businesses. In many markets, the number of sales transactions of similar businesses is fairly small; thus, little data may be available. In such cases, other methods of valuation will be more useful.

Asset Value

There are two approaches to valuing a business using value of assets as a base: book value and replacement value.

Book Value. The book value method lists the business at the net balance sheet value of its assets minus the value of its liabilities (Chapter 10 provides the fundamentals of balance sheet assets and liabilities). This method generally understates the value of the business by a significant amount. For this reason, the book value price may form a lower limit to determining the price of the business.

Replacement Value. The replacement value method lists the replacement cost of the assets as their value. Because the assets of an existing business typically are not new, the replacement value method tends to overstate the value of the business. When coupled with the liability side of the balance sheet, the replacement cost method may result in an upper limit for the price to pay for the business.

Earnings Value

The prospective purchaser is interested not only in asset value but also in how the business will perform in the future. Therefore, earnings potential is another factor to be taken into account in setting the price of a business. Pretax earnings or income should be used, as the tax rates vary by province or territory and by industry.

It is also important to use average earnings in calculating earnings potential rather than just the most recent year's net income figure. When using average earnings, extraordinary items that have affected income should be deleted in order to make the estimate a "true" average. This is called normalizing earnings. Many analysts will use the previous five years' average of earnings. If earnings appear to be unstable from year to year, a weighted-average calculation might be used. The determination of average earnings using the weighted-average approach is shown in Figure 5-2. This method gives a greater weight to the most recent year's earnings in arriving at average earnings.

Two specific methods of estimating the purchase value of the business use earnings as a base.

Capitalization of Earnings Method. This method is commonly used to arrive at a quick estimate of the price of a business. The capitalized value is found by dividing average earnings of the business by a specified rate of return expressed as a decimal. This specified rate of return figure can be obtained by using bank interest (a risk factor of a few percentage points should be added) or another required rate of return percentage for the investment. It can also be obtained by using average return on tangible net worth statistics from such sources as Dun and Bradstreet and Statistics Canada. Figure 5-3 illustrates the capitalization of earnings formula.

Figure 5-4 illustrates a calculation of capitalized earnings value using industry averages. This method measures the firm's ability to earn profits in relation to the capital invested. For example, for a book and stationery store, it will take $45,450 paid for the business to earn $10,000 after taxes if the store were run at the median level. Figure 5-4 also illustrates Dun and Bradstreet averages for various industries.

Dun and Bradstreet
www.dnb.com

Statistics Canada
www.statcan.ca

Figure 5-2	Calculating Weighted-Average Earnings for a Business

	Average Earnings		Weighted Average Earnings (Earnings × Weights Factor)			
Last year	$5,000	5,000	×	5	=	25,000
Two years ago	4,000	4,000	×	4	=	16,000
Three years ago	7,000	7,000	×	3	=	21,000
Four years ago	10,000	10,000	×	2	=	20,000
Five years ago	$14,000	14,000	×	1	=	14,000
	$40,000			15		96,000
	Average Earnings 40,000/5 = 8000			Weighted Average Earnings 96,000/15 = 6,400		

| Figure 5-3 | **Capitalization of Earnings Formula** |

$$\frac{\text{Average earnings}}{\text{Predetermined interest rate or}} = \text{Capitalized value}$$
rate of return required for investment

| Figure 5-4 | **Capitalized Earnings Value** |

Line of Business	Net Profits to Tangible Net Worth as a Percentage*	Capitalized Earnings Value†
Retail		
Book and stationery stores	22.0	$45,450
Clothing, men's	12.9	77,520
Clothing, women's	12.8	78,125
Drugstores	20.7	48,310
Food stores	10.8	92,595
Gasoline service stations	23.1	43,290
Hardware	14.5	68,965
Jewellery store	8.3	120,480
Manufacturers		
Appliances, small	18.4	54,350
Bakery products	17.8	56,180
Machine shops	19.7	50,760
Meat products	11.8	84,745
Sash, door, and millwork plants	29.0	34,480
Soft drinks	34.9	28,655
Sporting goods and toys	11.0	90,910
Construction		
Building contractors	23.3	42,920
Services		
Hotels	15.5	64,515
Agriculture, forestry, and fishing		
Agriculture	12.2	81,965

Sources: Adapted from Paul Harmon, *Small Business Management—A Practical Approach* (New York: D. Van Nostrand, 1979), p. 76. Figures updated from Dun and Bradstreet, *Key Business Ratios*.

* Tangible net worth is net worth less intangibles, that is copyrights, goodwill, trademarks, and patents. This figure can be found in Dun and Bradstreet, *Key Business Ratios*.

† Represents the investment or tangible net worth required to earn $10,000 in profits after taxes, assuming the firm is operating at median level, calculated in the following manner:

$$\frac{\$10,000}{\text{Net profit to tangible net worth as percentage}} = \text{Capitalized earning value}$$

Times Earnings Method. This method arbitrarily multiplies average earnings by a number, usually between 1 and 10, based on past sales and industry experience, to arrive at the price for the business. This is often called the price-earnings ratio. Small businesses are usually sold at between four and five times earnings, according to the U.S. Small Business Administration, although recently some Internet companies have sold at much higher multiples. This number can vary significantly for very small businesses. Therefore, the advice of an experienced business broker or accountant valuator should be sought.

Combination Methods

Because both the asset value and the earnings value are important components of the true value of the business, some methods attempt to combine both values to estimate an appropriate price. Two combination methods can be used to arrive at such a price. The first is an analytical approach and the second is a method based on historical transactions or experience in the industry. Each will be discussed briefly.

Analytical Method. This method combines three factors to arrive at the value for the business: adjusted net worth, past earnings, and future earnings.

To obtain adjusted net worth, take the market value of tangible assets, subtract liabilities, and then add goodwill. If the business's assets are worth $220,000 with liabilities of $60,000 and goodwill of $40,000, then the adjusted net worth is $220,000 − $60,000 + $40,000 = $200,000.

To arrive at a value for past earnings, these earnings (net income) are "capitalized" by multiplying earnings by a number usually between 5 and 10. If the firm is judged to be very solid, the factor used should be closer to 10, and if considerable risk exists, a factor of 5 would be more appropriate. If average past earnings are $40,000 and a capitalization rate of 8 is used, the earnings value is $320,000.

A future earnings value is established by discounting future earnings of the business. This is done by applying a discount factor to current earnings. Such factors reflect the fact that future earnings flows are worth more today than they will be in the future. If the business earns $40,000 today and a discount factor of 10 percent is applied, the future earnings flow make the business worth $400,000 today.

To combine the above factors into one value reasonable for the business requires experience, judgment, and insight. For example, if the business has considerable assets, more emphasis should be given to the net worth method, whereas if the business is a service business, the earnings methods will be given more prominence in the combination. In the above examples, if a 50 percent emphasis is used for assets and 25 percent for each of the earnings factors is used, the combined value for this business would be

$$(\$200,000 \times 0.50) + (\$320,000 \times 0.25) + (\$400,000 \times 0.25) = \$280,000$$

Historical Method. This method uses historical experience in determining relevant indicators of the components of the value of a business. Figure 5-5 illustrates such an example.

As mentioned previously, determining the price of a business by using a formula may provide a good estimate of a business's worth, but the unique characteristics of each situation may alter the price offered and paid for the business.

Figure 5-5	**Combination Methods for Pricing a Business**

Type of Business	Price Offering Range
Accounting Firms	100–125% of annual revenues
Auto Dealers	2–3 years' net income + tangible assets
Book Stores	15% of annual sales + inventory
Coffee Shops	40–45% of annual sales + inventory
Courier Services	70% of annual sales
Daycare Centres	2–3 times annual cash flow
Dental Practices	60–70% of annual revenues
Employment and Personal Agencies	50–100% of annual revenues
Florists	34% of annual sales + inventory
Food/Gourmet Shops	20% of annual sales + inventory
Furniture and Appliance Stores	15–25% of annual sales + inventory
Gas Stations	15–25% of annual sales + equip/inventory
Gift & Card Shops	32–40% of annual sales + inventory
Grocery Stores	11–18% of annual sales + inventory
Insurance Agencies	100–125% of annual commissions
Janitorial and Landscape Contractors	40–50% of annual sales
Law Practices	40–100% of annual sales
Property Management Companies	50–100% of annual revenues
Restaurants (non-franchised)	30–45% of annual sales
Sporting Goods Stores	30% of annual sales + inventory
Travel Agencies	40–60% of annual commissions

Source: Excerpted from 2003 *Business Reference Guide* (Wilmington, NC: Business Brokerage Press).

THE PURCHASE TRANSACTION

The entrepreneur should enlist the services of such professionals as lawyers and accountants to assist in the purchase decision. Once a purchase price and other terms and conditions have been agreed on, the buyer should enlist the services of a lawyer to draw up the purchase agreement and close the transaction. This helps ensure that clear title to the business is transferred and post-purchase difficulties are minimized. The purchase agreement should cover the following areas:

- The purchase price, including principal and interest amounts
- Payment date(s)—when and to whom payments are to be made
- A detailed list of all assets to be included in the purchase
- Conditions of the purchase—what nonfinancial requirements, if any, are part of the purchase (many purchase contracts are signed subject to the purchaser obtaining suitable financing)
- Provisions for noncompliance with conditions, including penalties for breaches of the contract
- Collateral or security pledged in the transaction (if the seller is financing the sale)

Negotiating the Deal

In purchasing a business, the first formal step is to make the offer to purchase. The offer may be made directly by the buyer or through a realtor or a lawyer. In either case, the offer to purchase should be made only after consulting a lawyer and an accountant. As part of the negotiating strategy, the potential buyer should have calculated (preferably financially) the maximum amount he or she can offer for the business using one or more of the methods previously cited. This value is generally somewhat higher than the original purchase offer. As negotiations continue, the purchase price or other aspects of the agreement may have to be altered.

Once the purchase price has been agreed on, the transaction is usually closed and legal transfer of title to the business takes place. Typically, this is carried out by both the buyer's and the seller's lawyers. The purchaser should exercise caution if the seller's lawyer is to close the deal. The buyer's lawyer should be permitted to review the details of the transaction in this case.

The buyer is normally required to make a deposit of 5 percent to 10 percent of the purchase price as a show of good faith. This amount should be minimized at least until the seller has met the conditions of the agreement.[2]

Summary

1. The potential advantages of buying a small business include the reduction of risk, time, set-up expense, and competition; capitalization of business strength; possible assistance from the previous owner; and easier planning. Potential disadvantages include problems with physical facilities, personnel, inventory, and accounts receivable; deterioration of the business's financial condition or market; and difficulty in negotiating a purchase price.

2. The common sources for locating a business for sale include classified ads, government departments, real estate brokers, word of mouth, and professionals such as lawyers, accountants, and bankers.

3. The key areas an entrepreneur should investigate in carrying out an industry analysis are sales and profit trends, degree of competition, state of the economy in the market area, legal

restrictions, and social concerns that may adversely affect the industry in the future. To evaluate the internal aspects, the following should be addressed: previous owner's reputation, why the owner is selling the business, validity of the financial statements, condition of the assets, personnel, external relationships of the business, and existing records.

4. There are three general approaches to valuing a business. The first method uses the asset value to determine the price. The second method uses the earnings of the business. The third method uses a combination of assets and earnings.

Chapter Problems and Applications

1. John Van Goegh wants to own his own business. His area of expertise is the sporting goods market. He has checked into opening his own store versus purchasing an existing store in the downtown area. The existing store is a seven-year-old proprietorship with sagging sales. There are four main sporting goods shops in the city (60,000 people). The existing business is in a prime location, and the market and product line are well established. The financial condition, however, includes a large number of accounts receivable. With this information, John turns to you as a consultant. What advice would you give John regarding whether to purchase the existing business or start his own? What additional factors should he consider? Justify your answer.

2. You are investigating the purchase of a fertilizer manufacturing plant. The results of your analysis of the firm are extremely positive, except for an unidentifiable annual payment of $100,000. On further investigation, you learn that the $100,000 is being paid in fines for dumping toxic waste. The previous owner has determined that it costs less to pay the fines than it would to properly dispose of the waste by deep-well injection. In light of recent government actions, how would this situation affect your decision to purchase? Explain.

3. Sally's Bar and Grill is available for purchase. Sally's earnings for the past five years were as follows:

Last year, $50,000   Four years ago, $40,000

Two years ago, $60,000   Five years ago, $25,000

Three years ago, $30,000

Determine the value of the business using the following methods (use current bank interest rates) using both general and weighted averaging methods.

a. Capitalized earnings formula

b. Times earnings method

4. Do an industry analysis for the existing grocery stores in your area. Complete your analysis using all the areas mentioned in the text. Refer to the checklist in Appendix 5A.

5. From an advertisement in the paper, contact the seller of a business.

Find out the price and other information pertinent to the sale. Does the asking price seem reasonable? Check with industry averages to evaluate the performance of the business.

6. Refer to Incident 5-3 and identify the potential problems that might have arisen with the purchase of this business.

Web Exercise

www.
rockymountainsoap.
com

Visit the website for the Rocky Mountain Soap Company and identify possible concerns about purchasing this company.

APPENDIX 5A

Checklist of Considerations in Purchasing a Business

The Industry

1. What are the sales and profit trends in the industry?

2. What is the degree of competition? What competitive changes have taken place?

3. What is the nature of competitor strategies?

4. What is the state of the economy in the market? How is the business's performance affected by changes in the economy?

5. What existing or pending legal restrictions affect the operations of the business?

6. What social or cultural concerns affect the industry?

7. Are there any potential competitive or trading area changes that might affect the business?

The Previous Owner

1. Why is the previous owner selling the business?

2. Has the reputation of the previous owner contributed to the success of the business?

3. Will the previous owner help you by providing assistance and advice after the sale?

4. Is the previous owner willing to finance all or part of the purchase?

5. Will the previous owner start a competitive business after the sale?

Financial Condition of the Business

1. Is the financial information provided accurate and indicative of the business's performance?

2. What is the history of profits going back at least five years?

3. Has the business gained or lost market share in the past five years?

4. How do the various financial ratios for the business compare with industry averages?

5. Does the business have a strong identity with customers or clients? Can this identity be maintained?

6. What prospects does the business have for increasing market share and profitability in the future?

7. If the business is currently unsuccessful, what are the chances of improving it with an infusion of capital or managerial expertise?

8. What value does the business place on goodwill?

Condition of Assets

1. Are any special terms or conditions associated with the liquid assets?

2. Are the accounts receivable collectible?

3. Is the inventory old or obsolete?

4. Are the building and equipment up to date and paid for?

5. Are taxes and service costs paid on land?

6. Is the location good? Is it increasing or decreasing in value?

7. Is the lease good? What are the terms and conditions of the lease?

8. Have you verified the value of assets with a qualified chartered business evaluator?

Quality of Personnel

1. Do the employees of the business compare favourably with the industry in productivity and expertise?

2. Will the employees stay on with the business after the sale?

3. Has the business been progressive in meeting competitive demands regarding wage rates and employee benefits?

Condition of External Relationships

1. Can favourable relations with suppliers be maintained?

2. Are financial sources appropriate and adequate? Can they be maintained?

3. Does the business have a strong support staff such as a lawyer, an accountant, and a consultant? Can these people be retained if needed?

Condition of Records

1. Can the purchaser obtain key records such as credit files, personnel files, customer lists, sales reports, and contracts?

Suggested Readings

Anthony, Joseph. "Maybe You Should Buy A Business." *Kiplinger's Personal Finance Magazine*, May 1998.

Business Development Bank of Canada—Business Ownership, Transition Financing Program—www.BDC.ca

www.mcgrawhill.ca/olc/balderson

Business Valuation Methods—www.home3.americanexpress.com/smallbusiness/resources/starting/valbuz.shtml

Buying A Business—www.cbsc.org/english/search/display.efm?

Gray, Douglas A., and Diana L. Gray. *The Complete Canadian Small Business Guide, 2nd Edition.* Toronto: McGraw-Hill Ryerson, 2003, pp. 79–103.

How to Evaluate A Proposed Business Acquisition—www.bdc.ca

Regimbald, Michel. "Your Business Acquisition Road Plan—www.bdc.ca

Shachter, Harvey. "Don't Grow it… Buy It." *Profit,* June 1998, p. 161.

Tulenko, Paul. "How to Buy Yourself a Job for Life." *The Globe and Mail*, July 24, 1995, p. B7.

Comprehensive Case *Sid Stevens: Part 3*

Although the numbers Sid had put together indicated that the Ladder Rail business might face several challenges, he decided to devote all his spare time to the venture. This was primarily because of the positive response that he had received from his co-workers, as well as from the local Home Hardware dealer, who thought that the product had a lot of potential. Within two months, this dealer sold five units of the Ladder Rail that Sid had made in his garage. Customer feedback was positive and this was encouraging to Sid.

One of the decisions that Sid is concerned with is whether to build a manufacturing plant or purchase an existing facility. He is aware of a small plant close to his home that is for sale. It has much of the metal-bending equipment that he needs and he could retrofit the plant to suit his purposes for $10,000. However, when he learned that the owner of the plant was asking $200,000 and that its net worth was only $180,000, Sid felt that it was just too much money and was leaning toward building his own plant.

Regardless of how he established the manufacturing facility, one thing that Sid had learned in his small business management class was that he should prepare a business plan. He therefore set to work preparing the plan and had Suzie type it for him. The outline of Sid Stevens' business plan for the Ladder Rail is found below.

Introduction

My objective in starting this business is to become independent and develop a business that will provide an adequate living for my family and me. I anticipate that within three years, the product will experience high awareness and demand throughout Southern Ontario. At that time, I will look to expand nationally and perhaps even internationally. I have considerable expertise in construction and roofing, which has allowed me to be knowledgeable about the safety and convenience concerns associated with the use of ladders.

Marketing

The product is a light metal handrail that will attach to most aluminum extension ladders commonly used in the construction industry and by many homeowners. It can be made inexpensively (estimated at $10 per unit) and has great profit potential (selling price estimated at $40 per unit). I anticipate that anyone who owns a ladder would see the Ladder Rail's benefit and would be interested in purchasing. I intend to advertise the product in the local newspaper at first and as sales bring in more money, I would be able to move into television advertising. There is currently no other product like it on the market.

Physical Facilities

Although I now can manufacture the ladder rail in my garage, as sales increase I will need to build or purchase a small factory to meet demand. I estimate that an adequate production facility, including the required equipment, will cost approximately $170,000. I already own the land that the plant would be built on.

Financial

I currently have $20,000 of my own money to invest in the business and will borrow the rest from the local bank. I am certain that the business will be able to generate the required income to make the interest payments on the loan plus provide a good living for my family.

Legal

I plan to operate the business as a sole proprietorship for the first few years until incorporation looks positive. I will need a business licence to operate the manufacturing plant.

Personnel

The business will employ three people initially, including me. I will be in charge of the production process, assisted by two others. I will also handle the marketing and financial aspects of the Ladder Rail with the help of my wife, Suzie.

Questions

1. What aspects about this situation would suggest that Sid should buy the plant instead of building it from scratch?
2. If Sid decided to purchase the building and estimated that income from the plant would be $20,000, is the asking price reasonable, assuming he wanted to make a 10 percent return on the investment? (Use the capitalization of earnings formula.)
3. Evaluate the business plan that Sid has prepared. Suggest improvements.

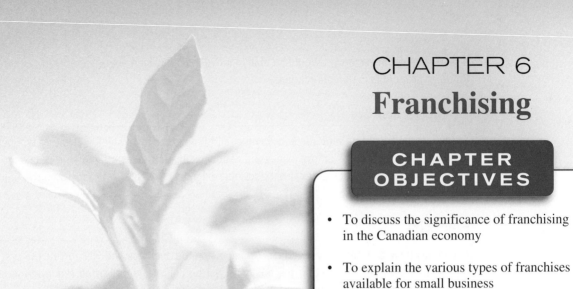

CHAPTER 6
Franchising

CHAPTER OBJECTIVES

- To discuss the significance of franchising in the Canadian economy

- To explain the various types of franchises available for small business

- To list the relative strengths and weaknesses of franchising as a method of starting a small business

- To explain how to evaluate a franchise opportunity

- To discuss how to organize a franchising system

SMALL BUSINESS PROFILE
Dale Wishewan

Booster Juice

Dale Wishewan grew up wanting to be a baseball player. After completing his degree in mechanical engineering at Portland State University, which he attended on a baseball scholarship, he founded Booster Juice with a partner, John Amack. Dale felt that there was a market for a healthy alternative to traditional fast food. Booster Juice provides a menu of juices and smoothies consisting of such nutritional ingredients as natural fruits as well as wheat grass and Acai berries. Booster Juice's mission statement is "To provide customers with an incredible, healthy alternative to fast food that's great tasting, convenient, and nutritious, making it perfectly suited for today's active lifestyle." The first Booster Juice outlet was opened in Sherwood Park, Alberta in 1999. Since then, the concept has grown with the aid of a well-developed franchise system.

Growth was rapid with 15 outlets added in the first year and 35 in the next. In 2002, however, Wishewan decided to reduce expansion to ensure that the business was on firm footing. "We consciously slowed down after our second year, wanting to be sure our concept grew into something solid," he reported. Wishewan and his management team spent about a year ironing out various kinks in the business plan. He secured better deals with food distributors and improved quality control by hiring permanent staff to visit each franchise on a regular basis. Wishewan understands that successful franchising is all about systems and Booster Juice provides good training and support for franchisees. This includes hands-on training as well as assistance in the marketing, legal, logistics, and real estate aspects of the franchise. To decrease competition, Booster Juice bought out two smaller smoothie chains. Today, Booster Juice is the top juice and smoothie franchise in Canada with 130 outlets operating across Canada (over twice as many as its nearest competitor.)

Booster Juice has also expanded internationally, with several outlets in the U.S. as well as successful franchises in Saudi Arabia and planned entrances into the United Kingdom and China. Expanding internationally has been a challenge, however. Wishewan indicates that it is a big hurdle to find suitable overseas partners. "It is challenging to qualify an individual franchisee in Canada, but it is 10 times as important to choose the right master franchisor in another country." Booster Juice's entry into the Saudi market has been a success as it has partnered with an established company there that has also brought other western companies to that country. Although there have been some logistics issues due to the distances involved, extra efforts to develop the brand, educating the public about the smoothie concept, and allowing more flexibility have paid off for both the franchisor and franchisee.

Source: Adapted from "Smoothie Chain Booster Juice Finds Expanding Globally Is Not Always Smooth," *Canadian Business*, Jan. 30–Feb 12; "The Persian Gulp," *Alberta Venture*, July/August 2005; and "CEO Report," *Alberta Venture*, May 2005 and Booster Juice website.

Booster Juice
www.boosterjuice.com

HISTORY AND BACKGROUND OF FRANCHISING

Franchising is becoming an increasingly popular method of establishing and operating a small business. Incident 6-1 provides an example of this growth. Many entrepreneurs find the opportunity to operate their own business with slightly less risk an attractive option. Others enter franchising out of necessity, having lost jobs with larger organizations. Franchising now occurs in most industries and is experiencing rapid growth in the service sector.

Franchising has not only been successful for the entrepreneur. Many large organizations also recognize that this method of doing business benefits their operations.

From the franchisor's point of view, franchising provides a source of capital and a stable and motivated workforce, usually leading to higher performance. For the franchisee, it offers a turnkey operation with valuable assistance from the franchisor (see Incident 6-2).

One dilemma the entrepreneur often faces is that as the business grows, funds are needed for expansion. Franchising is one solution to this financing problem.

INCIDENT 6-1   The Genius of Junk

1-800-GOT-JUNK is a junk removal company that does the dirty work for you. Brian Scudamore, the owner and CEO of the franchise chain, bought his first truck for $700 in 1989 as a 17 year-old high school dropout. After talking his way into university, and balancing both work and school for over three years, Scudamore again quit school to focus more fully on his growing business. Business continued at a slow and steady pace until 1998 when Scudamore changed the company name and decided to enter into a franchise.

The first franchise opened in Toronto in 1999, and between 1999 and 2003, 23 more franchise locations were opened. Business exploded after this and more than 150 locations opened within the next three years. Today, there are 25 franchise locations in Canada, 182 in the US, one in Australia, and one in England.

Scudamore expects his company to keep expanding. Company goals include generating sales of $100 million by the end of 2006, $420 million in sales by the end of 2009, and $1 billion in sales with franchises in 10 countries by 2012.

Source: Adapted from Stephanie Ponder, "The Genius of Junk," *The Costco Connection*, March/April 2006, pp. 26–28.

INCIDENT 6-2   A Growing Concern

Edmonton-based Grower Direct Fresh Cut Flowers is Canada's largest flower franchise. It began as a wholesale operation to stock the floral departments of IGA and Safeway. Skip Kerr, founder of Grower Direct, ran the operation out of the back of his car and sold the leftover stock to individuals. Word spread and Kerr soon found an increasingly large client base to which he responded by opening his first retail shop in 1990, offering cut flowers at wholesale price.

Alberta legislation in the early 1990s allowed the dealerships to become franchises. "In those early days, it cost a franchisee under $20,000 to go into business, which was $5,000 in franchise fees plus construction costs," says Kerr. Kerr says that successful franchising is about creating win/win propositions for the franchisee and franchisor. "You have to set things up so that your franchisee can make money. You also need to provide adequate training and support to help them be successful," he says. He says that the strength of the franchisor lies in the franchisees, meaning that you need good people to run your stores. The franchise now encompasses 65 franchise stores across Canada.

Source: Adapted from Elaine Davidson, "Words to the Wise," *Alberta Venture*, April 2004, p. 45.

INCIDENT 6-3   *Franchisor Using Innovative Methods to Inspire*

Ken Pattenden has taken the Canadian Taco Time franchise from 80 outlets to 110 in just a few short years. He has done this by using innovative and carefully researched marketing strategies and by converting his franchisees to his vision for the chain. Diane Hawkins, a 24-year veteran with Taco Time in Calgary remembers the first letter Pattenden sent to the franchisees. "It said something about change being invigorating, and he has certainly stuck to that!"

Edo Japan restaurants' president and CEO Tom Donaldson believes that the key to inspiring people into buying your franchise is first making sure that you're ready to franchise, and then finding the right people to inspire with your idea. In Donaldson's particular business, he ensures that the franchisees like working with the public, enjoy hiring and managing staff, and don't mind being on their feet all day before he begins to inspire them with how much they can expect to earn. In this way, Donaldson ensures that both the franchisee and the franchisor benefit in the long run.

Source: Adapted from Norma Ramage, "Gringo Goes Wild," *Alberta Venture*, October 2003, pp. 57–60 and "Words To The Wise," *Alberta Venture*, April 2004, pp. 43–46.

In addition, expansion of a business usually requires the addition of new employees. The new employees often lack the same incentive as the owner to make the business succeed. Some franchisors have used innovative methods to increase interest and motivation (see Incident 6-3).

Although the concept has been around for decades, franchising has experienced its most rapid growth in North America only since the 1950s. It began with the automobile manufacturers, oil companies, soft drink bottlers, and breweries and has since spread to many different industries throughout the world. Through franchising, many organizations with a proven concept or product were able to expand much more rapidly to meet demand. This growth was so rapid that toward the end of the 1960s, several problems developed in the industry that resulted in the formation of franchisee associations and the passage of legislation to protect the rights of both franchisees and franchisors. Currently several provinces are looking at requiring greater financial disclosure by franchisors to better protect potential franchisees.[1] Alberta and Ontario have already passed such legislation.

In the last decade, more than 40 percent of all retail sales resulted from franchising in North America.[2] Estimates are that this figure may be as high as 60 percent of sales by the year 2010.[3] Franchise growth in Canada has paralleled the rapid growth in the United States, with recent estimates indicating $185 billion in sales in 2005,[4] which accounts for 48 percent of total sales from more than 1,500 franchise systems and 75,000 franchised outlets.[5] This trend is shown in Figure 6-1 on page 166. Studies by Price Waterhouse and Peat Marwick Thorne show that franchising is growing faster than the general economy.[6] In addition, more than 100 Canadians are now franchising internationally, with the United States being the prime location,[7] whereas 500 of the largest U.S. franchisors have introduced their franchised systems into Canada.[8]

Figure 6-2 (on page 166) illustrates the industries in which franchising has had the most significant impact. The percentages denote industry sales as a percentage of total franchise sales. Traditional franchising includes motor vehicle, oil, and soft drink companies, which sell their products through franchises.

Canadian Franchise
Association
www.cfa.ca

| Figure 6-1 | Franchise Sales in Canada (in billions)* |

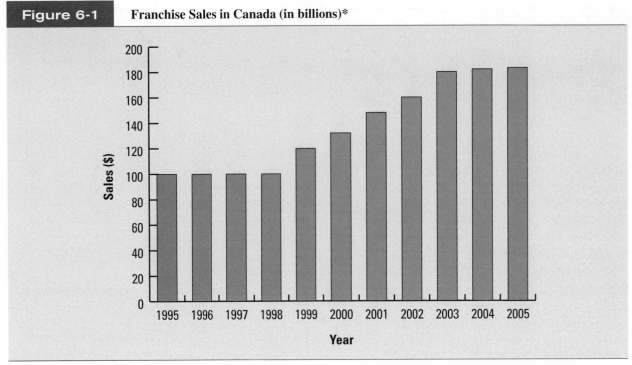

* Sales figures are estimates of the Canadian Franchise Association.

| Figure 6-2 | Franchising by Industry |

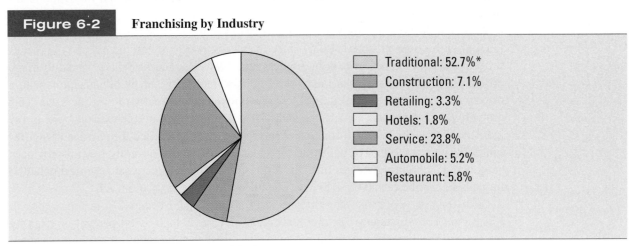

* Includes motor vehicles, oil companies, and soft drink bottlers.
Note: Percentages do not add to 100 because of rounding.

Source: *Market Research Handbook* (Ottawa: Statistics Canada, 2006), p. 191.

Franchises exist in almost all industries today. A major reason for the large recent increase in the number of franchises is expansion into the service sector, which is the fastest-growing sector in the Canadian economy. Figure 6-3 lists the largest franchises in Canada today.

Figure 6-3	**Canada's Leading Franchising Companies**			
Franchise	**Gross Revenue (000s)**	**Parent**	**Type of Business**	
Metro-Richelieu Inc.*	$10,944.0	Widely held	Convenience food	
Canadian Tire	$7,774.6	Billes Family	Retail hardware	
McDonald's Restaurants	$4,345.1	McDonald's Corp.	Fast food	

*Acquired A&P in 2005

Source: Taken from the 2005 and 2006 annual reports of these companies.

WHAT IS FRANCHISING?

Franchising is a system for selectively distributing goods or services through outlets owned by the franchisee. A common definition for a franchise arrangement is a patent or trademark licence entitling the holder to market particular products or services under a brand or trademark according to prearranged terms or conditions. In addition to products and services, the franchise may consist of or may include a "system" or method of providing the product or service. Today many applications of this definition translate into a broad range of franchising relationships. The brand identification is an important aspect of this form of distribution. It consists of standardization throughout the system. The various outlets in the system are similar as to class of trade, merchandise carried, or services rendered, and other factors that have a bearing on joint merchandising and management through common policies. Also, all the outlets in a franchise system are identified as members of the system. They operate under a common name or insignia, and the establishments often have a distinctive appearance common to all members of the system. This standardization is ensured and controlled by the terms of the franchise contract.

A franchise system is therefore a "voluntary" chain, that is, a chain of individually owned businesses. Franchising, in fact, has been the salvation of many independent wholesale and retail merchants in the face of increasing competition from corporate chains and discount operations. By joining a jobber-sponsored voluntary chain, for example, an independent retailer can get all the benefits that are available to a corporate chain store: central buying and assistance in merchandising, promotion, and management.

The franchising or licensing technique is more often utilized today, however, when a company comes up with an idea for a product or service and finds that it does not have adequate resources to market its own idea. By licensing prospective entrepreneurs to perform the marketing function for it, the franchising company is able to achieve rapid expansion at relatively low cost, with a substantial part of the investment being contributed by the franchise holder. The various types of franchises are grouped into three categories.

Manufacturer-Directed Franchise. In this type of franchise, the manufacturer (producer) of a product grants a dealer the right to sell the product. This right, which tends to be geographically exclusive, often requires no initial fee. (See Figure 6-4 for further details of this type of franchising.) Manufacturer-directed franchising is common in such industries as automobile sales, gasoline distributorships, and farm implement dealerships. This type of franchising is successful only when the manufacturer has an established name, a solid reputation, and considerable consumer loyalty.

| Figure 6-4 | Types of Franchises |

		Details of Agreement		Examples	
Title	**Method of Franchising**	**Franchisor Provides**	**Franchisee Provides**	**Industry**	**Company**
Manufacturer	Franchisee has right to sell product	Product sales support Exclusive territory	Selling function Facilities	Automobile Farm machinery Oil companies	Ford GMC Hesston ESSO GULF
Wholesaler–retailer	Franchisee owns equity in supplier company and purchases product from the franchise	Product and other technical assistance and service	Selling function Buys equity Board of directors	Retail grocery Hardware	Associated Grocers Home Hardware
Franchising company	Franchisee buys the right to sell service or product	Method of operations Training Location, building, and so on Financing Proven name Advertising	Fee Royalties Compliance with conditions of contract	Fast food Auto rental	McDonald's Kentucky Fried Chicken Avis Budget Hertz

Wholesaler–Retailer-Directed Franchise. In this arrangement, one member of the distribution channel, such as the wholesaler or retailer, initiates the organization of the franchise. The primary purpose of such an organization generally is to centralize many managerial and operational functions and take advantage of volume buying for a group of sellers. As with the manufacturer-owned franchise, there is usually no initial fee, but an equity investment in the franchise may be required. Figure 6-4 illustrates some of the other operating details for this type of franchise and the industries in which it is prevalent.

Franchising Company. This type of franchise usually involves a company (the master licensor) that sells a product or service in exchange for an initial predetermined fee and an ongoing royalty. The franchisee gains the right to sell under the franchisor's name and receives the franchisor's assistance and managerial expertise. Franchising companies are commonly found in the retail and service industries. In recent years, many companies using this method of franchising to expand their operations have experienced rapid growth. Figure 6-4 provides further details of the franchising company arrangement.

ADVANTAGES OF FRANCHISING

Compared with the other two methods of starting a small business (buying and organizing), franchising offers many specific advantages.

Proven Market for the Product or Service. Except for newly established franchises, a known market and instant brand recognition for the franchisor's product or service exists. Information about the performance of existing franchises is normally supplied or can be obtained by the franchisee. Such a track record makes it much easier to make projections for future operations.

The instant pulling power of the product also greatly helps the small business owner shorten the duration of the initial stage of the business, when the market is being developed and resulting revenues are low. A study by the University of Toronto showed that franchised businesses had higher sales per outlet than independents in almost all types of businesses.[9] Another study of franchisors found that during the last recession, franchised outlets were less affected than nonfranchised outlets.[10]

Services the Franchisor May Provide. A franchising company typically provides many valuable services to a franchisee. A description of franchisor services follows.

Selection of Location. Assistance in selecting the location can be very important, especially if location is critical to the success of the business, such as in retailing and often in the service industry. Often a franchisor has considerable site selection expertise that can be used in establishing the business.

Purchase or Construction of Site, Buildings, and Equipment. The franchisor's experience and financial resources in this area may mean considerable savings of time and money. In addition to providing expertise, the franchisor may even purchase or construct the facilities for the franchisee.

The Royal Bank
www.royalbank.com

Provision of Financing. Some franchisors will provide financing for franchisees, and their association with the franchisees often helps the franchisee obtain financing. For example, the Royal Bank, through its Franchise Assistance Program, allows favourable interest rates on franchisee loans because of a franchisee's association with a well-known franchisor.

Standardized Methods of Operating. Standardized operating procedures and manuals are often part of the services the franchisor provides in the areas of cost accounting, control systems, and customer service standards. Such methods can result in considerable savings for the small business.

Advertising. Most franchisors will provide national advertising that may benefit the franchisee. Such a level of promotion may be difficult and costly for the franchisee to develop unassisted.

Purchasing Advantages. Because the franchising company purchases large volumes of inventories for its franchisees, it can pass the resulting cost savings on to franchisees on purchases made from the franchisor.

Training. Most franchisors provide training to new franchisees. This may take the form of an instruction manual or thorough training at a franchisor's school. A McDonald's franchisee, for example, receives training at Hamburger University in Illinois and can even receive a bachelor's degree in Hamburgerology! Because of the extra training provided, franchising (as opposed to buying or organizing) is often more suited to someone who lacks experience in the industry. Recently, knowledge-based businesses such as consulting or research have experienced rapid growth in franchising. The capital investment to get established in these businesses is typically low and flexibility is high (see Incident 6-4).

Because of the foregoing advantages, a franchisee's chance of success in the business is higher than with the other two methods of starting a small business. The franchising industry advertises a failure rate of only 4 percent to 8 percent, which is much lower than the rate for nonfranchised businesses.[11] Some claim however, that this low failure rate is greatly exaggerated by franchising companies. In the United States and Canada an increasing number of franchisees are complaining—sometimes in court—about the problems incurred when they sign a franchise contract.

POTENTIAL DISADVANTAGES OF FRANCHISING

Because of the apparent advantages just discussed, many individuals have signed franchise contracts. However, many have suffered disillusionment and failure a short while later. The level of franchise litigation is growing. Often franchisees misinterpret the franchise agreement concerning such things as use of advertising funds, restrictions, and services provided by the franchisor. It is critical that the prospective franchisee be aware of the difficulties that can arise when one enters the world of franchising. There are several areas of potential conflict discussed in this section. The franchisee should have a clear understanding of how disputes will be resolved in the event that they occur. The following are some of the more common dangers.

Lack of Independence. In signing a franchise contract, the franchisee can expect to receive a certain amount of assistance from the franchisor. The franchisor will monitor the business, however, to ensure that the conditions of the contract are being met. This condition restricts the franchisee's freedom and independence.

Cost of the Franchise. Most franchises have a price that often consists of an initial fee and ongoing royalties based on operations. To enter most franchise organizations, individuals will have to accumulate a certain amount of capital either to pay the fee or to provide the facilities and the associated set-up costs. Appendix 6A provides details on this subject, including the financial requirements of some of the better-known franchises in Canada.

Unfulfilled Promises. Most franchising companies indicate they will provide such services as training and advertising. In some cases, however, this assistance does not materialize or is inadequate.

Restrictions of the Contract. The franchise agreement may contain some restrictions that inhibit the franchisee's freedom. Such restrictions include the following.

Product or Service Offered. The franchisee may not be allowed to offer for sale any products not procured by the franchisor.

Line Forcing. The franchisee may be required to offer the franchisor's complete line of products for sale, even if some are not profitable in the franchisee's market area.

Termination. The franchisee may not be able to terminate the franchise contract without incurring a penalty. The franchisee may also be prohibited from selling the business or passing it on to family members.

INCIDENT 6-4   A Cut Above

The ultimate goal of running a successful franchise operation is, according to Debbie Bertie, president of Beaners Fun Cuts for Kids, to love what you do. After a bad haircut experience in a salon with her young son, Bertie discovered Beaners, and in 1987 she bought a franchise. Bertie says, "It provided our family with a great secondary income. I worked 15 hours a week in my store and made a profit of $60,000 to $70,000 a year."

Bertie sold her store in 1999 and used the money to buy out franchise founder, Saundra Shapiro. "We have now linked our business with Canam Franchise Development Group and they are working with us to take Beaners across Canada and into the United States in about a year," says Bertie. Canam works to promote franchises like Beaners through a website, trade shows, and advertisements in magazines. It provides the sales team and corporate structure to help the franchise get ready for aggressive growth.

Source: Adapted from Elaine Davidson, "Words to the Wise," *Alberta Venture*, April 2004, p. 43.

Saturation of the Market. In some industries, franchising companies have allowed over-saturation to occur in a particular geographic market. Saturation in established markets is a growing problem in North America. Careful examination of the franchise contract should be made to ensure that this does not occur. This puts financial pressure on those franchisees operating within that market. If a franchisor has a large initial fee and no royalties, its major concern may be the selling of franchises rather than their ongoing success. Such franchises seem particularly vulnerable to oversaturation.

Lack of Security. A franchisor may elect not to renew a franchise contract once it has expired or may terminate the contract before its expiry if the franchisee has violated the terms or conditions. Many franchising companies operate company-owned outlets as well as franchised outlets. The number of company-owned outlets is only about 18 percent of total franchise outlets, but recent figures show slight increases in this percentage.[12] Some argue that franchising companies take over the outlets after the franchisees have successfully established them.

Cost of Merchandise. The cost of merchandise purchased from the franchisor may exceed the price the franchisee can obtain elsewhere. However, the contract may require the franchisee to purchase solely from the franchisor.

Effectiveness of Promotion. Most franchisors provide promotion and advertising for their franchisees. In some situations, however, the promotion is not effective for the franchisee's market and may be time-consuming and costly for the franchisee to participate in. Often a franchisee does not want to participate in these programs but is required by the contract to do so.

Exaggeration of Financial Success. Most franchising companies provide promotional literature for prospective franchisees. This information generally contains financial statements for the typical franchisee. In some cases, these estimates have been overly optimistic and the actual results for the franchisee are disappointing.

EVALUATION OF A FRANCHISE OPPORTUNITY

In view of the potential disadvantages just mentioned, it is critical that a thorough investigation of the prospective franchise be made before signing the contract. Several key areas should be examined in evaluating a franchise. Thorough investigation of the franchisor, the product or service, the franchise contract, and the market should be carried out. Sources of this information are reviewed briefly below.

Franchisor

The franchisor should provide a prospective franchisee with information in several areas (a more detailed list is found in Appendix 6B):

- A complete set of financial projections for the franchise should be provided. These should include indications of net income to be earned, when income will be made, what financial investment is required (franchise fee plus other costs), and when payments are required. The prospective franchisee should ensure that these projections are applicable to their own market area and personal situation.

- The franchisor should provide details on what financing is required and whether the franchisor provides financial assistance and at what cost.

- The proposed location should be calculated along with the number of other locations and protection against saturation of the market that will be provided.

- The extent of training, ongoing management support, and promotion that the franchisor will provide should be made available.

- The supplies purchasing arrangement and costs and level of mandatory purchasing from the franchisor should be identified.

Each of these areas should be analyzed carefully with professional help if necessary to ensure their accuracy.

Industry Associations

The Franchise Handbook
www.franchise1.com

Such organizations as the Canadian Franchise Association (Toronto), the local chamber of commerce, and various other industry associations may provide valuable information about a franchisor's history, reputation, operations, size, and number of operating franchises. In addition, considerable franchise information may be obtained on the Internet. *The Franchise Handbook* may be found online. Information about specific franchising companies may be found by searching the Net under the company name. Appendix 6B at the conclusion of the chapter lists several agencies that can provide assistance. Some publications also offer assistance, including the *Franchise Annual*, published by the Canadian Franchise Association in St. Catharines, Ontario; the *Franchise Yearbook*, published by *Entrepreneur Magazine*; and the *Info Franchise Newsletter*, published by Info Press in St. Catharines, Ontario. In addition, regular franchise shows are held in major cities in Canada. Such events allow the prospective franchisees the opportunity to evaluate and compare several franchise opportunities in a short time.

Professionals

A prospective franchisee is well advised to enlist an accountant to review the financial side of the franchise to ensure that the information provided is accurate. Often financial statements do not conform to Generally Accepted Accounting Principles (GAAP) or are unrealistic.

A lawyer's expertise should also be used in reviewing the terms and conditions of the contract. Because the franchising industry is becoming so specialized, it may be worthwhile to enlist a lawyer who is knowledgeable about franchising issues. The franchisee should ensure that his or her rights are protected and that there is a clear understanding of both franchisee and franchisor responsibilities regarding the following items:

- Initial fee—how much and when paid

- Royalties—how much and when paid

- Additional costs for training and management assistance

- The total investment required and how the balance will be financed

- Assistance offered by franchisor

- Product pricing fees

- Termination conditions—whether they are specific and realistic

- Advertising provided

- Any merchandise requirements and restrictions

- Liability insurance—who carries it and what is covered

- Geographic territory—the geographic territory of the franchise, and whether it is exclusive

In addition, lending institutions and other business organizations may be aware of attractive franchise opportunities.

Other Franchisees

One of the most valuable sources of information for the prospective franchisee is communication with other franchisees from the same organization. Because the largest incidence of fraud in franchising today is due to misrepresentation made by the franchisors, interviewing current franchisees can be helpful. Has the franchisee been happy in his or her association with the franchisor? Other specific questions to ask a franchisee are as follows:

- When was the franchise purchased?

- Why was this one selected?

- Have the franchisor's promises been fulfilled?

- What problems have developed?

- How have they been resolved?

Government Agencies

The Consumer and Corporate Affairs departments or their equivalents at the federal and provincial or territorial levels of government may also provide information about the practices of franchisors. The offer and sale of franchises is regulated in Alberta and Ontario. The Alberta Franchises Act sets the rules and specifies the amount of disclosure that must be provided to prospective franchisees in that province. Similarly, Ontario Bill 33—Franchise Disclosure Regulation requires disclosure of information before a franchise contract is signed in Ontario.[13] The industry division of Statistics Canada also offers a fraud checklist for potential investors.

Additional Areas to Investigate

Checking with the above sources can provide much valuable information to aid in the franchise decision. However, some final and critical questions remain. How much drawing power does the franchise name and product or service have? Is the franchise fee worth the drawing power and services provided? The latter may not be a critical question for well-established franchises such as McDonald's or Dairy Queen, but it may be very important for a lesser-known franchise. Market research obtained through secondary sources or even collected by the prospective franchisee may provide enough information for evaluating the strength of the franchise's drawing power. Specific areas to investigate include industry trends, consumer acceptance of the concept, and franchisability of the concept.

One should also evaluate whether they have the financial capacity, the willingness to accept direction from the franchisor, and the ability to manage the business. Because most franchises involve a fixed-term contract, one should be sure that they are ready to make a long-term commitment.

McDonald's
www.mcdonalds.com

Dairy Queen
www.dairyqueen.com

Because the signing of a franchise contract is a major step for the entrepreneur, the investigation should be thorough. Appendix 6C at the end of this chapter provides a comprehensive checklist for the prospective franchisee to use in this evaluation.

THE ENTREPRENEUR AS FRANCHISOR

An increasingly popular method of entrepreneurship in franchising is not being a franchisee but selling franchises and becoming a franchisor. Incident 6-5 illustrates this type of franchising.

Before a prospective franchisor attempts to sell franchises, several requirements must be met. Is the type of business franchisable? What information is required? How much capital is needed? All these questions should be addressed in the process of becoming a franchisor.

What Businesses Can Be Franchised?

Treats
www.treats.com

Franchises abound in many industries today. This phenomenon is reflected in the following statement by the U.S. Commerce Department: "Any business that can be taught to someone is being franchised."[14] The franchise business must have a sound concept. The franchise should be distinct, be practical, and fill a need. It must also be easy to teach and clearly communicate to others. It must be capable of being replicated and transferred to other geographical areas. Suzy Okun, a co-founder of the franchise Treats, which specializes in desserts, elaborates on this idea: "We sell a concept. We take what the palate already knows, and we make it electric! We take what the customer has already seen and do it differently."[15] Consumer research may be required to solidify the concept. Estimates based on sound research will be much more attractive to the prospective franchisee.

INCIDENT 6-5   The Idea that Keeps on Growing

Turning an innovative new idea into a successful franchise in under four years is not a common occurrence, especially for entrepreneurs as young as Jeremy Demont. Twenty-three-year-old Demont, along with two other partners, started PropertyGuys.com, a private home sellers market in New Brunswick.

The idea for PropertyGuys.com was devised when one of the partners saw a business opportunity in the "for sale by the owner" home sellers market. They then started an advertising and promotion service, which charged homeowners a flat fee, using the Internet, local print, and real-estate hotlines. Today their network offers legal, mortgage, home inspection, and appraisal services.

The company saw instant growth throughout New Brunswick and Dumont knew they had to expand their services. They joined the Canadian Franchise Association and started selling their services to people looking for business opportunities in the real-estate market. Their continued success can be attributed to the concept of the company itself, which appeals to clients who are reluctant to pay real-estate agents unnecessary fees. The company website also attracts upwards of 16,000 hits a day.

Because of the company's continued success, Jeremy's efforts earned him the Business Development Bank of Canada's (BDC) Young Entrepreneur Award for New Brunswick in 2002.

Source: Adapted from "The Idea that Keeps Growing," *Business Development Bank of Canada News Release*, www.bdc.ca/en/about/mediaroom/news_releases, October 21, 2002.

How Does One Become a Franchisor?

Once the prospective franchisor is satisfied that the business is franchisable, he or she must take several steps to develop the franchise. Some of the most important steps are the following.

1. Establish a Prototype. The franchisor should set up and operate a prototype business long enough to iron out the bugs and get a clear picture of market demand. This business can also serve as a reference point for prospective franchisees to use in their evaluations. To be useful, the prototype should be earning a consistent profit. Incident 6-6 illustrates the value of this.

2. Prepare the Necessary Information. Information prospective franchisees will require includes promotional literature regarding the franchise and detailed financial data not only for the company but for a typical franchise. A prospective franchisee requires information on capital needed, potential income, cash flow projections, and future trends in the industry to make an informed decision. It is recommended that someone with accounting expertise be retained to assist in preparing this information.

3. Investigate the Legal Requirements. The franchisor should investigate the legal requirements in setting up a franchising company. Some of these requirements might be

- Registration and disclosure with government agencies. As mentioned earlier, some provinces require detailed information before franchising can begin.

- The required business licences and incorporations.

- Other laws regulating the operations of franchises.

In addition, the franchise contract should be drawn up by someone with legal expertise to ensure that the rights of both parties are protected. The legal operations of the franchise and the responsibilities of both franchisor and franchisee are formalized in the franchise contract. The franchisor needs to decide which services and what assistance to provide, what restrictions to impose, and what to require from the franchisee in return. A more detailed listing of typical contract provisions appears in Appendix 6C.

INCIDENT 6-6   Steeped in the Tea Business

Entrepreneurs Brendan and Paul Waye of Edmonton developed the idea for a tea lounge while on a trip to Prague and Budapest. They loved the great atmosphere and high-end tea and teahouses in those cities. They wanted to create a tea lounge that offers an eclectic ambiance that is "hip, modern, funky, neoclassical, that includes antiques and rich and vibrant colors."

The brothers opened their Sherwood Park tea lounge in the spring of 1999 and allowed the concept to steep for over two years before opening their second location in Calgary. The business was finally ready for franchising in 2003, with two more locations added in Edmonton. "It took us that long to prove the concept, to make sure it works well, that it's easily duplicable, to work through all the franchise legislation and to show that there really is a market to fill," says CEO and co-founder Brendan Waye. The company is now set to open five to 10 more franchise locations per year across the country.

Source: Adapted from Elaine Davidson, "Words to the Wise," *Alberta Venture*, April 2004, p. 44.

Molly Maid
International Inc.
www.mollymaid.com

4. Develop a Planned and Standardized Program of Operations. Standardization of procedures is an essential part of a successful franchise and enables the franchisor to monitor operations more easily. The following quote about Molly Maid, a maid service franchise, illustrates the effective use of professionals in the development of the franchise system:

> *MacKenzie made full use of experts in setting up his company. He used two well-known accounting firms, one to develop an internal accounting system, and the second to construct a package for franchisees. A legal expert on franchising developed the franchise agreement, and a firm specializing in trademarks and patents set up the rules for use of the logo.[16]*

The operations manual is generally developed using the experience of the prototype business. As mentioned above, the methods or "system" used are typically the "service" that is franchised. The franchisor must ensure that the operations manual is understandable and easy to integrate into franchisee operations. The following quote about College Pro Painters shows the time and care taken in preparing the operations manual:

College Pro Painters
www.collegepro.com

> *After graduation in 1974, he took a year off to travel around the world, and started to put together a manual for the operation of College Pro Painters. Drawing on the knowledge he had acquired at school, he developed a chronology for starting a business and systematically attached every topic from "Business Plan" to "Close Down" in what would become his corporate bible.[17]*

5. Obtain Adequate Financing. To franchise successfully, the franchisor will need capital to set up the prototype business, do the necessary market research, prepare the promotional literature and financial estimates, and develop the system of operations. A rapid expansion program may even require outside equity financing from a venture capital company or other financial institution.

FRANCHISING IN THE FUTURE

Franchising is expected to continue its rapid growth as new types of businesses incorporate franchising principles into their operations. Several trends are expected to surface in the future. The retail food industry, the largest sector of Canadian franchising, is expected to continue its growth, but in more specialized areas such as ethnic foods. This growth will provide numerous opportunities for entrepreneurs but it also means greater competition for existing small businesses in certain industries. As mentioned previously, more and more service businesses are expected to become franchises. A high percentage of Canada's fastest-growing franchises are in the service industry.

Some franchises are experimenting with "piggybacking," in which two or more franchises operate in one outlet. This concept has been tried with gas stations/convenience stores and restaurants/video stores. The practice of converting existing chain outlets to franchises, or "branchising" is expected to continue as chains search for new sources of interest-free capital. Additional growth areas in franchising are "mini-franchises," which are small satellite versions of larger franchisees (McDonald's in Wal-Mart) and mobile franchises that move from location to location on a seasonal basis.

Wal-Mart
www.wal-mart.com

Recent trends show a more sophisticated group of franchisees participating in the industry. These individuals tend to have higher educational qualifications and more business management experience. This trend is not only leading to higher success rates for franchises but also to the creation of more organizations to protect franchisee rights. Other dominant franchising trends include the growth of master franchising, service and home-based franchises.

Summary

1. Franchising has enjoyed phenomenal growth in recent years. One reason franchising is popular is the increased incentives for franchisees. Franchising continues to allow many organizations with a proven concept or product to expand much more rapidly to meet demand.

2. The three types of franchises are (a) the manufacturer-directed franchise, in which the manufacturer of a product grants a dealer the right to sell the product; (b) the wholesaler–retailer-directed franchise, in which one member of the distribution channel, such as the wholesaler or retailer, initiates the organization of the franchise; and (c) the franchise company, in which a company sells a product, service, or system in exchange for an initial predetermined fee and an ongoing royalty.

3. Franchising offers the following advantages over the other two methods of starting a small business: a proven market, services such as selection of location, purchase or construction of the site, financing, standardized methods of operating, advertising, volume purchasing, and training. The potential disadvantages of franchising are lack of independence, cost of the franchise, unfulfilled promises, restrictions of the contract, saturation of the market, lack of security, cost of merchandise, and possible exaggeration of financial success.

4. Several key areas should be examined in evaluating a franchise. Information can be obtained from several sources including the franchising company, the Association of Canadian Franchisors, professionals such as lawyers and accountants, other franchisees, and government agencies.

5. Becoming a successful franchisor entails five steps. The first step is to develop a franchise prototype to iron out any difficulties. The second is to prepare the necessary information for the prospective franchisee. The third is to investigate the legal requirements in setting up a franchise company. The fourth is to plan and standardize the program of operation to facilitate the monitoring of operations. The last step is to ensure that adequate financing is available to keep up with possible rapid expansion.

Chapter Problems and Applications

1. Contact a franchisor and obtain information about becoming a franchisee. Using the procedures discussed in this chapter, evaluate the attractiveness of this opportunity.

2. What possible benefits does a franchise realize in franchising its businesses instead of expanding through company-owned outlets?

3. Discuss in detail the steps you would follow in developing a house-cleaning franchise system.

4. Visit a local franchise in your city and ask the manager what he or she thinks are the advantages and disadvantages of franchising.

5. Using the same franchise as in question 4, gather information from government agencies and other sources about that franchise. From your collected information and the results of question 4, would you invest in a franchise of this company? Justify your answer.

6. How could you determine whether obtaining a franchise is better than organizing a business from scratch, assuming the cost to get started was the same for both options?

Web Exercise

Access the website of one of the franchises listed in Appendix 6A and find as many details as you can about becoming a franchisee of this company.

APPENDIX 6A

A Sampling of Franchises Operating in Canada

Franchisor	Total Locations	Initial Fee	Total Investment	Total Royalty
Arbys	116	$42,500	$400,000	4%
Chem-Dry Carpet and Upholstery Cleaning	140	$15,950	$32,950	$285/month
Cullingan of Canada Ltd.	59	$1,000–$20,000	$75,000–$100,000	5%–10%
Curves International Inc.	600	$19,900	$19,900+	$395/month
Dairy Queen of Canada Inc.	504	$35,000	$450,000–1,200,000	4%
Jani-King Canada	9,000	$29,000–$33,000	$100,000–$250,000	–
Japan Camera	150	$20,000	40% of purchase price	7%
Kernals Popcorn	63	$25,000	$110,000–$125,000	9%
Kwik Copy	76	$25,000	$200,000	9%
Mail Boxes Etc.	211	$29,950	$120,000	6%
McDonalds Restaurants	1,062	$45,000	$600,000–$800,000	17%
Minute Muffler	126	$5,000–$25,000	$120,000–$150,000	4%
Molly Maid	160	$14,000	$14,000	6%
Mr. Lube	84	$50,000	$200,000	7%
Nutri-Lawn International	38	$15,000	$45,000	6%
Orange Julius Canada Ltd.	106	$20,000	$150,000–$200,000	6%
Pet Land	17	$25,000	$150,000–$250,000	4.5%
Sports Experts	280	$30,000	$300,000–$400,000	4.5%
Subway	1972	$10,000	$150,000	10.5%
The Great Canadian Bagel	166	$30,000	$260,000–$300,000	6%
Thrifty Car Rental System	157	$8,000–$150,000	$80,000–$250,000	8%
Tim Hortons	1525	$50,000	$275,000–$360,000	3%

Source: *2005 Franchise Annual*

APPENDIX 6B

A Checklist for the Potential Franchisee: Questions to Answer Affirmatively before Going into Franchising

The Franchisor

1. Has the franchisor been in business long enough (five years or more) to have established a good reputation?

2. Have you checked better business bureaus, chambers of commerce, government agencies, Association of Canadian Franchisors, industry associations, or bankers to find out about the franchisor's business reputation and credit rating?

3. Did the above investigations reveal that the franchisor has a good reputation and credit rating?

4. Does the franchising firm appear to be financed adequately so that it can carry out its stated plan of financial assistance and expansion?

5. Have you found out how many franchisees are now operating?

6. Have you found out the "mortality" or failure rate among franchisees?

7. Is the failure rate low?

8. Have you checked with some franchisees and found that the franchisor has a reputation for honesty and fair dealings among current franchisees?

9. Has the franchisor shown you certified figures indicating exact net profits of one or more going operations that you have checked yourself?

10. Has the franchisor given you a specimen contract to study with the advice of your legal counsel?

11. Will the franchisor assist you with
    a. a management training program?
    b. an employee training program?
    c. a public relations program?
    d. obtaining capital?
    e. good credit terms?
    f. merchandising ideas?
    g. designing store layout and displays?
    h. inventory control methods?
    i. analyzing financial statements?

12. Does the franchisor provide continuing assistance for franchisees through supervisors who visit regularly?

13. Does the franchising firm have experienced and highly trained management?

14. Will the franchisor assist you in finding a good location for your business?

www.mcgrawhill.ca/olc/balderson

15. Has the franchising company investigated you carefully enough to assure itself that you can successfully operate one of its franchises at a profit both to it and to you?

16. Have you determined exactly what the franchisor can do for you that you cannot do for yourself?

The Product or Service

17. Has the product or service been on the market long enough to gain broad consumer acceptance?

18. Is it priced competitively?

19. Is it the type of item or service the same consumer customarily buys more than once?

20. Is it an all-year seller in contrast to a seasonal one?

21. Is it a staple item in contrast to a fad?

22. Does it sell well elsewhere?

23. Would you buy it on its own merits?

24. Will it be in greater demand five years from now?

25. If it is a product rather than a service,
    a. is it packaged attractively?
    b. does it stand up well to use?
    c. is it easy and safe to use?
    d. is it patented?
    e. does it comply with all applicable laws?
    f. is it manufactured under certain quality standards?
    g. do these standards compare favourably with similar products on the market?
    h. if the product must be purchased exclusively from the franchisor or a designated supplier, are the prices for you, as the franchisee, competitive?

The Franchise Contract

26. Does the franchisee fee seem reasonable?

27. Do continuing royalties or percent of sales payment appear reasonable?

28. Is the total cash investment required and the items for financing the balance satisfactory?

29. Does the cash investment include payment for fixtures and equipment?

30. If you will be required to participate in company-sponsored promotion and publicity by contributing to an advertising fund, will you have the right to veto any increase in contributions to the fund?

31. If the parent company's product or service is protected by patent or liability insurance, is the same protection extended to you?

32. Are you free to buy the amount of merchandise you believe you need rather than required to purchase a certain amount?

33. Can you, as the franchisee, return merchandise for credit?

34. Can you engage in other business activities?

35. If there is an annual sales quota, can you retain your franchise if it is not met?

36. Does the contract give you an exclusive territory for the length of the franchise?

37. Is your territory protected?

38. Is the franchise agreement renewable?

39. Can you terminate your agreement if you are not happy for some reason?

40. Is the franchisor prohibited from selling the franchise out from under you?

41. Can you sell the business to whomever you please?

42. If you sell your franchise, will you be compensated for the goodwill you have built into the business?

43. Does the contract obligate the franchisor to give you continuing assistance after you are operating the business?

44. Are you permitted a choice in determining whether you will sell any new product or service introduced by the franchisor after you have opened your business?

45. Is there anything with respect to the franchise or its operations that would make you ineligible for special financial assistance or other benefits accorded to small business concerns by federal, provincial or territorial, or local governments?

46. Did your lawyer approve the franchise contract after studying it paragraph by paragraph?

47. Is the contract free and clear of requirements that would call on you to take any steps that your lawyer thinks are unwise or illegal in your province, county, or city?

48. Does the contract cover all aspects of your agreement with the franchisor?

49. Does it really benefit both you and the franchisor?

Your Market

50. Are the territorial boundaries of your market completely, accurately, and understandably defined?

51. Have you made any study to determine whether the product or service you propose to sell has a market in your territory at the prices you will have to charge?

52. Does the territory provide adequate sales potential?

53. Will the population in your territory increase over the next five years?

54. Will the average per capita income in your territory remain the same or increase over the next five years?

55. Is the existing competition in your territory for the product or service not too well entrenched?

56. Are you prepared to give up some independence of action to secure the advantages offered by the franchise?

57. Are you capable of accepting supervision, even though you will presumably be your own boss?

58. Are you prepared to accept rules and regulations with which you may not agree?

59. Can you afford the period of training involved?

60. Are you ready to spend much or all of the remainder of your business life with this franchisor, offering this product or service to the public?

APPENDIX 6C

Franchise Contract Clauses

The following are individual clauses commonly found in franchise agreements. The clauses are listed in the order in which they are most frequently found in a franchise agreement.

1. Term and Renewal
2. Site Selection
3. Franchisor Approval of Lease
4. Exclusive Territory
5. Trademark Restriction
6. Training by Franchisor
7. Franchisor Help with Operating
8. Operating Manual
9. Advertising by Franchisor
10. Advertising by Franchisee
11. Advertising, Control of
12. Royalty
13. Franchisor—Right to Inspect
14. Standard of Cleanliness
15. Standard of Operations
16. Franchisor—Right to Audit
17. Noncompetition
18. Confidential Information
19. Permitted Incorporation
20. Termination by Franchisor
21. Termination by Franchisee
22. Right of First Refusal
23. Sale Approval by Franchisor
24. Sale of Equipment to Franchisor

Suggested Readings

Canadian Franchise Directory (annually)
http://www.cgb.ca/directory.html

Canadian Franchise Handbook
http://www.cgb.ca/handbook.html

Franchise Annual. St. Catharines, Ontario: Canadian Franchise Association, yearly, (905) 688-2665

Franchise Canada (bi-monthly)
http://www.cfa.ca

Franchise Directory. *Entrepreneur* (annually)

Franchise Financing. Toronto: Canadian Imperial Bank of Commerce

Franchise in Canada. Industry Canada, (613) 941-1240

Franchising in Canada. CCH Publishing—www.cch.com

Franchise Handbook—www.franchise1.com

Franchise World—www.franchise.org/newsarea.asp

Opportunity Canada: Franchise and Dealership Guide (905) 277-5600.

Michelle Collins and Julie King, "So You Want To Buy A Franchise," Canada One Website—www.canadaone.com

Spinelli, Stephan Jr., Robert H. Rusenberg, and Sue Birley. *Franchising—Pathway To Wealth Creation*. Saddle Brook, New Jersey: Prentice-Hall, 2004.

Tomzack, Mary E. *Tips and Traps When Buying A Franchise*, *2nd Edition*. Oakland, California: Sourcebook Publications, 1999.

CHAPTER 7
Financing the Small Business

CHAPTER OBJECTIVES

- To discuss financing problems experienced by small businesses

- To identify the types of start-up capital the entrepreneur may require

- To illustrate a method for determining the amount of capital required

- To identify the sources of equity and debt funds available to start and operate a small business

- To explain the considerations in obtaining equity or debt financing

- To discuss what elements to include when preparing a proposal to obtain financing for the small business

SMALL BUSINESS PROFILE

Steve Smith

S&S Productions Inc.

Steve Smith was a teacher in Toronto who started his TV career with Smith & Smith, a self-financed series starring him and his wife, Morag. While writing and producing all 195 episodes, Smith created the character of the bumbling Red Green, based on real TV outdoorsman Red Fisher.

In 1990, the company, S&S Productions, launched *The Red Green Show*. Smith himself had to buy airtime and sell commercials to keep the show on the air. It bounced from independent stations to YTV to Global, until Red Green finally became a staple on both CBC and PBS.

Today S&S Productions is one of Canada's fastest-growing TV production companies. Smith's alter ego boasts a fan club of more than 100,000 members, a syndicated newspaper column, his own line of duct tape from 3M, and a website that sells Red Green books, hats, T-shirts, suspenders, and bumper stickers.

In 2002 S&S produced *Duct Tape Forever*, a movie that Smith spent years raising $3.5 million to finance. In the end, he put his own money on the line, deferring his salary and cutting a cheque as the movie's second biggest investor. He even got 3M to kick in some cash. In true entrepreneurial fashion, Smith cut costs by inviting fans to contribute their props: duct-tape sculptures that were essential to the plot.

In June 2003, the Banff TV Foundation recognized Smith as one of the 50 most famous personalities in Canadian television. Smith downplays his business skills, claiming he's mainly a writer, but his theory of comedy could be an entrepreneurial manifesto. "I learned a long time ago that unless you have a particularly unique way of looking at the world, you're going to have a tough time making it."

Used with permission of Steve Smith.

SMALL BUSINESS FINANCING

The inability to obtain adequate funding has often been cited as a major small business frustration, if not a primary cause of some small business failures. The entrepreneur may require financing not only to start the business but also to provide capital to fund ongoing operations.

One dilemma the entrepreneur often faces is that as the business grows, funds are needed for expansion. As the previous chapter illustrated, franchising is one solution to this financing problem.

Although many small businesses have experienced difficulties due to their inability to obtain needed funds, statistics show that financing woes are often a symptom of other management problems.[1] Lack of managerial competence and experience can often result in the following specific financial problems:

- Underestimating financial requirements. This typically leads to undercapitalization (shortage of cash) and is a major cause of failure. See Figure 7-1 for an illustration of the significance of this factor in business bankruptcies.

- Lack of knowledge of sources of equity and debt capital, leading to either an inability to obtain funds or the failure to obtain them at the lowest cost.

- Lack of skills in preparing and presenting a proposal for financing to a lender or investor.

- Failure to plan in advance for future needs, resulting in last-minute financial crises.

- Poor financial control of operations, leading to failure in payment of loan obligations.

| Figure 7-1 | Financial Management Problems Contributing to Bankruptcy |

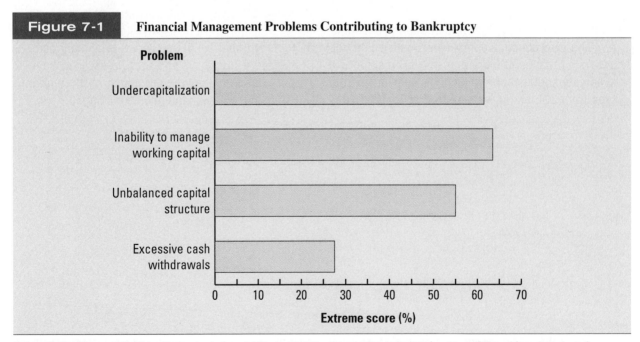

Source: *Failing Concerns: Business Bankruptcy in Canada* (Ottawa: Statistics Canada, November 1997), p. 26 and Office of Superintendant of Bankruptcy Canada Statistics, October 2006.

This chapter discusses each of these important areas to assist the entrepreneur in obtaining financing for establishing his or her business. Most of the information in this chapter is also applicable to the purchase of a business or for signing a franchise contract.

DETERMINING THE AMOUNT OF FUNDS NEEDED

The first step in securing capital (funds) for the business is to determine the amount of money needed. Any lender or investor will want to see evidence of a systematic and thoroughly prepared statement of fund requirements. In this regard, it is helpful to divide required funding into two categories: start-up costs and ongoing operating requirements. The entrepreneur's own funds available for the venture can then be subtracted from the projected required amounts to obtain the capital needed from outside sources, as shown in the following formula:

$$\text{Capital requirements} = \text{Start-up costs} + \text{Operating requirements} \\ - \text{Owner assets available for investment}$$

Start-up Costs

The Strategis Guide to Financing
www.strategis.ic.gc.ca/sc_x/engdoc/financing.html?guides=e_fin

Capital will be required to finance land, buildings, equipment, and other items needed to start up the business. Figure 7-2 on page 188 illustrates an example of a start-up schedule for a small retail store. Note the source provided for each number in the schedule. The owner should obtain and verify quotes from sellers of these assets with owners of existing similar businesses. Add a contingency factor for potential price increases during the planning and start-up phase.

Start-up capital will also be required to finance some of the operating costs during this period. Usually a delay in sales revenues occurs for a start-up business, but many operating expenses are incurred before the business begins operating. The entrepreneur will need to make estimates of these types of expenses and should include them in the capital requirements. The length of time until operations provide sufficient cash flow to finance expenses will vary, but it may be two to six months. Some of these types of expenses are

- Initial inventory

- First few months' payroll, including owner's salary

- First few months' utilities

- First few months' rent

- Initial advertising

- Prepaid items such as utility deposits, rent deposits, and insurance

- Licences and permits

- Other operating costs to be paid before revenues are generated

Start-up costs may be difficult to project. Note the sources of information used to prepare this statement. Also note that operations of the business in the first two months should provide some cash to offset the initial start-up requirements although this has not been included in this example.

Figure 7-2	Start-up Cost Schedule

Item	Cost	Source
Land and buildings	No cost—leased	If purchased, a similar business or quotes from suppliers
Equipment	$ 34,000	Other similar businesses or quotes from suppliers
Initial inventory	70,000	Other similar businesses or quotes from suppliers
		Use the formula Inventory = Projected sales/Inventory turnover (300,000/4.3)
Wages (first two months)	6,000	Other similar businesses or current wage rates
Utilities and telephone		
First deposit	100	Quotes from provider
First two months	680	Quotes from provider
Rent (deposit)	500	Quotes from lessor
First two months	3,000	Quotes from lessor
Advertising		
agency or media	960	Quotes from advertising agency or media
Insurance (prepaid)	975	Quotes from insurer
Licences and permits	200	Quotes from municipal agency
Other prepaids	285	Other similar businesses
Contingency	3,300	
Total start-up requirements	**$120,000**	

Ongoing Operating Costs

The entrepreneur should prepare a cash flow statement to calculate financial operating requirements after the start-up period. A cash flow statement, explained in more detail in Chapter 10, is simply a record of all projected cash inflows and outflows. An example of such a statement for the same business for which the start-up schedule appears is found in Figure 7-3 (on pages 190–191). In this monthly cash flow for a hypothetical business, it has been calculated that up to $34,000 may be needed to finance operations. This occurs in the first month.

If debt financing were used, the entrepreneur would most likely attempt to arrange a $35,000 line of credit (operating loan), with a lender to cover this amount when required. Such a method of financing would allow the business to withdraw and deposit funds on an ongoing basis as long as the total amount withdrawn at any point in time did not exceed $35,000.

The Owner's Net Worth

After estimating start-up and operating capital requirements, the owner should prepare a personal net worth and capability statement. Preparing this statement not only will help determine the amount of the owner's funds to invest in the business but will also probably be required by a lending institution if the owner needs to borrow the necessary capital. The essentials of the personal net worth statement are the same as those for a business's balance sheet. An example of a net worth statement appears in Figure 7-4 (on page 192).

DETERMINING TYPES OF FINANCING

Two general sources of funds can be used to finance a small business. The first is equity or ownership financing. The second is funds obtained from borrowing, usually referred to as debt financing (including trade credit). Many small businesses use both forms of financing to get established. A recent study of small business financing (see Figure 7-5 on page 192) shows the sources of funds from various sources to start or maintain small business operations.[2] This section discusses each of these types of financing.

Equity Financing

Equity financing involves giving up ownership of the business in return for capital. The three sources of equity financing are private investors, corporate investors, and government.

Private Investors. This source of financing may include one's own savings, which is cited as the most important source of financing for 54 percent of entrepreneurs.[3] Often entrepreneurs who are unable or unwilling to obtain financing elsewhere find that they are able to get the business established or continue operations through "bootstrapping." This involves using one's savings, factoring accounts receivable (discussed later), leasing rather than purchasing, developing arrangements with suppliers, and cutting back on expenditures. Other private financing sources include funds from friends, relatives, or private investors in exchange for share in an incorporated company or for a percentage of ownership in a sole proprietorship. It is especially critical from an investor's point of view that there be a clear understanding of conditions, authority, and responsibilities of all the investors under such an arrangement. The investor's degree of involvement can vary greatly. Some investors expect only a reasonable return on their investment, while others expect to be full operating partners in the business in addition to receiving a return on their capital.

An increasingly popular form of private financing is the selling of ownership interest to the employees of the business. Many companies have found that in addition to providing a source of funds, this method of financing results in dramatic increases in productivity. Incident 7-1 on page 193 illustrates such a situation.

Another form of private equity investment is the sale of shares in the business to anyone who is interested. This is known as going public, wherein shares in the company are sold on a public stock exchange. This form of financing, commonly referred to as an IPO (initial public offering), is discussed in detail in Chapter 15. Generally, small businesses are not large enough to seek public equity for the business start-up. For businesses that require smaller amounts of money, private investors (sometimes referred to as "angels") may be helpful. "Angels" are thought to invest some $3.5 billion per year in small businesses.[4]

Figure 7-3	Sample Cash Flow Statement

	Before Start-Up	Feb.	March	April	May	June
Opening balance	$ 0	$ (69,000)	$ (65,285)	$ (48,595)	$ (31,905)	$(55,173)
Bank loan	$ 35,000	0	0	0	0	0
Sales:						
Cash	0	12,000	12,000	12,000	13,750	13,750
Credit	0	0	12,000	12,000	12,000	13,750
Total receipts	$ 35,000	$ (57,000)	$ (41,285)	$ (24,595)	$ (6,155)	$(27,673)
Disbursements						
Furniture and fixtures	$ 34,000	$ 0	$ 0	$ 0	$ 0	$ 0
Rent		1,500	1,500	1,500	1,500	1,500
Utilities		200	200	200	200	200
Promotion (2% of sales)		480	480	480	550	550
Telephone		140	140	140	140	140
Wages and salaries		3,000	3,000	3,000	3,000	3,000
Inventory	70,000	0	0	0	41,820	0
Maintenance and repairs		240	240	240	270	270
Professional fees		330	330	330	330	330
Insurance		975	0	0	0	0
Interest and bank charges		1,420	1,420	1,420	1,208	1,208
Loan repayment						
Total disbursements	$ 104,000	$ 8,285	$ 7,310	$ 7,310	$ 49,018	$ 7,198
Cash (+/–)	$ (69,000)	$ (65,285)	$ (48,595)	$ (31,905)	$ (55,173)	$(34,871)

Note: 50% of monthly sales are cash and 50% are credit. The credit sales are collected in the next month.

National Angel
Organization
www.angelinvestor.ca

In October of 2002 the National Angel Organization was organized in Canada. The typical "angel" investment is $100,000 with an average holding period of five to eight years and an expected after-tax return of 30–40 percent annually.[5]

Corporate Investors. Many companies are interested in investing in a small business in the hope that the value of their investment will increase over time. Often they then sell their ownership interest back to the original owners when the owners are in a better position to finance the business independently.

Companies whose major activity is investing in smaller and medium-sized businesses are called *venture capital companies.* These companies use highly sophisticated evaluation techniques and accept only a small percentage of applications.[6] A venture capital company typically looks for a business within a growth industry, with sound management and the potential for a return on investment of between 20 percent and 40 percent.

Figure 7-3	Sample Cash Flow Statement (concluded)

July	Aug.	Sept.	Oct.	Nov.	Dec.	Jan.
$ (34,871)	$ (14,569)	$ (36,839)	$ (17,289)	$ 2,261	$ (20,311)	$ 1,467
0	0	0	0	0	0	0
13,750	13,750	13,750	13,750	13,750	14,250	14,250
13,750	13,750	13,750	13,750	13,750	14,250	14,250
$ (7,371)	$ 12,931	$ (9,339)	$ 10,211	$ 29,761	$ 8,189	$ 29,967
$ 0	$ 0	$ 0	$ 0	$ 0	$ 0	$ 0
1,500	1,500	1,500	1,500	1,500	1,500	1,500
200	200	200	200	200	200	200
550	550	550	550	570	570	570
140	140	140	140	140	140	140
3,000	3,000	3,000	3,000	3,000	3,000	3,000
0	41,820	0	0	43,350	0	0
270	270	270	270	270	270	290
330	330	330	330	330	330	330
0	0	0	0	0	0	0
1,208	1,960	1,960	1,960	712	712	712
0	0	0	0	0	0	35,000
$ 7,198	$ 49,770	$ 7,950	$ 7,950	$ 50,072	$ 6,722	$ 41,742
$ (14,569)	$ (36,839)	$ (17,289)	$ 2,261	$ (20,311)	$ 1,467	$ (11,775)

Canadian Venture
Capital Association
www.cvca.ca

In 2005, the 125 members of the Association of Canadian Venture Capital Companies invested some $2.21 billion in almost 700 small businesses in Canada, 80 percent of which were technology companies. The total pool of venture capital stood at $50 billion in 2005. The majority of the investments fell in the $3,000,000 range.[7] Incident 7-2 on page 193 provides an example of the difficulty a Canadian entrepreneur has had obtaining outside venture capital. An entrepreneur seeking venture capital assistance should be aware of the areas of the business to which investors will pay specific attention. Normally such factors as the abilities and expertise of the management team, the level of development of the product or service, and the industry trends are key elements in this evaluation.[8] Appendix 7D presents a list of some of the more active venture capital companies in Canada.

Government. Traditionally the government has hesitated to provide equity funding to small businesses. However, programs have been developed in recent years that permit government funding and incentives for venture capital firms or allow for direct equity investment by the government in the business. Some of these programs and agencies are described next.

Figure 7-4	**Suggested Format for a Personal Net Worth Statement**

Personal Net Worth Statement for _____

As of _____, 20_____

Assets		*Liabilities*	
Cash on hand and in banks	$ _____	Accounts payable	$ _____
Savings account in banks	_____	Notes payable to banks	_____
Canada savings bonds	_____		
Accounts and notes receivable	_____	Notes payable to others	_____
Life insurance—cash surrender value only	_____		
Other stocks and bonds	_____	Instalment account (auto)	
		Monthly payments $_____	_____
Real estate	_____	Instalment accounts (other)	_____
		Monthly payments $_____	_____
Automobile—present value	_____	Loans on life insurance	_____
Other personal property	_____	Mortgages on real estate	_____
Other assets	_____	Unpaid taxes	_____
		Other liabilities	_____
		Total liabilities	_____
		Net worth	_____
Total	$ _____	Total	$ _____

Figure 7-5	**Sources of Financing Used for Established Enterprises and Business Start-Ups**

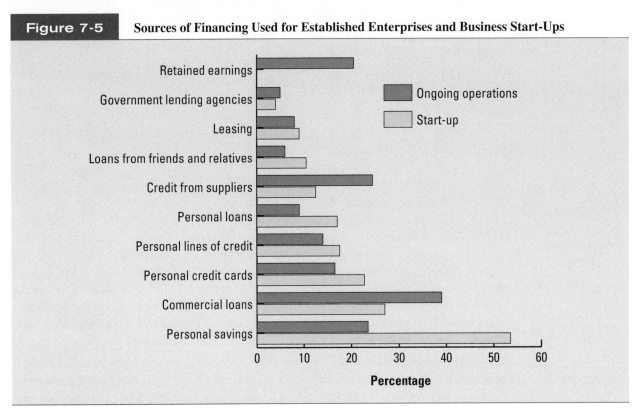

Source: "Sources of Financing Used by Small Business for Established Enterprises and Business Start-Ups," adapted from the Statistics Canada publication *The Daily*, Catalogue 11-001, Tuesday, October 1, 2002.

INCIDENT 7-1   Employee-owned Business

Calgary-based Alpine Environmental Ltd. received new ownership when Kathy Reich and executive partners Troy Bulbuck and Ranju Shergill led a successful management buyout. Reich says, "I was confident that this was the best way for the previous owners to exit the company and an ideal way for us to take advantage of an excellent business opportunity."

Because the new owners were previous employees, they brought first-hand experience to the fast-growing firm. This also enabled a smooth and rapid transition of responsibilities to the new owners.

BDC assisted in the transition of ownership with subordinate financing. Brenda Wall, manager, BDC Subordinate Financing, says, "Subordinate debt mimics equity financing because the investment is based on the cash flow of the company rather than on the tangible assets." Because Alpine Environmental Ltd. had a history of cash flow but lacked sufficient assets, they became the perfect candidate. The finance deal ensured a healthy amount of capital going toward company growth while making the transition to an employee-owned company.

Source: Adapted from, "Business Ownership Transition at Alpine Environmental Ltd," *Profit Newsletter*, Business Development Bank of Canada, Spring 2006, p.4.

INCIDENT 7-2   On the Line

Peter Szirmak has a great product that combines both tennis and technology. Auto-Ref, a computerized line-calling system, uses high-speed cameras and software to determine the location of the ball within four millimeters. Auto-Ref has been proven to work, and has been successfully demonstrated and tested by the International Testing Foundation. It also received a U.S. patent for its optical line monitor for tennis.

However, Szirmak faces a problem familiar to many Canadian entrepreneurs: He needs money to finance his product. Szirmak has been looking for outside backing for the past three-and-a-half years and has found that finding money for innovation in Canada is difficult. He has tried venture capital, banks, and government aid, which so far haven't given him the help he needs to get going. He has also talked to several private and public financiers. However, these financiers get thousands of applicants every year. Because there are no other companies Auto-Ref can compare itself with to judge potential revenues and pricing models, the task of finding financing is all the more difficult. "If you try to really revolutionize something, there really is no competition, and for any Venture Capital fund, that's a red flag," says Szirmak.

Source: Adapted from Andy Holloway, "On the Line," *Canadian Business*, pp.87–89.

Business Development
Bank of Canada
www.bdc.ca

Business Development Bank of Canada (BDC). The BDC will participate with other investors as a principal in the provision of investment capital in businesses it views as promising. Generally the purpose of such financing is to provide an adequate equity base for the firm to receive funding from additional sources. In July 1995 the Government of Canada changed the name of the old Federal Business Development Bank to Business Development Bank of Canada. The BDC continues to be an important source of equity capital for small and medium sized business, investing $106 million in 81 companies in 2006.[9]

Canada Development Corporation (CDC). CDC is a Crown corporation set up by the federal government to act as a venture capital company. This agency, however, provides funds primarily for larger businesses and large-scale projects.

Provincial Programs. Provincial governments have provided tax and rebate incentives for the formation of small business investment companies, which function similarly to venture capital companies. A listing of current provincial government equity capital programs appears in Appendix 7A at the end of this chapter.

Advantages and Disadvantages of Equity Financing. Before proceeding to obtain equity capital, the entrepreneur should be familiar with the advantages and disadvantages of equity financing versus debt financing.

Pan Canadian
Community Futures
Network
www.community
futures.ca

Western Economic
Diversification Canada
www.wd.gc.ca

Atlantic Canada
Opportunities Agency
www.acoa.ca

Equity financing offers the following advantages:

1. There is no obligation to pay dividends or interest. This flexibility allows the firm to invest earnings back into the business in its early years, when these funds are usually needed most.

2. Often the original owner benefits from the expertise the investor brings to the business in addition to the financial assistance.

3. Equity capital expands the borrowing power of the business. Most lenders require a certain percentage of equity investment by the owners before they will provide debt financing. Thus, the more equity a business has, the greater its ability to obtain debt financing.

4. Equity financing spreads the risk of failure of the business to others.

Disadvantages of equity financing include the following:

1. Equity financing dilutes the ownership interest of the original owner and leads to decreased independence. Because of this drawback, many owner-managers are hesitant to follow this route in obtaining capital.

2. With others sharing the ownership interest, the possibility of disagreement and lack of coordination in the operations of the business increases.

3. A legal cost may be associated with issuance of the ownership interest.

Debt Financing

Few small businesses are able to get established and continue operations without some sort of debt financing. About 30 percent of the money loaned to business in Canada is held by small businesses.[10] A national survey found that 85 percent of small- and medium sized businesses used a bank for financial support, 75 percent have lines of credit, and 50 percent have loans.[11] According to a survey carried out by Statistics Canada, the average debt outstanding for firms with fewer than five employees is $187,000 and for firms with 5–20 employees in 2006, it is $489,000.[12] Because of the high possibility that debt financing will be required, it is essential that the entrepreneur be aware of the advantages and dangers of using it. It is also important that he or she understand the sources of debt capital and the characteristics and requirements of various financial lenders.

Advantages and Disadvantages of Debt Financing.
Some of the positive benefits of using debt are as follows:

1. It is possible to obtain a higher return on investment by using leverage debt. If borrowed funds earn a higher return than the associated interest cost, it is possible to increase the overall return on investment for the business through debt financing. Figure 7-6 illustrates this concept. The $10,000 investment could be any productive asset or change in the business.

| Figure 7-6 | **Leveraging —Using Debt Financing and Return on Investment** |

Basic Information

Amount to invest = $10,000

Interest rate = 8%

Investment cost = $10,000

Estimated return per year = $2,500

Calculation of percentage return after one year

1.   If no debt was used:

$$\frac{\text{Return}}{\text{Investment}} = \frac{\$2,500}{\$10,000} = 25\% \text{ return}$$

2.   If debt was used (assuming only $2,000 was invested, $8,000 was borrowed to purchase the investment, and the interest on $8,000 is $640):

$$\frac{\text{Return}}{\text{Investment}} = \frac{(\$2,500 - \$640)}{\$2,000} = \frac{\$1,860}{\$2,000} = 93\% \text{ return}$$

Note: The potential investment income that could be earned on the $8,000 not invested in the project could be added to this amount.

2.   Interest costs in a business are tax-deductible expenses (assuming a profit is being made), whereas dividends paid as a result of equity ownership are not tax deductible.

3.   Debt financing may allow greater flexibility in that there is no loss of ownership control.

4.   Many small businesses have found it is often easier to obtain debt capital than equity capital.

Some of the potential negative aspects of debt financing are as follows:

1.   Interest must be paid on borrowed money. Interest costs can be high, and high interest expenses are a common problem in many failing businesses. Interest rates have been high in the past in Canada and this caused serious hardship for many small businesses. The inability to pay interest costs resulted in the foreclosure or bankruptcy of many businesses. Although interest rates are currently low, the small business owner must monitor rate changes closely.

2.   Debt financing creates additional paperwork requirements for the entrepreneur, and the lender may monitor the business.

3.   When using debt financing, the total risk of the venture lies squarely on the owner's shoulders. There are no other partners or shareholders to assume some of this risk.

Sources of Debt Financing. Several sources of debt financing are available to small businesses, including private lenders, corporate lenders, private lending institutions, and government agencies.

Private Lenders. One increasingly common source of debt capital for small business is the borrowing of funds from the owners of the business. These funds are called shareholders' loans, and they offer some unique advantages. It is estimated that approximately one-third of small business owners make a start-up loan to their own businesses.[13] Although the interest paid is a tax-deductible expense for the business, the repayment terms are often flexible. In addition, lenders often view shareholders' loans as equity as long as the funds are left in the company. Some believe this method combines the advantages of equity and debt financing.

Another source of private debt is borrowing from other individuals such as friends or relatives. As with shareholders' loans, it may be possible to structure flexible repayment terms.

Corporate Lenders. In some circumstances, other companies may lend funds to a small business. Often these are larger firms that have established some connection or working relationship with the small business. One example of such funding would be the granting of trade credit by a company to a small business that purchases merchandise from that company. Most small businesses use this source of financing wherever possible. Trade credit for inventory is normally financed for 30, 60, or 90 days, with discounts for prompt payment. Equipment is usually financed for up to five years, with a 20 percent to 30 percent down payment required.

Another type of lender associated with accounts receivable is a factor. Factor companies purchase accounts receivable from a business at a discount. The business obtains needed cash, and the factor collects the accounts receivable. An increasing number of businesses in Canada are enlisting factoring companies to obtain short-term financing.

The sale and leaseback is another form of financing involving other businesses. In this arrangement, the business sells an asset to another company, which in turn leases it back to the seller. The advantage of the sale and leaseback is that the seller not only has the use of the funds of the sale but also benefits from the tax deductibility of the lease payments.

Recently a private foundation has been established in Canada to provide start-up financing and mentorship to young entrepreneurs. This organization is the Canadian Youth Business Foundation (see Appendix 7B).

Regular Private Lending Institutions. This category includes companies whose major purpose is the lending of funds. The most common of these firms are the following. (See Figure 7-7 for an indication of the share of bank financing to small business.)

- *Trust companies.* Trust companies are geared primarily for mortgages on long-term capital assets such as land, buildings, and equipment.

- *Credit unions.* Credit unions are usually locally owned. They tend to be concerned primarily with personal loans, but in some communities they also provide significant financing to small businesses.

- *Finance companies.* These are high-risk lenders that charge a higher rate of interest than other agencies. As with credit unions, the majority of their loans are personal loans.

- *Chartered banks.* A major source of small business financing is Canada's chartered banks. A survey of Canadian small businesses indicated that 78 percent use bank financing.[14] At present, six major Canadian chartered banks and a multitude of foreign-controlled banks operating in Canada account for the majority of all small business lending. Chartered bank loans to small- and medium-sized businesses in Canada in 2004 totalled $80.6 billion.[15] In many larger cities, some of these banks are even creating specialized business branches. The majority of small business loans range from $20,000 to $50,000.

Canadian Youth
Business Foundation
www.cybf.ca

Canadian Bankers
Association
www.cba.ca

Bank of Montreal
www.bmo.com/
business/business
.html

Royal Bank
www.royalbank.com/
sme/index.html

Canadian Imperial
Bank of Commerce
www.cibc.ca

Scotiabank
www.scotiabank.com

TD Canada Trust
www.tdcanadatrust.
com/smallbusiness

Business Development
Bank (BDC)
www.bdc.ca

Small Business
Information Canada
www.sbinfocanada.
about.com

Figure 7-7   Small Business Market Share, 2003

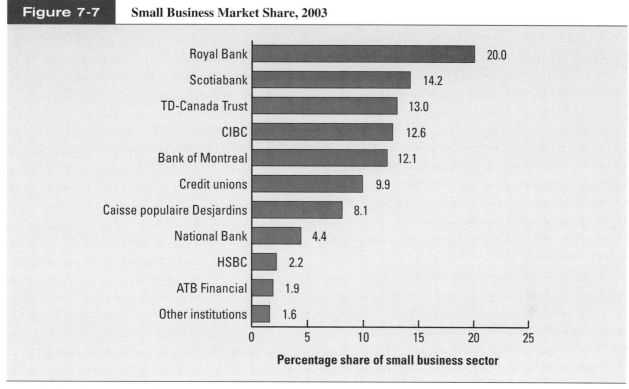

Source: *Banking Survey,* Canadian Federation of Independent Business, October 7, 2003.

An additional source of small business financing that seems to be increasing is the entrepreneur's use of their credit cards to provide temporary assistance. The Canadian Bankers Association states that 59 percent of small businesses help finance their start-up in this way,[16] and 23 percent of start-up entrepreneurs report credit cards as their most important source of financing.[17]

Government Lenders. Government agencies at both the federal and the provincial or territorial levels lend money, provide grants, and give counselling assistance to small businesses. At the federal level, the major small business lender is the Business Development Bank (BDC) of Canada, which currently has more than $9.7 billion in loan authorizations with small business. Initially government lending agencies were established to assist those small businesses unable to obtain financing from conventional sources because of high risk. In recent years, however, they have relaxed this attitude and become more similar to other lending institutions (see Incident 7-3 on the next page).

The potential advantages of approaching a government agency are the following:

1. The agency may finance higher-risk or lower-equity ventures, which characterize many small businesses.

2. Government lenders may be more willing to rewrite loan terms and conditions if the business gets into trouble. They also tend to be less quick to foreclose on a failing business.

3. Government agencies may provide a lower interest rate than the chartered banks. Many provincial and territorial government lenders fall into this category. BDC rates, which are adjusted periodically, are usually similar to chartered bank rates.

INCIDENT 7-3   Government Funding Helps Launch Retail Business

Heather Boyd, owner of Boyd's Basics of Your Day Store, has gone from being a stay-at-home mom to the proprietor of the thriving retail business located in Warren, Manitoba. In 1998, Warren, with a population of 800, had only one small variety store. Other businesses were at least 25 kilometres away. Boyd began researching and learning retail and doing the groundwork to launch her business.

After being turned down by local banks, Boyd went to the federal government-sponsored Super Six Community Futures Development Corporation (CFDC) for funding. Unlike local banks, the CFDC were interested in Boyd's idea and helped to develop her business plan while loaning her $125,000. In 1999, the store was launched and today is a regular destination for residents. In the beginning, Boyd worked 17-hour days but now she has been able to cut it down to a meager 12. The store now encompasses the entire strip mall and employs 18 of Warren's 800 residents.

Source: Adapted from "$125,000 Government Funding Helps Launch Retail Business," *Small Business Funding Centre*, www.cdnloans.grants, August 2006.

4. Government lenders may provide some equity capital in the form of temporary ownership or grants, depending on the type of business and its location.

5. Government lenders may provide management counselling along with funding to assist the business.

Although the above advantages may make borrowing from government agencies attractive, there are some potential disadvantages of which the small business owner should be aware:

1. A government agency usually requires more information to review a loan application than other lending institutions do.

2. The time required for approval of a loan tends to be a longer than with private lending institutions.

3. Most government agencies exert more monitoring and control over the businesses they lend to and often require regular reports on operations.

In addition to the government agencies established to provide both debt and equity financing, several specific federal government programs also provide financial help for the small business. Appendix 7B at the end of this chapter briefly reviews those most helpful for the small business.

Most provinces and territories also have various programs designed to provide financial assistance to the small business community. Appendix 7C at the end of the chapter reviews some of these programs.

DETERMINING THE TERM OF FINANCING

The small business owner should carefully evaluate the characteristics of the above sources of financing to ensure their suitability to the needs of the business.

The length of term and type of financing required may assist in making the decision among lenders, as Figure 7-8 shows. This figure also illustrates the typical assets covered by the various terms of financing. The length of the term allowed by a lender is normally equivalent to the useful life of the asset, except in the case of land, which is often carried on a 20-year term.

Figure 7-8	**Matching Financing to Assets**

Type of Loan	Sources	Use	Security	Loan Characteristics
Short-term (demand) loans (3–6 months)	Banks, private sources, factoring houses, confirming houses	Receivables, line of credit, inventory (working capital items)	Assignment of receivables and inventory, personal guarantees, assignment of life insurance	Can be withdrawn on short notice; no fixed payment terms; interest, principal rates fluctuate
Medium-term (3–10 year) loans	Banks, term lenders, financial houses, leasing companies, foreign banks, private sources, and government programs	Equipment, furnishings, vehicles, leaseholds, and new business investments	Chattel mortgages, conditional sales contracts, or assignment of equipment insurance	Specific repayment terms; interest either fixed or floating with prime rate
Long-term (15–25 year) mortgages, bonds, debentures	Trust companies, foreign banks, private sources	Property, land, and buildings, new business investments	Collateral mortgages, assignment of property insurance	Fixed repayment terms; fixed interest rates

An often costly mistake that some owner-managers make is to use funds obtained for long-term purposes to get them through short-term crises. Inevitably, this practice creates a more serious financial crisis a short while later. If capital requirements were underestimated, the owner should approach the lender again with this information and attempt to have the lender adjust the funds provided.

PREPARING A PROPOSAL TO OBTAIN FINANCING

Industry Canada
www.strategis.ic.gc.ca

Incident 7-4 on page 200 describes an all too common situation for the small business. Industry Canada reports that 16 percent of small business requests were denied financing in 2003.[18] In attempting to obtain financing, a small business owner should be aware of those areas about which the lender requires information. In addition to completing the loan application, the owner should include the financial projections. A detailed and well-prepared loan proposal goes a long way toward ensuring the approval of a loan application.

Criteria Used in the Loan Decision

Dun & Bradstreet Canada
www.dnb.ca

Most lenders make the loan decision by evaluating the following three criteria.

1. The Applicant's Management Ability. The lender will want to be sure the applicant has the skills, education, experience, and ability to make the business succeed. To evaluate the applicant's managerial ability, the lender will specifically want to know the following.

How Much the Applicant Knows about the Business. The lender will probably ask questions about the business or industry to ascertain the applicant's level of knowledge. The lender will also be interested in any previous experience the applicant has had that relates to the proposed business.

INCIDENT 7-4   Reclino-Bath

Harold Taylor had a problem. He had withdrawn his total savings of $20,000 to purchase the mould required in the manufacture of a plastic bathtub accessory he had invented. To begin production, he needed additional funds but had been turned down by both chartered banks and government agencies. The lenders not only were unconvinced there was a market for the product but could also see Taylor's lack of planning in estimating his financial requirements. They wanted him to prepare detailed information on what he needed and a projected statement of income based on objective research to estimate consumer demand for his product. Taylor didn't know where to turn. He lacked both the expertise to prepare the statements or do the research and the funds to hire an outside agency to do it.

Source: D.W. Balderson, University of Lethbridge.

How Much Care Was Taken in Preparing the Proposal. The lender will want to see a detailed plan of what the loan is for, as well as a listing of the other sources of financing for the project. The steps of a business plan outlined in Chapter 4 should provide the basis for the financing proposal. Several statements will be required, and it is important that the applicant document the source of the information in those statements. The first statement is the lending proposal, which typically follows the format shown in Figure 7-9.

In addition to the lending proposal, the lender will probably want to see a proposed income and cash flow statement for at least the first year of operations, and probably longer. A balance sheet may also be required. These statements should be carefully prepared following the formats discussed in Chapters 3 and 10. As mentioned above, each item on the statement should be well researched and documented. The lender will want to know what provision has been made for the owner's salary and for potential contingencies. Often an entrepreneur is advised to enlist an accountant if he or she is weak in financial statement preparation. Incident 7-5 discusses the work involved in preparing a successful loan proposal.

2. The Proposal. Obviously the lender will assess the idea or proposal itself. Using the income statement and cash flow projections, the lender will assess the chances of repayment of the loan. The lender will evaluate not only the specific business but industrial trends, including the extent of competition and the experiences of similar businesses. The lender may also check with experts in the industry. Many chartered banks now have industry specialists on staff to assist in this type of evaluation.

Some specific types of evaluation used in the lending industry are

- *Level of working capital*—the dollar difference between current assets and current liabilities. Working capital should be sufficient to meet current obligations as they become due and to finance delays in revenue caused by such items as accounts receivable.

Figure 7-9	Loan Proposal Format

Program		Financing	
Land	$20,000	Bank loan	$60,000
Building	50,000	Own funds	20,000
Equipment	10,000	Total	$80,000

INCIDENT 7-5   Woo Investors

Most business plans fail to answer important questions and are turned down by potential investors. When these tough questions go unanswered, investors have every right to be skeptical, says business plan specialist David Gumpert. Gumpert also says that a realistic plan must convincingly answer the tough questions such as, "What's the opportunity?" "What special advantages do you have?" "What is the secret of your expected sales success?" "What have you learned from the competition?" "How will you use the funds you raise?" and finally, "What are the risk factors?" Confidently answering these questions will allow potential investors to see what sets your business above others.

Source: Adapted from "Woo Investors," *Profitguide.com*, October 28, 2004.

- *Current ratio*—current assets compared with current liabilities. A healthy current ratio is 2:1.
- *Quick ratio*—current assets less inventories compared with liabilities. A healthy quick ratio is 1:1.
- *Debt-to-equity ratio*—percentage of owner's equity compared with debt. A minimum debt-to-equity ratio is 4:1 (25 percent equity). For smaller businesses, most lenders prefer to see 50 percent equity.

Chapter 10 discusses each of these ratios in detail.

The lender will also want to see projections for the basic financial statements such as the balance sheet and income statement. The fundamentals of these statements are also covered in Chapter 10.

Collateral. Because of the security position on the loan, the lender will want to know whether another lender is also providing funding for the project and, if so, what collateral it has taken as security for the loan. The lender will also want to ensure that the funds loaned will be secured by some form of saleable collateral. On capital assets, a lender generally allows no more than 80 percent of the value of the assets as security. The reason is that if the lender needs to realize on (repossess) the security, obsolescence, selling, and administration costs will reduce its value. The level of collateral may also vary by industry type, reflecting risk and type of asset.

At this point the entrepreneur may realize that he or she does not possess the required equity to secure adequate financing. In such cases an investigation of the possibility of leasing instead of buying could be made. An increasing number of businesses are leasing assets to free up capital for other purposes. A recent study carried out by Trimark Seg Fund found that more than one-half (53.5 percent) of small business entrepreneurs have given personal guarantees to secure loans. Forty percent have used their homes, while 20 percent have used their savings.[19]

3. The Applicant's Background and Creditworthiness. In addition to the project itself and the applicant's managerial ability, the lender will require some additional information in judging the applicant's creditworthiness.

Personal Information. In filling out a loan application, an applicant is usually required to file information typically included in a personal résumé—items such as age, marital status, education, and work experience. (Be careful to check the legal implications of certain questions.)

Present Debt and Past Lending History. The lender will want a list of the current state of any loans outstanding and may require information about the applicant's past loan history as well. Most lenders are members of credit bureaus that can provide a complete credit history of the applicant. Lenders will generally use this source to verify the information provided by the applicant.

Amount of Equity the Applicant Has Invested. All lenders want to know the amount of the applicant's personal funds going into the project. Usually cash equity is required, but occasionally capital assets or even "sweat equity" may be acceptable. The amount of equity funds required will vary depending on the risk associated with the project, but as mentioned above, few lenders will provide financing if the applicant has less than 20 percent to 25 percent equity to invest in the business.

Will the Applicant Bank with the Lender? Many lenders will request that the applicant's business accounts be transferred or opened with the lending bank. They may also require that a compensating balance be held in the account as collateral. If the loan request is turned down, it is important that the entrepreneur find out the reasons for the refusal and make adjustments to the proposal. Alternatively, several lenders should be visited to secure the necessary funding.

Lender Relations

Once financing has been obtained, it is important that the business provide up-to-date information to the lender regarding current operations and future plans. Regular financial statements and lease contracts can help establish trust between the banker and the owner-manager. Many businesses have found that maintaining a close working relationship with lenders helps ensure adequate levels of financing in the long run. An example of how to do this is found in Incident 7-6.

What do entrepreneurs do if they have investigated both equity and debt sources and are unable to obtain the needed capital? Probably the first thing to do is find out the reasons for

---

INCIDENT 7-6   Get More from Your Bank

For Fred Mohr, the relationship he has with his bank has been the lifeline of his business. Mohr, the owner of Jeet Contracting Limited and Cartier Kitchens Ltd. in Brampton, Ontario, was in real trouble when his investment property in Germany went from being valued at $300 per square foot to $85 per square foot during the year of the German reunification. Mohr ended up using all his business funds to keep the investment alive and in doing so, he eventually maxed out a $1.5 million line of credit and drained all the equity from his Canadian businesses. This left Mohr in a dire financial situation, with his banks ready to drop him any day.

At this point Soumaya Baker, a new addition to the Royal Bank, entered the situation. She listened to Mohr's story and trusted his promise that, with the appropriate financing, he would be back on his feet within a year and banks would be borrowing from him. To test the heath of his Canadian business, she asked for financial information on Mohr's accounts receivables and payables and his income statements. Baker then went to work trying to convince the Royal Bank lenders that they should continue to back Mohr through his financial difficulties. They did, and it paid off. Mohr saw revenues of $10 million in 2002 and was able to repay more than half his debt.

Baker's testament is that banks should stick with their clients through thick and thin. In return, she wants her clients to keep the lines of communication open and to let her know when they are experiencing difficulties. By following Baker's guidelines regarding open communication, Mohr found support and, later, success, proving that working closely with your lender can have rewards.

Source: Adapted from "Get More From Your Bank," *Profit* Magazine, April–May 2003, p. 26.

refusal and possibly rework the proposal to bring it more in line with the lender's requirements.

Changes may be necessary to make the proposed business more attractive to lenders or investors. One option that is increasingly being used to reduce the amount of funds required for capital purchases is to consider leasing or renting the asset. Leasing the asset generally does not require a down payment. The ability to obtain the lease is usually based more on the earning power of the asset and the business than on the background of the owner. Later, when the company is in a more stable condition, the owner may succeed in obtaining funds to make a purchase if he or she desires. Specific conditions of leases are discussed in Chapter 4.

Summary

1. Lack of managerial competence and experience can often result in such financing problems as underestimation of financial requirements, lack of knowledge of sources of capital, lack of skills in preparing and presenting a proposal for financing to a lender, failure to plan in advance for future needs, and poor financial control in payment of loan obligations.

2. Start-up capital includes initial inventory, deposits, and first month's payments for payroll, utilities, rent, advertising, insurance, licences, and permits. Accounts receivable and any other operating costs that need to be paid before revenues are generated should also be planned for.

3. An essential step in determining the amount of capital needed is to calculate the owner's net worth. This helps determine the amount of funds the owner(s) has to invest in the company and will probably be required by a lending institution.

4. Three general sources of equity financing are private investors, corporate investors, and government programs. Sources of debt financing include owners of the business, corporate lenders, regular lending institutions, and government agencies.

5. The advantages of equity capital over debt financing include interest obligation, expertise of the investor(s), expanded borrowing power, and spreading of risk. The disadvantages of using equity financing include dilution of ownership, increased potential of disagreements, and the cost incurred in the issuance of the ownership interest. The potential advantages of debt financing over equity capital are a possible higher return on investment, deductibility of interest, flexibility, and ease of approval. The disadvantages include interest expense, additional paperwork, and lack of diversification of risk to other investors.

6. Criteria most lenders use in making the loan decision are the applicant's managerial ability, the proposal itself, and the applicant's background and creditworthiness.

Chapter Problems and Applications

1. Indicate whether each of the following is a start-up cost (S), an ongoing operating cost (O), or both (B).

   a. $1,000 for first month's rent

   b. $25,000 for store fixtures

c. $1,000 for third month's rent

d. Weekly cleaning fee of $250

e. Purchase of $50,000 of inventory

f. Payroll expense

g. $50,000 for TV advertising

2. Discuss the advantages of the type of financing used in Incident 7-1.

3. What are some potential drawbacks of the financing system as explained in Incident 7-2?

4. Imagine you are preparing a business plan for a small manufacturing firm in your province or territory. Using Appendixes 7A and 7B, determine what programs are available for possible assistance. How could each program help your client's business?

5. a. Using Figure 7-8 as a reference, match the following list of assets to the type of financing, source, and loan characteristics needed:

   (1) Capital for building of manufacturing plant

   (2) Company car

   (3) Inventory purchase

   (4) Equipment (life expectancy two to three years)

   b. Why is it important to match financing to your assets?

6. Interview an employee at one of the government agencies that offer equity or debt financing to small businesses. Determine the purpose, the merits, and the weaknesses of that program.

7. Interview a banker to determine what he or she looks for in a loan application.

8. Using Figure 7-4, calculate your personal net worth.

Web Exercise

www.bdc.ca
www.cvca.ca

Access the websites for the Business Development of Canada and the Canadian Venture Capital Association and review the financial and consulting services these organizations offer to small business.

APPENDIX 7A

Provincial Equity Capital Programs

Canada
Canadian Venture Capital and Private Equity Association
http://www.cvca.ca

Alberta
Small Business Equity Corporation

British Columbia
Small Business Venture Capital

Manitoba
Venture Capital Program

New Brunswick
Venture Capital Support Program

Newfoundland and Labrador
Venture Capital Program

Nova Scotia
Nova Scotia Venture Corporations

Ontario
Small Business Development Corporations Program
Venture Investments Corporations

Prince Edward Island
Small Business Development Corporations
Venture Capital Program
http://www.acoa.gc.ca/e/financial/venture.shtml

Quebec
Societés de placement dans l'entreprise Quebecoise
Societés de developpement de l'entreprise Quebecoise

Saskatchewan
Community Bond Program
Equity financing available through SEDCO
(Saskatchewan Economic Development Corporation)
Labour-Sponsored Venture Capital Program

Source: "Provincial Venture Capital Corporations: A Comparative Analysis," *Journal of Small Business and Entrepreneurship—Canada*, vol. 4, no. 5, (Fall 1986), p. 22.

APPENDIX 7B

Federal Government Assistance Programs for Small Business

Program	Type of Assistance	Limits	Purposes	Contact Offices
Canadian Small Business Financing Act http://laws.justice.gc.ca/en/c-10.2/	Provides guarantees on loans for a variety of capital purposes.	No refinancing of existing debt. Annual revenues can't exceed $5 million. Interest: prime plus 1 percent. Maximum 10-year repayment period.	Improve and modernize equipment and buildings; purchase land.	All approved lenders
Program for Export Market Development http://pemd-pdme.info export.gc.ca/pemd//menu-en.asp	Shares costs of specific export marketing efforts. Encourages and assists export.	Provides up to 50 percent of the costs incurred by a company in penetration of new markets. Repayable if sales are made.	Specific project bidding; market identification; participation in trade fairs abroad; bringing in foreign buyers; export consortia development; sustained export market development.	Industry Canada regional offices
Self-Employment Incentive Program	Provides temporary grants while entrepreneurs establish business.	$200 per week.	To assist with living expenses while an entrepreneur establishes a business.	Employment and Immigration Canada
Atlantic Canada Opportunity Agency http://www.acoa.ca	Financial assistance for economic development and capital costs.	Varies by type of project and industry.	Improve the economic viability of businesses in Atlantic Canada and encourage entrepreneurship.	ACOA offices in Atlantic Canada

Federal Government Assistance Programs for Small Business

Program	Type of Assistance	Limits	Purposes	Contact Offices
Western Economic Diversification Fund http://www.wd.gc.ca	Financial assistance through grants.	Maximum amount of assistance depends on which tier the applicant is in. Level of support depends on nature of the project, need for support, value, and government economic objectives.	Promote industrial and regional development in Western Canada.	Industry Canada regional offices
Industrial Research Assistance Program http://irap-pari.nrc-cnrc. gc.ca	Financial assistance through grants and technical assistance.	Varies according to which aspect of the program is applied for.	Increase the calibre and scope of industrial research and development through the use of available technology.	Industrial Research Assistance
Small Business Development Bond	Assistance through reduced interest rates on loans.	Eligible small business corporations that use all their assets in an active business. One-to-five-year loan. Specific time restrictions on past loans to qualify.	Relieve the financial burden of interest rates on the small businessperson.	All approved lenders
Technology Outreach Programs	Financial assistance.	Small businesses can access information, receive grants and loans for implementing new technology.	Promote innovation and use of new technology.	Industry Canada
Business Development Bank http://www.bdc.ca/	Loans and equity investment.	Extend debt financing to small businesses. Can also extend venture capital to small firms wanting to expand.	Increase viability of small business.	BDC offices
Patient Capital Program	Financial assistance.	$230,000 for early-stage technology companies.	Improve chances of success for new companies.	Industry Canada
Micro Business Program http://www. vtmicrobusiness.org	Financial assistance.	$25,000 for very small companies.	Improve chances of success of new companies.	Industry Canada
Canadian Small Business Financing Program	Loan guarantee of up to 85 percent of lender's losses on defaulted loans.	$250,000 for equipment, property, improvements.	Improve chances of success for small companies.	Industy Canada

Federal Government Assistance Programs for Small Business

Program	Type of Assistance	Limits	Purposes	Contact Offices
Aboriginal Economic Economic Programs	Financial assistance.	Up to 40 percent equity and 75 percent for marketing, innovation and R&D for aboriginal businesses.	Support and encourage formation and growth of aboriginal businesses.	Aboriginal Programs, Industry Canada
Co-Vision Financing Program	Financial assistance.	Up to $100,000 and counselling.	To help start-up entrepreneurs start a business for the first time.	Business Development Bank of Canada
Canadian Youth Business Foundation http://www.cybf.ca	Financial assistance and mentoring.	Up to $15,000 to candidates 18–29 unable to raise funding elsewhere.	To help youth start businesses.	Private

APPENDIX 7C

Provincial and Territorial Government Financial Assistance Programs and Agencies for Small Business

Alberta

Alberta Economic Development Department. This department administers several financing programs for small businesses in the province. The AOC is a lender of last resort. It can be accessed through the following website, www.Albertafirst.com.

Small Business Assistance Program. This program provides access-fixed-term loans (3 to 10 years) with fixed rates to qualifying small businesses throughout the province. Loans can be for refinancing or consolidating business debt or for improving, constructing, or acquiring capital assets. Limit $150,000.

Small Business Equity Corporation Program. Essentially this program provides a cash grant of 30 percent of the capital invested by a resident of Alberta or a refundable tax credit of 30 percent of capital invested by a corporation with a "permanent establishment in Alberta."

British Columbia

B.C. Development Corporation. The BCDC is a provincial Crown corporation set up to further economic development in British Columbia through financial, advisory, and information services. Under its low-interest loan plan, the BCDC provides funds for establishing, modernizing, or expanding manufacturing and processing industries.

Small Manufacturers Assistance Program and Assistance to Small Enterprise Program. These programs create jobs by assisting with the establishment, expansion, or modernization of small manufacturers. They also give other assistance to small enterprises in the province. These programs provide interest-free, forgivable loans to British Columbia companies that may be used for start-up, expansion, or modernization.

Manitoba

Design Assistance for Small Projects. This cost-shared program will pay up to 50 percent of design costs to improve product, graphics, and packaging to a maximum contribution of $1,000.

Venture Capital Company Program. This program aims to stimulate the flow of equity capital into Manitoba businesses by providing an investment vehicle for the private sector. The province participates jointly on a 35/65 percent basis with private investors, who must contribute $25,000 at the time the venture capital company is registered and a minimum of $65,000 within one year.

New Brunswick

Department of Commerce and Development. The Minister of Commerce and Development may provide financial assistance to aid and encourage the establishment or development of manufacturing or processing industries in the province. Assistance may take the form of a direct loan, bond guarantee, or acquisition of shares in a company.

Financial Assistance to Small Industry. This program makes interest-free, forgivable loans to new or existing industries for start-up, modernization, or expansion. Loans are calculated on the basis of approved capital costs.

Newfoundland and Labrador

The Newfoundland and Labrador Development Corporation. This Crown corporation is funded jointly by the federal and Newfoundland and Labrador governments. It is mandated specifically toward small business. The NLDC offers both term loans and equity finance, but it does not guarantee loans.

Northwest Territories

Small Business Loans and Guarantees Fund. This program gives loans and guarantees to small businesses in the territory that are not eligible for the Eskimo Fund or the Indian Business Loan Fund. Funds may be used for purchase and for improvement or expansion of land, buildings, equipment, and inventory.

Nova Scotia

Industrial Estates Limited Financing Program. This program provides appropriate loan financing to new or expanding manufacturing operations. The minimum loan financing available is $250,000. Repayment is normally by way of a 20-year amortization.

Product Development Management Program. This program assists manufacturers in developing new products and upgrading the design quality of existing products. Grants under the program provide up to 75 percent of the product development costs submitted by a consultant designer. The maximum grant is $15,000 per project.

Small Business Development Corporation. This program provides loans to businesses with annual sales of less than $2 million or employing fewer than 50 people. Interest rates are fixed for the life of the loan, and repayment terms are flexible.

Ontario

New Ventures. This program offers loans to new companies to a maximum of $15,000 if approved by a participating financial institution. These loans are guaranteed by the Ontario government (Ontario Ministry of Industry, Trade and Technology) and matched by the owner's equity.

Ontario Development Corporation. This agency and its complementary development corporations within Ontario stress the importance of small business and the desirability of a private sector share in small business financing. Although commencement of repayment may be deferred, loans may be interest free or at a rate lower than the ODC's prevailing rate.

Small Business Development Corporation Program. This program acts as a private sector investment firm in which individuals and corporations are encouraged to buy equity. These firms then invest in small businesses eligible under the act. Money invested may be issued only for expansion or improvement of fixed assets, development, or start-up debt. Corporations that invest in SBDCs are granted a credit of 25 percent against Ontario corporations' income tax.

Prince Edward Island

Department of Industry and Commerce. The PEI Department of Industry and Commerce administers five general assistance programs. Those occupied with direct assistance are run jointly with the Department of Regional and Economic Expansion. Eligible recipients of these programs are manufacturers and services in the small business sector. http://www.gov.pe.ca/development/peibdi-info/index.php3

Quebec

Quebec Industrial Development Corporation. This Crown corporation aims at spreading economic power within the population, improving and rationalizing the business structure. Assistance may come in the form of a rebate on the company's borrowing cost, a loan at the usual market rate, a loan guarantee, or acquisition of a minority interest in a company.

Small Business Assistance Program. This program was established to assist firms that are usually profitable and well managed but face temporary working capital shortages. Financial assistance takes the form of an interest subsidy and loan guarantee.

Saskatchewan

Community Bond Program. This program provides financing for communities in the area of economic development.

Labour-Sponsored Venture Capital Program. This aims to stimulate growth of the province's small business sector. It provides provincial tax incentives to both individuals and corporations that are willing to invest in Saskatchewan small businesses. http://www.finance.gov.sk.ca/programs-services/

Saskatchewan Economic Development Corporation (SEDCO). This Crown corporation is a major internal provincial government vehicle of economic development and as such deals with enterprises of all sizes and sectors. There is no upper limit on loans, and interest rates are set according to type of loan and current market conditions.

Yukon

Yukon Small Business Assistance Program. This program offers both financial and non-financial assistance to entrepreneurs wishing to start a new business as well as those seeking to expand an existing business. Financial assistance takes the form of loans and loan guarantees.

APPENDIX 7D

Venture Capital Firms in Canada

ACF Equity Atlantic Inc.—www.acf.ca

BG Acorn Capital Fund
Toronto
Focus: all sectors

Business Development Bank of Canada
Venture Capital Division
Several offices across Canada
Focus: small businesses
http://www.bdc.ca/en/home.htm

Canadian Medical Discoveries Fund Inc.—www.cmdf.com

Canadian Venture Founders
Oakville, ON
Focus: environmental and high tech/information management

Canadian Venture Capital Association—www.cvca.ca

DGC Entertainment Ventures Corp.
Toronto
Focus: entertainment, communications, primarily Ontario-based

Discovery Capital Corporation—www.discoverycapital.com

Fonds De Solidarite Des Travailleurs De Quebec
Montreal
Focus: all sectors, preference for small and medium-sized businesses in Quebec
http://www.fondsftq.com

Grieve Horner Brown & Asculai
Toronto
Focus: technology related to health care, information processing, communications

Helix Investments (Canada) Ltd.
Toronto
Focus: technology

Horatio Enterprise Fund L.P.
Toronto
Focus: Toronto-area telecommunications services, education

Innovatech Grand Montreal
Montreal
Focus: information technology, biotech, pharmaceuticals, telecommunications

Innovation Ontario Corp.
Toronto
Focus: all sectors; high-tech R&D ventures based in Ontario

MDS Discovery Venture Management Inc.
Vancouver
Focus: medical and biotechnology
http://www.mdsintl.com/index.asp

MDS Health Ventures Inc.
Etobicoke, ON
Focus: health care and biotech
http://www.mdsintl.com

Native Venture Capital Co. Ltd.
Edmonton
Focus: Alberta ventures operated by aboriginal peoples

Ontario Teachers' Pension Plan Board—www.otpp.com

Saskatchewan Government Growth Fund
Regina
Focus: Saskatchewan-based ventures
http://www.sggfmc.com

Soccrent
Jonquiere, PQ
Focus: aluminum, forest products

Societe En Commandite Capidem Quebec Enr.
Quebec City
Focus: manufacturing

Soquia Inc.
Quebec City
Focus: agri-food technology
http://www.sgfqc.com

Vencap Equities Alberta Ltd.
Calgary
Focus: all sectors

Ventures West Management Inc.
Vancouver
Focus: technology
http://www.ventureswest.com/

Vision Capital Fund
Winnipeg
Focus: all sectors, Manitoba-based preferred

Wesport Capital Inc.
Toronto
Contact: D. T. Waite
Focus: small businesses

Growth Works WV Canadian Fund
Toronto
Contact: David Levi
Focus: small businesses
http://www.growthworks.ca/funds/canadian

Suggested Readings

"Canada's Best Bankers." *Profit Magazine*, April–May, 2003, p. 26.

Canada Small Business Financing website—http://strategis.ic.gc.ca

Canadian Bankers Association website—http://www.cba.ca

Csordis, Mark D. *Business Lessons For Entrepreneurs*. Mason, Ohio: Thomson Learning, 2003.

Government Assistance Manual For Canadian Small Business Financing and Tax Planning Guide—
www.cch.ca

Gray, Douglas A., and Diana L. Gray. *The Complete Canadian Small Business Guide, 2nd Edition*.
Toronto: McGraw-Hill Ryerson, 2003, pp. 145–63.

Lister, Kate, and Tom Harnish. *Finding Money: The Small Business Guide to Financing*. New York:
Wiley.

Money Book—Guide To Sources of Financing. *Alberta Venture*, October, 2006.

Rogers, Steven. *The Entrepreneur's Guide to Finance and Business*. New York: McGraw Hill,
2003.

Small Business Funding Centre—http://www.cdnloans.grants-loans.org/

SME Financing in Canada. Industry Canada, Ottawa, 2003.

Sources of Venture Capital in Canada. Ottawa: Department of Industry, Trade and Commerce, 2005.

"The Online Definitive Guide to Small Business Financing." Royal Bank of Canada,
http://www.rbcroyalbank.com/sme

Ward, Susan. "8 Sources of Business Startup Money," *Small Business Canada*, June, 2006, pp. 1–3.

Watson, Thomas. "How To Shake The Money Tree." *Canadian Business*, November–December,
2003, pp. 147–149.

Your Guide To Government Financial Assistance For Business—www.productivepublications.ca

Comprehensive Case *Sid Stevens: Part 4*

Sid was quite proud of his business plan and realized that he had learned a lot in preparing it. He also realized, however, that in order for the business to get off the ground, he would need financing. Suzie would only let Sid use $20,000 of their savings for the venture, but Sid was of the opinion that this would at least help them get started. Once the business was up and running additional funds would be generated through sales of the Ladder Rail.

Sid decided that he would rather establish the manufacturing facility from scratch than purchase the plant that was for sale. This way he could arrange the facility in the way that suited him and he would not have to spend money to retrofit. In addition, Sid lived on an acreage and he already owned enough property on which to construct the building. He estimated that to construct a small building of 2000 square feet would cost about $100,000. Although he could use some of the metal-cutting and -bending equipment that he already had, another $30,000 would be required to obtain the equipment required to move to commercial production of the Ladder Rail. Sid also thought that he would need a good truck to haul inventory to the plant and to deliver the finished product to purchasers. The estimated cost for a good used truck was $30,000. Initial inventory of aluminum was estimated at $10,000. The financing requirements totalled $170,000 (see Figure 4-A).

Figure 4-A	Ladder Rail Start-up Costs	
	Building	$100,000
	Equipment	30,000
	Truck	30,000
	Inventory	10,000

Armed with his business plan and his estimate of start-up costs, Sid went to his local bank to obtain the required financing. He was surprised that his banker was less than enthusiastic about his proposal. His banker's response was clear. "First, you need more equity than this before I could advance a loan to you. Second, you will need more detail on your costs. Third, I will need some indication that your business has the ability to make the loan payments." With his banker's words ringing in his ears, Sid was determined to show how this business could repay a loan. He went home and started to work up a proposed income statement, which is shown in Figure 4-B.

Figure 4-B	Ladder Rail Income Statement	
	Revenue: 5,000 units @ $40	$ 200,000
	Cost of goods sold: 5,000 units @ $10	50,000
	Wages (Sid: $50,000; 2 workers @ $30,000 each)	110,000
	Utilities and phone	15,000
	Net income	$ 15,000

When Sid took this statement to the banker, he was still told that more work needed to be done. Sid went home to Suzie feeling pretty discouraged and was not sure what to do next.

Questions

1. What items have been overlooked by Sid in both the start-up costs and the income statements for the Ladder Rail?
2. What additional statements would the banker likely require?
3. What other sources of equity (or debt) financing might help Sid get established?

Video Cases for Part 2

Beer Mitts   Bulldog Interactive Fitness
Cottage Cheesecake Industry

PART ENDING VIDEO CASE & QUESTIONS   *Beer Mitts**

(Appropriate Chapters—3, 4, 7)

Some people spend a lifetime trying to come up with the "perfect product," the idea that should sell itself. Others just stumble right into it, but as Colin King discovered from a couple of guys who found their "big idea" sipping beer, the idea's the easy part.

1. What can be learned from this example about the importance of preparing a feasibility analysis?
2. Discuss the start-up problems that occurred with this business.
3. What type of approach to starting a business was utilized in this example?
4. What can be learned about partnerships from this example?

*Source: CBC *Venture* #720, running time 8:24.

PART ENDING VIDEO CASE & QUESTIONS   *Cottage Cheesecake Industry**

(Appropriate Chapters—1, 7, 11, 15)

Brad Miller bakes cakes in his garage in Sydney, Nova Scotia. At least he did until the business grew so big that Brad decided to move the bakery into a full-sized factory. But growing up is hard to do.

1. What aspects of Brad Miller's background would be positive for him to obtain financing for his business? What aspects would be negative?
2. What are the advantages and disadvantages of equity financing for this business?
3. What other sources of financing might he have accessed?
4. What does this example show about family business?

*Source: CBC *Venture* #726, running time 9:04.

www.mcgrawhill.ca/olc/balderson

PART ENDING VIDEO CASE & QUESTIONS   *Bulldog Interactive Fitness**

(Appropriate Chapters—1, 3, 6, 15)

1. Discuss the research that James and Holly Bond did before starting Bulldog Interactive Fitness.

2. What should James and Holly do to ensure success in selling enough franchises to meet their goal?

3. Discuss the suitability and importance of the partnership with Sony.

4. What are some of the difficulties Bulldog may experience competing with larger companies? How could they minimize the risk of failure?

*Source: CBC *Venture* #15569, running time 9:08.

Cases for Part 2

Clark's Sporting Goods   Kelly's Grill
Jensen Roofing   Second Cup
Conrad's Photographer's Supplies

CLARK'S SPORTING GOODS

D. Wesley Balderson, *University of Lethbridge*

Dave Clark plans to open a sporting goods store in London, Ontario, as soon as he graduates from university there in the spring. He did a market demand analysis for such a store for one of his course projects and is confident the opportunity exists.

Dave's major problem is determining the amount of funds he will require. His father, who is quite wealthy, will give him $30,000 as a graduation gift to invest. He has located a store that rents for $2,000 per month (in advance) and has made an itemized list of the start-up costs as follows:

Merchandise (4 months)	$100,000
Shelves, racks, displays	5,000
Remodelling	4,000
Cash register (used)	800
Check-out counter	500
Office supplies (4 months' supply)	200
Telephone: $50/month, $100 deposit, $25 installation fee	
Utilities: $200/month, $200 deposit	

Dave has made the following estimates:
- He can completely turn over his inventory every four months.
- In the first year, he plans a 60 percent markup on cost of merchandise.
- He can get by on a salary of $2,000 per month.
- He plans to hire one full-time employee at $1,500 per month and one at $1,000.

- He plans to spend $2,000 in opening promotion in the first month and $500 a month after the grand opening for advertising.
- He estimates that 50 percent of his sales will be on credit and will be paid in 30 days.
- The interest rate is 10 percent, payable every four months.
- The depreciation rate is 10 percent.

Questions

1. Estimate how much money Dave will need from outside sources to start his business.
2. Assuming Dave receives start-up financing from a bank, as calculated in question 1, will he require an operating line of credit during the first four months of operation? If so, how much?
3. Should Dave pursue debt or equity sources of funds to get started?

JENSEN ROOFING

D. Wesley Balderson, *University of Lethbridge*

Robert Jensen had just completed a short entrepreneurial course at a local college as preparation for establishing his own roofing business. One of the main things that he learned in the course was the necessity of preparing a business plan for the enterprise. As a result Robert went to work and within a few days had put together the following business plan for Jensen Roofing.

Background

I, Robert Jensen, will be the sole owner of this proprietorship, which will install and repair roofs in the Lethbridge, Alberta, market area. I have completed an entrepreneurial course at the Lethbridge Community College and have had several years experience in the roofing business working for Charles Hill Roofing, the largest roofer in the Lethbridge area.

I am desirous of starting my own business in order to be independent and to obtain a higher financial compensation than I am currently receiving. I want everyone in Lethbridge and surrounding areas to know my company and the quality work we do.

Market Approach

The target market will be every person who owns a house, apartment building, warehouse, condo, or office building. The services we provide will cater to all people who own buildings that need roof repair or construction. We will provide all types of roofing materials and services. Eavestroughing will also be included in our business. Quality workmanship will be the building block of our business. We will ensure a one-year guarantee on all workmanship.

Because the service Jensen Roofing will provide is of high quality, I will charge a slightly higher price on our product. I will try to maintain a 20 percent markup over costs to keep our prices fair to every customer. Jensen Roofing will utilize several forms of promotion. Brochures and pamphlets will be prepared and sent through direct mail to every homeowner in Lethbridge. Newspaper ads and the Yellow Pages will also be used to promote the business.

Physical Facilities

The business will be located in my home at first. This will save a considerable amount of money until the business gets established. Equipment, supplies, and opening inventory will be purchased from local suppliers. The following schedule provides a listing of the equipment and supplies that will be needed to get started.

Physical Requirements

1 work truck (used half ton)	$ 5,000
3-tonne dump truck	5,000
1 hoist	500
4 ladders (25 foot)	1,500
Computer system	3,000
Office equipment and supplies	1,000
Total	$17,000

Financial

To estimate potential revenue for Jensen Roofing for new houses, I have multiplied the average roofing job for new houses ($8,000) by the number of new houses constructed in Lethbridge (400) in 2004 for a total of $3,200,000. For repair jobs I have taken the average dollar expenditure per household for the Lethbridge area (Urban Family Expenditure Data) of $100 and multiplied it by the number of homes (26,000) for a total of $2,600,000. Of this total of $5,800,000 I estimate that Jensen Roofing will obtain a 10 percent market share for a total revenue of $580,000. There are currently eight other roofers in the city, but because of my quality workmanship, I hope to increase the market share of Jensen Roofing to 20 percent within five years.

Projected income based on these estimates are found below:

Jensen Roofing Projected Income—Year 1

Sales	$580,000
Cost of goods sold (45%)	261,000
Wages	100,000
Depreciation	2,000
Advertising	2,600
Insurance	1,200
Repairs and maintenance	5,000
Licences and permits	200
Professional fees	800
Interest (8% on $15,000)	1,200
Total	374,000
Net Income	$206,000

Jensen Roofing will obtain a loan from a local bank to finance $15,000 of the start-up requirement. The remaining $2,000 will be supplied by me, the owner. The financial records of the business will be prepared and maintained by an accountant.

www.mcgrawhill.ca/olc/balderson

Legal Requirements

The necessary business licences and permits will be obtained from the City of Lethbridge. Initially the business will be operated as a proprietorship, and when the business becomes more established I will consider forming a limited company.

Personnel

The personnel required to keep Jensen Roofing operating will vary from season to season. Due to the uncertainties of the weather, part-time employees will be utilized. Ads will be placed in the local newspaper to find workers for the business. I will also utilize the government employment agency of Canada Manpower. During the summer months I may also look at hiring students. I estimate that on average I will have about five workers on the payroll. Training will take place on the job which is appropriate for this type of work.

Question

1. Evaluate the Jensen Roofing business plan from an investor's and a lender's point of view.

CONRAD'S PHOTOGRAPHER'S SUPPLIES

D. Wesley Balderson, *University of Lethbridge*

Richard and Karen Bingley are interested in going into a business related to their hobby—photography. For the last year, they have been good customers of Conrad's Photographer's Supplies, a sole proprietorship, owned by Shelley Conrad. Although the store is relatively new, they have become well acquainted with Shelley who is a well-known photographer in the community. Shelley told the Bingleys that the store was doing well considering she opened it just over year ago. More and more people have gotten involved in photography and with the introduction of digital cameras the industry, was in a growth position. An increasing number of people seemed to prefer an outlet at which they could get advice about taking pictures as apposed to buying only for low prices.

However, one day Shelley confided in Karen that although she enjoyed operating the business, it was taking much more time to run than she had expected, and she was considering selling the business to devote more time to her professional photography. Shelley thought Richard and Karen might be interested in purchasing the business, since they were such good customers and knew a lot about photography.

Richard and Karen were quite excited about the idea and met with Shelley to go over the entire business. They were impressed with the operation as all the equipment and fixtures were new and they were especially impressed with the extensive customer list. As they discussed the financial information (see below), Shelley indicated that she would sell the business for $80,000, slightly above the value of the assets of the company. Richard and Karen currently had $20,000 in equity and Shelley indicated that she was prepared to finance them over four years at 8 percent per annum, which was 2 percent less than Shelley was paying on her business debt. Because of her stature in the industry and her numerous connections in the community, Shelley has been able to develop a good working relationship with her suppliers, which typically includes them granting 30-day credit on inventory. The store is located in a strip mall at the north end of the city of Winnipeg and has two years remaining on the three-year lease.

Conrad's Photographer's Supplies Income Statement for 2006		Conrad's Photographer's Supplies Balance Sheet at Dec. 31, 2006	
Sales	252,000	**Assets**	
Cost of Goods Sold	171,000	Cash	1,000
Gross Margin	81,000	Accounts Receivable	8,000
		Inventory	40,000
		Fixtures	15,000
		Goodwill	12,000
		Total	76,000
Expenses			
Wages	38,000	Liabilities and Owner's Equity	
Promotion	4,000	Accounts Payable	27,000
Rent	15,000	Debt	20,000
Utilities	6,000	Equity	29,000
Miscellaneous	2,000	Total	$76,000
Depreciation	5,000		
Net profit	$11,000		

Questions

1. Suppose the Bingleys decided to organize a photography store from scratch. Discuss how this decision would compare with the other two methods of getting into the business on (a) independence, (b) risk, and (c) information requirements.
2. In evaluating this business in order to purchase it, discuss concerns you would have about (a) the previous owner, (b) financial information, and (c) assets of the business.
3. Assuming the information in the financial statements is accurate, is Shelly Conrad's asking price a reasonable one? Use book value and capitalization of earnings methods to help you answer this question.
4. There is at least one adjustment to the balance sheet and two to the income statement that should be made to make these statements more accurate, which will affect the calculation of the price of the business. Make the adjustments and reevaluate the asking price based on your adjustments.

KELLY'S GRILL

D. Wesley Balderson, *University of Lethbridge*

Kelly Orr worked as assistant department manager in the ladies' wear department of a large department store in Kingston, Ontario. She enjoyed her work but saw that chances of further advancement in her $35,000-a-year job were limited. For the past few years, Kelly had been thinking about starting her own business. As a teenager, she had worked summers in a fast-food franchise and had always desired to own her own restaurant. As she had two children, she resented having to work Thursday and Friday evenings and Saturdays and thought that by owning her own business she could more easily take time off to be with her family. Her husband, a schoolteacher, had supported her working in the past but was a bit hesitant about Kelly risking her savings of $20,000 to go out on her own. They agreed, however, that Kelly should investigate a few possibilities and obtain as much information as she could about the restaurant industry in Kingston.

For the past six months, Kelly has visited with several of her friends, looked at some prospective businesses, and checked with public officials to find out what information was available. She has obtained the following information:

Population of Kingston	95,000
Per-family away-from-home food expenditures	$80/month
Number of families in Kingston	28,000
Number of restaurants in Kingston	110
Average square footage per outlet	1,500
Cost of goods sold as percentage of gross sales	50%
Bank's lending rate	10%

Operating expenses, excluding rent, interest, and franchise advertising royalties, are estimated to be 35 percent of gross sales.

From several restaurant possibilities, Kelly has narrowed the decision down to three: a site in a new shopping mall, a downtown restaurant that is for sale, and a fast-food franchise. All three involve a greater investment than Kelly was planning on. To get sufficient funds, the Orr's may have to remortgage their house.

Possibility A

The first potential site is a new shopping centre just nearing completion in a new and growing part of Kingston. The centre is anchored at each end by two national department stores. The space Kelly is considering contains 3,000 square feet and carries a rental of $10 per square foot, plus a royalty of 2 percent of gross sales. Although the rental costs would be high, Kelly is confident that the mall would generate considerable customer traffic, which would outweigh the rental costs. Also, the mall location is within a few minutes' drive from her home. However, the space is unfinished, and Kelly estimates she would need a minimum of $40,000 in equipment and $20,000 in leasehold improvements to get the restaurant started. Since not all the space was leased out, she was not able to find out how many other restaurants were planning to locate in the mall.

Possibility B

The second potential site is a 1,500-square-foot, busy downtown lunchtime café that is for sale. The present owner is asking $50,000 for the restaurant and is willing to finance the sale at $25,000 down and $10,000 per year for three years. The space had been leased at $12,000 annually and was due to be renegotiated in three years. The location of this restaurant makes it attractive to lunchtime and late-afternoon customers. The restaurant has operated successfully for six years and is located close to several large office buildings.

Possibility C

The third possibility is to sign a franchise contract with a national fast-food franchise chain that wants to expand into Kingston. The typical outlet size is 2,000 square feet. The initial franchise fee is $20,000, plus an additional $50,000 to be financed through Kelly's bank with the franchise guarantee, which would lower the interest rate by 2 percent. Kelly would also pay 6 percent of gross sales as a royalty. They would train Kelly in one of its company-owned outlets at no charge and help with the start-up of her own outlet. She would, of course, be constantly monitored by the franchise—a point that makes her a bit uneasy.

Kelly needs to make a decision soon. All three prospects might be lost if she waits too long.

Questions

1. How well has Kelly thought out and prepared for her decision to start her own restaurant?
2. Based on the information provided, which of the choices open to Kelly would you advise her to make?
3. What additional information should she obtain before making this decision?

SECOND CUP

D. Wesley Balderson, *University of Lethbridge*

Ken and Mary Hatch are in the process of making a major career change. Ken has been caretaker for a local high school in Markham, Ontario for 20 years, rising to the position of supervisor. Mary has worked in a coffee shop for eight years since their children entered school. They are considering opening their own coffee shop and are interested in a Second Cup franchise.

Second Cup is a successful nationally known Canadian franchise that was established in 1975 in Toronto and has grown to more than 400 outlets across the country. Mary became aware from her employer that Second Cup was looking for franchisees in the Markham area and she has collected the following information from the company. The franchise fee is $20,000 and there is a promotional royalty of 9 percent of gross sales. Second Cup estimates that the total investment for an outlet is Markham to be an additional $200,000 for equipment and other start-up costs. This cost does not include the building, which Second Cup builds and then rents back to the franchiser.

Although the Hatches don't have $200,000, they have saved $20,000 and have been assured by Second Cup that the bank will finance the remainder at 5 percent by being signed up with the franchising company. One of the Hatches' concerns is that they haven't managed a restaurant before, although Ken has supervised people in his caretaking job and Mary has worked in the coffee shop for eight years. The Hatches take some comfort in the fact that Second Cup offers a three-week course at their Coffee College to teach the fundamentals of the coffee and retail business.

They are both tired of taking orders from supervisors and see this opportunity as a way to be their own boss with minimal risk. There are currently five other Second Cup outlets in Markham and three Starbucks coffee houses, which are their major competitors. There are also many other independent coffee shops and other fast-food outlets that sell coffee. However, with the city and coffee sales growing, the Hatches are optimistic about their chances for success. They cite the fact that they will save considerably by purchasing all of their supplies from the parent company and the fact that the well-organized operating and monitoring system will ensure that they operate at peak efficiency as reasons for optimism.

Second Cup has supplied the following sample financial statement to help the Hatches in their planning.

Opening cash balance	$20,000
Sales	600,000
Cost of goods sold	320,000
Total	$ 300,000

Expenses

Advertising royalty	$ 54,000
Other advertising	6,000
Rent ($30 @ 1000)	30,000
Insurance	5,000
Repairs and maintenance	5,000
Telephone and utilities	15,000
Salaries	100,000
Miscellaneous	10,000
Total	$ 245,000
Net income	$ 75,000

The Hatches were most happy with the projections because the business would make $55,000. Ken estimates that half the salary total would be their own wage for working in the business. Ken and Mary have noted that combining these two would almost double what they are earning in their current jobs.

This couple is about to make the final decision to leave their employment and sign this franchise contract.

Questions

1. What further analysis should be done before making this decision?
2. What specific questions about the financial information as presented by Second Cup should be asked?

PART THREE

Managing the Small Business

Part 2 of this text dealt with issues relating to the organization and establishment of a small business. Once the business has been established, the owner-manager should follow several management fundamentals to ensure that the business stays viable and competitive. Part 3 discusses five of these management areas. Chapter 8 focuses on the marketing principles essential for understanding the market and getting the product or service to the consumer. Chapter 9 explores a relatively new phenomenon: electronic commerce. Chapter 10 covers the recording and controlling of the financial aspects of the business. Both marketing and finance are areas in which many entrepreneurs lack training and competence. Chapter 11 discusses some fundamental components of the internal operations or production aspects of the business. Chapter 12 reviews the principles of personnel management applicable to the small organization. Chapter 13 outlines the most relevant tax considerations for the small business.

CHAPTER 8
Marketing Management

SMALL BUSINESS PROFILE

Ben Varadi, Anton Rabie, and Ronnen Harary

Spin Master Toys

The history of Spin Master Toys is part Wright brothers, part Roots—a tale of what happens when innovation meets savvy marketing. Childhood pals who met at summer camp a few years after their families moved to Toronto from South Africa, Anton Rabie and Ronnen Harary both attended the University of Western Ontario in London, where they met fellow biz student Ben Varadi. The three established a business under the name Sieger Marketing, selling a locally sponsored frosh-kit calendar as their first product. Their success with this project allowed them to build up enough money so that in 1994, when Harary's grandmother brought back a novelty gift from Israel—a sawdust-filled stocking with a face that sprouted grass for hair—they knew they had found a new product. The Earth Buddy was born.

In the years that followed, the company continued to identify and successfully market interesting novelty and toy products. After the Earth Buddy came Devil Sticks, a three-rod juggling game, which went on to become Canada's number one non-promoted toy for 1995. The company's success owed much to the grass-roots approach to marketing and promotion, combining innovative point-of-purchase displays, highly visible promotions, and intense PR campaigns.

In 1997, the company was approached by a group of British inventors with the idea that would change its course and establish it as a legitimate player in the international toy marketplace. The concept was simple—an air-pressure-powered toy airplane that relied on a theoretically sound, yet unproven, engine design. All the major companies passed on the idea, but Rabie, Harary, and Varadi saw something special—a chance to corner the market on flight, delivering a great flying toy at a great price point. It took more than a year, a sink-or-swim course in Far East manufacturing, and close to $1 million in development costs before they had a plane that would fly. The Air Hogs line was born, and it was a huge hit, eventually cracking the top three best-selling toys of the year.

The success of the Air Hogs stemmed from two main drivers—innovative product development and powerhouse PR and marketing. If developing the product was tough, the Air Hogs press campaign was only slightly less difficult. By generating a legitimate success story, spinning it for the media, and packaging it all in a series of eye-catching press kits (an Air Hog along with a bag of airline peanuts and a sickness bag), the company became the darling of the media. Over the past several years, the company has continued its record of major successes with trend-setting items like Flick Trix extreme sports toys, Key Charm Cuties, dozens of Air Hogs spin-offs, and a new lineup that includes an R/C airplane, Shrinky Dinks, Mighty Beanz, Aqua Doodle, and the McDonald's McFlurry ice cream maker.

Now, with annual sales of $300 million, Spin Master has become Canada's largest toy manufacturer and one of the largest in North America. Licensing with companies such as Disney, McDonald's, Marvel, and Nickelodeon has become an integral part of its marketing program. Although it has accordingly stepped up its marketing techniques by cultivating these relationships, it has also developed innovative, interactive in-store displays designed to show off what are. after all, new, unseen, and inherently complex, must-try products. The results from the merchandising have increased sales by more than 40 percent in some instances. At the same time, PR remains the backbone of the company—a throwback to their days of super-low-budget, most-bang-for-the-buck strategizing—though through reputation alone, the founders have had to up the creative ante with every new campaign. Recently, Spin Master has moved into the marketing of children's furnishings as the toy market stagnates. The owners see the company not as a "toy company" but a "children's entertainment lifestyle company."

Adapted from: "Inside the Tornado," *Profit*, December 2005, pp. 41–47, and the Spinmaster website.

Photo: Laura Arsie Photography

Spin Master Toys
www.spinmaster.com

THE ROLE OF MARKETING MANAGEMENT IN THE SMALL BUSINESS

Marketing activities are often overlooked by owner-managers after the business has been established. Some possible reasons for this are that (1) owner-managers do not fully understand what marketing is; (2) owner-managers may not think it is necessary—that is, they may believe that if they have a good enough product, it will sell itself; or (3) owner-managers tend to be so busy with the day-to-day activities and problems of the business that they do not take the time to assess the market and develop a marketing plan.

www.
businessgateway.ca

Regardless of the reasons for failing to apply marketing principles in the small business, it is critical that the owner-manager understand and apply those principles. The business will likely be unable to hire a specialist in marketing. Therefore, the owner-manager will have to do a considerable amount of marketing, not only to potential customers but also to suppliers, employees, bankers, and perhaps even government agencies. The Small Business Profile of Spin Master Toys Inc. illustrates how important marketing and meeting consumer needs was to the successful establishment of Spin Master Toys.

The major purpose of this chapter, then, is to introduce the fundamentals of marketing that can help sustain the growth of the business. Some of the principles also apply to establishing a business and were mentioned briefly in Chapter 3. Other marketing principles form an important part of a business plan and were discussed in Chapter 4.

An owner-manager may become involved in the following marketing activities:

- Defining the target customer (market niche), target customer characteristics, and information concerning that customer's product or service wants and needs

- Understanding those influences outside the business that will affect its operations

- Developing the product or service

- Developing the channel(s) of distribution

- Setting price levels for the product or service

- Providing information or promoting the product or service to those who are influential in its purchase

This chapter will discuss the relevant aspects of each of these components of marketing separately. It is important to note, however, that these components need to be coordinated to prepare a marketing plan and managed together as a system to be most effective.

THE TARGET CUSTOMER

In preparing the feasibility analysis in Chapter 3, we stressed the need to define the target customer. The ability of the entrepreneur to clearly identify the specific market is critical to success, as the Small Business Profile that opens this chapter shows. This is important in calculating a quantitative estimate of the size of the market. The small business owner might attempt to reach and collect information about the following target markets:

1. The consumer market
2. The organization market
3. The export market

Each of these markets has unique characteristics that must be taken into account in developing the marketing program.

The Consumer Market

The owner-manager should obtain information about several characteristics of the consumer market. Some characteristics that may be most helpful in developing the marketing program are the following:

Ideasite for Business
www.
ideasiteforbusiness.
com

1. *Demographic characteristics.* These include items such as age, income, education, occupation, and location of residence.
2. *Lifestyle characteristics.* This category includes such things as activities, interests, opinions, media habits, and personalities of target market individuals.
3. *Purchase characteristics.* These include what, when, where, and how much of the product or service the market purchases. Figure 8-1 gives a general example of purchase characteristics for various age groups.
4. *Purchase motivations.* This area contains one of the most important items of information: It explains the reasons behind consumer purchases. In addition to understanding the "why" of the purchase, the entrepreneur should attempt to understand the factors that might influence the purchase. Common sources of influence are members of the consumer's reference group, social class, and family. Current prominent motivations are service and value of the price/quality relationship.

Figure 8-1	Purchase Characteristics for Various Ages

In Their Teens

This group has an increasing amount of money to spend on clothing, cosmetics, and entertainment products. They also have a major influence with family purchases.

In Their 20s

This group is not yet financially secure. It demands instant gratification, lasting values, and tangible benefits. Purchase decisions are often based on subjective factors.

In Their 30s and 40s

These people have high incomes and high debt. They are individualistic, striving for self-fulfillment, and concerned about social and environmental issues. They look for information before buying.

In Their 40s and 50s

Prosperous and facing retirement, they purchase for sentimentality, brand loyalty, and convenience.

In Their 60s and 70s

They tend to have lots of leisure time. They seek financial security, quality, and value. They rely on knowledge and experience.

In Their 80s

This group spends heavily on health care, travel, and security products.

Once this type of information has been obtained, the development of the marketing program—including product characteristics, pricing strategy, distribution channels, and method of promotion—becomes much easier, and the program is usually more effective.

Much of the above information about the target customer can be obtained through secondary data or primary research, as discussed in Chapter 3. It is important for the small business owner to realize that collecting information about the target consumer is not a one-time event used only as the business is getting established. It should be used continually to help the owner stay responsive to changes in consumer needs and wants.

Most successful companies, whether large or small, stay that way because they are close to the consumer and incorporate consumer wants and needs into their marketing programs.[1] This philosophy, called the marketing concept, has been taught in introductory marketing courses for a number of years. Incident 8-1 illustrates how two entrepreneurs applied the marketing concept in meeting a consumer need. Many small businesses are successful initially because they fill a consumer need, but as they grow they often fall out of touch with their customers. This situation usually leads to difficulties, particularly in competitive markets. A recent survey of Canadian entrepreneurs who have been nominated for Canadian Entrepreneur of the Year awards indicated that customer relations was their most important issue.[2]

Other companies define their consumer markets too broadly. As a result, their marketing programs may fail to satisfactorily meet the needs of any one group in the market. The practice of tailoring the marketing program to each specific market is known as market segmentation.

Figure 8-2 illustrates the target market information for a distinct market segment for a hypothetical small restaurant. In this example, the owner-manager has selected a specific

---

INCIDENT 8-1 Child's Play

Youthography, a youth marketing consultancy based in Toronto, works to understand youth culture in order to assist marketers in selling their products to this most complex age group. The company, founded in 2001 by 26-year-old president Max Valiquette, deals directly with youth, as its research is based on the idea of simply asking youth what products they want marketed. Over 25,000 surveys were completed in 2003, 2,500 of them in-depth interviews and 10,000 Internet surveys.

Youthography's upfront approach also does not try to hide the fact that youth are being marketed to, as most youth are already well aware of this. Marketing is being taught in schools and youth are becoming more and more sophisticated in the ways of the world.

With the help of Youthography, companies like Bell Mobility, Molson Canada, CIBC, and McDonalds, among others, have boosted their market share among youth aged 16 to 24. Bell Mobility has raised its market share for this age group by fully eight points in the past three years. Part of this increase was due to the launch of an All-In-One Lunchtime & After School Calling Plan, inspired by the research done at Youthography. This plan originated from asking youth what they wanted in a phone rate plan and offers youth unlimited calling during lunchtime and after school.

Youthography has quickly become one of Canada's leading players in the field of selling expertise on marketing to people ages 13–29.

Source: Adapted from "Child's Play," *Canadian Business*, March 2004, pp. 42–45.

| Figure 8-2 | **Target Market for a Hypothetical Small Restaurant** |

The typical consumer has the following characteristics:

Demographics

> Age: 30–49
>
> Income: higher than average ($40,000–$80,000)
>
> Occupation: professionals, managers
>
> Education: university graduates

Lifestyle (Psychographics)

> Activities: exercise and participation in sports, high social interaction; low TV usage and high reading; husband and wife both work, enjoy the outdoors, attend cultural events
>
> Interests: appearance, health, fashion
>
> Opinions: conservative economically, liberal on social issues
>
> Personality: achievement-oriented, outgoing, independent

Purchase Characteristics

> What: higher quality and higher priced menu items
>
> Where: higher class restaurant, international cuisine
>
> When: evenings and weekends
>
> How much: frequently eat away from home, 50 percent higher than national average

Purchase Motivations

> Benefits sought: superior quality of food, service, atmosphere, variety of the menu
>
> Influencers: reference groups and social class the main influencers in choice of restaurant, through word of mouth

group of consumers toward whom to direct the marketing strategy. The demographic information needed to prepare quantitative estimates of feasibility (see Chapter 3) can be obtained from such secondary sources as government census reports. The information on lifestyles, purchase characteristics, and motivations might be obtained from industry marketing research reports, or the owner-manager may need to collect this data. This thorough consumer profile allows the restaurant owner to develop a market strategy that responds to the consumers' characteristics and needs. For instance, a high-quality, nutritious menu should be provided. Higher prices reflecting this level of quality would probably not affect demand negatively. Advertising showing young, socially active, and successful models might be effective. Testimonial endorsements may also have some influence. Incidents 8-2 and 8-3 on the next page illustrate how two entrepreneurs identified the needs of their target market in developing a business plan and thus were able to develop an appropriate competitive strategy in launching their businesses.

Another consumer market issue that the entrepreneur must not overlook is that consumer demographics and lifestyles are constantly changing. It is therefore important that a continual monitoring of consumer characteristics be carried out.

INCIDENT 8-2   The Unbackable Sewer

Gabe Coscarella's simple plumbing invention has saved thousands of Canadian homes from potential flood damage, as well as a great deal of money and distress. This former contractor for the City of Edmonton came up with the idea eight years ago after seeing first-hand the damage a sewer backup can cause. After spending 10 minutes drawing up the plans, Coscarella spent about 40 hours building a simple valve prototype out of Tupperware and Plexiglas. This newfound sewer valve soon became the patented Fullport Backwater Valve. Today, Coscarella's company, called Mainline Backflow Products, sells more than 50,000 sewer valves a year.

This much needed and much valued valve has made an instant impression with plumbing supply dealers and is responsible for changing Canada's national plumbing code. Sales are expected to jump to 100,000 as Mainline introduces new products. Coscarella's valves are now going into about 95 percent of new homes built in western Canada. He says, "You have a choice between the old, flapper type of valve that doesn't work well and ours. We've never had a valve failure in a new home."

Source: Adapted from "The Unbackable Sewer," *Alberta Venture*, April 2006, p. 38.

INCIDENT 8-3   Anatomy of a Marketing Campaign

Mountain Crest Brewing Co. took a marketing approach like few other beer companies. They identified a market for a lower cost but still high-quality beer and developed their business plan and marketing strategy around this target market. The brewing company, started in 2002 by 25-year-old Ravinder Minhas and his sister Manjit, used a low-budget, straightforward campaign that focused solely on the quality of the beer. Ravinder says, "You're not going to catch a sasquatch and you're not going to be a better cowboy. So let's quit the antics and let's talk about the quality of beer itself." Along with the Mountain Crest slogan of "Damn Good Beer!," the campaign protests against the reality of high beer prices. The campaign also conveys that, although Mountain Crest beer might be cheaper (about $10 less for a 24 pack compared to leading brands), it is still a premium lager. The quality aspect of the product was developed based on the un-met market need for a low-priced quality beer.

After starting the company in 2002, the Minhases travelled to liquor stores around the province, giving free samples of their beer. Billboards were the next step, followed by promotional tactics such as giving away one-year leases for six PT Cruisers. Finally in the summer of 2004, the Minhases felt it was time for TV. The "Damn Good Beer" commercial was shot on a low budget, with much of it filmed at the Minhases' home. Ravinder would also call or email television stations everyday to see if he could get last minute advertising spots at bargain prices. This saved up to 60 percent per advertisement. Ravinder says, "We have a lower budget because we are passing on savings to the consumer. Not because they are getting an inferior product." The marketing strategy of Mountain Crest Brewing Co. has certainly paid off—they made $40 million in 2004.

Source: Adapted from Anthony Davis, "Anatomy of a Marketing Campaign," *Alberta Venture*, January/February 2006, pp. 80–83.

The Organization Market

The second type of market the small business might attempt to reach is the organization market. This market includes companies, institutions, or even individuals who purchase the product to assist in the manufacture of other products. Government purchases, an ever-increasing market for small business, are also classed as an industrial market.

In consumer markets, buying influences include the emotional as well as the rational. Industrial goods, conversely, are purchased primarily for rational reasons. Such characteristics as price, quality, dependability of supply, ability to manufacture to specification, speed of manufacture and delivery, and services offered are commonly considered in making industrial purchases. The purchasers, often acting as a committee, are well informed about the product category and are also aware of competitive offerings. Generally the information the purchaser requires is of a technical nature, requiring a well-trained and knowledgeable sales staff on the part of the small business.

In attempting to reach the industrial market, the following areas should be investigated: (1) which companies and government agencies purchase from small businesses, (2) the influences on industrial demand, and (3) how the bidding-tendering process works.

Canada Business
Service Centres
www.cbsc.org

Contracts Canada
(Government of Canada)
www.contractscanada.
gc.ca

Companies and Government Agencies That Purchase from Small Businesses. Many large organizations purposely look to small business to fill their product and service needs. Such businesses find that the efficiency and service of the small enterprise meet their needs adequately and the price is competitive. Another form of selling to other businesses is through barter—the trade of goods or services. Bartering has grown to a $50 million business in Canada and may benefit the small business by opening new markets and reducing the need for higher levels of cash.[3]

Influences on Industrial Demand. Demand for industrial goods is derived from demand for the final product. Because of this relatively delayed response, industrial demand changes can be easier to predict than consumer demand changes. Some of the key indicators of industrial demand changes are

- The state of the economy and its effect on the purchase of the end product

- Government legislation or regulations

- Potential competition for the purchasing company

- Specific bodies or agencies that exert influence on the purchases

The Bidding-Tendering Process. The small business owner should be aware of how the purchase decision is made and which criteria or specifications are used to make the decision in the industrial market. Because many industrial goods, particularly those purchased by the government, are purchased on a tender-bid basis, it is essential that the small business owner know how to prepare and submit bids within such a system.

The Export Market

Canada has always been known as a trading nation. The value of exports has contributed an estimated 20 percent to Canada's employment and 41 percent to GDP.[4] Export sales increased from $40 billion in 1977 to $429 billion in 2004.[5] The importance of exports to the Canadian economy is underscored by the fact that for every billion dollars worth of exports, 9,000 new jobs are created.[6] Further, recent studies have shown that businesses that export create more new jobs per business than non-exporting companies.[7] In the past, a large portion of exports have come from the primary and resource industries, which consisted of large companies and government agencies. Recently, however, many small businesses have successfully exported manufactured goods to foreign countries (see Incident 8-4). The number of small- and medium-sized businesses that export has increased to over 40,000 businesses and the share of small business exports is estimated to be close to 25 percent of total Canadian exports.[8] It is also estimated that 85 percent of Canadian exporters are small businesses.[9] A significant contributor to this increased exporting activ-

---

INCIDENT 8-4 Digigraph Systems Inc.

Ten years ago, during a trade mission to Latin America, architect Bernard McNamara realized that there was a market for quality, affordable housing. He also noticed that traditional construction methods appeared insufficient to meet the growing demand.

With this in mind, McNamara, president and managing director of Digigraph Systems Inc., set to work designing a product that would draw on Canadian industrial know-how and be made of materials readily available in Central and South America. By 1996, he had developed an affordable, lightweight polyvinyl chloride (PVC) house frame that is made in Canada, shipped in segments, and easily assembled at the building site. His company focuses exclusively on export markets.

Digigraph has filled orders for homes in Chile, Colombia, and Costa Rica and is in the process of developing products in Ghana and Nigeria. It has established a network of distributors in Latin American countries, the West Indies, and Africa and had export sales of $2.7 million in 2002.

Source: "Readiness for Exporting," *Profit*, vol. 17, no. 2, Spring 1997, p. 3; and Digigraph website, http://www.digigraph-housing.com, July 2004.

---

ity and its beneficial effect on entrepreneurs was the signing of the North American Free Trade Agreement in 1994.[10]

Because of both the vast potential in these foreign markets and the considerable encouragement and assistance provided by the government, the small business owner should not overlook this option. The North American Free Trade Agreement among Canada, the United States, and Mexico (as mentioned above) is rapidly opening up new markets for Canadian small businesses,[11] as is the current direction of policy formation by the World Trade Organization. Recent surveys indicate that Canadian entrepreneurs expect exports to increase significantly in the next few years.[12] The top international markets that Canadian entrepreneurs export to are the United States (85 percent), Asia (85 percent), Western Europe (44 percent), and South America (38 percent).[13] To determine the readiness for exporting, several questions should be answered. A brief review of some of these questions is shown in Figure 8-3. In addition, it is estimated that a certain amount of money will be required for such things as travelling to markets, drafting brochures, working tradeshows, and meeting potential customers. Estimates range from $10,000 to $15,000 to cover these expenses.

The small business owner who plans to export needs to investigate (1) the forms of government assistance available for exporting, (2) the unique characteristics of the foreign market, and (3) the mechanisms of exporting.

Government Assistance Available for Exporting. Many government programs are designed to encourage and assist the entrepreneur who desires to export a product or service to another country. Some of the more active agencies and programs follow.

Department of Industry Canada. This federal government department provides assistance in designing marketing plans, offers information and liaison with other government departments, and administers specific programs such as the following:

1. *Promotional Projects Program.* This program promotes Canadian goods and services abroad through trade fairs, missions, and other foreign contacts.

2. *Program for Export Market Development (PEMD).* This program shares part of the financial risk associated with foreign trade by providing grants to the entrepreneur for

World Trade
Organization
www.wto.org

Industry Canada
www.strategis.ic.gc.ca

Figure 8-3	**Readiness for Exporting**

Some of the questions that should be asked to determine readiness for exporting include the following:

1. Are you entrepreneurial?
2. Do you have a reliable, service-oriented character?
3. Are you a natural networker, building and maintaining relationships?
4. Do you see yourself as highly organized and research-oriented?
5. Do you have good communication skills?
6. Do you pride yourself on your strong negotiating skills?
7. Are you experienced in handling complex documentation?
8. Are you an avid follower of global politics?
9. Can you speak and write more than one language?
10. Are you sensitive to different cultures?
11. Do you adopt ideas easily, even under pressure?
12. Are you well travelled or curious about other cultures?

travel to identify foreign markets, participate in trade fairs, and bring foreign buyers to Canada. Recently the emphasis for this program was changed to target firms with sales of less than $10 million.

Export Hotline
www.exporthotline.com

3. *World Information Network for Exports (WIN Exports).* This computer-based information system is designed to assist in matching foreign needs to Canadian capabilities.

4. *Technology Inflow Program.* This program is designed to help locate, acquire, and adopt foreign technologies by promoting international collaboration.

Team Canada Inc.'s
Export Source
www.exportsource.
gc.ca

5. *New Exporters to Border States (NEBS)—to U.S. South (NEXUS)—to overseas (NEXOS).* This program provides counselling assistance as well as organizes trade missions to businesses planning to export to these areas.

6. *New Exporters Overseas (NEXPRO).* This is a training and counselling program for new exporters provided by Industry Canada. The 1998 Team Canada trade mission led to the signing of 306 agreements for a total value of $1.78 billion of which 90 percent were concluded with small and medium-sized Canadian businesses.[14]

Export Development Canada (EDC). As mentioned previously, the EDC is a Crown corporation of the federal government that essentially provides three services to exporters:

Export Development
Canada/Exportation et
développement Canada
www.edc.ca

1. *Export insurance.* This is a protection service for the exporter to ensure payment for export sales in the event of buyer default or detrimental foreign government action. The required screening to obtain the insurance assists small business in selecting creditworthy partners in foreign countries.

2. *Export guarantees.* Guarantees can be provided to financial institutions to assist exporters in obtaining financing for the export operations.

3. *Export financing services.* The EDC also has authorization to provide medium- and long-term financing for exporters to help them compete in the international marketplace.

EDC also provides a 1-800 number to help smaller firms get instant access to financial and insurance assistance for goods and services abroad.

Canadian Commercial
Corporation
www.ccc.ca

Canadian Trade
Commissioner Service
www.infoexport.gc.ca

Royal Bank Small
Business Exporting
Guide
www.rbcroyalbank.
com/business/
definitiveguide/
exporting.html

Canadian Commercial Corporation (CCC). CCC is another Crown corporation that responds to requests from foreign governments and international agencies seeking Canadian goods and services by attempting to match those requests with suitable sources of supply.

Canadian International Development Agency (CIDA). CIDA is a federal government agency that administers Canada's development cooperation programs around the world, many of which employ private consultants, contractors, suppliers, and manufacturers in underdeveloped countries.

Department of Foreign Affairs and International Trade—Trade Commissioner Service. This referral service maintains an extended network of more than 134 trade offices around the world. Its primary focus is to assist Canadian companies seeking export markets. A directory of the trade offices throughout the world may be obtained through the Department of Foreign Affairs or the Department of Industry Canada. In addition, entrepreneur exporters who register with WIN Exports have free access to more than 600 market reports.

Forum for International Trade Training (FITT). This agency offers training for entrepreneurs in international trade.

Canadian Export Association (CEA). The CEA is a national nonprofit association concerned with improving the environment for Canadian exporters. It provides information, contacts, education, and lobbying support for exporters.

Export Clubs. Many cities have established export clubs that meet regularly to exchange ideas and information about exporting.

Provincial and Territorial Government Programs. Most provincial and territorial governments actively encourage exports and may offer specific incentive programs to assist in this regard. The Department of Industry, Trade and Commerce or its equivalent in each province or territory can provide information about their programs. In addition to the above, trade missions facilitate the creation of a large number of agreements.

As we have seen, considerable assistance is available for a prospective exporter. Addresses for the above agencies are given in Appendix 8A.

Unique Characteristics of the Foreign Market. A second requirement for success in exporting is to understand the peculiarities of the foreign market. Many companies experience difficulties in marketing internationally because they fail to obtain enough information about the various markets. Several of the agencies mentioned above can provide information to answer the questions listed in Figure 8-4.

Figure 8-4	**Key Questions for Developing a Foreign Marketing Strategy**

1. What needs does the product fill in this culture?
2. What products (if any) currently meet these needs?
3. What are the differences in the way the product is used (consumed)?
4. What are the characteristics of the consumers who will buy the product?
5. Can the consumers afford to purchase the product?
6. What are the political or legal restrictions to marketing the product?
7. How stable is the political situation in this country?
8. What are the distribution and media capabilities in the culture?
9. What language differences exist?
10. What nonverbal communications should be noted?
11. What information-collecting restrictions might exist?

Figure 8-5 illustrates the areas that in the past have constituted the greatest barriers to international markets. Additional analysis may be required in these areas. Incident 8-5 (on the next page) illustrates how one company was lucky enough to avoid the major barriers discussed.

Because of the volatile conditions existing in many countries and the implications of foreign exchange fluctuations, the entrepreneur will need to constantly monitor the conditions of the foreign market. Hedging is a way the entrepreneur can achieve foreign exchange protection.

Mechanisms of Exporting. The agencies discussed earlier can also provide information about the mechanisms of exporting. Some of the essential features of an exporting arrangement are as follows:

- *Documentation.* Contracts, invoices, permits, insurance, and bills of lading must be drafted or obtained.

- *Methods of credit offered.* Letters of credit, accounts receivable, and consignment sales are often a part of the process.

- *Physical distribution.* The type of shipment, transfer of title, and inspection points will have to be determined.

- *Channel of distribution.* Sales representatives, government agencies, export agents, and trading houses will need to be identified and contacted.

- *Security.* Export insurance and guarantees must be obtained.

| **Figure 8-5** | **Major Barriers to Success Abroad** |

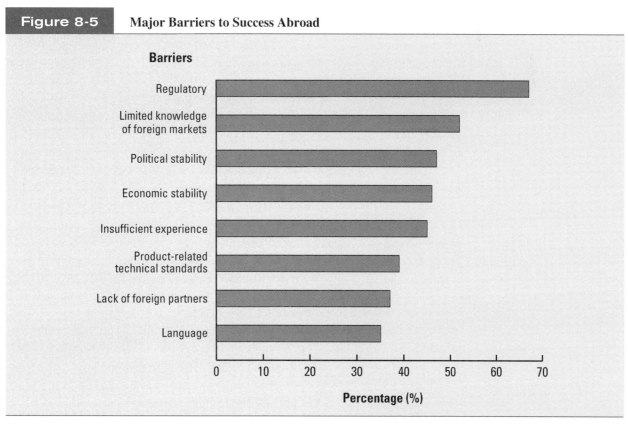

Source: First Annual Survey of Canadian Entrepreneurs as reported in *The Globe and Mail,* June 24, 1995, p. B7.

INCIDENT 8-5   Ani-Mat Inc.

Owners Rosaire Croteau and Ange-Albert Allard have a whole lot riding on recycled tires. Since its establishment in 1983, Ani-Mat Inc. has become a business that handles everything from manufacturing to installation of their rubber mat product line. Being in the right place at the right time, offering a low-cost, versatile product, and knowing how to make the most of a niche market have contributed greatly to the success of this Quebec-based company.

Specializing in rubber mats designed for animal comfort has been largely responsible for tripling Ani-Mat's sales in the past three years. Narrowing the company's focus, from tools that help increase farm animal productivity to the production of mats made from recycled rubber tires, permitted the exploitation of a niche market. Although Ani-Mat's niche marketing strategy has allowed them to target key clients in the dairy industry, the company's products have proved to be useful as protective arena coverings. Croteau and Allard attribute the majority of Ani-Mat's success to offering a turnkey product and service that has simplified the lives of their dairy farm clientele.

Ani-Mat's president forecasts a substantial sales increase in the next year. These ambitious figures are not going to be reached relying solely on the company's niche marketing strategy. In fact, Ani-Mat's past exponential growth has been due to its rapid exploitation of international markets. A Productivity Plus Loan from BDC enabled the upgrading of Ani-Mat's manufacturing equipment. This allowed the company to deliver more products faster and meet the large demand of U.S. clientele. Developing a sound export strategy was key to meeting international demand for Ani-Mat's products and services. Today, 50 percent of Ani-Mat's products are delivered to the United States and 10 percent to Europe.

Source: Adapted from "A Whole Lot Riding on Recycled Tires." *Profit*, Fall 2000, p. 3; and Ani-Mat Inc., *Annual Report*, July 10, 2004.

Because many of these items are complex, it is recommended that the entrepreneur seek assistance from the agencies mentioned earlier to ensure that he or she follows safe and proper procedures in carrying out the mechanics of exporting. Many Canadian exporters have found that one of the most effective ways to do business in another country is to strike a partnership with firms in that country.

A recent study by Neil Abramson of successful Canadian exporters to the United States found the following five factors being followed.[15] Successful Canadian exporters

1. *Are larger or appear larger.* According to Abramson, "Americans seem to prefer to do business with larger suppliers because the American buyers have a greater confidence that a larger suppler is more likely to remain in business." Some successful small companies in the researcher's survey had formed strategic alliances or joint ventures in order to appear larger or to have more product than their competitors.

2. *Have built effective relationships.* The ability to resolve conflicts, acquire trust, and develop shared goals results in higher overall performance and more effective channels of distribution in the United States. The less-successful smaller companies surveyed were not always noted for their conflict resolution skills. For example, the CEO of one company surveyed, convinced that the Canadian way of selling software was the only way, insisted that U.S.-based sales representatives take training on Canadian sales methods. When the U.S. sales manager's complaints that sales declined after each training program went unanswered, she tried, unsuccessfully, to have the CEO removed. The CEO closed the manager's sales office and began using a few local representatives. Sales fell off dramatically.

3. *Have sales and service offices in the United States.* Abramson's research found that transferring to the United States any R&D, manufacturing, marketing, sales, or service was related to higher gross sales. Transferring R&D was related to the greatest

increase in sales, and the companies that did so had 2.95 times the U.S. sales of the companies that did not.

4. *Have experience in the market.* More experience in the United States and more commitment to American markets was related to higher performance. However, the researcher notes that companies with negative U.S. experience were more likely to have negative views about American customers and were, therefore, less likely to commit themselves extensively to U.S. markets.

5. *Sell higher-priced products.* Products priced at the higher end of the scale were more likely to result in increased sales. "This may be because American customers equate higher prices with leading-edge products." Although Canadian customers seem to want "tried and true" products, their U.S. counterparts are looking for a competitive edge. "American customers were perceived to be fairly price insensitive when new innovations were available."

Incident 8-6 shows a company that has been successful by effectively developing export markets.

INFLUENCES EXTERNAL TO THE ORGANIZATION

In any market, several conditions exist that may have a significant impact on the small business but are outside the control of the owner of that business. Nevertheless, the owner-manager can do some things to effectively respond to these external influences:

- Identify which external conditions affect the business.

- Set up a system to continually monitor the relevant external influence(s). For the owner-manager, this might mean regularly obtaining reports, newsletters, and studies that contain up-to-date information on these conditions.

- Adjust internal operations to respond to changes in these external influences most effectively.

INCIDENT 8-6   Business, African Style

In a country where nothing is guaranteed, Iristel Inc. has proven its worth in providing long distance services to the Ivory Coast. Iristel Inc. is a wholesaler of Internet-based long distance capacity to Telecos in North America, Europe, and Africa. Providing service to a country where land lines are rare and long distance service is both unreliable and expensive requires more than just a willingness—it requires an open mind and flexibility with the African way of doing business.

Samar Bishay, president and CEO of Iristel faced his share of challenges in bringing the service to the Ivory Coast. Just prior to the launch of Iristel in Africa, a 1999 coup caused Iristel's much-needed government connections to flee the country. Bashay had to spend an entire year building new relationships in order to proceed. In Africa, it is not "what you know" but "who you know," so the firm had to enlist the help of bureaucrats and local business partners, which meant flying to the Ivory Coast for another year as business has to be done face-to-face, not over the phone. Bashay then had to pay "bonuses" to ensure his partners' cooperation. Bashay says that when dealing with another country, you must have a local partner who knows who to pay and how much, otherwise you will end up either overpaying or underpaying, with little assurance that the job will even get done. Bashay's flexibility has paid off, as Iristel has done so well in Africa they are now expanding into more countries.

Source: Adapted from "Business, African Style," *Profit*, Fall 2005, p.17.

Some of the most common external influences that can affect the small business and thus affect the information to be collected are the economy, the competition, legal restrictions, and the social and cultural environment.

The Economy. The state of the economy in the market area is a critical external condition. For most products and services, market demand is directly related to upturns and downturns in the economy. Small businesses often are able to react more quickly than large businesses to changes in the economy.

Competition. As mentioned in Chapter 1, a small business usually finds itself competing against larger firms over which it has no control. New technology used by competitors is another factor in assessing competition, especially in many growth industries. In some cases, the small business may gain competitive advantages because of its size. The North American Free Trade Agreement among Canada, the United States, and Mexico has not only opened up new markets for Canadian entrepreneurs but has also increased competition for Canadian businesses as U.S. companies continue to enter Canadian markets. These situations were also discussed in Chapter 1. By accurately identifying prospective competitors and their strengths as well as weaknesses, the entrepreneur can develop a more effective strategy. Attempts should be made to clearly identify the competitive advantage for the business. Many entrepreneurs have found that studying their competitor's website is a helpful resource in analyzing their strategy and future plans.

Legal Restrictions. This potential influence includes the laws and regulations with which the business is required to comply. The owner-manager should keep up to date with any legislation that might affect business operations.

Social and Cultural Environment. This factor encompasses trends in the culture in which the business operates that may affect demand. The culture may dictate norms that the population is generally hesitant to violate or suggest new growth industries that can be attractive opportunities.

Technology. New technology can be a significant factor in the success of a small business. Failure to recognize and adopt technology can spell disaster for the entrepreneur. Likewise, developing and utilizing it can be an important competitive edge.

Figure 8-6 illustrates how the owner of a small business can work with all these uncontrollable conditions.

DEVELOPING THE PRODUCT OR SERVICE

As we mentioned at the beginning of this chapter, the product or service to be offered should be designed to meet target market demand. To ensure responsiveness to consumer demand, the owner-manager should think of the product or service in terms of the ways and extent to which it satisfies consumer need. A prototype of the product should be prepared and tested with a representative sample of the market. This type of information should be collected before finalizing the production decision.

Some major decision areas about which the small business owner should be knowledgeable when developing a product strategy are discussed next.

Develop Product or Service Policies. Product policies should cover such items as quality level, product or service depth and width, packaging, branding, level of service, and warranties.

Decide How the Product Will Be Manufactured. For many small businesses, contracting with another firm to manufacture the product is advantageous. This may be an especially viable alternative during the early stages of a business, when the risk is usually higher.

| Figure 8-6 | Management of the External Influences | | |

External Influence	Possible Characteristic	System to Monitor	Possible Internal Adjustment
Economy	Inflation rate Unemployment level	Collect relevant government and industry reports regularly	Lower prices Increase advertising
Competition	Competitor strengths and weaknesses Competitor's use of new technology	Competitor's new products Competitor's reaction to your strategies	Product or service alterations Selection of specific target market
Legal	Laws affecting your business What changes in laws are pending	Regular receipt of legislative changes from government documents and industry reports	Product or service alterations Promotional changes
Social and cultural	Lifestyle trends Demographic studies Purchase patterns	Industry and government reports recording social statistics and purchases	New products or services Distribution channel changes Promotional themes and levels
Technology	Trends	New product reports Fast-growing company literature	Product alterations

Once the product has achieved market acceptance and the volume of production has increased, it may be more cost effective to acquire the manufacturing capability.

Understand the Product Life Cycle. All products and services have a life cycle, as Figure 8-7 on the next page shows. As the product moves from the introduction to the decline stage in its life cycle, the marketing strategy for the product and even for the business may also change. This means changes may be required in pricing, in distribution, in promotion, and even in the product or service. Knowing that the product or service has a life cycle helps the owner-manager plan for any necessary adjustments to the marketing strategy when the maturity stage is reached. Such modifications can help prolong the life cycle of the product or service. Strategies include the following:

- Appeal to a new target market.

- Adjust the product or service to meet changes in customer needs.

- Increase promotion to enhance frequency of purchases.

- Emphasize different uses or characteristics of the product or service.

- Offer a new product or service.

Product life cycles in many industries, notably the high-technology areas, are getting shorter. This has an impact on the long-term planning of the entrepreneur.

| Figure 8-7 | **Product Life Cycle** |

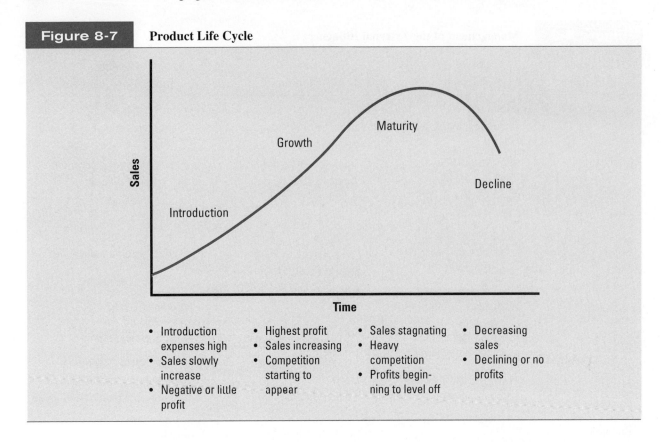

- Introduction expenses high
- Sales slowly increase
- Negative or little profit

- Highest profit
- Sales increasing
- Competition starting to appear

- Sales stagnating
- Heavy competition
- Profits beginning to level off

- Decreasing sales
- Declining or no profits

Determine Factors That May Accelerate Product or Service Adoption. Research shows that consumers generally adopt new products or services at different rates. Those who purchase first are the innovators or early adopters. These people often are the opinion leaders in a social group. The innovators and early adopters typically make up about 15 percent of the market, but they have a far greater influence because the rest of the market usually looks to this group before purchasing.[16]

After the small business owner has identified the innovators and early adopters within the target market, every attempt should be made to test market the product or service to that group first. If the early adopters accept the product or service, they may even do much of the initial promotion. Early adopters and opinion leaders also tend to be very vocal about the products and services they try and use. In addition, they tend to have higher income and educational levels, be more socially active, be more willing to take risks, and have greater exposure to printed media.

In addition to understanding the characteristics of innovators and early adopters, the small business owner should be aware of the factors that can speed up product adoption and attempt to capitalize on them. The following are some of the more important factors.

Relative Advantage. If the product or service appears to have a significant advantage over existing ones, and if this advantage can be communicated effectively, it is more likely to have a faster adoption.

Complexity. If the product or service is difficult to understand, the adoption rate is typically longer. In such a case, promotion should have an informational or educational content.

Divisibility. A product or service that can be purchased in small amounts with a minimum of social or financial risk usually has a quicker adoption rate.

Communicability of Results. If the results of using the product or service are quickly evident and easily communicated to others, its adoption will be more rapid.

In summary, the less risk associated with the purchase decision, the more rapid the adoption rate. The owner-manager therefore should do whatever is possible to reduce such risk when introducing a new product or service. Providing information and offering a guarantee or warranty as part of the purchase are commonly used methods for reducing risk.

Understand How the Consumer Classifies the Product or Service. Marketers use a standard classification system in categorizing consumer products. This system can be valuable in developing the marketing strategy for the small business. The classifications are as follows:

- *Convenience products.* Convenience products are purchased with minimal effort. They may be necessities, unplanned purchases, or emergency goods.

- *Shopping products.* Shopping products are purchased only after comparison with similar products. Comparisons may be made on the basis of price if competing products are viewed as similar or in terms of quality or style if competing products differ.

- *Specialty products.* Consumers have substantial brand or product loyalty with specialty products or services. As a result, they are willing to spend considerable effort to locate and purchase the brands and products they desire.

Figure 8-8 illustrates strategy implications for each of these classifications. The focus of the marketing strategy is determined by how the target consumer classifies the product or service.

Figure 8-8	**Strategy Implications for Product Classifications**		
Type of Product	**Price**	**Distribution**	**Promotion**
Convenience	Although usually lower priced goods, the markups tend to be high.	They should be located close to consumers, either in relation to where they live or within the store.	Promote availability. Use point-of-purchase displays for impulse goods.
	Within a certain range, price is not important to consumer.	Availability is important to the customer.	
Shopping	For similar products the price must be competitive, as consumers are price sensitive.	They should be located close to competing products to aid comparison.	Promote price advantage for similar products or quality/style advantage for dissimilar products.
	For dissimilar products that are still competitive, price is not as important to the consumer.		
Specialty	Within a certain range, price is not important to the customer.	Location is not important to the customer.	Promote the outlet that carries the product or or brand.

DEVELOPING THE DISTRIBUTION SYSTEM

Many entrepreneurs develop an excellent product but lack the knowledge about the best way to get it to the consumer. Such a situation is illustrated in Incident 8-7. An effective distribution system should provide the product or service to the right consumer, at the right place, at the right time, and in the right quantity.

The distribution channel is the path the product or service follows from the producer to the consumer. It includes the different organizations or individuals who will assist in this movement toward consumption.

The small business owner needs to address three main distribution decision areas: the type of channel to use, the length of the channel, and the number of distributors authorized to sell the product.

Channel Options

A small business can follow essentially two channel paths, although various combinations of these types of channels are possible.

Manufacturer to Consumer (Short-Direct Channel). This type of channel involves distributing the product or service directly to the consumer. The transportation and selling functions are carried out by the owner-manager or the sales staff. Often small businesses lack the financial capacity or expertise to hire and train their own sales forces.

Manufacturer to Wholesaler/Retailer to Consumer (Long-Indirect Channel). In this type of distribution channel, the wholesaler or retailer purchases the product and resells it to another channel member or to the consumer. The manufacturer assumes less risk with this method but generally has a lower profit margin and less control over the distribution. The small business may use this type of distribution channel by going to a retailer or wholesaler directly or visiting a tradeshow attended by these intermediaries. Many products receive their initial start from successful tradeshow experience.

INCIDENT 8-7   The Candy Men Can

Chris Emery and Larry Finnson, executives of Krave's Candy Co. and makers of the famous "Clodhoppers," know how to create a successful business. However, it was difficult getting retailers to buy their product in the beginning. Chris and Larry personally visited the buying offices of some of Canada's leading department and food stores, with limited success. Then contracts with Wal-Mart started the distribution ball rolling. Now that they've solidified Canadian distribution, the duo plans to expand and is now marketing their goods to the U.S. "We want to see (Krave's) as a global brand doing over $100 million in sales," Finnson explains.

Emery and Finnson have also set their sights on public relations to improve their business. The pair have become masters at gaining media coverage and free publicity. Krave's has received an inordinate amount of newspaper and magazine coverage during its brief history. Emery and Finnson also hope to notch a spot in *The Guinness Book of World Records* as they attempt to make a clodhopper as big as an average-size garage. The duo has also embraced the hip-hop culture by buying appropriate threads, footwear, toques, jewellery, and designer shades. They have recently bought a modified 1947 Chevrolet Fleetline hot rod which they tenderly call the "Clodhoppermobile."

Source: Adapted from David Menzies, "The Candy Men Can," *Marketing*, January 2005, p. 9.

Channel Length

The decision regarding channel length will depend on the concerns of the manufacturer mentioned above. It also involves examining the product and market characteristics listed in Figure 8-9.

Channel Intensity

Another channel decision is how many distributors/dealers will be allowed to sell the product. Generally speaking, products that require greater selling effort, seller knowledge, and sales expertise are best distributed through a more exclusive type of arrangement. Standardized or convenience-type products usually call for a more intensive channel system. Because product availability is important in such a system, many dealers are allowed to carry the product.

Multi-Level Marketing

An increasingly popular form of distribution channel used by small and large organizations is the multi-level system. In a typical multi-level marketing or network marketing arrangement, individuals associate with a parent company as an independent contractor or franchise and are compensated based on their sales of products or service, as well as sales achieved by the people they bring into the business. This type of selling is typically through personal contacts or at group social gatherings. Multi-level marketing organizations typically provide the entrepreneur with well-prepared training manuals and motivational meetings. The attractions of this type of marketing to the individual entrepreneur include flexibility, the ability to work from home, and the promise of high income. Careful evaluation of MLM's should

| Figure 8-9 | Deciding Channel Length |

Direct-Short Channel (Manufacturer to Consumer)	Indirect-Long Channel (Manufacturer to Wholesaler/Retailer to Consumer)
Implications for Manufacturer	
More expensive to set up	Cheaper to set up
Greater potential return	Least return
More risk	Less risk
More expertise needed	Less expertise needed
Product Characteristics	
Perishable	Standardized
Technical	Inexpensive
Large, bulky	Proven demand
Expensive	
Market Characteristics	
Geographically concentrated	Geographically dispersed
Low product awareness	High product awareness
Sales effort required	Less sales effort required

be carried out, however, because with many of these organizations, the promised income is never realized and some systems are illegal. More and more products and services have been added to multi-level marketing systems in recent years and expansion to the Internet has vastly increased the market average for organizations and entrepreneurs. Despite the potential difficulties, multi-level marketing may be an excellent distribution method for the entrepreneur.

SETTING THE PRICE FOR THE GOOD OR SERVICE

Another marketing strategy variable within the control of the owner-manager is the setting of price for the product or service. Pricing is a critical part of the marketing strategy; the small business cannot afford to make a pricing mistake in a competitive industry.

To approach price setting effectively, one must understand the factors that affect prices. These factors can be classified as either external or internal. External influences, as discussed earlier, include the state of the economy in the market area, the extent of competition, possible legal restrictions, cultural or societal attitudes toward certain price levels, and target market demand. Typical internal influences on pricing policy are internal costs, the firm's long-run objectives, and pricing policies as set by the owner-manager.

In setting price levels for the product or service, one may find that some of these factors are more influential than others. As a result, businesses use three general bases for price setting that take these influences into account: cost, demand, and competition.

Cost-Based Pricing

In cost-based pricing, the major influence is the cost of producing the product for the manufacturer, of purchasing and selling the product for the retailer, and of providing the service for the service firm (internal influence). Figure 8-10 illustrates the use of cost-based pricing in each of these types of business.

Once the costs have been determined, a percentage markup is added to reflect the profit objective of the firm. The owner-manager should realize, however, that the initial markup is seldom achieved. Markdowns and inventory shrinkage should be estimated (see Figure 8-10) and built into the markup calculation.

Demand-Based Pricing

Demand-based pricing uses consumer sensitivity to price as the major factor in arriving at the final price level (external influences). Usually primary research in the form of surveying will be required to assess acceptable prices for new products. Figure 8-11 on page 246 illustrates the results of such a survey incorporated into a demand curve. Each point on the line shows the quantity demanded at the related price. For example, at a price of $30, demand would be 10 units; at $20, demand increases to 16 units. In this example, the total revenue at the $30 price is $300 (30 × 10), whereas at $20 the total revenue is $320 (20 × 16). This situation can be described as price elastic. In price-elastic situations, price increases result in a negative effect on demand. For some types of products (convenience and specialty) and some industries (those with little direct competition), price may be less important to the purchaser, and thus a change in price may not significantly affect demand. If this condition exists, it means the business has much more freedom and flexibility in setting prices than it would in a more competitive and price-sensitive situation.

Figure 8-10	**Cost-Based Pricing Methods**

Manufacturing Firm

Direct material cost per unit	$ 18.00
Direct labour cost per unit	21.00
Variable overhead (manufacturing)	10.00
Fixed overhead (factory)	30.00
Total manufacturing cost per unit	79.00
Selling cost per unit	3.00
General overhead (allocated per unit)	5.00
Total cost per unit	87.00
Desired profit	13.00
Selling price	$100.00

Retail Firm

Cost of merchandise	$ 50.00
Selling and storage (estimated)	20.00
Estimated markdowns	5.00
Desired profit	25.00
Selling price	$100.00

In retailing, the difference between the price and the cost of inventory is known as *markup*. In this example, it is $50 and is usually expressed as a percentage in the following manner:

$$\text{Percentage} = \frac{100 - 50}{100} = 50\%$$

Service Firm

Estimated cost of providing service per customer	$ 60.00
Estimated overhead costs per customer	20.00
Desired profit per customer	20.00
Selling price	$100.00

For products and services already on the market, existing price levels and industry experts may provide valuable information to assist in setting demand-based prices.

Competition-Based Pricing

Firms in a growing number of industries are using competitive pricing in which the major considerations in setting prices are the price levels and policies of competitors (external influences). Many firms conduct ongoing price checks on the competition to guide their own pricing. The small firm may want to set prices at a fixed percentage above, equal to, or below competitors' prices.

The small business owner should not rely too heavily on only one of the above methods of pricing. All these methods are important in most industries, and each should be taken into account when setting the final price for a product or service.

| Figure 8-11 | **Consumer Price Sensitivity: Demand Pricing** |

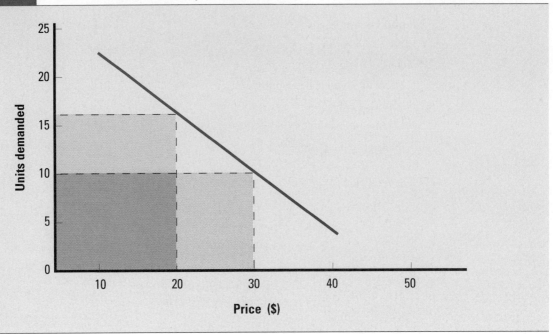

PROMOTION

Gone are the days of the philosophy "build a better mousetrap and the world will beat a path to your door." Today most businesses must actively provide information to the purchaser. For the entrepreneur, finding low-cost but effective ways to promote the business or product is a challenge. Knowledge of the options and the use of creativity can help stretch the promotional dollar. Examples of these options are described below.

Types of Promotion

A small business can use essentially four methods to provide information about its product or service: advertising, sales promotions, public relations, and personal selling.

Advertising. Advertising is a nonpersonal form of promotion. It is directed at a mass audience through various forms of media such as television, radio, newspapers, magazines, billboards, the Internet, and direct mail. A small business owner should be aware of the strengths and weaknesses of each of these types of media and exactly when each is appropriate. This information is presented in Figure 8-12. One of the most rapidly growing vehicles for small business advertising is through the Internet. Recent surveys carried out by the Canadian Federation of Independent Business and Deloitte and Touche found that an increasing number of small business owners used the Internet regularly.[17] The Advertising Bureau of Canada estimated that online ad sales in Canada for 2006 are over $800 million and predicts increases of 40–50 percent per year.[18] The Internet is not only an effective means of advertising but also an excellent tool for securing customer feedback. More will be discussed about small business and the Internet in the next chapter.

Because the small business typically does not have a lot of money to spend on advertising, it is important that the entrepreneur find effective ways to promote the business economically. Co-op and shared advertising are two ways of doing this.

Canadian Federation of
Independent Business
www.cfib.ca

| Figure 8-12 | Advertising for Small Business | | | |

Media Type	Advantages	Disadvantages	Particular Suitability	Typical Costs
Newspapers	Flexible Timely Local market Credible source	May be expensive Short life Little "pass along" Nonselective audience	All general retailers or for definable market areas similar to circulation	One-page ad: large market ($1,800–$3,000) small market ($500–$800) (prices dependent on length of contract)
Television	Sight, sound, and motion Wide reach	Cost Clutter Short exposure Less selective	Definable market area surrounding the station's location for certain products	30 seconds of prime time: large local market ($750–$1000) small local market ($200–$300)
Direct mail	Selected audience Personalization Flexible	Relatively expensive per contact High "throwout" rate	New and expanding businesses; those using coupon returns or catalogues	Approximately $1 per contact
Radio	Wide reach Segmented audience Inexpensive	Audio only Weak attention Short exposure	Business catering to identifiable groups: teens, commuters, housewives	30 seconds of prime time: large local market ($175–$250) small local market ($35–$60)
Magazines, including trade publications and catalogues	Very segmented audience Credible source Good reproduction Long life Good "pass along"	Inflexible Long lead times Costly	Restaurants Entertainment Identifiable target markets Mail order Chains	Approximately $30,000 for one-page, four- colour ad in *Chatelaine* (French and English)
Outdoor	Flexible Repeat exposure Inexpensive	Mass market Very short exposure	Amusements Tourist businesses Brand name retailers	One month of prime location billboard, large market ($2,500–$3,000)
Telephone directories	Users in market for goods or services Continuous ads Costs relatively low	Limited to active shoppers Limited visibility Not dynamic	Services Retailers of brand name items Highly specialized retailers	Inexpensive— depends on size of ad
Internet	Inexpensive Requires computer hardware and expertise	Limited market (but growing) Can't see and try Lack of privacy Viruses	Products that do not require trial Information products	"Sign on" fee varies by type of ad
Tradeshows	Many buyers High exposure Time saving	Cost	Product sold in chain stores	Varies

With co-op advertising, the manufacturing company shares the cost of advertising with the small retailer, if the retailer features the manufacturer's products in those ads. Both the manufacturer and the retailer get more advertising per dollar by sharing expenses. Co-op advertising is used most frequently by small retailers, but unfortunately, many small retailers do not take advantage of this type of assistance.

In shared advertising, a group of similar businesses forms a syndicate to produce generic ads that allow the individual businesses to dub in local information. This technique is especially suitable for small businesses that sell relatively standardized products or services. The result of this form of advertising is higher quality ads and significantly lower production costs.

Sales Promotions. Sales promotions are also nonpersonal forms of promotion but are directed at a much more restricted audience than is advertising. Examples of sales promotions are point-of-purchase displays, coupons and discounts, tradeshows and exhibitions, and contests. The tradeshow may be an especially cost-effective method of promotion for the small business. Research indicates that more than 80 percent of visitors at tradeshows are decision makers and more than 60 percent plan to make a purchase.[19] All these mechanisms are very effective forms of advertising for the small business, and some are relatively inexpensive.

Public Relations. Public relations, or publicity, can be a very effective form of promotion for the small business. This is particularly the case when the product or service is innovative or extraordinary in some way. The profile at the beginning of this chapter illustrates how Spin Master Toys was successful in utilizing public relations to launch new products. This form of promotion may involve public-interest news stories, publishing a newsletter, involving celebrities, interviews with the media, sponsorship by the business of community projects such as sporting teams or events, or specialty advertising such as calendars, pens, hats, and the like. Public relations is generally inexpensive and can be very helpful in promoting not only the product or service but the business itself. Incident 8-8 illustrates the successful use of public relations.

Personal Selling. The conditions conducive to a short distribution channel or an emphasis on personal selling are discussed earlier in this chapter. Most businesses will require some

---

INCIDENT 8-8   How To Get On Oprah

Brian Scudamore, founder and CEO of 1-800-GOT-JUNK, had always wanted to be on the Oprah show so he made being on her show a company goal. Eighteen months later, and after sending numerous emails to Oprah producers, GOT-JUNK finally got the call. Scudamore was thrilled, and even more thrilled with the results. The day after the program aired, the firm fielded 3,000 calls, about 300 percent more than usual, and over the next few months, over 500 franchise inquiries followed.

Clearly, the fact that having a well-known talk show host gush about your business to people in 105 countries helps the growth of your firm. However, Scudamore also found other ways to spread publicity. During the Vancouver Canucks' 2002 playoff run, GOT-JUNK distributed 1,000 blue clown wigs to spectators. This brought the company a lot of media attention and they became known as "the blue-wig guys."

In 2003, GOT-JUNK scored at least 340 media hits in North America. System-wide revenue climbed from $10 million in 2002 up to $17 million in 2003 and is now expected to reach $32 million in 2004.

Source: Adapted from Susanne Baillie, "How To Get On Oprah," *Profit*, March 2004, pp. 77–79.

personal selling as part of their marketing strategy. Owner-managers will undoubtedly be required to promote themselves, their businesses, and their products to customers, bankers, suppliers, and government agencies through personal selling. If salespeople are employed, they will need to be trained, not only with respect to product or service knowledge, but also in selling skills. Other aspects of training, supervision, and motivation of a sales force are discussed in detail in Chapter 12. A type of personal selling that is significant for small business is the use of direct marketing. Common methods of direct marketing are mail, phone, cable television, and the Internet. Blogs, as discussed in Chapters 3 and 9, have become increasingly used as informal personal selling tools by many entrepreneurs to market products and services.

STEPS IN A PROMOTIONAL CAMPAIGN

How does the owner-manager prepare the promotional program for the product, service, or business? The following are the essential steps in carrying out a promotional program that can be used as a guide for the small business.

1. Set promotional objectives. Specific objectives should be set before the promotion. Typical examples are the desired percentage increase in sales, the amount of traffic to be generated, and the percentage of awareness increase desired.

2. Determine the target of the promotion. Although in many cases the target will be the ultimate consumer, often it will be an intermediary in the distribution channel or another group that has considerable influence over the purchase.

3. Understand the target's needs and perceptions of the product or service. Once the target of the promotion has been determined, it is essential that information be gathered about members of that group with regard to their needs, media habits, and perceptions of the product category or specific product or service. This information is very similar to the consumer profile discussed earlier.

4. Develop the relevant theme. The next step is to develop a theme for the promotion that will reflect responsiveness to target needs and perceptions and help achieve the promotional objective. It is important that only one theme be used, since too many themes or too much information can confuse the consumer and lead to unsatisfactory results. Research has shown that the most important factor in the success of a small business is to promote credibility.[20]

5. Determine the method or media to use. The decision about which promotional type to use often depends on the relative importance of creating awareness or closing the sale. Figure 8-13 lists the strengths of each previously mentioned type of promotion with respect to these purposes. As the figure illustrates, advertising, public relations, and some sales promotions tend to be more effective in creating awareness, whereas personal selling tends to work better for achieving or closing the sale.

6. Develop a specific promotional message. Once the theme and medium have been determined, it is possible to develop the specific type of message to be used. As Figure 8-13 points out, some types of information are not appropriate for certain types of media. Care should be taken to ensure that the benefits of the product are clearly communicated.

7. Set the promotional budget. Once the method of promotion is determined, it is possible to estimate the cost of the promotion. Several methods are used to determine amounts to spend on promotion. The most common approach is the percent of sales method.

Figure 8-13	Effectiveness of Promotion Types

	Personal Selling	Sales Promotions	Public Relations	Advertising
Create awareness of product or business	Weak	Weak	Strong	Strong
Develop interest in product	Weak	Medium	Weak	Strong
Increase desire to purchase product	Medium	Medium	Weak	Medium
Achieve product purchase	Strong	Medium	Weak	Weak

Standard percentages for various businesses can serve as a guide in using this method. (See Appendix 8A for examples.) The percent of sales method is theoretically weak but simple to apply, which explains its high rate of use by small businesses. A business owner should remain flexible in using these percentages, however, as market and product conditions may necessitate a deviation from the averages.

8. Implement the promotional program. An essential feature of implementing the program is proper timing. Certain times of the year, the week, and even the day may be inappropriate for promoting the product or service to the target market.

9. Evaluate the effectiveness of the promotion. The owner-manager should attempt to evaluate the promotional effectiveness to aid in future promotions. Evaluating effectiveness is much easier if specific objectives such as those mentioned earlier are set. Observations of results and surveys may be used in this evaluation. The mechanics of using primary research methods were discussed in Chapter 3.

As this chapter illustrates, many aspects are involved in the marketing plan of a small business. The way all these aspects are integrated so that they compose a clear and coordinated strategy often spells the difference between a successful and an unsuccessful business. Appendix 8B at the conclusion of this chapter provides a marketing plan checklist.

CUSTOMER RELATIONSHIP MANAGEMENT FOR THE SMALL BUSINESS

This chapter has illustrated the importance of the consumer to the success of an organization. Throughout the process of identifying the target consumer and developing an effective strategy the relationship that the organization develops and maintains with the consumer is of prime importance. As more organizations realize the value of this, greater emphasis has been placed on customer relationship management (CRM). Although effective CRM systems tend to be technology dependant, reduction of technology costs are allowing more and more small businesses to also integrate such systems.

Customer Relationship Management is defined as a marketing method in which business consistently maintains two way communication with their prospective, current and inactive customers in order to gain a deeper understanding of their needs while delivering personal and compelling marketing throughout their lifecycle. Increasingly small businesses are using CRM techniques to be more successful and to obtain a competitive advantage in their market.

The Database Information System

A critical part of most effective CRM's is the development of a database information system focused on the consumer. The emergence of database marketing is based on the premise that past behaviour is the best indicator of future purchase patterns. The increase in computer power and storage capabilities coupled with decreasing costs now enables organizations to deal directly with customers on an individual level.

Database Marketing for the Small Business

A customer database is an organized collection of comprehensive data about individual customers or prospects, including geographic, demographic, psychographic, and behavioural data. The database can be used to locate good potential customers, tailor products and services to the special needs of targeted consumers, and maintain long-term customer relationships. Database marketing is the process of building, maintaining, and using customer databases and other databases (products, suppliers, resellers) for the purpose of contacting and transacting with customers. (See Incident 8-9.)

A small business can use databases for both business-to-business as well as business-to-consumer marketing. In business-to-business marketing, the salesperson's customer profile may contain such information as the products and services the customer has bought, past volumes and prices, key contacts, competitive suppliers, status of current contracts, estimated customer expenditures for the next few years, and assessments of competitive strengths and weaknesses in selling and serving the account. In consumer marketing, the customer database may contain a customer's demographics, buying behaviour, and other relevant information. Several simple and inexpensive database software programs are now available to assist small businesses in being more responsive to their customers.

INCIDENT 8-9   Kinder, Gentler Software

Want to know your customers better? Want to keep your customers coming back? Putting all your client data in one place and focusing marketing so that you never forget another birthday has now been made available through increased customer relationship management technology. In the late 1990s, CRM came out as a new tool to track every interaction with your customer through centralized data processing and powerful software. However, these CRM software solutions proved costly and complex. Today, big players such as Siebel, SAP, and Oracle are breathing life back into the CRM. These companies are introducing more molecular technology aimed at specific sectors and smaller businesses. It takes both time and money to find the perfect CRM technology to meet the needs of your company but such a solution has been proven to retain customers, boost sales, and reduce costs.

Another new technology that has allowed for increased customer service is wireless salesforce automation. These powerful wireless "smart" phones and handhelds can do almost as much as a notebook computer as they deploy fast and secure wireless data networks. FingertipWare president Tim Grimes says, "It's about having customer information and product data always available. You provide more service to your customers, and you close more business."

Source: Adapted from Rick Spence, "Growth by Technology," *Profit*, December 2004, pp. 54–60.

There are five steps in developing a database information system.

1. Begin with the customer information that the organization already has. Such information might include sales records, requests for information, credit files, and other customer data.

2. The next step is to obtain more information. The might be received through warranty cards, surveys, mail-in coupons, rebates and contests. One caution regarding the collection and use of information to be used in a database has to do with privacy issues. Customers may be unwilling to provide sensitive information and may object to this information being supplied to others. Care should be taken in obtaining information and permission should be sought for this information to be shared with other organizations.

3. Organizations may be able to supplement this data by accessing information available from a variety of public and private sources. Government, and private market studies may profile different types of consumers and their purchase behaviours. Other data bases might be obtained from credit card companies and banks.

4. The organization must then process the information. The acquisition of a data base software system will be required. There are now a number or inexpensive systems available or the business may need to have a customized model developed to suit its purposes. Such a system should allow the business to see the relationship between the data and the behaviour of the customer.

5. The last step in the development of a database system is to use the data to develop a highly specific profile of the company's customers.

Applications of Customer Relationship Management and Databases

There are four applications of CRM and Databases for the small business. Each will be discussed briefly below.

1. *Nurture The Customer*—Much has already been said in this chapter about the importance of this. Database management can be used to identify the target market and obtain their loyalty. Creating a detailed profile on each customer is viewed as a method of establishing a collective memory that recreates the close relationship with customers. In this way the profile can be used to target new customers for the business's products or identify potential customers in partnership with other businesses where cross promotions might be effective.

   Once this has been done a dialogue can be initiated with prospective customers through surveys requesting their suggestions, advertising, and other direct contacts. It is important that the business let customers know that they are not mere targets but also valuable business assets. They require nurturing and investment over time and the information database allows this to occur.

2. *Grow The Customer*—Most businesses realize that satisfied customers become more profitable for the organization over time. Therefore as the customer is nurtured and becomes more loyal the business should use the CRM to solidify and expand the relationship. Databases allow businesses to recommend additional products or services to customers based upon their past purchase behaviour. Notification of events, inventory clearances, and price reductions are also ways of capitalizing on the customer relationship.

3. *Retain The Customer*—Many of the above mentioned suggestions can also increase retention of the customer.

One of the most critical keys to the success of the small business is retaining its customers. (See Incident 8-10.) An increasing number of organizations are realizing that the cost is much higher to attract a new customer than to retain an existing one. As a result, expenditures for customer retention activities have now surpassed expenditures on customer attraction in North America.[21] The entrepreneur needs to identify the reasons why customers do not return to their business, and then work to rectify problems that contribute to loss of patronage. Marketing studies show that the perceptions of those who have a high level of satisfaction with a business only have a loyalty rate of 40 percent or less.[22] Several studies show that by far the most common reason given for a customer terminating business with a company is because of a negative experience with, or bad attitude of, a staff person.[23] Furthermore, North American business, in general, is not given a very positive evaluation in the area of customer service. This problem is even more serious for a small business because of the small customer pool available to the business. In addition, when a current customer switches to a competitor because of poor service, the business not only loses that person's sales but also additional sales of those that this person influences. It is a well-known fact that customers tell more people about a bad experience that they have had with a business than they do about a good experience.

The small business should have a natural advantage over large businesses in the area of customer service and retention because of the ability to develop a more personal relationship with the customer. Many large businesses, in their attempts to increase volume of sales, simply cannot provide the level of service that a small business can. This is because service tends to be individualized and time consuming to provide. The small business needs to remember that in most situations the offering of excellent service is what will set it apart from large business and provide an important competitive advantage.

In order to provide effective customer service and retention, the small business should do the following:

- Identify the types of service to offer. These service activities, of course, should be tailored to the needs of the target market of the business.

INCIDENT 8-10   All in the Family

Olivier Soapery has created a unique family approach to business from the beginning. The New Brunswick-based company manufactures eco-skincare that combines the therapeutic properties of essential oils, traditional soap making, the history of olive oils, and the science of plants and flowers to create biodegradable long-lasting skin care products.

Isabel Gagné, founder and president of the company, believes that the secret of a successful business lies in creating long-lasting relationships with customers. Her family approach to selling is what makes her business different than others. "Whenever you call, you get a real live person and never a machine. And that's fundamental to my company," Gagné says. The firm sells quality products through retail stores, a company website, a comprehensive distribution network, and through loyal clients.

Source: Adapted from "All In the Family," *BDC Success Stories*, p. 3.

- To provide effective service, the business needs to budget adequate funds for this activity. Employee training, guarantees, and other service activities will require a financial investment.

- The small business should be sure to handle customer concerns and complaints effectively. Research has shown that if a business handles a complaint quickly and satisfactorily, 70 to 95 percent of customers will continue to patronize the business.

- It is important that the service level does not disappoint the consumer. Although the business may need to advertise the service, many have found the the best policy is to provide better service than their customers expect. Christine Magee, founder of Sleep Country Canada, reflects this point of view. "When a customer comes in the door, we want to exceed their expectations."[24]

- The chances of retaining a customer primarily depend on the level of satisfaction received through the experience with the business. Specific activities that can be utilized to increase the chances of satisfaction are quality products and services, rebates and rewards, follow up contacts and thank-yous, requests for suggestions, and guarantees.

- Any program such as for customer service and retention should be regularly evaluated to ensure its effectiveness and that it meets the needs of customers.

4. *Win Customers Back*—Contrary to common belief, it is more likely that a lost customer can be won back than it is that a new customer will be obtained. Many customers change patronage from a business for no apparent reason. The small business may be able to utilize the database system to achieve success in this area by: evaluating the value of the lost customer, attempting to understand reasons the customer left, improve on attributes most valued by these people if possible, track the competitors, offer an enticement to return and stay in touch with this customer.

Summary

1. Marketing activities include defining the target customer's needs and wants, monitoring the relevant outside influences, developing the product or service, selecting the channel of distribution, setting the price, and developing the promotional program.

2. The three types of target markets a small business may attempt to reach are consumer markets, industrial markets, and export markets. It is important that the entrepreneur identify the needs of the target market in developing the marketing strategy.

3. Some of the most common external influences affecting the small business are the economy, the competition, legal restrictions, and the social and cultural environment. In dealing with external influences, the owner-manager must identify which external conditions affect the business and then set up a system to monitor and effectively respond to changes in those influences.

4. The classifications of consumer goods include convenience, shopping, and specialty goods. The marketing strategy will differ for each type. The major decision areas in distribution include being aware of the channel options, deciding on the length of the channel, and determining the channel intensity. The three methods of setting price are cost-based, demand-based, and competition-based pricing. There are four methods of providing information about a product or service: advertising, sales promotion, public relations, and personal selling.

Chapter Problems and Applications

1. Define the target market for the business in Incident 8-2. What are the target market demographics, lifestyle characteristics, purchase characteristics, and purchase motivations (see Figure 8-2)?

2. Illustrate how Ani-Mat Inc. (Incident 8-5) developed an export market in comparison to the three steps outlined in the chapter.

3. Discuss the uncontrollable variables that might affect Digigraph Systems Ltd. (Incident 8-4) in the development of its overseas markets.

4. Develop a marketing mix (i.e., product, promotion, price, distribution) for a bakery.

5. Where is Kellogg's Corn Flakes in the product life cycle? What has Kellogg done to prolong the life cycle of this product?

6. What could a new cereal company do to speed up the adoption rate for its cereals?

7. How would you classify the following products (see Figure 8-8)? How would you promote and distribute these products? Explain.
   a. Discount clothes
   b. Quality furniture
   c. Chocolate bar
   d. Bread

8. How can Kraves Candy Co. (Incident 8-7) develop an effective distribution system?

9. Which pricing system would you use for the following products? Why?
   a. Campbell's Soup
   b. Toronto Blue Jays season tickets
   c. Patio furniture
   d. Automobiles

10. If the cost of merchandise is $100 and it is sold for $150, what is the markup on cost? on selling price?

11. You have been approached to develop an advertising campaign for a new local discount golf franchise. The owners realize they need to develop awareness among consumers but have a very limited amount of funds available for advertising. Using Figure 8-12 as a guide, decide which media type to use for the advertising campaign. Justify your decision to use or not use each media type.

12. Interview a local small business owner and find out what his or her marketing strategy is. Determine the promotional strategy. Are these strategies similar to those discussed in the chapter?

13. Segmentation is the process of breaking a population down into smaller groups. Is it possible for a small business to oversegment? How might that be detrimental to the success of the business?

Web Exercise

Using the website for Spin Master Toys, develop a marketing plan for one of this company's new products.

www.spinmaster.com

APPENDIX 8A

Advertising as Practised by Selected Small Businesses

Type of Business	Average Ad Budget (percent of sales)	Favourite Media	Other Media Used
Gift stores	2.2	Weekly newspapers	Yellow Pages, radio, direct mail, magazines
Hairdressing shops	2.0–5.0	Yellow Pages	Newspapers (for special events), word of mouth
Home furnishing stores	1.0–3.2	Newspapers	Direct mail, radio
Pet shops	2.0–5.0	Yellow Pages	Window displays, shopper newspapers, direct mail
Restaurants and food services	0.3–3.2	Newspapers, radio, Yellow Pages, transit, outdoor	Television for chain or franchise restaurants
Shoe stores	0.5–0.8	Newspapers, direct mail, radio	Yellow Pages (especially for specialty shoe vendors)
Bars and cocktail lounges	1.0–1.2	Newspapers (entertainment section), local magazines, tourist bulletins	Specialties
Bookstores	1.5–1.6	Newspapers, shoppers, Yellow Pages	Direct mail
Building maintenance services		Direct mail, door-to-door, Yellow Pages	Signs on company vehicles and equipment
Camera shops (independent)	2.0–3.5	Direct mail, handouts, Yellow Pages	Newspapers (except large urban)
Drugstores (independent)	1.0–3.0	Local newspapers, shoppers	Direct mail (list from prescription files)
Dry cleaning plants	0.9–2.0	Local newspapers, shoppers, Yellow Pages	Store front ads, pamphlets on clothes care
Equipment rental services	1.7–4.7	Yellow Pages	

Sources: Adapted from Dennis H. Tootelian and Ralph M. Gaedeke, *Small Business Review* (Sacramento, Calif.: Goodyear Publishing Company), pp. 154–155; and Dun and Bradstreet Operating Statistics, (Toronto: Dun and Bradstreet).

APPENDIX 8B

Checklist for a Marketing Plan

The Target Market

1. Has the target market been clearly defined geographically?
2. Has the target consumer been clearly identified?
3. What are the target consumer's characteristics—age, income, education, occupation?
4. What are the target consumer's lifestyle characteristics—activities, interests, opinions, media habits, personalities?
5. What are the target consumer's purchase characteristics—what, when, where, how much of the product or service does he or she purchase?
6. What are the reasons the target consumer purchases the product?
7. Are there any government programs that can assist in marketing to the target consumer?

The Environment

1. What economic forces will affect the business?
2. What is the competitive situation? How many competitors? What are relative market shares? What is the nature of competitors' strategies? What are competitors' strengths and weaknesses?
3. What legal restrictions will affect the marketing of the product or service?
4. Are there any social or cultural trends that will affect the business?
5. What adjustments have been made to accommodate any of the above environmental constraints?

The Product

1. What are the objectives and policies for the product?
2. How will the product be manufactured?
3. What is the estimated length of the life cycle for the product?
4. What can be done to increase the rate of adoption of the product?
5. How does the target consumer classify the product?
6. What will be the product quality, depth, and variety?
7. What warranty and service standards will be set?
8. Does the product or service possess the features or characteristics the target consumer wants?

Distribution

1. What channel options are available to reach the target consumer?
2. Can the product be marketed better through a short-direct channel or a long-indirect channel?

3. Who are potential buyers for the product?

4. What tradeshows exist for the industry?

5. What level of intensity should exist in the distribution channel?

6. Will the selected distribution channel provide the product to the target consumer at the right place, at the right time, and in the right quantities?

Price

1. What price policies have been set?

2. What price is the target consumer willing to pay?

3. How important is price to the target consumer?

4. What levels of markup are required to cover selling and overhead costs?

5. What are competitors' prices, and how do they compare with our product price?

Promotion

1. What are the objectives of the promotional program?

2. Does the theme reflect the target consumer's needs and attitudes?

3. What specific media will be selected to carry the message to the target consumer?

4. Does the product require personal selling?

5. How much will be spent on promotion?

6. What is the timing of the promotional program? Has a calendar timetable been prepared for this?

7. How will the results of the promotion be evaluated?

8. Will the business offer credit to the target consumer? If so, what procedures will be followed to screen, monitor, and collect accounts?

Suggested Readings

Buskirk, Bruce, and Molly Lavik. *Entrepreneurial Marketing*. Mason, Ohio: Thomson Learning, 2004.

Canada Business website—information on small business marketing and exporting— www.canadabusiness.gc.ca

Canadian Manufacturers and Exporters website—http://www.cme-mec.ca/

Carroll, Jim. *Opportunities for Canadian Business*. Scarborough, Ont.: Prentice-Hall, 1995.

"Customer Service Strategies That Get Results," Business D.C. Newsletter—March, 2006— www.bdc.ca

"Cut Through The Clutter." *Profit*, March 2003, p. 24.

Davidson, Hillary. "Why Canadians Can't Market." *Profit*, April, 2001, pp. 18–22.

Foot, David, and Daniel Stoffman. *Boom, Bust, and Echo 2000: Profiting from the Demographic Shift in the New Millennium*. Toronto: MacFarlane, Walter and Ross, 1998.

Freedman, David H. "Can You Survive The E-Bay Economy?" *Inc. Magazine*, March 2000.

International Trade Canada website—www.international.gc.ca/menu.asp

Lewis, Herschell Gordon, and Robert D. Lewis. *Selling On The Net—The Complete Guide.* Lincolnwood, Ill.: NTC Business Books, 1996.

Marketing Entrepreneur website—www.marketing.entrepreneur.com

Roadmap to Exporting (2nd ed.). Ottawa: Government of Canada, 2000.

Statistics Canada. Assistance For Surveying: http://www.statcan.ca/english/edu/power/toc/contents.htm

Team Canada Inc. *A Step-by-Step Guide to Exporting.* Ottawa: Government of Canada, 1999.

Ward, Susan. "4 Ways To Provide Customer Service That Outshines Your Competitors"—Small Business Canada: August 14, 2006—http://sbinfocanada.about.com/cs/marketing

Comprehensive Case   *Sid Stevens: Part 5*

Although Sid was discouraged by his encounter at the bank, he was successful in securing more equity from Suzie's parents ($20,000), and the bank counted the land that the factory would be built on as having a value of $50,000, which was also treated as equity. These adjustments allowed Sid to obtain the financing to at least get started with the construction of the building to make the Ladder Rail. He received a 10-year loan of $130,000 with an interest rate of 8 percent and payments due annually.

One concern expressed by the banker in their discussions was that Sid needed to be sure that the positive comments he had received about the Ladder Rail were shared by potential customers. He suggested that Sid obtain some sales orders before he advanced all the funds that Sid had requested.

Sid was not sure which would be the best way to market the product. He had thought about selling the Ladder Rail door to door but was unsure of how many salespeople he would need and whether the product would sell well in this manner. He also thought of advertising in the newspaper or television and selling the Ladder Rail from his manufacturing plant. He could always do a direct mailing of brochures. He could visit hardware tradeshows and try to sell the ladder to contractors or even ladder manufacturers.

The option that he felt would be the best was to sell the Ladder Rail to retail hardware chains. He felt that this would provide better market coverage for the least amount of effort and expertise. He therefore visited the buying offices for one regional and one national chain of hardware stores with some samples of the Ladder Rail. At these visits, Sid learned that the buyers thought the product had promise but that he would have to package it more professionally for their stores. They were not interested in using his homemade display unit. He also learned that although they thought his retail price of $40 was reasonable, they would only pay Sid $30 as they needed to make a profit on the merchandise that they sold. Sid was disappointed with this turn of events and went home very discouraged. "I've done all this work to develop the Ladder Rail and if I market it through the hardware stores I will hardly make any money," he lamented to Suzie.

Suzie suggested that he try marketing to firms in the United States. "It is a much larger market. I'm sure that companies down there would be more positive about the Ladder Rail," was Suzie's conclusion.

Sid was facing a dilemma. He was not sure which was the best way to market the Ladder Rail. The construction of the manufacturing plant was proceeding. However, to receive the remainder of the funding from the bank, he needed confirmed orders for the Ladder Rail.

Questions

1. Evaluate Sid's marketing options. Which distribution channel would you recommend?
2. What aspects about the product has he overlooked?
3. How can he solve the pricing dilemma should he decide to proceed with the hardware chains?
4. If he decided to export to the United States, what aspects should be explored?

CHAPTER 9

Small Business and Electronic Commerce

CHAPTER OBJECTIVES

- To explain what electronic commerce is and how a small business can utilize it

- To identify the forms electronic commerce can take

- To describe the advantages of electronic commerce to a small business

- To discuss the potential difficulties associated with establishing electronic commerce

- To describe how to construct an electronic commerce website, select a web host, and attract customers to it

- To discuss recent innovations in web tools

- To discuss ways to advertise on the web

SMALL BUSINESS PROFILE
Steven Edwards

EMI Holdings Inc.—Music City

Steve Edwards learned to play piano and guitar when he was young and began to tune pianos at age 17. He was soon working in a retail music store In St. John's, Newfoundland and displayed great talent for selling musical instruments, in addition to his expertise as a piano tuner.

In 1997 Steve opened his own retail music store and since then has developed it into a very successful business. This success earned Steve the Business Development Bank of Canada's 2004 Young Entrepreneur Award for Newfoundland and Labrador.

Steve Edwards' skill as a marketer was not only evident on the sales floor of his business but also in understanding the demographics of his customers and being responsive to their needs. A part of this marketing savvy and a key to Music City's recent success was the development of a website for the business. At the time Steve realized that nobody in Canada was really offering an online music store. Initially he received assistance from the Business Development Bank's e-business experts. When developed, Music City's website was able to not only sell music, instruments, and accessories online but also provide superior customer service.

The website offers its customers a pleasant, user-friendly online shopping experience, much like a musical "Starbucks." Customers can easily browse for instruments by category or brand, or for music by style, artist, or title. As Steve is quick to point out, "you can do so much more than simply sell on the web. You can give your clients more insight into your products and help them use them. Our business is not about price but customer service. That's where we have to shine."

Although the initial website software was designed for the music industry, BDC staff and Steve also custom designed some aspects of it to provide the look, feel and functionality of the site. Additionally, Steve has realized that there is a need to be continually adjusting the site. "It's not a static thing, but an evolving part of your business." He also offers advice to entrepreneurs. "Whoever is leading your company has to give your web initiative the time it needs. You have to focus on it and make sure that you're getting what you want," he stresses.

In the future Steve is planning a number of additional business applications of the web: the development of an online community with music associations, industry people and musicians, building an auction site where clients can sell musical instruments to one another, as well as the possible development of online video demonstrations. All of these initiatives would be impossible without the capabilities of the web being an integral part of the business.

Source: "Steve Edwards Strikes the Right Note with Music City," BDC Newsletter, October 2004, and the Music City website.

EMI Holdings Inc.—Music City
www.musiccitycanada.com

SMALL BUSINESS AND ELECTRONIC COMMERCE

internet.com
www.internet.com/
home-d.html

Electronic commerce (e-commerce) is pervasive in society today. A person cannot pick up a newspaper or magazine, or turn on the television or radio, without being flooded with information about some aspect of e-commerce. Business managers are given the impression that they must get on the e-commerce bandwagon or risk being left behind by their competitors. Many small business owners recognize the need to incorporate e-commerce into their operations but do not know how to do so. This chapter will provide information to guide the small business owner in evaluating the merits of e-commerce and establishing it in their organization.

WHAT IS ELECTRONIC COMMERCE?

Electronic Commerce
in Canada
www.e-com.ic.gc.ca/
english/index.html

Electronic commerce, or e-commerce, refers to the use of computers and electronic communication networks to connect with other relevant organizations. E-commerce covers a wide range of activities from electronic mail (e-mail) and Internet-based sales to transactions and web-based marketing. E-commerce is a worldwide phenomenon that will significantly affect national economies, businesses, and consumers over the next few years. It is a new way of conducting business that will supplant many traditional commercial relationships.

The majority of people think e-commerce means online shopping. However, web shopping is only a small part of the e-commerce portrait. The term also refers to online stock-and-bond transactions, and buying and downloading software without ever going near a store. In addition, e-commerce includes business-to-business connections that make purchasing easier for large and small organizations.

E-commerce can help small business improve the ways it does business with customers, other businesses, and the government. Small business involvement in e-commerce can take a number of forms, with varying levels of cost and complexity, depending on the business's needs. The basic use of e-mail by small business can provide a rapid and reliable way to communicate with suppliers, to receive and respond to customer queries, or even to initiate customer contact. For example, product information and quotations can be e-mailed, manufacturers and wholesalers can accept orders online, and businesses can quickly and easily put potential customers in touch with their retail outlets.

A small business can improve its operations by greater use of electronic bookkeeping and records management. The Internet offers a means for business to order its supplies online, resulting in faster and more efficient provision of goods and services, potentially reducing the need for the physical warehousing of inventory. Small businesses can also improve their efficiency by making use of a wide range of online banking services, such as electronic bill payment, funds transfer, and payroll management, all now offered by most large financial institutions.

E-commerce has also uncovered many small business opportunities and threats, as many industries deal with "disintermediation." Disintermediation is a buzzword that describes the effects of e-commerce networks, marketing products, and services directly from the producer to the final consumer and bypassing intermediaries, including marketing and distribution channels. Opportunities abound, as small businesses can distribute their products and services to their target market directly without paying middlemen to get their product to their customers. The threats come from the fact that many small businesses are intermediaries for the producers and may be cut out of the distribution channel as producers interact directly with their final consumers.

GROWTH OF E-COMMERCE

Small Business Canada
www.sbinfocanada.
about.com/cs/
ecommerce/index.html

Grocery Gateway
www.grocerygateway.
com

Over the past decade, e-commerce has seen a dramatic growth. Forrester Research estimates that worldwide e-commerce was $12.8 trillion in 2006.[1] Although North American activity represents most of this trade, its domination will continue to fade as Asian-Pacific and Western European countries experience increased growth.

Canadian expenditures on the Net have also increased dramatically over the last five years. Combined public and private Internet sales stood at $39.1 billion in 2005.[2] The growth in Internet transactions has risen at least 38 percent or more four years in a row. In addition, more Canadians appear to be plugged into the Internet than almost any other country, with estimates pegging Internet access at close to 70 percent of the population.[3]

The major growth areas of e-commerce, in terms of tangible goods, are computer products, consumer products, books, magazines, and music and entertainment products. Although significant portions of Canadian consumer expenditures in these areas were made from non-Canadian companies mostly from the United States, an increasing number of Canadian companies have begun to enter the market. As of 2005, the proportion of Canadian businesses using the Internet is 82 percent, firms with a website, 38 percent, and firms engaged in online sales, 7 percent.[4] One successful Canadian e-tailing business is Grocery Gateway, which combines the expertise of several organizations to sell groceries online. Figure 9.1 illustrates the extent of Internet usage in Canada while Figure 9-2 shows the extent of Internet usage among small businesses.

Although Internet purchases receive a lot of attention, other important uses of e-commerce for small businesses are also experiencing growth. Other types of Internet use include firms with a website, firms engaged in online banking, and firms engaged in online selling.

TYPES OF E-COMMERCE

There are several types or methods that a small business can follow to utilize e-commerce in their operations. The following paragraphs describe these options.

Figure 9-1	Online Buyers in Canada, 2005–2009 (millions and percentage of Internet users)

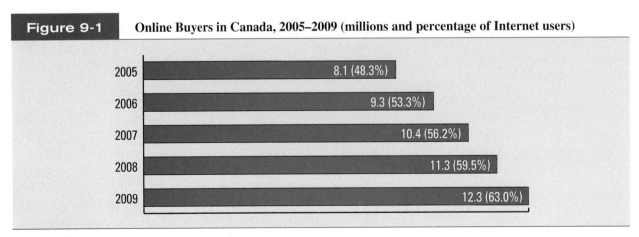

Note: ages 18+

Source: *eMarketer*, December 2006.

Figure 9-2	**Extent of Internet Usage among Small Business**

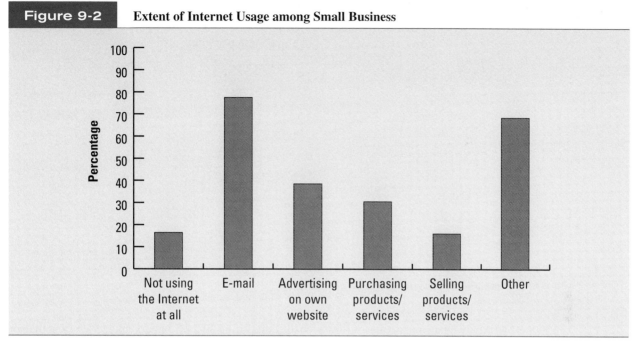

Source: Canadian Federation of Independent Business, June 2005.

Business to Consumer (B2C)

With this type, the focus is on the business-to-consumer transaction processes. This type of e-commerce has experienced very rapid growth recently, as has just been discussed. Consumers are increasingly going online to procure goods and services, arrange delivery and financing, and acquire after-sale service. B2C e-business includes retail sales (e-tail) and other online purchases such as software, music, entertainment venue tickets, airline tickets, travel products, and financial products. Many existing brick-and-mortar retailers (including many small businesses) are now also e-retailers with a web storefront. These combined brick-and-mortar/online businesses are known as "brick and click." Those businesses whose whole channel is online are known as "pure play" e-commerce businesses. The largest business-to-consumer e-tailers are shown in Figure 9-3. There are a number of business models that B2C businesses use to generate revenue. These models will be covered in the next section.

Business to Business (B2B)

Although B2C is the most familiar type of e-commerce at present, B2B is expected to represent a much larger share in dollar terms in the future. Recent statistics indicate that 75 percent of the total value of online sales results from the B2B type.[5] There are a number of methods that businesses use to conduct B2B online. Many businesses use intranets to allow employees to view and access websites that are only for internal organizational use and not for the outside world. The use of intranets, which use Internet technology, can add value to small business in a number of ways. These include increased productivity and decreased costs. Small businesses are also using extranets, which connect a business intranet to selected suppliers and buyers. This can improve a small business's procurement in B2B exchanges. Since both intranets and extranets use web technologies, end users need very little training to become proficient in their use.

Figure 9-3	Top Online Shopping Destinations on November 25, 2005

Site	Unique audience (000)
eBay	10,324
Amazon	4,189
Wal-Mart	1,543
Target	1,196
BestBuy.com	1,196
Overstock.com	1,092
Circuitcity.com	872
Dell	1,739
Shopping.com	1,168
Shopzilla.com	1,156

Source: Nielsen/NetRatings 11/18/2005—http://www.netratings.com/pr/pr_051128.pdf.

Many small businesses utilize websites that bring several buyers and sellers together in a digital market space. B2B exchanges can add value to small business by allowing small businesses to buy goods and services from and sell them to each other at dynamic (market-driven) prices. Their purchases and sales can be aggregated with other small and large businesses so that they can compete in the market on an equal footing with businesses and markets that are much larger.

B2B e-commerce sites work in various ways and are broken into two major groups: the verticals and horizontals. Verticals are B2B sites designed to meet the needs of a particular industry, such as retail. Vertical sites are the most likely to contain community features like industry news, articles, and discussion groups. Horizontal sites provide products, goods, materials, or services that are not specific to a particular industry or company. Horizontal B2Bs provide services and products that any industry could use. Horizontals might provide travel, transportation services, office equipment, or maintenance and operating supplies. Horizontals and verticals can perform as intermediaries that facilitate transactions or connect buyers and sellers together directly. There isn't one predominant model for B2B electronic commerce. B2B sites vary from those providing simple lead generation, to multifaceted marketplaces serving a diversity of buyers and sellers, to private extranets.

Business to Government (B2G)

The primary focus with this type of e-commerce is on government agencies at the national, provincial or territorial, or local level. The method is similar to the B2B exchange type but focuses on the government procurement model. This is a very large market in Canada. Before the establishment of e-commerce, many small businesses were unable to obtain access to this market because of the significant barriers of entry. The Canadian federal government estimates that it procures $8 billion to $9 billion in goods and services per year. Most provincial, territorial, and federal agencies and departments across Canada are required to advertise potential purchases over $25,000, with many others choosing to post contracts under that dollar value to ensure open competition. Experts estimate that as government agencies and departments streamline processes and amalgamate departments, governments will look increasingly to the private sector to provide goods and services.

Merx
www.merx.com

E-commerce tools have opened the way for small business to enter this market on a more equal footing with larger business. Merx is one B2G exchange on which Canadian federal government contracts are advertised.

Consumer to Consumer (C2C)

In this method consumers sell directly to one another via online exchanges and auctions. A good example of this model is ebay Canada. Ebay has been very successful at generating repeat business. Some dealers of antiques and collectibles are, in fact, making a living using ebay as their sole storefront. Many people, who started off as consumers, have turned these auction C2C models into a business.

ebay Canada
www.ebay.ca

Consumer to Business (C2B)

This type of e-commerce is called a reverse auction. This method lets consumers name the product or service they are interested in and the attributes they want in the product or service. The consumer might dictate such things as quantity, physical attributes, and price. Businesses are then able to match their offerings with what the consumer wants in order to complete the transaction. Examples of this type of e-commerce are priceline.com and reverseauction.com.

priceline.com
www.priceline.com

E-COMMERCE MODELS

Within the types of e-commerce discussed previously, there are many e-commerce business models. A business model is the way a business conducts business in order to generate revenue. A good business model is an important part of a business plan for a brick-and-mortar business. It is just as essential in the world of e-commerce. For a firm to be successful, it needs to be able to describe how it can generate revenues that exceed costs in order to be profitable over the long term. There are nine basic business models that can be used on the Internet.[6] These will be discussed below.

Brokers

Brokers are market makers in that they bring buyers and sellers together and facilitate transactions. They can be business-to-business (B2B) or consumer-to-consumer (C2C) markets. A broker charges a fee for each transaction it enables. Brokerage models can take a number of forms. An example of this model is eTrade, which allows consumers to buy stocks on the Internet.

Advertising Model

The web advertising model is an extension of the traditional media-broadcasting model. The broadcaster, in this case a website, provides content (usually free) and services (like e-mail, chat forums) mixed with advertising messages in the form of banner ads. The banner ads may be the major or sole source of revenue for the broadcaster. The broadcaster may be a content creator or a distributor of content created elsewhere. The advertising model only works when the volume of viewer traffic is large or highly specialized. Examples are ExciteCanada.com and Google. More will be discussed about specific methods of advertising on the web later in this chapter.

Google
www.google.com

Infomediary Model

Neilson/netrating
www.neilson-
netratings.com

Data about consumers and their buying habits is extremely valuable, especially when that information is carefully analyzed and used to target marketing campaigns. Some firms are able to function as infomediaries by collecting and selling information to other businesses Neilson/netrating measures the online audience market which adds value to businesses looking for market intelligence.

Merchant Model

chapters.indigo.ca
www.chapters.indigo.ca

The merchant model is a classic model of wholesalers and retailers of goods and services, one with which most people are very familiar. An example is chapters.indigo.ca, an online seller of books.

Manufacturer Model

Flowerbud.com
www.flowerbud.com

This model relies on the power of the web to allow manufacturers to reach buyers directly and thereby compress or disintermediate the distribution channel. It is important to remember that the services performed by the intermediaries in the distribution channels are just being transferred somewhere else. It is likely that the manufacturer or the consumer now has to provide the intermediary's functions. An example of this type of model is Flowerbud. com, a fresh flower distribution company.

Affiliate Model

amazon.com
www.amazon.ca

The affiliate model provides purchase opportunities wherever people may be surfing. This model gives financial incentives to other websites to promote products and services. An example is Amazon, which gives a commission for sales resulting from other sites referring people to Amazon.

Community Model

National Public Radio
www.pbs.org/npr

The viability of the community model is based on user loyalty (as opposed to high-traffic volume). Users have a high investment in both time and emotion in the site. In some cases, users are regular contributors of content or money. Having users who visit continually creates advertising, infomediary, or specialized portal opportunities. The community model may also run on a subscription fee for premium services. An example of a community model site is National Public Radio.

Subscription Model

Slate
www.slate.com

With the subscription model users pay for access to the site. High-value-added content is essential for this model to be effective. An example is *Slate*, a magazine that regularly publishes online news and information.

Utility Model

Slashdot
www.slashdot.org

The utility model is a metered usage or pay-as-you-go approach. This works very much like an electric bill in that the more electricity that is used, the higher the bill. An example of this is Slashdot, which is one of the largest IT news sites on the web.

In utilizing an e-commerce model there may be overlaps with some of the models mentioned above. As a result, a firm may combine different models as part of its web business strategy. A brokerage model may be blended with a subscription model to yield an overall strategy that is profitable. It is likely that in the future new and innovative models will be introduced to the e-commerce landscape.

ADVANTAGES OF E-COMMERCE FOR THE SMALL BUSINESS

Although some of the advantages of e-commerce use for a small business have already been mentioned briefly, this section will discuss some of the major reasons that small businesses should give consideration to this tool.

Expand Markets

E-commerce can give a small business greater visibility and the possibility of expanding existing markets and finding new customers. This is a great attraction for many small businesses. An example of such a business is found in Incident 9-1. The Internet overcomes many of the challenges of geographic location for small businesses to achieve access to geographically dispersed domestic and foreign markets. By using the web, customers all over the world will have access to the business. Many organizations were caught off guard by this sudden international presence and have not planned for it.

For many Canadian small businesses, it may be something as simple as gaining access to the large U.S. market in an inexpensive way. A web presence can provide visibility without

---

INCIDENT 9-1   Axiom Storms the U.S. Marketplace

Can everything sell online? Axiom Canada Inc. produces high-end stereo speaker systems. You would think an expensive product like that would first have to be heard and experienced in person before investing. Axiom has proved this notion wrong and has gone online to sell its products. President Ian Copquhoun states that annual revenues now are greater than $10 million annually. This figure represents average annual growth exceeding 35 percent over the last five years. This compares to the industry average of just 16 percent during the same time period.

Axiom was founded in 1980 in out-of-the-way Dwight, Ontario. Axiom's marketing model was to do business by the traditional method of using sales agents to get placement and distribution on retail store shelves. Consumers would then come to the store and test out the speakers. It was hoped that consumers would then decide to purchase Axiom speakers. Axiom used this model until 2000. Almost its entire product line was sold in Canada because that is where its retail store network was located. Axiom wanted to get into the enormous U.S. market where it had no retail placement and sold just a small amount of product by word of mouth.

Axiom entered the U.S. market by means of the web; it used a very simple and inexpensive website for the U.S. only. Axiom sales to this new market skyrocketed. Sales to the U.S. market now make up 75 percent of Axiom's revenues. This phenomenal growth led Axiom to make a major marketing decision. It has shut down its distribution channel in Canada and now all of Axiom's sales take place on the web.

Source: Adapted from Gerry Blackwell, "Everything Sells Online: Music Equipment," *Canadian Business,* Feb 27, 2006.
http://www.canadianbusiness.com/after_hours/lifestyle_products/article.jsp?content=20060227_74687_74687

the expense of physically setting up in these markets. For the Canadian small business, the U.S. market has the advantage of a common language, banking, and legal systems.

A web presence makes entering and having a visibility in foreign markets a real possibility, with a reduced investment and expertise. However, having a web presence and conducting business in foreign markets still bears considerable risks that a small business must be prepared for, such as legal, logistical, and currency exchange differences and problems. These were discussed in detail in Chapter 8.

Maximize Customer Relationships

Experience has shown that it is much less expensive to service existing customers than it is to find new ones, as was discussed in Chapter 8. For this reason many firms concentrate on satisfying and developing existing relationships with their customers. E-commerce technologies can help the small business maximize customer relations and improve customer responsiveness, such as quick turnaround in answering customer queries. Through the use of a website and e-mail, a small business can have a 24/7 presence and access for its customers. Product information and a frequently asked questions (FAQ) section on a business website can provide first access for customers to satisfy concerns or answer questions before, during, and after purchase of the product or service. E-mail is also an important tool for achieving customer satisfaction through the answering of queries and concerns. One frequently used area of software development is a web-based software tool called a CRM package. CRM is the initialism for customer relationship management. These packages allow large and small businesses alike to keep better track of their customers and to better satisfy their needs and wants. CRM software is designed to leverage existing customer relationships, increase sales, and reduce the cost of finding new customers.

Create New Services

The materialization of e-commerce has permitted many small businesses to add new digital products and services to their product line in a cost-effective manner. Examples of this are adding information products, or adding value to existing products and services. Many small businesses use websites or e-mail to help customers in their information search by highlighting those attributes or comparing their product with that of their competitors. Mass customization is made much easier by the use of e-commerce.

Although mass production of standardized goods was the source of a business's economic strength for generations, this is changing. The new paradigm of management is mass customization, which allows for large production runs while at the same time customizing each product for each customer. A good example of this is Dell Computer's website. Each customer selects or designs what he or she wants his or her individual computer to look like, and then Dell is able to assemble that computer in a low-cost way on an assembly line. This is made possible by the use of information technology using computers and the web.

Reduce Costs

Small business can achieve substantial cost reductions using e-commerce technologies. These reductions can be achieved in many of the core business processes such as purchasing, production, marketing, and human resource management. The selection of suppliers, cost comparison, aggregation of purchases online with similar business buyers, order, and reduction of delivery time are examples of purchasing advantages. Incident 9-2 discusses a firm that reduces costs in the supply chain using e-commerce tools. In the area of produc-

---

INCIDENT 9-2   Dropshipper

The area of B2B e-commerce is the largest type of e-commerce. E-commerce has the promise of lowering costs of purchasing for small business. Jay and Shweda Chopra created an online business to fulfill that promise for other small online businesses. The Chopras moved to Canada from India in 2001 and started a Calgary-based online dropshipping business called Save Instant Trading Inc., www.ewis.ca. They have based their warehouse in Calgary and target corporate customers anywhere in the world. Most of their clients use the web to resell the Chopras' goods online on their own websites or on auction sites such as ebay.

Jay and Shweda provide three basic marketing functions. They source, purchase, and store the inventory. They assume all the risks entailed in those marketing processes. A small business customer will then retail the item at the retail price; it sells the product to the customer, collects payment, then emails the order to the Chopras. Jay and Shweda then ship the item directly to the final retail customer using the small business's name and address as the shipper. The final retail customer has no idea that it came from the dropshipper directly instead of from the small business.

Jay and Shweda search the world over to find products, which they buy in bulk, or discontinued lines to obtain deep discounts. Most of their products come from Austria, India, China, and the U.S. The Chopras then sell the items to their wholesale small business customers with a small margin. The small business customer has already sold the product at something approaching the retail price.

The Chopras add value to small businesses by assuming the risks of purchasing, financing, and storing inventory. They get the word out about their service in many ways. If you type in "dropshipper" on Google, their business is listed first. This Canadian dropshipping business is facilitated and made possible by the e-commerce tools of online websites and email.

Source: Adapted from Danyael Halprin, "E-Tales," *Alberta Venture*, March, 2006, p. 120.
www.ewis.ca

---

tion, a small business can develop more accurate forecasting and order delivery times, and monitor work in progress, resulting in less cash tied up in inventory. Marketing savings might include less expensive advertising messages which are achieved in digital format. Costs such as recruiting, hiring, and training can also be reduced and improved for small businesses by using Internet-based tools.

PROBLEMS WITH E-COMMERCE FOR SMALL BUSINESS

Even though statistics show that the e-commerce market is rapidly growing, there are still many problems that can result from the attempt to adopt it. Figure 9-4 illustrates the results of a survey conducted by Statistics Canada that indicates many of the perceived concerns that nonuser businesses have with e-commerce. Among businesses that did not buy or sell over the Internet, 44 percent believed that their goods or services did not lend themselves to Internet transactions. Thirty-six percent preferred to maintain their current business model. Smaller proportions of these enterprises felt that security was a concern (17 percent), or that the cost of development and maintenance was too high (14 percent).

Other frequently mentioned concerns with the adoption of e-commerce include Internet availability, complexity of getting started, inconsistent tax laws, and legal issues. Incident 9-3 describes a company that found success using e-commerce by creating trust with the target market. Some small businesses may also find that e-commerce is not suitable for them.

Figure 9-4	Why Businesses Have Not Adopted E-Commerce

	% of Enterprises That Do Not Buy or Sell Online
Goods and services do not lend themselves to Internet transactions	44
Prefer to maintain current business model	36
Security concerns	17
Development and maintenance costs too high	14
Customers not ready	11
Lack of skilled employees	10
Concerns about competitors analyzing company	7
Uncertain about the benefits	7
Internet available to us is too slow	5
Suppliers not ready	5

Source: Statistics Canada, *The Daily*, April 20, 2006, http://www.statcan.ca/Daily/English/060420/d060420b.htm

---

INCIDENT 9-3 Out Front

Edmonton's Larry Yakiwczukk has joined the online auction service known as eBay and is finding much success with it. Formerly a garage-sale seller, Yakiwczukk started Backaru Auctions quite literally from his kitchen table with a laptop and a few goods, after using eBay in 1998 while earning his master of business administration at the University of Alberta. Yakiwczukk works only five or six hours a week finding undervalued items from inventory sales, liquidation sales, garage sales, retailers, and on eBay itself. He then posts the items on eBay where they are subject to a seven-day auction by over 157 million registered eBay users. Yakiwczukk now has two warehouses and has hired two full-time employees who clean and test new acquisitions, prepare written descriptions and digital photos, then prepare everything for shipment.

Yakiwczukk says that the key to success is establishing a positive track record, as eBay monitors both positive and negative reports from consumers. Yakiwczukk now offers instructional courses based on eBay basics.

Source: Adapted from Ian Doig "Out Front," *Alberta Venture*, October 2005, pp. 11–12.

Three factors that appear to be major stumbling blocks to a more successful experience with e-commerce are security concerns, protection of property, logistics problems, and payment systems. These will be discussed in more detail below.

Security Concerns

For many consumers, security is a major reason for not using the Internet. Once a business is connected to a public network such as the Internet, it is exposed to security risks that are associated with that network. E-commerce security is the protection of assets from unauthorized access, use, alteration, or destruction. Any act or object that poses a danger to computer assets is known as a threat. Although this section will identify major threats and countermeasures being used today, new threats to network security are emerging with surprising frequency.

When a small business encounters security concerns, the display of security measures and privacy policies can alleviate some of the reservations consumers may have about conducting online transactions. A small business should start with a security plan or policy. Generally, the plan should state what is to be protected, who is to be allowed access, and what resources will be allocated to e-commerce safety. There are trade-offs that a small business must make with regard to security. The greater the security that a business desires for its electronic commerce assets, the greater the cost to protect those assets will be. There is no foolproof system of security, and there will always be some degree of security risk in the digital world just as there is in the physical world. A security policy should address the following specific concerns.

Authentication is the process of determining whether someone or something is, in fact, who or what it is affirmed to be. In private and public computer networks (including the Internet), authentication is commonly done through the use of log-on passwords. Knowledge of the password is assumed to certify that the user is authentic. The weakness in this system for transactions that are significant (such as the exchange of money) is that passwords can often be stolen, inadvertently revealed, or forgotten.

Access control or authorization is the process of giving someone permission to do or have access to the e-commerce system. Different users may have different degrees of access to e-commerce assets. Managers must make important decisions regarding, for instance, the extent to which internal workers and customers have access to information.

Data integrity determines who will be able to change or modify data. Obviously a business wouldn't want employees able to change their wage information at random, or customers to change price information.

To assess the existence of e-commerce threats, it is useful to look at the entire e-commerce process, beginning with the consumer and ending with the business server. The three general e-commerce assets to protect are client computers, electronic commerce channels, and the commerce server. Key security provisions in each of these areas include secrecy, integrity, and available service. Encryption provides secrecy, and there are several types or forms available for e-commerce. Encryption includes the use of codes that only certain parties may be aware of.

Digital certificates provide both integrity controls and user authentication. The idea and process are much like an individual going into the bank to cash a cheque. A teller would want to authenticate one's identity by requiring some I.D. such as a driver's licence or birth certificate. The same sort of trust of proof is needed to make people secure with e-commerce transactions. Trusted third parties, known as certification authorities, provide digital certificates to users and organizations. Verisign is a leader in the certification authority industry. The two most heavily used Internet browsers, Explorer and Navigator, have built-in protocols to protect electronic commerce channels. There are several Internet protocols that provide secure Internet communication channels such as Secure Sockets Layer (SSL) and Secure HTTP.

The commerce server must also be protected. Protections for the server include access control and authentication, which are provided by user name and password log-in procedures and client certificates. Firewalls provide a hardware and software solution that separates the trusted inside computer networks and clients from the untrusted outside networks.

Copyright and Intellectual Property Threats

Copyright and intellectual property rights are security threats and risks that should be understood and managed by the small business. Copyright law secures for the originator of a creative effort the exclusive right to control who can make copies, or make works derived from the original work. There are a lot of subtleties and international variations of copyright law. If a person creates something, and it fits the definition of a creative work, that person receives control of who can make copies of it and how these copies are made. Under the Berne copyright convention, which almost all major nations have signed, every creative work is copyrighted the moment it is fixed in tangible form. No notice or registration is necessary, though these are helpful in legal cases. The copyright lasts 50 years after the author dies.

An intellectual property is any product of the human intellect that is distinctive, new, and unobvious. Intellectual property is defined as any new and useful process, machine, composition of matter, life form, article of manufacture, software, copyrighted work, or tangible property. Intellectual property may or may not be patentable or copyrightable. It is created when something new and useful has been conceived or developed, or when unusual, unexpected, or nonobvious results, obtained with an existing invention, can be practised for some useful purpose. Intellectual property can be created by one or more individuals, each of whom, to be an inventor, must have conceived a critical element or have contributed considerably to its theoretical development.

These two issues are of great concern in e-commerce because the material on the Internet is in a digital format. This characteristic makes copying, theft, and the distribution of one or numerous copies of the information very quick and of high quality. This was not the case with other analogue products such as cassette or VHS tapes for which the quality of copies was usually quite inferior to the original.

The financial loss caused by breach of use of copyright and intellectual properties usually has a smaller impact on a business or an individual than other e-commerce security breaches. However, if the business depends on the marketing of copyright material of intellectual property, it can have a significant effect. An example is organizations that "share" music files on the web. Napster was a pioneer in this area and instantly had millions of users "sharing" files over the Internet. The recording industry has recently shut down the free sharing of music files on the Napster website through legal methods. However, many more sites and technologies have emerged that still make this "sharing" possible and are presently out of reach of the recording industry.

Logistics Problems

Delivery and logistics problems are an often overlooked problem for entrepreneurs who start e-commerce businesses. These can be costly and complicated and require thorough planning to be effective. Many small e-commerce enterprises have been unsuccessful due to their failure to manage this aspect of the business adequately.

Payment Systems

In the physical world when an item is purchased, there are a number of options for payment—cash, cheque, credit, or debit cards. The e-commerce industry is trying to duplicate the attributes of these payment systems in the digital world. There have been many companies attempting to introduce electronic payment systems that they feel will increase e-commerce purchase activity. Many of them have not been successful. Effective implementation of electronic payment systems is still developing. When customers access a website and are ready to make a purchase, it is important that they feel it is safe, convenient, and widely accepted. The small business must provide the choices that are best suited to their target market.

Some of the options that are available to the small business include electronic cash, electronic wallets, stored value cards, and credit and debit cards. Each of these will be discussed briefly below.

Electronic Cash. Electronic cash has not yet seen widespread use in North America. For electronic cash to be functional, it must have certain characteristics in common with real money: a person must be able to spend e-cash only once and it must be anonymous. The business must be able to determine that e-cash is not counterfeit or being used in two different e-commerce transactions at once. There are many e-cash systems on the market, including checkfree, clickshare, Digicash, ecoin.net, Millicent, Paypal (very popular with eBay users), Beenz, and Flooz.

Electronic Wallets. As customers shop online, one of the negative aspects includes the amount of personal information that is required in order to purchase a product. Research has shown that many people abandon their purchase screen or digital shopping cart because of the need to fill out this information repeatedly as they go to various sites. An electronic wallet is encryption software that works like a physical wallet during electronic commerce transactions. To speed up transactions, a wallet can hold a user's payment information, a digital certificate to identify the user, and shipping information. The consumer benefits because the information is encrypted against piracy and because some wallets will automatically input shipping information at the merchant's site and will give the consumer the option of paying by digital cash or cheque. A merchant benefits by receiving protection against fraud. Most wallets reside on the users' computer but recent versions, called "thin" wallets, are placed on the credit card issuers' server. Netscape and Microsoft now support wallet technology on their browsers.

Electronic wallets hold a great deal of promise both on the consumer and on the business side of the transaction. For the consumer, the advantages include saving the time and effort required to type in information in order to purchase an item. For the business, the advantages include a better chance of the information being accurate, the authentication of the buyer, and a decreased rate at checkout of abandoned shopping carts filled with digital purchases.

The biggest problem facing the use of wallets is the standard that is used. There are a number of vendors attempting to establish themselves in the e-wallet market. This fragmentation of standards has made adoption and use of this promising technology slow. Consortiums are now working to standardize the wallet technology across the industry.

Smart Cards. Smart cards are plastic cards (like a credit card) with an embedded microchip that contains large amounts of information. At present, a smart card can store more than 100 times the information that the typical magnetic strip credit card will hold. Smart cards are much more secure than current credit cards because the information is encrypted on the embedded microchip rather than being visible.

The adoption of smart card technology and standards has been very successful in Europe, Japan, and Australia. It has been slower to catch on in North America. Mondex has been a pioneer in this area and has many years of experience in the industry. Recent developments such as the entrance of Visa and American Express into the smart card market should contribute to more rapid adoption in North America in the future.

Credit and Debit Cards. Credit and debit cards are still the most popular forms of payment on the Internet. They are universal, convenient, and simple to use. There is a large installed base of users of these cards, and they are in use on a global basis. The incidence of credit card fraud over the Internet, however, is a major problem. Recent research estimates that e-commerce fraud totalled $60 billion in 2005.[7]

In order for a small business to accept credit or debit cards over the Internet, it must obtain what is called a merchant account. A small business will receive a numbered account into which they deposit the accumulated card sales amount. There are also several third-party Internet- and web-based businesses that are available to handle all the details of processing payment card transactions. PayPal has been successful for its credit card services. In such a system the business simply inserts PayPal Web Accept buttons on its site. Members can also use PayPal to request payments. Fees are charged on a per-use basis, making the service a cost-effective solution for small companies that are still in the developing stage.

PayPal
www.paypal.com

PLANNING AND BUILDING A WEBSITE

Canadian Internet
Registration Authority
www.cira.ca

One of the challenges that the small business owner faces in establishing e-commerce is developing the website. A good website should answer the following four questions about the firm.[8]

1. Who are we?

2. What do we do?

3. How do we do it?

4. How can consumers contact us?

Figure 9-5 illustrates an example of an effective website for a small Canadian specialty business. Figure 9-6 (on page 278) shows the information that is quickly accessed by clicking on the What Is "Everything Garlic"? icon.

Identifying Objectives

The small business owner who wants to use e-commerce alone or in conjunction with a brick-and-mortar business must first identify the objectives of using e-commerce. The following questions should be answered in order to determine such objectives as the first step in website development.

Will the website

- allow customers to order products and services over the Internet?
- advertise and promote products and services?
- provide technical support for the firm's products and services?
- create or support brand or image development?
- conduct market research online about current and potential customers?
- give links to related websites that will help the customer?
- provide general or industry information?
- recruit new employees?
- serve international customers?
- serve multiple or single market segments?

It is probable that the website will have multiple objectives. As with most aspects of small business, it is important to keep the target market or customer at the centre of the strategy. Currently 54 percent of Canadians have high-speed access at home.[9] It is therefore important that the site be constructed so that it downloads very quickly as the time it takes for a visitor to leave a site for the competitor site is less than ever before. Understanding who the target customers are and what their characteristics are in relation to e-commerce,

Figure 9-5	An Effective Internet Site

EVERYTHING GARLIC

Your One-Stop Shop For Garlic Lovers!

What Is "Everything Garlic"?

Sizzling New Garlic Tidbits & Facts

How To Order (2)

Garlic Cookbooks (17)

Garlic Oils (5)

Garlic Vinegars (3)

Pickled Garlic and Garlic Olives (3)

Garlic Salsas and Sauces (4)

Garlic Spreads (4)

Garlic Mixes and Seasonings (4)

Garlic Condiments (5)

Garlic Bread Mixes

Garlic Braids, Wreaths and Swags (4)

Garlic Keepers (9)

Garlic Bakers (6)

Garlic Baker & Keeper Gift Sets (2)

Garlic Tools (4)

Garlic Presses (6)

Garlic T-Shirts and Linens (3)

Great Gift Ideas (6)

On Line Response Form - SAVE 10% !

Hot Garlic Info Links

such as their level of experience and what type of technology they currently use, is very important in website development.

Another issue in strategy development is the business's ability to handle the estimated increase in business generated by being on the web. Resources should be allocated to deal with this growth. This situation is illustrated in Incident 9-4 on page 279.

By defining the objective of the business's e-commerce strategy, the firm can determine which website level would be most appropriate to incorporate. There are three levels of e-commerce that a small business may utilize.

Figure 9-6   An Example of a Menu for an Internet Site

about our company

call or fax toll free: 1-800-668-6299
9:30 am - 6 pm pacific standard time
p.o. box 91104, west vancouver, b.c.
v7v 3n3 canada
tel: (604)926-3154 fax: (604)926-3154

everyone's garlic specialty store...
fresh garlic, specialty garlic food
products, supplements, utensils, books,
gifts, and more!

some things are worth making a big stink about!

you've found it! whether your interests lie in gourmet foods, improving your
health or finding a garlic press that actually works, everything garlic is the place
for you.

you're even sure to find something for the hard-to-buy-for person on your list. after
all, everyone appreciates a gift of food, and our products are always in good taste!

we have the most complete and varied supply of garlic products you'll find anywhere.
check us out for everything from garlic mist to garlic t-shirts. in this web site you
will find some of our best sellers and personal favourites.

if you're in the vancouver, b.c. area, please take the time to visit our retail store at
lonsdale quay market in north vancouver. we carry a wide array of unique products,
including many unavailable elsewhere.

please note: all prices are in canadian dollars ($1.00 canadian is equal to
approximately $.75 us).

check out the garlic information hotline:
1-800-330-5922 9 am - 5 pm e.s.t.

cornell university provides information on research findings regarding garlic's
preventative and therapeutic qualities.

how to order in canada

how to order in the u.s. and internationally

INCIDENT 9-4   Images for Everyone

When photographer Bruce Livingston, simply looking for his own creative outlet, published his own photographs to a website in 2000, he had no idea of the impact he would have on stock photography. People from around the world soon began downloading the pictures and photographers began asking to publish their material on his website. Livingston soon created the Calgary-based iStockPhoto.com, a site where photographers and graphic designers could exchange images at no cost. Before iStockPhoto, people who wanted to download something such as an annual report or PowerPoint presentation were required to pay large royalties to media companies. By creating iStockPhoto.com, millions of images became available and revealed a huge demand for affordable imagery.

Because of the popularity of his site, Livingston soon created a micro-credit system, which allowed people to purchase royalty-free images for a small one-time fee.

This Internet-based company has revolutionized stock photography. It has grown to include over 600,000 member/customers and 23,000 contributors. It is on track to sell 10 million images and is among the 300 busiest Internet sites in the world. In February 2006, Getty Images Inc. purchased the company for $50 million.

Source: Adapted from "Images for Everyone," *Alberta Venture*, April 2006, p. 34.

Level 1—Read Only. This is a static site on which to post company and product information. Providing a toll-free number (linked to the company's call centre) encourages visitors to call in and request products and other information.

Level 2—Electronic Request Capability. Sites at this level provide level-1 features as well as e-mail communication. Organizations typically use this type of site to improve customer service. For example, software companies may allow customers to download software files. Airlines provide flight schedules, and manufacturers of all kinds may provide product specification and price lists. Visitors can ask questions and request information electronically.

Level 3—Transaction Capability. Sites at this level have firewalls and secure socket layers installed to protect information. Customers can place orders and make electronic payments. "E-commerce programs" can be used to build this kind of interactive site. Predictions about the future of e-commerce point strongly to integrated business systems and increasingly complex subsites that offer a higher degree of customization and self-service capabilities for customers. As the business website's self-service capability and complexity increase, it becomes more operational and able to do e-commerce. Ability to reach out to customers is strengthened, and web revenues are likely to grow as well. Likewise, the costs of building and maintaining a site increase to the next level.

Strategies for Website Development

Once the website objectives and levels have been determined, the next step is to start developing the site. There are three options to examine with this step.

Buy a Ready-Made Solution. This is an off-the-shelf solution. Therefore, one would attempt to choose an e-commerce package that most closely matches the features needed to achieve the objectives. The advantage of this option is that development can be very quick. Most of such services state that they employ best business practices in the various industries in which they compete. For example, an industry might have a preset package tailored to that industry. The disadvantage is that these solutions are typically not very flexible. This option may meet the business objectives in the early stages but may not be flexible enough to meet the changing needs and objectives as the business grows. Examples of these types of packages are Intershop or IBM WebSphere. Incident 9-5 provides an example of a small business that has successfully developed a web presence.

Rent Space in a Network-Based E-commerce Solution. Depending on the business objectives, this solution has many common e-commerce features and is relatively inexpensive. This solution is fast because there is no need for additional software. The site is administered over the web. One selects a look, configures some settings, and enters product information for an instant storefront. These services would include a customer storefront that can be built in the browser, tools to design, manage, and promote the business, a user-friendly shopping cart, secure credit card processing, and competitive monthly pricing with tech support for merchants. The disadvantage is that these services may not support the features or the look and feel that are wanted. They save the small business from having to deal with the complexities of installation and configuration, but they only offer a few ways to do these things. This may be acceptable if there exists a good match between what they provide and what is needed. Examples of these types of packages are Yahoo Stores or Escalate Direct.

Build the System from Scratch. This option will give the small business the exact solution it needs but will require expertise, time, and a sizable budget to implement. The advantage is that the business can build into the system the required features and functions that may be necessary to be unique and competitive in the marketplace. When taking this route, the

---

INCIDENT 9-5   From Snowboards to Storefront Software

Scott Lake and Tobias Lutke from the Ottawa area just wanted to sell some snowboards online. As they proceeded down this slope, they found it very slippery and difficult to facilitate. The experience gave the two entrepreneurs an idea for a product to solve this problem.

Scott and Tobias had extensive experience in working in information technology. Scott was VP for a software company that eased collaboration, while Tobias created software for setting up blogs. They felt it it would be easy to set up an online store to sell their snowboards from their company Snowdevil. But they ran into a problem a lot of small business owners find when they try to go online: the tools were intended for very large companies. They were also expensive and complicated and simply did not meet the requirements of the small business market.

Scott and Tobias decided to solve the problem by creating the technological tools from the ground up, by developing a service called Shopify. This service is designed to simplify and integrate setting up a small business Web site. Scott feels the biggest obstacles to setting up a small business site are hosting the site and providing security for the site.

Shopify solves these two obstacles by integrating the payment gateway and handling the hosting of the small business Web site themselves. You don't need to install any software as everything is handled online. Shopify's business model is to charge a very small commission on all sales through the website. If you don't sell anything online, then you don't pay anything for the Shopify service. This service from Shopify makes it easy to get an online presence but it does not guarantee success. You still have be creative in your marketing and merchandizing in order to be successful. http://shopify.com

Source: Adapted from Shane Schick, "Small Business Needs On-line Savvy for Success," *The Globe and Mail*, May 18, 2006
http://www.theglobeandmail.com/servlet/story/RTGAM.20060518.smb-einsider18/BNStory/

organization will need to design databases from scratch and then integrate tax, shipping, and payment processing software modules with the mail application. The small business needs to be comfortable developing applications on this level. If not, professional e-commerce systems developers can be hired to get the website developed. Examples of these types of packages are Macromedia's ColdFusion, Intershop 4, and Microsoft's Site Server Commerce Edition.

When evaluating these solutions, one should consider not only the cost of the package but also how much it will cost to customize it to suit the individual needs of the business. What may look like an inexpensive set-up at the outset can end up being very expensive if it becomes necessary to add new features or redo the design.

CHOOSING A WEB HOST

Once the site has been developed, the small business owner must next decide on how to get the site onto a computer that is connected to the Internet or web host. An Internet service provider (ISP) or a web host provides access to a host computer. Many large businesses, colleges, universities, and government agencies may already have a computer network that is part of the Internet. For most small businesses the cost of having their own computer host connected to the Internet can be a large financial barrier.

To be a self-web-hosting organization, the business will need hardware, electronic commerce software, and a T-1 connection just to get started. The cost of setting up an in-house web-hosting capability can cost in excess of $75,000, which is beyond the budget of many small businesses.

Types of Web Hosts

There are a number of other options the small business can select to obtain the web host. They are discussed briefly below.

Shared Hosting. In shared hosting the website resides on a web host's server with several other websites. It is inexpensive, requires very little of the business's time to maintain, and may have a very fast connection to the Internet. Shared hosting can have some disadvantages also. There might be a loss of direct control; at times updates are slow due to the large quantity of traffic to the server's other online businesses. There could also be some security problems resulting from numerous businesses sharing the same server.

Dedicated Hosting. Dedicated hosting occurs when an ISP or web host provides a server just for the small business in question. The advantages include more web and commerce options, a high-speed connection, and more decision-making and site design control. Disadvantages include higher software costs, higher maintenance costs, and very little control over the hardware containing the site.

Colocated Hosting. This form is closer to self-hosting. The server is owned by the online small business but is located at the ISP or web host's site. Even though the server is dedicated, it is necessary to have a secure, environmentally controlled location in which to house it. The web host will provide the needed space along with fast, reliable connectivity and full UPS (uninterruptible power supply) backup. The business gets the benefit of a direct connection to the Internet backbone at dramatically reduced costs. The web host of the ISP provides maintenance. Advantages are the same as self-hosting. The disadvantages include maintenance costs that are higher than self-hosting, occasional difficulty getting access to the server to implement changes, and more expensive software.

Advantages of Using a Web Host

For the majority of small businesses, the advantages of using a web host far outweigh the disadvantages. Most business owners find that setting up a web server infrastructure is both complex and costly. But the web host already has the infrastructure in place. A web host can combine a dedicated server with management and monitoring service. A web host can provide a reliable, stable, continuous, and secure system. The website content can be updated at any time. Disk space is available for the website and can be provided with a unique domain name. The cost is usually reasonable and the contracts can be very short term (as short as one month), and payment for services is usually on a monthly basis. This helps the small business with cash flow and does not require the capital investment of self-hosting.

A domain name is registered with a central registrar for one to ten years and costs about $50 to $65 per year. The easiest way to register is through the web-hosting service when the web space is purchased. To register the name before finding a web host, the small business can utilize a service like Network Solutions or register.com. When the site is ready, the web-hosting provider can arrange the transfer. The web host or ISP costs range from $30 to a few hundred dollars per month. For a business that decides to host its own website, that cost could reach more than $1,000 per month.

ATTRACTING CUSTOMERS TO THE WEBSITE

Once the site has been developed and the host determined, the small business must plan how to attract customers to the website. Traditional methods of advertising such as printed or broadcast media may be effective but expensive for the small business. Other methods that are related to the technology tend to be more effective and less expensive. Some of these methods are listed below.

Register with a Search Engine

Many people go to search engines to find what they are looking for on the web. Registration with the search engine will provide exposure of your business when people do searches. Some service companies will register the site with the top search engines for a fee. Many businesses also buy advertising space on the home pages of search engines or other companies.

Request Links on Industry Sites

This type of promotion involves contacting the industry association related to the small business and allowing the business to be listed on their website. Although there may be a cost to do this, it is usually worth the contact that can be made.

Include URL on Stationery, Business Cards, and Literature

Although it seems like an obvious way to promote the business, many small businesses fail to include their website address on printed materials of the business.

Request Reciprocal Links

The small business could request that their link be placed with suppliers' and customers' websites.

Issue News Releases

The small business can find newsworthy events (such as launching new products or services) and send news releases to print and web periodicals in the industry.

Capture Visitor E-mail Addresses and Request Permission to Send Updates

On the website, include a checkbox where a visitor can provide permission to receive e-mail updates about products or services. The e-mails to visitors are not "spam" because they have been requested.

Publish an E-mail Newsletter

Although it can be very time consuming, publishing a weekly, monthly, or quarterly newsletter is one of the best ways to keep in touch with current and potential customers. It also allows the small business to build brand awareness, trust, and future business. The newsletter can be distributed by using an e-mail program, or by people subscribing on the website directly.

Set Up a "Signature" in the E-mail Program

Most e-mail programs allow the customer to choose a "signature" to appear at the end of each message that is sent. It should be short and include such things as the company name, address, phone number, URL, e-mail address, and a one-phrase description of unique business offerings.

Promote the Site in Mailing Lists and Newsgroups

The Internet offers thousands of very targeted mailing lists and newsgroups made up of people with very specific interests. Helpful messages about the product or service when a related discussion is taking place can be an effective way to find new business. Do not use hard-line marketing and be sure to place the "signature" at the end of the e-mail message.

Begin an Affiliate Program

An affiliate program pays a commission to those sites whose links result in an actual sale. This commission acts as an incentive to provide more prominent placement of the website.

ADVERTISING ON THE WEB

A business can advertise its products or services on the web in several specific ways, such as by using banner ads, cookies, full-page ads, "push" technology ads, and e-mail ads. Each will be discussed briefly below.

Banner Ads

Banner ads, which account for two-thirds of online advertising expenditures, are small, rectangular ads that promote a company's product or service. When visitors click on the banner ad, they go straight to the advertiser's home page. The cost of a banner ad to an advertiser depends on the volume of the website.

Banners ads do not have to be expensive, however. Many small business owners increase exposure of their banner ads by joining a banner exchange program. In such a program, member companies post their banners on one another's sites. These programs work best for companies selling complementary products or services.

The primary disadvantage of the banner ad is the low click-through rate, which is below 2 percent.

Cookies

Cookies are small programs that attach to users' computers when they visit certain websites. These programs track the locations that users visit while on the site and use this electronic footprint to send pop-up ads that would be of interest to the user. For instance, a web user who frequently visits garden sites might find ads for garden tools and seed companies popping up on their screen. Because cookies record a person's web use, their use has become somewhat controversial, and many sites require users to register before the sites can collect information to create cookie files.

Full-Page Ads

Full-page ads are those that download to web users' screens before they can access certain websites. They are common on popular game sites that attract a high volume of web traffic.

Push Technology Ads

Push technology ads appear on users' screens when they download information such as news, sports, or entertainment from another site. For example, a web user downloading sports information might receive an ad for athletic shoes or T-shirts along with the information.

E-mail Ads

With more than 135 million users, e-mail is the most common application on the Internet. E-mail advertising has grown rapidly. With e-mail advertising, the company broadcasts its advertising messages via e-mail through permission e-mail (the company receives permission to send the message) or spam (unsolicited e-mail). Despite the growth of e-mail ads there are still challenges firms face in their use. (See Figure 9-7.)

| **Figure 9-7** | **Greatest Challenges in Conducting E-Mail Marketing Campaigns according to U.S. E-Marketers, 2006 (% of respondents)** |

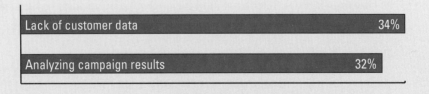

Note: n=422

Source: JupiterResearch commissioned by Silverprop, December 2006. www.eMarketer.com

CUTTING EDGE E-COMMERCE WEB TOOLS

Using the Internet for business is becoming more and more important. As a result, many exciting applications and tools that take advantage of this constantly changing environment are being developed. Small business has been an early adopter of many of these new technologies. In many cases, small business has been ahead of the curve and has gained an early competitive advantage from being able to quickly implement these new web tools and strategies. Some of these methods are discussed below.

Blogs

A blog is a web page made up of short, often updated web posts. These posts are arranged chronologically, like a journal. A business blog is a business tool for communicating with stakeholders in a small business. This would include customers and employees with whom the small business wants to share information and expertise. Blogs' simplicity is one of the reasons that small business is adopting this tool earlier than larger business. The potential benefits to a small business are:

1. *Ease of Use.* Blogging software is easy to use. If you can type, you can blog. Blogging software companies such as Movable Type, Blogger.com, and Radio Userland provide easy blogging tools to get started.

2. *Low Cost.* Blogging is a low-cost alternative to communicating to your customers and employees on the web. Many small business owners don't have the time or expertise to learn web languages like html. Hiring outside web expertise can be expensive. Blogging can be a very inexpensive alternative to getting the company's brand and reputation up on the internet

3. *Fast Publishing.* Updating the blog yourself is much quicker and easier than having to communicate your changes to a webmaster and doing the uploading.

4. *Relationship Management.* Blogs provide an excellent opportunity to share your expertise and knowledge with your customers and employees. Blogging can also be a very effective marketing tool to establish the small business owner as an authority in his or her field. This can generate leads and create positive word of mouth about the owner's qualifications in the market. Blogging can also be used to talk directly with customers and collect valuable and immediate feedback.

Wikis

A wiki is a web application that allows a small business owner to add content on an Internet page or forum, but it also allows anyone to edit the content. The most well-known wiki example is Wikipedia, an online encyclopedia that is written and maintained by anyone who feels like writing entries on the site. This sounds like a formula for chaos, but that is not the case. Entries are typically well-written and well-researched.

A small business can create its own Wiki, which focuses on their particular business. The small business can designate who can add and access content and make changes. This would typically be employees and customers.

Why Create a Small Business Wiki?

Ease of Use and Cost. If you can use a Web browser, you can use a wiki. It is based on web browser technology, so most people can quickly learn how to use this tool.

You don't need to know any programming or html. Set-up and maintenance are very low cost. For small business, that can be anywhere from free to $200. Wiki software companies such as Social Text, Project Forum, and Jotspot provide easy wiki tools so small businesses can get started.

Increases Collaboration and Teamwork. A wiki is a central place where small businesses can put all their notes, plans, operating procedures, and email, etc. in one central place on the Web. The wiki can be accessed anywhere in the world with Internet access. It cuts down on email overload and is also a living intranet for small business. Unlike traditional intranets that are expensive to set up and very difficult to update, the wiki is inexpensive and can be constantly updated by those in the know.

This information can be updated and searched by everyone in the organization. This leads to improved teamwork, creativity, and productivity in the firm, as everyone is working from the same updated information, knowledge, and best practices.

Webcasting

A Webcast is an online conference or web seminar. Webcasting can be an effective tool for B2B marketers and small business is discovering webcasts can boost sales and save money. Webcasts use the Internet to broadcast a live or delayed audio and/or video transmission to a target market who log-in for the session. The online meetings are interactive and collaborative. Small businesses can communicate directly with customers or employees all over the world. The online meetings are interactive and collaborative.

A small business wanting to participate in this technology would subscribe to a webcast hosting service to run the webcast. Examples of firms that provide this service to small business are companies such as Webex, Gotomeeting, and Microsoft Office Live. Participants need only a phone, a computer, and an online connection. Webcasts can be archived for later listening and viewing.

Webcasts can be used for a variety of applications, such as training staff or customers, introducing products or brands, informing investors, researching markets, generating leads, rewarding loyal customers, and driving participants to the small business's website. Webcasting can provide some of the following benefits:

- Less travel

- Increased productivity

- Reduced costs

- Easily collaborate with customers and employees

- Increase of customer base by reducing geographic boundaries

- Collaborate in real time

The cost of using webcast technology is a fraction of the cost of setting up live meetings. Webcasts are also a good way to reach clients or influential buyers who may be unwilling or unable to meet face to face.

THE FUTURE OF E-COMMERCE AND SMALL BUSINESS

E-commerce is still in the embryonic stages of development. Despite its rapid growth, the industry is still struggling with many problems and challenges that affect a small business.

It appears, however, that most successful new businesses are embracing e-commerce as a vital part of their operations.

E-commerce is an exciting and dynamic area in which products, services, and ideas have very short life cycles. It is widely recognized that any book attempting to describe and instruct on e-commerce is somewhat outdated by the time it is published. It is therefore necessary that the small business owner be aware of current news articles, trade publications, and stories on the web to keep up to date on the trends relating to e-commerce.

Summary

1. Electronic commerce involves the use of computers and electronic communication networks to perform business such as electronic mail, marketing, and making transactions.

2. Electronic commerce can take the form of business to consumer, business to business, business to government, consumer to consumer, and consumer to business.

3. Advantages of small businesses using e-commerce include expanded markets, maximization of customer relationships, creation of new services, and reduction of costs.

4. Some of the challenges of using e-commerce include security issues, copyright and intellectual property rights, and payment systems.

5. The small business owner should use a well-planned approach to building a website, choosing a web host, and attracting customers to the site.

6. A small business can use several methods to advertise on the web, including banner ads, cookies, full-page ads, push technology ads, and e-mail ads.

7. New web tools include blogs, wikis, and web casting.

Chapter Problems and Applications

1. Briefly describe what is meant by electronic commerce.

2. Which of the e-commerce types as described in the text are employed by the following?

   A. Amazon.com

   B. Priceline.com

   C. Save Instant Trading Inc. (Incident 9-2)

   D. Axiom (Incident 9-1)

3. Describe how a small business can benefit by implementing e-commerce.

4. Briefly describe the potential problems for a small business of establishing an e-commerce system.

5. How could you determine whether a business should proceed with each of the three levels of e-commerce: Level 1—advertise only, Level 2—communication ability, and Level 3—transaction ability?

6. How could one go about selecting a web host?

7. Interview a small business owner who has a website to determine which of the "methods of attracting customers" the business is using.

8. What are the characteristics of an effective website?

9. Interview a small business owner who has a website about the problems and challenges he or she experienced in establishing e-commerce.

10. Interview a small business owner who has a website to determine the steps he or she followed in establishing the site.

11. What are some of the new web tools that could help a small business?

12. What are some of the factors that may affect the future growth of e-commerce for the small business?

Web Exercise

Access the e-business website for the Business Development Bank of Canada (Suggested Readings) and review the services provided.

Suggested Readings

Reynolds, Janice. *The Complete E-Commerce Book: Design, Build, & Maintain a Successful Web-based Business, Second Edition.* Berkeley, CA: CMP Books, October 2000, pp. 2–10.

Laudon, Kenneth and Carol Traver. *E-Commerce: Business, Technology, Society, Third Edition.* Upper Saddle River, NJ: Prentice Hall, 2006, pp. 1–53.

McGarvey, Robert and Melissa Campanelli. *Start Your Own E-Business.* Newburgh, NY: Entrepreneur Press, 2005, pp. 53–64.

Rayport, Jeffrey F. and Bernard J. Jaworski. *Introduction to e-Commerce, 2nd edition.* New York, New York: McGraw-Hill/Irwin, 2003, pp.71–149.

Chaston, Ian. *Small Business E-Commerce Management.* New York, New York: Palgrave Macmillan, 2004, pp. 42–83.

Nabeel, A. Y. Al-Qirim and Brian J. Corbitt. *E-Business, E-Government & Small and Medium Size Enterprises: Opportunities & Challenges.* Hershey, PA: IGI Global, 2004, pp. 19–45.

Brown, Bruce Cameron. *How to Use the Internet to Advertise, Promote and Market Your Business or Website with Little or No Money.* Ocala, FLA: Atlantic Publishing Company, 2006, pp. 36–64.

Hanson, Ward and Kirthi Kalyanam. *Internet Marketing and E-Commerce.* Scarborough, ON: Thomson Nelson, 2006, pp. 184–197.

Chaston, Ian. *E-Commerce for Small Business.* New York, New York: Palgrave Macmillan, 2004, pp. 62–84.

Comprehensive Case   *Sid Stevens: Part 6*

After reviewing his options, Sid was able to secure a tentative deal with a national hardware chain. On this basis, Sid received the remainder of his funding. The manufacturing plant was completed and production began making 30 units per day. The hardware chain had helped him develop a packaging and display unit that appealed to the consumer, and they had ordered 1000 units initially to place in their stores. The agreement was for payment to Sid of $30 per unit, and they listed the Ladder Rail at $39.95. They also prohibited Sid from selling the Ladder Rail to any competing hardware store. They did allow him to sell by direct mail should be choose to do so.

After a few months, sales through the hardware chain were not what Sid had projected. It was taking some time for potential customers to become aware of the Ladder Rail. Some of the best advertising appeared to be word of mouth from satisfied customers, but this would also take time to yield results. The hardware chain was willing to continue with the Ladder Rail but expressed some concerns. Sid wondered if he should attempt to enhance sales of the Ladder Rail through another method. A friend suggested that he get a website and sell over the Internet. "This is the marketing tool of the future," encouraged his friend.

So, Sid began exploring this option for improving sales.

Questions

1. Evaluate the use of the Internet to market the Ladder Rail.
2. If Sid decided not to use the Internet to sell the Ladder Rail, how might the Internet still be of value to his business?

www.mcgrawhill.ca/olc/balderson

CHAPTER 10
Financial Management

CHAPTER OBJECTIVES

- To review the fundamentals of small business accounting

- To discuss the various types of accounting systems a small business can use

- To describe the considerations in purchasing a computer for the small business

- To show how to develop and use budgets and financial planning tools

- To illustrate how to evaluate the financial operations of the small business

- To discuss the important aspects of credit management for the small business

SMALL BUSINESS PROFILE

Mark Chaplin

Disc-Go-Technologies Inc.

In 1996, Mark Chaplin and his friend Ron Haufler started a CD-ROM repair business in their garage in Langley, B.C. to supplement their incomes. The disc-repair expertise had been developed through Ron's work as an auto detailer and Mark's studies in engineering at British Columbia Institute of Technology. The number of customers grew rapidly and by 1999 included video-rental companies such as Movie Gallery, Blockbuster Canada, and Rogers Video. In 2000, Mark and Ron established Disc-Go-Technologies Inc.

However, they realized that they would need to develop an automated system to make their business a full-time commercial enterprise. To do this they would need a considerable amount of funding. They struggled to obtain this financing but finally, with the aid of a business plan, angel investors, and family members, they were able to secure close to half a million dollars in startup capital. This allowed them to design and build the Disc-Go-Mech, the industry's first automated disk-repair machine.

A key aspect of the company's early success was the partners' ability to understand and manage the finances of the business. For example, during the company's startup phase, Chaplin and Haufler went without pay cheques on more than one occasion so the company could pay suppliers and employees and remain solvent. Now that the business is established, continual development and monitoring of budgets and financial projections is part of their business operations.

Over the next few years, Ron and Mark had their ups and downs but learned from their mistakes and developed a marketing system which yielded per-disk royalties on each machine they sold. The system has provided the company with the cash flow to develop new markets and products. Disc-Go-Tech now has distributors in Europe and Australia. In addition, the company also introduced the Disc-Go-Cube for smaller commercial markets and the Disc-Go-Pod and Disc-Go-Pod Plus for the consumer market.

Chaplin reviews his business plan every six months and revises it to meet changing customer requirements. Because downloading will one day make CDs and DVDs virtually obsolete, he is investigating Internet-based opportunities for Disc-Go-Tech.

Disc-Go-Tech is now profitable, with 22 employees and revenues of over $5 million. Because of his creative talents and business acumen, Chaplin was named one of Vancouver's Top 40 under 40.

Source: *Costco Connection*, Nov/Dec 2005, pp. 23–24, *Canadian Business*, Oct/Nov 2005, pp.139–141.

Disk Go Technologies Inc.
www.discgotech.com

THE NEED FOR FINANCIAL RECORDS

Canada Revenue
Agency
www.cra-arc.gc.ca

Incident 10-1 illustrates why financial management skills are important for a small business. However, as the example shows, such skills are frequently lacking. One survey found that from 24 percent to 45 percent of Canadian small business owners did not understand basic financial measurement ratios used in evaluating their businesses.[1] Failure to understand and manage the financial aspects of a business can be disastrous for the small business owner. The need for competence in this area is continually growing as new technology and greater competition in many markets necessitate closer monitoring of operations and quicker decision making. Keeping proper records can warn the owner-manager in advance of future financial difficulties and assist in planning the growth of the business.

Another reason for proper record keeping is to satisfy government requirements. Although most owner-managers don't revere the Canada Revenue Agency (CRA), the fact that this agency requires accurate record keeping to calculate a business's tax liability may actually benefit the small business.

Record keeping is also necessary if a business must borrow money. Lenders will require that proper record keeping be followed to ensure that debt obligations are met. Incidents 10-2 and 10-3 illustrate how two Canadian entrepreneurs could have benefited from a better understanding of the financial implications of debt and rapid growth.

The availability of accurate and current records of the operations of the business is also essential for the evaluation and control of business operations. Figure 10-1 (on page 294) illustrates the various uses of accounting information.

Small business owners may be tempted to neglect the financial aspects of the business in favour of the day-to-day operational aspects such as production, personnel management, and marketing. Often this is because they have an incomplete understanding of how to manage the record-keeping system effectively. Understanding the managerial aspects of record keeping requires reviewing some basic accounting fundamentals.

INCIDENT 10-1   Alex Tilley

Alex Tilley sold his first wide-brimmed hat on a boat show over 25 years ago. His cotton creation became an instant success and today he sells 280,000 hats a year. Tilley's products have grown to include shorts, skirts, jackets, vests, and underwear, and have penetrated the market in 17 countries.

However, Tilley admits that there have been some desperate times. He says there was a time when he was in desperate need of $5,000 and the bank wouldn't lend it. After trying everything, he went to his parents where he cried like a child. "Dad went with me to the bank, said something to the guy, I got my five grand and paid it back a week later after we went to a boat show," he says. Tilley also says that he had to cash in his RRSPs twice. He indicates that more skill in financial management would have saved him a lot of stress in the early years of his business.

Source: Adapted from, Andy Holloway, "Alex Tilley," *Canadian Business*, January 2005, p. 66 and small business profile, Chapter one, from the 6th edition of this textbook.

INCIDENT 10-2   How to Open Your Own Restaurant

Nico and Karri Schuermans spent four stressful months getting their Belgian cuisine restaurant ready to open in downtown Vancouver. By the time the doors were ready to open, the husband and wife duo were flat broke and only had $11 in the bank a month into operating. The restaurant, called Chambar, is a modern twist on classic Belgian cuisine that has quickly become a hot spot in Vancouver and has proven popular enough to turn a profit in just five months.

Karri and Nico estimated they'd need about $400,000 to get the restaurant up and running. The couple ran into some problems when two of their investors pulled out, one taking $200,000 during construction and one two weeks before opening. The couple managed to get another $200,000 although they ended up $100,000 short of their plan.

Based on her frenzied experience at Chambar, Karri recommends restaurant owners to have at least six months' worth of cash flow before opening their doors. She also recommends not signing a lease or starting construction until the money is in the bank.

Source: Adapted from Omar El Akkad, "How to Open Your Own Restaurant," *Report on Small Business*, Summer 2006, p. 30.

INCIDENT 10-3   Nuytco Research Ltd.

Dr. Phil Nuytten's passion for undersea diving has led to a life-long career in deep-diving technology and one-atmosphere systems (pressure-proof mini-submarines and armoured diving suits). Nuytten founded Can-Dive Services Ltd. in 1966 and in 1969, it and two small American diving companies cofounded Oceaneering International Inc. (OII), which became one of the largest underwater technology companies in the world (currently measuring annual revenues in excess of a half billion U.S. dollars). Nuytten sold his interest in OII in 1984 and reacquired Can-Dive from the American parent, now in its 36th year of commercial diving operations. He is currently the majority shareholder.

In 1984, Nuytten patented a flexible rotary joint, and Can-Dive spun off a company called International Hard Suits Inc. (IHS) to exploit that technology. Nuytten led a skilled team to produce the world famous "Newtsuit." The Newtsuit allows commercial and military divers to work at depths in excess of 1,000 feet with no need for lengthy decompression to avoid the potentially crippling or fatal "bends." In 1996, Hard Suits was the subject of a hostile takeover. Nuytten's Newtsuit (now called "Hardsuit") and the submarine rescue system "Remora" are still being successfully manufactured by Hard Suits today.

Nuytten continued the development of one-atmosphere work systems through his wholly owned Nuytco Research Ltd., which currently builds and sells the manipulator-equipped "DeepWorker 2000" (a 2,000-foot, Lloyd's-certified, mini-submersible) along with new underwater lighting, communications, manipulators, and life-support items. One of Nuytco's most anticipated new developments is the lightweight Exosuit™. Nuytco is currently booked to capacity on "DeepWorker" orders—which only goes to show that success sometimes involves sales being "down." Critical to Nuytco's success has been Phil Nuytten's understanding of the accounting and financial aspects of the business. This has allowed the company to remain on solid ground as it has experienced rapid growth.

Source: Courtesy of Nuytco Research Ltd.

Figure 10-1   **Uses of Accounting Information**

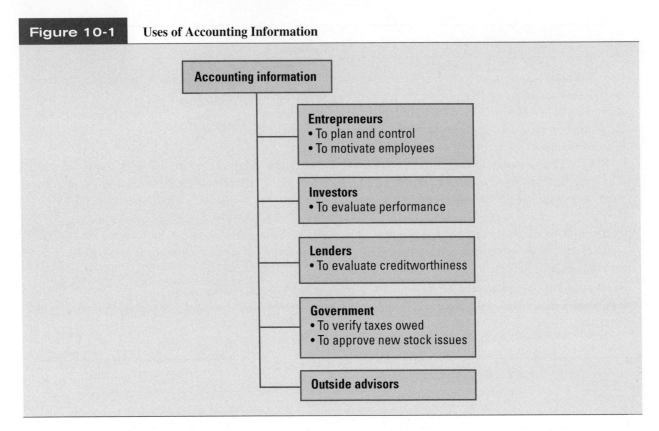

Figure 10-1   Uses of Accounting Information

THE ACCOUNTING CYCLE

Figure 10-2 illustrates the basic process by which transactions of the business are translated into financial statements.

Recording Transactions

Transactions are recorded chronologically (as they occur) in a record called a *journal*. Many types of journals are used. In a business in which few transactions occur, these entries may be made manually. In many retail businesses, the daily cash register tape total may be used to record the revenue journal entries. The cheque register can be used to record payments or disbursements. In businesses with a large number of transactions, the journal may be kept mechanically by a bookkeeping machine or by a computer.

Accounting uses double-entry recording. This means the amounts of each transaction are recorded twice. This procedure accurately reflects the fact that each transaction affects two parts (accounts) of the business. Often a decrease in one means an increase in another.

Figure 10-2   **The Accounting Cycle**

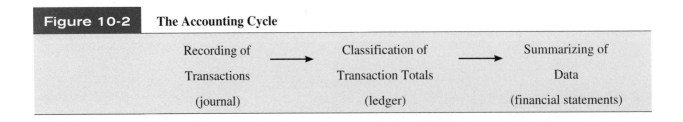

For example, if a desk costing $400 is purchased and paid for in cash, the amount of cash in the business decreases by $400 and the value of the office furniture in the business increases by $400. The use of double-entry accounting also allows for double-checking of the accuracy of the entries.

Figure 10-3 illustrates how some typical recording entries might appear in a small business journal. In each of these transactions, for every increase in one account, a corresponding decrease occurs in another account. At the end of the period, the totals of increases and decreases at the bottom of the page for a number of transactions should be equal.

Classifying Transaction Totals

Once the transactions have been accurately and properly recorded, the next step is to group or classify similar transactions together. These groupings or classifications are called accounts and are entered into a book called a *ledger*. The ledger keeps a running balance of the dollar amounts in each account so that the net totals may be known at the end of each period. Like journal entries, a ledger may be kept manually or by computer. Figure 10-4 on the next page shows some accounts of a typical ledger for service, retail, and manufacturing firms. The recording and classifying steps of the accounting cycle are usually referred to as

Figure 10-3	**Typical Journal Entries**		
		DR.	**CR.**
Jan. 1, 2007	Cash	2,000	
	Accounts receivable		2,000
	Received from Bill Smith on account.		
Jan. 5, 2007	Equipment	4,500	
	Cash...		4,500
	Purchased equipment for cash.		
Jan. 20, 2007	Inventory..	2,000	
	Accounts payable		2,000
	Inventory is purchased on account.		
Jan. 31, 2007	Accounts payable.....................................	500	
	Cash...		500
	Liabilities of $500 are paid with cash.		
Jan. 31, 2007	Cash	8,000	
	Sales revenue..............................		8,000
	Sales of $8,000 are made during the month.		

| Figure 10-4 | Typical Ledger Account Titles Utilized for Some Types of Businesses |

Service Firm	For a Retail Firm Add These Accounts	For a Manufacturing Firm Add These Accounts
Sales	Sales returns and allowances	Machinery
Cash	Sales discounts	Accumulated depreciation: Machinery
Accounts receivable	Furniture and fixtures	
Accounts payable		
Land	Accumulated depreciation: Furniture and fixtures	Cost of goods sold: Raw materials Direct labour Factory overhead
Building		
Accumulated depreciation: Building	Merchandise inventory	
Office equipment		
Accumulated depreciation: Office equipment Office supplies inventory Retained earnings Salaries expense Telephone expense Advertising expense Office supplies expense	Cost of goods sold: Purchases Purchase returns Purchase discounts Transportation in	
Depreciation expense: Building		
Depreciation expense: Equipment		
Miscellaneous expense		
Salaries payable		
Utilities expense		
Licences and taxes expense		
Insurance expense		
Accounting and legal expense		

bookkeeping. Many small businesses have found it valuable to hire an accountant to set up the bookkeeping system most appropriate for their businesses.

Summarizing Data

The third step in the accounting cycle (which is usually carried out by an accountant) involves taking the account totals from the ledger and putting them together to form the financial statements. These statements indicate the past success and current position of the business. It is important that the small business owner understand what financial statements mean and how to use them.

Essentially three financial statements are important to the small business owner: the balance sheet, the income statement, and the cash flow statement.

Balance Sheet (Statement of Financial Position). The balance sheet presents, in summary form, a snapshot of what the business owns and owes at any point in time. Those items the business owns are termed assets, and those owed are either liabilities (owed to sources outside the business) or equity (owed to owners). Figure 10-5 illustrates a balance sheet for a hypothetical small business. Assets and liabilities are generally listed in order of liquidity, with the most liquid being first. Usually assets and liabilities are divided into current (to be consumed in one year) and noncurrent (in more than one year).

Figure 10-5	Balance Sheet

Small Business Corporation
Balance Sheet
As of December 31, 2007
Assets

Current assets:		
Cash	$ 3,449	
Accounts receivable	5,944	
Inventories	12,869	
Prepaid expenses	$ 389	
Total current assets		$22,651
Fixed assets:		
Land, buildings, and equipment cost	26,926	
Less accumulated depreciation	$13,534	
Total fixed assets		$13,392
Other assets:		
Investments	$ 1,000	
Total other assets		$ 1,000
Total assets		$37,043

Liabilities and Shareholders' Equity

Current liabilities:		
Accounts payable	$ 6,602	
Other current liabilities	$ 825	
Total current liabilities		$ 7,427
Other liabilities:		
Mortgage payable	3,000	
Total liabilities		10,427
Shareholders' equity:		
Common stock	15,000	
Retained earnings	11,616	
Total shareholders' equity		26,616
Total liabilities and shareholders' equity		$37,043

Income Statement (Statement of Profit and Loss). The income statement shows the results of the operations of the business for a given period. This statement, introduced in Chapter 3, is an integral part of the feasibility analysis and the business plan. The profit or income is determined by taking revenue from operations and subtracting expenses incurred in earning that revenue. Figure 10-6 illustrates an income statement for a hypothetical small business.

Cash Flow Statement or Statement of Changes in Financial Position. The importance and format of the cash flow statement was discussed in Chapter 7. This statement is similar to the income statement except that only cash inflows and outflows are shown.

In recent years, it has been common to examine not only the cash flow position of a firm but all the asset and liability accounts over time. This practice has led to the popularity of a statement called "the statement of changes in financial position." As the name implies, this statement presents balance sheet account changes from one period to the next. It can help explain why a business has a positive net income but a decrease in cash for the same period of operation, a situation that mystifies some small business owners. The examination of the statement of changes in financial position can be complex. An example of a cash flow statement for a hypothetical small business appears in Figure 10-7.

Figure 10-6	Income Statement

Small Business Corporation
Income Statement
For the Year Ended December 31, 2007

Net sales	$197,000
Cost of goods sold	123,000
Gross margin on sales........................	74,000
Operating expenses	
Selling expenses	
Advertising expense	1,200
Sales salaries expense	18,300
Depreciation expense—store equipment.....	2,000
Total selling expenses	21,500
General expenses	
Depreciation expense—building...........	3,000
Insurance expense	675
Miscellaneous general expenses	425
General salaries expense	7,200
Total general expenses	11,300
Total operating expenses.................	32,800
Net operating margin	41,200
Other expenses	
Interest expense...........................	2,750
Net income before income taxes...............	38,450
Income taxes................................	14,350
Net income	$ 24,100

Figure 10-7	Cash Flow Statement

Small Business Corporation
Cash Flow Forecast 2007

	Jan.	Feb.	Mar.	Apr.	May	June
Cash receipts:						
Sales in 2005.............	—	$ 5,000	$ 7,500	$10,000	$10,000	$ 10,000
Accounts receivable for 2004..	$19,000	13,000	6,000			
Other:						
Equity funding		10,000				
Total cash receipts...........	$19,000	$28,000	$ 13,500	$10,000	$10,000	$ 10,000
Cash disbursements:						
Cost of sales						
Labour	$ 5,000	$ 5,000	$ 5,000	$ 7,000	$ 7,000	$ 7,000
Materials	400	800	800	1,000	1,100	1,100
Transport	300	400	400	500	400	400
Accounts payable from 2004....	12,000	10,000	10,000	6,000		
Selling expense	400	800	800	800	800	800
Administration..............	250	550	550	550	550	550
Fixed-asset investment						
Long-term repayment			2,500			2,500
Income tax installment			3,000			3,000
Interest on debt						
Long-term debt			680			640
Bank loan (other cash source) .	$ 400	$ 350	$ 270	$ 370	$ 430	$ 440
Total cash disbursements.......	$18,750	$17,900	$ 24,000	$16,220	$10,280	$ 16,430
Monthly cash surplus (deficit) .	$ 250	$10,100	$–10,500	$–6,220	$ –280	$–6,430
Accumulated cash surplus .... **(deficit) for 2005**	250	10,350	−150	−6,370	−6,650	−13,080

ACCOUNTING SYSTEMS FOR THE SMALL BUSINESS

Small businesses use several types of accounting systems today. Variations occur because of differences in size, type of business (retail, service, manufacturing), industry, number of transactions, and expertise of the owner. The following is a brief description of some of the more common general systems used.

One-Book System

The one-book system is most appropriate for the very small business with few transactions. It combines the recording and classifying steps of the accounting cycle into one step and presents this information on one page in a typical columnized ledger. Figure 10-8 illustrates a typical one-book system. In this example, the journal entry is recorded in columns 1 through 5 and the ledger accounts are entered in columns 6 through 10. The double-entry procedure is followed, and column totals at the end of the period are taken to prepare the financial statements.

One-Write System

A simplification of the one-book system is the one-write or "pegboard" system used by many small businesses. The format is the same as that for the one-book system. However, special carbon cheques are used so that when a disbursement cheques is made out, it automatically enters the name and amounts into columns 2, 3, and 5 of the journal. This eliminates one operation and reduces the potential for error in transcribing the information from the cheque register to the journal columns. The ledger part of the entry is the same as that for the one-book system.

One-write systems are commercially available and are usually reasonably priced.

Multi-journal System

For businesses that are larger or have a large number of similar transactions, the journal and ledger entries may be separated into two books. It is common for the business to use more than one journal, such as a sales journal, a disbursement journal, a payroll journal, and others. This practice can simplify the entry procedure and allow easy transfer of the journal totals to the ledger accounts.

The multi-journal system, along with the one-book and one-write systems, are manual systems whose use is decreasing as more and more small businesses adopt automated systems. However, a recent survey found that nearly 1 million Canadian small businesses still do their accounting manually.[2]

Outsourcing Financial Activities

A business can outsource such financial activities as cash receipts and disbursements, payroll, accounts payable, bank reconciliations, general ledger maintenance, budgeting,

Figure 10-8	Illustration of a One-Book Accounting System

1	2	3	4	5	6	7	8	9	10
			Bank		**Revenue**		**Expenses**		
Date	Description	Cheque Number	In	Out	Sales/Miscellaneous		Wages/Advertising/Other		
Sept. 1/07	Wages paid for August	25		5,000			5,000		
Sept. 8/07	Sales for week 1		8,000		8,000				
Sept. 12/07	Paid utility bill	26		800					800
Sept. 15/07	Sales for week 2		6,500		6,500				
Sept. 19/07	Paid advertising bill	27		400				400	

preparing interim financial statements, and information technology activities. Some small businesses have found that this option can be quicker, easier, and less costly and does not require financial expertise.

Another outsourcing option for many small businesses that cannot afford their own computerized accounting system is to use a computer service bureau. Most of these services are offered by accounting firms. For a monthly fee, a small business can take its journal or ledger totals to such a bureau and within a few days receive detailed financial statements for the period (usually monthly). Much of the bookkeeping will still need to be carried out by the business, but a good portion of steps 2 and 3 of the accounting cycle can be provided by the service bureau. The big advantage is that the details contained in the reports can be valuable in operating the business.

Small Business Computer Systems

In the previous chapter the use of electronic commerce was discussed. Another valuable use of technology is in the management of the financial aspects of the business. Recently, many software programs have been developed that are written specifically for small businesses. This software may maintain bookkeeping and accounting of transactions, maintain a database of inventories, assist in making capital investments, and allow financial performance evaluation.

These applications allow for increased speed and accuracy of maintaining records, improved service to customers, improved and more timely information to managers, and reduced operating costs. Note that the selection of software is the most important aspect of the computer decision. Software that will carry out the operations the small business requires should be selected first, followed by the hardware on which the software will run. This ensures that the hardware is powerful enough to handle the demands the software places on the computer.

Despite the benefits, purchasing a computer may not automatically solve an owner-manager's financial problems. It is important that the software match the needs of the business (see Incident 10-4). Some of the potential disadvantages include the following.

Cost. Although computer prices are coming down, an adequate total system for most small businesses could still cost more than $2,500.

INCIDENT 10-4   From "Spreadsheet and Luck" to State of the Art

When Ron Routledge took over as production manager at Springland Manufacturing Ltd. just two years ago, he says it was run "by spreadsheets and luck." Springland Manufacturing Ltd. makes grain-handling equipment for markets all over the world. Accounts for the company were handled by an off-the-shelf accounting package, inventory was done by paper on a clipboard, and job estimating was done by spreadsheets.

Today, Springland supports a state of the art enterprise resource planning (ERP) system. The software handles everything from ordering parts to customer follow-up. The system was relatively inexpensive, costing only $11,200 when compared to the $50,000 to $200,000 that many small business owners pay. The new software has considerably lightened the administrative load of the company. "We now have tremendous control over what we do and it is starting to show up in increased profit margins. It paid for itself within just a few months," Routledge says. Clearly, a new software system can give small businesses planning power at an affordable cost.

Source: Adapted from Terrence Belford, "From 'Spreadsheet and Luck' to State of the Art," *The Globe and Mail*, October 13, 2005, p. B16.

Obsolescence. The rapid changes in the computer industry are resulting in very short life cycles for most computers. Often, by the time a computer is purchased and operating, new, improved versions hit the market.

Employee Resistance. Employees within an organization may resist the introduction of a computer. The owner may need to involve such employees in the decision and purchase process to help dispel any such resistance.

Capabilities. Many types of computers are available, all with different capabilities and characteristics. Some computers cannot do what the small business owner requires them to do. Thorough investigation of the business's needs and computer capability is required to avoid this situation. Business owners should purchase computers with future growth and expansion in mind, recognizing the possible need to add to existing capacity.

Set-up Time. Installing a computer system, educating those who will use it, and eliminating the bugs will take time. It is recommended that the system previously used by the small business be continued for a short period in case such a problem arises.

Failure to Compensate for Poor Bookkeeping. Some small businesses purchase a computer hoping it will clean up their bookkeeping systems. However, a computer will not help a bookkeeping system that is sloppy and inaccurate. After all, the same information entered on a manual basis must be entered into the computer. A common rule of thumb used in the computer purchase decision is that if the information generated by a manual system is accurate but takes a long time to prepare and retrieve, a computer may be of great assistance.

As the preceding discussion shows, the decision to purchase a computer is not one to be made haphazardly. It should be approached systematically and with thorough investigation.

MANAGEMENT OF FINANCIAL INFORMATION FOR PLANNING

The first part of this chapter deals with the fundamental aspects of collecting and maintaining the financial information within the business. This information is of minimal value, however, unless it is used to monitor, evaluate, and control current operations as well as plan for the future. Incident 10-5 illustrates how sound financial management can allow a firm to adopt to rapidly changing trends.

Short-Term Financial Planning

Short-term financial planning consists of preparing an estimated future financial result of operations of the business. Such pro forma (projected) financial statements serve as a blueprint for planning operations. The projected income statement is generally referred to as a budget and was described in Chapter 3 in the preparation of the feasibility analysis. Although budgets can provide many benefits to an organization, relatively few small businesses prepare or work with budgets. A budget, however, can be a very valuable financial tool for the following reasons.

Clarification of Objectives. A budget forces an organization to anticipate future operations and set goals and procedures to accomplish them.

Coordination. The budgeting process draws employees and departments together and brings them into the planning process to input into the budget information relevant to their responsibilities.

Evaluation and Control. A budget allows the owner-manager to quickly determine discrepancies that may require investigation. Such an investigation is often called variance analysis. It also allows comparison of planned (budgeted) amounts with actual results, which can

---

INCIDENT 10-5   Orient Express

In 1976 Rita Tsang and her fiancé, Andrew, found a niche in the travel industry. Tsang had come to Canada from Hong Kong for an education, as had many others. She understood the need to regularly fly home to visit family. From that, Far East Holidays was born.

Based out of Chinatown in Toronto, Tsang targeted homesick students from Hong Kong and China. The strategy was to purchase tickets in bulk and then sell them at prices lower than those imposed by the International Air Transport Association. Within the first 18 months, the company had broken even. In 1976, China was opened up to Westerners. The demand to travel to China was there; however, there were many regulations and red tape to get through. Tsang persevered and expanded the business to open another office in New York's Chinatown in 1980.

By 1982 Far East was grossing $10 million a year. Far East began organizing multicity tours to Asia and then selling them to other retailers. This remains the bulk of their sales today. After the Tiananmen Square massacre in 1989, demand for travel to China dwindled, and in its place Far East began offering European tours, ski packages, and cruises and increased bookings to other Asian destinations. When demand for travel in China rebounded, Far East was there. By opening an office in Beijing, they have been able to free themselves from a lot of red tape.

Far East expects to have revenues of over $300 million this year. The key to their success has been Tsang's forward thinking and ability to adapt financially to current trends.

Source: Adapted from Allan Tong, "Orient Express," *Canadian Business*, October 28, 2002, p. 47 and Far East Holidays website, 2006.

---

improve effectiveness in the long term. Figure 10-9 on the next page shows how a budget might be established and used. After the comparison of budgeted (planned) and actual results, attempts can be made to explain the reasons for any differences. Consequently, changes might be made to correct the differences or refine the budgeting process.

Long-Term Financial Planning

Three types of long-term financial planning decisions could affect the small business—decisions regarding capital investment, capacity, and expansion.

The Capital Investment Decision. Most long-term planning includes the question of future capital purchases. This may involve the acquisition of land, buildings, equipment, or even another business. The small business owner needs to have a simple but accurate way to determine whether the decision will be financially sound. Some of the more commonly used methods of estimating future return for capital investments are discussed below.

Rate-of-Return Method. This method estimates the annual rate of return of the new investment. After this value has been determined, it can be compared with alternative investments. Figure 10-10 (on page 305) shows how a rate of return for a capital asset is determined.

Present Value Method. This method employs the time value of money in looking at future cash inflows and outflows. Future inflows and outflows of cash are discounted because cash held today is worth more than cash received or paid in the future. Present value rates are collected from present value tables, which most accounting and finance texts provide. The rate required to equalize discounted outflows (for the purchase of the assets) and discounted inflows (income from the assets) represents the discounted rate of return of the asset.

Payback Method. This method, which is similar to the rate-of-return method, estimates the number of years required for the capital investment to pay for itself. Figure 10-11 illustrates how the payback method is used.

Figure 10-9 **Use of a Budget**

Small Business Corporation
Income Statement
For the Year Ended December 31, 2007

	Budgeted	Actual	Difference	Explanation
Net sales	$197,000	$180,000	$17,000	Sales targets not reached
Cost of goods sold	123,000	120,000	3,000	Material costs increase
Gross margin on sales	74,000	60,000	14,000	
Operating expenses				
Selling expenses				
Advertising expense	1,200	1,200	0	
Sales salaries expense	18,300	18,300	0	
Total selling expense	19,500	19,500	0	
General expenses				
Depreciation expense—store				Additional equipment
equipment	2,000	4,000	2,000	purchased
Depreciation				
expense—building	3,000	3,000	0	
Insurance expense	675	1,200	525	Premium increase
General salaries expense	7,200	7,200	0	
Miscellaneous general				
expenses	425	600	175	
Total general expenses	13,300	16,000	2,700	
Total operating expenses	32,800	35,500	2,700	
Net operating margin	41,200	24,500	16,700	
Other expenses				
Interest expense	2,750	3,200	450	Rate increase
Net income before income	38,450	21,300	17,150	
taxes				
Income taxes	14,450	7,455	6,995	Marginal rate decrease
Net income	$ 24,000	$ 13,845	$10,155	

The Capacity Decision. Another important financial planning decision for the small business, especially the small manufacturer, is the size and extent of operations. Financial management techniques related to capacity help answer such questions as how many units should be produced and how large the plant should be. A useful technique for answering these questions is break-even analysis.

The *break-even point* is the point at which the level of output (in units or dollars) is equal to fixed and variable costs. By applying break-even analysis, the small business owner can determine the minimum level of operations required to financially break even. The use of

Figure 10-10	**Rate-of-Return Method**

Steps	Example
1. Calculate total cost of investment.	$50,000
2. Estimated depreciable life of investment.	5 years
3. Calculate average value of investment over life. Beginning value ($50,000) plus end value (0) divided by 2 equals average value.	$\frac{\$50,000}{2} = \$25,000$
4. Estimate average annual profit over depreciable life (net of depreciation).	$10,000
5. Average profit divided by average investment.	$\frac{\$10,000}{\$25,000} = 40\%$

A reasonable rate of return on a capital investment is between two and three times the prime rate of interest. Using this criteria, the 40 percent rate of return in this example represents an attractive investment.

Figure 10-11	**Payback Method**

Steps	Example
1. Calculate total cost of investment.	$50,000
2. Estimate depreciable life of investment.	5 years
3. Calculate annual depreciation charge.	$10,000
4. Estimate average annual profit over depreciable life.	$10,000
5. Cost of investment divided by cash inflow (profit + depreciation)	$\frac{\$50,000}{\$10,000 + \$10,000} = 2.5$ years

The payback period for the capital investment would be 2.5 years. As this is considerably less than the depreciable life of the asset, it appears to be an attractive investment.

break-even analysis could form an important part of the feasibility analysis discussed in Chapter 3. The formula for break-even analysis is shown below.

$$BEP = \frac{\text{Fixed costs}}{\text{Profit per unit}} = BEP \text{ in units}$$

or

$$BEP = \frac{\text{Fixed costs}}{\text{Profit as percent of sales}} = BEP \text{ in dollars}$$

where

Fixed costs = Costs that will not vary as production increases (e.g., costs of plant, equipment, and some overhead expenses)

Profit per unit = Selling price − Variable costs

The resulting graph (Figure 10-12 on the next page) illustrates at what price and output the break-even point occurs given fixed and variable costs.

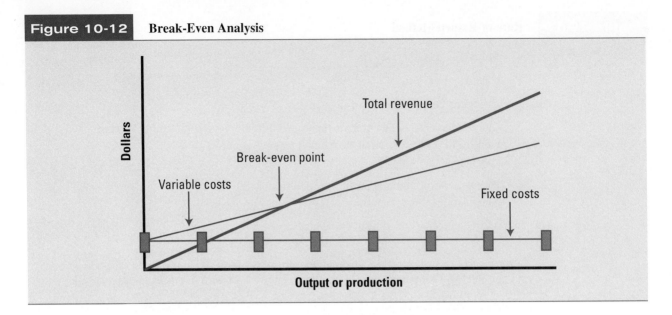

Figure 10-12   **Break-Even Analysis**

The Expansion Decision. Break-even analysis can also be used to help the owner-manager decide whether to expand the scope of operations. The same formulas can be used but only on an incremental basis, as follows.

The Effect of Fixed-Cost Adjustments

$$\text{BEP} = \frac{\text{Additional fixed costs}}{\text{Profit per unit}} = \begin{array}{c}\text{Additional unit volume needed to}\\\text{cover additional fixed costs}\end{array}$$

$$\text{BEP} = \frac{\text{Additional fixed costs}}{\text{Profit as percent of sales}} = \begin{array}{c}\text{Additional sales volume needed}\\\text{to cover additional fixed costs}\end{array}$$

The Effect of Variable-Cost Adjustments. Another use of incremental break-even analysis is to measure the effects of changes in the components of the formula, such as variable costs. The following example illustrates this calculation:

$$\text{BEP} = \frac{\text{Fixed costs}}{\text{New profit/unit}} - \frac{\text{Fixed costs}}{\text{Old profit/unit}}$$

= Additional unit volume needed to cover additional variable cost

$$\text{BEP} = \frac{\text{Fixed costs}}{\begin{array}{c}\text{New profit as}\\\text{percent of sales}\end{array}} - \frac{\text{Fixed costs}}{\begin{array}{c}\text{Old profit as}\\\text{percent of sales}\end{array}}$$

= Additional sales volume (in dollars) needed to cover additional variable costs

EVALUATION OF FINANCIAL PERFORMANCE

Quantitative evaluation of the performance of the business is an essential management task. Because they lack a financial background, many small business owners rely on their accountants to look after the complete financial end of the business. An accountant may be essential for preparing year-end financial statements, but few small businesses can afford ongoing financial management advice from this source. The small business owner is well advised to acquire a basic working knowledge of some key financial evaluation components of the business. This can enable the owner to monitor and control operations throughout the year, not just at year-end.

Several measures also can be used to evaluate the results found in the financial statements. Some of the more common techniques are described next.

Management of Current Financial Position

One critical problem many small businesses face is a shortage of cash to finance operations. Some small business owners find it hard to understand that as their businesses become successful and grow, this tends to create a strain on operating funds. Equally hard for many to understand is the situation in which the income statement shows a profit, but the cash position of the business has deteriorated.

The reason these situations occur is that most small businesses do not operate on a cash basis of accounting. (Some service businesses, farmers, and fishermen do use cash basis accounting methods, however.) The system used is called an accrual-based accounting system. With an accrual system, a transaction need not involve a cash transfer to be recorded. For example, a sale of merchandise is recorded as revenue for income statement purposes whether it is paid for in cash or purchased on credit. Likewise, many noncash transactions may affect the income statement, whereas some cash transactions may not.

The above discussion illustrates the need to closely monitor the cash position of the business. As indicated, this is difficult to do by examining only the income statement. The balance sheet and cash flow statements are essential components of monitoring cash position.

If the cash position of the business needs to be improved, an effective way to do so is to reduce the length of time from payment for inventory to receipt of payment for the inventory once it is sold. This cycle has three essential components:

1. Time taken to pay accounts payable

2. Time taken to sell inventory

3. Time taken to receive payment for inventory

Figure 10-13 (beginning on the next page) illustrates how to use these components in reducing this cycle for a hypothetical business. Additional information about estimating cash requirements for an increase in sales is provided in Chapter 14.

Evaluation of Financial Statements

Once the financial statements have been prepared, several relationships between various account totals can assist in evaluating the operations of the business. This evaluation of relationships is called ratio analysis. It can be used to compare the financial performance of the business with those of other similar businesses or with previous results for the same business.

Statistics Canada
www.statcan.ca

Reports of financial ratios for other businesses are prepared by industry associations and Statistics Canada, and can be found on the Statistics Canada, Strategis, or G.D. Sourcing websites. These reports are collected from many businesses across the country; thus, when using them it is important to use comparable businesses from the same industry.

Financial ratios can also help in isolating and analyzing weaknesses within the business. Four categories of ratios are commonly used in evaluating a small business. Each is discussed next with a general statement regarding whether the ratio is acceptable. The ratios of certain industries, however, may deviate from these averages. Illustrations of these ratios for a small business appear in Appendix 10A.

| Figure 10-13 | Financial Management |

Small Business Co. Ltd.
Balance Sheet
at Dec. 31, 20—

Assets		Liabilities	
Accounts receivable	$100,000	Accounts payable................	$ 40,000
Inventory	50,000	Bank loans.....................	100,000
Fixed assets	$140,000	Shareholders' equity	$150,000
		Total liabilities and shareholders'	
Total assets	$290,000	equity.......................	$290,000

Small Business Co. Ltd.
Income Statement
for Year Ended Dec. 31, 20—

Sales...	$750,000
Cost of goods sold...	500,000
Gross profit...	250,000
Expenses	200,000
Net profit	$ 50,000

1. Time taken to pay accounts

$$= \frac{\text{Accounts payable}}{\text{Cost of goods sold}} \times \text{365 days}$$

$$= \frac{\$40,000}{\$500,000} \times \text{365 days}$$

$$= \text{29.2 days}$$

This means that, on average, it takes 29.2 days to pay for inventory purchased.

2. Time to sell inventory

$$= \frac{\text{Inventory}}{\text{Cost of goods sold}} \times \text{365 days}$$

$$= \frac{\$50,000}{\$500,000} \times \text{365 days}$$

$$= \text{36.5 days}$$

This means that, on average, it takes 36.5 days to sell the inventory.

3. Time to receive payment

$$= \frac{\text{Accounts receivable}}{\text{Sales}} \times \text{365 days}$$

$$= \frac{\$100,000}{\$750,000} \times \text{365 days}$$

$$= \text{48.67 days}$$

This means that, on average, it takes 48.67 days to receive payment for inventory sold. The business cycle for this company is:

$$36.5 \text{ days} + 48.7 - 29.2 = 56 \text{ days}$$

Figure 10-13	continued

To increase the cash position, suppose the business was able to increase the accounts payable and decrease the turnover and receivable day totals for each component by five days. The result of these actions is shown in the paragraphs below.

1. *Time taken to pay accounts:* A five-day increase substituted in the formula would increase accounts payable from $40,000 to $46,849 with a resulting increase in cash of $6,849 (46,849 – 40,000) by using the above formula. This five-day increase might be accomplished by obtaining extensions from suppliers or simply not paying accounts payable until absolutely required.

2. *Time to sell inventory:* A five-day decrease substituted in the formula would decrease inventory from $50,000 to $43,150 with a resulting increase in cash of $6,850 (50,000 – 43,150). Such a decrease might be a result of increased advertising, more careful purchasing, or greater incentive to salespeople.

3. *Time taken to receive payment:* A five-day decrease substituted in the formula would decrease accounts receivable from $100,000 to $89,733 with a resulting increase in cash of $10,267 (100,000 – 89,733). Such a decrease might be accomplished by increasing the intensity of collection procedures or submitting charge card receipts more often.

The total effect of these measures on the cash position of the company would be $6,849 + $6,850 + $10,267 = $23,966 increase. The owner-manager, of course, would have to balance this increase in cash against the costs of accomplishing the five-day increases or decreases.

Liquidity Ratios. Liquidity ratios assess the business's ability to meet financial obligations in the current period. Two liquidity ratios are commonly used: the current ratio and the acid test or quick ratio. The calculations for these ratios are as follows:

$$\text{Current ratio} = \text{Current assets:Current liabilities}$$

This figure, expressed as a ratio, should be higher than 1:1 and usually between 1:1 and 2:1.

$$\text{Acid test or quick ratio} = \text{Current assets} - \text{Inventories:Current liabilities}$$

The quick ratio is more suitable for businesses that have a high level of inventories. A ratio of 1:1 is considered healthy. If the liquidity ratios are lower than they should be, the business may have difficulty meeting obligations within the year and will have a hard time raising further debt capital. Actions that could improve the liquidity ratios are increasing current assets without a corresponding increase in current liabilities such as equity financing or increased long-term debt.

Productivity Ratios. Productivity ratios measure the efficiency of internal management operations. They include the inventory turnover ratio and the collection period ratio.

The calculation of the inventory turnover ratio is as follows:

$$\text{Inventory turnover} = \frac{\text{Cost of goods sold}}{\text{Average inventory at cost}}$$

or

$$\text{Inventory turnover} = \frac{\text{Sales}}{\text{Average inventory at retail price}}$$

Inventory turnover reveals the number of times the inventory is turned over (sold) in a year. Average turnover rates vary considerably by industry but usually should not be lower than two to three times. An inventory turnover that is too low may reflect poor inventory buying in terms of either being overstocked or buying low-demand inventory.

The collection period is calculated as follows:

$$\text{Collection period} = \frac{\text{Accounts receivable}}{\text{Daily credit sales}}$$

This ratio reflects the average number of days taken for purchasers to pay their accounts to the business. Normal collection periods are in the 20-day to-40-day range. If the collection period is too long, it may mean the credit-granting policy is too loose, the administration of billing is too slow, or the collection of accounts is too lax. Solutions to poor productivity ratios include better buying and more emphasis on selling and collections.

Profitability Ratios. Profitability ratios measure the effectiveness of operations in generating a profit. There are four ratios in this category.

The first ratio is gross margin:

$$\text{Gross margin} = \text{Sales} - \text{Cost of goods sold}$$

This figure, usually expressed as a percentage of gross sales, can be used for comparisons. Gross margin for an individual product is calculated by subtracting cost from selling price and is commonly called markup. Average gross margins usually range from 20 percent to 50 percent. If gross margins are lower than they should be, the cause may be poor buying, failure to emphasize high-margin items, theft or spoilage, or price levels that are not current.

The profit-on-sales ratio measures profit as a percentage of gross sales:

$$\text{Profit on sales} = \frac{\text{Net profit (before tax)}}{\text{Sales}}$$

Typically the average percentages fall within 1 percent to 5 percent. A lower than average profit-to-sales percentage can reflect a problem with either pricing or expenses. Pretax profits are normally used, since the tax rates may vary by jurisdiction and industry. In addition, reporting agencies that publish industry standards may use pretax profits as a comparison.

The third profitability ratio is the expense ratio:

$$\text{Expense ratio} = \frac{\text{Expense item}}{\text{Sales}}$$

Many specific expenses on the income statement may be expressed as a percentage of gross sales. These figures can then be compared with those for similar businesses.

The return-on-investment ratio reflects the profitability of the owner's investment:

$$\text{Return on investment} = \frac{\text{Net profit (before tax)}}{\text{Owner's equity}}$$

This ratio may be compared not only with those for other similar businesses but also with alternative investments. If compared with the bank rate of interest, it is important to remember the risk associated with the business. Thus, the return on investment should be higher than the bank rate to compensate for this.

Debt Ratio. The debt-to-equity ratio measures the solvency of the business, or the firm's ability to meet long-term debt payments:

$$\text{Total debt to equity} = \text{Total debt} : \text{Owner's equity}$$

Acceptable debt ratios vary, but generally speaking it should not be greater than 4 to 1. A lender normally will not provide further financing to a firm with a higher ratio. To improve the debt ratio, the small business may need to increase the equity investment or reduce debt through operations.

CREDIT AND THE SMALL BUSINESS

A major concern for many small businesses in their attempt to reduce the length of the business cycle is control of credit. The owner-manager should understand the fundamentals of credit granting and management to effectively control receivables. Before deciding to extend credit, the owner-manager should be aware of the costs and potential difficulties involved in granting credit as well as the advantages of its use. The attractiveness of such a program is less today, since the majority of consumers can use bank credit or debit cards for their purchases.

Advantages of Credit Use

The advantages of offering credit include the following:

- A credit program will undoubtedly result in increased sales and will probably be necessary to remain competitive.

- Credit customers are more likely to be loyal to the store or business.

- Credit customers tend to be more concerned than are cash customers with quality of service as opposed to price.

- The business can maintain information about and a record of credit customers and their purchases that can help in formulating future plans.

Disadvantages of Credit Use

A credit program can also create certain difficulties:

- There will generally be some bad debts when using a credit program. The number of bad debts depends largely on how strict the credit-granting policy is and how closely accounts are monitored.

- Slow payers cost the business in lost interest and capital that could be used for more productive investments. It is estimated that in many businesses, losses resulting from slow payers are greater than losses from bad debts.

- A credit program increases bookkeeping, mailing, and collection expenses. Purchase records need to be kept, statements mailed, and accounts monitored and collected. As a result, many small businesses decide against offering their own credit programs.

Management of a Credit Program

If the small business owner decides to use a credit program, some essential steps should be followed to ensure maximum effectiveness.

Determine Administrative Policies. This includes such items as application forms, credit limits for customers, procedures to follow on overdue accounts, determining which records to keep, and deciding when to send statements.

Dun and Bradstreet
Canada
www.dnb.ca

Set Criteria for Granting Credit. A small business owner-manager may want to assess many of the same areas a lender would evaluate in considering a small business loan, although perhaps not in the same detail. Some essentials would be past credit history, other accounts held, monthly income, references, and bank used. A small business is well advised to use the services of a credit bureau located in most cities or a commercial agency such as Dun and Bradstreet to evaluate customers' creditworthiness.

Set up a System to Monitor Accounts. Proper management of accounts receivable involves classifying accounts by the length of time they have been outstanding. This process is called aging of accounts receivable. Common categories used are under 30 days, 30 to 60 days, 60 to 90 days, and over 90 days. Experience shows that the longer an account is outstanding, the smaller is the chance of collecting it. Therefore, special attention should be paid to overdue accounts.

Establish a Procedure for Collection. A uniform procedure should be set up regarding the use of overdue notices, phone calls, credit supervision, legal action, and a collection agency. Lax supervision of accounts has led to many small business failures, so this is an area of credit management that cannot be ignored. An example of such a collection policy appears in Figure 10-14.

One form of collection sometimes used by small businesses is a factoring company, which, as discussed in Chapter 7, can also be a source of small business financing. This type of company purchases accounts receivable for cash and attempts to collect them. In some cases, a factoring company handles the overall credit program for the business and even provides debt financing.

Use of Bank Credit Cards

Visa Canada
www.visa.ca

MasterCard
www.mastercard.com/
canada

Because of the high costs and risks involved in operating their own credit programs, many small businesses find the most effective way to offer credit is to use bank credit cards such as Visa and MasterCard. The use of credit cards and electronic banking by consumers has now surpassed that of cash and cheques in Canada. The credit card companies assume the risk of bad debts and cover much of the administration costs of bookkeeping and issuing of statements in return for a fee—usually from 2 percent to 6 percent of sales, depending on

---

Figure 10-14	An Example of a Collection Policy				
	30 Days	**45 Days**	**60 Days**	**75 Days**	**90 Days**
Communication	Letter, telephone; copy of statement	Letter, telephone; copy of statement	Letter, telephone	Letter, telephone	Registered letter or lawyer's letter
Message	Overdue account, please remit	Pay in 15 days or deliveries will be stopped	Deliveries stopped; pay immediately	Pay in 15 days or account will be turned over for collection	Action is being taken
Action	None	None	Stop deliveries	None	Use collection agency or small claims court

Source: *Small Business Review,* pamphlet (Toronto: Thorne Riddell Chartered Accountants).

volume. Because of the high ownership of these cards by consumers today, most retail and service firms find their use essential to enhancing sales.

Many businesses allow the use of debit cards, such as Interac. Much like the bank credit card, the debit card automatically transfers the sale amount from the customer's account at the bank to the business's account. The obvious advantages of debit cards are the quick repayment and reduction of accounts receivable. For a monthly fee the business can be assured of on-the-spot transfers to their bank for a transaction. The costs of offering this service are approximately $50 per terminal per month.

Summary

1. The three-step process of the accounting cycle includes (1) recording the transactions (journal), (2) classifying the transaction totals (ledger), and (3) summarizing the data (financial statements). The three financial statements important to the owner-manager of a small business are the balance sheet, the income statement, and the cash flow statement.

2. The common types of bookkeeping systems used by small businesses today are the one-book system, the one-write system, the manual multi-journal system, outsourcing certain functions, computer service bureaus, and small business computers.

3. Some of the more common operations computers can perform are word processing, general ledger, database files, payroll, financial planning, and capital investment decisions. Some potential disadvantages of computer ownership are cost, obsolescence, employee resistance, restricted capabilities, and set-up time.

4. Short-term financial planning consists of preparing an estimated future financial result, or a budget, and comparing it with actual results. The three types of long-term financial planning decisions are capital investment, capacity, and expansion decisions.

5. Ratio analysis enables the small business owner to compare the financial performance of the company with that of other firms in the industry and with the company's own past performance. Common financial ratios include liquidity ratios, productivity ratios, profitability ratios, and debt ratios.

6. The advantages of offering credit are a likely increase in sales, increased store loyalty, and improved information about purchases. The disadvantages are bad debts, slow payers, and administration costs. Essential aspects of administering a credit program are defining administrative policies, establishing credit-granting criteria, setting up a system to monitor accounts, and establishing a procedure for collection.

Chapter Problems and Applications

1. For the following transactions, indicate which accounts are changed and by how much.

    a. Feb. 14, 2007—Received $1,000 from Frank Johnson on account.

    b. Feb. 14, 2007—Purchased equipment for $1,500 (paid cash).

    c. Feb. 15, 2007—Paid owner Bill Cartwright $2,000 for January's salary.

    d. Feb. 18, 2007—Paid telephone bill of $90.87.

    e. Feb. 19, 2007—Bought ice cream on account, $395.00.

2. Discuss what can be done to ensure the purchase of the right computer for a small business.

www.mcgrawhill.ca/olc/balderson

3. Calculate the rate of return for the following investment. The total cost of the investment is $250,000, the depreciable life of the investment is 10 years, and the annual profit (net of depreciation) is $30,000. What considerations other than financial ones exist?

4. Assume the annual depreciation charge for the investment in Problem 3 is $25,000. Determine the payback period of the investment.

5. Determine the break-even point, in dollars, for an investment with fixed costs of $100,000 and an estimated contribution of 60 percent. How much revenue would it need to produce before you would invest?

6. a. From the balance sheet and income statement of Sam's Paint and Drywall, determine the following ratios.

   (1) Current

   (2) Inventory turnover

   (3) Profit to sales

   (4) Return on investment

   (5) Total debt to equity

   b. From Dun and Bradstreet's *Key Business Ratios* on industry norms, evaluate each of the above ratios.

SAM'S PAINT AND DRYWALL
For Year Ended December 31, 2007 (in thousands of dollars)

Assets		Liabilities and Net Worth	
Cash	$ 12	Accounts payable	$ 15
Inventory	41	Notes payable—bank	4
Accounts receivable	18	Other	20
Total current assets	71	Total current liabilities	39
Fixed assets:		Long-term liabilities	41
Vehicles	10		
Equipment	15		
Building	22		
Land	23	Total net worth (owner's equity)	61
Total fixed assets	70		
Total assets	$141	Total liabilities and net worth	$141

Income Statement
December 31, 2007
(in thousands of dollars)

Sales	$280
Less: cost of goods sold	186
Gross margin on sales	94
Less: operating expenses	81
Net profit	$ 13

7. Conduct an informal survey with three small businesses to find out which accounting system they use. Determine whether their systems are working effectively.

8. Dick's Draperies has gross sales of $15,000 per month, half of which are on credit (paid within 30 days). Monthly expenses are as follows: wages, $3,000; utilities and rent, $2,000; advertising, $300; and miscellaneous, $500. Inventory is purchased every three months and totals $30,000 for each order. Yearly expenses paid for in advance are insurance of $1,000 and a rent deposit of $700. Prepare a six-month cash flow statement for Dick's Draperies. What advice would you give this business based on the cash flow statement?

Web Exercise

Find the website for a book retailer and calculate what ratios you can. Use the Statistics Canada Small Business Profiles site.

APPENDIX 10A

Use of Financial Ratios for a Small Business (Automotive Dealer)

| Ratio | Method of Computation | Motor Vehicle Dealer | | | Explanation |
		Last Year	Previous Year	Industry Average	
1. Liquidity a. Current	Current assets:Current ratio	1.09 times liabilities	1.05 times	1.1 times	Satisfactory: This dealer has the same ability as is common in this industry
b. Quick ratio	Current assets – inventories: Current liabilities	0.33 times	0.45 times	Not available	
2. Productivity a. Inventory turnover	Cost of goods sold/Average inventory (at cost) or Sales/ Average inventory (at retail)	7.41 times	7.41 times	6.0 times	Good: This dealer has a higher turnover rate than the average dealer. This may indicate a higher sales level or lower inventory levels.
b. Collection	Average inventory at retail/Daily credit sales	13.56 days	16.01 days	12 days	Fair: The collection period is longer than average, which may indicate the need to tighten the credit policy; however, it seems that some action has already been taken.

3. Profitability a. Gross margins	Gross sales – Cost of goods sold as a percent of sales	10.71%	12.28%	16.70%	Poor: The inventory may be obsolete or company prices may be too low.
b. Profit on sales	Net profit (before tax)/Gross sales	0.85%	– (0.6%)	0.6%	Good: Expenses are being kept in line
c. Expense ratio	Expense item/ Gross sales	11.69%	13.59%	Not available	Good: The company is making an effort to cut expenses.
d. Return on investment	Net profit (before tax)/ Owner's equity	10.49%	– 1.74%	9.0%	Good: This company is more profitable than most in the industry. It is clear that action is being taken to improve profitability of this firm.
4. Debt a. Total debt to equity	Total debt/ Owner's equity	325.89%	376.09%	398.20%	Good: This dealer depends less on debt financing than is common in this industry. An intentional move has been taken in this direction.

Note: The symbol / denotes division.

Suggested Readings

"Accounting Software: What's New?" *Small Business Canada*, vol. 2, no. 4, Fall 2000, pp. 31–34. Business Development Bank of Canada Ratio Calculations, www.bdc.ca

Managing Your Business's Finances—CCH Business Owner's Toolkit, www.toolkit.cch.com/text/P06_0100.asp

Fundamentals of Record Keeping and Finance for Small Business. New York: Center for Entrepreneurial Management, 1986.

G.D. Sourcing—Sample Business Plans, Startup Cost and Cash Flow Calculator, http://www.gdsourcing.ca/SBDC.htm#plans.

Gray, John. "Ten Accounting Warning Signs You Need To Know." *Profit*, April 2002, p. 28.

Luciw, Rome. "Bookkeeping Drags Down Small Biz Owners." *The Globe & Mail*, October 2, 2006, p. 1.

McNamara, Carter. "Basic Guide To Financial Management in Small For Profit Business," www.authenticityconsulting.com

Ward, Susan. "Accounting Software For Small Business," Small Business Canada, August 14, 2006—www.sbinfocanada.ca

Comprehensive Case *Sid Stevens: Part 7*

Despite the problems identified with marketing the Ladder Rail, Sid persevered and within a few months he was able to secure enough orders to keep production steady. Sid was especially pleased to see that sales through the hardware chain were increasing and that it had placed repeat orders. Sid had also been successful in selling several Ladder Rail units to contractors in the area.

Although Sid had underestimated many of his expenses and start-up costs, he had provided much of the labour and expertise himself to defray part of this shortfall. As the year progressed, orders for the Ladder Rail continued to increase and Sid began to think that the business had turned the corner.

Suzie had kept track of the receipts and disbursements and at the end of the first year of operations took all the financial information to their accountant. A couple of weeks later the accountant called them in, and they were very disappointed in the results (see Figure 7-A). While reviewing the statements with their accountant, he provided some industry averages to help them in planning for the next year (see Figure 7-B). They were quite nervous about taking the statements to their banker, but even though they were negative, Sid's banker agreed to postpone the principal payment on the loan if Sid paid the interest, because sales were increasing.

Figure 7-A

The Ladder Rail Income Statement: Year 1

Sales	4500 @ $30	$135,000	
	250 @ $40	10,000	$145,000
Cost of Goods Sold	4750 @ $12	57,000	
Wages		80,000	
Employee Benefits		6,000	
Utilities		17,000	
Repairs & Maintenance		4,500	
Insurance		1,000	
Amortization		17,000	
Interest and bank charges		10,400	$192,900
Net Income			($ 47,900)

The Ladder Rail Income Statement: End of Year 1

Assets

Cash	$ 2,250
Accounts Receivable	3,800
Inventory	10,250
Building & Equipment	153,000
Land	50,000
Total Assets	$219,300

Liabilities & Owner's Equity

Accounts Payable	$ 36,800
Bank Loan—Current Payable	23,400
Bank Loan—Long Term	117,000
Owner's Equity	42,100
Total Liabilities & Owner's Equity	$219,300

Figure 7-B

Selected Ratios for Metal Fabricating Companies

Current Ratio	1.52:1
Gross Margin	23.2%
Profit on Sales	6.1%
Profit on Net Worth	21.13%
Collection Period	59 days
Inventory Turnover	4.2
Debt to Equity	1.1:1

Before Sid had seen the statements, he had been contemplating expanding his small factory by building an addition and adding some new equipment at a cost of $80,000 with a life of 10 years. He had estimated that this addition would bring in an additional income of $10,000 per year. With the first year's performance, however, Sid was not sure whether he should make this investment.

Questions

1. Evaluate Sid and Suzie's financial management practices.
2. Using the ratios provided by the accountant, evaluate Sid's business and make suggestions for improvement.
3. Using the financial information provided, calculate a break-even point and rate of return for the new addition. What additional information would Sid need to do a payback analysis of the proposed expansion?

CHAPTER 11

Operations Management

CHAPTER OBJECTIVES

- To review the methods of planning the production process

- To discuss the management of the components of the physical facilities of a small business

- To explain the types of layouts used in small businesses

- To describe the factors to consider in planning the layout of a store

- To illustrate methods of purchasing and controlling inventories in the small business

SMALL BUSINESS PROFILE

John Stanton

The Running Room

The idea for John Stanton's career as an entrepreneur began in 1983 when the Toefield, Alberta, native (employed as a vice-president in the grocery sector) agreed to join his youngest son in a three-kilometre run in Edmonton. Weighing about 230 pounds (90 kilograms), the two-pack-a-day smoker barely made it to the finish line. Embarrassed by his performance and his lack of stamina, John took up running, lost 60 pounds (27 kilograms), and ran in more than 60 marathons and many other road races and triathlons. He also started a retail store that specializes in running equipment as well as instruction. His concept took off and within a year The Running Room needed more room. Stores opened almost yearly. Today, the company boasts 90 stores across Canada and the United States.

John credits several factors for his company's success. First, he attempts to improve each day. This applies to his running and to the performance of the employees of his company. They are expected to improve on a regular basis. John is aware that when everyone in the organization is improving, the overall performance of the operations of the company will also improve.

Second, Stanton feels that a key to The Running Room's success is that the business is specialized.

Some of his larger competitors are involved in several categories of products, while The Running Room has expertise in running. Its employees know about the products and training, and they can give customers tips on whom to talk to, such as a local sports medicine doctor or a good nutritionist. Part of The Running Room's customer service strategy is to provide The Running Room clinics to help runners prepare for events.

Third is the location and layout of the Running Room outlets. They are located in areas that are conducive to runners and the interior of the stores make someone who is in the middle of their jog or run feel comfortable dropping in to chat or make a purchase. The broad range of products requires effective inventory control. Relationships with suppliers are actively managed and lead times are short. The company also uses a point-of-sale system that allows it to maintain contact with their customer base.

Finally, the last key to the success of The Running Room is John Stanton's hands-on approach to managing the business. He travels extensively, visiting both stores and customers. The Running Room is very involved in the community, sponsoring many fitness-related events, which also improves communication between the business and its customers.

Used with the permission of John Stanton.

The Running Room
www.runningroom.com

MANAGEMENT OF INTERNAL OPERATIONS

The management of internal operations is part of the physical facilities section of the business plan (see Chapter 4). Operations management is one area in which many small business owners have their greatest strength. They know how to produce a quality product or provide a quality service, and their primary interest often lies with this aspect of the business. Incident 11-1 illustrates the potential problems of inefficient management and production. Although they may have production expertise, many entrepreneurs lack the management skills of maintaining quality and control. Typical areas needing attention might be cash flow, production costs and product quality, inventory management, and physical facilities issues. As mentioned in earlier chapters, the entrepreneur is typically weaker in the areas of marketing and financial management than in managing the production process. As a result, many entrepreneurs find it advantageous to outsource some of these services. A recent study by Price WaterhouseCoopers found that 73 percent of Canadian businesses outsource one or more business processes.[1] Some of the typical services are financial management, human resource management, income tax preparation, marketing, call centre and customer care, and mail-room operations.

THE PRODUCTION PROCESS

The production process involves the conversion of inputs such as money, people, machines, and inventories into outputs—the products or services provided. Figure 11-1 illustrates this application for manufacturing, wholesaling, retailing, and service businesses. The owner-manager's task is to organize the production process of the business so that the outputs

---

INCIDENT 11-1   Back From the Brink

Linda Lundstrom's amazing business turnaround came after three years of declining sales and escalating costs. Lundstrom, a producer of women's fashions in Toronto, started the company in 1974. Lundstrom Inc. enjoyed sales of $12 million. Sales gradually dipped and by 2001 Lundstrom owed creditors over two million dollars.

Lundstrom then decided on an action plan to refinance the ailing firm, trim its production line, and overhaul its manufacturing methods to reduce waste and improve productivity. Lundstrom diversified into other types of clothing as well as fragrances but these ventures quickly died due to the lack of marketing muscle or distribution partners. The turning point in Lundstrom's business came when the firm adopted a different manufacturing process, lean marketing. Components were now produced and assembled on the fly, instead of being produced in large batches for subsequent assembly.

Lundstrom also slashed her supply–chain management and inventory costs. The value of the firm's work-in-progress inventory dropped from $250,000 to $16,000. Changes on staff included employees moving from sewing assembly lines to being organized in production cells, where they could complete an entire garment. The turnaround time for garments became just five days, instead of up to five weeks, allowing for new production targets. Lundstrom trimmed her line of 1,000 styles by 40 percent and renegotiated her lease, cutting back on square footage.

The transition to a new marketing system took just two months. After five years in the red, in 2004 Lundstrom Inc. achieved sales of 10.6 million.

Source: Adapted from Deena Waisberg, "Back From the Brink," *Profit*, November 2005, p. 55.

Figure 11-1   **Examples of Production Systems**

Type of Business	Inputs	Process	Outputs
Apparel manufacturer	Cloth, thread, buttons	Store—Cut—Sew—Press—Ship	Dresses
Wholesaler	Large volume per order of each product	Store—Sort—Package—Ship	Smaller volume of a product in each order
Retailer	A volume of each of many products to the ultimate customer	Store—Customer display—Package	Low volume of a few products to each customer
Laundry (service firm)	Dirty clothes	Sort—Wash—Press—Store	Clean clothes

Source: Adapted from Curtis E. Tate, Jr., Leon C. Megginson, Charles R. Scott , Jr., and Lyle R. Trueblood. *Successful Small Business Management,* 3rd ed. (Georgetown, Ont.: Irwin-Dorsey of Canada, 1982), p. 244.

(products) can be produced efficiently. Incident 11-2 illustrates how one Canadian firm is accomplishing this.

The priority evaluation and review technique (PERT) and other flowchart systems have been developed to assist in organizing the production process. A simple example of such a system is shown in Figure 11-2 for a manufacturing firm. By visually plotting the tasks and required time, the owner-manager can minimize down time and ensure the most efficient production. Continual efforts should be made throughout the process to ensure quality control.

Total Quality Management

Many small businesses have been able to develop a competitive advantage by ensuring superior quality in their products and services. This is referred to as total quality management.

INCIDENT 11-2   *Production Line Undergoes Extreme Makeover*

After a period of low productivity and floundering sales, Jean-Guy Doucet, President of Doco Enterprises, decided something had to change. The leading cabinet door manufacturer went to BDC Consulting to see how he could turn things around. "To compete in our market, we needed to be sure that our operations could be streamlined, increase production volume and ultimately generate more profits down the line," says Doucet.

The advice he received was to change his production to lean manufacturing. This means eliminating unnecessary work that adds no value to the product or service, thereby simplifying the production process. The company was able to make key improvements to its production line, such as creating new workstations that reduced assembly time. Also, special carts were designed to easily carry materials from one station to another to reduce the number of hands-on manipulations.

The changes have paid off as evidenced by the tripled revenue, reduction in delivery time, and improved productivity.

Source: Adapted from "Doco Enterprises Opens the Door for "Continuous Improvement," *BDC,* Spring 2005, Volume 25, No. 1.

| **Figure 11-2** | **Priority Evaluation and Review Techniques (PERT)** |

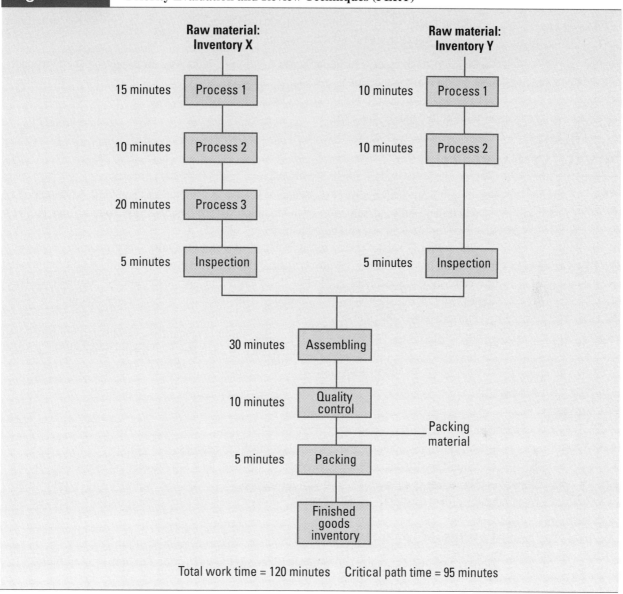

Total work time = 120 minutes   Critical path time = 95 minutes

Total quality management (TQM) is a philosophy of management focusing on problem solving and control. An organization that focuses on TQM uses such factors as consumer driven product quality, efficient distribution, quick response, continuous improvement, elimination of waste, and top management leadership and commitment as measurement tools.

To achieve such a standard, the business must meet several requirements:

- Realize that the business is going to exist in the long run. Therefore it is more concerned with long-term performance than short-term profits.

- Involve employees in decision making so that they also see the need to ensure overall superior quality.

- Invest time and effort in training employees adequately.

- Develop standards by which quality performance can be measured.

- Continually measure internal performance through internal systems and externally by surveying customers and other key parties.

Some small businesses, particularly those who are interested in exporting their products, have found it advantageous to get their products quality certified through the International Standards Organization (ISO 9000). Although costly for the small business, certification can be an effective marketing tool.

PHYSICAL FACILITIES

Planning the physical facilities is discussed briefly in Chapter 3 as part of the preparation of the feasibility analysis. Selection of the location for the business is introduced in Chapter 4 as one of the steps in organizing a business.

Although it is not necessary to review that information again, it is critical for the owner-manager to recognize that the physical facilities must be closely monitored and maintained to ensure they are efficient and up to date. Locations are never static—populations, businesses, and traffic patterns shift continually. This trend has caused many excellent locations to deteriorate over the years.

Some aspects of the physical facilities that should constantly be evaluated are illustrated in Figure 11-3. The figure ranks the importance of each physical facility characteristic based on the type of small business.

LAYOUT

Effective management of the interior layout of the business can greatly enhance productivity. Small businesses use several types of layouts. The layout selected varies by industry and by scope of operations. In determining layout, it is advisable to draw up a floor plan to better utilize available space.

Layouts for Manufacturing Firms

Here are some key areas to consider in planning the interior of a manufacturing plant:

- Location of utility outlets for machines

- Location of receiving and shipping areas for raw materials and finished goods

- Safety aspects

- Adequate lighting capability throughout

- Provision for ease of maintenance and cleaning of the plant

Essentially three types of layouts are used by small manufacturing firms: product layout, process layout, and fixed-position layout.

Product Layout. The product layout is suitable for the business that manufactures just one or only a few products. It closely resembles the production line of a large factory. Figure 11-4 (on page 326) illustrates the floor plan of a typical product layout. The product layout generally allows for economy in both cost of and time required for production, as each part of the manufacturing process is carried out in sequence.

| Figure 11-3 | **Business Building and Site-Rating Table** |

Factors	Retailing	Service	Manufacturing	Wholesaling
Building feature:				
Age	1	4	3	4
Space	1	3	1	4
Configuration	1	4	4	3
Appearance	1	3	3	4
Frontage	1	4	4	4
Access	1	2	1	1
Interior utilization:				
Floor space	2	3	1	1
Room dimensions	1	3	1	4
Ceiling heights	2	2	2	4
Stairways, elevators	3	3	1	1
Window space	1	3	4	4
Utility services	3	1	1	3
Improvement potential:				
Building exterior	1	3	4	4
Building interior	1	3	2	2
Site	1	2	3	4
Surrounding	2	2	3	4
Streets and walks	2	3	3	3
Access	1	3	2	1
Expansion	2	1	1	1
Site and environment:				
Street and service areas	1	2	2	3
Setback and frontage	1	3	4	4
Parking	1	2	2	3
Surrounding businesses	2	3	4	4
Area environment	2	3	4	4

Key to ratings: 1 = critical; 2 = very important; 3 = not ordinarily important; 4 = minimum importance

Source: John B. Kline, Donald P. Stegall, Lawrence L. Steinmetz, *Managing the Small Business* (Homewood, Ill.: Richard D. Irwin, 1982).

Process Layout. The process layout is designed for factories that manufacture many different or custom-made products. In this layout, similar processes are grouped together and the product moves back and forth among those areas until completed. The process layout is often more expensive and requires more management time to ensure efficiency. Figure 11-5 (on page 326) illustrates a process layout for a small factory.

Figure 11-4 Product Layout

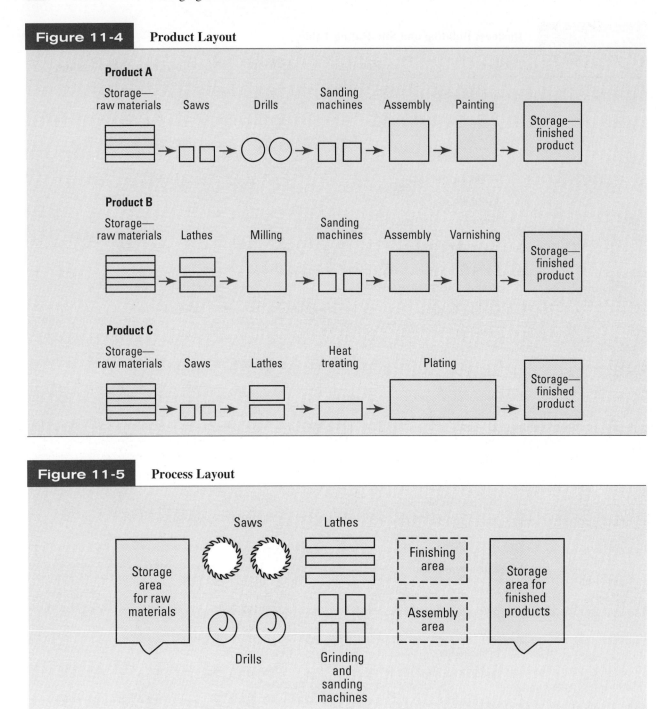

Figure 11-5 Process Layout

Fixed-Position Layout. In the fixed-position layout, the product remains in a fixed position throughout its manufacture. The production processes move to the product. As one might expect, this type of layout is used for very large and cumbersome products and is used infrequently by the small business. Figure 11-6 illustrates the fixed-position layout. Also see Incident 11-3.

Figure 11-6   **Fixed-Position Layout**

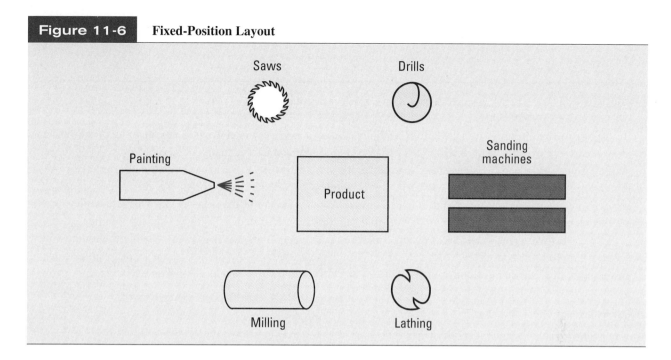

INCIDENT 11-3   MacNeil Wash Systems

MacNeil Wash Systems increased its production capacity 50 percent by improving its manufacturing facility. After conducting a manufacturing review, MacNeil Wash Systems, a leading manufacturer of innovative car wash equipment, saw the need to become better prepared for extensive growth. The Ontario-based company set about changing the layout of the plant to improve operational efficiency and drive productivity.

A large part of the manufacturing review included finding creative ways to keep materials moving more fluidly in the plant. Experts evaluated a detailed diagram of the production floor and focused on specific aspects such as equipment and racking. The review has paid off for the company: productivity has improved and the company is driving more growth. Improving operational flow means fewer errors, faster production, improved employee morale, and a better product.

MacNeil Wash Systems builds over 100 car wash systems annually and exports 80 percent of its products through a network of over 40 distributors throughout North America and Europe.

Source: Adapted from "Manufacturing Review—How MacNeil Wash Systems Made a Clean Win," *BDC*, retrieved Jan 12, 2004 from www.bdc.ca.

Layouts for Retail Firms

As noted in Figure 11-3, interior layout and creative display are important factors in the success of a retail store. (See Incident 11-4 on the next page.) Sensitivity to consumer needs and shopping patterns is critical to the development of an effective layout. In planning the layout, the retailer will need to analyze several key areas.

Allocation of Selling versus Nonselling Space. Experience in retailing shows that some areas of a retail store are more productive and draw more traffic than others. This phenomenon is illustrated in Figure 11-7 (on the next page). Generally, the space at the front and to the right is more productive space. Obviously, selling space should be planned for the most productive areas of the store.

INCIDENT 11-4   Eye-catching Design Beckons Customers

People passing by the newly designed Telus Mobility store at the Scarborough Town Centre mall in Toronto have been so captivated by the displays that they have leaned in too far and have actually hit their heads on the window. With a bright purple and lime green colour scheme, the store offers a variety of funky and unique displays. An illuminated lime platform displays the latest digital wireless phones and accessories. To attract early-morning browsers, the lights are left on when the store is closed. Another feature of the store includes numerous pods that elevate the latest products. As well, all of the in-store handsets are active so that customers can test out the features.

Bruce Herscovici, vice-president of channel marketing for Telus, says that the key to creating the ultimate in service is to provide a completely accessible store. With the two live computer stations in the store, customers can go online to hook up and customize their phones. People are also able to take care of their accounts right there instead of having to wait until they get home.

Source: Adapted from Rosalind Stefanac, "Eye-catching Design Beckons Customers," *Canadian Retailer*, September/October 2004, pp. 8–9.

Figure 11-7	Rankings of Space Importance in a Typical Retail Store

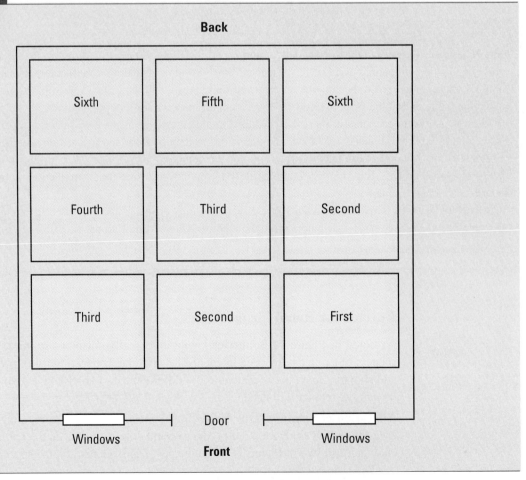

Allocation of Space among Departments and Products. The same principle discussed above should be applied in allocating space among departments and products, with the most profitable being placed in the high-traffic areas if possible.

Classification of Merchandise. Chapter 8 discusses the classification of consumer goods—convenience, shopping, and specialty goods. Each merchandise classification may require a slightly different placement in the retail store based on the purchase motives associated with that class of goods. For example, convenience items are often found close to heavier customer traffic flow. Shopping goods might be placed by competing brands, and specialty or demand items at more inaccessible parts of the store.

Location of Displays and Products on the Shelf. The small retailer should acquire expertise in a number of display techniques. Placement of merchandise on the shelf or counter can lead to increased sales, as certain areas are more productive than others. Merchandise placed at eye level and at the ends of aisles generally sells better. Two types of layouts are used by retail stores: the grid layout and the free-flow layout.

Grid Layout. The grid layout is organized with customer convenience and retailer efficiency in mind. Grid layouts have traditionally been used in stores like supermarkets and hardware stores. Figure 11-8 illustrates a grid layout.

Free-Flow Layout. Some types of merchandise are purchased in a more relaxed atmosphere that allows customers more time to browse. For such merchandise it is common to use the free-flow layout, illustrated in Figure 11-9 on the next page. This type of layout is suitable for clothing and many specialty types of merchandise.

Figure 11-8	Grid Layout

| Figure 11-9 | Free-Flow Layout |

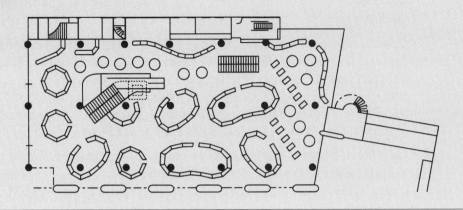

Many larger retail stores use combinations of the grid and free-flow layouts. Most small retailers, however, generally use one or the other type. Incident 11-5 describes the innovative layout of a well-known retailer.

Layouts for Service Firms

Because the operations of service firms are so diverse, it is difficult to provide standard information on layouts. Some service firms, such as restaurants, more closely approximate

---

INCIDENT 11-5   Navigating Ikea

Although it may seem odd to talk about a store solely in terms of its layout, if anyone deserves the honour, it's Ikea. Most people who have visited the store, whether or not they enjoyed the experience, can say that if there is anything that makes Ikea different, store layout is high on the list. Most will admit even further, however, that Ikea has some awesome information architecture going on.

In the main lobby, you'll find an array of sensible and well-marked services. There are restrooms and payphones, and even phone numbers for local buses and taxis. In the lobby, you can also find a huge diagram of the store.

On the first level, Ikea has everything laid out for people who know what they are looking for. As well, you can browse bins of "take-me-home-now" items. Here you will also find self-serve furniture aisles and a bistro. But of course, Ikea would prefer you to move up the stairs, to the second level, where things really get interesting.

The second level is devoted to those people who aren't exactly sure what they want. All Ikea's merchandise has been laid out in context or, as some have called it, in "room displays." For those who aren't decorator savvy, this is perfect, as Ikea provides them with an Ikea vision of "real life." As well, on this level you are guided to move in one direction. And in case you get confused, just look down! There are arrows on the floors and even signs at critical junctures that explain that you're moving through the store in the planned, straightforward manner. All of this, of course, is on purpose. And while you can certainly move around in Ikea in your own manner, chances are you'll feel odd doing so. But that's all part of Ikea's plan, proving that, if any store has an edge when it comes to retail layout, it's Ikea.

Source: Adapted from Kat Hagedorn, *Ramblings: The IA of Ikea Stores*, http://www.kathagedorn.com/ikea.html, October 16, 2001; and S.L. Wykes, "Navigating Ikea: Tour of Emeryville Store Provides Tips For Future P.A. Shoppers," *The Mercury News* http://www.mercurynews.com/mld/mercurynews/news/local/6606519.htm?1c, August 24, 2003 and IKEA website 2006.

the layouts of retail stores. Many of the principles discussed earlier for retailing apply here. For those service firms that are more similar to manufacturing firms, such as repair shops, the principles of manufacturing layouts may be more appropriate.

PURCHASING AND CONTROLLING INVENTORIES

The cost of purchasing and holding inventories can be substantial. Because a small business generally has limited economic resources, it is critical that such a firm give inventory management a high priority. The following sections discuss areas about which the small business owner should be knowledgeable in purchasing and controlling inventories.

Sources of Supply

Chapter 8 discusses various aspects of the distribution channel from the seller's point of view. The same principles apply in this section, but from the buyer's position. The owner-manager should know which suppliers are available. Purchases can usually be made directly from the manufacturer, from an agent of the manufacturer, from a wholesaler, or from a retailer. Although sources vary considerably among industries, most small businesses purchase their inventories from wholesalers. Many owner-managers import merchandise that uses sources of supply from other countries. In this case, many of the concepts discussed in Chapter 8 with respect to the exporting section may be applicable.

One question most small businesses face is whether to purchase from one supplier or many. In purchasing from only one supplier, the buyer is assured of consistent quality and will probably receive favourable treatment, such as discounts and guaranteed supply in case of shortages, although orders may be too small to divide. Conversely, other suppliers may offer lower prices periodically. The business may also spread risk by purchasing from many suppliers. The small business owner must weigh these pros and cons in making this decision. Incident 11-6 illustrates the possible consequences of making the wrong supplier decision.

www.upgc.com/
contact.cfm

Many small business owners find it advantageous and cost effective to pool purchases with other companies. This may be done on an informal basis but usually involves the business joining a purchasing group or franchise system. This type of arrangement may also be used to purchase group insurance and benefit plans for employees.

Other methods of achieving potential savings on purchasing include buying in large quantities, seasonal buying, consignment buying, and receiving price discounts for paying in cash.

INCIDENT 11-6   Bill's Service Station

Bill Andrews, owner of Bill's Service Station in Montreal, Quebec, had a dilemma. He had run out of antifreeze early in the winter, and most of his regular customers were growing impatient and going elsewhere to winterize their cars. In the past, Bill had prided himself on shopping competitively for antifreeze. To obtain the lowest prices, he frequently changed suppliers and had been able to pass some of this saving on to his customers. With the onset of the antifreeze shortage, however, this practice had come back to haunt him. Suppliers were providing the scarce product only to the retailers who had been loyal to them and had previously purchased larger volumes. Bill's Service Station was one of the first outlets to be cut off. Now Bill wished he had stayed with one supplier, even if it meant paying a few dollars more.

Source: D.W. Balderson, University of Lethbridge.

Evaluating Suppliers

Small business owners generally use certain criteria to evaluate suppliers. The following are some of the more common criteria.

Dependability. The owner-manager should evaluate how dependable the prospective supplier will likely be. Dependability will undoubtedly be more important for some companies and even for some types of products than for others.

Cost. Obviously the cost of inventories will play a major role in supplier selection for the small firm.

Services Offered. Typical services offered by suppliers are delivery, discounts, credit, promotion, promotional support materials, return policies, guarantees, and technical assistance. Willingness and ability to provide these services at all hours may be an important factor in the selection of a supplier.

Determining Order Quantities

Estimating the quantities of inventories to order will require several essential items of information.

Order Lead Time. The time taken to process the order at both shipping and destination points, as well as to transport the item(s), should be estimated. This is called order lead time and is illustrated by the distance between points B and C in Figure 11-10. An increasing number of businesses have instituted a just-in-time inventory policy. In this approach, the order is placed so that the inventory arrives "just in time" to be utilized in the production process. This system is appropriate for manufacturers that have computer capabilities, are confident of the dependability of suppliers, and require large amounts of inventory.

Figure 11-10	Order Points

The basic idea of JIT is to reduce order sizes and time orders so that goods arrive as close to the time they are needed as possible. The intent is to minimize a business's dependence on inventory and cut the costs of moving and storing goods. JIT is used more by producers than by retailers. There are notable differences between a JIT approach and a more traditional approach. Figure 11-11 illustrates these differences.

Sales or Production Estimate. The owner-manager will need to make a realistic projection of inventories to be sold or consumed in the manufacture of the finished product for the period. Methods of obtaining this type of information are discussed in Chapter 3. Such a rate of sale throughout the period is shown by the diagonal line A–C in Figure 11-10.

Minimum Inventory Levels Required. No business wants to run out of inventory, especially if the inventory consists of important items. It is therefore common to carry a minimum basic inventory for many items. Such inventory is often called safety stock and is shown as the distance between D and E in Figure 11-10. The size of safety stock usually depends on such factors as the importance of the inventory, volatility of demand, and dependability of sources of supply.

Inventory Currently on Hand. The owner-manager should have an accurate estimate of inventories on hand. To monitor current inventory levels on a continual basis, a perpetual inventory system can be used. Details of this type of system will be discussed later in this chapter. For many businesses, a perpetual system requires a computerized inventory system. As mentioned in Chapter 10, an increasing number of small businesses can now afford such systems. Once current inventory levels have been determined, the owner-manager can incorporate those amounts into various methods to determine order quantities.

Methods for Determining Order Quantities. Some of the more common methods used to determine order quantities follow.

Minimum Turnover Method. This method uses the inventory turnover formula (discussed in Chapter 10) for the business in determining amounts of inventory required. For example,

Figure 11-11	**JIT and Traditional Inventory Comparison**

JIT Inventory	Traditional Inventory
Small orders and frequent deliveries	Large orders and infrequent deliveries
Single-source supplier for a given part with long-term contract	Multiple sources of suppliers for same part with partial or short-term contracts
Suppliers expected to deliver product quality, delivery performance, and price; no rejects acceptable	Suppliers expected to deliver acceptable level of product quality, delivery performance, and price
Less emphasis on paperwork	Requires more time and formal paperwork
Delivery time and quantity can be changed with direct communication	Changes in delivery time and quantity require new purchase orders

Source: Sang Lee and Marc Schniederjams, *Operations Management* (Houghton Mifflin, Boston, 1994), p. 256.

if inventory turnover for the business is 4 (four times per year) and projected sales for the period are $200,000, the required inventory is calculated as follows:

$$\frac{\text{Sales}}{\text{Inventory}} = \text{Inventory turnover}$$

$$\frac{\$200,000}{\text{Inventory}} = 4$$

$$\text{Inventory} = \frac{\$200,000}{4} = \$50,000$$

Hence, the minimum required inventory at retail value for the period is $50,000.

Maximum and Minimum Method. Some small businesses set acceptable maximum and minimum limits on inventory levels. Whether inventory is measured in dollar amounts or number of units, reaching these limits indicates when it is time to order and specifies the amount to order. This method is used frequently by small businesses for merchandise of lower unit values.

Open-to-Buy Method. This method of calculating order quantities, used extensively in retailing, uses the following formula (the components are discussed earlier):

Open to buy = Maximum inventory – Merchandise on order – Merchandise on hand

where

Open to buy = Inventories that can be purchased
Maximum inventory = Expected sales + Safety stock required

Economic Order Quantity (EOQ). This formula is used infrequently in small businesses but may be helpful for important items or in manufacturing businesses. It allows for the calculation of the minimization of the ordering and storage costs of inventory. Generally speaking, if ordering costs are higher (more frequent orders), storage costs are lower (less inventory required). Through this formula, the owner-manager can arrive at the least-cost combination of ordering and storage costs. The EOQ formula for dollar amounts is as follows:

$$\text{EOQ} = \sqrt{\frac{2AB}{i}}$$

where

A = Annual or period demand in dollars
B = Costs of making an order in dollars
i = Inventory carrying costs (storage costs) expressed as a percentage of inventory value

For obtaining the economic order quantity in units, the formula is

$$\text{EOQ} = \sqrt{\frac{2AB}{Pi}}$$

where

Pi = Unit price

Although this formula has proved unwieldy for many small businesses in the past, the increasing accessibility of computers and the ability to enter the formula into the appropriate software has allowed more businesses to take advantage of the EOQ formula.

A-B-C Analysis. This method of inventory management recognizes that some items of merchandise are more important to the business than others. The level of importance is influenced by such factors as higher sales, high unit value levels, higher profitability, or importance in the manufacture of the finished product.

With A-B-C analysis, the most important inventory (A items) is watched more closely to ensure it is managed efficiently. The B and C items, being less important, may require less detailed monitoring and control. Figure 11-12 gives an example of A-B-C analysis.

Administration of the Buying Process. The owner-manager should be familiar with the mechanics of purchasing. Knowledge of the different kinds of discounts and purchase terms and conditions is essential, as are efficient receiving, checking, and marking of merchandise to minimize inventory costs and reduce shrinkage.

Inventory Control

As discussed earlier, efficient purchasing requires proper monitoring and control practices. Three essential aspects of inventory control are determining the unit of control, the method of valuing inventories, and the method of monitoring inventory levels.

Unit of Control. Most firms keep track of their inventories by dollar amounts. This approach is called dollar inventory control. Dollar inventory control is suitable for firms with large amounts of inventory at a relatively low per-unit value.

Some businesses that have relatively small amounts of inventory keep track of inventories in numbers of units. This method is called unit control.

Valuation. Generally accepted accounting principles allow inventories to be valued at the lower of cost or market value. It is very important that an accurate valuation of inventory levels be calculated, because, as Figure 11-13 shows, inventory levels directly affect the net income of the business at the end of the period.

Monitoring. There are essentially two methods of monitoring inventories. The first, periodic inventory, involves physically counting and recording the merchandise to determine inven-

Figure 11-12	A-B-C Analysis		
	A Items	**B Items**	**C Items**
Percent of total inventory value	65%	25%	10%
Percent of total list of different stock items	20%	20%	60%
Inventory method used	Minimum turnover EOQ Maximum turnover	Minimum turnover	Eyeballing
Time allocation	Time-consuming and precision needed	Less time-consuming estimates	Rough estimates only

Figure 11-13	**Valuation of Inventories**

Sales – Cost of goods sold – Other expenses = Net income

where

Cost of goods sold = Beginning inventory + Purchases – Ending inventory

Using the relationships in these formulas, one can see that if ending inventory is overstated, cost of goods sold will be understated by the same amount and net income overstated by that same amount. Therefore, a valuation error of $100 will translate into either an overstatement or an understatement of net income by $100.

tory levels. Periodic inventory calculation is required at least once each year for income tax purposes. It is costly and time-consuming to carry out, however, so most businesses use this method no more frequently than required.

The second type of inventory monitoring, perpetual inventory, involves continuous recording of inventory increases and decreases as transactions occur. Historically this system was feasible only for a small business with low levels of high-unit-value inventory. Recently, however, microcomputer database management programs have made the perpetual inventory system a reality for many small businesses. These systems utilize the bar codes that identify inventory purchases and sales. By using this system, sales can be tracked, inventory levels can be monitored, and orders can be made. Inventory software programs that small businesses can use are Peachtree Complete Accounting and QuickBooks Pro. These programs are relatively inexpensive and are regularly updated. Some small businesses find that developing a customized program, even though more costly, better suits their needs to manage inventory effectively. Inventory control is also enhanced by performing various evaluation analyses such as calculating turnover, comparing budgeted amounts with actual inventories, and analyzing inventory disappearance (shrinkage). Incident 11-7 illustrates how the use of computer technology can help the small business to be competitive.

INCIDENT 11-7   The Next Wave

An example of how technology can help inventory management is demonstrated at McNairn Packaging. Sales are growing 10 to 15 percent a year because of the company's new wireless technology. McNairn is a submarine, hamburger, and French fry wrapper manufacturer with more than 600 types of finished products and up to 2,000 rolls of raw material. With this entire product, inventory accuracy remains at 98 percent, thanks to the new wireless technology.

McNairn's system comprises six wireless bar-code scanners and six ceiling-mounted receivers at each location, a cost of just $35,000 per faculty. Employees are continuously scanning bar codes at each station, and the location of each roll is known at all times. This is a considerable improvement over the method used previously in which inventory was recorded by hand.

The results show that despite a 25 to 30 percent surge in production volume, McNairn has been able to hold its warehouse staff steady at six. Inventory accuracy has climbed from 88 percent to 98 percent.

Source: Adapted from "The Next Wave," *Profit*, September 2004, p. 95.

Security of Inventory. Preventing loss of inventory (shrinkage) is a major challenge for most small businesses. The business should develop a detailed procedure for ordering, receiving, marking, handling, and monitoring all inventories. The system selected will vary depending on the type of business.

The Small Business-Supplier Relationship

One critical key to the success of operations management is the relationship that the business maintains with its suppliers. Because of the size of the business and resulting relatively small volumes of purchases, the small business tends to be at a disadvantage compared with large businesses in receiving favourable treatment from suppliers. It is therefore important that the owner-manager implement policies and procedures that can ensure a successful relationship with the supplier. Examples of such policies and procedures are as follows:[2]

1. Define clear, identifiable, and measurable objectives for your supplier management strategy.

2. Be prepared to work with the supplier to identify and define the roles that each will perform. Consider your relationship a partnership to achieve the goals stated in number one above.

3. Attempt to employ technology to share data relating to forecasting, product movement, and financial evaluation.

4. Evaluate suppliers regularly with an objective standardized framework that is both quantitative and qualitative.

Summary

1. The production process involves the conversion of inputs such as money, people, machines, and inventories into outputs—the products or services provided.

2. The physical facilities must be continually monitored as the conditions that contribute to their effectiveness will not remain static.

3. The three types of layouts used by small manufacturing firms are the product layout, process layout, and fixed-position layout. The product layout is used when the business manufactures large numbers of just one or a few products. The process layout is designed for factories that manufacture smaller numbers of many different or custom-made products. The fixed-position layout is used for very large or cumbersome products.

4. In planning the interior layout of a retail store, the retailer needs to analyze the allocation of selling versus nonselling space, the allocation of space among departments and/or products, classification of the merchandise, and the location of displays and products on the shelf. The two types of layouts used by a retail store are the grid layout and the free-flow layout. The grid layout, typically used in a supermarket, is organized with customer convenience and retail efficiency in mind. The free-flow layout has a more relaxed atmosphere that is conducive to browsing. This type of layout is suitable for clothing and many specialty types of merchandise.

5. In estimating the quantities to order, the essential items of information required are the order lead time, the sales or production estimate, minimum inventory levels required, and the inventory currently on hand. Some methods used to determine order quantities include the mini-

mum turnover method, which uses inventory turnover calculations; the maximum and minimum method, which indicates the time and amounts to order; the open-to-buy method, used in retailing; the economic order quantity, which calculates the minimization of the ordering and storage costs of inventory; and A-B-C analysis, which prioritizes types of inventory.

Chapter Problems and Applications

1. What kind of layout should be used for the following manufacturing firms?

   a. Golf club manufacturer

   b. Independent bottler

   c. Bob's Machine Shop

2. What kind of layout should be used for the following retail firms?

   a. Clothing store

   b. Motorcycle shop

   c. Small grocery store

3. Answer the following questions regarding the location of food items in a grocery store.

   a. Where are the bread and milk located? Why?

   b. Where are the chocolate bars and other candy located? Why?

   c. Where on the shelf are the top name-brand items located? Why?

   d. Where are the high-margin items positioned in the store and on the shelf? Why?

4. Visit a small retail store or manufacturing plant and evaluate the layout.

5. Frank Newhart is opening a new DVD electronics store, but has not determined which DVD supplier to use. Frank has narrowed the choice to two sources. Supplier 1 is newly established and sells the units for $60 apiece. Supplier 2 is a well-established firm and sells the units for $75 each, with a 7 percent discount on orders over 50 units. Evaluate each supplier from the information given. With this information, develop different scenarios in which Frank would choose supplier 1 or supplier 2.

6. Interview three business owners to determine which inventory ordering system they use and why.

7. Interview a small business owner to learn why he or she selected a particular supplier. Find out what criteria were important to the owner in making the choice.

8. How could a small business improve the quality of a product or service that it offered? Discuss the information provided in this chapter.

Web Exercise

Access the website for the company profiled at the beginning of this chapter. Identify any aspects mentioned in the profile that are discussed in the chapter.

www.runningroom.com

Suggested Readings

Barter Network, http://www.bnibarter.com.

Berman, Barry, and Joel R. Evans. *Retail Management: A Strategic Approach.* New York: Macmillan, 2006, pp. 392–416.

Business Development Bank of Canada. "15 Steps to ISO 9000"—*BDC Newsletter*, June 2004, pp. 1–2.

Hatten, Timothy S. *Small Business Entrepreneurship and Beyond.* Saddle River, New Jersey: Prentice Hall, 2006, pp. 423–442.

Levy, Michael. *Journal of Retailing.* Babson College, Wellesley, Ma.

Lewison, Dale, and D. Wesley Balderson. *Retailing* (Canadian ed.). Scarborough, Ont.: Prentice Hall, 1998, pp. 236–259.

Longnecker, Justin G., and Carlos W. Moore, J. William Petty, and Leslie E. Palich. *Small Business Management—An Entrepreneurial Emphasis.* Toronto: Thomson, January, 2005.

Varnicchio, David. "Affordable Computer Solutions to Help You Market." *Small Business*, vol. 4, no. 2, Fall, 2000, p. 10.

Zimmerer, Thomas W. and Norman M. Scarborough. *Essentials of Entrepreneurship and Small Business Management* (3rd ed.). Upper Saddle River, N.J.: Prentice Hall, 2002, p. 200.

Comprehensive Case   *Sid Stevens: Part 8*

Sid worked long and hard to improve the financial condition of the business as a result of the statements received at the end of the first year of operations. He was able to make some adjustments in operations, move some short-term debt to long term, and obtain additional equity that allowed the business to receive adequate financing for the second year. His banker was also influenced positively by the upward sales trends for the Ladder Rail.

In addition to allowing the existing operation to receive stable financing, the bank also agreed to finance the addition to the building that Sid had been contemplating. It was felt that this building was needed to meet the growing demand for the product. With the new addition, Sid was now considering revising the interior space of the plant. Until now, he had employed an assembly-line type of production process, as he made only one product. However, Sid was starting to get orders for different-sized ladders (which required a variation in the size and type of Ladder Rail), as well as for other accessories such as safety braces to prevent ladders from moving sideways when placed against a building or roof. Given the possibilities for increasing his line of products in the future, Sid was wondering whether his current manufacturing layout was still effective.

Another concern Sid was dealing with was inventory levels. Sid had started out using the industry average for manufacturing plants to order initial inventory, but he soon realized that the industry average did not apply to a small plant like his. He then tried to order high volumes of inventory to get a better price, but he found that if the metal was sitting too long in inventory, it was costing him in interest expenses. Conversely, Sid did not want to run out of metal and cause a stoppage in the production process.

Sid was currently purchasing the metal that was used in fabricating the Ladder Rail from a local plant in Hamilton. He was, however, continually receiving calls from salespeople from outside the area offering better prices. This was also a concern for Sid. All these dilemmas were weighing heavily on Sid and were taking him away from making the Ladder Rail units. He often thought how nice it would be to be just involved in the manufacturing part and not have to worry about buying the metal and selling the Ladder Rail.

Questions

1. Discuss the layout options for Sid's company, considering the increased space and changes in product line.
2. What advice could you give to Sid regarding his inventory ordering and management practices?
3. Discuss the criteria that Sid could use to evaluate suppliers for metal.

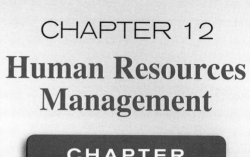

CHAPTER 12
Human Resources Management

CHAPTER OBJECTIVES

- To explain the importance of human resources management to the small business

- To illustrate the methods of planning for hiring and training employees

- To discuss skill areas the owner-manager can strengthen to improve personal leadership and people skills within the organization

- To illustrate principles of effective human resources management for the small business

- To review the procedures of administering a small business payroll

- To review the legal requirements relating to personnel of the small business

SMALL BUSINESS PROFILE

Clive Beddoe

WestJet Airlines Inc.

In 1995, Clive Beddoe was a successful businessman who spotted what he thought was an opportunity for a low-cost airline in Western Canada. Despite considerable advice to the contrary by industry experts who thought there was no room for another airline, Beddoe's team member Mark Hill developed a solid business plan that showed an opportunity in the market for a discount airline patterned after Southwest Airlines, one of the most successful low-cost airlines in the United States. Plans were drawn up in early 1995 for an equity-based operation with no debt and limited overhead, and Beddoe consulted extensively with David Neeleman, president of Morris Air, which was purchased by Southwest Airlines.

WestJet was up and running with its first commercial flight on February 29, 1996. It shuttled 388,000 passengers in the first six months, exceeding its own projections. Since then WestJet has revolutionized travel in Western Canada, radically changing the rules of competition in every market in which it has flown. Some of the reasons for WestJet's success include careful planning, innovative employee programs, extensive research, economic circumstances, and the desire of Westerners to see it succeed.

WestJet is considered to possess the "most admired corporate culture" in Canada by many. Some of the features of this culture include the following: profit sharing and employee share purchase options, open communications between employees and executives, efforts to recognize and reward employee performance, employee empowerment to make judgment calls, and treating all employees as equals. Even WestJet's television commercials stress the philosophy of employees as "owners" as a reason for superior service. The underlying philosophy of the company is to treat employees as #1. When this is done Beddoe is convinced that WestJet's good relationship with employees translates into good relationships with customers.

WestJet also saves money by providing a ticketless reservation system and offering no meal services. The company flies only one type of aircraft, which cuts expenditures on maintenance crews, pilot training, and inventory, and operates with roughly 75 employees per aircraft. It also owns its own planes rather than leasing, and because of its high equity content, incurs little in interest expenses.

Today WestJet operates more than 60 aircraft, flying to many destinations across Canada, with revenues of close to $1 billion. Beddoe, along with co-founders Don Bell, Mark Hill, and Tim Morgan, were honoured with a national Entrepreneurs of the Year award and WestJet was recently judged the second-most admired Canadian corporation through an Ipsos Reid survey. Clive Beddoe himself was recently honoured by *Canadian Business Magazine* as the most outstanding executive in the country.

Adapted from: "Sky High," *Profit Magazine*, March 2004, pp. 22–26, "People Power," *Canadian Business*, Oct. 10–25, 2005, pp. 125–6, and the WestJet website.

WestJet Airlines Inc.
www.westjet.com

HUMAN RESOURCES MANAGEMENT AND THE SMALL BUSINESS

Management in an organization has often been defined as getting things done through other people. The small business owner is a personnel manager even if his or her main strength or interest lies in the production, financial, or marketing aspects of the business.

Often the small business owner is reluctant to learn personnel administration fundamentals because he or she believes these principles apply only to larger organizations. The result is often personnel problems, such as frequent turnover of staff, lack of motivation and initiative, lack of harmony among employees, high absenteeism, frequent grievances, and high overall employee costs. The incidence of these problems appears to be high in small business. A recent study by Industry Canada found that successful entrepreneurs believe that owner-managers' number one challenge and most time-consuming activity is personnel.[1] Another study pointed out that the demands of running the business usually prevented owner-managers from paying as much attention to their employees as they should.[2] A third study, conducted by the Canadian Federation of Independent Business, found that more than half of small businesses had difficulty finding qualified labour at a reasonable wage.[3] Moreover, the Conference Board of Canada predicts that business will experience employee shortages of 1 million by the year 2020 due to the retirements of "Baby Boomers."[4] Despite these predictions and trends CFIB has also found that employees in small companies are significantly more likely to rate their workplace as "good" than those in large firms, as shown in Figure 12-1. The reasons for this apparent high level of satisfaction are increased flexibility in the workplace and a closer relationship with the owner.[5] Small businesses have a natural advantage over large businesses in these areas. It is critical that the entrepreneur use the techniques described in this chapter to maintain that advantage.

As the business grows, the owner-manager's workload generally expands. Because there is a limit to what one person can do, the business may suffer if the owner fails to hire new employees and delegate responsibilities to them.

Canadian Federation of
Independent Business
www.cfib.ca

Figure 12-1　　**Job Satisfaction among Employees at Small and Medium-Sized Enterprises and the Self-Employed Is High**

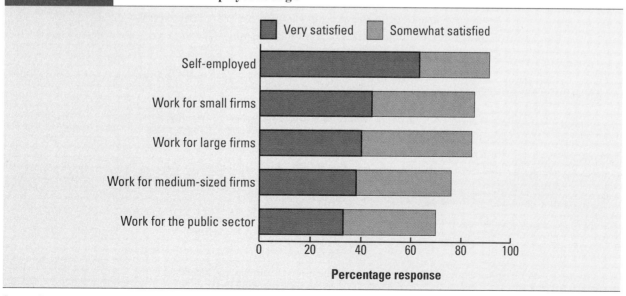

Source: Canadian Federation of Independent Business, *Small Business Primer,* January 2002, p. 2.

The reputation of a business in the community can be affected by employees' satisfaction with their jobs. The level of employee satisfaction can be enhanced or lowered by the owner-manager's use of personnel management principles. This is especially true in the retail and service industries. Motivated and competent personnel are one characteristic of a business that the competition may find difficult to duplicate.

A recent survey found that from 2000 to 2003, 56 percent of small business owners increased the time and money invested in employee training, with only 2 percent indicating a decrease.[6] The majority report that the responsibility for training employees lies mainly with the owner.

Given all these factors, it is essential that the owner-manager have some knowledge of personnel administration principles to sustain the success of the business. This chapter covers planning for personnel, hiring, and ongoing personnel management in the small business.

PLANNING FOR HUMAN RESOURCES

There are essentially four human resource planning steps in an organization. This section discusses each of these steps briefly.

Determine Personnel Requirements. The first step in planning for personnel is to determine the number of jobs or tasks to be done, shift schedules if applicable, the level of expertise required, and the number of people needed to perform those tasks. This process may already have been carried out as part of the feasibility analysis discussed in Chapter 3.

Set Organizational Structure. The second step in personnel planning is to integrate tasks and employees so that the owner can visualize how the different parts of the plan will work together. This formalized plan is commonly called an organizational chart. In the very small (two- or three-person) business, the organizational chart may simply be a division of responsibilities, as in Figure 12-2. In a larger business, the organizational chart shows the lines of responsibility for each member of the organization. An organizational chart for a small retail store appears in Figure 12-3 on the next page. Each business possesses unique characteristics that dictate how to set up the organizational chart. Some of the more common approaches are to organize by (1) function performed, such as sales, purchasing, or promotion; (2) type of merchandise or department, as in Figure 12-3; and (3) geographic territory.

In setting up the organizational structure, some rules of thumb have been found to contribute to a successful operation:

- Each employee should report to only one supervisor. This arrangement is called unity of control or command.

- Similar functions should be grouped together if possible.

Figure 12-2	Division of Responsibilities for a Very Small Business

Partner A	Partner B	Partner C
↓	↓	↓
Marketing	Production	Finance

Figure 12-3   **Organizational Chart for a Retail Furniture Store**

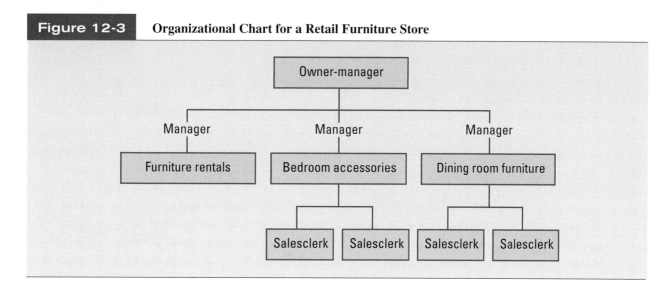

- There is a limit to an individual's span of control. Span of control is the number of people who can be directly supervised by one person. The proper span of control varies according to the combined characteristics of the manager, the subordinates, and the job.

Prepare Job Descriptions. The third step in personnel planning is the preparation of job descriptions and specifications. Before hiring employees, a detailed listing of the job or task duties (job descriptions) must be made. The job description briefly explains what is to be done, how it is to be done, and why it is done. This information goes into the job specification—a statement of the skills, abilities, physical characteristics, and education required to perform the job. As mentioned earlier, part of the job description may be included in the policy manual. Figure 12-4 (on the next page) illustrates a job description and specifications for an employee of a small business.

Develop Personnel Policies. The fourth step in personnel planning is to formally develop personnel policies. Including these policies in an employee policy manual can help prevent many personnel problems. For the very small business, this may simply be a list of some dos and don'ts; a larger business may provide a booklet to each new employee.

Policy manuals are used infrequently in small businesses. The uncertainty that can result may create serious employee difficulties. The common areas to be covered in a policy manual are described below. Minimum standards for many of these areas are set by government labour departments in each province and territory.

- Job descriptions clearly outline the duties, responsibilities, and reporting lines for employees, as mentioned previously.

- Working conditions include such things as hours of work, coffee breaks, and other expectations of management.

- Holidays and leaves outline statutory holidays, paid vacations, and procedures for taking a leave of absence.

- Remuneration and pay consist of a listing of details of the payroll, such as date of payment, time periods included, and reviews of pay levels.

Figure 12-4	Job Descriptions and Specifications Sales Manager, Hardware Store

Job Duties Description

Reports to the general manager

Directly responsible for floor salespeople

Suggests markdowns on slow items

Controls inventory

Authorizes merchandise returns

Occasionally meets with suppliers to learn about new products

Maintains good customer relations at all times

Takes care of written correspondence concerning sales

Does any other task relevant to the job as requested by the general manager

Personal Requirements Specifications

High school diploma or equivalent

At least two years' experience in a similar job

Initiative; "instinct" for sales; convincing manner; aptitude for managing people

Self-disciplined; good appearance; willing to work overtime

- Employee benefits provided by the firm, such as bonuses, profit sharing, medical-dental insurance plans, and employee discounts should be clearly stated.

- The grievance procedure consists of a description of the procedure employees are to follow if they have a concern or grievance within the organization.

THE HIRING PROCESS

Once the personnel plan has been developed, the next step is to review various sources for potential employees and make the selection.

Sources of Employees

A recent study by the Canadian Federation of Independent Business indicated that the most common methods of recruitment for small businesses were referrals from friends and employees (used by 69 percent of companies), media ads (used by 41 percent), unsolicited applications (used by 37 percent), and government agencies (used by 17 percent).[7] The following are some other potential sources of employees for the small business.

Recruitment from Within. For most organizations, recruiting from within the firm is the most common course if current employees have the qualifications. Hiring an outsider to perform a supervisory job instead of someone within the organization usually has a negative and disruptive effect on the business.

Other Businesses. To reduce training costs, employees from competing firms or similar industries can be hired. Such employees generally will have some background in the industry or business that can be easily transferred. The recruiter, however, will have to use this approach carefully to avoid a negative reaction from the competition, particularly in smaller markets.

Employee Referrals. Present employees may be asked to recommend acquaintances to fill available jobs. This method has the advantage of some prior knowledge of the individual's background. It may have a negative effect, however, if the new employee proves unsatisfactory.

Advertising. Some small businesses advertise for employees in local newspapers. The cost of this type of advertising is minimal.

Employment Agencies. Employment agencies sponsored by provincial governments are one source. Human Resources Development Canada offices also have lists of employees looking for work. This can be a potentially valuable source of employees, particularly for positions that do not require highly technical expertise. Private employment agencies typically are not used by small businesses to recruit employees, but they may be helpful in recruiting highly skilled employees.

Educational Institutions. Some small businesses that require employees with technical expertise use universities or colleges as sources. These sources can be helpful in manufacturing, some service businesses, and retailing.

Human Resources
Development Canada
www.hrdc-drhc.gc.ca

The Screening Process

Once potential employees have been identified from one or more of the above sources, the owner-manager faces the task of selection. Several screening devices can be used to aid in the selection of employees.

Application Form. Many small businesses do not use an application form. If new employees are hired infrequently, such a formal document may be unnecessary. However, the application form can be a valuable screening tool and a time saver for the owner. An application form need not be lengthy to be useful, as Figure 12-5 (on the next page) illustrates. The owner-manager must be careful not to violate provisions of the Human Rights Act in preparing the application form.

Human Rights Act
http://laws.justice.
gc.ca/en/H-6/

The Employment Interview. Although the application form may screen out several potential employees, an interview is usually required in making the final decision. The employment interview is particularly important for jobs requiring interpersonal contact, as it allows the interviewer to judge appearance, poise, and communication ability. A helpful tool in interviewing is an interview guide, which focuses the discussion and provides a constant base of information with which to compare applicants. Again, human rights legislation precludes the use of certain questions during an employment interview, and the owner-manager should be aware of such legislation.

Checking References. The third screening device is the checking of references. Most application forms require the applicant to list both personal and business references. As might be expected, business references are more valuable because they provide information regarding the individual's past work record. Incident 12-1 on page 349 illustrates the value of checking references for one small business.

Checks made by telephone or in person with business references are preferred to written responses. The writer of a letter of reference may have little or no idea of the requirements of the job. Also, past employers are sometimes reluctant to write uncomplimentary letters of reference. Specific questions should be asked about the candidate's performance, as well as about whether employers would consider rehiring the person.

| Figure 12-5 | **Application for Employment for a Small Business** |

Name_____   First Name _____

Address (Home) _____   Tel. _____

Address (Work) _____   Tel. _____

Social Insurance No._____

Languages: Spoken_____   Written _____

Secondary Education

_____

Years   School   City   Diploma

Post-Secondary Education

_____

Years   School   City   Degree

Work Experience
(begin with most recent)

From _____ To _____   Employer _____

Title_____   Nature of Duties _____

Salary _____

Reason for Leaving_____

_____

Work Experience

From _____ To _____   Employer _____

Title_____   Nature of Duties _____

Salary _____

Reason for Leaving_____

Other Information

References	Name	Address	Title
1.			
2.			
3.			

Signature   Date

INCIDENT 12-1   Home Hardware

Home Hardware
www.homehardware
dealers.com

The owner of the Home Hardware store in Magrath, Alberta, was looking for an assistant manager for hardware. After interviewing several applicants, the owner decided to hire an individual who had several years' experience in a hardware store in a distant town. All indications were that this individual was the best choice. Before making the offer of employment, the owner decided to check with the previous employer. He was grateful he did, because he found out that the chosen applicant had an unsatisfactory work record as well as questionable honesty. As a result of this reference check, another applicant was chosen and proved to be an excellent employee.

Source: D.W. Balderson, University of Lethbridge.

Tests. Many large businesses use various types of intellectual, ethical, and physical tests as part of the screening process. Some specific tests being used increasingly in small businesses are proficiency and skill tests (to perform a particular trade, craft, or skill), vocational interest tests (to assess long-term interest in the job or company), aptitude tests (to determine how a person might perform on a given job), and polygraph tests (to measure level of honesty). Because some of these tests are technical, the owner-manager should seek professional assistance in administering them.

Notification of the Hiring Decision

Once the hiring decision has been made, an offer of employment should be made to the successful applicant. This notification should be in writing, with a clear indication of the terms and conditions associated with the job. Most businesses require written confirmation of acceptance of the offer by the applicant.

All unsuccessful applicants should also be notified. Failure to provide this courtesy can have a detrimental effect on the reputation of the business.

PERSONNEL MANAGEMENT

Once the employee has been hired, the owner-manager's responsibility is to see that he or she is properly trained, satisfied enough with the working conditions to continue working there, and—probably most important—motivated to work hard and show initiative. Most small businesses are not in a position to hire a professional personnel manager to ensure that these desirable conditions exist. However, the owner-manager can foster these conditions by using the concepts of personnel management discussed in this section.

The Introduction Period

The first few months on the job are crucial to the employee's overall satisfaction and length of stay with the business.

The First Week. One of the most frequently mentioned characteristics of good working conditions is the way the owner-manager makes the employees feel like part of the organization.[8] Much can be done in the first week to communicate to the employee that he or she is a valued member of the business. The new employee should be introduced to co-workers, shown the locations of employee facilities, informed of any company regulations, and encouraged to ask for additional information needed. The employee should be talked to frequently during the introductory period, not simply left alone to read the company policy manual as larger companies sometimes do.

Many employers find it helpful to set some short-term goals toward which the employee can work within the first week or two. These goals can be discussed at the conclusion of the agreed-on time. This communicates not only that the employer is interested in the employee but also that the business is results- and goal-oriented.

The Probationary Period

Most employers find it advantageous to use a probationary period of three to six months for new employees. The probationary period allows the employer to further assess the new employee's suitability for the job. At the conclusion of a satisfactory probation period, the employee becomes permanent and may be entitled to a pay increase and other benefits of a permanent employee.

Training

The purpose of the training program is to increase productivity. In addition, successful training programs can reduce employee turnover, allow for less supervision, and increase employee morale. Properly trained employees acquire a sense of worth, dignity, and well-being, as well as increased skill levels. Businesses use many forms of employee training. Two of the more common are discussed next.

On-the-Job Training. This is the least structured and most frequently used method by small businesses. It is perhaps the best method of training for routine and repetitive types of work. The business may assign another worker to work closely with the new employee in a buddy system or apprenticeship.

Just In Time (JIT) Training. One of the more common types of employee training that is becoming particularly suitable for small business is short term or project training. Because of rapid advances in technology, many jobs are changed or displaced every three to five years.[9] It is predicted that in the future an organization's core workforce will need to be continually training as new skills are required. This just-in-time (JIT) training may be provided by professional training agencies or simply downloaded onto employee computers.

Formal Classroom Training. Businesses use many varieties of formal classroom training, but only a few have been used by small businesses. One such system is a cooperative type of program with an educational institution. This allows the employee to attend classroom instruction and training on a part-time basis. In Canada, the government provides financial assistance for employee training programs. These programs are discussed later in this chapter. Some businesses hold periodic seminars in which they bring experts from various fields to the business. Recent research indicates that 43 percent of small businesses in Canada utilize a combination of the above methods, while 43 percent use only informal on-the-job training.[10]

The Owner-Manager as Personnel Manager

Leadership Style. The first step in this process is a self-evaluation to obtain an understanding of one's own leadership or management style. Sometimes the owners are so preoccupied with running the technical or market side of the business that they give little thought to the kind of leadership example they set for employees.

Among leadership styles of entrepreneurs, several styles appear to be successful. A recent study of Canadian entrepreneurs found five different types of leadership. Figure 12-6 describes each type.[11]

The effectiveness of the owner-manager's leadership style may vary depending on the characteristics of the business and its employees. However, certain styles generally are more successful in the long run. Whatever the owner-manager's style, concern for both the people within the organization and the production process is important. The resulting team management approach, found in many Japanese companies, is particularly adaptable to the small business.

Time Management. A second critical aspect of successful people management is efficiently managing one's own time. Time management is often difficult to apply in the small business. So many operating crises and interruptions take place in the normal course of a day that the owner-manager may feel that much of the advice in time management literature is impossible to employ. However, some basic time management concepts can be used successfully in the small business. Some of the more important concepts are discussed next.

Recognize the Importance of Time. Much time wasting results from a failure to recognize the importance of one's time. The first step in improved time management, therefore, is to have a sincere desire to use time more efficiently.

Reexamine and Clarify Priorities. Priority planning may be long or short term. Long-term planning involves setting objectives that the owner and business are projected to meet over a period of months or years. Long-term objectives, which are a part of the business plan, as discussed in Chapter 4 as part of the establishment plan of the business, provide direction for the firm. This strategic plan serves as the guideline for all operations of the business.

Short-term priority planning deals with the utilization of time on a daily or weekly basis. It involves prioritizing tasks and working on those that are most important.

Analyze Present Time-Consuming Activities. This step requires keeping a diary of the daily activities of the owner-manager. Most people find the results of this step surprising. Often they find they spend time on less important items at the expense of more important ones. One small business owner spent several hours arguing over a $25 increase in building rental instead of using that time to evaluate the suitability of the overall location.

Figure 12-6   **Leadership Styles in Canadian Small Business**

Solo	Osmosis	Managerial	Systems	Figurehead
Does everything	High level of control over business, but does spend time developing managers	Sets objectives and lines of authority	Develops systems and direction	Owns business but has little to do with it
Little delegation				
Very small firms		Controls results but delegates more on procedures	Allows employees to set some objectives and determine how they are met	Complete delegation
	High level of contact with employees	Less employee contact		

Implement Time Management Principles. The owner-manager may be able to eliminate common time-wasting traps and become more efficient in his or her use of time by implementing the following practices:

- Avoid procrastinating on difficult but important decisions in favour of easier but less important ones.

- Use the most productive time of the day for the more important decisions or analyses. For some people this may be early in the day, and for others it may be later. Many have found it beneficial to schedule routine or enjoyable tasks during their least productive time.

- Read only relevant information. Stop reading and start searching. Use travel, waiting, or otherwise unproductive times for reading.

- Use letters less and the telephone more. If possible, handle letters only once in a given period of time.

- Operate with a minimum of meetings. Make sure meetings are results-oriented and have definite starting and ending times.

- Delegate as much work as possible, recognizing that the owner-manager is still ultimately responsible for the decision or action. A more detailed discussion of delegation in small businesses appears in Chapter 14.

Motivation and Loyalty

Employers Online
http://employers.gc.ca

Successful managers are able to generate strong loyalty from their employees. They also succeed in motivating employees to work hard and be creative. They have open communication lines and creative benefits that provide a comfortable work environment (see Incident 12-2). It is no accident, however, that these conditions exist in some companies and not in others. In a recent Angus Reid survey, reasons for employees' dislike of their jobs were examined. The results are shown in Figure 12-7. Some owner-managers understand and are able to

---

INCIDENT 12-2   A Special Touch

Sandra Avery, owner and manager of A Special Touch, knows how to treat her employees well. The Newfoundland gift store sells extraordinary gifts, collectibles, fine china, and housewares. It also sells specialty products such as the Katherine Karnes Munn collegian of prints, STORM Watches, and a line of Willowtree figurines as well as offering an array of services. Avery and her husband opened the gift store in their basement in 1987 and after a couple of years they moved the gift store into the Avalon Mall.

Today, A Special Touch is facing tough competition from larger giftware stores both in products and in hiring staff. "With the big-box stores, there are more products fighting for the same number of consumer dollars," Avery says. "They're also hiring my staff away. It's hard for a small person like me to offer staff what the larger companies can."

However, Avery works hard to keep her employees motivated and happy. She offers flexible work hours, special bonuses and incentives for those who do well, and uses a team approach. She is now researching a potential health benefits program.

Source: Adapted from Talbot Boggs, "Newfoundland Gift Store Has A Special Touch," *Canadian Retailer*, September/ October 2004, pp. 31–32.

| Figure 12-7 | Reasons Employees Dislike Their Jobs |

Reason

A horizontal bar chart showing reasons employees dislike their jobs with the following approximate percentages:

- Dislike boss or co-worker: ~6.5%
- Deadend job, no career opportunities: ~7%
- Not getting enough hours or work: ~7%
- Restructuring or layoffs: ~7%
- Poor management: ~8%
- Company treats employees poorly: ~10%
- Heavy workload: ~11%
- Low wages: ~20%

Percentage (%)

apply these critical principles in human relations management. Two important principles concern working conditions and employee needs.

Working Conditions. Employee satisfaction with general working conditions has been shown to reduce employee turnover. Although these factors may have minimal motivational impact, they are important in developing loyalty to the organization.[12] Some working conditions that may have this effect are the physical characteristics of the workplace, the level of supervision, relationships with co-workers, and company policies.

Employee Needs. Understanding employee needs and providing the means whereby employees can fulfill unmet needs can be a powerful motivational tool for the owner-manager.[13] Employees' needs include adequate pay, feeling they are a valued part of the organization, the possibility for advancement, extra responsibility or authority, recognition and praise by management, esteem of peers, a sense of achievement, and the challenge of the job. Incident 12-3 on the next page provides a good example of how Apex Public Relations utilizes several methods to meet employee needs.

One real challenge to the owner-manager is to encourage employees to have the same interest and enthusiasm for the business that she or he has. A recent Angus Reid survey found that 46 percent of Canadian workers are encouraged and expected to think of new and innovative ways of doing things.[14]

Paying Employees

Small business owners face stiff competition from large companies and even the government in paying their employees. In 2005, people in companies with fewer than 100 employees earned an average of $650 a week, compared with those in companies with upward of 500

INCIDENT 12-3   Employees First

Pat McNamara knows the meaning of putting her employees first. Since she created Apex Public Relations six years ago, McNamara has catered to her staff, offering them benefits to motivate them to work hard, deliver results, and remain loyal. Rewarding employees effectively is necessary to keep turnover down, especially in businesses such as public relations that have long-term relationships with clients.

One of McNamara's motivation tactics includes dedicating $1,000 each year to each employee for professional training. She has also included an anniversary program which celebrates yearly milestones. For example, at five years an employee gets five extra vacation days as well as $5,000 for a vacation. Once a month, Apex employees gather for drinks in the boardroom and free food is always available to them in the kitchen. McNamara says that the key is to look for personal touches; if someone is working hard, they are rewarded with days off and a free massage or a night at a hotel.

Along with rewarding her staff, McNamara consistently involves employees in decision making and frequently asks their advice and opinions. "I want Apex to have a legacy that goes beyond my tenure," she says. Keeping her employees happy earned McNamara PR Professional of the Year and Mentor of the Year by the Toronto chapter of the Canadian Public Relations Society.

Source: Adapted from Rebecca Gardiner, "Employees First," *Profit*, November 2004, p. 60.

---

workers who earned an average of $785.[15] In addition, a recent CFIB study found that the federal government is the fastest growing sector among all industries with a 23 percent wage and benefits advantage over its private sector counterparts.[16] Many think they cannot afford to meet this competition. However, the value of a key employee cannot be overstated for many small businesses. As a result, many owner-managers have recognized that they must be competitive in paying key employees.

Employees are concerned not only about absolute but also relative wage levels. This means employees are usually aware of and concerned about their level of pay relative to those of their co-workers. Employee pay levels are very difficult to keep confidential in a small business. Often a wage increase for one employee will be seen by other employees not as a reward for that employee but as a decrease in pay for themselves. This, of course, can cause unrest within the organization.

Wage levels are generally set using external and internal factors as a guide. Externally, the owner-manager may want to assess wage levels in similar or competing industries. Many provincial governments publish wage survey data that can assist in this regard. Most owner-managers can find out what the wage levels are in their communities through an informal survey. Other external considerations in arriving at wage levels might be cost-of-living increases, the demand/supply situation for employees, and government regulations. Internally, considerations employers use in setting salary levels are ability to pay, employee performance levels and requirements, and, as just mentioned, relative pay relationships.

Remuneration for employees can offer employees security and also have a motivational effect. There are many methods of paying employees, each with advantages and disadvantages. The owner-manager needs to tailor the pay plan to meet the needs of employees and the goals of the organization. An example of how one Canadian entrepreneur did this effectively is found in Incident 12-4. Figure 12-8 lists some of the more common methods of paying employees in small businesses and describes their advantages and limitations. Many organizations use combinations of these plans. A recent survey of top employees who left large organizations to work for smaller companies revealed that the main reason was the possibility of owning equity in the firm.[17]

INCIDENT 12-4   The Big Idea

Entrepreneur Eveline Charles demonstrates the importance of personal marketing practices within her Edmonton-based hairstyling service. Starting from a one-person cut and colour operation 20 years ago, EvelineCharles Salon Spas (No. 48) now offers hair styling, esthetics, massage, body treatments, and water therapy at six different locations in Edmonton, Calgary, and Vancouver. The firm employs 150 full-time and 55 part-time staff and in 2003 achieved revenues of $ 8.6 million.

Success came when Charles decided to pull herself away from the floor seven years ago to enable the company to grow like a corporation. Charles realized the firm needed quality control, systems, and structure. Almost four years ago, EvelineCharles Salon Spas switched its strategy from commission to salary. This reduced payroll from 65 percent to 45 percent of revenue and helped boost profits from 2–3 percent in the mid-1990s to 15–20 percent today. Charles also implemented quarterly performance reviews as well as rigorous employee training programs. These programs attempt to improve quality through employee training and education.

Because Charles has made her business successful through personal marketing strategies, she became the first women inducted into the Alberta Business Hall of Fame.

Source: Adapted from Jacqueline Louie, "The Big Idea," *Profit*, November 2004, p. 58.

Figure 12-8   Salary Plans for a Small Business

Type of Plan	How Calculated	Advantage	Limitation	Businesses Using the Plan
Salary	Per hour or per month	Security Simplicity	Lack of incentive	Many businesses—routine tasks
Commission	Percentage of sales	Incentive	Lack of control Lack of security Lack of simplicity	Automobile sales Housing industry Some retail products requiring extra selling effort
Cash bonus on individual performance	Bonus on reaching objectives or quota	Security Incentive	Can be complicated	Retailing Manufacturing
Profit sharing on company performance	Percentage of profits distributed	Incentive Cooperation in organization	Can be complicated Amounts too small to motivate	Manufacturing Retailing Knowledge based/service
Stock bonus	Predetermined percentage to employees based on objectives	Long-term interest in organization Incentive	Some employees want only cash	Manufacturing Knowledge based/service

Fringe Benefits

Although one survey found that fewer than half of Canadian small businesses offer incentive plans,[18] increasingly a small business needs to provide fringe benefits to attract and retain employees. A recent survey of the 100 fastest-growing small businesses in Canada indicated that only 65 percent to 75 percent of employee compensation should be salary. The rest can be made up of bonus, profit sharing, stock options, and commissions.[19] Some benefits becoming common in industry today are employee discounts, pension plans, disability and life insurance, and dental insurance. If the small business has enough employees, it may be able to qualify for group insurance plans that reduce the cost of providing this benefit. Frequently these plans are available through industry associations.

Other work-related fringe benefits the business might offer to increase employee satisfaction and motivation are discussed next.

Job Rotation. With job rotation, employees are periodically allowed to exchange jobs with other employees. Used in factory situations, this program can not only increase employee interest and motivation but also assist in training workers.

Job Sharing. Some firms have found success in allowing employees to share their jobs. The possibility of two part-time workers may satisfy the job requirements and increase the satisfaction of those who may not want to work full time. It is estimated that over 170,000 Canadians job-share, according to Statistics Canada.[20]

Statistics Canada
www.statcan.ca

Working from Home. An increasing number of businesses are allowing employees to complete some or all of their work at home. This may not be appropriate for all types of small business but may be viewed as a valuable benefit to some employees. Statistics Canada has found that close to 10 percent of working Canadians do at least part of their jobs from home.[21]

Flexible Hours. Some firms have experienced increases in productivity by allowing employees a work schedule other than the nine-to-five schedule common in many industries. A recent survey found that 60 percent of Canadian employers offered flexible work schedules in 2003, up from 47 percent in 2001.[22]

Employee Suggestion Systems. Many companies have some form of employee suggestion system. Recently some companies have taken this idea a step further by offering employees money to implement their suggestions. The National Association of Suggestion Systems reports that some 3,000 formal suggestion systems operate in the United States, generating more than 300,000 ideas and saving companies more than $800 million annually.

Benefits Interface Inc.
www.benefits.org

Figure 12-9 provides a description of five fast-growing employee benefit programs. Additional assistance benefit programs may be available through a number of private companies that specialize in this area. An example is Benefits Interface Inc.

Controlling and Evaluating Employee Performance

Many of the practices previously mentioned may contribute to a more motivated and loyal workforce. It is essential, however, that this motivation be directed toward the achievement of the firm's objectives. In this regard, the owner-manager needs to effectively evaluate progress toward goals and objectives and inform employees of their progress. This can be done through a regular performance appraisal.

Zigon Performance
Group
www.zigonperf.com

Another method for accomplishing this is the management by objectives approach (MBO), which is used in many organizations. A simplified version of MBO that is suitable for the small business is described in *Putting the One Minute Manager to Work.*[23] The five steps in this method (called the PRICE system) are as follows:

Figure 12-9	**Five Hottest Employee Benefits**
1. Spending Accounts	Many firms that can't afford flexible-benefit plans are turning to spending accounts, funded by company or employee contributions. They can be used to cover a range of health or dental expenses. When employees contribute a portion of their salaries (say 2 percent) to these funds, that income isn't taxed.
2. Health Promotion	More employers offer non-medical benefits aimed at "wellness." Staff are allowed certain sums for such items as gym memberships, health-risk assessments, psychological counselling, and personal training.
3. Increased Choice	There's more choice in structuring benefit plans. Staff choices depend on how much they wish to spend, or on other variables such as their state of health or access to other benefits.
4. Flexible Work Hours	To help families juggle increasingly complex schedules, more firms let workers set their own hours. It could be 9 to 5, 7:30 to 3:30, or four 10-hour days.
5. Employee Input	More employees are being asked for their input on operational matters, but at a cost. Staff who suggest benefits changes, for instance, are held responsible for the program's success. If costs exceed plan, they must make up the balance.

Source: Daphne Woolf and William M. Mercer, *Profit*, September 1998, p. 38.

- *Pinpoint:* Define the performance area to be evaluated (i.e., sales for a retail clerk).
- *Record:* Set up a system to monitor and record performance in that area (i.e., the cash register tape).
- *Involve:* Manager and employee jointly set goals and a strategy for reaching those goals in that performance area (i.e., dollar sales per month).
- *Coach:* The manager observes performance periodically, perhaps making suggestions but allowing the employee considerable freedom to work toward the agreed-on goals.
- *Evaluate:* At the end of the agreed-on period, an assessment of performance is made; positive results are rewarded, and future goals are set.

The value of the PRICE system is the clear line of communication between employer and employee in directing the employee toward goals and evaluating his or her progress.

HANDLING GRIEVANCES

Employee grievances, or concerns, arise in most organizations. They can have a negative effect on the morale of the organization, but they can also be positive and helpful if handled properly. The following are some principles for effective grievance management:

1. Implement a precise method whereby employees can express grievances. It is important that the organizational lines of authority be followed in this case.

If at all possible, the grievance should be expressed to the immediate supervisor. This procedure should be laid out in the policy manual.

2. Employees need assurance that expressing their concerns will not jeopardize or prejudice their relationship with the employer. A wise employer will recognize that many grievances are legitimate and, if acted on, can help the organization.

3. There should be minimal red tape in processing complaints. Employees need to feel that someone is really listening to their concerns.

4. Owner-managers need to understand that some employees may be hesitant to raise a concern directly. In these situations, the suggestion box is effective.

Unionization and the Small Business

Most small businesses do not have unions operating within the organization. As the firm grows, however, and as employees become farther removed from the owner, the possibility of union-related activity increases. The owner-manager should recognize that unions are formed when a majority of employees believe that a union would better serve their employment needs than the existing system. Effective human relations policies can go a long way toward discouraging union establishment in the firm. Some small businesses in certain industries may be required to hire unionized employees.

In both of these situations, there are certain requirements for both the employer and the union as set out in the Labour Relations Act in each province and territory. Some of the more common aspects of collective bargaining that may affect the small business owner are the following:

- The contents of an agreement must deal with wages, benefits, and working conditions.

- Both parties must meet and bargain in good faith. However, an employer need not reveal company data that he or she prefers to keep confidential.

- The owner cannot discriminate against an employee for union involvement.

- Both employers and unions are bound by the terms and conditions of the collective agreement.

- Disputes concerning interpretation of the agreement must be resolved by an arbitrator.

GOVERNMENT REQUIREMENTS AND ASSISTANCE

The owner-manager should be aware of relevant government labour laws and programs that affect the management of personnel. A brief discussion of such laws and programs for all levels of government follows.

Federal Government

The federal government provides training and employment programs to 400,000 Canadians each year. Through the Canadian Jobs Strategy program, approximately $1.7 billion is spent to increase training and expand opportunities.[24] Some specific programs of Jobs Strategy include the following:

- *The job entry program* provides training for unemployed or undertrained people for up to one year.

- *Skill shortage and skill investment programs* provide financial assistance and training for up to three years for skill upgrading as a result of technological change within the company.

- *The job development program* provides training and financial assistance for the unemployed, disadvantaged persons, women, persons with disabilities, mature people, and visible minorities.

- *Innovation programs* provide funds to test new solutions to labour-market-related problems.

- *The Community Futures Program* helps finance local committees for development training and employment initiatives in areas experiencing economic hardship.

For more information on each of the above programs, contact the local Canada Employment Centres.

The federal government also has some legislation in the areas of employment standards, employment and pay equity, and hiring practices. Because of some overlaps in jurisdiction with the provinces and territories, details are discussed in the next section. Appendix 12A at the end of this chapter illustrates these jurisdictions for the various programs and standards.

Provincial and Territorial Governments

Each province and territory in Canada, through its human resources or labour department, has set labour standards with which every owner-manager should be familiar. Appendix 12B (on the website) lists the agencies that administer these standards in each province and territory. Some of the more important areas are discussed briefly below.

Job Discrimination. Each provincial and territorial government has passed legislation concerning human rights in the workplace. Entitled Bills or Codes of Human Rights, they are administered by provincial and territorial human rights commissions; this legislation has jurisdiction over businesses not federally owned or regulated. Like their federal counterparts, these regulations are designed to prevent discrimination in the workplace.

Pay and Employment Equity. Recently, some provinces and territories have enacted legislation to ensure equality of pay and employment opportunity regardless of gender, race, religious affiliation, or ethnic origin.

Working Conditions and Compensation. Numerous legal requirements govern the conditions under which retail employees work. Of importance to the small business owner are wage and hour requirements, restrictions on the use of child labour, provisions regarding equal pay, workers' compensation, unemployment benefits, and the Canada Pension Plan.

Employment Standards. Both the federal and provincial or territorial governments administer a considerable amount of legislation related to employment standards and labour relations. At both levels of government, ministries of labour have primary responsibility in this field of regulation. In addition, both levels have legislation that allows for the establishment of unions and collective bargaining agents in the form of provincial or territorial labour relations acts and the federal Canada Labour Code. The Canada Labour Code also deals with many aspects of fair labour standards, labour relations, dismissal procedures, severance allowances, and working conditions. Similarly, each province and territory enforces statutes covering minimum wage rates, hours of work, overtime,

Canada Labour Code
http://laws.justice.
gc.ca/en/L-2/index.
html

holidays and leaves, termination notices, employment of young people, and information requirements on the statement of earnings and deductions.

Employment Safety and Health. Employment safety and health programs are designed to reduce absenteeism and labour turnover. Most provinces and territories have passed industrial safety acts to protect the health and safety of workers. These laws govern such areas as sanitation, ventilation, and dangerous machinery. In addition to legislation, provincial and territorial governments, as well as employers, provide programs and training designed to accomplish similar purposes.

Workers' Compensation. Workers' compensation is an employee accident and disability insurance program required under provincial and territorial law. It covers the employees who are accidentally injured while working or are unable to work as a result of a disease associated with a particular occupation. Although these programs vary, they generally provide for medical expenses and basic subsistence during the period of disability. Employers help pay for the program through assessments from the Workers' Compensation Board or Workplace Safety and Insurance Board. The assessment rates represent a substantial operating expense; thus, they must be planned for and managed with considerable care.

Wage Subsidy Programs. These programs provide financial assistance for up to six months for small businesses that hire unemployed persons.

Provincial and Territorial Training Programs. These programs provide job training and skill development incentives to upgrade the labour force. Often such programs include a wage subsidy to small businesses that hire new employees. Contact a local labour department (see Appendix 12B on the website) for details of these programs.

Municipal Governments

Local or municipal government regulations related to industry generally are confined to such areas as licensing, zoning, hours of operation, property taxes, and building codes. For example, one issue of current debate in some areas relates to Sunday openings of retail stores. Generally authority has been left to the municipal government. This issue has significant implications in terms of operating costs and competitiveness.

Municipal authorities also exercise an especially strong influence over food establishments. For instance, a municipal licensing system for restaurants and other food services establishments may be in effect. Health inspectors may make periodic and sometimes unannounced inspections. (Any store that sells wine, beer, or liquor may require a licence from provincial or territorial liquor-licensing authorities.)

RECORD KEEPING FOR EMPLOYERS

Every employer should maintain an employee file that includes such information as the employee's original application form, work record, salary level, evaluation reports, and any other pertinent information. One of the most important employee record-keeping tasks for the owner-manager is completing the payroll. There are several essential steps in managing a payroll system for employees.

Employee Remittance Number. As an employer, the owner-manager collects employee income tax on behalf of the government as a deduction from the employee's wage. Before remitting this amount to the Receiver General, the employer must obtain a remittance number,

Canada Revenue
Agency
www.cra-arc.gc.ca

available by contacting the nearest office of the Canada Revenue Agency. Along with the remittance number, the appropriate tax-deduction tables and forms will be provided.

Payroll Book. The employer should obtain a payroll book or record that contains space for recording time worked as well as all the required deductions. These books can be obtained from most business supply or stationery stores.

Monthly Remittance. As mentioned above, each payday the employer is required to make the appropriate deductions and remit them, as well as the employer's share of Canada pension (2 times the employee's share) and unemployment insurance (2.4 times the employee's share), to the Canada Revenue Agency. This remittance is made on a prescribed form similar to that in Figure 12-10. This form contains the remittance number, the current payment amount, and a cumulative record of payments to date.

Year-End Statements. At the end of the calendar year, the employer is required to total and reconcile the year's remittances with the Canada Revenue Agency's totals. This is done on a T4-A summary form provided by the Canada Revenue Agency.

It is also the employer's responsibility to fill out for each employee a record of earnings and deductions for the year on the T4 slip. The T4 slip (see Figure 12-11) is completed by reviewing totals from the payroll book and is required to be sent to the employee by the end of February of the following year.

Figure 12-10   Remittance Form

Figure 12-11   **T4 Slip**

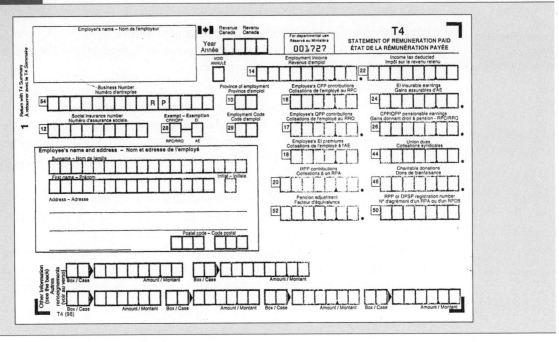

An increasing number of small businesses have found it to be cost effective to hire another firm to handle the payroll function. This is called outsourcing and has extended into other areas as well because of the increasing complexity of some of these functions.

Contract Employees

A growing number of small businesses owners may utilize a contract employee to meet part or all of the business's labour requirements. This form of outsourcing was utilized in the amount of $1.7 billion in 2003 and is expected to reach $2.8 billion by 2008.[25] These workers are considered independent contractors and as such are not employees of the company. The contractor or the contracting company simply invoices the small business for services rendered. Contract employees may be hired for a particular project and could be long term. They could also be hired for temporary purposes and paid a fee to provide a short term service. Although the owner-manager still manages these people, the calculation of CPP, EI, or other benefits are not required. This typically results in a reduction in costs to the small business of about 10 percent to 15 percent. However, some companies have experienced increased costs.[26] It must also be remembered that some positions and tasks may not be suitable for the contract employee, and issues of motivation and loyalty may be a problem for contract workers. Therefore, a contract employee may be more appropriate for temporary or project-type jobs. Other difficult issues relating to contract employees involve new privacy legislation, labour standards, performance appraisal, and terminations. The owner-manager should be aware of the legal differences in managing contract and traditional employees.

Summary

1. Sound personnel management is a key to the success of a small business, because motivated and competent personnel is one aspect of a business that may be unique and difficult to duplicate.

2. The organizational chart integrates tasks and employees so that the owner can visualize how the different aspects of the plan will work together. An effective way to prevent many personnel problems is to have a policy manual covering such areas as job description, working conditions, holidays and leaves, remuneration, and employee benefits.

3. The owner-manager should apply the following concepts of personnel management: assess his or her leadership style, work on time management by avoiding procrastination on important decisions or tasks, assess priorities, and use the most productive time of the day for the more important decisions.

4. The screening devices used in hiring employees include an application form, the employment interview, references, and various kinds of tests. An interview guide helps focus the interview and provides a constant base of information with which to compare applicants.

5. The steps in administering a payroll system are to obtain an employee remittance number, obtain a payroll book, make the appropriate deductions and remit them with the employer's share to the Canada Revenue Agency, total and reconcile the year's remittance at the end of every calendar year, and send out T4s.

6. Legal requirements for the personnel aspects of small business are applicable from federal, provincial or territorial, and municipal governments.

Chapter Problems and Applications

1. Discuss the relative advantages and disadvantages of the various compensation plans used in small businesses.

2. What industries can you think of in which profit sharing would be less successful? Why?

3. Discuss the relative advantages and disadvantages of the different types of fringe benefits for a small manufacturing company. If possible, interview employees of such a business to find out which of these benefits are the most attractive.

4. Recently, a small business increased the wages of its employees, but its productivity is still inadequate. What could be some possible reasons for this low level of productivity?

5. ABC company employee deductions for July are EI $98.72 and CPP $110.17. For what amount would the employer be liable?

6. Interview two small business owners to find out their personnel policies and how they communicate those policies to their employees.

7. Ask three employees of small businesses what they like and dislike about their jobs. What personnel policies could be used to remedy the dislikes?

8. Determine how three employees of various small businesses were recruited for their present positions. What seems to be the most popular source from which to recruit employees for small businesses? Why?

9. After reading this chapter, what do you believe will be the most critical small business personnel problem in the future?

Web Exercise

Access the website for your provincial or territorial government labour standards department and review the standards that would apply to a small business in your area.

www.mcgrawhill.ca/olc/balderson

APPENDIX 12A

Labour Legislation Jurisdiction

Topic	Comments	Municipal	Jurisdiction Provincial/ Territorial	Federal
Minimum age: contact provincial or territorial Department of Labour	Varies among provinces and territories		X	
Minimum wage: contact Minimum Wage Commission	Each province or territory has its own industrial relations legislation		X	
Hours of work; annual vacations, holidays: contact provincial or territorial Department of Labour	Varies among provinces and territories; general standard is two weeks; other holiday depend on the province or territory		X	
Workers' compensation: contact provincial or territorial Workers' Compensation board or Workplace Safety and Insurance Board	Contributed by employer		X	
Industrial safety and health: contact provincial or territorial Department of Labour	Major jurisdiction from provinces and territories; some federal jurisdiction		X	
Unemployment insurance: contact Canada Employment and Immigration Commission	Contributed by employer			X
Canadian pension plan: contact Canada Customs and Revenue Agency, District Taxation Office	Except in Quebec, where contributions are made to Quebec Pension Plan and both employer and employee contribute			X
Employment equity: contact provincial or territorial Department of Labour	Ontario has legislation; some federal guidelines		X	
Hours of operations	Contact city hall	X		

Suggested Readings

Barrier, Michael. "Leadership Skills Employees Respect." *Nations Business*, January 1999.

Canadian Council of Human Resource Associations (CCHRA), http://www.chrpcanada.com.

"Why Human Resources Management Is An Excellent Investment," Business Development Bank of Canada website, June, 2006.

Gray, Douglas, and Diana Lynn Gray. *The Complete Canadian Small Business Guide*, 2nd Edition, McGraw-Hill Ryerson, 2005.

Leiber, Ronald. "Why Employees Love Their Companies." *Fortune*, January 12, 1998.

Small Business Administration—Personnel Management Series—Small Business Administration website, Washington, D.C.

"The Definitive Guide to Managing Human Resources for Small Business Owners." *Profit*, October 1998, p. 20.

Ward, Susan. "Determining Your Personnel Return On Investment." Small Business Canada website, May, 2006.

Comprehensive Case   *Sid Stevens: Part 9*

Sid was able to resolve the inventory and layout concerns with the help of a consultant whom his banker had suggested. With the expansion of the plant, Sid was able to meet demand for orders of the Ladder Rail and some additional products. Sales were increasing and the problems with finances and marketing that had caused concern earlier seemed to be less troublesome.

However, partway through year two an additional problem began to surface. It involved his personnel. With increased demand and plant expansion, Sid had hired four additional employees. Three were put to work in the metal fabricating part of the business, and the other was hired to work full time with marketing and distribution. The two employees who had started with Sid had both left for higher paying jobs and so Sid had hired a total of six new employees in a short time. The first couple of hires had been found through ads in the local newspaper, but lately Sid had simply gone down to the local Canada Manpower office and found the required workers.

Sid was becoming increasingly discouraged with the time and hassle involved in managing employees. On many occasions, he would have liked to have fired an employee, but the hiring and training process seemed to take so long that Sid felt that he could not afford a slowdown of the production process with demand being what it was. He realized that the type of employee he was hiring possessed little education, but as a small business owner, he simply could not afford—nor did the job require—better trained employees. He currently paid employees $1 above minimum wage, which was well below union rates, but he increased the wage as the employee finished the on-the-job training. He also intended to give all employees a raise each year based on seniority. Because the business was losing money, however, Sid did not feel that he could afford raises to employee wages at this time.

Some of the employee problems that particularly bothered him were employees wanting more money and better benefits; workers threatening to leave for higher union steelworker wages if he did not increase their wages; work slowdowns when he was not physically present at the plant; poor quality work and too much wasted metal as a result of fabricating errors; and the appearance and conduct of some of the younger workers. This last problem had especially annoyed Suzie who was frequently in the plant working on the finances.

In addition, on some occasions Suzie had been in the plant and had given some direction to the workers when Sid was away. The employees simply ignored her because she was not the boss.

Questions

1. Evaluate Sid Stevens's personnel procedures.
2. How could Sid motivate his employees?
3. What should be done differently for the marketing person? Why?
4. What outside assistance might be available to help Sid with his personnel problems?

www.mcgrawhill.ca/olc/balderson

CHAPTER 13
Tax Management

CHAPTER OBJECTIVES

- To explain the importance of understanding the nature of the Canadian tax system

- To discuss key tax management principles the owner-manager can follow

- To describe specific tax-related programs that apply to small business

SMALL BUSINESS PROFILE
Doreen Braverman

The Flag Shop

In 1974 Doreen Braverman's career had been anything but entrepreneurial. She had worked as a telephone operator, a receptionist, and a teacher. Her decision to purchase a small promotional products business changed the direction of her working life.

The company that she purchased—Vancouver Regalia, located in downtown Vancouver—did reasonably well, but Braverman soon realized that one of its products, flags, had more potential than the rest. She decided to focus on selling flags of all kinds to a ready market. She hired seamers and sewed flags. She renamed the company The Flag Shop and soon found, because of the growing demand, she would have to start printing her own flags to ensure an adequate supply. She bought a screen-printing factory to provide the expertise.

Growth of the company has been steady. Average growth per year since 1975 has been 17 percent. The Flag Shop topped $6 million in sales last year. It employs 57 people in its 13 shops.

Braverman realized early in her entrepreneurial career that she would have to understand how to macro-manage her business to ensure its continued success. To this end, she earned an MBA degree by correspondence from the Canadian School of Management in Toronto. This training helped her maintain tight financial control over The Flag Shop. She receives weekly sales and operations reports from her managers and prepares monthly reviews on the company's progress. Braverman also recognized the value of financial planning. Annual plans are prepared every year, with a three-year forecast. This allows the company to effectively manage its tax situation.

Doreen Braverman has always believed in being active in industry associations. While contributing considerably to these organizations, she also gains valuable contacts and assistance from them. She is a strong advocate for free enterprise and believes that governments should not subsidize business. She also believes in having a board of directors with outside directors. Her board has seven directors: three family members, four outside directors, and one employee representative. Through profit sharing, 15 employees have shares in the company.

For the past three years, Braverman has worked on succession plans. Her daughter, Susan Braverman, who had worked at the Flag Shop for about 15 years, both full and part time, has now taken over the general management of the Vancouver operations. Today, Doreen Braverman still works 50 hours a week. She is the chair of the board and handles franchise sales and marketing for the Flag Shop chain.

Used with the permission of Doreen Braverman.

The Flag Shop
www.flagshop.com

TAXATION AND SMALL BUSINESS

Chapter 4 presented a brief outline regarding the tax requirements of a small business. It was noted that various types of business and property taxes are levied by federal, provincial, and municipal governments. The calculation of and liability for most of those taxes are relatively straightforward and are not discussed again in this chapter. Income taxes, however, can be more complicated, be more subject to interpretation, and have a greater impact on the planning and cash flow of the business. This chapter therefore focuses primarily on this area.

The income tax was instituted in Canada as a "temporary" measure in 1917. But as Incident 13-1 illustrates, income taxes are not only here to stay but are also becoming increasingly complicated and generally more burdensome for most Canadians. A 2005 study by Toronto Dominion Bank, the Vanier Institute and the Fraser Institute concludes that

> *the average Canadian family pays more than 48 percent of its income in taxes. In addition, this situation has not improved in the last decade as the tax bill to Canadians has risen at a much higher rate than the growth in incomes.[1]*

Canadian Federation of Independent Business www.cfib.ca

The Canadian Federation of Independent Business reports that the total tax burden is the top concern of small and medium-size enterprises (SME). This is shown in Figure 13-1. Individuals who reside and corporations that operate in Canada are liable for federal and provincial income taxes. These taxes are applied on income that is received or receivable during the taxation year from all sources, less certain deductions. Federal and provincial or territorial tax agreements govern the procedures by which the federal government is empowered to collect taxes and remit portions to the provinces and territories.

INCIDENT 13-1   The Little Shoebox of Horrors

Karen Yull, a tax specialist at Grant Thornton LLP and author of *Smart Tax Tips*, describes the little shoebox of horrors as being an experience where a client arrives with a box or bag full of receipts. It is then the accountant's job to make sense of the business expenses while keeping the tax payable and the accountant's fees to a minimum. Yull knows the frustration that can accompany this task and suggests that a little organization can go a long way in managing personal and business expenses for tax purposes. Small business owners are usually the ones who pay for things with cash and often have all their personal and business expenses coming out of the same account. A lot of time and money can be saved by simply keeping their business affairs separate from their personal banking and by keeping track of all expenses. Although it may sound like a simple solution, time and time again Yull has seen small business owners mixing their professional and personal expenses, leaving the difficult task of sorting expenses to the accountant.

Yull offers a few suggestions to business owners to help at tax time. Because small business owners don't usually have their own pension plans, it is important to plan for retirement. If members of your family are working in your business, consider paying them a salary, which will help the tax situation. By using small business credit cards solely for business purposes, you can separate personal and business expenses. Also, maintaining your own ledger will make the accountant's job easier and will save money in accounting fees. The last piece of advice is perhaps the most important and suggests that if you are unsure about what you are doing, seek the help from a professional.

Source: Adapted from Sasha Nagy, "The Little Shoebox of Horrors," *Globe and Mail Update*, March 21, 2006, www.theglobeandmail.com.

Figure 13-1	**Total Tax Burden Remains Top SME Concern**

Source: Canadian Federation of Independent Business, Our Members' Opinions (OMO #56) 2nd quarter results, January 1–June 30, 2005.

Some provinces and territories, including Quebec and Alberta, now collect their own corporate income taxes.

Because of the complexity of tax principles and the frequency of legislative changes concerning taxes and the provincial differences in application, a detailed treatment of tax management for small business is beyond the scope of this book. This chapter briefly discusses some general tax management principles and programs. Although it is essential for owner-managers to have some knowledge of these principles in managing and planning their businesses, they are strongly advised to seek professional advice in preparing tax returns and investigating methods of minimizing tax liability. A basic knowledge of tax principles may assist the entrepreneur in avoiding many difficulties.

The income of the organization that the government requires the small business owner to report refers to the profits the business makes (for tax purposes). This should not be confused with the income the owner makes from the business, which may or may not be taxable depending on the legal form of the organization. This chapter deals primarily with the income tax considerations of the organization.

Some owner-managers may not be overly concerned with income taxes and thus may do little tax planning. This lack of concern may be due to one of two factors. First, the business may currently have no tax liability; in other words, it is losing money. This situation, of course, will be only temporary because the business will eventually become profitable or cease to exist. Second, the owner-manager may not understand the impact of taxes on the cash flow of the business. As Figure 13-2 on the next page illustrates, an increase in the tax rate of only 10 percent translates into a tax liability that would require an additional $100,000 in sales to offset. When the owner-manager understands the full effects of a lower or higher tax liability, he or she will want a working knowledge of tax principles and programs.

Figure 13-2	**Impact of Tax Rate on a Business**
Taxable income	$50,000
Increase in tax rate from 20% to 30%	20% of 50,000 = $10,000
	30% of 50,000 = $15,000
Increased tax liability	15,000 − 10,000 = $5,000
Profit as a percentage of sales	5%
Sales required to offset tax	5,000/5% = $100,000

Note: The extra $100,000 in sales would also incur an additional $1,500 tax liability.

GENERAL TAX MANAGEMENT PRINCIPLES

The owner-manager should be aware of ten fundamental areas of tax management.

Continual Tax Planning

One of the most disturbing aspects of tax statement preparation for the owner-manager is learning that he or she has incurred an unnecessary tax liability. This situation usually arises because the accountant received and prepared the return too late to take advantage of favourable programs and deductions.

It is critical, therefore, that the owner-manager be aware of the tax consequences of business operations throughout the year, not just at or after the year-end. Up-to-date income statements (as discussed in Chapter 10) can assist in forecasting income trends, allowing some advance tax planning. Many simple software programs are now available that can assist the entrepreneur in the information and tax management function. Incident 13-2 stresses the importance of record keeping to manage taxes effectively.

Canada Revenue Agency
www.cra-arc.gc.ca

The Canada Revenue Agency (CRA), formerly Revenue Canada, requires that income tax be paid in instalments throughout the year. Individuals operating proprietorships and partnerships are required to remit quarterly installments for the amount of taxes they incur. Corporations must submit monthly installments based on their estimated tax liability. Again, prior planning will be required to allow compliance with this regulation.

Tax Deferral

One unwritten rule of tax management concerns tax deferral. This means that one should attempt to put off paying taxes as long as legally possible. There are at least two good reasons to defer taxes. First, one has the use of the tax money for the period of the deferral. This money can be put to productive use in the business or other investments. Second, tax laws may change, resulting in a decreased liability in the future.

Several specific programs facilitate deferral of tax liability. Some of these programs are discussed later.

Income Splitting

The tax system for individuals in Canada is a progressive system whereby a higher taxable income results in a higher percentage tax liability (see Appendix 13A (on website) for cur-

INCIDENT 13-2   Keep It in the Family

Income splitting, a form of tax management, is an ideal way for small business owners to pocket more of their hard-earned income rather than give it up to the Canada Revenue Agency. Hiring a family member to work in your business is an easy and legitimate way of saving tax dollars by legally redistributing your income to your kin. Robert Gold, a CA and partner with Bennett Gold LLP suggests that many small businesses may not realize there is a benefit to bringing family members into the company and paying them properly.

To qualify for income splitting, rules must be followed. For example, the spouse or child must provide services to the paying entity and must be receiving compensation that is commensurate to their services. It is important to keep a paper trail, documenting everyone on the payroll and deductions, attendance, and duties. Without proper documentation, you could be hit up for the missing funds, plus penalties and interest. Also, the CRA will devote extra scrutiny to your tax returns, which could lead to other claims being examined. To avoid such problems, it is advisable to consult a professional and manage tax documentation carefully.

The payoff from income splitting can be pretty impressive. Because you are distributing part of your income to a spouse or children, your income becomes lower, qualifying you for a lower marginal tax rate. For instance, in Ontario, hiring a family member who makes about $20,000 will make that money he or she earns have a tax rate of just 25.9 percent, rather than 43.4 percent, if you had earned it. This could help your family save $3,500 in taxes. Also, since teenage children pay almost no income tax, the money they earn can be pretty much tax-free.

Source: Adapted from Rick Spence, "Keep It in the Family," *moneysense.ca*, May 2006, pp. 23–25.

rent tax rates for individuals in Canada and Appendix 13B (on website) for tax rates for corporations). Because of the progressive nature of taxes, splitting incomes between spouses and other family members or among partners will result in a reduced overall tax liability, as Figure 13-3 shows. If done within a family, the spouse and children will likely be taxed at lower rates, which would further reduce this tax liability.

Care should be taken when splitting income within the family to ensure that wages paid to the spouse or children are a reasonable amount considering their contribution to the business and that payroll withholding taxes, if applicable, are deducted.

Figure 13-3   **Income Splitting—Federal Perspective**

Business income = $40,000

A. If one person declared the income:

Income = $40,000

Tax rate = $4,921 + 22% of $9,246

Tax liability = $6,955.12

B. If two people split the income:

Income = $40,000

Partner A = $20,000

Partner B = $20,000

Tax rate for each = 16% of $20,000

Tax liability A = $3,200

Tax liability B = $3,200

Tax liability for A & B = $6,400

Tax savings by splitting income = $6,955.12 − $6,400 = $555.12

Marginal Tax Rates

The marginal tax rate is the tax rate applied by the Canada Revenue Agency to the next dollar of income earned. Knowledge of an individual's marginal rate can be helpful in planning income and expenses. For example, if an owner-manager has a marginal tax rate of 30 percent, he or she knows that each dollar of income earned will incur a tax liability of 30 cents, whereas each dollar of expense incurred will save 30 cents in tax liability. Thus, awareness of the current marginal rate allows the owner-manager to calculate the after-tax effects of extra income and expenses.

Another benefit of knowing the marginal rate is the possibility of moving that rate to a lower bracket by incurring some additional expenses before year-end—provided, of course, that the expenses are necessary. Like income splitting, this principle has the most value for the proprietorship and partnership.

Deductibles

The small business owner should be familiar with those expenses that are deductible in the calculation of taxable income. The onus is on the taxpayer to keep proper records, since the burden of proof for these expenses lies with him or her. This means the owner-manager must keep receipts of business expenses. An often neglected aspect of this practice is the failure to obtain or keep receipts of expenses for which the owner-manager paid personally on behalf of the business. These expenses may seem too small to justify keeping track of them. However, if the tax rate is 25 percent, a mere $4 expense unrecorded can result in an increased tax liability of $1. According to Generally Accepted Accounting Principles, an expense is defined as a payment or a liability created to earn income. To determine whether certain expenses are deductible, the owner-manager should consult an accountant, CRA, or such publications as the *Master Tax Guide* published by Commerce Clearing House. Some of the more common small business expenses that may require explanation follow.

Accounting and Legal Expenses. Only those expenses incurred to earn income are deductible. Expenses incurred to incorporate the business or prepare a personal tax return are not deductible.

Advertising. Advertising expenses are deductible only if used in Canadian media and targeted to Canadian consumers.

Business Entertaining. Business entertaining expenses incurred in one's home are not deductible. Neither is the purchase of club memberships or yachts. Other types of legitimate business entertaining, however, are deductible.

Automobile Expenses. For a personal auto, the portion of expenses used for business purposes is deductible, but records must be kept to verify those amounts. Usually the business portion is the number of kilometres expended on business travel. In addition, automobile lease costs are also deductible business expenses.

Interest Expense. Interest expense is deductible for business loans but not for personal loans. Some experts counsel that to maximize this deductible, personal savings should be used to finance personal expenses if possible, rather than business expenses.

For a corporation, another interest-related matter is a loan to the business by a shareholder. This is a fairly common form of financing a business, because it offers some significant advantages. The interest is a deductible expense to the business, but the repayment terms may remain flexible depending on the ability of the business to pay and the wishes of the owner-lender. In a sense, the shareholder's loan combines the advantages of both debt and equity financing.

Repairs and Improvements. Repairs are deductible expenses, but improvements should be depreciated at the specified CCA rates. CCA (capital cost allowance) rates are percentages that can be subtracted from a capital asset cost and allocated as a business expense. It is often unclear what portion of the expenditure is a repair and what portion is an improvement. An accountant should be consulted in making this allocation.

Office Expenses. Office expenses are deductible and can be an important area for the owner-manager whose office is in the home. In such a case, a portion of household expenses such as utilities, mortgage interest, insurance, repairs, and taxes can be listed as business expenses. The portion to deduct depends on the size of the office relative to the size of the house. Care should be taken in including depreciation as an office expense, since it could be deemed to be recaptured and added to taxable income. A small business owner should consult with an accountant to verify the level of home expenses that qualify as a deduction.

An increasingly popular way of taking advantage of these expenses is contracting out. Many employees have left employment with an organization and have contracted out their services to that company. Although this may allow them to take advantage of some of the above deductions, care must be taken to be sure that it is not an employment arrangement. Discussion with a tax accountant should be held if such a plan is being contemplated.

Government Tax-Related Programs

Numerous government programs and policies in Canada affect the tax management practices for the small business. It is important that the entrepreneur be aware of these programs in order to take advantage of their benefits as Incident 13-3 advises. The following is a summary of some of the more important items for the owner-manager.

Special Tax Rate Deductions
Small Business Deduction (SBD). The small business deduction is 16 percent (from 28 percent to 12 percent) of active business income for an incorporated, Canadian-controlled, private business. This special rate applies to the first $300,000 of income. For income above this limit, the federal tax rate is 22 percent (28 percent minus 6 percent). Figure 13-4 illustrates the significance of this program for a small business. In addition provincial tax rates for

---

INCIDENT 13-3   Can a Computer Solve Tax Problems?

The answer is no. Software can't do your thinking for you, although it can keep accurate records and work more efficiently. At CFIB, horror stories are shared about how business owners didn't understand the tax rules or their software so they ended up in all sorts of trouble. This can be avoided by hiring a bookkeeper to handle day-to-day affairs, or by hiring an accountant to set up your system and answer questions. An accountant is completely liable to give you accurate advice so you will be insured against any loss.

If you do make a mistake, all is not lost. Simply contact your accountant and follow their instructions. It is also a good idea to get expert advice before contacting the Canada Revenue Agency so that you can describe the situation accurately.

Source: Adapted from Catherine Swift, "Ask Catherine," *Report on Small Business*, Summer 2006, p. 41.

Figure 13-4	Effect of the Small Business Deduction

Business income = $50,000

No small business deduction:

Tax rate = 38%

Tax liability = $19,000

Small business deduction:

SBD = 38% − 16% = 22%

Tax liability = $11,000

Difference in tax liability = $8,000

small businesses range from 4 percent to 9 percent. These lower rates allow small businesses to retain more of their earnings in the business for reinvestment.

Manufacturing and Processing Deduction. This program provides for an additional reduction of 7 percent in tax liability for any business involved in the manufacturing or processing industries. This deduction is available for income that is not eligible for the SBD mentioned above (only for income over the $300,000 limit cited above).

Investment Tax Credits. Only the Atlantic provinces and the Gaspé are eligible for investment tax credits on purchases of qualified property. All taxpayers are eligible for tax credits on qualified scientific research expenditures (SRTCs). Canadian-controlled private corporations may apply for a 35 percent SRTC, while all other taxpayers may apply for a 20 percent SRTC. In the Atlantic provinces and the Gaspé, the rates for SRTC are 35 percent and 30 percent, respectively.

Deferral Programs. Some programs that allow tax deferrals have been very popular with owner-managers of small businesses:

1. *Deferred profit sharing.* DPS allows for a deferral of part of the business profits that have been registered for payment in the future to employees. The payment amount is taxable to employees only when received but is a deductible expense in the year in which it is set aside or registered.

2. *Registered retirement savings plan.* RRSPs allow the owner-manager to put money into a registered plan that will be taxed only when received at a future date, presumably when the taxpayer is in a lower tax bracket. Budget changes have increased the contribution limits of RRSPs.

3. *Bonus deferral.* This program permits the business to deduct as an expense an accrued bonus or wage but allows a certain time period (180 days) to pay the amount. This amount is not taxable until received. The bonus deferral thus may effectively allow the business an expense in one year, but defer tax liability in the hands of the recipient to the following year.

Accelerated Capital Cost Allowance. This program allows an increased depreciation rate (capital cost allowance) to be applied as noncash expenses to certain classes of assets in calculating taxable income. Capital cost allowance rates can be obtained from an accountant or the tax department or by consulting the *Master Tax Guide.*

Small Business Financing Programs. For the incorporated business, these programs allow the business to borrow money from a chartered bank at a reduced interest rate. This is made possible because of special tax treatment these banks receive from the CRA. Only businesses unable to obtain ordinary debt financing are eligible for this program.

The Incorporation Question

One decision regarding the establishment or growth of the business that owner-managers face is incorporation. Chapter 4 discusses the relative merits and weaknesses of the proprietorship, the partnership, and the incorporated company. Some significant differences in tax treatment also exist among these different forms of business.

As mentioned above, with the small business deduction the tax rate for an incorporated business is about 25 percent. If the business is a partnership or a proprietorship, the business income is brought into the owner-manager's personal tax return. This return includes various other personal deductions and exemptions. The individual's personal rate (see Appendix 13A on the website) may be higher or lower than the rate for an incorporated business (see Appendix 13B on the website). If the minimization of tax liability were the major concern, the owner-manager would pursue incorporating when the tax rate for the business was lower than the personal rate. The incorporation question is influenced by more than just the tax liability for the different legal forms of business; many government programs are available only to incorporated businesses. Examples of the tax consequences of the different legal forms of business are shown in Figure 13-5.

The Remuneration Question

Another difficult decision owner-managers must make is how to be paid by the business. In the proprietorship and the partnership, payment to the owner is treated as a drawing from the business and is not a deductible expense (or taxable income). In the corporation, an owner can be paid with a salary or with dividends. These methods of payment receive significantly different tax treatment, as Figure 13-6 on page 376 illustrates. The owner-manager should consult with an accountant before making a decision in this area, as federal budgets have changed the difference in tax treatment of salary and dividends. Currently surtaxes imposed by the federal and some provincial governments result in a slightly higher income tax paid when remuneration is taken in dividends if the owner's taxable income exceeds $55,000. Beginning in 2000, dividends paid to children became taxable, although a family trust can still be used. This change reduces the effectiveness of income splitting with family in an incorporated business.

Figure 13-5   **Income Tax for Different Legal Forms of a Business**

	Bob Johnson Ltd. Corporation	Bob Johnson Proprietorship	Bob and Sue Johnson Partnership
Revenue	100,000	100,000	100,000
Expenses	80,000	80,000	80,000
Net Income	20,000	20,000	20,000
Tax Consequences	Taxed at the corporate rate. (Bob's salary is a business expense.)	Income brought into and taxed at personal rate. (Bob's salary not a business expense.)	One-half of income partner's income and rates. (Salary to Bob and Sue not business expenses.)

Figure 13-6	Dividend versus Salary Income		
		Salary	*Dividend*
Corporate income		$ 1,000	$ 1,000
Salary		21,000	—
Taxable income of corporation		—	1,000
Corporate tax @ 23%		—	230
Available for dividend payment		—	770
Income to shareholder		1,000	770
Dividend gross-up @ 25% of dividend received		—	193
Net income		1,000	963
Personal tax @ 29% on salary or dividend		290	279
Less: dividend tax credit @ $13^1/_3$ of grossed-up dividend		—	128
Net federal tax		290	151
Plus: Provincial tax (50% of net federal tax)		145	75
Total personal tax		435	226
Corporate tax		—	230
Personal tax		435	226
Total tax		$ 435	$ 456

Transferring the Business: Capital Gains

Many small business owners wanting to transfer their businesses to others have encountered considerable difficulty. Some tax considerations significantly affect how the business is transferred. Tax changes involving capital gains exemptions have made it much easier to transfer the business to family members or others. Currently CRA allows a $750,000 lifetime capital gains exemption on the shares of a small business corporation. This topic is discussed in more detail in Chapter 15.

Goods and Services Tax (GST) and Provincial Sales Taxes (PST)

Although the GST and PST are value-added taxes that are not levied on the income or profits of the small business, they are taxes on sales revenues achieved by the small business and require a significant amount of effort on the part of the small business. The federal GST is currently set at 5 percent of the sale price whereas the PST rates vary by province or territory. The amount of both taxes (Harmonized Sales Tax (HST)) is added to the retail price of the product. Accurate record keeping is required to collect, record, and remit GST amounts to the government. Figure 13-7 illustrates the type of information required for submission to the Canada Customs and Revenue Agency by the small business. If the small business has sales of less than $30,000 per annum, no GST collection and remittance is required. The small business owner should consult the CRA or the provincial or territorial revenue department for information about how the GST and PST applies to his or her business.

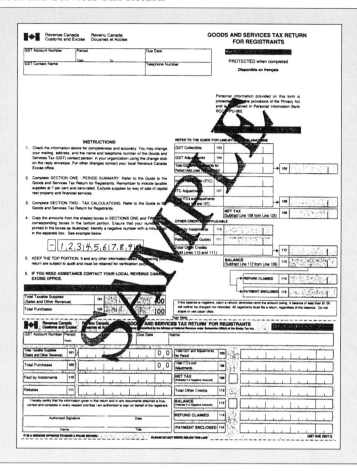

Figure 13-7   **Goods and Services Tax Return**

Summary

1. Basic tax knowledge allows the small business owner to save money that would otherwise be paid in taxes. Continual tax planning ensures that the owner-manager is aware of the tax consequences of business decisions throughout the year rather than just at the year-end.

2. The ten fundamental areas of tax management of which the owner-manager should be aware are (a) continual tax planning, (b) tax deferral, (c) income splitting, (d) marginal tax rates, (e) deductibles, (f) knowledge of government tax-related programs, (g) the incorporation question, (h) the remuneration question, (i) capital gains, and (j) GST and PST.

3. Some of the more important government tax-related programs are the small business deduction, manufacturing and processing deductions, investment tax credits, deferral programs, accelerated capital cost allowances, and small business financing programs.

Chapter Problems and Applications

1. Explain why the year-end date is significant in tax planning.

2. The year-end for Wave Waterbeds is soon approaching. The proprietor, Tom Newcombe, estimates that the company currently has taxable income of $5,500. He would like to purchase a new

cash register worth $2,000. Determine the tax liability if Newcombe purchases the cash register before or after year-end (use Appendix 13A on the website); cash registers are depreciated at 20 percent. When would you advise Newcombe to purchase the cash register? Why?

3. The owner-manager of L.A. Construction has just incurred the following expenses. Which expenses are tax deductible?

   a.   Incorporation expenses

   b.   Advertising expense in the United States and in Canada

   c.   Truck repairs of $2,000

   d.   Costs of maintaining a residential phone used for business purposes

4. What is the tax liability for the following proprietorship's taxable incomes?

   a. $5,496

   b. $10,942

   c. $34,999

   d. $63,000

5. Which variables affect the decision to incorporate?

6. Determine the federal tax liability for the following companies using Appendix 13A (on the website).

   a.   A Canadian-controlled incorporated company with $25,000 taxable income

   b.   A Canadian-controlled incorporated company with $25,000 taxable income that qualifies for a small business deduction

   c.   Same as part *b*, but the business qualifies for the 5 percent manufacturing credit

   d.   A proprietorship with taxable income of $25,000

7. Ask a consultant or an accountant when a business should incorporate. What are the important considerations?

8. Discuss with an accountant the advantages and disadvantages of the different owner compensation methods in a corporation.

9. Calculate the marginal tax rate for you or for someone you know.

10. For the small business highlighted in the profile at the beginning of this chapter, discuss the pros and cons of this business incorporating. Give reasons for your answer.

Web Exercise

Canada Revenue Agency
www.cra-arc.gc.ca

Look at the website for the Canada Revenue Agency and review the details of the GST as it applies to small businesses.

Suggested Readings

Canadian Master Tax Guide. Don Mills, Ont.: Commerce Clearing House, yearly.

Canadian Tax Journal. Canadian Tax Foundation. CCH Canada.

Carter, Robert. "Insure Your Retirement." *Profit,* May 1999, p. 622.

CICA Handbook. Canadian Institute of Chartered Accountants.

Cohen, Bruce. "A Taxing Proposal." *Profit,* April 1999, p. 84.

Government Assistance Manual For Canadian Small Business Financing and Tax Planning Guide, www.cch.ca

KPMG. Federal and Provincial Tax Rates on Active Business Income, www.KPMG.ca

Krishna, Vern. *Fundamentals of Canadian Income Tax* (8th ed.). Toronto: Thomson Carswell, 2004.

Smith, Robert A., and Michael Cavanagh. *Dollars From Change.* Markham, Ontario: Albert Street Press Ltd., 2005.

Ward, Susan. "The Truth About Small Business Deductions," Small Business Canada, www.sbinfocanada.com

"When Entrepreneurs Don't Know Tax Rules, Results Can Be Costly." *The Globe and Mail,* October 20, 2003, p. F2.

Video Cases for Part 3

High Flyers   Lulu
Baron of Beer   Red Paper Clip

PART ENDING VIDEO CASE & QUESTIONS   *High Flyers**

(Appropriate Chapters—4, 8, 13)

Back in 1993, Anton Rabie was just 23 years old but already a born entrepreneur. Anton and two buddies from business school were manufacturing Earth Buddies, little grasshead guys similar to the Chia Pet.

1. What inexpensive forms of promotion have been used by Spin Master?

2. What are the advantages and disadvantages of an Air Hog section in a toy store?

3. What are the risks associated with operating a business in this industry?

4. What lessons can be learned about partnerships from this case?

*Source: CBC *Venture* #748, running time 10:24.

PART ENDING VIDEO CASE & QUESTIONS   *Baron of Beer**

(Appropriate Chapters—1, 3, 7, 8, 11)

Winnipegger Gary DePape developed a taste for premium ales and lagers while playing hockey on the pro circuit in Germany. These days, he's playing a tough new game—building a million-dollar microbrewery in Winnipeg's highly competitive specialty beer market.

1. Briefly discuss the problems of starting from scratch, as illustrated by the Aggasiz Brewing Company.
2. How could Gary DePape have avoided these problems?
3. What would have been the advantages and disadvantages of Gary purchasing a micro-brewery instead of starting from scratch?
4. What risks would Gary have faced if he had dropped the price of his product?
5. What does this example show about the importance of financial management?

*Source: CBC *Venture* #729, running time 16:58.

PART ENDING VIDEO CASE & QUESTIONS   *Lulu.com**

(Appropriate Chapters—2, 8, 9)

Bob Young cut his teeth on Red Hat, an open source software company, now chief rival to Microsoft. He founded Lulu so people could create their own content on the Web and bring their work directly to their audiences.

1. Discuss the characteristics that would suggest that Bob Young is a true entrepreneur.
2. What improvements did Bob Young make to similar competing products?
3. Discuss the implications of this product to Internet customers.

*Source: CBC *Venture* #15567, running time 3:12.

PART ENDING VIDEO CASE & QUESTIONS   *Red Paper Clip**

(Appropriate Chapters—2, 8, 9)

Kyle McDonald had a dream: to trade a paper clip for a house. In an improbable series of events, he did just that and his quest became an international phenomenon.

1. Discuss the characteristics that suggest that Kyle McDonald is an entrepreneur.
2. What are the advantages of publicity as illustrated by this video example?
3. How has the Internet contributed to the growth of this type of business venture?

*Source: CBC *Venture* #15566, running time 11:39.

Cases for Part 3

ALLIANCE COSMETICS

Gordon McDougall, *Wilfrid Laurier University*

Alliance Cosmetics, a small cosmetics manufacturer in Manitoba, has a well-positioned set of mid-price-range facial cosmetic products. The quality of this product line, which retails in the $4 to $7 price range, is slightly above that of the major competitors such as Max Factor and Bonne Belle. The firm had sought and gained distribution through major pharmacy stores in Ontario and Manitoba, and chains such as Shoppers Drug Mart had responded well to its product line.

The line's success was due to more than just the slightly higher quality–price relationship. The firm had initially contracted representation from an aggressive set of manufacturer's agents. This was necessary to get quick high-volume distribution, which appeared to be possible only through the drug mart chains. The majority of the agents had long-term relationships with the chain buyers and were able to open the doors for the firm's products. This rapid and fairly intensive distribution was a key factor.

Drug mart chains are interested in high turnover and good margins. Therefore, above-average retail markups—in the neighbourhood of 120 percent versus the more typical 100 percent on cost to retailer—were offered. In addition, the firm spent $200,000 on advertising in the introductory three-month launch of the initial product line three years ago and has spent about $600,000 per year on advertising.

With the success of the current mid-price-range product line, three drug chains had recently expressed an interest in the firm's producing top-of-the-line facial cosmetics. The firm had the following major facts to consider in pursuing this opportunity:

1. The plant had ample capacity. It could produce an extra 1,000,000 product units without overstraining the capacity of the equipment.
2. The fixed costs the company now faces per year are estimated at $650,000. This would likely increase by $175,000 with an additional product line.
3. The current average retail price of the company's product is $5.50. The company has an average selling price to retailers of $2.50 per unit.
4. The direct manufacturing costs per unit for the current line are $0.80. The direct overhead costs of the new line would be $1.00 per unit. Agent's commissions are 4 percent of the company's selling price.
5. Total advertising for all lines would be in the neighbourhood of $1 million in the year the product is launched.

6. The average retail price of the line would have to be a minimum of $7.75 for it to be perceived as a high-quality good.
7. Some product samples had been produced and these were very well accepted by cosmeticians and models who had tried them.

This firm faces some interesting pricing problems. Price is often equated with quality in products like cosmetics. Here the consumer is purchasing, in a very real sense, "the total product concept." Cosmetics represent much more than the physical attributes of the product to the consumer. They represent glamour, beauty, and hope! Many buyers see price as a significant determinant of the quality of a product. To signify a premium-range product, a premium price has to be set. Unfortunately, as this premium price strategy is constrained by the firm's advertising budget, it cannot match the dollar volume of the large competitors in the industry. The higher the price, the greater the need for heavy and extensive advertising and promotional push. The company must have an advertising budget that will allow it to convince the public to pay the high price. The basic question is whether the planned $1 million in advertising expenditures is enough to support both product lines.

Questions

1. What pricing approach would you recommend for the new product line?
2. What price would you set for the new line? Why?

BIOSTAR INC.

D. Wesley Balderson, *University of Lethbridge*

In 1992 Stephen Acres was a successful veterinary scientist at the University of Saskatchewan in Saskatoon. At 49 he was at the top of his career, running an internationally recognized research institute in infectious diseases. Because of his position many were surprised when he left the university to start his own business—Biostar Inc. Dr. Acres had no reservations about leaving academia. "You always worry a little that you may not be successful, but it's the same with any undertaking. If you're not prepared to take those risks, you probably shouldn't be doing anything."

Biostar develops and holds the commercial rights to animal health products, which have a place in the world marketplace. Biostar is building on two broad technology platforms: vaccines to prevent infectious disease and enhance protection in animals, and biological mechanisms to deliver vaccines and drugs to specific cell types or organs.

Dr. Acres sees his company as a player in a global biotechnology race. "Because this is a relatively young industry, everyone is trying to get improved products to the market before their competitors do," says Acres. By 1996 Biostar had developed, received regulatory approval, and marketed three genetically engineered animal health products which provided revenues of $1.5 million.

Biostar's 21 employees carry out their research and product development close to the university, which still provides financial and research support to the venture. Additional financial support has come from the provincial government and a private share placement that was made in 1993. Several venture capital firms invested in Biostar at that time and this money is provided on a gradual basis as the company grows.

Stephen Acres is faced with several major decisions that will affect the future success of the company. The first challenge is one of marketing. It currently has eight new products in development, including a contraceptive vaccine for livestock and house pets. (Because of the staggering cost of regulatory approval for human health products, Biostar plans to stick mainly to animal health.) Although the domestic market appears lucrative (preventable disease costs the Canadian livestock industry alone more than $750-million a year), Acres is also considering the development of the international market. Therefore, Dr. Acres is contemplating the development of a Canadian and an international marketing strategy that the company can follow to be successful in the future.

The second decision flows from the first. If the company continues to grow, it will require a major expansion of physical facilities, its organization, and its financial resources. In the past Biostar has attempted to remain organizationally compact by forging alliances with other companies to provide certain services. As Dr. Acres puts it, "Very few companies today are fully integrated and can do everything that's required to get a product from the concept stage to the market." However, some growth would take place and Acres is uneasy about how best to manage such an organization.

Acres is also contemplating which would be the best method to finance this expected growth. He is considering selling shares on the public stock exchange to finance its growth. Although Acres will profit from such a sale, he realizes that considerable ownership of the company may move outside of his control.

Questions

1. What considerations should be made for the development of a marketing strategy for Biostar?
2. Discuss the implications of a public stock offering as a way of obtaining financing.

DEROCHER'S MARKET

D. Wesley Balderson, *University of Lethbridge*

Derocher's Market opened a new store in Quebec City in January 2006. Although the firm had been in business for three generations, the neighbourhood in which the original store stood had become shabby, and many of its loyal clientele had moved to the suburbs. The present owner, Claude Derocher, decided to follow the population move. The new store was located in a small shopping centre adjacent or close to more than 70 four-storey apartment buildings that housed more than 400 families. Many more apartment buildings were under construction, as well as three- and four-bedroom, single-family homes in several nearby housing developments. The nearest competition was located approximately two miles northeast of the present shopping centre.

In preparation for the grand opening, Claude Derocher purchased many varieties of canned juices, fruits, and vegetables. In addition, he carried a number of varieties and lines of cheeses, frozen foods, other dairy products, fruits, vegetables, and meats. To display and sell all the stock, it was necessary to use valuable aisle space as islands for various bulk cheeses, canned fruits, and dry groceries such as potato chips, pretzels, and the like. The store size was 17 by 27 metres. The store layout, shown in Figure 1, is as follows:

Figure 1	**Present Store Layout—Derocher's Market**

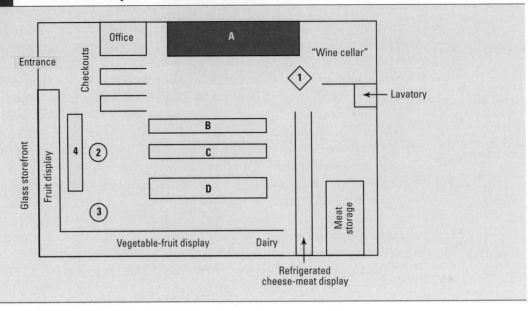

- A: display area for crackers, breads, and cookies
- B: refrigerated area for frozen foods, frozen desserts, and packaged cheeses
- C: display area for olives, pickles, other condiments, canned fruit, and fruit juices
- D: display area for canned vegetables, canned fish, breakfast cereals, and dried fruits.
- 1: island display for bulk cheeses
- 2, 3: island display for soft drinks
- 4: area for shopping carts

The store employed eight full-time people. These consisted of six clerks and two assistant managers—one manager for meat and dairy and the other for grocery, produce, and frozen foods.
During the first four weeks of operation, it was found that

1. There were far too many employees for the type of work needed.
2. There was far too much congestion of shoppers at certain in-store locations.
3. There was a build-up of customers at the check-out stations.
4. Many customers inquired as to where to find various food items.
5. Several of Derocher's employees indicated that some changes needed to be made to the interior layout of the store.

After receiving this input, Derocher was not sure what to do. The present layout seemed unsatisfactory, but he did not want to spend a lot of money making changes.

Questions

1. Based on Figure 1 and the observations of the first four weeks, what are the weaknesses of the present store layout?
2. Develop a layout that might solve these problems.

HOME MART HARDWARE STORE

D. Wesley Balderson, *University of Lethbridge*

Home Mart is a small hardware store located in Weyburn, Saskatchewan, an agricultural community with a population of about 9,000. Merchandise stocked includes automotive and farm supplies, furniture and appliances, sporting goods, plumbing and electrical supplies, and giftware.

The owner is David West, a prominent businessman in the community who also owns another business that occupies a large portion of his time. Because of this, West has delegated considerable authority to the manager of the store, John Burns. In July 2000, West and Burns decided to hire a new employee to be trained as an assistant manager. They first discussed the possibility of promoting one of the store's existing employees, but Burns thought none of them would be suitable as assistant managers because they were either too old or did not want the extra responsibility. Doug Burns, John's uncle, was already 63 years old and, though working full time, had indicated he wanted to work fewer hours and begin to ease into retirement. Sue Mikita, 52, had been with the company for 12 years but had concentrated on the giftware side of the department. Burns did not think she had an adequate knowledge of the farm supply side of the business, which produced the most revenue in the store. Ruth Huddy, 61, had worked for the company for only six years, mostly part time, and although she was very competent and knowledgeable, Burns felt she was also too old to fill the position. The only other employees were part-time students who worked Saturdays and summers.

West and Burns decided to advertise for an assistant manager in the local paper. This resulted in a few enquiries but no applicants who met the two criteria Burns and West considered most important: familiarity with the people in the community and a knowledge of agriculture. West and Burns met again in August to discuss the lack of prospects. West suggested that he might contact Noel Branlen, an acquaintance who lived in Weyburn, about coming to work for the company. Branlen currently worked in a town some 25 miles away, and perhaps he could be attracted back to his home town. Branlen was young—only 25—and knew the people in the community. West approached him and found out he was interested in working for him but required a salary higher than West and Burns had planned for this position. If they agreed to pay the salary he requested, Branlen would be paid a higher wage than the other hardware department employees except Burns himself. Although West and Burns were worried about this, they decided to hire Branlen and requested that his salary be kept confidential. Branlen would be in a training position for approximately six months and would then assume the position of assistant manager of the store.

Things went smoothly at first, but after a few months it was evident to West that some problems were surfacing. West noticed antagonism between Branlen and the other three regular employees, and so did the store's customers. In discussing Branlen's progress with Burns, West learned that Branlen was frequently late for work, his appearance was unsatisfactory, he was very slow in gaining essential product knowledge, and Burns had had several complaints from customers about him. In addition, Branlen himself had contacted West directly and expressed his disillusionment with the job and with his supervisor, John Burns. He indicated that Burns was not providing adequate training for the products or the authority to order inventory, set prices, and so on. Also, when Burns had his day off, several sales were lost because none of the employees knew the information customers required. Branlen also mentioned that as assistant manager he shouldn't have to sweep the floors as he had been required to do on several occasions. He further requested that he be granted time off two afternoons a week to take a management course at a local college to help him prepare for the managerial aspects of his job.

West discussed the problem again with Burns, who said that as soon as Branlen proved himself he would be given the requested authority—and he was very opposed to letting Branlen take time off for a management course, so this request was turned down.

Toward the end of November, Branlen contacted West to see if he could take some of his holidays just before Christmas. When West mentioned this request to John Burns, Burns was very opposed to it because this was the busiest time of the year for the store; furthermore, in the past employees had worked for a year before they took their holidays. However, West allowed Branlen to take the holiday.

The store got through the Christmas rush and inventory taking without serious incident, but things got progressively worse thereafter. Nine months after his hiring, Branlen handed in his resignation, saying he was going back to university. West was relieved that this problem employee was leaving and hoped that the same problems would not recur next time.

Questions

1. Comment on the possible reasons why Noel Branlen's employment did not turn out successfully.
2. How could Home Mart successfully compete against the threat of competition from Wal-Mart or Home Depot?

MARTHA'S DESIGNS

D. Wesley Balderson, *University of Lethbridge*

Martha Millwork needed to make some important decisions regarding her clothing manufacturing business. Started as a hobby in the 1980s, the business had grown to the point where she had opportunities to expand the scale of operations so that it could become a full-time commercial enterprise. She was unsure of which markets to pursue, which marketing channels to utilize, and the extent of product line that would be the most effective.

Martha lived in Grenfel, Saskatchewan, and had started sewing clothing for herself and her children in the 1980s. Her skill and talents were first shown publicly during the summer agribition celebration at Regina in 1992 at a fashion show she organized. As a result of this initial show she had received orders from interested buyers, and the hobby soon became a part-time business, which she operated out of her home in Grenfel. Company sales had grown steadily since that time and reached close to $30,000 in the latest fiscal year. Although this only brought a profit of $5,000, Martha had fine-tuned the business so that an increase in sales would also mean a larger profit percentage.

Martha's Designs specializes in high-quality, fashionable women's and men's coats made from canvas, denim, and Hudson's Bay and Pendleton wool blankets. The coats were designed to be comfortable, sophisticated, and original. They also featured fur and leather trims. Several coat designs were available and Martha modified existing designs and created new ones on an ongoing basis. The coats were well made, with high-quality materials, and were priced from $300 to $600. The clothes were fashionable and modern. This blend of fashion, function, and tradition made a unique finished product that she had successfully sold to buyers from across North America and Europe.

As the owner-manager, Martha designed the coats and cut the fabric. She usually ordered materials only after receiving an order for a particular coat. The cut pieces, trim, and notions were sent to one of two part-time local seamstresses who did the sewing in their own homes. Martha carefully inspected each garment upon completion. The purchasing of materials was an important aspect of the production process, since the cost of materials was such a large part of the cost of goods. Fabric was purchased at the lowest possible price, but Martha was aware that better prices would be available as she increased the size of her orders. The unique trims used on the coats were purchased primarily from local suppliers.

Recently, Martha was approached by the town of Wolseley (estimated population 1,000), which is about 10 miles from Grenfel, to be a part of a sewing plant that the village was planning to establish. The village intended to purchase sewing machines and other equipment and contract out the sewing services of the workers to interested firms such as Martha's Designs. Martha realized that to make such a change in operations worthwhile, Martha's Designs would have to increase its production volume dramatically. This proposal was attractive because of its low financial risk, the opportunity for increased production efficiencies, and the flexibility to produce a greater volume of coats.

Martha's marketing efforts to date consisted primarily of fashion shows, displays at events, some newspaper advertising and a brochure. Each year she organizes several fashion shows in Alberta, Montana, North Dakota, and Saskatchewan. In the past, some of these were in conjunction with other events such as the agricultural exhibitions, rodeos, and athletic events. Each show is the result of coordinating the individual efforts of models, commentators, hairdressers, make-up artists, sound specialists, musicians, and publicity staff. Displays have been set up at various trade shows and even such events as the Calgary Winter Olympics. A small amount of advertising has been done in newspapers such as the *Regina Leader Post* and other local papers. Martha uses advertising to promote general awareness and to promote good community relations.

With a potential increase in production capacity, Martha had to plan the company's future marketing strategy. She was confident that demand for her company's unique clothing existed, and that volume could be increased enough to result in significant material purchase savings, which would lower production costs. A major decision was which marketing channel to use. Until now, sales had been made directly to purchasers of the clothing. Martha thought she might achieve an increase in volume by selling through retail stores or clothing wholesalers, but she was unsure which type of retail store would most effectively reach her target customer. An alternative would be to continue selling directly to customers, and expand on these efforts by distributing a mail-order catalogue.

Another important decision was where to focus the firm's marketing efforts. Her sales to date had been mainly through buyers from Alberta, Saskatchewan, and North Dakota but there was also the possibility of increasing sales to other parts of Canada, the United States, and Europe. Martha was also thinking about increasing the sales of men's and children's coats. Although this strategy would add to her product line and create additional design work, it could also make the line more marketable by broadening its appeal.

A final decision to be made was how to support the sales efforts. Should she use more advertising, or should she concentrate on setting up sales booths at trade shows? There were many trade shows, and deciding which to attend would be difficult.

As Martha considered the alternatives available to her, she was beginning to realize that her company was at an important crossroads—in order to continue its growth it would have to enter new markets and expand production capacity. Martha's Designs was a cottage industry on the verge of becoming a small manufacturer.

Questions

1. Discuss the implications of Martha Millwork's potential expansion.
2. Evaluate the distribution channel options and promotional implications associated with them if Martha's business expanded.

SADIE'S COUNTRY N' WESTERN STORE

D. Wesley Balderson, *University of Lethbridge*

Sadie Rogers is the owner of a western-wear clothing and gift store located in Champion, Alberta. Champion is a small town of 500 located about 150 km south of Calgary and 100 km north of Lethbridge Alberta. There are several other smaller communities within a 100 km radius of Champion, as well as numerous rural farmers. Champion is located on one of two major highways from Lethbridge (and the United States) to Calgary. Other amenities located in the small town include a school, bank, post office, restaurant, hotel, grocery store, hardware store, farm machinery dealership, and services such as insurance, beauty salon, and a small library.

Sadie established her store two years ago after a successful five-year experience owning the town's grocery store. With this first venture, she had been pleasantly surprised that such a small community could support a grocery store and she was especially pleased that she had been able to draw residents from some of the other communities to her store. The margins in the grocery industry, however, were not very high and she had contemplated using her experience, expertise, and knowledge of the community with a clothing and gift store. She reasoned that if she could have the same success in drawing customers with higher margin merchandise, the business could really be profitable. She therefore sold the grocery store and started her current business. She named it Sadie's Country n' Western Store.

Sadie's Country n' Western is located on the main street and is part of a mini-mall with a beauty salon, grocery store, and bank. Sadie's features a huge selection of clothing for men, women and children (including jeans, shirts, jackets, footwear, hats, and accessories), gifts, collectibles, toys, furniture, jewellery, cards, and gift wrap. She has maintained a close working relationship with Wrangler, which has become her most profitable brand. The store also carries a line of rancher supplies such as saddles, bridles, and other cowboy accessories. She imports many of these products from the United States, which allows her to carry products that are exclusive to Southern Alberta.

Sadie defines her target market as customers within a 90-minute drive of her store. Interestingly the majority of her market comes from outside the town of Champion. There are few direct competitors to her store in many of the towns within the 100 km radius. However, Sadie feels that the main reason she is able to draw customers from outside her community is because of her marketing efforts and low prices.

Because of her low overhead Sadie makes sure that her prices are lower than her competitors'. She regularly visits these stores in other communities and does price checks. Sadie's promotion includes direct mail flyers distributed throughout southern Alberta, highlighting low prices on standard products and some of her unique products. Sadie's also offers discounts to 4H and rodeo club members, guest appearances by well-known rodeo professionals, and various contests and giveaways.

Sadie has been very pleased with sales as she nears the end of her second year of operations. Results have been remarkable considering the small size of the community in which she is located. Although sales have exceeded expectations, she has some concerns about the profitability of the business and is anxiously awaiting the year-end results.

Questions

1. How do you account for the ability of Sadie's Country n' Western Store to attract customers from outside of the local community?

2. Evaluate Sadie's marketing strategy. What additional things might be done to enhance sales?
3. Evaluate Sadie's pricing strategy. Relate your evaluation to the classification of consumer goods.

DALE'S SPORT PURSUIT

D. Wesley Balderson, *University of Lethbridge*

Dale Jorgensen has developed a new board game for sports enthusiasts similar to Trivial Pursuit except that the questions are about sports. The game involves asking questions about various players, teams, statistics, and records in all of the major North American professional and amateur sports. As the participants answer the questions correctly, they move around the board, which is patterned after a racetrack. The first participant to cross the finish line is the winner.

Dale has made a few prototypes of the game in his home and is now in the process of developing the marketing plan. Dale currently works for a national sporting goods chain in Toronto as a retail sales associate. Dale is now 38, and he would like to turn this idea into the type of business that would allow him to leave retailing and be his own boss. Dale has an extensive background in athletics, having played major junior hockey for three seasons and participated in amateur baseball until he was 16. He enjoys attending professional sporting events and most of his good friends meet often to discuss various sports. He has tested the prototype of his game with these friends and they have indicated to him that he has the makings of a million-dollar product if he can market it effectively.

Assume that Dale has come to you for guidance in developing the marketing plan for his product. As Dale has little experience in marketing or managing a business, he has come to you to assist him in developing a marketing strategy for Sport Pursuit.

Questions

1. Discuss how the concept of product classification would provide Dale direction regarding price, distribution, and promotion strategy.
2. What considerations would help Dale determine whether personal selling on the Internet or selling to a national chain like Toys-R-Us would be the most effective distribution method?
3. What factors could help determine whether to emphasize personal selling or advertising as the major promotional method?
4. Give an example of how public relations could work with this product and mention an advantage and disadvantage of using this promotion.
5. If Dale wanted to export the product, briefly discuss some things that he should know about each country he planned to market to.

SUSIE'S FASHIONS

D. Wesley Balderson, *University of Lethbridge*

As part of his course requirements in completing his MBA at Simon Fraser University in British Columbia, Darren Richards had received a student consulting assignment with a small clothing manufacturer in Vancouver. The firm had been in operation a little over a year and had received funding from the government agency funding small businesses. However, it was experiencing cash flow problems. There was a concern that the business, Susie's Fashions, would have to either close or obtain additional funds. Richards spent considerable time wading through the financial data and finally came up with the approximate statements shown in Figure 1.

Susie Mikado had emigrated to Canada from Hong Kong about five years earlier. Being a hard worker and having worked in a clothing factory in Hong Kong, she got a job immediately at a dress-manufacturing factory. After three-and-a-half years, she accumulated some funds and decided to start her own small business making selected clothing primarily for the large Asian population in the Vancouver area. Mikado had an obvious talent for selecting fabrics and

Figure 1	Susie's Fashions

Susie's Fashions
Balance Sheet
As at January 31, 2006

Assets		Liabilities and Owner's Equity	
Current assets:		Current liabilities:	
Cash	$ 95	Accounts payable	$ 8,450
Accounts receivable	3,815	Current portion of debt	1,000
Inventory	4,765	Total current liabilities	9,450
Prepaid expenses	275	Long-term liabilities	
Total current assets	8,950	Debt	4,000
Fixed assets:		Total liabilities	13,450
Equipment	3,500	Owner's equity	(1,000)
Total assets	$12,450	Total liabilities and owner's equity	$12,450

Income Statement
For Year Ended January 31, 2006

Sales:		
352 dresses	$17,600	
298 robes	11,920	
Other miscellaneous	5,200	
Total sales		$ 34,720
Cost of goods sold:		
Dresses	6,336	
Robes	7,152	
Other miscellaneous	2,500	
Total cost of goods sold		15,988
Expenses:		
Wages (including Susie's)	20,400	
Rent	4,800	
Utilities and phone	3,200	
Interest	1,000	
Repairs and maintenance	3,000	
Total expenses		32,400
Total cost of goods sold and expenses		48,388
Net profit (loss)		**$(13,668)**

designing garments and, through her family and friends, developed a reputation as a skilled seamstress.

Mikado located her business in the Chinatown district of Vancouver in a leased space of about 1,800 square feet. To make renovations, buy equipment, and pay other initial expenses, she had borrowed $5,000 and put $2,000 of her own funds into the venture. She had hired two full-time employees, paying them $6 per hour to assist in sewing the clothing items. The production process was simple: Each employee and Mikado would make a garment from beginning to end.

Darren Richards visited Susie's Fashions to assess the situation and determine what could be done to solve the cash flow problem. He was impressed with the product line, which exhibited quality craftsmanship. Susie's produced primarily two garments. The first was a Chinese-style dress retailing at $55, and the second was a kimono-like robe retailing at $45. Sales were based almost entirely on word of mouth, as Mikado spent no money advertising. In examining the production process, Darren noticed numerous interruptions occurred as family and friends of the workers frequently came by to visit. He estimated, however, that on average the dresses took four hours to make and the robes took three hours. The average dress took about three yards of material, and the robes averaged four yards. The fabric for both items cost Mikado about $6 per yard.

Richards was concerned about the management of the firm. Although Mikado had hired two full-time employees, she often hired family or friends to help for a few days at a time when they, as she put it, "needed some money." He was most concerned, however, with the financial procedures Susie was following. Because there was no record-keeping system, he had difficulty determining paid and unpaid bills from the assortment of receipts, scraps of paper, invoices, and notes Mikado kept. Deposits and withdrawals from the bank account had been made but not recorded. Mikado's salary was not recorded, but Richards learned that she withdrew $200 per week. Credit sales were frequent and informal, with Mikado allowing customers to take garments without leaving a down payment.

Questions

1. Briefly evaluate Susie Mikado's approach to starting her own business.
2. Examine the pricing system for Mikado's clothes.
3. Assuming miscellaneous clothing and robe sales stay the same, how many dresses would Susie's have to sell to break even?
4. Evaluate the financial statements prepared by Darren Richards in both form and content.
5. What kind of financial record-keeping system would you advise for Susie's?

TAYLOR CONSTRUCTION COMPANY

D. Wesley Balderson, *University of Lethbridge*

In September 2006, George Taylor realized a lifelong dream by starting his own construction company. He had worked for several construction firms in the province of Quebec over the years, and prior to the time he started his own firm, he had been a foreman on several large projects. He was a hard worker and had developed a reputation as a capable and sought-after foreman by many companies. Since starting Taylor Construction Company, George succeeded in obtaining several profitable contracts, which kept him very busy.

One day he was visiting with a friend, Rob Dumont, over lunch. The following conversation revealed that things were not so great at Taylor Construction.

Rob: How is your business doing, George? You've sure been busy lately.

George: Yes, we've got lots of work, but you can't imagine the problems I've had with employees. I never dreamt it would be such a hassle.

Rob: What kinds of problems are you talking about?

George: Take your pick! When we started up and got our first contract I needed six labourers, so I ran an ad in the paper. I got 19 applicants, and I was surprised that most hadn't finished high school. Even the ones I hired were lazy and undependable. I spent half my time replacing those who quit or whom I fired. Since then things haven't really improved much.

Rob: Maybe you should spend more time training them.

George: More time? As it stands now, I have to be with them almost constantly on a job and tell them what to do every step of the way. If I leave one of them in charge when I have to be away, the others resent it. It seems like they're always bickering with each other.

Rob: I wonder if you should train a foreman to supervise the workers.

George: I tried that. The work that he supervised was poorly done, and on top of that he padded his hours. I even noticed a few tools missing. When I confronted him with it, he up and quit.

Rob: Can't you spend a little more money and find some better-qualified and motivated employees?

George: My labour costs are too high already! Even though I don't hire union workers, I have to pay pretty close to those rates, and they are high. Once in awhile a hard worker will come along, but before long peer pressure from the others seems to drag him down to their level.

Rob: It sounds pretty hopeless.

George: The worst part is that just last month I gave all my employees a bonus. I distributed it based on how long they had worked for me and thought I had explained it to them. However, after I gave it out, several of them were upset, and I even had two quit on the spot. Can you believe that? I'm seriously considering shutting down the business and going back to work for my old firm.

Questions

1. Why do you think George has gotten into this situation?
2. What recommendations would you make to George?

THE BARREL BRACKET

D. Wesley Balderson, *University of Lethbridge*

Gary Anderson operates an accounting firm in Fredericton, New Brunswick. Although his accounting business is successful and he enjoys it, Gary has always wanted to invent a product and take it to market. In his spare time Gary recently developed a metal bracket that, when attached to a wall, allows one to hang a wheelbarrow on the wall of a garage or shed. Gary feels that this simple metal product could provide wheelbarrow owners with a major saving of space. Named the "Barrel Bracket," Gary has received positive comments about the product from several friends and some retail hardware store owners. Gary has obtained a patent on the product and has made a number of them in his garage. He believes that the Barrel Bracket would be an ideal product for most homeowners who own wheelbarrows, and it may even be of interest to some businesses and retail stores.

With his steel press located in his garage, Gary can make 100 Barrel Brackets per day with the material cost to him being $5.00. He is hoping that he can sell the product for $10.00 and that eventually sales would increase to the point that he could build his own manufacturing facility and retire from his accounting practice.

The major decision facing Gary at this time is to determine the most effective way to market the Barrel Bracket. He has identified three distribution channel options, which all seem viable. The first is to sell to a national retail hardware chain such as Canadian Tire or Home Depot. This method would guarantee substantial sales, but Gary is unsure of the profit margin he could make on each bracket. The second option is to hire manufacturer representatives to sell the Barrel Bracket. Manufacturer representatives are independent salespeople who sell to retail stores and receive a commission on these sales. These type of salespeople typically represent several manufacturers as they travel around to various retail stores. The third option is to hire some salespeople himself and sell the product door to door.

Since Gary does not have a lot of expertise in marketing, the decision of the appropriate marketing channel is especially troublesome to him. In addition, Gary does not want to spend a lot more money on the venture because he has already invested most of his spare cash to develop the product and obtain the patent.

Questions

1. Evaluate the three distribution options for Gary using the information provided in the textbook regarding long and short channels.
2. Discuss the implications for setting the price of the Barrel Bracket for each of the three distribution options mentioned.
3. What other marketing costs may Gary have overlooked?

THREADZ

D. Wesley Balderson, *University of Lethbridge*

Threadz is a small independent retail women's clothing store located in London, Ontario. London is a city of 336,000 in southwest Ontario and has a large young adult population due to the university and colleges that are located in the area. The owner-manager of the store is Jennifer Byers. Byers established Threadz eight years ago after graduating from university with a bachelor's degree in business management. During her high school and college days she had worked in various retail clothing stores and had gained valuable experience for this kind of business. Her father, a successful entrepreneur, provided start-up capital and other assistance for the venture.

Although sales have increased steadily each year, Jennifer has been concerned recently that this success is starting to fade and would be short-lived unless something was done soon. Last year, sales were virtually the same as the previous year and the rate of growth in sales has declined in each of the last three years. Because Threadz is an independent retailer, Jennifer is concerned that stiff competition from the well-known chains is luring away her customers, due to lower prices, greater choice, and large advertising budgets.

The Threadz outlet contains 500 square meters of selling space and targets the 20–35-year-old aspiring professional woman. Jennifer's competition comes from such stores as Benetton, Mexx, Esprit, Banana Republic, Club Monaco, Savannah, and Suzy Shier. In addition, there are many other clothing retailers that are somewhat competitive but Jennifer is of the opinion that they are not focused on the exactly the same customer that Threadz targets. Byers describes her target market as the upper-middle-class woman who is "on the go" and requires clothes that are easy to "mix and match" and are "for any occasion." Threadz's target market comprises a decreasing circle of women who enjoy the shopping experience. Because of career obligations, women in this market tend to shop during lunch breaks or in evenings and on weekends. Threadz is located in a large mall in downtown London and is accessible to a large work population as well as the residential market. The downtown has many eating places and night clubs which also contribute to mall patronage at midday and in the evenings.

Jennifer has operated the store in the past with herself as manager, an assistant manager, and two sales clerks. Recently, she hired a new assistant manager, Sarah Hetherington, who had graduated from a retail management diploma course at a local college. As she was discussing Threadz's current sales dilemma with Jennifer, Sarah asked her if she had thought of establishing a database program in an attempt to retain the customers she suspected she was losing. Sarah indicated that such a system would help in better customer relationship management, something that successful retailers were recently giving much more attention to. Although she was aware of CRM, Jennifer had thought that such systems were far too expensive for a small, independent retailer like Threadz. She was not sure that she could afford another marketing cost as she was already spending four percent of sales on promotion, above the industry average.

Threadz's promotion budget comprises special events, newspaper advertising, and participation in various mall promotions. In the past, Jennifer had also considered developing a website to further advertise the business but felt the costs did not outweigh the expected benefits. However, Sarah explained that technology costs had come down and that a website and a database system might help Threadz to provide better service to its existing customers. Such a system could profile these customers and monitor their purchasing behaviour in order to tailor special offers to them. As the system was developed further, Sarah explained that it could also be used to target new customers.

Another use would be to exchange this information with other organizations such as restaurants, jewellry stores, and shoe stores that had the same target market as Threadz. A main benefit, according to Sarah, would be that this system could provide in-store sales personnel with immediate information about its customers so that the store could provide more personal treatment to them. Jennifer could see some of the advantages of the system that Sarah was suggesting but was unsure whether it was worth the financial investment.

Questions

1. Evaluate the advantages of the system that Sarah Heatherington is suggesting.
2. What concerns should be explored with this system?
3. What steps should be followed in setting up a CRM system for Threadz?
4. What other promotional suggestions might improve Threadz's performance?

GARNER MEN'S WEAR

D. Wesley Balderson, *University of Lethbridge*

Garner Men's Wear is a relatively small independent men's wear retailer located in Oshawa, Ontario, that has been operating for more than 20 years. The owner, Adam Garner, had previously worked for 10 years at Tip Top Tailors, a national chain of men's formal clothing, before starting his own store. Although the first few years were difficult as the business was getting established, Adam was eventually able to develop the business and provide superior service while offering high-quality men's clothing at competitive prices. His target market is made up of middle-aged executives and professionals, most of whom he knows on a first-name basis. Adam has always felt that if he took care of his best customers, the financial part of the business would take care of itself. He was comfortable with this philosophy because he really didn't enjoy all the bookwork that was part of running a business.

Recently, however, he was becoming concerned with the performance of the business. One of his concerns included the financial aspects of the business. He seemed to always have lots of customers but when he got his financial statements from his accountant about two months after the year-end, he was surprised and disappointed to find that the net income of the business had dropped to $10,000 and there was no cash in the business bank account. Assume that you have been called in to evaluate Adam's business. He provides you with the following financial statements for the last two years.

Garner Men's Wear Ltd. Balance Sheet

Assets	2006	2007
Cash	$ 10,000	$ 0
Accounts Receivable	90,000	120,000
Inventory	50,000	80,000
Fixed Assets	140,000	130,000
TOTAL	$290,000	$330,000

Liabilities		
Accounts Payable	40,000	50,000
Long Term Debt	100,000	120,000
Owner's Equity	150,000	160,000
TOTAL	$290,000	$330,000

Garner Men's Wear Ltd. Income Statement

	2006	2007
Sales	$750,000	$720,000
Cost of Goods Sold	500,000	490,000
Gross Profit	250,000	230,000
Expenses	200,000	220,000
Net Profit	$ 50,000	$ 10,000

Questions

1. Comment on the financial management practices of Adam Garner in managing Garner Men's Wear.
2. Calculate and discuss the significance of each of the following for Garner Men's Wear.
   - i) current ratio
   - ii) inventory turnover
   - iii) debt ratio
   - iv) return on investment
   - v) return on sales
3. How many days are there in this company's business cycle? (That is, how long is it taking to convert cash spent back to cash available?)
4. Where did the $10,000 cash from the 2006 statement go in 2007 even though the business made $10,000 income during 2007?

BOOMERANG BOUNCERS ENTERTAINMENT

Jim Clark, *University of Lethbridge*

As Cam Bean sat at his desk on March 1st 2006, he felt he needed to make some decisions about his strategy for using e-commerce tools to take his business to the next level. Cam had decided that April 1st 2006 would be his last day as a tax trust lawyer for a firm that employed 175 other lawyers just like him. He was not enjoying this profession but it paid the bills. After three years of running a small part-time business, Cam and his wife/business partner felt the time was right to take the business on fulltime and devote all his energies into making his business a full time endeavour.

Cam Bean was 32 years old. His wife Janet was also his business partner. They had four young children. Cam had a joint law/MBA degree and Janet had an education degree. Cam had grown up in a family which had a small-business and entrepreneur background. Janet's parents worked for very large aerospace firms. Three years ago, Cam decided to make some extra income on weekends by renting out air bouncers to people for recreational activities. Bouncers are large inflatable tent-like structures. They are sometimes known as moonwalks, spacewalks, jumps, inflatables, among several other names. They come shaped in themes such as Barney, Spiderman, Cinderella etc. Cam had gotten the idea for the air bouncers from a college friend who had a thriving business in bouncers in Kansas City, Kansas. Cam lived in Calgary and thought this might be a nice way to bring in extra income on the weekends.

Cam and Janet called their small part-time venture Boomerang Bouncers Entertainment. The bouncers were usually rented for five hours at a time at a cost of $225. Boomerang Bouncers Entertainment would deliver and set up the jumps. They would make sure everything was safe, clean, and dependable. At the end of the rental time, Boomerang would then pick up the jump and take it back to inventory to be rented out again. The market for theses jumps included daycares, schools, family parties, church and club socials, and corporate parties. Weekends are usually the busiest time. The business is seasonal and things slow down from November to February each year.

In their first year, Cam and Janet invested in two bouncers at a cost of $4,500 each. With these two bouncers, they generated sales of $32,400 on 72 unit bookings. The next year, Cam thought they would expand this business with two more bouncers and another $9,000 investment. In year two, they generated sales of $72,000 on 320 bookings. In year three, they went to a total of six bouncers and sales went to $108,000 on 480 bookings. They almost always had multiple requests for bouncer rentals on weekends which they could not fulfill because all the bouncers were already booked out. Cam found that he really enjoyed the business and could hardly wait for his work day as a tax lawyer to end so he could take time for Boomerang Bouncers Entertainment. He decided to quit his tax job and operate Boomerang Bouncers fulltime, with a total of 20 bouncers.

This decision to go fulltime with 20 bouncers meant Cam had to make a number of other decisions. He would have to hire more drivers for delivery and increase his marketing efforts to keep all the bouncers rented as much as possible.

Cam advertised in local community papers read by moms of school-aged kids, used word of mouth, and also made some person-to-person sales. Most orders were received over the phone with Janet. She would make sure the particular jump the customer wanted was available. As these jumps are visually stunning, it was hard to describe them adequately over the phone. Cam knew that keeping these jumps rented out as much possible was the key to expansion. He felt he needed a Web strategy of some sort to increase his marketing and sales efforts to keep his jumps booked at a high capacity. Cam and Janet felt the Web would graphically show the potential customer the variety of products that they had in inventory.

Cam was a fairly sophisticated computer user, skilled with PCs and networking. He felt that with his business growing, he could use the Web for marketing and sales. He also wanted to use a database to keep track of sales and human resource needs.

Cam knew he had to make a number of decisions regarding his use of e-commerce tools and that he needed to make them very soon. In 30 days, his whole livelihood depended on making Boomerang a success.

Questions

As a consultant to Cam, answer the following questions:
1. What are the advantages of a Web presence for Boomerang Bouncers?
2. Identify what Boomerang Bouncer's website objectives should include.
3. Which of the three strategies found below for website development should Cam proceed with? Why?
4. Cam will need to host his website once it is developed. What would you recommend he should do about choosing a Web hosting strategy? Why?
5. What are the five top ways that Boomerang Bouncers could attract customers to their website? Why did you choose them?

PART FOUR

Looking to the Future

Part 4 focuses on management of the small business for the long term. If a business is being managed effectively and increasing sales and profitability have resulted, the owner-manager will face the question of expansion. If growth of the business is desired, some changes will be required within the organization. Chapter 14 discusses the preparations needed in such a situation.

Chapter 15 discusses the methods of transferring ownership of the business to someone else. Many key considerations in this regard have legal and tax implications with far-reaching consequences for the owner-manager. An option other than transferring ownership to another person is involving family members in the business. The majority of small businesses are, in fact, family owned and operated. Thus, Chapter 15 also examines the special characteristics of such businesses.

CHAPTER 14
Managing Growth

CHAPTER OBJECTIVES

- To describe the potential problems that success and growth can bring to the small business

- To review the characteristics of the stages in the business life cycle

- To discuss how to sustain the business despite the difficulties created by growth

- To illustrate the importance of planning for growth

SMALL BUSINESS PROFILE

Joyce Groote

Holey Soles Holdings Ltd.

Joyce Groote is an experienced entrepreneur with a strong business management background. Her career evolved from being an academic scientist in genetics to a CEO in the private sector. In the transition time between these two extremes, she worked in government regulation and was president of a Canadian biotechnology industry association. In 2002, she formed a venture capital corporation to invest in life science companies and chaired the Life Science Angel Investor Network of British Columbia.

Shortly after establishing the venture capital organization, she became aware of a company that her neighbour Anne Rosenberg had started, called Holey Soles. Holey Soles' product was an injected-foam shoe which was at the leading edge of a hot footwear trend. Recognizing that she was out of her financial and business depth, Anne asked Joyce to help her manage and grow Holey Soles. In early 2004, Joyce joined Holey Soles and invested in the company. Later in the year, she bought the company from Anne.

Since buying Holey Soles, Joyce has moved the company from its original focus on shoes to becoming an innovative lifestyles products company. Each lifestyle collection has a different model shoe as its base and accessories have been developed that use the foam and also meet the needs of that lifestyle segment. Joyce's vision and business plan are based on using the foam material and incorporating it into innovative products that meet targeted lifestyle needs. Her vision is that Holey Soles will be a world leader in the use of injection foam molding as the basis for a new generation of lifestyle products that are comfortable, functional, stylish, and affordable.

As a result of Joyce Groote's clear focus and expertise, Holey Soles was named the #1 fastest growing company in Canada by *Profit Magazine* in 2006. This distinction was earned by increasing sales from $52,000 per year in the first year (2003) to $3.5 million two years later representing a two-year growth rate of 6568 percent. Sales of the Vancouver-based company jumped even further, to almost $12 million in 2006, with markets growing to almost 50 countries around the world.

Some of the challenges Joyce has had to face in growing the company were: dealing with competitors who are larger and use litigation as a business strategy; responding to continually changing lifestyle market segments; adjusting distribution channels to accommodate the expanding product line and new markets; and obtaining the financing to handle the rapid growth. In addition, procedures and processes were required to handle employee growth, from 2 to over 50, in a short period of time. As these challenges were being met, the company has also had to continually deliver on its mandate of excellence in customer service.

Source: Used with permission of Joyce Groote, Holey Soles Holdings Ltd.

Holey Soles Holdings Ltd.
www.holeysoles.com

SMALL BUSINESS AND GROWTH

As Incident 14-1 illustrates, short-term success and subsequent growth do not always lead to a trouble-free business operation. Often success and growth may compound the complexities and difficulties of managing the business.

To avoid the pitfalls of growth and changes in the market, the owner-manager should try to ensure long-term viability early in the life of the business. First, the owner-manager needs to understand the life cycle of the business to effectively plan for the future. Second, he or she should be aware of some of the more common growth problems a business is likely to face. Finally, the owner-manager should take specific steps in planning for growth of the business.

THE BUSINESS CYCLE

The business cycle of the small enterprise is similar to the product life cycle discussed in Chapter 8. For many small businesses that have only one or two products, the business cycle and the product life cycle may be the same.

Figure 14-1 illustrates the shape and characteristics of a life cycle for a small business. The vertical axis represents the growth index, usually measured by gross sales, market share, or profitability. The horizontal axis measures the time taken to pass through the stages of the cycle. The length of time a business stays in one stage depends on several variables. Many small businesses take several years to move through the life cycle, while others pass through all four stages within a couple of years. This shorter life cycle is common in high-technology industries. The characteristics of the stages of the business cycle are discussed next.

Introduction. Stage 1 is the start-up stage of the small business. It is characterized by expenditures made for both product development and introductory promotion and by low profits, particularly at the beginning. Stage 1 also usually includes a narrow market, a very limited

---

INCIDENT 14-1   The Wheels of Fortune

Steep and sweet could describe Louis Garneau's ride to the top of the corporate cycling world. Garneau's sports designs are founded on a single product he made 23 years ago in his father's garage. Today, he distributes hundreds of high-quality sports items such as cycle wear, cycling helmets and accessories, cross-country ski clothes and accessories, children's clothing, personalized team equipment, and bike and fitness equipment. Garneau currently has six factories in both Canada and the U.S., and the company employs about 450 people, with revenues of $50 million annually from around the world.

Garneau became hooked on cycling at a young age and after years of training and perseverance, he rose to be among the world's best. After his cycling career was over, Garneau began making cycling shorts. Although growth was slow at first, with Garneau's perseverance business exploded. Soon, Garneau moved to a bigger venue, hired more seamstresses, and introduced more products. The introduction of the Louis Garneau helmets had a slow start but sales soon skyrocketed. "They made us famous," says Garneau. The company now handles a range of bikes as well. The expanded product line has helped Garneau's company to grow.

Louis Garneau Sports has become one of the world's largest manufacturers of top-line cycling helmets, as well as a major sponsor of elite international racing teams and cycling athletes.

Source: Adapted from Mark Cardwell, "The Wheels of Fortune," *The Costco Connection*, May/June 2006, pp. 18–21.

product line, and involvement in most aspects of the business by the owner-manager. The owner's role tends to be more technical and entrepreneurial in this stage.

Growth. Stage 2 of the business cycle, growth, is usually characterized by the establishment of a market share, or acceptance, and expansion of the product line or markets. It may also take the form of internal or external expansion, such as a merger or franchising. During this period, sales grow at an increasing rate. At the end of the growth stage, however, competitive pressures begin to take their toll, necessitating changes in business strategy. Promoting the business to customers, investors, and employees is important at this stage of the business life cycle. Most small businesses find that this stage requires increased capital to finance the expansion. The business may have orders to purchase but only receives payment when the product or service is delivered. Therefore, financing to cover inventories, equipment, and employees is required before sales occur. Most high-growth firms indicate that this is the stage at which the most severe cash flow problems occur in the life of the business.

Maturity. Stage 3 is characterized by a levelling of sales due to increased competition or a decrease in demand. During this stage, the owner-manager must make some important strategic decisions to avoid moving into stage 4, decline. Of necessity the strategy of the business will become more competitive. Such a strategy may involve adding new products, expanding to new markets, or adjusting or improving existing products in some way. The goal of such actions is to lengthen the life cycle, as illustrated by the increase in sales during the decline stage of the adjusted life cycle in Figure 14-1. The owner's responsibility becomes much more managerial during this stage.

Decline. As Figure 14-1 shows, stage 4 involves a decrease in both sales and profits. Unless action is taken to reverse this trend, the business will fail.

Figure 14-2 on the next page shows an example of the growth of a business and subsequent operational and strategy changes that should take place. The actual dollar level of sales relating to the stages of the life cycle will vary depending on the growth of the market,

| **Figure 14-1** | **The Life Cycle of a Business Concept** |

Figure 14-2	Stages of Growth

Approximate Sales Level	Market	Product	Owner-Manager
$0–$1,500,000	One market	One or limited line	Involved in day-to-day aspects of the business such as buying, selling, and financial management
$1,500,000–$4,000,000	Expanding into new markets	Adding new products in same category	Some organizational change allowing supervisor to oversee greater part of day-to-day operations
			Greater need for financial evaluation
			Greater need to obtain capital to finance growth
			Some delegation required
			Development of managers
$4,000,000+	Established markets: continued expansion to new markets	Adding new products in different categories	Managers run day-to-day operations and report to owner Communication and information important Training for management development
			Establishment of proper controls

Source: Ronald W. Torrence. *In the Owner's Chair: Proven Techniques for Taking Your Business from Zero to $10 Million,* © 1986, p. 259. Reprinted by permission of Prentice Hall, Inc., Englewood Cliffs, New Jersey. Updated 2005.

the type of industry, and the owner's objectives. However, Figure 14-2 points out the need to deal quickly with the changes that growth in sales can create.

PROBLEMS CREATED BY GROWTH

To be able to anticipate growth difficulties and make plans to minimize them, the owner-manager should be aware of some of the problems that can be expected to accompany growth. Figure 14-3 illustrates the importance of some of these obstacles to growth. Some of these are discussed below.

Owner-Manager Fatigue and Stress. Stress levels rise when the scope of the business and the magnitude of its problems increase.

Lack of Communication. As the scope of operations grows, the former closeness between owner and business dissipates. Many owner-managers resent this loss of closeness and even curb their growth objectives as a result.

Lack of Coordination. Various aspects of the business may become specialized and less integrated with the overall operation as a business grows. This often results in increased conflicts among departments and individuals within the organization. Employees who in the

| Figure 14-3 | Perceived Obstacles to Business Growth and Development by Management Capacity (Percentage), 2004 |

Source: SME Financing Data Initiative, Statistics Canada, *Survey on Financing of Small and Medium Enterprises*, 2004.

early stages of the company life cycle performed many duties are often reluctant to give up some of those responsibilities to specialists. Such resentment often leads to conflicts within the organization.

Shortage of Cash. Growth and expansion often require financing that the business has not yet generated. Merchandise may have been sold but cash not yet received, even though cash is still needed to acquire new inventories. It is important that the owner-manager estimate the case requirements of an increase in sales. See Figure 14-4 for an illustration of how to do this. Incidents 14-2 and 14-3 illustrate the cash flow difficulties caused by growth for two Canadian companies.

Low Profitability. Low profitability is common in rapidly growing businesses. Several of the fastest-growing companies in Canada lost money in 2000, and others earned small profits.[1] Considerable expenses are incurred in research and development of markets during the growth period.

Breakdowns in Production Efficiency. Declining production efficiency, as evidenced by unmet schedules, increases in quality assurance problems, and consumer complaints, are common in rapidly growing companies.

Lack of Information. Lack of information with which to evaluate the business's performance often accompanies rapid growth. As the owner-manager becomes increasingly removed from day-to-day operations and the scope of the business outgrows manual infor-

| Figure 14-4 | How to Estimate the Cash Requirement for an Increase in Sales |

To make the calculation, a business needs the following information:

- The increase in sales planned ($)
- The timeframe for adding new sales (days)
- The company's gross profit margin, gross profit ÷ net sales (percent)
- The estimated additional expenses required to generate additional sales ($)
- The company's average collection period (days)

To calculate the amount of additional cash needed, use the following formula:

Extra cash required = [(New sales – Gross profit + extra overhead) × (Average collection period × 1.20*)] ÷ (Time frame in days for adding new sales)

*The extra 20 percent is added as a cushion.

Consider the following example:

The owner of Ardent Company wants to increase sales by $75,000 over the next year. The company's gross profit margin is 40 percent of sales (so its gross profit on these additional sales would be $75,000 × 30 percent = $22,500), its average collection period is 47 days, and managers estimate that generating the additional sales will require an increase in expenses of $21,300. The additional cash that Ardent will need to support this higher level of sales is:

Extra cash required = [($75,000 – $22,500 + 21,300) × (47 × 1.2)] ÷ 365 = $11,404

Ardent will need $11,404 in extra cash to support the additional sales of $75,000 it plans to bring in over the next year.

Source: Adapted from Norm Brodsky, *Paying for Growth: How Much Cash You Need to Carry New Sales*, inc. Online Tools & Apps: Worksheet.

INCIDENT 14-2   The Digital X-Ray

In 1991, Robin Windsor built his first digital radiology system to improve the use of x-rays in his wife's veterinary clinic. After many modifications, this new x-ray unit has become the backbone behind Imaging Dynamics Company. Because this new technology is able to produce the highest-resolution x-ray images in the world, health care costs are being cut due to the decreased need for expensive film, chemicals, and imaging plates. With $30 million in sales in 2005, and a 500 percent increase within one year, Imaging Dynamics Company is one of the fastest growing technology firms in Alberta.

However, the road to success wasn't always an easy one and the company struggled with growth in its early stages. "The first five years were hell. We never had enough money, we never had the science where we wanted it to be, we were feeling our way through the world in terms of distribution, we couldn't attract money," says Darryl Stein, CEO.

Although the company struggled at first, it knew it had an incredible product and persevered in the technology industry. Competitors General Electric and Philips are now on the market with their new digital machines, although their machines cost more than twice the price of the Imaging Dynamics system. Because of this price difference, sales have continued to increase steadily, moving from only 7 units in 2002, to 32 in 2003, 90 in 2004, 300 in 2005, and a projected 1,000 this year.

Source: Adapted from "The Digital X-Ray," *Alberta Venture*, April 2006, p. 50.

INCIDENT 14-3   Rostar Precision Inc.

Growth is a goal that many small businesses strive for, but it calls for careful and informed business decisions.

When Rostar Precision Inc., a manufacturer of mechanical components for the aerospace industry, decided to try to spur more dynamic growth, it meant restructuring the company. Although Rostar had grown at a respectable rate through much of its 21-year existence, it wanted to be considered for high-profile aerospace, satellite, and International Space Station projects run by companies such as Spar, Boeing, and Allied Signal. "We didn't want to be thought of as a small company that couldn't meet the requirements of these large contracts," says the director of marketing Roman Kuczynski.

Exporting is crucial to the growth of some companies almost from the very beginning, but getting the support needed to pay for and manage an expensive export and marketing program can be extremely difficult. The problem is a common one for many start-up software companies, which not only have to sell their specialized products globally in order to survive but also have to foot the bill for high research and development costs.

"Cash flow is always a challenge," says Tony Harris, president and CEO of Comdale Technologies (Canada) Inc., a manufacturer of advanced software for the industrial automation marketplace. "We never had trouble paying employees, but we had to delay some payments to suppliers." He added that the period when a software company is trying to "shrink wrap" its product to sell in higher volume is financially one of the toughest.

Source: "Controlling Growth," *Profits Magazine*, vol. 17, no. 3 (Business Development Bank of Canada), p. 4.

---

mation retrieval, a more automated system is often required to generate the required data. Incident 14-4 illustrates how one small business recognized the value of communications technology for growth.

Decreasing Employee Morale. Lower employee morale results in higher employee turnover and absenteeism. New people are added to the firm to accommodate growth, but they often receive insufficient training. Existing employees work harder in growth companies and may not receive adequate recognition for their efforts. This situation can lead to employee discontent.[2]

INCIDENT 14-4   Deadly Optimism

In 1996, Kids Only Clothing Ltd. was riding high with revenues of around $16,000,000. Founded in 1987 by Cindy Eeson, the Calgary-based company got its start when Eeson began selling some of the high-end clothes she'd designed for her kids at home parties. This strategy worked well for almost a decade. After that, Kids Only was battered by unfriendly demographic trends, as Eeson struggled to recruit sales agents. Rising competition from mega-brands such as Gap and Club Monaco and unsustainable sales structure furthered the decline in sales.

As Cindy and husband Ralph, who is also her managing partner, struggled to agree on the direction to take the business, marital problems ensued. Ralph felt that the business lacked managing experience and suggested selling the firm. Communication between the two diminished as Cindy put her whole self into restoring the company. Ralph opted out of both the marriage and the business in 1999. In 2000, revenue dropped $13.9 million and there wasn't enough money left in the firm's line of credit to pay for fabric for the upcoming season. Finally in 2001, Eeson began the process of closing Kids Only, a move that cost her almost $1.1 million, out of her own pocket.

Source: Adapted from "Deadly Optimism," *Profit*, September 2004, pp. 25–26.

Any one of the above problems can spell disaster for an otherwise potentially successful small business. To prevent such problems, the wise owner-manager can prepare himself or herself and the business to handle growth in several ways.

Owner Lifestyle. An often overlooked contributor to business failure due to growth relates to personal lifestyle decisions of the owner as the business begins to be successful. A larger house, car, or exotic vacations based on the expectation of continued growth often leave the owner unable to meet personal obligations.

EVALUATING THE GROWTH QUESTION

The owner-manager should answer four important questions before proceeding to expand the business.

Is the Business One That Can Grow? A preliminary step in dealing with the question of growth is to evaluate whether the product or business is one that can grow. Restricted markets or products that have volume production restrictions are difficult to expand. Many service businesses that rely on the special expertise of their owners also fit into this category. Rapidly changing industries such as those found in high technology suggest concerns of rapid obsolescence. This is particularly critical if the capital investment of growth is large.

Is the Business Owner Prepared to Make the Effort? Expanding a business will require additional time and effort on the part of the owner-manager. The decision the owner-manager must make is whether he or she is ready to increase effort and prepare for the stress or be content with a smaller but less demanding business. Many successful small businesses have chosen not to grow for precisely this reason.

Does the Owner-Manager Have the Capabilities to Grow? The owner-manager should assess whether the needed capital, labour, and expertise can be obtained to deal effectively with growth. Some of these specific areas will be discussed in the following section.

How Should the Owner-Manager Pursue Growth? If growth is desired, several approaches may be taken in pursuing it. The most common strategies (some of which were already mentioned) are as follows:

- Pursue new markets for the product or service. This may involve different geographic (domestic or foreign) or demographic markets.

- Increase sales of existing products or services by increasing the frequency of use. This can be done through increased promotion.

- Add new products or services or modify existing ones to increase sales.

- Find new uses for the product or service and promote these uses to the market.

- Acquire other small companies or merge with another organization.

PLANNING FOR GROWTH

Once the decision to expand has been made and the method of expansion has been determined, a plan for growth should be developed. A growth or strategic plan is a blueprint of future actions. Planning is an essential but often overlooked part of management. One survey found that only 5 percent of all companies do formal short-term and long-term planning, and almost 50 percent do little or no formal planning.[3]

Some small business owners fail to plan for the future because they do not understand what a plan is. A plan is more than short-term sales forecasts and budgets. It includes setting long-term objectives and outlining procedures for reaching those objectives.

In addition, most small business owners feel snowed under by the daily operations and often think planning is a nuisance. However, small business owner-managers who are able to periodically step back from the organization and objectively assess its overall direction are generally better able to cope with the environmental changes that will affect the business.

Finally, in many industries conditions change so rapidly that plans have to be altered frequently. The need for constant adjustment discourages many small business owners.

The Expansion Plan

Chapter 4 discusses the essential elements of the start-up business plan. Many similarities exist between the start-up plan and the expansion plan. The business plan as introduced in Chapter 4 includes projecting for growth and expansion as well. The steps in the expansion plan are as follows.

Set Objectives. The first step in the planning process is to set the objectives the business is to accomplish. As mentioned previously, it is important to set objectives specifically so that the outcomes can be measured. Objectives may include dollar sales, market share percentage, or dollar profits.

Determine Alternatives. The second step includes identifying possible strategies to achieve the set objectives. It also involves forecasting the possible outcomes of different alternatives.

Select the Best Alternatives. Alternatives should be selected with a view toward long-term success. The components of this success are the company's capability and the potential growth of the area.[4]

Understanding the Requirements of Growth

Rapid growth will necessitate some fundamental changes within the organization. Some of the requirements of growth are discussed next.

Greater Management Depth. The owner-manager must realize that an expansion of management depth must accompany the expansion of the business. This will require more skills or harder work on behalf of the owner-manager. Because he or she may already be stretched to the limit, such expansion usually consists of training subordinates to handle some of the managerial responsibilities. This involves training and delegation, two personnel practices owner-managers are often hesitant to incorporate into their management styles. As the business grows, the owner must spend more time thinking and less time doing. This also means he or she must move from task delegation to functional delegation, allowing key people to manage various functional areas of the business. Greater management depth can also be achieved through the use of functional specialists outside the company such as accountants, lawyers, directors, or mentors.

Intelligent Expansion. A common problem among small business owners is that in their effort to succeed, they start too many diverse projects. They often do so without evaluating whether they have the productive or marketing expertise and resources to accomplish the expansion. They may also ignore the potential effects of unplanned expansion on their existing products. The decision to expand should incorporate continuity, experience, and intelligence. Incident 14-5 illustrates the need for this for one of Canada's most successful entrepreneurs.

INCIDENT 14-5   Watch Your Growth

Roots Canada Ltd.
www.roots.com

In some instances, a company's distribution channels can't handle the volume. A classic example relates to Roots, a Canadian clothing and apparel company, which at one time had an immensely successful advertising campaign. Unfortunately, their distribution infrastructure wasn't able to cope with the level of demand.

Don Green, co-founder of the highly successful Roots chain concurs. "Between 1987 and 1989, before sports-licensed merchandising appeared, there was a major fad for logo sweatshirts. Our product filled a void in the market and we caught the wave beautifully," he says. "But we had a problem in meeting demand."

Green explains that suppliers secured additional production capacity soon after, and things went more smoothly. Roots has since continued its expansion and now boasts 100 outlets and 1,000 employees across Canada, as well as stores in the United States and Asia. "We now try to plan well ahead of time," he adds. "We also own two factories in the Toronto area, which is really key in terms of ensuring supply."

Source: "Watch Your Growth," *Profits Magazine,* vol. 17, no. 1 (Business Development Bank of Canada), p. 6.

Additional Capital. Any expansion in the business will require additional money to finance added productive capacity, inventory, or personnel. Unless the business has a solid debt-equity ratio and a steady cash flow, it may have difficulty obtaining this needed financing. Chapter 7 discusses sources of financing. Incident 14-6 shows how one Canadian firm grew rapidly because of its ability to obtain the needed capital.

One way to achieve high growth even with limited capital may be to franchise the business or the idea. Although becoming a franchisor requires a certain amount of capital (see Chapter 6), franchising may allow a firm to expand rapidly without needing large amounts of funds.

Financial Information. Often increased sales obscure the fact that the profitability of the business is declining or even negative. As the business grows, it is increasingly difficult—but more important—for the owner-manager to obtain accurate information about the profitability and productivity of the business. The use of computers by many small businesses has greatly helped in this area. As the business grows there is a greater need to utilize information technology. Owner-managers should regularly project future financial requirements so that cash shortages do not occur.

INCIDENT 14-6   VAW Systems

Winnipeg's VAW Systems manufactures noise-control systems for commercial buildings and industrial plants. The privately owned company is a world leader in sound and noise control technology and exports 90 percent of its production. "From 1980 to 1992, we were a small regional player," says Robert Jackson, the company's president. "In 1992, we decided to expand our market to include the United States and we have grown a lot since then."

VAW Systems's sales grew from $2.7 million in 1992 to $6 million in 1996. Customers include Motorola, Advanced Micro Devices (the world's second-largest computer chip manufacturer), and the Diamond Back, a new dome stadium in Phoenix, Arizona. "The main challenge to our growth is finding and training enough technical employees," says Jackson.

Source: "Growing Companies Create The Most Value," *Profits Magazine*, vol. 17, no. 1 (Business Development Bank of Canada), p. 4.

Organizational Change. As the owner-manager realizes he or she can no longer be involved in every aspect of the business, the organizational structure will require alteration. This is necessary to establish a clear understanding of reporting and responsibility centres in the business. The aim is to reduce the owner's span of control and allow more of his or her time for the planning and long-term strategy development of the business. It can also allow the owner more time to foster coordination within the firm. Incident 14-7 illustrates how one entrepreneur found that organizational change and delegation were required for the firm to grow. As the firm grows, the owner can also make greater use of advisory boards and professionals.[5]

At the same time, the owner-manager must resist the temptation to "overdo" the bureaucracy of the organization. An entrepreneurial culture (which likely contributed to the business's success in the first place) must be retained if growth is to continue.

Implementing Managerial Controls. As a business grows, it becomes more difficult to control. Through the use of informational and organizational methods, a system of goals, performance levels, and evaluations must be put into place. As discussed in Chapter 11, the integration of new software into the small business's operations has greatly enhanced the owner-manager's ability to control all aspects of the business. Such measures as ratio analysis, bench marking, inventory turnover, margins, and cost controls are examples.

Monitoring the External Environment. The final growth requirement is that the owner-manager focus greater attention on the external environment of the business. These external forces serve as a guide to the long-term strategic planning in which the owner-manager now must engage. Important external forces, discussed in Chapter 8, are technological change, competition, consumer demand, social and cultural norms, legislation, and the state of the economy.

To keep their companies strong and encourage growth, managers need to

- Invent new applications for products and services
- Find new sales and distribution channels
- Rethink internal processes
- Enhance technological content
- Provide employees with upgradeable, saleable skill sets
- Disseminate internal information effectively[6]

INCIDENT 14-7   The Value of Outside Help

During tumultuous times, external advice could be what you need to get your business back on track. Family-owned Richards-Wilcox Custom Systems went through a trying year when the death of the founder caused instability and change within the company. The Ontario-based company designs, develops, and manufactures custom-fit doors, platforms, mezzanines, and staircases.

President Kathryn Rhamey went to BDC Consulting to get advice about human resources and management issues. BDC looked at the company's strengths and weaknesses and offered a fresh perspective on how to do things. Because Richards-Wilcox Customs Systems had also reached a plateau in growth, BDC did a thorough assessment of the firm, and picked 12 employees to run monthly meetings to tackle important issues. The company also received assistance in letting go a number of employees, a job that can be emotionally trying. BDC also encouraged the company to focus on management coaching as a way of training and to communicate openly about problems or issues.

Source: Adapted from "Success Story—HR Advice Opens the Door to Tangible Results," *BDC*, www.bdc.ca, May 2006.

Summary

1. Problems to anticipate as a result of growth are the owner-manager's increased fatigue and stress, lack of communication, lack of coordination, shortage of cash, low profitability, a breakdown in production efficiency, lack of information, and possible decreases in employee morale.

2. The four stages of the business cycle are the introduction, growth, maturity, and decline stages.

3. To acquire the knowledge to deal with growth problems, the owner-manager should address three areas. First, the owner-manager must review the business life cycle. Second, the owner-manager should be aware of the common growth problems that arise. Third, the owner-manager must know the steps he or she can take to plan effectively for growth.

4. Growth planning is often overlooked because of the failure to understand the planning process, lack of time, and the constant changes occurring in the industry. The three steps in developing an expansion plan for a small business are (1) setting objectives, (2) identifying all the possible strategies or alternatives for achieving the objectives, and (3) choosing the best and most viable alternative.

Chapter Problems and Applications

1. Describe the business cycle for Garneau Sports (Incident 14-1).

2. What problems should the owners be aware of when expanding Garneau Sports? How might these problems be dealt with?

3. The owner-managers of a small, successful hair-cutting company want to expand their business. Their growth objective is to have 35 percent of the local hair-cutting market in two years' time.

   a. What steps could they take to determine the feasibility of their expansion?

   b. Outline a brief expansion plan.

4. What recommendations for expansion would you make for the following companies? Justify your answers. How does your recommendation differ from what actually happened? Why does it differ?

   a. Imaging Dynamics (Incident 14-2)

   b. Rostar Precision Inc. (Incident 14-3)

   c. Kids Only Clothing (Incident 14-4)

   d. Garneau Sports (Incident 14-1)

5. What requirements for growth would be necessary for further expansion of Garneau Sports?

6. Interview the owner-manager of a successful small business, and evaluate the potential for further growth. Would you recommend expansion for this firm? Why or why not?

7. Visit three small businesses that you suspect have varying sales levels. Determine the market, product, and degree of owner-manager involvement in each business. Are your results significantly similar to those in Figure 14-2? Explain.

Web Exercise

www.profitmagazine.ca

Access the website for *Profit* Magazine's fastest-growing companies and identify what advice the owners provide about achieving success. What percentage of these fast-growing businesses are profitable?

Suggested Readings

"Canada's Emerging Growth Companies." *Profit*, September 2003, p. 19.

"Canada's Fastest Growing Companies." *Profit*, June 2003, p. 24.

"The Definitive Guide to Understanding Business Cycles for Growing Companies." *Profit*, June 1999, pp. 1–27.

El Akkad, Omar. "When Running Things Like A Small Business No Longer Works." *The Globe and Mail*, Oct.12, 2005, p. B13.

Pearson, Kalli. "Growth Secrets of Canada's Hottest Startups." *Profit*, September 2002, p. 27.

"Plan Your Growth Step By Step," Business Development Bank of Canada website, June 2006.

"Profit Hot 50 Top Growth Firms," *Profit*, October, 2006.

Spence, Rick. "The Enemy Within." *Profit*, May 2004, p. 17.

Zimmerer, Thomas W., and Norman M. Scarborough. *Entrepreneurship and Small Business Management.* New Jersey: Prentice Hall, 2002, pp. 483–532.

Comprehensive Case   *Sid Stevens: Part 10*

Despite the personnel problems, Sid was able to persevere and keep the plant running. Toward the end of the second year of operations, Sid's business seemed to be really taking off. Sales had reached $400,000 by October, mainly because of distribution of the Ladder Rail and accessories across Canada as well as a growing number of sales from the United States. He had added some accessory products and their sales were also contributing to the positive company performance. This expansion had necessitated renting additional manufacturing space nearby and doubling production. Sid had secured patent protection for the Ladder Rail and its accessories and now had several ideas for new but related products.

However, the major concern that Sid has is that the business had grown to the point that he is putting in 18-hour days. It seemed that every day new crises arose and he was the only one who had either the expertise or the interest to deal with these problems.

Despite the sales success, the business continually experienced cash flow problems. Sid had to pay for the metal C.O.D. but the retail hardware chain that had exclusive rights for his products would only pay him once per month. This resulted in a continual operating deficit until this payment was received.

The plant personnel problems continued to cause a lot of stress and with the additional plant, this was compounded. Sid found that he was going from one plant to the other to try to ensure quality production. Times when he had been on the road, the quality had slipped and a number of customer complaints had been received. Although his marketing person was a hard worker and capable, Sid had to oversee marketing as well as review the financial condition of the business. Finally, he had to ensure that the loan payments to the bank were made.

His family life had essentially disappeared. The dream of owning his own business and having the freedom to do what he wanted was turning into a nightmare. All the problems of trying to run the business seemed to be compounded when Suzie announced that something had to be done or they were through. Sid realized that he didn't want to lose Suzie. He was contemplating selling the business or altering the organization somewhat to allow for more time for his family.

Question

1. Identify the problems that growth has caused with Sid's business and discuss possible solutions.

www.mcgrawhill.ca/olc/balderson

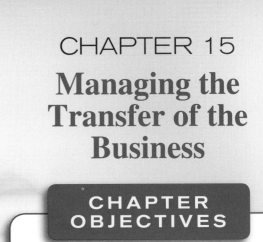

CHAPTER 15
Managing the Transfer of the Business

CHAPTER OBJECTIVES

- To discuss the importance of planning for the long-term and the possible transfer of ownership of the small business

- To review the unique characteristics and problems of owning a family business and passing it on to family members

- To explain the critical considerations in selling the business to someone outside the family

- To discuss information pertaining to the closing down of the business

SMALL BUSINESS PROFILE
Moira and Lindsay G. Merrithew

Merrithew Corp.

In just over a decade, husband-and-wife entrepreneurial team Lindsay G. Merrithew and Moira Merrithew, co-founders of Merrithew Corporation, have parlayed their passions for fitness and business into an exercise empire. Blending his business savvy with her fitness expertise, they established Merrithew Corporation as the world's only fully integrated company of its kind specializing in Pilates education, equipment manufacturing, and video production, and established STOTT PILATES as the world's most respected mind-body fitness brand.

Forced to end her dance career because of a foot injury, Moira applied for and received a grant from Toronto's Dancers in Transition Centre to retrain as a Pilates instructor at Joseph Pilates's original studio in New York City. Lindsay, meanwhile, spent time in New York completing a second degree at the Juilliard Theater School before launching a successful acting career. When the two returned to Toronto in 1987, they began their entrepreneurial venture in Pilates. Moira began offering private sessions in their Toronto apartment, attracting such celebrity clients as prima ballerina Karen Kain. Lindsay focused on the business side of their small but high-potential business while also working in film and television. The proceeds of his acting work were used to help finance the fledgling company's growth. Early positive media exposure, a demand for mind-body exercise among dancers, athletes, and the massive aging baby-boom market, and an incredible sense of ambition on the part of Lindsay, inspired the couple to think big.

Today the two former struggling artists have their own line of Pilates equipment and an independent brand of Pilates exercises marketed under the STOTT PILATES banner. They have built a manufacturing facility in east Toronto, moved classes into a mid-town studio near Yonge and Eglinton, and expanded into instructor training and certification as well as a line of videos.

Merrithew Corp. was ranked as one of the fastest-growing companies in Canada five years in a row by *Profit* Magazine. Merrithew's revenues grew 742 percent between 1998 and 2003, while the number of staff grew almost four-fold during the same period.

One challenge of making this business successful has been the working relationship with a spouse. The Merrithews have had to learn how to divide management duties and responsibilities to make a good partnership. As president and CEO, Lindsay handles the firm's sales and management. Moira, the company's executive program director of the company's education division, oversees program content and education. The current delineation of roles didn't come without significant growing pains. In hindsight, says Lindsay, they were blissfully ignorant about the challenges of building a business together. "We didn't know any better at the time."

"Despite the firm's early success, growth experts say taking Merrithew to the next level will be a real challenge," says Maneesh Mehta, a Toronto-based partner with accounting firm Deloitte & Touche LLP. "Having a clear game plan, understanding their markets, their customer needs and their product development strategy goes before anything else."

Lindsay and Moira agree. "We've got these growth pillars in place and are now focused on expanding our professional management team to ensure continued strong growth," says Lindsay. Building on this strong foundation, the Merrithews look forward to tackling the challenges and seizing the opportunities that will undoubtedly come their way with the growing demand for health and wellness products and services.

Used with the permission of Lindsay G. and Moira Merrithew.

Merrithew Corp.
www.stottpilates.com

LONG-RANGE PLANNING

As mentioned in Chapter 14, relatively few owner-managers engage in formal long-range planning. One reason is the unpredictability of the future due to changes in the economy, technology, consumer demand, and legislation. However, one outcome that is predictable for small business is the fact that the owner-manager will not be able to manage the business forever. Someday the business will be transferred to others or be closed down. Because of the time, effort, money, and commitment owner-managers have put into their ventures, they generally want the business to continue to grow and prosper and hope to realize a financial gain for their efforts in starting and building the organization.

To ensure this continuity for the business, the owner-manager needs to plan early for the time when he or she will no longer be in charge. Many small business owners are uncomfortable about this prospect. As a result they often procrastinate, avoiding the issue until shortly before the transfer of ownership is a necessity. Most succession experts advise that planning should be done several years in advance.[1] Unfortunately, it has been estimated that 60 percent of entrepreneurs aged 55–64 have not yet discussed succession with family members or partners.[2] Given today's legislation and tax laws, such a lack of planning can be extremely costly and damaging to both the owner-manager and the new owners of the business.

In addition, succession problems are predicted to be at a high level in the near future as many business owners who started their businesses following the Second World War are now retiring. According to a recent study, 41 percent of family-owned businesses expect a succession within the next five years, and only one-third admit to having a succession plan.[3] The experience with Canadian small businesses confirms this trend, with an estimated 71 percent of small and medium sized businesses expecting a leadership change in the next 10 years with only 48 percent having a succession plan in place.[4] Further, this phenomenon will mean an estimated $1.2 billion in assets will change hands—and up to two million jobs are at risk when this happens.[5]

The entrepreneur should be familiar with the possible outcomes for the business, the relative merits of those outcomes, and some key implications of each.

ALTERNATIVE OUTCOMES FOR THE BUSINESS

The owner-manager can anticipate four possible outcomes for the business: transferring ownership to family members, selling the business to an employee, selling the business to outsiders, and closing down the business or declaring bankruptcy.

Transferring Ownership to Family Members

Keeping the business in the family is a common method of transferring the business. Many Canadian family businesses have been successful and many small business owners desire to pass the business they have inherited or built up to their children. In most cases, this transfer occurs with considerable tension.[6] Because a family-owned business has many unique characteristics, it is important to review the problems and potential solutions in managing this type of organization.

Canadian Association
of Family Enterprise
www.cafecanada.ca

Estimates of the extent of ownership within a single family indicate that approximately 90 percent of all businesses in Canada are family owned and operated[7] and employ close to 60 percent of the Canadian workforce. The Canadian Association of Family Enterprise (CAFE) exists to provide assistance to family businesses relating to many areas discussed in

---

INCIDENT 15-1   Watch and Learn

Ruth Maran is one of North America's busiest and best-selling authors. Maran is the principal writer for maranGraphics, a family-owned company out of Mississauga, Ontario, which produces the *Teach Yourself Visually* books. These books are built around a two-page, four-panel lesson format and teach consumers everything from computer software to yoga.

The company had sold more than 14 million copies as of mid-April 2005, and published in more than 25 languages. The Marans learned the business from their father, Richard. He founded the company and developed the teaching techniques found in the books. Maran started by producing training manuals for banks and insurance companies. He then produced his first consumer book, after which he found a U.S. distributor, IDG Books. He then tripled his sales in a single year. Meanwhile, Maran groomed his children to succeed him by giving them part-time jobs while they attended high school and university. They each joined him, one by one, as they finished their degrees. The siblings' formula for running the family business follows their "make the complex simple" book approach. They each have well-defined areas of responsibility of absolute control.

Source: Adapted from D'Arcy Jenish, "Watch and Learn," *The Costco Connection*, July/August 2004, p. 17.

---

this chapter. Although a majority of these firms are small businesses, a significant number of family-owned large companies exist. Almost 35 percent of the Fortune 500 companies are owned or controlled by a single family.[8] In Canada, family involvement in business is also significant as approximately 40 percent of the largest 100 companies on the Toronto Stock Exchange (TSX) have handed down control to a second or even later generation.[9] One survey of the 500 fastest-growing private corporations in America undertaken by *Inc.* and *USA Today* found that 33 percent of spouses and 28 percent of children are involved in family business operations.[10]

Despite the predominance of family businesses in Canadian society, relatively few survive into the second and third generations. It is estimated that only 30 percent continue into the second generation and 10 percent into the third.[11] This succession problem also appears to be occurring more frequently today as many entrepreneurs who launched in an economic boom 30 years ago are now nearing retirement.[12] What are the reasons for this apparent lack of continuity? Observation shows that if some unique considerations in operating the family business are not recognized and planned for, they can cause considerable difficulties for the enterprise. Family involvement in a business may have a detrimental effect not only on the business but also on family relationships. Additionally, unique challenges result when spouses own and operate a business together. Statistics Canada estimates that 30.7 percent of all self-employed persons have their spouses as a partner.[13] The profile at the beginning of this chapter illustrates some of these considerations.

Planning for Succession in the Family. The owner-manager has both a difficult task and an excellent opportunity in preparing children to become involved in the business. See Incident 15-2. Some difficulties include providing proper training, adequate motivation, and a supportive atmosphere so that the child is able and wants to come into the business. Research shows that fewer than 50 percent of children who worked in family businesses expect to return after receiving their college or university education, and only 20 percent plan to return to the business within five years of their graduation.[14] Other studies indicate that 70 percent of family businesses are either liquidated or sold after the founder retires.[15] It is

---

INCIDENT 15-2   Alex Tilley

Alex Tilley sold his first wide-brimmed hat on a boat show over 25 years ago. His cotton creation became an instant success and today he sells 280,000 hats a year. Tilley's quality products have grown to include shorts, skirts, jackets, vests, and underwear, and have penetrated the market in 17 countries.

Tilley's daughter Alison is now the vice president of marketing and merchandise at Tilley Endurables. Alison has expanded the business to include more than 2,000 dealers who carry Tilley products. She also reconfigured the company catalogue to cater more to the target market of age 50 and up.

The younger Tilley remarks, "I guess I am what you would call a chairman-in-training. My father is giving me a level of trust that he used to give the creative director, which is nice."

Source: Adapted from, Andy Holloway, "Alex Tilley," *Canadian Business*, January 2005, p 66. Also Diane Stegmann, "Tilley Junior Redesigns Tilley Endurables," *Multichannel Merchant*, multichannelmerchant.com, July 1, 2000, retrieved September 25, 2006.

---

apparently difficult for the parent to instil in the child the personal interest in the business the parent has. One school of thought is that parents may take too passive a role in attempting to interest their children in the business. They assume the children will find a profession more interesting and rewarding for them.[16] A common scenario is that of the parent-owner who is unwilling to give up control or allow the child a say in the business. Conversely, it is also common for the inexperienced child to want to make changes the parent believes will be detrimental to the business. Incident 15-3 illustrates such a situation.

Running a family business also offers a great opportunity to provide on-the-job training and background for the child that is not otherwise possible. The parent-owner can also assess the child's progress and level of preparation over a longer period than would be possible if hiring an outsider to manage the business. In addition, the owner-manager's business philosophy and style may be taught to the child who is apprenticing for management and ownership of the business.

Figure 15-1 provides questions that should be asked before transferring the business to an heir.

INCIDENT 15-3   Charles Northstrup

Life in a family business has its ups and downs, but Brett Northstrup knew more about the downs. He had worked for his parents in the family furniture store all his life. "I grew up with the idea that I was going to work in the business; my parents told me the business was for me," said Brett. So there was never any leeway or choice as to what he was going to do as an adult. He was going to work there, so he did. But when it came time for his dad, Charles Northstrup, to retire, he wouldn't. He wanted Brett to take over the business, yet he didn't want him to do it because it was taking something away from him. Charles Northstrup now said, "I don't know if I ever will want to retire. I'd just take it a little easier someday, because I know I'd miss all the friends I've made, all the customers—they're just like friends. Besides, I'm not sure Brett can handle the business yet; he just doesn't run the business my way."

After 15 years with the business, Brett had finally had enough. He left and started over, leaving his parents to run the business their way.

Source: Rick Heyland, University of Lethbridge.

| Figure 15-1 | Mom and Pop Quiz: How Succession-Ready Is Your Company? |

Consider this a final exam that your family business should take before it advances from one generation to the next. Developed by Scott E. Freidman, an attorney, author, and consultant specializing in family-business issues, the Family Business Scorecard is a comprehensive, 100-question survey designed to identify problem areas, especially those that can directly impact a planned succession. "Three types of people should take this quiz," Friedman explains. "Adult family members who work in the business, adult family members who don't work in the business but are stakeholders, and key non-family employees and advisers, such as the firm's lawyer, accountant, and financial planner. How much of a consensus there is among the participants can be as revealing as the answers themselves."

We've adapted 10 "yes" or "no" questions from the quiz to help give readers a quick take on how they're doing.

1. Our family has customized its decision-making process to require various levels of consent (by different family members or outside advisers) for issues of varying significance.
2. Our key non-family employees are satisfied with the manner in which family members are brought into and employed by our business.
3. All family members, regardless of sex or birth order, will be considered as possible successors for the business.
4. Our succession criteria include formal education, job experience outside our business, and job experience inside our business with increasing responsibility.
5. A written agreement establishes rules for buying, selling, and transferring ownership interest in our business.
6. If our business leader suffered a catastrophe, our family would be prepared to react.
7. Spouses of family members have a meaningful form in which to air their views on subjects affecting the business.
8. Adult family members have begun working on their estate plan.
9. Senior family members approaching retirement age look forward to pursuing interests outside our business.
10. Our family has considered the merits of adopting an alternative dispute-resolution mechanism in the event of family conflict.

If you answered "no" to five or more of these questions, or if the people in your company who took the test gave different answers to the same questions more than four times, your business would benefit from a more complete analysis by an adviser. Freidman's law firm, Buffalo-based Lippes, Mathias, Wexier, and Friedman LLP (716-853-5100; sfriedman@lippes.com), charges for a complete survey and follow-up analysis.

Source: "Mom and Pop Quiz: How Succession-Ready is Your Company?" *Success*, December 1998, p. 80.

Tax and Legal Implications of Transferring the Business to Family Members. An increasingly complex consideration in transferring a business to heirs is the legal and tax implications. One specific tax consequence of transfers of business ownership within a family concerns capital gains. In Canada one-half of the capital gain (defined as the increase in value of the asset since acquisition of the business or since 1972, whichever is shorter) on the sale is added to the income of the person disposing of the asset (business). This rule applies a "deemed disposition" rule (to family) in that the business is "deemed" to have been sold at market price whether or not the market price was actually paid.

In the past, the federal government allowed a tax-free rollover or capital gains deferral to a spouse and children up to a maximum capital gain of $200,000. This applied to Canadian-controlled private corporations. If the heir sold the shares (or business) to someone outside the family, the capital gain would be realized and a resulting tax liability incurred. Canadian tax law also allows for a $750,000 lifetime capital gains exemption. This provision allows for the transfer of ownership of the business with little capital gains consequence, whether or not the business is an incorporated company.

Obviously these changes have affected the tax consequences of transferring the business to heirs. Although most of these changes have been positive from the point of view of the small business, they are complex and may differ by province and territory. Therefore, counsel should be sought from a legal or tax expert before making a decision in this area.

Another important task when considering transferring or selling the business is determining its value. Assistance should be sought from an accountant or member of the Canadian Institute of Chartered Business Valuators in this regard.

Methods of Transferring the Business to Family Members. In deciding which method to use in transferring all or part of the business to the heirs, the owner-manager first needs to clarify his or her own objectives in making the transfer. Some common transfer-related objectives are the following:

- The owner-manager wants to keep a reasonable amount of control over the business until the heirs are of an age and competence level to assume their responsibilities.

- Although the owner-manager wants to maintain control of the business, he or she also wants the heir(s) to maintain their interest in and commitment to the business.

- The owner-manager desires to distribute the business assets (ownership) so that the heirs (if more than one) will recognize this distribution as fair.

- The owner-manager wants sufficient access to income or assets from the transfer of the business to maintain an adequate standard of living.

- The owner-manager wants to achieve an orderly transfer of the business to minimize the tax consequences for both parties.

Some of the most common methods of transferring ownership to the heir(s) are discussed next.

Through a Will. When the transfer is made through a will, ownership of the business does not pass to the heir until the owner dies. This method may satisfy the owner's objective of maintaining control of the business, but it fails to address any of the other objectives mentioned. For example, serious tax consequences may arise if the business is unincorporated. In such a situation, the previous owner's income is calculated at the date of death. If the business has an irregular business cycle and a death occurs at the wrong time of the year, a large income (and higher tax liability) may result. The heirs would then have to deal with this tax liability.

Purchase and Sale of the Business. This method may not satisfy the owner's objectives unless it takes place gradually over a number of years. Such an agreement can remain flexible within the family to accomplish the objectives of both the owner and the heirs (see Incident 15-4). A "deemed disposition" is viewed to have taken place at market value whether or not that amount was actually paid. Purchasing the business gradually may provide an incentive for the heir and also allow the parent to maintain the desired control for the required period of time.

INCIDENT 15-4   Customizing the Right Succession Plan

When it came to choosing a successor for his business, Fred Lai decided to get an early start and plan ahead. Lai is the president of Amazing Custom Fabricators, a Mississauga-based manufacturer of custom sheet metal components. In 2000, Lai drew up a strategic plan to help the company identify its market and work out some issues. "Planning for my retirement was a natural extension of this," says Lai. Working closely with a consultant, Lai was able to work out a few options. One option was to pass the company on to either of his two sons, aged 26 and 30. He wanted to give them time to gain experience in the business world before they took over the company, if they chose to do so.

Lai says it is important to have an external consultant to help negotiate family matters, because they offer an unbiased opinion. A second option that Lai has planned for is to eventually sell the business. Lai has demonstrated that early planning can allow business entrepreneurs to make better business decisions and can alleviate the problem of succession.

Source: Adapted from "Success Story: Customizing the Right Succession Plan," *BDC*, 2006, www.bdc.ca/en/my_projects/.

Gifting Program. In the absence of gift taxes, part or all of the business may be gifted to the heir(s). The most common method of doing this is gradually, over several years. This option is likely feasible only if the owner is not dependent on proceeds of the sale for his or her income.

Life Estate. A life estate is used primarily when the significant assets are real property. This method transfers the ownership or title of land or buildings to the heir, with the condition that the previous owner has a position of control until he or she dies. The extent of control can diminish as the heir becomes more involved in the business. Immediately on the parent's death, the title automatically passes to the heir. This method accomplishes many of the aforementioned objectives.

Joint Ownership of the Business. In this method of succession, the parent can transfer shares of the business to the child (if the business is incorporated) or transfer an ownership interest to the child in the form of a partnership (if it is not incorporated). In both situations, the parent can retain control over the business by providing the child with a different form of ownership such as a different class of share (corporation) and a limited partnership interest (not incorporated).

In a corporation, this type of arrangement may also provide the beneficial tax advantage of freezing the value of the shares. In both methods, the voting or controlling interest may be transferred gradually as the interests, abilities, and conditions warrant.

Potential Problems in a Family Business. Several problems may surface in the family-owned business. Recognition of these potential difficulties is essential for the owner-manager and even for the other family members so that they can take steps to prevent problems.

Overreliance on the Founder. Most family businesses remain highly dependent for their success on their leader, who is typically the founder of the business. Most have no contingency plan covering the disability or death of this person.

Higher Emotional Level. Because of existing family relationships, some of the business decisions and evaluations may be more emotionally charged than they would be in a nonfamily setting. For example, the evaluation of performance or supervision affecting a family member employee may be biased positively or negatively because of the relationship. Family members often bring their personal feelings and stress to the business, which often precludes them from making objective decisions.

Blurring of Roles. In many family-owned businesses, the personal and business roles of individual family members may become blurred. For example, the chief executive officer of the business may in practice not really be in control because of his or her subordinate role in the family. This often occurs when children have "taken over" the business but their parents still exert informal control over both the children and the business.

Incompetence. The problem of incompetence may arise in the family business in two areas. The first situation involves the relative who assumes the position of chief executive simply because of birthright. The experience, education, intelligence, and work ethic required to manage the business successfully may be lacking. The second situation involves hiring incompetent family members. Helping out an incompetent family member not only may lead to disappointment and damage to the business but can also have a disruptive effect on the nonfamily employees.

Nonfamily Employee Attitudes. One common characteristic of family-owned businesses is high turnover of nonfamily employees. Many young employees see no chance for promotion to management in the company because they are not part of the family. As a result, they may gain experience in the business and then leave for other organizations that offer the opportunity for promotion.

Objectives of Family Owners. In most family businesses, more than one member of the family owns shares or has an ownership interest in the business. Because these owners may be from different generations, have different levels of involvement in the business, and have various backgrounds and needs, differences of opinion regarding the operations of the business are common.

For example, owners who are actively involved in building up the business often want to reinvest more of the earnings in the business. The nonactive owners or shareholders, however, may want their share of the profits to be distributed as dividends or payments to themselves.

Objectives regarding the growth of the business may also differ. Sometimes younger members of the family want to expand the business or make capital expenditures that older family owners are more conservative or cautious about making. Both situations can lead to conflicts that have a detrimental effect on the long-term progress of the business.

Principles of Success for Family Businesses. The preceding section has demonstrated the many difficulties that can arise in a family business. As was illustrated, these difficulties can be detrimental to the success of the business and damaging to family relationships. If the owner-manager is concerned about succession, planning for it should commence immediately rather than waiting until health or other circumstances force or prevent action. If one is involved in a family business or is contemplating bringing family members into the business, the following practices may help prevent some of the aforementioned difficulties from arising.

Recognize the Importance of Objectivity. Evaluations and supervision involving family members should be done on an objective basis. Even if tempted to do otherwise, the owner-manager must attempt to separate family discussions and emotions from business activities. Care should be taken to ensure that consistent policies are followed for both family and nonfamily employees. Many owner-managers have found it essential to separate their children physically and functionally from themselves and one another to prevent such difficulties from arising.

Create Clear Role Structures. The solution to the problem of the blurring of roles may be difficult to implement, as much of the control may be exerted informally. A clear definition of the roles, objectives, and responsibilities of all associated family members may help solve the difficulty. Separation of business and family goals and systems has also been recommended to alleviate this problem.[17]

Ensure Competence. Because an incompetent owner-manager can spell disaster for the business, providing the heir with technical and practical training, along with increasing decision-making authority, is vital. This may involve encouraging the family member to acquire some necessary skills outside the business at a college, a university, or another business before returning to become fully involved. Many potential inheritors of businesses appear to follow this route to the ownership of the family business.[18] If a competent family member is not available, the remaining family owners may be able to persuade the owner-manager to let a more capable individual run the day-to-day affairs of the company.

If training does not improve the performance of incompetent relatives, but for family reasons it is not possible to let the employee go, some owner-managers place such an employee in a position in which he or she can do the least harm to the company.

Provide Incentives for Nonfamily Employees. To maintain the loyalty of nonfamily employees and ensure that they stay with the company, the owner-manager will need to devise various rewards and incentives. These incentives can be financial or may involve including employees in decision-making and educational programs. It may still be impossible to retain an energetic young employee who desires to eventually rise to the top of the organization unless the owner-manager is prepared to give up some of the ownership or authority of the business.

Clarify Objectives of Family Owners. To prevent disharmony resulting from differing objectives of family members, it is important to formally clarify the long-and short-term objectives of the company. These might include objectives for such areas as expansion and distribution of profits. Some firms distribute a set percentage of profits in dividends or reinvest a specified amount back into the business annually.

Keep Communication Lines Open. Perhaps the most effective aspect of operating a family business successfully is open communication. Given many potential areas of conflict, differences of opinion must be communicated to the relevant parties before they develop into a serious problem. Formalized objectives, plans, roles, and procedures can accomplish this. Incident 15-5 illustrates how one couple has worked out their roles in the business.

INCIDENT 15-5   Husband/Wife Duo

Susan Birnie and her husband own Golden Hardware and Building Supplies, a member of the Home Hardware chain, in Golden, British Columbia. Susan says, "I walked into a position that is traditionally a man's role. That was my second challenge. My first was walking into a hardware business I knew nothing about and telling myself that I can turn this around."

The husband-wife duo works well together. Birnie's husband manages relationships with contractors and Birnie manages the store operations. Birnie likes the freedom and independence that retail has given her. "If you're willing to work hard, I think you can make retail into anything you want it to be," she says.

Source: Adapted from "Refining Retail," *Canadian Retailer*, March–April 2006, p. 30.

Selling the Business to an Employee

It may be that the owner of the business has no family members available or able to take over the business. However, family members may still have a desire to see the business progress successfully even though they have decided to leave the organization. Advance planning is still crucial for this type of succession. The following steps should be a part of the succession plan for an employee.

- Identify the timeframe and exit strategy.
- Develop a plan to maximize the value of the business and minimize the tax effects before the transfer date.
- Choose the successor.
- Make yourself replaceable. Install the procedures that will allow the company to grow without you.
- Find a way to fund the transition, such as debt financing or subordinate financing.
- Introduce the successor to clients, suppliers, and other contacts.
- Make sure that the new owner's vision ensures the continuity of the business.
- Manage the possible financial, fiscal, legal, and other impacts of the transition process, drawing on the support of professionals.

Selling the Business to Outsiders

If the owner-manager is not able or does not want to keep the business in the family, he or she may decide to sell all or part of the business to someone outside the family. This action, of course, could be taken at any time, not just when the owner-manager is ready to retire. Regardless of when the business is sold, however, the owner-manager should realize that the last few years' performance will affect the purchase price. Therefore, careful planning should be done to ensure that the business's performance is as positive as possible before the sale.

Many aspects of selling a business are discussed in Chapter 5, including the informational requirements of the prospective purchaser. The seller of the business must now prepare this information and make it available to a prospective buyer. Particularly important is information on the financial condition of the business as represented by the financial statements. A listing of any hidden assets or capabilities that do not show up on the balance sheet should be made. The asset valuation and earnings methods discussed in Chapter 5 can assist in setting an asking price for the business. Most buyers will thoroughly review these statements, particularly the earnings record, to determine how accurately they portray the business.

Another critical area in selling the business includes the terms of the sale. Timing of payments may have considerable tax consequences. Some of these consequences have been reduced, however, by the alternative minimum tax provisions. Often the purchaser wants the previous owner to remain in the business in an advisory capacity. This arrangement (with appropriate compensation) can be included in the purchase agreement.

One possible outcome of selling the business may apply to a partner or other owner. As mentioned in Chapter 4, a buy/sell clause should be a part of the partnership agreement. This clause should be carefully worded to account for future differences in the value of the firm.

Sometimes small businesses are purchased by larger companies in the form of a merger. The acquiring company is usually looking to expand or capitalize on some unique advantage or capability the small business has. For example, purchasing a small business may allow a company to capitalize on such strengths as a unique product, market access, or expertise it could not otherwise obtain. In many such situations, the owner-manager of the smaller business is retained in the organization. Incident 15-6 is an example of such an arrangement. Often, however, this relationship is short-lived because the former owner is uncomfortable with his or her lack of independence in the new arrangement.

The owner-manager may want to sell only a part of the business. This is accomplished much more easily if the business is incorporated to allow a share transfer to take place. In such a case, the owner-manager may be able to retain control over the business while obtaining capital needed as payment for the shares.

Going Public. Sometimes a small business that has been successful but has a need or desire for a significant amount of capital sells shares to the public. (See Incident 15-7.) This is called an initial public offering (IPO) and the corporate status changes from a private to a public company. The advantages and disadvantages of this form of equity investment are discussed in Chapter 7. Sometimes owners regret the move to go public rather than selling shares privately. Figure 15-2 illustrates a comparison of public versus private placement. Going public may also allow control of the business to remain with the owner-manager if more than 50 percent of the shares are not sold. The business should address the following issues if it is planning an IPO.[19]

- Improve the company's overall capital structure and financial performance.

- Review staff needs including the need for a strong management team.

- Strengthen the organization through purchase or sale of particular business units.

- Structure the board to include strong outside directors.

- Plan for effective distribution of earnings.

INCIDENT 15-6   Microsoft Buys Out Ontario Gamers

Microsoft Corporation
www.microsoft.com

Two Waterloo couples who developed a computer game business in late 1997 have sold the company to Microsoft Corp. and are moving to Washington state to work for the software giant.

When Microsoft officials made that pitch to the founders of ShadowFactor Software Inc. in April, they didn't spend a lot of time agonizing over whether they should hang onto their brainchild, which lets people playing computer games talk to each other by voice over the Internet.

Paul Newson, his wife, Isabella Carniato, and Rod and Joanne Toll established the business two years after trying out a voice-over Internet communications system called Battlefield Communicator. They knew they were on to something when an announcement seeking "beta testers" to try out an early version of the product drew 1,000 email responses in 48 hours.

When the four quit their jobs to work at the company full time, "it was a leap of faith," Newson said. "We knew there was potential there, but it wasn't going to be there forever."

Microsoft wanted both the technology and the people behind it, thinking, "if they could do it once, they could do it again," Newson said.

Microsoft has incorporated the product into DirectX 8.0, a multimedia technology that is part of the Windows operating system. ShadowFactor software has expanded to such products as SideWinder, and GameVoice under the direction of Carniato.

Source: Adapted from the *Toronto Star,* June 11, 1999, p. E4; and "GameVoice: Avid Gamer Helps Launch Latest Version of Gaming Product She Helped Devise," Microsoft Press release, July 11, 2004, pp. 1–6.

INCIDENT 15-7   Crossing the Chasm

Thanks to WaveRider, a wireless Internet company based in Toronto, rural consumers can finally get high-speed Net access. Founded by Steve Grant and Rich Antoine, WaveRider went public on NASDAQ in 1997 through a reverse takeover of a shell company. WaveRider sells cheap transmitting antennas and specialty modems that receive the wireless Internet protocol signals. The company is a $100 million-year market in North America and it is expected to grow between $2 billion and $5 billion in the next few years. It has already grown to $13.1 million in 2003, up from $206,000 in 1998.

Affordability and flexibility is what set Waverider apart from its competition. WaveRider uses an inexpensive indoor antenna that consumers can set up themselves. The company plans on concentrating on building its revenue, especially in developing markets in Asia and Central and South America—regions that don't have competing systems. WaveRider's biggest achievement showed a 50 percent revenue growth and 50 percent reduction in expenses at the same time.

Source: Adapted from Charles Mandel, "Crossing the Chasm," *Profit,* June 2004, p. 48.

Figure 15-2	**Implications of Selling Shares**		
		Going Public	**Private Placement**
	Shareholders	Many new shareholders	Few investors
	Importance of earnings	High	Low
	Importance of stock performance	Short term	Long term
	Investor communication required	Extensive	Limited
	Board of directors	Independent members	Strategic members

Source: *The Globe and Mail,* June 12, 1996, p. B7.

One or more of the following characteristics may indicate that the small business is in a favourable position to go public:[20]

- The company is in a popular specialized market.
- The company is in an above-average growth position.
- The business has a strong market niche and proven sales appeal in an emerging rather than a mature industry.
- The business can and does generate a return on equity of at least 20 percent to 25 percent.
- The company has at least $10 million in annual revenues.
- The company has strong management.
- The company has reached the point at which it needs a substantial amount of capital for growth and expansion.

If the owner-manager finds it necessary or desires that the firm's shares be offered to the public, the services of an investment dealer may be helpful. An investment dealer (or underwriter) will assist the owner by acting as the marketer for the stock. The investment dealer can use an over-the-counter market, one that includes securities that are not sold on the stock exchange. If this method is followed, a reputable investment dealer with substantial connections throughout the investment community should be selected.

Closing Down or Going Bankrupt

The third possible outcome for the business—generally a result of unsatisfactory performance—involves closing down, being placed into receivership, or going bankrupt. These are, of course, the least desirable outcomes for the small business. As discussed in Chapter 2, however, each year many small businesses end up in this situation because of lack of profitability. Closing down is much easier for an unincorporated business than for a limited company. In theory, the incorporated company is required to file dissolution forms and notify government agencies. Although this is the case if the company does not have a large debt load, the incorporated company has more protection in a debt situation because of its limited liability.

Business Bankruptcy. In 2005, a total of 7,519 business bankruptcies were declared in Canada.[21] The majority of those failures were small businesses. If the business debts are significantly greater than assets and the earning power of the business is inadequate to service future obligations, the owner-manager may face two options.

First, a major creditor may appoint a receiver and the business is placed in receivership. When a company is in receivership, the receiver enlists the services of another agency in an attempt to manage it out of financial difficulty. As this may be difficult to do, receivership is often a forerunner to bankruptcy.

The second option is to consult an accountant. If the accountant's recommendation is to see a licensed trustee for bankruptcy, an assignment usually takes place. When this happens, the debtor (the small business) assigns its assets to the trustee, who in turn meets with the creditors. The assets are converted to cash and distributed to the creditors to repay as much of the debt as possible. These assets are distributed using a priority system. Secured creditors, such as Canada Revenue Agency (unpaid taxes, CPP, or EI premiums) as well as those who have signed security for some of the debt (including the trustee)—have first priority to proceeds of the deposition. Preferred creditors such as employees, landlords, or government departments have second priority, followed by ordinary unsecured creditors.

Frequently, ordinary creditors receive little or none of the money owed them. This is a significant point, since most small businesses themselves are ordinary creditors in their business dealings. Thus, they often lose out when a business with which they are dealing goes bankrupt.

If a proprietorship or a partnership of individuals goes bankrupt, the owner-manager is allowed to retain certain necessary assets. It is also possible for an owner of an incorporated business to declare personal bankruptcy in order to be protected from the liabilities of a failing business. It is still possible for a bankrupt individual to start another business at a later date. In fact, some businesses enter into voluntary bankruptcy, which allows them to dissolve quickly and get reestablished. Once bankrupt, however, a person's credit rating is weaker than before, and obtaining debt financing may be difficult. There are also significant "human" costs for a company that goes bankrupt. A lawyer should be consulted if this type of bankruptcy is being contemplated.

Although bankruptcy is becoming more common, it can be a difficult and damaging experience that could have been avoided in 70 percent to 90 percent of the cases had financial difficulties been spotted and acted on early.[22] Owner-managers who have developed and are using financial management concepts as discussed in Chapter 10 should be in a better position to avoid bankruptcy.

Summary

1. Planning for the eventual transfer of the business is an important component of small business management. Some of the more common methods of transferring ownership of a business to family members are through a will, a sale of the business to the heirs, a gifting program, a life estate, and joint ownership.

2. The unique problems of a family business are higher emotional levels, blurring of roles, incompetence, nonfamily employee turnover, differing objectives among family owners, and planning for succession.

3. Sometimes a small business that has been successful but needs a significant amount of capital may sell shares to the public to meet financial needs while retaining control of the company.

4. A business that cannot be transferred can be closed down, be placed in receivership, or file for bankruptcy.

Chapter Problems and Applications

1. How could Charles Northstrup have satisfied both his son's career demands and his own desires and still effectively run their furniture store (Incident 15-3)?

2. Jim Duncan is the owner-manager of a local restaurant chain. In its earlier years, the three local family restaurants were very successful. Then a recession came, and the businesses did not do as well. Jim is 60 years old and is thinking about retirement or semi-retirement. He has a son who has managed one of the restaurants, but he is not sure Jim Jr. is ready for the problems of the whole operation. If you were Jim Sr. how would you transfer ownership? Explain your decision.

3. Your father has just made you president of the family sand and gravel company. You want to computerize the payroll and the accounts payable and receivable, but your father doesn't see the need for the extra expense when expenses are already too high. What two problems exist here? How would you resolve this conflict as the newly appointed president?

4. Your parents have just made you the manager of your family's grocery store. Since the transition, problems have seldom been brought to your attention, and you have received little feedback on your instructions. What problems might be evident? How would you solve these problems?

5. Hamilton Rogers is the owner-manager of a successful machine shop. In the last year, he has promoted his sons to floor managers. Recently, several employees have also left the company. What factors could be responsible for the employees leaving their jobs? How could Hamilton have prevented this problem?

6. Interview the manager of a family-owned and operated business. What unique problems are evident?

7. Interview someone who is a future heir of a family business and is now going to school or gaining business experience. What problems are evident from his or her perspective? Does this person want to go back to the business? Why or why not?

8. Pomaona Fastener Company has suffered several years of operating losses. Because of the unfavourable outlook for the firm, it filed for bankruptcy and was dissolved. On liquidation $570,000 was received, to be split among the following creditors:

Accounts payable	$100,000
Secured loans from bank	400,000
Accrued wages	10,000
Rent due on building	20,000
Government loan	300,000
Trustee's fee	10,000

What would be the priority of payment, and how much would each class of creditor receive?

9. Interview the owner-manager of a small business that recently went public, and find out what he or she learned through the experience.

10. Assume you owned a company that you wanted to keep in the family. One of your three children has been working in the business and is interested in taking over. However, the other two feel that they are entitled to their one-third share of the value of the business. What would you do?

Web Exercise

www.familybusiness.com

Go to the website of an organization that provides information about family businesses and review the information provided about succession of a business.

Suggested Readings

Bellow, Adam. *In Praise of Nepotism*. Knopf Publishing Group, 2004.

"Business Succession." Business Development Bank of Canada website, 2006.

Church, Elizabeth. "Leadership Crisis Forseen for Family Business." *The Globe and Mail,* January 18, 1999, p. B13.

"Combine Family Harmony With Long Term Survival of The Business," Business Development Bank of Canada website, 2006.

"Family Run Companies Consider Themselves Unique." *The Globe and Mail*, October 8, 2002, p. B7.

Leach, Peter, Bruce Ball, and Garry Duncan. *Guide to the Family Business, Canadian Edition*. BDO Toronto: Dunwoody, 2000.

Mahaffey, Cheryl. "Generations: Family Business." *Alberta Venture*, May 2002, pp. 32–36.

Miller, Donny. *Managing For The Long Run*. Harvard Business School Press, 2005.

www.mcgrawhill.ca/olc/balderson

Moore, Janet. "Like Father, Like Daughter." *Upstate Business*, October 8, 2000.

Pooley, Erin. "Family Values." *Canadian Business*, May–June 2005, pp. 55–56.

Poza, Ernesto J. *Family Business*. Mason, Ohio: Thomson Learning, 2004.

Rimler, George. "How To Professionalize the Family Business." *Air Conditioning, Heating & Refrigeration News*, June 19, 2000.

Stern, Deborah. "Giving Your Kids the Business." *Canadian Grocer,* February 1999, pp. 39–45.

"Transition Planning," Business Development Bank of Canada website, June 26, 2006.

Video Cases for Part 4

Sugar High   Fields of Seeds

PART ENDING VIDEO CASE & QUESTIONS   *Sugar High**

(Appropriate Chapters—4, 7, 8, 14)

Winnipeggers Chris Emery and Larry Finson have a lot to smile about. Their company, Krave's Candy, has been tagged Manitoba's fastest-growing company—growing 938 percent and hitting annual sales of close to $1 million in just three years, due to their Clodhoppers candy. But the founders of Krave's don't want to stop there. Chris and Larry want Krave's to become Canada's premier candy company, taking on Hershey and Nestlé.

1. What are some of the growth problems of Krave's Candy Company?
2. What could Chris Emery and Larry Finson do to solve these problems?
3. What are the advantages and disadvantages of diversifying to other products besides Clodhoppers?

*Source: CBC *Venture* #732, running time 10:00.

PART ENDING VIDEO CASE & QUESTIONS   *Fields of Seeds**

(Appropriate Chapters—8, 12, 15)

Alberta's Spitz Sunflower Seeds has one barrier between it and a national distribution deal with a major retail chain. Owner Tom Droog has to find a distributor in Quebec and crack a market and culture that finds public spitting deplorable. *Venture* follows the adventures of the acerbic Alberta entrepreneur as he tries to conquer the Quebec market.

1. How do husband and wife complement each other in managing Spitz Sunflower Seeds?
2. What does this case show about the problems that rapid growth creates?
3. What might be the best strategy for Spitz to move into the Quebec market?

*Source: CBC *Venture* #734, running time 9:24.

Cases for Part 4

BAILEY'S OFFICE SUPPLY

D. Wesley Balderson, *University of Lethbridge*

In 1966, John Bailey left a major department store chain where he worked as the hardware department manager to open his own office supply store. John had worked for the chain for more than 15 years and had become very knowledgeable about the business. He felt, however, that he could develop a successful business by offering more personalized customer service than the larger stores could. By 1976 the firm, Bailey's Office Supply, had become a large and well-known establishment in Toronto with three outlets. The firm had no particular specialties but did carry a very extensive line of all basic office supplies, typewriters, and adding machines and a limited line of office furniture. Its strength was, as John Bailey had intended, its superior customer service. John was careful to properly train his employees to know not only their products but also their customers' needs.

In 1986, John Bailey's son Marty was finishing college in business administration and had decided to join his father in the business. Marty had worked from time to time for his father and thought that he might enjoy the business. John had told Marty, however, to get an education first and that if he decided to work at Bailey's, he would have a job. Although John had made this offer to Marty, he was concerned because he had a younger son and an older daughter and wondered how they would react to Marty being brought into the company.

Marty joined Bailey's as assistant sales manager with the understanding that he would be given the job of sales manager on the retirement of Kenneth Harker, which was due to take place in another three years. At the same time Marty's brother and sister along with Marty were placed on the board of directors for Bailey's. Although the board met only sporadically, it did have the authority to ratify major management decisions.

During the late 1980s both Baileys observed the phenomenal growth and development of the high-technology firms that occupied the "Golden Triangle" area in and around Toronto, Ottawa, and Montreal. This boom not only spawned the creation of many successful firms, but it also signalled the introduction of many strong competitors for Bailey's. Some of these were warehouse stores, which offered a large assortment of office merchandise at very low prices. John Bailey still maintained that if Bailey's continued to offer its personal "down home" service this new competition would not seriously affect Bailey's.

It was tempting for the Baileys to invest in newly created firms, knowing that the investments of several of their friends had been very successful. John Bailey, however, was fairly conservative, and having built the business to a success was now looking forward to enjoying the fruits of his hard work by playing more golf and travelling with his wife for a month or two every year. He still retained controlling interest in the business and was opposed to making any outside investments. Marty, on the other hand, was anxious to take advantage of some of these opportunities and felt strongly that by adding lines of computer hardware and software to their merchandise line, Bailey's could increase sales. He felt, in fact, that Bailey's would have a difficult time competing with the office supply warehouses if they didn't move into this area. As this would require a rather major reinvestment of earnings back into the firm, John and his other son and daughter were reluctant to move in this direction. These disagreements were a source of frustration for Marty and he contemplated leaving the family business and starting his own high-tech office supply store.

By 2005 the effects of the competition and a cutback in building construction had reduced the total income of business and the profit of Bailey's by some 20 percent. It was a sobering turn of events for a firm that had experienced a long, steady expansion. In thinking about this, John Bailey felt that it might be wise to turn the management of the business over to Marty along with some of his ownership interest. Under John's proposal he would retain majority ownership of the company and still come in to work part time, but Marty would be responsible for the day-to-day operations. When John approached Marty with the proposal, he was shocked to hear that Marty had decided to leave the firm. John felt that he had given Marty a tremendous opportunity to learn about and then take over the business that he had built into a success. He could not understand why Marty could turn down such an offer.

Questions

1. Why would Marty want to leave the firm instead of accepting his father's offer?
2. What could be done now to salvage the situation and keep Marty with the company?
3. Assuming that Marty remained with the firm, what suggestions could be made to turn the business around?

BAKER HARDWARE LTD.

D. Wesley Balderson, *University of Lethbridge*

Baker Hardware Ltd. is a hardware store in the town of Souris, which is located in an agricultural area of southern Manitoba. Souris is 48 km south of Brandon (population 55,000), which is the major trading centre for many smaller towns within a 100 km radius.

Mr. Baker, the owner of Baker Hardware, is contemplating expanding his merchandise offering to include lumber and building supplies. Currently Baker's, in addition to a standard selection of hardware merchandise, carries paint and building tools; therefore, Mr. Baker thinks this new line would be fairly compatible.

Baker Hardware was a part of the Home Hardware network of dealers, a nationwide group of hardware stores and home centres located primarily in smaller towns and cities. For the past few years, Home Hardware had been encouraging its dealers to expand into building supplies. Concerned that there was another lumber yard in Souris (which happened to be next door to Baker Hardware), Mr. Baker had shown little interest in such a move in the past.

Recently, however, he became aware that this lumberyard, Banner Building Supplies, was for sale or would be closed down. Mr. Baker gathered information from both the owners of Banner as well as from Home Hardware and was in the process of making a decision. As Mr. Baker saw it, he had three choices: (1) purchase Banner Building Supplies, (2) expand into building supplies through Home Hardware on his own premises, or (3) maintain current operations (not expanding into building materials).

The Market

As previously mentioned, Souris was a small town of about 2,000 located in an agricultural area of southern Manitoba. The estimated population of surrounding area farms was 500. The town was located 48 km southwest of Brandon, the major trading centre for the area. Over the years, the retail communities in most of the small towns close to Brandon had deteriorated because of the strong competition of retailers there and the increased mobility of consumers. The building supply industry was no exception. Such chains as Canadian Tire and Beaver Lumber, which had outlets in Brandon, had attracted numerous customers from these rural communities.

The population of Souris consisted mainly of farmers, commuters who worked in Brandon, and professionals such as teachers who worked in the town. The town had experienced some growth in recent years because of its relaxed atmosphere and excellent recreational facilities. Projections indicated the population could reach 2,500 by the year 2008.

Baker Hardware

Baker Hardware had operated successfully in Souris for many years. Mr. Baker had purchased the store from his father, and with changes and modernizations, increased sales from $450,000 in 1980 to $800,000 in 2005. Although sales showed a significant increase, profits did not. The strong competition from hardware chains in Brandon in recent years had eroded Mr. Baker's profit margin. Baker Hardware's competitive strength had always been that it catered to the agricultural community. Unfortunately, farm incomes had experienced considerable volatility in recent years, and this trend directly affected Baker Hardware's profit performance.

Baker Hardware currently had 4,000 square metres of selling space and a large (2,700-square-metre) warehouse. Mr. Baker believed that if he went into building supplies he could, with some renovations, free up about half of the warehouse space to house the new merchandise.

Baker Hardware's current financial situation, while not serious, was such that if a capital investment were made, Mr. Baker would have to borrow to finance it. At the current interest rate of 8 percent, this was a concern for Mr. Baker.

Home Hardware

Home Hardware Ltd. is a well-established franchise system of dealer-owners located across Canada. Originating in southern Ontario, it has expanded to become a dominant small-town retailer of hardware merchandise. Recently Home Hardware moved into the building supply industry in an attempt to capitalize on the growth of the home centre concept. Home has been encouraging its dealers to branch into this area, and many have done so.

Mr. Baker obtained from Home Hardware a list of the recommended product assortment for a home building supply dealer. A summary of this list, along with space requirements and markups, appears in Figure 1. Home Hardware also suggested that Mr. Baker would need a forklift (estimated cost $15,000, used), a delivery truck (estimated cost $10,000, used), and a shed of at least 5,000 square feet (estimated cost $5,000).

Banner Building Supplies

Banner Building Supplies was a family-owned business that had operated in Souris for more than 40 years. It was owned by two brothers, both close to retirement age, who also owned a window and door manufacturing plant. As the manufacturing plant was much larger in size and scope of operations, the Banners had devoted most of their time and energy to this business. The retail building supplies outlet had, over the years, taken second priority in their business interests, although it provided a stable and needed outlet for the town.

Interest in selling the retail outlet resulted from two major factors. First, both brothers wanted to cut back on their work responsibilities, as both were approaching retirement age and had no family members interested in taking over the business. However, one brother had a son-in-law who was interested in the manufacturing part of the business. Second, the profitability of the retail outlet had suffered in recent years due to strong competition from larger hardware chains and home centres in Brandon. Some of these competitors could sell certain types of lumber and other supplies at lower prices than Banner's costs. The estimated profit and loss statement Mr. Baker obtained from Banners for 2005 is shown in Figure 2. Currently Banner Building Supplies has approximately $75,000 in inventory (see Figure 3) and owns a large lot containing some sheds and a showroom next door to Baker Hardware. The estimated value of real estate and buildings is approximately $25,000. The company has no debt.

| Figure 1 | Recommended Home Building Supply Full Product Assortment |

Product	Cost	Suggested Markup on Cost	Estimated Turnover	Space Requirement
Insulation	$4,000	25%	4.0	600
Doors and mouldings (complete assortment)	6,000	30	2.5	900
Plywood (complete assortment, 2 pallets each)	10,000	15	5.5	2,100
Drywall (complete assortment, 2 pallets each)	6,000	15	4.5	600
Cement	2,000	30	5.0	180
Roofing materials	5,000	25	3.5	600
Nails	1,000	30	5.0	120
Siding, soffit, facia	6,000	30	2.0	900
Dimensional lumber, 2 by 4, 2 by 6, etc. (complete assortment, 2 pallets each)	20,000	15	6.0	3,000
	$60,000			9,000

In looking at the merchandise requirements recommended by Home Hardware, Mr. Baker noted that Banner's inventory levels were different. Mr. Baker discussed this with the previous manager of Banner's and learned that some building supplies did not sell well in Souris. He informed Mr. Baker that the standard types of lumber (plywoods, 2 by 4's, etc.) were the steady sellers, although warpage caused considerable waste in dimensional lumber. He also mentioned that it was very difficult to compete with the city building centres for the large contractors' business. The major market for Banner's had been the small contractor (renovators) and the do-it-yourself customer.

Armed with the above information, Mr. Baker was determined to make a decision.

Figure 2

Banner Building Supplies
Estimated Income Statement for 2005

Sales	$ 230,000	
Cost of goods sold (85%)	195,500	
Gross profit		$ 34,500
Expenses:		
Wages	22,500	
Taxes and licences	2,000	
Insurance	1,000	
Professional fees and admin.	500	
Utilities	2,000	
Fuel (trucks, etc.)	1,200	
Bad debts	1,000	
Depreciation	1,800	
Repairs and maintenance	1,000	
Misc. supplies	$ 500	$ 33,500
Net income before taxes		$ 1,000

Figure 3

Banner Building Supplies
Inventory Estimate

Insulation	$ 6,000
Doors and mouldings	24,000
Plywood	12,000
Drywall	7,000
Cement	1,000
Roofing materials	2,000
Nails, etc.	1,200
Siding	2,000
Dimensional lumber	35,000
Paints	2,500
Tools and hardware	2,500
Carpet and linoleum	$ 1,800
	$97,000

Questions

1. What other information should Mr. Baker obtain before he makes this decision?
2. Using the information provided, evaluate the alternatives Mr. Baker has identified. Be sure to evaluate the attractiveness of the proposed merchandise lines.
3. What other alternatives has Mr. Baker not explored?

BRIAN LUBORSKY—PREMIER SALONS INTERNATIONAL INC.

D. Wesley Balderson, *University of Lethbridge*

Brian Luborsky started out his business career as a chartered accountant with Coopers and Lybrand. It didn't take long for him to realize, however, that he wanted to be part of something that was more growth-oriented and that allowed him to be more entrepreneurial. He still remembers the day he decided to quit. His boss wanted him to write a memo, but Luborsky, who was building and buying houses on the side, was working to save $50,000 on a property to buy. "The deal was worth more than my annual salary," he laughs, "I wasn't doing myself any favours and I wasn't being fair to the company so I resigned."

Meanwhile he became interested in a new hair salon franchise called Magicuts. Magicuts had been established in 1981 as a discount haircut chain that attempted to bring the McDonald's efficiency principles to hair salons. Luborsky joined Magicuts as a franchisee, purchasing four franchises in 1984. What lured him was the math. "There is such a high ratio of sales to assets in haircutting it was hard to go wrong," he says. "Say it costs $50,000 to set up shop. I can do $250,000 in sales in a year out of that store. Now, say I make 10 percent on that: I'm getting a 50 percent return on investment, and that's hard to beat."

In 1993 Luborsky considered expansion to the United States. He felt that his company was in a position to grow and he became aware of a chain of hair salons that he felt could fit in with the system that he had developed for Magicuts. After difficult negotiations for financing, he was successful in acquiring a large financially troubled Minneapolis-based chain of hair salons —MEI Salons. MEI had 1,600 outlets, three times as many as Magicuts, but was in need of financial and management stability, which Luborsky could provide.

Luborsky's goal for growth is now centred on three areas. First he wants to continue to emphasize superior service in order to compete with the independent mom-and-pop salons that dominate the industry. Because of the size of the company, it can take advantage of economies of scale, and this allows investment in employees. As a result, Premier (as the salons were renamed) has invested heavily in extensive employee training. Premier's 76 trainers teach the latest styles and trends, as well as soft skills such as dealing with clients. Luborsky's second push involves "partnerships" with well-known retailers, most of which are department stores. Magicuts is now installed in more than 100 Zellers stores. "The price fits well with our customers," says Zeller's Vice-President Garnet Kinch. Luborsky's third growth strategy is to seek out compatible chains and purchase them, similar to what occurred with MEI. Recently, Premier purchased 22 Boscov's salons in Pennsylvania.

Questions

1. What are some of the problems that Brian Luborsky will likely face with the expansion to the United States? What solutions can be suggested?
2. What questions should he have evaluated prior to the U.S. expansion?

ITI EDUCATIONAL CORPORATION

D. Wesley Balderson, *University of Lethbridge*

The idea for ITI began in 1984, when Gary Blandford, an MBA dropout, was studying computers at a failing private college in Halifax, Nova Scotia. When Gary learned that the college was in financial difficulty and was up for sale, he wondered if he could make it successful. Because computer training was a growing market and rather than lose a chance to graduate, the 28-year-old scraped together $60,000 to buy the school. Gary worked hard at improving the school and by 1995, the renamed Information Technology Institute boasted annual sales of more than $2 million.

Exploding demand for information technology workers told Blandford that it was time to expand to meet this growing demand. ITI went public in 1995, raising $3 million over the next two years to fund school openings in Moncton, Ottawa, and Toronto. The company also switched from a strictly technical program to a mixed curriculum aimed at arts grads. Gary was able to partner with large organizations so that tuition for the course was often paid by many of these firms as they were interested in upgrading the skills of their employees. This type of arrangement ensured that ITI's classrooms were full. By the end of 1997, ITI was producing 1,500 grads a year.

ITI continued its rapid expansion and by mid-2000, students in seven Canadian and three U.S. cities were each paying ITI $25,000 for its crash course in technology. Due to market growth, the ITI short course seemed to have unlimited potential. However, ITI's rapid expansion eventually stirred up rivals such as DeVry Canada, which was much larger and offered a more complete and longstanding training program. Aggressive competition from DeVry and others began taking sales from ITI, which devastated the bottom line.

In 1999, ITI lost $11.6 million on sales of $35.4 million. To revive the company Blandford developed an $8 million marketing campaign to fight back, but his rivals were spending four times as much and ITI's message didn't get effective exposure.

After the dot-com bubble burst, new enrolments plummeted. Suddenly, ITI was big and bloated. Blandford disbanded ITI's expansion team and slashed marketing, accounting, and curriculum spending by the millions, but ITI still lost $12 million in 2000 on sales of $50 million. By August, 2001, Blandford was forced to close down the business.

Questions

1. Identify the problems that led to ITI's demise.
2. What could Gary Blandford have done to prevent the failure of ITI?

COMPANY'S COMING COOKBOOKS

D. Wesley Balderson, *University of Lethbridge*

Cooking has always been an important part of Jean Paré's life. In 1963, when her four children had all reached school age, Jean volunteered to cater the 50th anniversary of the Vermillion School of Agriculture, now Lakeland College. Working from her home, Jean prepared a dinner for more than 1,000 people. The dinner was so successful that Jean decided to start a catering business. This business developed into a flourishing catering operation that has continued for more than 18 years.

At first Jean single-handedly ran the business with part-time assistance from family members. It gave her an opportunity to try new recipes, and she soon wrote a cookbook that included some of her best ones. Jean also travelled across Alberta opening retail accounts to handle the book. As the business grew, Jean teamed up with her son Grant Lovig to form Company's Coming Publishing Limited. Between sales trips and publishing her second cookbook, she managed shipping and receiving, invoicing, and accounts receivable collections for her growing publishing venture.

Jean's first cookbook, entitled *150 Delicious Squares* was very successful, and soon the company was publishing several cookbooks each year. By 2003 the company had published more than 60 titles and sold more than 20 million cookbooks worldwide for sales of more than $10 million annually. The head office is now a specially constructed building in Edmonton, where Grant oversees business operations in his role as president.

Printed in both English and French, Company's Coming cookbooks are available in more than 6,000 retail stores across Canada. The cookbooks are also distributed in the United States and various overseas markets. A Spanish-language edition of Jean Paré's familiar and trusted recipes can even be found in Mexico.

Jean credits much of the company's success to the sales savvy of her son Grant, who was fresh from marketing school when he developed the retail plan for the cookbooks. Grant feels the family connection is one of their great strengths. Although Jean is the primary creative force behind Company's Coming, she confides that some of her best material comes from yet another son, Brian, who lives in Kelowna, B.C. Her daughter Gail Lovig has also been a part of the company since its inception and currently oversees all marketing and distribution efforts, leading a team that includes marketing personnel located in major cities across Canada.

Questions

1. Which success principles for operating a family business discussed in the text does Company's Coming appear to be following?
2. As Jean Paré looks to the future what concerns might she have about family members being involved in the business? How could she address these concerns?

Directory of Supplementary Cases

THE FRAMEMAKERS

D. Wesley Balderson, *University of Lethbridge*

Robert and Teresa Norman faced a big decision. They were contemplating Robert leaving his job managing his father's painting business to set up their own retail picture-framing store. As they thought about this dilemma, their minds wandered back to the events that had led up to the impending decision. Robert had been raised in a small town about 20 miles south of Brandon, Manitoba. His father was a painter, and Robert had worked in the painting business part time for several years. Upon graduating from high school, he completed a two-year business administration in interior design course at a college in the United States. It was there that he met and married his wife, Teresa.

Teresa had studied interior design at college. She came from a small farming community near Robert's hometown. One of her favourite pastimes when she was growing up was taking pictures of the beautiful scenery and making frames for them. Teresa, an only child, had always been very independent. Her parents, farmers, spent a lot of time tending to the farm. Teresa started helping them when she was very young by doing the bookkeeping and other administrative jobs.

Although Robert had always thought he might come back to take over his father's painting business, he wanted to obtain some outside business experience first. As a result, he found a job in a Zellers store in Winnipeg after his graduation. Robert enjoyed working with people in the retail setting but felt frustrated working for a larger company. He wanted to be on his own and dreamed of someday running his own business. While Robert worked at Zellers, Teresa had been developing her photography skills, working for local retailers preparing catalogues. Though she was fairly busy with this, she did not feel as if she were being challenged.

Finally, after two years with Zellers, the Normans decided to leave Winnipeg and return to Brandon where they could begin to take over the painting business. Robert's father was pleased with their decision and, since he was approaching retirement age, allowed his son to assume a major role in the business. Norman managed the business for six years with Teresa doing the bookkeeping. But although it provided a steady income, he could see that the growth possibilities in terms of income and challenge were limited. In addition, he soon realized he didn't like painting as much as he thought he would. As a result, he and Teresa started looking around for sideline opportunities to earn a little extra money. One they particularly enjoyed was assembling and selling picture frames.

One day, while in Winnipeg to obtain some water-seal paint, Robert ran across a small retail store called U-Frame-It. He went in to look around and talk to the manager about the business. He was impressed by the manager's enthusiasm and noticed that the store was extremely busy. Robert immediately began wondering about the possibility of starting his own picture-framing store.

Excited by what he had seen, Robert returned to Brandon without even buying his paint and told Teresa what had happened. She was extremely enthusiastic about the idea. Robert's father was skeptical and, as Robert had expected, disappointed that they wanted to leave the family business.

Robert and Teresa needed to make their decision quickly. The manager of the U-Frame-It store had indicated that the franchise chain was looking at Brandon as a possible site for another outlet sometime in the future.

After a few days of evaluating their small business decision, Robert and Teresa Norman decided to open the picture-framing retail outlet in Brandon. Robert had learned a great deal about the business from his visit with the U-Frame-It franchise in Winnipeg. He convinced his father that the opportunity had promise. Both were aware that many people were now becoming do-it-yourselfers in home decorating.

His college training had taught Robert the importance of thorough investigation before starting a business. He realized he should do this even before deciding whether to start the business on his own or to become a franchisee. He contacted the Professional Picture Framers Association (PPFA) and learned that the average customer spends $32 per visit at a framing store. In checking framing costs with the U-Frame-It manager in Winnipeg, he confirmed this information. A typical per-customer profit statement for a framing shop was as follows:

Revenue	$32	(100%)
Materials	15	(47%)
Overhead (rent, utilities, wages, etc.)	9	(28%)
Profit per customer	8	(25%)

Robert knew there was one other framing store in Brandon, a city of 35,000. Using Winnipeg as an example, Robert calculated that a framing store could service a population of approximately 25,000 people and earn an acceptable profit.

While Robert was collecting his information, Teresa was conducting some of her own market research. She visited the only picture-framing store in Brandon and noted that the store was the busiest between the hours of 11 a.m. and 3 p.m. She also observed that many customers had some time to wait for available workstations and for the glue to dry. During this time, they browsed around the store looking at the merchandise.

Robert also attended an industry supplier seminar in Minneapolis. He was encouraged to learn that the do-it-yourself framing business was experiencing rapid growth throughout North America. While there, Robert learned about several picture-framing trade magazines and bought subscriptions for them. He also made valuable contacts with suppliers and other dealers.

Things looked more positive each day, so Robert closed down the painting business, and he and Teresa began preparing to open their new store, which they would call The Framemakers.

Robert and Teresa Norman immediately went to work organizing their new business. They had contemplated signing a franchise contract with U-Frame-It but decided against it when he found out he would have to pay a $20,000 franchise fee and royalties of 10 percent of sales just for the name and set-up assistance. In addition, the franchisor required that the stores follow a set format and that all supplies be purchased from them.

Robert's college training had taught him the importance of drawing up a business plan, so they prepared the following outline for their business:

- *Target market.* They thought the new store should cater to the price-conscious individual who wanted to save a few dollars by doing his or her own framing. What he had learned about the do-it-yourself market seemed particularly suitable for the new business. They judged that the target market was between the ages of 35 and 60 and could spend up to an hour in the store. This was based on their observations of the other framing store in Brandon.

- *Financial.* Based on data from the U-Frame-It franchise, Robert estimated start-up costs to be about $100,000. Since they were planning to lease space for the store, the capital requirements included only the purchase of shelves, fixtures, initial inventory, and tools. Because he and Teresa had $25,000 in equity to put into the venture, they expected to be able to borrow the remaining $75,000 from a local bank.

- *Personnel.* Robert and Teresa were hesitant to hire any employees until they were sure the business would be successful. In addition, they wanted to be totally involved in the business to better learn about all aspects of framing. The two would work full time, each doing whatever needed to be done.

- *Regulations.* They knew The Framemakers would need a business licence, which they would obtain from the city hall. They would operate the business as a proprietorship until the need to incorporate became evident.

- *Layout.* After looking at the U-Frame-It shop in Winnipeg, Robert drew up an interior lay-out plan he believed allowed efficiency and convenience for the store.

- *Location.* Although there weren't many available locations in Brandon, Robert recognized the need to locate in a high-traffic area of the city. This would not only be convenient for regular customers but, they hoped, would attract some walk-in customers as well.

After developing this business plan, Robert and Teresa began making contacts to get the business going. Within the next month, Robert was busy negotiating with suppliers, landlords, his banker, and the city hall to get the business started as soon as possible.

After selecting their location, Robert and Teresa Norman began securing merchandise for their initial inventory in earnest. They soon learned, however, that suppliers wanted to be paid before making deliveries. Therefore, Robert approached his local bank's manager to obtain the money he needed to get started. Although he had known his banker for a long time, he was surprised to find a less than positive reaction toward his proposal. Robert requested a $75,000 business loan, with he and Teresa contributing $25,000 of their own money to the estimated $100,000 cost of the venture.

The bank manager asked Robert to go home and prepare a detailed description of their needs, as well as a projected operating statement for the first year's operations. The Normans were upset by this negative reaction and decided to visit other banks to obtain the funds they needed. But they found out they would need to provide the requested information to obtain the money no matter where they went. Robert and Teresa spent two days working feverishly and came up with the statements shown in Figure 1.

Figure 1

The Framemakers Financial Requirements, Year 1		
Item	**Amount**	**Source of Information**
Inventory	$ 45,000	General estimate
Equipment and fixtures	35,000	Approximation
Opening promotion (trade show)	2,000	Price of booth
First month's rent	2,000	From landlord
Three months' salary (Robert and Teresa)	12,000	Estimated $4,000/month
First three months' advertising and	3,600	One ad on TV and radio, in newspaper
Miscellaneous	400	Estimate
Total	$100,000	

	The Framemakers Projected Income Statement, Year 1		
	Per Customer (Professional Picture Framing Association Figures)		20 Customers a Day for 240 Days
Sales	$32	100%	$153,600
Expenses	24	75	115,200
Profit	8	25	38,400

When Robert took the proposals to the bank, the manager seemed impressed but still would not give approval for the loan. Some uncertainties about the statements still bothered the banker. Finally, after two weeks of collecting information—and pleading—the Normans' loan for $75,000 was approved. A major reason for the approval was their past dealings with the bank and their good credit standing. Now they could begin purchasing supplies to get started.

Before long, however, the Normans realized that they had underestimated many of their expenses. They learned, for example, that utilities, rent, and telephone all required initial deposits of $200. They also needed some additional supplies, even though they had overbought some unnecessary supplies from especially persistent salespeople. The landlord required the first and last months' rent before letting them move in. The equipment costs and inventory levels were higher than they had estimated. Finally, since the Normans had decided it would be better to incorporate their business, they faced additional legal costs for which they had not planned. The result of all these additions was that The Framemakers needed another $10,000—and the Normans hadn't even opened the doors!

Robert and Teresa didn't know what to do. They were hesitant to go back to the bank and ask for more money because of the difficulty they had had obtaining the first loan. However, they knew their chances of obtaining funding elsewhere were slim. On top of that, the time for the grand opening was rapidly approaching.

Questions

1. What aspects of Robert and Teresa Norman's backgrounds will contribute to their success with the picture-framing store?
2. What positive things have Robert and Teresa done in investigating the feasibility of the new store and what additional information might they have collected? From what sources could this information be obtained?
3. From the information provided, evaluate the business plan they have prepared for their new business.
4. Weigh the relevant pros and cons for the Normans of operating a U-Frame-It franchise instead of starting their business from scratch.
5. Evaluate the Normans' initial approach to obtaining financing for The Framemakers.
6. Assuming you are the banker, evaluate the financial requirements and projections Robert and Teresa prepared.

CLOVIS JEWELLERS

D. Wesley Balderson, *University of Lethbridge*

Clovis Jewellers is a small jewellery store located in Brandon, Manitoba.[1] You have been called on by the owner to prepare an analysis of the business. The owners have supplied you with a detailed description of their operation and strategy. Critically evaluate each area described in the case.

Structure

Legal Structure. Clovis Jewellers is an incorporated company under the name of Clovis Jewellers (1988) Limited. It is a privately held corporation. The only shareholders are Mr. and Mrs. Neudorf, each of whom owns 50 percent of the outstanding shares. As a corporation, Clovis Jewellers is authorized to issue an unlimited number of Class A, B, and C common shares. The only outstanding shares are 100 Class A shares. In the case of Clovis Jewellers, the shareholders are the owners, directors, and managers.

Financial Structure. The capital structure of Clovis Jewellers is financed by a combination of debt and shareholder's equity. The debt constitutes roughly 75 percent of the capital and the shareholder's equity the other 25 percent. The shareholder's equity is made up of both class A share capital and retained earnings, of which the latter is by far the larger.

The debt financing is held with the Bank of Montreal and is in the form of a long-term loan. This loan is approximately $190,000. The first $150,000 is guaranteed through a provincial government small business assistance plan and therefore carries an interest rate of 9 percent; the remaining $40,000 carries a rate of prime plus 1 percent. This long-term debt is covered by personal guarantees of Fred Meyer, a business associate of Mr. Neudorf, and by a mortgage on the Neudorfs' house.

The bank of Montreal has also authorized an operating line of credit to Clovis Jewellers with a ceiling of $20,000. This line of credit is used to assist Mr. Neudorf in managing the cash flow in the slower summer months.

Organizational Structure. There are four levels of employees in Clovis Jewellers' organizational structure (see Appendix 1 on page 464). The first level is the manager and is filled by Mr. Neudorf. The duties of this position include accounting and financial management, management of day-to-day store operations and gemologist/diamond expert. Mr. Neudorf works together with both the assistant manager and the sales staff.

The second level in the organization is the assistant manager and is filled by Mrs. Neudorf. She works as the assistant manager approximately 50 percent of the time and as a salesperson the remaining 50 percent. The duties of the assistant manager include purchasing of merchandise and control of inventory. The inventory control function is done on a very informal basis, usually by a simple visual check.

The third level in the organization includes the sales staff and the repair service administrator. The job of overseeing the repair service is held by one of the full-time salespersons and requires approximately 20 percent of her time. The number of salespersons varies with the time of year, ranging from six to seven at Christmastime to two or three during the summer months.

The fourth level in the organization is the goldsmith and repairperson. This position is filled by Mr. Neudorf and requires a great deal of his time. Mr. Neudorf works together with the repair service administrator when acting as goldsmith.

---

1 Although this case describes an actual business, the names of the business and owners, as well as the location, have been changed.

There are two positions outside of the four-level organization. One is an accountant, and the other is a lawyer. Mr. Neudorf hires these two professionals on a part-time basis as demand calls for them. Both the accountant and the lawyer interact only with Mr. Neudorf.

Personnel

Clovis Jewellers experiences very little employee turnover (one staff member every two or three years) and therefore does not engage in recruiting procedures on a regular basis. When a new staff member is needed, a small advertisement is placed in the classified section of Brandon's daily newspaper. Although an advertisement is always placed, most hiring results through word of mouth and other contacts with neighbouring businesspeople.

When selecting a new employee, Mr. and Mrs. Neudorf look for individuals with an outgoing, friendly personality. Usually the person is middle-aged and has sales experience. Application forms are screened based on these qualifications, and the applicant who best meets the qualifications is asked to come in for a personal interview. Unless there is more than one "ideal" applicant, the new employee is hired after only one interview.

The training supplied to new employees comes in two forms: product training and operations training. The product training requires the employee to learn a great deal about jewellery—a very complex area. The individual must gain knowledge about watches, diamonds, gemstones, and qualities of gold. This product training occurs as the person works in the showroom selling jewellery and takes approximately one month.

The operations training is less involved than the product training and is completed in the first week or two of employment. This training involves learning the daily routine carried out at Clovis Jewellers, as well as cash register and receipt-writing operations.

The method of employee remuneration is a straight hourly wage; no commissions are paid. Employees' hours are recorded in a payroll register, and employees are paid every two weeks based on the number of hours worked. Mr. Neudorf tried to introduce a commission pay plan in the past, but employee resistance forced him to shelve the plan.

Employee morale appears relatively high compared with other retail stores. Mr. Neudorf believes this is because he and his wife treat the sales staff with respect and as friends. The employees know the importance of selling to the company's well-being, and Mr. Neudorf continually reinforces this by verbally acknowledging an individual for his or her sales efforts. A further indication of high morale is the fact that Clovis Jewellers experiences an extremely low rate of absenteeism and lateness.

Marketing

Product. A majority of Clovis Jewellers' yearly sales consists of ring and precious stone jewellery; for this reason, its product mix heavily favours these two items. Ring sales are responsible for the single highest sales total; therefore, great emphasis is placed on the ring inventory when the product mix is evaluated. Clovis Jewellers is known for carrying good-quality merchandise; this is reflected in the purchasing habits and quality control employed at Clovis. However, Clovis has shifted to a lower-quality selection of rings and jewellery to compete with the competition. This shift appears to be temporary, as the better-quality lines remain.

Mr. Neudorf believes seasonal fluctuations in sales do not seriously affect the product mix. Relative sales of most items remain constant throughout the year.

Distribution. Clovis Jewellers is in the middle of a transition from using a traditional manufacturer-retailer distribution channel to a more direct channel. Jewellery and ring manufacturers are actually intermediaries in the supply of diamonds and precious gems (the manufacturers buy the gemstones from large diamond and gemstone suppliers). This method of purchasing was more convenient for Mr. Neudorf but inevitably meant higher-priced merchandise. Mr. Neudorf has now made arrangements to buy diamonds directly from the source of supply and therefore has greatly reduced merchandise costs. This shift also gives Mr. Neudorf much greater control over diamond and gemstone quality.

Pricing. Mr. Neudorf uses several different methods in calculating the retail prices of the merchandise. Brand-name items such as watches are priced according to the manufacturer's suggested retail price, because Mr. Neudorf thinks customers will base their purchase decisions solely on price when shopping for brand names.

Merchandise whose quality the customer cannot differentiate easily, such as gold chains, are priced very competitively. Comparisons are often made with other jewellery stores to ensure that these items are priced competitively. Jewellery items such as earrings and pendants are priced according to a standard markup of keystone (50 percent), plus an additional 10 percent to make up for markdowns, which are often needed to sell the jewellery.

Mr. Neudorf finds rings the hardest items to price, as they carry no brand names or identifying trademarks. Each ring is priced individually, based on special features (or lack of them). A general markup formula is still used, but individual factors dictate the final selling price of the ring. For example, everyday solitaire engagement rings are priced below the standard markup, whereas individual modern engagement rings are priced above that markup.

Promotion. Clovis Jewellers uses a wide range of media in its advertising program, including a daily newspaper, a local television station, AM and FM radio stations, and flyers. Advertising is used to convey both a specific promotional method and corporate image advertising. Mr. Neudorf prepares much of his own advertising, especially radio and newspaper ads. He also gives the ads a personal touch by recording many of the radio ads himself and including his picture in several newspaper advertisements. Mr. Neudorf claims that Clovis Jewellers targets its selling toward middle-aged women, but this target is not evident in the advertising; rather, the advertising appears to be general, with no real objectives or target market in mind. The advertising budget is prepared by taking a percentage of projected sales. This target percentage is between 4 percent and 5 percent.

Mr. Neudorf uses many different forms of sales promotion throughout the year. These include diamond remount plans, jewellery repair sales, graduation promotions, Mother's Day promotions, and other general markdown sales. The number of sales promotions has increased over the past few years due to an increase in competition. The trend in promotions has switched from using them to enhance slow selling periods toward bettering higher selling periods. That is, they are now timed in conjunction with a month of already higher-than-average sales.

Personal selling is heavily used at Clovis Jewellers. Mr. Neudorf believes jewellery requires a substantial selling push and therefore uses in-store personal selling as a major marketing tool. Emphasis is on making every sale count, large or small. Monthly sales totals are updated every day and then compared with the projected sales for the month. This information is then passed on to the salespeople to keep them aware of the importance of selling.

Public relations can also be an effective marketing tool, especially in a close-knit community such as Brandon. Mr. Neudorf is involved with many community clubs and events, which give him a fair amount of low-cost public relations. Clovis Jewellers sponsors sporting events for persons with disabilities and is a member of both the Rotary Club of Brandon and the Brandon Chamber of Commerce (of which Mr. Neudorf has been president and is currently a director). Mr. Neudorf gives talks to local women's groups and at high school career days. He has also had much interaction with the Brandon City Council and has served on committees such as the Brandon Parking Commission.

Location and Layout

Location. Clovis Jewellers' trading area consists of the city of Brandon, surrounding towns and farmlands, and small communities that extend to the Ontario and Saskatchewan borders. The population of the area is slightly greater than 200,000, of which 55,000 live in the city of Brandon. The primary trading area (approximately 70 percent of the business) includes the entire city of Brandon and the surrounding towns of Virden, Souris, Minnedosa, and Neepawa.

The economy of Clovis Jewellers' trading area relies heavily on its two industries, farming and oil. Clovis Jewellers' sales experience large fluctuations due to the characteristics of each of these industries. The downturn in the oil industry has had a significant impact on the firm's profitability; sales have dropped significantly in the past three years.

Clovis Jewellers leases its site from a management firm located in Winnipeg. The basic rent is approximately $2,400 per month. On top of this expense, Clovis pays a yearly management, property tax, and insurance fee for the building. The building is a single-storey structure located on Brandon's main downtown artery. The physical characteristics of the site follow the image Clovis is trying to portray; the storefront is pleasant and modern looking.

The buildings surrounding Clovis Jewellers host mostly banks and other independent retail stores. Several retail stores on the same city block appeal to Clovis's target market, including the Roset by Reid jewellery store located across the street. There is one vacant space on the street, located right next to Clovis Jewellers. The vacancy was caused by a fire over a year ago, and the building remains boarded up.

Clovis Jewellers is located on Ross Street, which is the centre downtown street. Ross Street has angle parking on both sides and is busy every weekday from 9:00 a.m. until around 6:00 p.m. This heavy vehicle traffic is due to the large number of banks in the area that deal with a high volume of customers every day. Ross Street also experiences a high volume of pedestrian traffic during the day, as it is situated in the heart of Brandon's retail and office sector.

Layout. Clovis Jewellers' present location is 1,000 square feet. Eight hundred square feet are used as selling space and the remaining 200 for office and storage space. The showroom is divided among rings, gold chains, watches, gift items, diamond jewellery, and regular jewellery. Although space is allocated to each section according to proportion of total sales, the allocation is based on rough estimates of both percentage of sales and space used.

The layout of the store is designed to make efficient use of high-traffic areas. The engagement rings, which are classified as specialty goods, are located at the back of the store, a spot that would normally see low-traffic volume. The shopping goods such as watches and gold chains are located in high-traffic areas around the cash register and front entrance.

Merchandise is displayed in either a locked showcase or behind a showcase out of the customer's reach. This method of displaying is necessary due to the high value and small size of individual pieces of merchandise. Each display case is lighted by two spotlights dropped from the ceiling. Florescent lights light the general-purpose areas of the store; other lamps are suspended from the ceiling as part of the decor. The lighting appears adequate, as the store gives a "bright" first impression.

Purchasing and Inventory Control

Purchasing. Mrs. Neudorf is responsible for purchasing the majority of the required merchandise. The salespeople often assist her, especially when the purchasing is done in Clovis Jewellers' showroom. Purchasing is done through a combination of jewellery and gift show attendance and meetings with individual supplier representatives.

The tradeshows Mr. and Mrs. Neudorf attend are held throughout Canada and the United States and include cities such as Hawaii, Vancouver, Brandon, Calgary, Winnipeg, and Toronto. Roughly 20 percent of total purchases are made at these tradeshows. Mr. and Mrs. Neudorf attend them for the purpose of obtaining new products and ideas as well as the actual purchasing.

Eighty percent of purchasing is done in-store and with the help of the salespeople. Mrs. Neudorf prefers in-store purchasing because it gives her the undivided attention of the company representative and allows her to compare items with Clovis's existing merchandise. Each company representative visits Clovis Jewellers two or three times a year, usually in the spring and early fall.

Mr. Neudorf has arranged special payment terms with approximately 75 percent of his suppliers. The credit terms are usually 30/60 days, 30/60/90 days, 30/60/90/120 days, or even up to six months; most companies will give these terms free of any interest charges. Mr. Neudorf finds these terms necessary for cash flow management, as the majority of purchases are made during slow sales periods.

Mr. Neudorf maintains a tight level of quality control, inspecting each piece of jewellery before it is put on sale. Each item is checked for diamond or gemstone quality, quality of stone settings, and adequate stamping of gold quality. Items that do not meet the strict quality standards are returned to the supplier for exchange.

A purchasing budget is prepared by multiplying the target gross margin percentage by the budgeted sales figure. This total purchase figure is then spread out throughout the year according to monthly sales, with the majority of purchases made in the pre-Christmas season.

Inventory Control. No formal inventory control method is used at Clovis Jewellers. Mr. and Mrs. Neudorf rely on experience when it comes to controlling inventory levels. Visual inspections determine whether inventory levels are sufficient or need replenishing. No automatic reorder procedure is used; Mr. and Mrs. Neudorf believe automatic reordering would hurt rather than enhance sales because customers expect to find unique pieces of jewellery at Clovis.

Mr. Neudorf has insurance to cover fire, loss of merchandise stored in the safe, loss of customer goods stored in the safe, and business interruption (up to six months). Insurance to protect against theft of merchandise not stored in the safe is either not available or too expensive. All of the rings and diamond jewellery are placed in the safe after business hours; therefore, most of Clovis's inventory is insured in the event of a break-in. The business interruption insurance is related to inventory; a major loss or damage of inventory would not force Clovis Jewellers out of business, as the firm would continue to have a daily cash flow.

Accounting and Financial

Recording and Classifying. The daily and weekly recording and classifying done by the staff at Clovis Jewellers basically follows a one-write system, with the addition of certain journals and a daily cash summary. The one-write system, kept by Mr. Neudorf, is used to maintain all of the sundry (nonmerchandise) accounts as well as the company payroll. The nonmerchandise accounts are paid as they arise and therefore require almost daily attention; the payroll is calculated every two weeks.

A daily cash summary is prepared by Mr. Neudorf every weekday morning (Friday's and Saturday's are prepared on Monday). This cash summary includes a summary of the day's sales, both cash sales and charge sales; a summary of how the cash flow is distributed, including cash expenses and bank deposits; and a record of returned merchandise and cheques. The main purpose of this cash summary is to ensure that the cash transactions balance on a day-to-day basis.

Mr. Neudorf also keeps an accounts payable ledger, which he updates weekly. Proper managing of the accounts payable is important to Clovis Jewellers because it relies on trade credit to purchase all of its inventories. A journal of monthly purchases is kept to maintain control over the inventory and the merchandise purchases. Mrs. Neudorf is responsible for keeping this journal up to date; usually she adds all of the invoices to the journal at the end of the month, when a total can be calculated.

One final area in which recording is done on a day-to-day basis is the jewellery repair journal and record of ring sales. Clovis Jewellers has an extensive jewellery and watch repair department. The repair department is run by the sales staff and involves entering every repair job into a journal for easy reference. Because of the quick turnover of repair jobs (usually one to two days), they must be entered into the journal the same day they are received to prevent any bottlenecks in the system. Individual ring sales are also recorded in a book for quick reference as needed.

Budgeting. Five years ago, the budgeting process was almost nonexistent at Clovis Jewellers. Except for some very rough, off-the-top-of-the-head figures, no budgets were prepared. This has changed in the last few years, and although the budgetary process still needs improvement, it has taken a definite shape and form.

The process starts with a sales budget. This budget is prepared by looking at last year's sales and then updating them based on any special considerations for the upcoming year. The budget is prepared monthly and used to make regular comparisons with actual sales figures.

Once the sales budget is complete, a merchandise purchases budget is prepared based on the specific level of monthly sales. The purchases budget includes all shares of merchandise purchases, including the cost of repairs.

An expense budget is prepared by Mr. Neudorf. Again, previous years' expense totals are used. These expense totals are evaluated as being too high, too low, or correct over the past year and are then changed accordingly for the upcoming budgeted year. The budgeting of all the expense totals is very important, as it allows for better control of these expenses as they are incurred.

The final budget prepared is the cash flow project budget. This is done by combining the projected sales, merchandise payments, and expense budgets. This cash flow projection is very important for Clovis Jewellers, because the seasonal cash inflows it experiences often creates cash shortages; the cash flow analysis allows Mr. Neudorf to plan for these shortages.

Financial Statements. Clovis Jewellers has a complete set of financial statements prepared once a year by a certified general accounting firm (see Appendix 2 on pages 465–467). The statements are prepared after January 31 of each year, which Mr. Neudorf has chosen as the year-end date due to the low volume of business and low inventory count that occur at this time. All financial statements are prepared showing the previous year's figures for purposes of easy comparison.

The balance sheet is prepared in the traditional format, with assets on the left side of the statement and liabilities and equity on the right. Current assets constitute roughly 75 percent of the total assets; inventory is the largest and most important part of the current assets. Clovis Jewellers has a long-term loan payable, which makes up the largest part of the total liabilities. This loan contract is held with the Bank of Montreal and carries personal guarantees from both Mr. Neudorf and his business associate, Fred Meyer.

An income statement is prepared based on sales and expense figures supplied by Mr. Neudorf. This statement does not include a detailed list of the operating expenses. For this purpose, a detailed statement of operating expenses is prepared. This statement lists each expense totalled for the year and in alphabetical order.

A statement of changes in financial position is also prepared at year-end. This statement explains how funds were generated and used throughout the year. The purpose of this statement is to indicate any changes in the working capital of the business and explain how those changes occurred.

Planning

Long-Term Planning. Management at Clovis Jewellers appears to be typical of most small businesses in that a serious lack of any long-term planning exists. The only long-term planning that has occurred is the signing of a five-year lease. Although this means of planning is extremely informal by even a liberal definition, it indicates that some consideration has been given to the long-range plans of Clovis Jewellers.

Short-Term Planning. Mr. Neudorf engages in a number of forms of short-term planning. Among them are budgeting for the upcoming year, planning promotions, and cash flow planning. Budgets are prepared early in the fiscal year and extend to the end of the year. The budgets include a sales budget, a purchases budget, and an expense budget. The budgetary process is still in the early stages of development, but an increased awareness on the part of Mr. Neudorf ensures that it will be an effective form of short-term planning in the future.

Promotions are planned on an informal basis; no concrete goals or objectives are stated. Most of the promotions are planned based on the success of the previous year's promotions. If a promotion proved successful one year, it is automatically considered for the next year. This method produces mixed results, as some promotions are successful one year and quite unsuccessful the next.

One area of short-range planning that requires attention is the planning of future cash flows. Mr. Neudorf prepares a complete cash flow analysis for the upcoming year based on projected sales, merchandise purchases, and expenses. This cash flow analysis does not always prove accurate due to extraordinary items that arise in the course of the year, but at least it gives Mr. Neudorf a plan for goals for which to aim.

Appendix 1

Clovis Jewellers: Organizational Structure

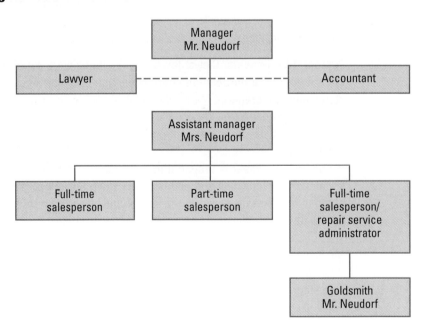

Appendix 2

Clovis Jewellers: Financial Statements

CLOVIS JEWELLERS (1988) LTD.
Balance Sheet
(Unaudited)
January 31, 2007

	2007	2006
Assets		
Current		
Cash	$ 24,886.15	$ 32,834.17
Accounts receivable (trade)	4,885.34	5,725.74
(shareholders)	18,186.40	18,462.84
Inventory	190,612.90	197,318.70
Prepaid expense	8,437.01	9,150.01
	247,007.80	263,491.46
Assets		
Investments	1,045.00	—
Fixed	10,853.69	13,566.69
Other		
Goodwill less amortization	56,672.20	59,228.20
Incorporation costs	—	373.54
Due from Neudorf holdings	15,448.95	15,448.95
	$ 331,027.64	$ 352,108.84
Liabilities		
Current:		
Accounts payable and accruals	$ 70,987.17	$ 92,214.96
Employee remittance payable	1,447.75	1,539.07
Corporation taxes payable	925.40	834.85
Current portion of long-term	11,316.00	8,000.00
	84,676.32	102,588.88
Long-Term	199,961.77	214,156.14
	284,638.09	316,745.02
Shareholders' Equity		
Share Capital	$ 100.00	$ 100.00
Retained Earnings	46,289.55	35,263.82
	46,389.55	35,363.82
	$ 331,027.64	$ 352,108.84

CLOVIS JEWELLERS (1988) LTD.
Statement of Income
(Unaudited)
Year Ended January 31, 2007

	2007	**2006**
Sales	$ 420,559.99	$ 472,035.50
Cost of Sales	218,332.01	261,016.36
Gross Margin	202,227.98	211,019.14
Selling Expenses	192,626.33	210,073.57
Operating Income	9,601.65	945.57
Other Income:		
Interest earned	350.48	213.63
Gain from sale of assets	—	1,133.00
Income before Taxes	9,952.13	2,292.20
Income taxes	925.40	834.85
Net Income	$ 9,026.73	$ 1,457.35

CLOVIS JEWELLERS (1988) LTD.
Statement of Operating Expenses
(Unaudited)
Year Ended January 31, 2007

	2007	**2006**
Operating Expense:		
Accounting	$ 761.20	$ 1,039.30
Advertising	11,024.93	33,250.03
Amortization	4,556.00	4,556.00
Auto expenses	1,794.77	3,146.33
Bank charges and interest	4,318.90	4,549.10
Canada Pension Plan	1,201.94	1,296.32
Donations	350.00	350.00
Depreciation	2,713.00	3,391.00
Employment insurance	2,492.46	2,539.19
Equipment rental	4,200.00	2,700.00
Interest	28,016.38	30,747.77
Insurance	3,047.00	3,079.41
Legal expenses	448.54	80.09
Memberships and dues	510.00	587.74
Postage and stationery	1,382.82	2,388.12
Rent	28,965.29	28,175.00

CLOVIS JEWELLERS (1988) LTD.
Statement of Operating Expenses (*continued*)
(Unaudited)
Year Ended January 31, 2007

Repairs and maintenance	432.41	464.59
Salaries	82,180.91	74,505.54
Security	711.39	681.25
Supplies	2,224.87	2,308.94
Taxes	2,603.75	3,144.88
Telephone	983.67	1,104.04
Travel and promotion	3,764.89	1,621.14
Utilities	3,818.71	4,092.59
Workers' compensation	122.50	245.00
Total expenses	$ 192,626.33	$ 210,073.57

THOMSON GREENHOUSE

D. Wesley Balderson, *University of Lethbridge*

Background

Thomson Greenhouse is located just outside Sudbury, Ontario, and is owned by Earl and Lisa Thomson. It is a seasonal operation, offering many different types of bedding plants, vegetables, annuals, perennials, and specialty plants and arrangements. The business also has a two-acre tree nursery and garden offering a wide range of trees from pines to fruit trees.

Earl and Lisa Thomson have been operating the business for 17 years after taking over the business from Lisa's parents. The original business was located on land on the outskirts of Sudbury that was annexed by the city. It was at that time that Earl and Lisa decided to move from the city to a small acreage, so that they could continue the business and set up a new location. The structures were taken down and reassembled on the new acreage just northeast of Sudbury.

Much of the knowledge of the greenhouse business has been passed down from Lisa's parents and as Earl and Lisa have three sons working in the business it continues to be a solely family-run operation. Many of the aspects of the business have remained the same since it was established. Thomson Greenhouse has been serving the city of Sudbury and surrounding area for many years and has been fairly successful in establishing a name for quality products and good customer service.

Thomson Greenhouse is a form of second income to the Thomsons due to its seasonal nature and because Earl is the chief accountant for a local manufacturing company. It also has allowed the Thomsons' three sons to work in the business to help finance their schooling. The oldest son, Derek, is currently about to graduate with a bachelor's degree in business from the local university while the other brothers (Ryan and Russel) are in Grades 10 and 12 respectively. Lisa's parents, Morris and Anna Slemko, also work in the business during the busy times.

Due to the success of the business and the fact that their sons are getting to the age where they are about to leave home the Thomsons are faced with some long-term decisions about the business.

Organization

Thomson Greenhouse is a general partnership with the two partners being Earl and Lisa Thomson. Earl feels that although they have unlimited liability under this arrangement, the tax and flexibility advantages of a partnership outweigh this risk. Both partners own an equal share of the business, although Lisa spends more time working in the business because Earl has a full-time job in Sudbury.

Earl and Lisa have equal authority with regard to the employees. Both are knowledgeable regarding horticulture and care for trees and plants. Earl is more responsible for the accounting, advertising, deliveries, and seeding. Lisa handles orders, daily operations in the greenhouse, transplanting, sales, and customer service. Both Earl and Lisa know their strengths and weaknesses, and tend to do the things they each do well. Some overlapping occurs, but this is advantageous in some ways because some operations are too big to handle by themselves.

Over the years there have been few conflicts in the management of the operation or with employees as it has all been within the family. All three of the Thomson sons have worked in the business throughout the summer as well as evenings and weekends for a number of years. During the busy season Lisa's parents, from whom Earl and Lisa purchased the business, help out. Because of the fact that the business is family owned and operated, no formal personnel policies or training programs have been developed. Management of the company has been carried out on an informal basis. The employees are paid on a straight salary basis with considerable flexibility available for the sons as things come up that they need to do.

One of the major concerns that Earl and Lisa have is the future of the business when the children finish their high school and university studies. The business is not currently large enough to be a full-time occupation unless a considerable capital investment is made to expand the operation. Another difficulty is that the second-oldest son, Ryan, has expressed interest in becoming involved in the business but the Thomsons are concerned about how to make this transition should it take place. They are wondering what effects such a move would have on their other two sons.

Location and Physical Facilities

Thomson Greenhouse is located just northeast of the city limits of Sudbury. The market area not only includes the city of Sudbury (population 90,000) but also many of the small communities around the city, which is estimated to have another 60,000 people. This location serves Thomson well because of its proximity to the city; as well, its rural location allows for plenty of space for production and expansion, if required. Distribution is carried out primarily by truck, and the highways and roads in the area are very well maintained.

Thomson Greenhouse is located on 20 acres of which 5 are used for the greenhouse and the Thomsons' residence and the other 15 are rented out to a local farmer. The greenhouse building covers approximately 800 square metres. Although most of the area is taken up with plants and could be referred to as selling space, a small area at the front is devoted to customer service and a cash counter. A small greenhouse at the back is used for personal items and the holding of special orders. The building's age is a concern, and it has begun deteriorating. The frame is made of wood and the aging process has damaged many of the wooden glass frames. Much of the material for this greenhouse came from the original greenhouse that was moved from the previous site.

Recently Thomson Greenhouse purchased a new computer system. The Thomsons are in the process of converting their manual record keeping and inventory control over to the computer. Other equipment owned by the business are a small front-end loader/garden tractor, a truck used to deliver plants to commercial customers, roto tiller, dirt mixer, and dirt purifier, and other miscellaneous garden tools and greenhouses devices.

Purchasing for Thomson Greenhouse is carried out by both Earl and Lisa. They purchase their supply of inventory from various seed processors located primarily in Southern Ontario and the United States. Quality, dependability, and price are all used to evaluate suppliers. Lead times for ordering are about 30 days for most items. No formal inventory-ordering method is used as the business is small enough that Earl and Lisa are able to adjust their inventory levels from visual inspection and from previous experience.

Marketing

The target market for Thomson Greenhouse consists of consumers who come to the greenhouse as well as some large retail accounts to supermarkets such as Superstore and A&P. The consumer market tends to be older, those who have the resources and time to spend on their yards and gardens. The supermarket or commercial accounts purchase vegetables and some flowers while those customers who come out to Thomson Greenhouse make greater purchases of bedding plants and trees. In terms of quality and price, the commercial accounts tend to be interested in low price. As a result, the margins that Thomson achieves with the commercial accounts are much lower than with the customer accounts. Those who come out to the greenhouse desire high quality and customer service even if it means paying a slightly higher price. Earl Thomson realizes this and sets prices to meet these preferences and also to ensure that the business is able to achieve a profit. The profit margin has to be high enough to include the discounts that inevitably occur at the end of the season due to the perishability of the product.

The busy time of year for bedding plants is during May and June as most people are preparing their yards and gardens. During the summer and fall, produce sales increase, and during the winter months very little business is done.

There are several other greenhouses in the Sudbury area and many customers do price shopping. Thomson Greenhouse has always prided itself on superior customer service and despite the competitive nature of the industry seems to retain a fairly loyal following. The commercial contracts also add to the stability of operations for Thomson. Earl has an informal idea of Thomson Greenhouse market share through the monitoring of sales of their various products.

One of the trends the Thomsons have noticed is the increasing market share that has been obtained in the gardening-nursery product category by department stores such as Wal-Mart and Canadian Tire. Thomson Greenhouse currently has contracts with only two supermarkets and although these have provided steady volumes, purchases from these sources have not grown over the past few years. The Thomsons are considering attempting to obtain contracts with some of these department stores as a means of increasing sales. They realize that margins would be thin, however, and that price would be a major purchasing factor for the consumer. Many of the other greenhouses in the area are actively competing for the business of these stores and the Thomsons realize that they would have to be very competitive to be successful in obtaining a contract. If they were able to secure new purchasers, expansion of their current operation would seem to be necessary.

Thomson Greenhouse uses several forms of promotion. It places some ads in the local newspaper and utilizes the Yellow Pages. It also purchases a booth at the Home and Garden Tradeshow, which is held in Sudbury each spring. Occasionally, direct mail promotion is used to highlight special sales or end-of-season discounts. Thomson uses business cards and has been actively involved in sponsoring minor hockey teams and karate schools as part of its public relations promotion. Earl and Lisa realize, however, that word of mouth is their most effective form of promotion so they ensure that they and their sales staff are knowledgeable about the product and courteous to the customer.

Financial Situation

Thomson Greenhouse has been profitable since its establishment, earning about $10,000 per year on about $40,000 in sales. (See Exhibit 1 for the latest income statement.) Although sales haven't increased over the past five years, Earl and Lisa have not been concerned about this because there has been an increase in competition and they are currently operating at capacity with their present facilities. They have been using a one-book system for accounting but are currently switching over to an accounting software program in conjunction with their computer purchase.

One of the concerns that Earl and Lisa have is the state of their current greenhouse, which is getting old. They are considering constructing a new one in addition to the current greenhouse. This would increase the capacity of the business and would allow for increased sales but would also increase the workload for the Thomsons, something that they are not sure they want. Alternatively, they could replace the existing greenhouse and maintain current operations but at a more efficient level.

A new greenhouse of a similar size to the current one would cost approximately $12,000 and would last about 10 years. If the Thomsons decided to go ahead with this, they would finance $8,000 at the local bank at 8 percent interest. They estimate that the annual sales for a greenhouse of this size would be $30,000.

Exhibit 1

Thomson Greenhouse
Income Statement
For the Year Ended December 31, 2006

Revenue		$37,000
Expenses		
Cost of Goods Sold		
Seed and materials	$3,560	
Containers	3,150	
Fertilizer	290	
Water	305	
Soil	90	
Direct labour	3,000	$10,395
Contribution Margin		26,605
Occupancy and Selling Costs		
Building repairs	130	
Truck costs	2,300	
Office expenses	1,015	
Property taxes	1,560	
Heat and power	3,450	
Advertising	2,150	
Selling labour	3,150	
Depreciation	$3,800	$17,555
Profit before Income Taxes		$ 9,050

Thomsom Greenhouse
Balance Sheet
As at December 31, 2006

Current Assets		
Cash	$ 1,000	
Accounts receivable	1,500	
Inventory	3,000	
Fixed Assets		
Land	26,000	
Buildings	58,000	
Equipment	$ 21,000	
Total Assets		$110,500
Liabilities and Owner's Equity		
Liabilities		
Accounts Payable	1,500	
Owner's Equity	$109,000	
Total Liabilities and Owner's Equity		$110,500

Questions

1. Discuss the implications of the Thomsons' attempt to obtain additional commercial contracts (the department stores) for their products.
2. Evaluate the decision to construct another greenhouse from a financial as well as organizational point of view. (Use rate of return, payback, and break-even analysis in your evaluation.)
3. Comment on the financial health of the Thomson Greenhouse through a review of the financial statements.
4. Discuss the implications for succession of the business if the decision were to
   a. pass the business to one of the sons
   b. sell the business to someone outside the family

Endnotes

Chapter 1

1. John Naisbitt, *Global Paradox* (New York: William Morrow and Company, 1994).

2. As reported in *Success*, February 1999, p. 12.

3. *Growing Small Business* (Ottawa: Industry Canada/Statistics Canada, February 1994).

4. G.E.M. Report, as reported in *Business Research Newsletter*, June 18, 2007.

5. *Small Business Quarterly*, Industry Canada, August 2006, p. 1.

6. As reported in *G.D. Sourcing*, CIBC, October 2003.

7. Canadian Economic Observer, November 1997, CAICS 11-010-XPB, January–December, V-10, Statistics Canada.

8. "The Entrepreneurial Numbers Game," *Inc.*, May 1986, pp. 31–36.

9. "Small Businesses Fuel Growth," *Success*, July/August 2000, p.16.

10. "Canadian Small Business—A Growing Force," *CIBC World Markets*, September 2003, p. 4.

11. *Small Business Quarterly*, Industry Canada, August 2006, p. 1.

12. *Small Business Quarterly*, Industry Canada, May 2007, p. 6.

13. CIBC Study as reported in Business Research Newsletter, February 27, 2006.

14. *Small Business Quarterly*, Industry Canada, February 2007, p. 6.

15. *Small Business in Canada—A Statistical Overview* (Ottawa: Industry Canada, January 1996).

16. *Statistics Canada Survey of Employment*, September 2004, p. 4.

17. *Small Business Quarterly*, Industry Canada, May 2007, p. 5.

18. Ibid.

19. *Growing Small Business*, p. 1.

20. David Smith, *Why Small Business Is So Important* (Budget Brochure, Ministry of State for Small Business and Tourism, Government of Canada, 1984).

21. "Entrepreneurship Education," *Technological Entrepreneurship and Engineering in Canada, Canadian Academy of Engineering Report*, Chapter 9, Ottawa, 1997, pp. 149–160.

22. Harvey Schachter, "I Was A Teenage Capitalist," *Canadian Business*, December 24, 1998–January 8, 1999, pp. 58–60.

23. Thomas Peters and Robert H. Waterman, Jr., *In Search of Excellence* (New York: Harper and Row, 1982).

24. Ibid.

25. Stephanie Melita, "Small Talk," *Wall Street Journal*, May 21, 1998, pp. 28–29.

26. *Canadian Federation of Independent Business Report*, November 18, 2003.

27. *The Globe and Mail*, June 12, 1995, p. B7.

28. Code of Federal Regulations 13:121, *Standard Industrial Classification Codes and Size Standards* (Washington, D.C.: U.S. Government Printing Office, January 1, 1994), pp. 354–367; and *Growing Small Business*.

29. R. Peterson, *Small Business—Building a Balanced Economy* (Erin, Ont.: Press Porcepic Ltd., 1977), p. 64.

30. Canadian Federation of Independent Business, *Small Business Profile*, December 2005, p. 1.

31. Key Small Business Statistics, July 2005, p. 1.

32. *Growing Small Business*, p. 5.

33. *Small Business Quarterly*, Industry Canada, vol. 2, no. 3, March 2001, p. 1.

34. *Growing Small Business*, p. 5.

35. *Small Business Profile*, CFIB, December 2005, p. 5.

36. Ibid.

37. *Small Business Quarterly*, February 2007, p. 7.

38. "The Young and the Restless," *Profit*, June 1993, p. 48.

39. R. Lucien, "Canada's Small Business Owners Getting Greyer," *The Globe and Mail*, September 11, 2006, pp. 1 and 2.

40. As reported in *Costco Connection*, March–April 2005, p. 16.

41. "Women Entrepreneurs Leading the Charge," *CIBC World Markets*, 2005, p. 1.

42. Ibid.

43. *Small Business Quarterly*, Industry Canada, February 2005, p. 1.

44. *Small Business Quarterly*, Industry Canada, August 2006, p. 2.

44. *Self-Employment in Canada—Trends and Prospects*, CIBC Economics Division, December 2000, p. 7.

45. *Women in Management 9*, no. 2 (University of Western Ontario, December–January 1999), p. 2.

46. See footnote 41.

47. *Self-Employment in Canada—Trends and Prospects*, CIBC Economics Division, December 2000, p. 7.

48. "Canadian Small Business—A Growing Force," *CIBC World Markets*, September 2003, p. 3.

49. Bank of Nova Scotia Economic Survey, September 2005, p. B-7.

50. CFIB Small Business Profile, December 2005, p. 2.

51. Peters and Waterman, *In Search of Excellence*.

52. Ibid.

53. *Statistics on Foreign Ownership, Small versus Large* (Ottawa: Statistics Canada, Inter-Corporate Ownership, 1984), p. 252.

54. "Would You Want Your Son to Marry a Marketing Lady?" *Journal of Marketing*, January 1977, pp. 15–18.

55. Ivan I. Stefanovic, "Sidestepping Socialism in Yugoslavia," *Venture*, September 1984, p. 60.

56. *Global Entrepreneurship Monitor*, London Business School, Summer 2000.

57. Randall Litchfield, "Turn Change into Advantage," *Small Business*, June 1989, p. 19.

58. "Canadian Small Business—A Growing Force," *CIBC World Markets*, September 2003, p. 2.

59. *Self Employment in Canada—Trends and Prospects*, CIBC Economics Division, December 2000, p. 7.

60. North America Free Trade Agreement, Chapter 10.

61. North America Free Trade Agreement, Chapter 3.

62. North America Free Trade Agreement, Articles 1202 and 1204.

63. "Sunshine in the South," *Forbes*, September 16, 1991, p. 205.

64. Jason Myers, "In Praise of Open Markets," *Canadian Business*, November 13, 1998, p. 132.

65. Joe Dangor, "Thriving on Change," *Small Business Magazine*, June 1989, p. 32.

66. Cathy Hilborn, "Recession Startups Not So Risky Business," *Profit*, July–August 1991, p. 8.

67. "Canadian Small Business—A Growing Force," *CIBC World Markets*, September 2003, p. 2.

68. "Canadian Small Business—A Growing Force," *CIBC World Markets*, September 2003, p. 2.

69. GEM Report in Business Research Newsletter, February 28, 2005, p. 2.

70. *Growing Small Business*, p. 1.

71. John Bulloch, "Policy Guidelines to Help Make Your Venture Work," *The Financial Post Special Report*, November 24, 1984, p. 53.

72. CFIB, "Making Red Transparent....."

73. *Growing Small Business*.

74. CFIB, "Rated R: Prosperity Restricted by....," December 2005.

75. *Profits*, Business Development Bank of Canada, Winter 1999, p. 2.

76. "Canadian Small Business—A Growing Force," *CIBC World Markets*, September 2003, p. 2.

Chapter 2

1. "*Inc.* and *U.S.A. Today* Survey of 500 Fastest Growing Private Companies," Inc., June 1986, p. 48.

2. *The Globe and Mail*, July 17, 1995, p. B5.

3. *Canadian Economic Observer*, November 1997, Statistics Canada, Catalogue #11-010-XPB, p. 21.

4. CIBC World Markets, January 2005, p. 4.

5. "*Inc.* and *U.S.A. Today* Survey of 500 Fastest Growing Private Companies."

6. Pat Thompson, "Characteristics of the Small Business Entrepreneur in Canada," *Journal of Small Business and Entrepreneurship*, vol. 4, no. 3 (Winter 1986–87), p. 5.

7. *The Globe and Mail*, April 17, 1995, p. B4.

8. Karl Vesper, "Freedom and Power: What Every Entrepreneur Craves," *Success*, May 1988, p. 48.

9. As reported in *Costco Connection*, September/October, 2003.

10. Thompson, "Characteristics of the Small Business Entrepreneur in Canada."

11. "Fostering Flexibility, Work, and Family," CFIB, September 2004, p. 1.

12. GEM Report as reported in Business Research Newsletter, February 2005, p. 6.

13. "Size Comparisons of Bankrupt Firms versus Non-Bankrupt Firms," *The Canadian Small Business Guide*, February 22, 1985, p. 5013.

14. *The Canadian Business Failure Record*, 1994 (New York: Dun and Bradstreet, 1994), pp. 1– 19.

15. David P. Boyd and David E. Gumpert, "Coping with Entrepreneurial Stress," *Harvard Business Review*, March–April 1983, pp. 44–64.

16. "Inc. and U.S.A. Today Survey of 500 Fastest Growing Private Companies."

17. RBC Study, as reported in Business Research Newsletter, February 2005, p. 5.

18. *Statistics Canada Survey of Employment*, September 2004, p. 15.

19. *Small Business Quarterly*, vol. 5, no. 3, November 2003, p. 6.

20. *Small Business Quarterly*, Industry Canada, February 2006, p. 5.

21. Ibid.

22. *Small Business Quarterly*, vol. 5, no. 3, November 2003, p. 6.

23. *Profit*, June 1993, p. 49.

24. *The Globe and Mail*, June 17, 1995, p. B5.

25. *Self-Employment in Canada—Trends and Prospects*, CIBC Economic Analysis, December 2000, p. 16.

26. *Small Business Quarterly*, Industry Canada, August 2006, p. 5.

27. Amex, December 2005, as reported in G.D. Sourcing, January 2006.

28. Charles A. Garfield, *Peak Performers* (New York: William Morrow, 1985).

29. Thompson, "Characteristics of the Small Business Entrepreneur in Canada."

30. "A Nation of Entrepreneurs," *Report on Business Magazine*, October 1988.

31. *Self-Employment in Canada—Trends and Prospects*, CIBC Economic Analysis, December 2000, p. 16.

32. *Canadian Economic Observer*, November 1997, Statistics Canada, Catalogue #11-010-XPB, p. 19.

33. Carter Henderson, *Winners: The Successful Strategies Entrepreneurs Use to Build New Businesses* (New York: Holt, Rinehart and Winston, 1985), p. 178.

34. Jeffry Tannenbaum, "On Their Own," *Wall Street Journal*, May 21, 1998, p. R20.

35. Joel Corman and Robert Lussier, *Entrepreneurial New Ventures* (Cincinnati, Ohio: Thomson Learning, 2001), pp. 1–18.

36. Ibid.

37. *Small Business Quarterly*, Industry Canada, May 2006, p. 4.

38. Ibid.

39. Statistics Canada, February 2005, as reported in *Business Research Newsletter*.

40. Jeffrey A. Timmons, Leonard E. Smollen, and Alexander L. M. Dingee, *New Venture Creation: A Guide to Entrepreneurship* (Homewood, Ill.: Richard D. Irwin, 1985), p. 28.

Chapter 3

1. National Federation of Independent Business, "Bright Ideas," *USA Today*, May 11, 1987.

2. Small Business Canada, October 2006, pp. 1–2.

3. Micro-Enterprises Survey 2000, A Progress Report. Industry Canada, June 7, 2001, p. 10.

4. The Financial Post, October 29, 1994, p. S24.

5. As reported in *Maclean's*, October 9, 2006.

6. *The Globe and Mail*, June 5, 1995, p. B5.

7. *National Business Incubator website*, January 2007.

8. "Incubator Update," *Inc.*, January 1993, p. 49.

9. *Canadian Association of Business Incubators website*, January 2007.

10. "Business Incubators Come of Age," *Entrepreneurial Manager's Newsletter*, May 1986, p. 5.

Chapter 4

1. *Business Research Newsletter*, G. D. Sourcing, vol. 3, no. 12, November, 2000, p. 9.

2. Joe Mancuso, president of the Centre for Entrepreneurial Management.

3. Donald Rumball, *The Entrepreneurial Edge* (Toronto: Key Porter Books, 1989), pp. 225–33.

4. Jerry White, "Canada's Free Trade Winners," *Small Business Magazine*, July–August 1990, p. 38.

5. *Ipsos-Reid SOHO Syndicated Study*, 2001.

6. Statistics Canada, "Perspectives on Labour and Income," as reported in *The Globe and Mail*, September 10, 1998, p. B12.

7. *Profit*, December–January 1998, p. 46.

8. *The Globe and Mail*, April 10, 1995, p. B6.

9. *Small Business Quarterly*, Industry Canada, February 2007, p. 7.

10. *The Globe and Mail*, June 19, 1995, p. B7.

Chapter 5

1. Harvey Schachter, "Don't Grow It… Buy It," *Profit*, June 1998, p. 161.

2. Peter Thomas, "Negotiate to Win," *Profit*, October 1991, p. 34.

Chapter 6

1. *The Globe and Mail*, October 1995, p. B7.

2. *Franchise Annual* (St. Catharines, Ont.: Info Press, 1988).

3. Faye Rice, "How to Succeed at Cloning a Small Business," *Fortune*, October 28, 1985, p. 60.

4. Canadian Franchise Association estimate, October 2006.

5. *Franchising in Canada website*, October 2006, p. 1.

6. *Franchising in the Canadian Economy 1990–92*, Canadian Franchise Association and Price Waterhouse, 1992.

7. *Canadian Capabilities: Key Facts about Canadian Franchise Expertise*, Industry Canada, March 4, 1998, p. 1.

8. Franchising in Canada website, October 2006.

9. Gordon Brockhouse, "The Franchise Advantage," *Small Business Magazine*, July–August 1990, p. 48.

10. *Franchising in the Canadian Economy 1990–1992* (Toronto: Canadian Franchise Association and Price Waterhouse), p. 3.

11. Rice, "How to Succeed at Cloning a Small Business."

12. U.S. Department of Commerce, *Franchising in the Economy, 1977–79* (Washington, D.C.: U.S. Government Printing Office, 1981), Table 3, p. 34.

13. *Alberta Franchises Act*, Queens Printer, Edmonton, and Ontario Bill 33, Toronto.

14. Rice, "How to Succeed at Cloning a Small Business."

15. Kenneth Barnes and Everett Banning, *Money Makers: The Secrets of Canada's Most Successful Entrepreneurs* (Toronto: McClelland and Stewart, 1985), p. 84.

16. Ibid., p. 72.

17. Ibid., p. 144.

Chapter 7

1. *The Canadian Business Failure Record, 1999* (Toronto: Dun and Bradstreet Business Education Division, 1998).

2. Statistics Canada, *Survey on Financing of Small and Medium-Sized Enterprises*, 2000.

3. *CFIB Banking Study*, October 7, 2003.

4. *Small Business Quarterly*, Industry Canada, November 2005, p. 1.

5. Ying Liu, "An Overview of Angel Investors in Canada," July 2000.

6. "Venture Capital: More Money, Still Choosy," *The Magazine That's All about Small Business*, May 1984, p. 49; Canadian Venture Capital Association website, October 2006.

7. Canadian Venture Capital and Private Equity Association, *Profit*, April 2006, p. 38.

8. Stanley Rich and David E. Gumpert, "Business Plans That Win $$$: Lessons from the MIT Enterprise Forum," *Venture*, June 1985, p. 72.

9. *BDC Report*, June 2006.

10. *Canadian Year Book 2006*, Statistics Canada, p. 443.

11. Ibid.

12. Statistics Canada Survey on Financing, as reported in *The Globe and Mail*, March 24, 2006.

13. "Venture Survey—Financing," *Venture*, October 1986, p. 24.

14. "Small Business Magazine's First Annual Survey of Canadian Entrepreneurs," *Small Business*, June 1987, pp. 49–50.

15. Canadian Bankers' Association website, August 2006, p. 1.

16. Ibid.

17. *CFIB Banking Study*, October 7, 2003.

18. CFIB Survey, Spring 2003, as reported in *CBA Newsletter*.

19. *Business Research Newsletter*, G. D. Sourcing, vol. 4, no. 1, June 2001, p. 8.

Chapter 8

1. Thomas J. Peters and Robert H. Waterman, Jr., *In Search of Excellence* (New York: Harper and Row, 1982), p. 156.

2. *The Globe and Mail*, May 15, 1995, p. B7.

3. *Ontario Business Journal*, January 1995, p. 15.

4. *Small Business Quarterly*, Industry Canada, November 2004, p. 1.

5. *Statistics Canada website*, October 2006.

6. *Growing Small Business* (Ottawa: Industry Canada/Statistics Canada, February 1994), p. 38.

7. *Small Business Quarterly*, February 2006, p. 6.

8. *Small Business Quarterly*, Industry Canada, November 2004.

9. See footnote 7.

10. Business Development Bank of Canada Newsletter, Fall 2004.

11. Canadian Federation of Independent Business, *Federal/Provincial Action Report*, 1986.

12. *The Globe and Mail*, May 29, 1995, p. B6.

13. *Business Research Newsletter*, G. D. Sourcing, vol. 2, no. 8, June 1999, p. 1.

14. *Profits* 18, no. 2 (Business Development Bank of Canada), p. 5.

15. *Small Business Quarterly*, Industry Canada, vol. 5, no. 4, February 2004, p. 1.

16. Everet M. Rogers with F. Floyd Shoemaker, *Communication of Innovation* (New York: Free Press, 1971), p. 270.

17. *Lethbridge Herald*, March 3, 1996, p. 27.

18. Costco Connection, November/December 2006, p. 10.

19. Center for Exhibition Research Study as reported in *Profit*, vol. 23, no. 2, Fall 2003.

20. *Business Research Newsletter*, G. D. Sourcing, vol. 2, no. 6, May 1999, p. 5.

21. *Marketing—Fourth Canadian Edition*, Irwin-Times Mirror Higher Education Group, (Toronto: McGraw-Hill Ryerson), 1997.

22. *BDC Newsletter*, March 24, 2006, p. 1.

23. *Canadian Retailer*, May/June 2000, p. 17.

24. Lawrence N. Stevenson, Joseph C. Shlesinger, and Michael R. Pierce, *Power Retail: Winning Strategies from Chapters and Other Leading Retailers in Canada* (Toronto: McGraw-Hill Ryerson, 1999), p. 67.

Chapter 9

1. "The Estimates and Forecasts of Worldwide E-commerce," http://delivery.acm.org/10.1145/1090000/1089564/p52-yang.pdf?key1=1089564&key2=0485216611&coll=GUIDE&dl=GUIDE&CFID=8918714&CFTOKEN=85132278

2. "Internet World Stats," http://www.internetworldstats.com/am/ca.htm

3. Statistics Canada, *The Daily*, April 20, 2006, http://www.statcan.ca/Daily/English/060420/d060420b.htm

4. Statistics Canada, *The Daily*, April 20, 2006, http://www.statcan.ca/Daily/English/060420/d060420b.htm

5. Statistics Canada, *The Daily*, April 16, 2005, http://www.statcan.ca/Daily/English/051116/d051116b.htm

6. Michael Rappa, "Business Models on the Web," *Managing the Digital Enterprise*, http://digitalenterprise.org/models/models.html

7. "Statistics for General and Online Card Fraud," http://www.epaynews.com/statistics/fraud.html

8. *Small Business Canada*, March/April 2001, p. 21.

9. Statistics Canada, *The Daily*, July 8, 2004, http://www.statcan.ca/Daily/English/040708/d040708a.htm

Chapter 10

1. "Small Business Magazine's First Annual Survey of Canada's Entrepreneurs," *Small Business*, June 1987, pp. 49–53.

2. Intuit Canada, as reported in *G.D. Sourcing*, February 27, 2006.

Chapter 11

1. *Profit*, December/January, 1999, p. 48.

2. Naomi Levinson, "7 Steps to a Successful Relationship," *Canadian Retailer*, May/June 2000, p. 15.

Chapter 12

1. Grant Thornton, L.L.P., October 2001 as reported in *G.D. Sourcing*, April 2003.

2. *Small Business in Canada, 1990* (Ottawa: Industry, Science and Technology Canada), p. 19.

3. Canadian Federation of Independent Business, News Release, April 6, 2006.

4. *Profit Guide*, April 6, 2006, p. 4.

5. Linda Duxbury and Christopher Higgins, as reported in *The Globe and Mail*, September 21, 1999, p. B1.

6. Canadian Federation of Independent Business, News Release, Nov. 18, 2003.

7. Ibid.

8. Robert Levering, Milton Moscowitz, and Michael Katz, *The 100 Best Companies to Work for in America, 1984* (Scarborough, N.Y.: New American Library, 1985).

9. Cyberspace Industries 2000 Inc. website, 2007.

10. Canadian Federation of Independent Business, News Release, November 18, 2003.

11. For a complete discussion, see Donald Rumball, *The Entrepreneurial Edge* (Toronto: Key Porter Books, 1989), pp. 159–179.

12. Frederick Herzberg, *Motivation to Work* (New York: John Wiley and Sons, 1959).

13. Abraham H. Maslow, *Motivation and Personality* (New York: Harper and Row, 1970).

14. Angus Reid Group Survey for Royal Bank, September 1997, as reported in *Profit*, October 1998, p. 16.

15. *Industry Canada: Key Small Business Statistics*, March 2006, p. 5.

16. CFIB Mandate Newsletter, December 2003, p. 4.

17. *The Globe and Mail*, February 20, 1995, p. B6.

18. "Small Business Magazine's First Annual Survey of Canada's Entrepreneurs," *Small Business*, June 1987, pp. 49–53.

19. Work Arrangements in the 1990's, Statistics Canada, May 1998, as reported in *Profit*, October 1998, p. 14.

20. Ibid.

21. Ibid.

22. Mercer Human Resources Consulting as reported in *Alberta Venture Magazine*, November 2003, p. 12.

23. Kenneth Blanchard and Robert Lorber, *Putting the One Minute Manager to Work* (New York: Berkley Books, 1984).

24. *Small Business in Canada*, 1990, p. 61.

25. *Outsourcing Institute Study*, 2005, Jericho, New York.

26. *Profit*, December 2003, Advertising Supplement.

Chapter 13

1. "Totalling Canada's Tax Bill," TD Bank, Vanier Institute, and Fraser Institute, January 2005 and September 2006.

Chapter 14

1. "Canada's Fastest Growing Companies, 2000," *Profit*, June/August, 2001, pp. 32–72.

2. Paul Weinberg, "Growing Pains," *The Magazine That's All about Small Business*, May 1984, p. 26.

3. Donald L. Sexton and Philip M. Van Auken, "Prevalence of Strategic Planning in Small Business," *Journal of Small Business Management*, July 1982, p. 20.

4. Richard M. Hodgetts, *Effective Small Business Management*. Reproduced by permission of Academic Press Inc., 1982, p. 197.

5. *The Globe and Mail*, October 12, 2005, B13.

6. *Profits* (Business Development Bank of Canada, Winter 1999), p. 4.

Chapter 15

1. Myles Marchison, "Successful Succession Planning," *Profit*, September 2005, p. 75.

2. Ibid.

3. Jeff Wuorio, *Success*, December 1998, p. 76.

4. CFIB Study, June 2005.

5. "Are Canadian Entrepreneurs Ready for Retirement?," *CIBC Report*, February 2005.

6. P. C. Rosenblatt, L. deMik, R. M. Anderson, and P. A. Johnson, *The Family in Business* (San Francisco: Jossey-Bass, 1985), p. 5.

7. "Succession Planning for Small Businesses," Grant Thornton, October 2006, p. 1.

8. S. I. Lansberg, "Managing Human Resources in Family Firms: The Problem of Institutional Overlap," *Organizational Dynamics*, Summer 1983, pp. 39–46.

9. *Canadian Business*, May–June, 2005, p. 55.

10. Curtis Hartman, "Main Street Inc.," *Inc.*, June 1986, pp. 49–54.

11. See footnote 7.

12. *The Globe and Mail*, October 9, 1995, p. B7.

13. Statistics Canada, *Small Business Quarterly*, January 2001.

14. S. Birley, "Succession in the Family Firm: The Inheritor's View," *Journal of Small Business Management*, vol. 24, no. 3 (July 1986), p. 36.

15. Low, "Dad, When Are You Going to Let Go?" p. 28.

16. Marshall Paisner, "Myths about Succession," *Inc.*, October 1986, p. 146.

17. Rosenblatt, deMik, Anderson, and Johnson, *The Family in Business*, p. 274.

18. Birley, "Succession in the Family Firm."

19. "Your Going Public Checklist," *Profit*, November 1998, p. 47.

20. Mark Stevens, "When to Take Your Company Public," *Entrepreneurial Manager's Newsletter*, vol. 7, no. 4 (1986), p. 4.

21. *Small Business Quarterly*, Industry Canada, vol. 3, no. 1, May 2006, p. 4.

22. William V. Curran, C.A., "Bankruptcy—What It Means," in *Running Your Own Business* (Ontario: Gage and The Financial Post, 1982), pp. 104–107.

Index